The FATAL SHORE

The epic of Australia's founding

ROBERT HUGHES

The Fatal Shore

The Fatal Shore

Robert Hughes

Vintage Books
A Division of Random House
New York

First Vintage Books Edition, February 1988

Copyright © 1986 by Robert Hughes
Maps copyright © 1986 by Raphael Palacios

All rights reserved under International and Pan-American
Copyright Conventions. Published in the United States by
Random House, Inc., New York, and simultaneously in
Canada by Random House of Canada Limited, Toronto.
Originally published, in hardcover, in Great Britain
by William Collins PLC and in the United States
by Alfred A. Knopf, Inc., in 1986.

Library of Congress Cataloging-in-Publication Data
Hughes, Robert, 1936–
The fatal shore.
Bibliography: p.
Includes index.
1. Australia—History—1788–1900.
2. Australia—Exiles—History.
3. Penal colonies—Australia—History.
I.Title.
[DU115.H78 1988] 994   87-40089
ISBN 0-394-75366-6 (pbk.)

Manufactured in the United States of America
10 9 8 7 6 5 4 3 2 1

For my godson

ALEXANDER BLIGH TURNBULL, B. 1982

a seventh-generation Australian

and for my son's godparents

ALAN MOOREHEAD, 1910–1983
LUCY MOOREHEAD, 1908–1979

che 'n la mente m'e fitta, e or m'accora,
la cara e buona imagine paterna
di voi . . .
e quant'io l'abbia in grado, mentr'io vivo,
convien che nella mia lingua si scerna.

—Dante, *Inferno*, XV, 82–87

I have been studying how I may compare
This prison where I live unto the world:
And, for because the world is populous,
And here is not a creature but myself,
I cannot do it;—yet I'll hammer't out.

—Shakespeare, *Richard II*, V. v.

The very day we landed upon the Fatal Shore,
The planters stood around us, full twenty score or more;
They ranked us up like horses and sold us out of hand,
They chained us up to pull the plough, upon Van Diemen's Land.

—Convict ballad, ca. 1825–30.

Contents

Illustrations follow pages 194 and 450.

Introduction

THE IDEA for this book occurred to me in 1974, when I was working on a series of television documentaries about Australian art. On location in Port Arthur, among the ruins of the great penitentiary and its outbuildings, I realized that like nearly all other Australians I knew little about the convict past of my own country.

I grew up with a skimpy sense of colonial Australia. Convict history was ignored in schools and little taught in universities—indeed, the idea that the convicts might *have* a history worth telling was foreign to Australians in the 1950s and 1960s. Even in the mid-1970s only one general history of the System (as transportation, assignment and secondary punishment in colonial Australia were loosely called) was in print: A. G. L. Shaw's pioneering study *Convicts and the Colonies*. An unstated bias rooted deep in Australian life seemed to wish that "real" Australian history had begun with Australian respectability—with the flood of money from gold and wool, the opening of the continent, the creation of an Australian middle class. Behind the bright diorama of Australia Felix lurked the convicts, some 160,000 of them, clanking their fetters in the penumbral darkness. But on the feelings and experiences of these men and women, little was written. They were statistics, absences and finally embarrassments.

This sublimation has a long history; the desire to forget about our felon origins began with the origins themselves. To call a convict a convict in early colonial Australia was an insult certain to raise colonial hackles. The approved euphemism was "Government man." What the convict system bequeathed to later Australian generations was not the sturdy, skeptical independence on which, with gradually waning justification, we pride ourselves, but an intense concern with social and political respectability. The idea of the "convict stain," a moral blot soaked into our fabric, dominated all argument about Australian selfhood by the 1840s and was the main rhetorical figure used in the movement to abolish transportation. Its leaders called for abolition, not in the name of an independent Australia, but as Britons who felt their decency impugned by the survival of convictry. They were transplanted Britons but Britons still, *plus royalistes que la reine*. The first signs of Australian social identity had appeared as early as the 1820s among the "Currency lads and lasses," most of whom were native-born children of former convicts. In the name of abolition, this picture had to be severely edited in the 1840s; and for decades to come, the official voices of Australia would continue to stake their claim to respectability on their Britishness. If the end of transportation had been brought about in the name of the convicts' own descendants, this might not have happened. But the fight was on behalf of free emigrants and their stock; it was this side of Australia which most fervently brandished the myth of corrupted blood and "convict evil." After abolition, you could (silently) reproach your forebears for being convicts. You could not take pride in them, or reproach England for treating them as it did. The cure for this excruciating colonial double bind was amnesia—a national pact of silence. Yet the Stain would not go away: the late nineteenth century was a flourishing time for biological determinism, for notions of purity of race and stock, and few respectable native-born Australians had the confidence not to quail when real Englishmen spoke of their convict heritage.

Thus local imperialists, who believed that Australia could only survive as a vassal of Great Britain, held that the solvent for the Birth Stain was blood—as much of it as England needed for her wars. Below the propaganda of the Boer War and World War I, voices (usually working-class, and commonly Irish) were heard "unpatriotically" pointing out that, having been shipped out of Britain as criminals, we were shipped back as cannon fodder; so that, when peace came, the survivors could return to their real mission as Australians—growing cheap wool and wheat for England. But to dwell on the Stain did not promote that sense of national dignity which, our grandfathers and great-grandfathers believed, got the lads over the wire. Amnesia seemed to be a condition of patriotism, and this pervaded attitudes toward the writing and teaching of Australian history, at least up to the appearance of the first volume of Manning Clark's *History of Australia* in 1962. One of the reasons why Australians after 1918 embraced with such deep emotion the mythic event of Gallipoli, our Thermopylae, was that there seemed to be so little in our early history to which we could point with pride. "History" meant great men, stirring deeds, useful discoveries and worthy sacrifices; our history was short of these. This made us even more anxious about our worth as Australians living in Australia—the root of the "Cultural Cringe" which would continue to plague us until long after World War II. The idea that whether or not England should feel ashamed of creating the System,

Australians certainly had cause to be proud of surviving it and of creating their own values despite it, was rarely heard.

Australian historians up until the 1960s succumbed to this pressure; hence the textbooks' silence about convictry. It was as though some collective delicacy in American historians had persuaded them to play down the Civil War, so as not to open old wounds.

Denied its voice as history, convict experience became the province of journalists and novelists. The general public never lost its curiosity about these "dark" years in which so many of its roots lay tangled; and a vivid, trashy Grand Guignol, long on rum, sodomy and the lash but decidedly short on the more prosaic facts about how most convicts actually lived and worked, sprang up to supply its demands. So did one national novel, that powerful, meandering awkwardly framed and passionately felt magnum opus of Marcus Clarke's, *For the Term of His Natural Life*. All the popular literature of transportation focussed on the horrors of the System, the outer penal settlements to which recidivists were condemned—Port Arthur, Macquarie Harbor, Moreton Bay and, especially, Norfolk Island. It presented convict life as a wretched purgatory, relieved only by stretches of pure hell.

This folklore of the System kept its memory alive. But it was one-sided and, especially in its treatment of Port Arthur, sometimes luridly exaggerated. It did not bother with the general experience of convicts. Only a fraction of the men and women transported to Australia spent any time in these "secondary" settlements, which were as a rule reserved for prisoners who had committed second crimes while in the colony. Most served a few years of their sentences in assignment to a free settler or in Government labor, never wore chains, got their tickets-of-leave and in due course were absorbed into colonial society as free citizens. Most of them (if one can judge by the surviving letters) wanted to stay in Australia and rejected the idea of going back to England.

For assignment worked. Despite all its imperfections and injustices, and the abuses of bad masters and the general harshness of antipodean life, it did give a fresh start to many thousands of people who would have been crushed in spirit or confirmed in crime by long stretches in an English prison. And, despite the number of bigots in our grandfathers' day deriding Australians as the children of criminals, remarkably few Australians pointed out the obvious contrary fact that, whatever other conclusions one might draw from our weird national origins, the post-colonial history of Australia utterly exploded the theory of genetic criminal inheritance. Here was a community of people, handpicked over decades for their "criminal propensities" and for no other reason, whose offspring turned out to form one of the most law-abiding societies in the world. At a time when neo-conservative social idealogues are trying to revive the old bogey of hereditary disposition to crime, this may still be worth pondering.

From the 1960s onward, when Australian historians—inspired, though slowly at first, by Manning Clark's *History of Australia* and L. L. Robson's *The Convict Settlers of Australia* (1965)—began to draw the System out of folklore and into the light of inquiry, they focussed on the majority of convicts: those in assignment, not those on Norfolk Island. It was from them, not from the double-damned incorrigibles, that one could learn the actual workings of colonial society, the often-exotic ways in which convicts claimed rights and functioned as a class in relation to the free. Colonial Australia was unique in its mingling of the free and the bond, in its attitudes toward work and its definitions of servitude. It was also a more "normal" place than one might imagine from the folk-loric picture of a society governed by the lash and the triangle, composed of groaning white slaves tyrannized by ruthless masters. The book that best conveys this, and has rightly become a landmark in recent studies of the System, is J. B. Hirst's *Convict Society and its Enemies* (1983).

Though Hirst and other "normalizing" historians have not ignored the lower depths of the System, epitomized by Norfolk Island, they may have underestimated the moral and human significance of these places in their laudable desire to avoid sensationalism. It is true that relatively few convicts were pitched into these hellholes. It is also true that only a small fraction of the total population of Russia has suffered in the Gulag, and that relatively few Cubans have undergone the atrocities visited on dissidents by Fidel Castro's torturers on the Isle of Pines. Yet, just as it is impossible to read a book like Armando Valladares' *Against All Hope* without losing one's illusions about the true nature of Castro's regime, so it is difficult to reflect on places like Norfolk Island and Macquarie Harbor without adjusting some of one's views of British colonialism. They held a minority of convicts but they were absolutely integral to the System: they provided a standard of terror by which good behavior on the mainland of New South Wales (or so the authorities hoped) would be enforced.

The missing element in most accounts of the System has been the voices of the convicts themselves. The System left a mountain of official paper behind it. We hear a great deal from the administrators, the wit-nesses in the select committees, the parsons, the jailers, the masters; from the convicts themselves, very little. Accordingly I have tried, as far as possible, to see the System from below, through convicts' testimony —in letters, depositions, petitions and memoirs—about their own expe-riences. Much of this material is hitherto unpublished, and much more awaits study. It turns out that one common assumption is quite wrong: far from being a mute mass, the convicts did have a voice, or rather many voices. This book is largely about what they tell us of their suffering and survival, their aspiration and resistance, their fear of exile and their reconciliation to the once-unimagined land they and their children would claim as their own.

Friends gave me moral support and encouragement while I was writing this much-delayed book. Among these I should like particularly to thank Joanna Collard, who helped assemble a first list of Australian sources; Brendan Gill, whose initial enthusiasm for the idea back in 1975 sustained mine; Jerry Lieber, Barbara Rose and Lucio Manisco, on whom readings were inflicted; and Robert Motherwell, whose response to the first few chapters helped keep me going through the rest.

As anyone must who attempts to write on Australian history from primary sources, I owe my main debt to the Librarians and staff of the Mitchell and Dixson Libraries and the Archives Office of New South Wales in Sydney, the National Library of Australia in Canberra, the Allport Library and the Archives Office of Tasmania (Tasmanian State Archives) in Hobart. In particular, Catherine Santamaria (head of Australian Studies) and John Thompson (in charge of Australian Manuscripts) at the National Library, and Geoffrey Stillwell of the Allport Library steered me through the documentary labyrinth.

I must also record my gratitude to the Librarians and staff of the Latrobe Library, Melbourne; the New York Public Library; the State Paper Office and the National Library of Ireland, Dublin; the Bibliothèque Nationale, Paris; the British Library, London; the London Library, without whose lending service the early research for this book could not have begun; the Public Record Office, London; the Army Museums Ogilby Trust; the Religious Society of Friends; the Bedford County Record Office; the Derby Central Library; the Estate Office at Catton Hall, Staffordshire; the Lancashire Record Office; the William Salt Library, Stafford. For field trips in Tasmania in 1981, a car was supplied by Telford Motors, Hobart; and Dick Edwards of Strahan provided the boat in which I got around Macquarie Harbor.

The unwieldy manuscript was cuffed and licked into shape, through its various drafts, by Charles Elliott, my editor at Knopf, backed up by Christopher Maclehose and Stuart Proffitt of Collins Harvill. Gillian Gibbins at Collins and Sharon Zimmerman at Knopf helped gather material. Stephen Frankel, the copy editor, pounced on more inconsistencies than I thought possible. I offer heartfelt thanks to them all, and especially to Professor Michael Roe of the University of Tasmania, Hobart, for his generosity and care in reading the penultimate draft of the manuscript and pointing out its various sins of omission and commission. Though my interpretation of certain aspects of penal history differs from his, any surviving errors of fact are mine.

Finally, and most of all, I thank my beloved wife, Victoria Hughes, whose faith and levelheadedness kept me going through years of research and writing, and never for a minute let me down; this is her book too.

Maps

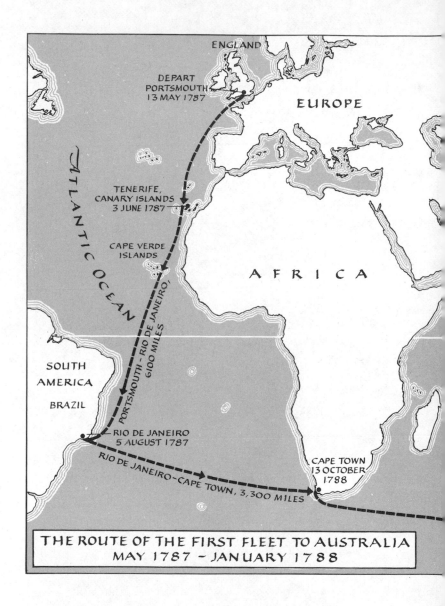

THE ROUTE OF THE FIRST FLEET TO AUSTRALIA
MAY 1787 – JANUARY 1788

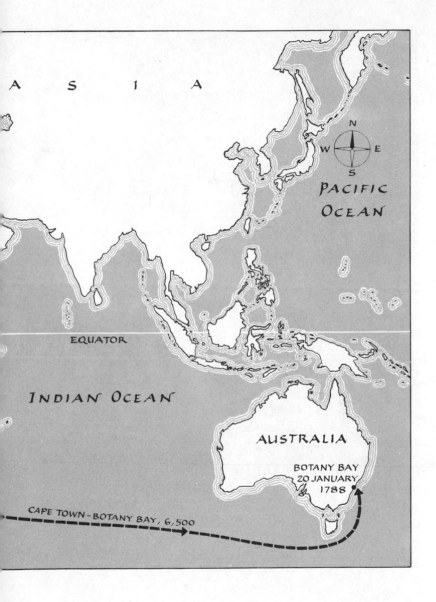

ASIA

PACIFIC
OCEAN

EQUATOR

INDIAN OCEAN

AUSTRALIA

BOTANY BAY
20 JANUARY
1788

CAPE TOWN - BOTANY BAY, 6,500

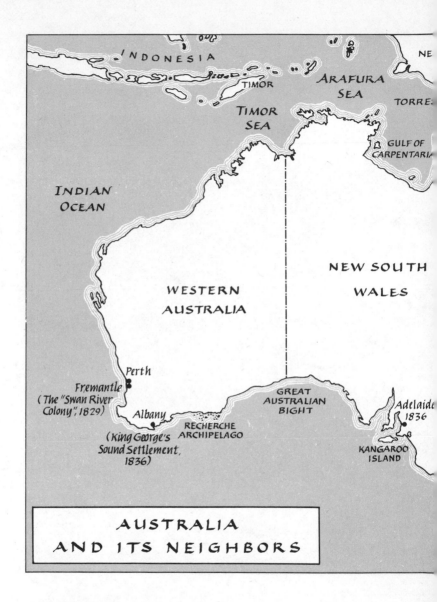

INDONESIA

TIMOR

ARAFURA
SEA

NE

TORRE

TIMOR
SEA

GULF OF
CARPENTARIA

INDIAN
OCEAN

NEW SOUTH

WALES

WESTERN

AUSTRALIA

Perth

Fremantle
(The "Swan River
Colony", 1829)

Albany

(King George's
Sound Settlement,
1836)

RECHERCHE
ARCHIPELAGO

GREAT
AUSTRALIAN
BIGHT

Adelaide
1836

KANGAROO
ISLAND

AUSTRALIA
AND ITS NEIGHBORS

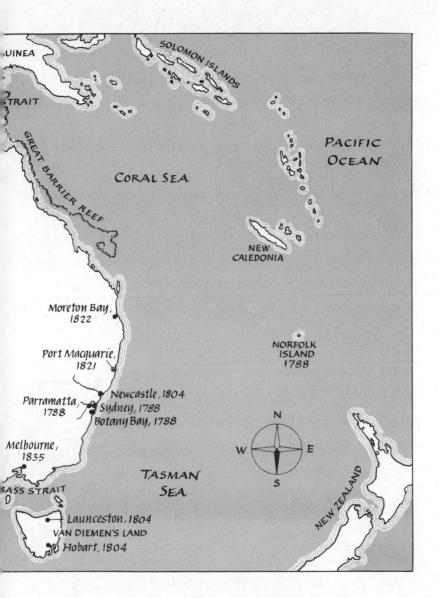

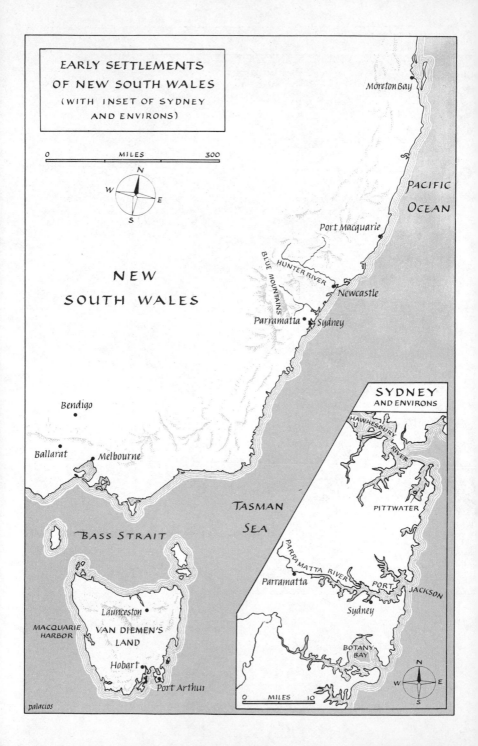

EARLY SETTLEMENTS
OF NEW SOUTH WALES
(WITH INSET OF SYDNEY
AND ENVIRONS)

0   MILES   300

N
W   E
S

NEW
SOUTH WALES

Moreton Bay

PACIFIC
OCEAN

Port Macquarie

BLUE MOUNTAINS   HUNTER RIVER

Newcastle

Parramatta   Sydney

Bendigo

Ballarat   Melbourne

TASMAN
SEA

SYDNEY
AND ENVIRONS

HAWKESBURY   RIVER

PITTWATER

BASS STRAIT

PARRAMATTA RIVER

Parramatta   PORT   JACKSON

Sydney

MACQUARIE
HARBOR   VAN DIEMEN'S
LAND

Launceston

BOTANY
BAY

Hobart

Port Arthur   0   MILES   10

N
W   E
S

palacios

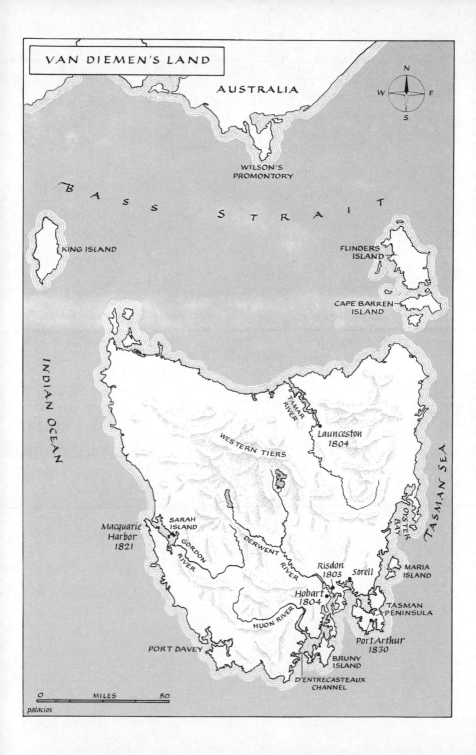

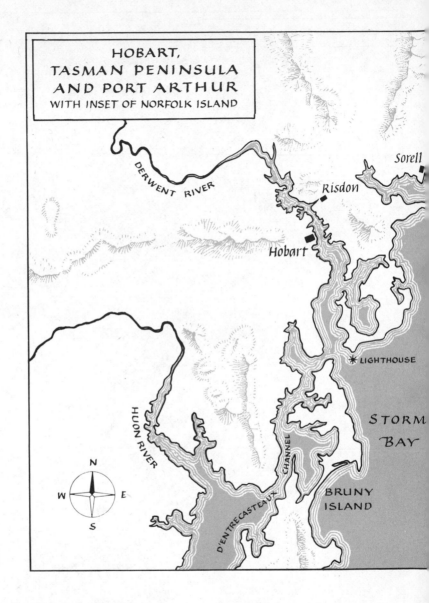

HOBART,
TASMAN PENINSULA
AND PORT ARTHUR
WITH INSET OF NORFOLK ISLAND

DERWENT RIVER

Sorell

Risdon

Hobart

HUON RIVER

LIGHTHOUSE

STORM
BAY

D'ENTRECASTEAUX CHANNEL

BRUNY
ISLAND

N
W   E
S

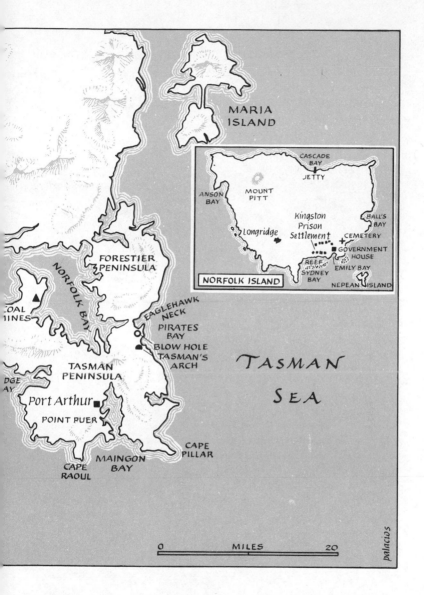

MARIA
ISLAND

NORFOLK ISLAND

CASCADE
BAY
JETTY

ANSON
BAY

MOUNT
PITT

Longridge

Kingston
Prison
Settlement

BALL'S
BAY

CEMETERY

GOVERNMENT
HOUSE

REEF
SYDNEY
BAY

EMILY BAY

NEPEAN ISLAND

FORESTIER
PENINSULA

NORFOLK BAY

COAL
MINES

EAGLEHAWK
NECK

PIRATES
BAY
BLOW HOLE
TASMAN'S
ARCH

TASMAN
PENINSULA

DGE
AY

Port Arthur

POINT PUER

CAPE
RAOUL

MAINGON
BAY

CAPE
PILLAR

TASMAN

SEA

0   MILES   20

palacios

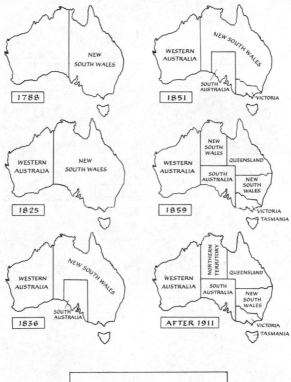

1788

1825

1836

1851

1859

AFTER 1911

WESTERN AUSTRALIA

NEW SOUTH WALES

SOUTH AUSTRALIA

NORTHERN TERRITORY

QUEENSLAND

VICTORIA

TASMANIA

HISTORICAL BOUNDARIES
OF AUSTRALIA,
1788 – PRESENT

The Fatal Shore

The Harbor and the Exiles

i

IN 1787, the twenty-eighth year of the reign of King George III, the British Government sent a fleet to colonize Australia.

Never had a colony been founded so far from its parent state, or in such ignorance of the land it occupied. There had been no reconnaissance. In 1770 Captain James Cook had made landfall on the unexplored east coast of this utterly enigmatic continent, stopped for a short while at a place named Botany Bay and gone north again. Since then, no ship had called: not a word, not an observation, for seventeen years, each one of which was exactly like the thousands that had preceded it, locked in its historical immensity of blue heat, bush, sandstone and the measured booming of glassy Pacific rollers.

Now this coast was to witness a new colonial experiment, never tried before, not repeated since. An unexplored continent would become a jail. The space around it, the very air and sea, the whole transparent labyrinth of the South Pacific, would become a wall 14,000 miles thick.

The late eighteenth century abounded in schemes of social goodness thrown off by its burgeoning sense of revolution. But here, the process was to be reversed: not Utopia, but Dystopia; not Rousseau's natural man moving in moral grace amid free social contracts, but man coerced, exiled, deracinated, in chains. Other parts of the Pacific, especially Tahiti, might seem to confirm Rousseau. But the intellectual patrons of Australia, in its first colonial years, were Hobbes and Sade.

In their most sanguine moments, the authorities hoped that it would eventually swallow a whole class—the "criminal class," whose existence was one of the prime sociological beliefs of late Georgian and early Victorian England. Australia was settled to defend English property not from the frog-eating invader across the Channel but from the marauder within. English lawmakers wished not only to get rid of the "criminal class" but if possible to forget about it. Australia was a cloaca, invisible, its contents filthy and unnameable. Jeremy Bentham, inveighing against the "thief-colony" in 1812, argued that transportation

> was indeed a measure of *experiment* . . . but the subject-matter of experiment was, in this case, a peculiarly commodious one; a set of *animae viles*, a sort of excrementitious mass, that could be projected, and accordingly was projected—projected, and as it should seem purposely—as far out of sight as possible.[1]

To most Englishmen this place seemed not just a mutant society but another planet—an exiled world, summed up in its popular name, "Botany Bay." It was remote and anomalous to its white creators. It was strange but close, as the unconscious to the conscious mind. There was as yet no such thing as "Australian" history or culture. For its first forty years, everything that happened in the thief-colony was English. In the whole period of convict transportation, the Crown shipped more than 160,000 men, women and children (due to defects in the records, the true number will never be precisely known) in bondage to Australia.[2] This was the largest forced exile of citizens at the behest of a European government in pre-modern history. Nothing in earlier penology compares with it. In Australia, England drew the sketch for our own century's vaster and more terrible fresco of repression, the Gulag. No other country had such a birth, and its pangs may be said to have begun on the afternoon of January 26, 1788, when a fleet of eleven vessels carrying 1,030 people, including 548 male and 188 female convicts, under the command of Captain Arthur Phillip in his flagship *Sirius*, entered Port Jackson or, as it would presently be called, Sydney Harbor.

ii

ONE MAY LIKEN this moment to the breaking open of a capsule. Upon the harbor the ships were now entering, European history had left no mark at all. Until the swollen sails and curvetting bows of the British fleet came round South Head, there were no dates. The Aborigines and the fauna around them had possessed the landscape since time immemorial, and no other human eye had seen them. Now the protective glass of distance broke, in an instant, never to be restored.

To imagine the place, one should begin at North Head, the upper mandible of the harbor. Here, Australia stops; its plates of sandstone break off like a biscuit whose crumbs, the size of cottages, lie jumbled 250 feet below, at the surging ultramarine rim of the Pacific. A ragged wall of creamy-brown sandstone, fretted by the incessant wind, runs north to a glazed horizon. To the east, the Pacific begins its 7,000-mile arc toward South America. Long swells grind into the cliff in a boiling white lather, flinging veils of water a hundred feet into the air. At the meetings of its ancient planes of rock, sea and sky—mass, energy and light—one can grasp why the Aborigines called North Head *Boree*, "the enduring one."

The sandstone is the bone and root of the coast. On top of the cliff, the soil is thin and the scrub sparse. There are banksia bushes, with their sawtooth-edge leaves and dried seed-cones like multiple, jabbering mouths. Against this austere gray-green, the occasional red or blue scribble of a flower looks startling. But further back to the west, the sandstone ledges dip down into the harbor, separating it into scores of inlets. In 1788 these sheltered coves were densely wooded. The largest trees were eucalypts: red gums, angophoras, scribbly gums and a dozen others. Until the late eighteenth century no European had ever seen a eucalypt, and very strange they must have looked, with their strings of hanging, half-shed bark, their smooth wrinkling joints (like armpits, elbows or crotches), their fluent gesticulations and haze of perennial foliage. Not evergreens, but evergrays: the soft, spatially deceitful background color of the Australian bush, monotonous-looking at first sight but rippling with nuance to the acclimatized eye.

In the gullies, where streams of water slid from pool to pool leaving beards of rusty algae on their sandstone lips, giant cabbage-tree palms grew, their damp shade supporting a host of ferns and mosses. Yellow sprays of mimosa flashed in the sun along the ridges, and there were stands of blackboy trees, their dry spear of a stalk shooting up from a drooping hackle of fronds.

Most of the ground was sandy and thin, but parts of the harbor fore-shores held, to the relief of Captain John Hunter, Phillip's second-in-command,

> tolerable land . . . which may be cultivated without waiting for its being cleared of wood; for the trees stand very wide of one another, and have no underwood; in short, the woods . . . resemble a deer park, as much as if they had been intended for such a purpose.[3]

The comparison of the harbor landscape with an English park is one of the more common, if startling, descriptive resources of First Fleet diarists. Partly it came from their habit of resorting to familiar European stereotypes to deal with the unfamiliar appearance of things Australian; thus it took at least two decades for colonial watercolorists to get the gum trees right, so that they did not look like English oaks or elms.[4] Partly, no doubt, it arose from the simple fact that any land looks like

Eden after months at sea. But it also had a basis in fact, since the land-scape was often burned by aboriginal hunters; their firesticks kept the big trees isolated and promoted the growth of grass.

So there was a mingled note of relief and aesthetic pleasure in Arthur Bowes Smyth's journal entry for January 26, 1788, as his transport *Lady Penrhyn* glided up the harbor, past the dangerous reef with outlying rocks that would later be called the Sow and Pigs, past the tilting, wind-gnarled, peach-colored sandstone ledges of Vaucluse and Parsley Bay, toward the wide, light-flushed notch of water now spanned by the Sydney Harbor Bridge:

> The finest terras's, lawns and grottos, with distinct plantations of the tallest and most stately trees I ever saw in any nobleman's ground in England, cannot excel in beauty those wh. Nature now presented to our view. The singing of the various birds among the trees, and the flight of the numerous parraquets, lorrequets, cockatoos, and maccaws, made all around appear like an enchantment; the stupendous rocks from the sum-mit of the hills and down to the very water's edge hang'g over in a most awful way from above, and form'g the most commodious quays by the water, beggard all description.[5]

He was wrong about macaws, which do not exist in Australia. But the density and range of bird life along the harbor was still amazing. Several dozen kinds of parrot thronged the harbor bush: Galahs, bald-eyed Corellas, pink Leadbeater's Cockatoos, black Funereal Cockatoos, down through the rainbow-colored lorikeets and rosellas to the tiny, seed-eating budgerigars which, when disturbed, flew up in green clouds so dense that they cast long rippling shadows on the ground. The Sulphur-Crested Cockatoos, *Cacatua galerita*, were the most spectacular—big birds with hoarse squalling voices, chalk-white plumage (dusted with yellow under the wedge-shaped tail), beaks the color of slate, obsidian eyes, and an insouciant lick of yellow feathers curling back from the head. When excited, they would flirt their crests erect into nimbi of golden spokes like Aztec headdresses. These raucous dandies assembled in flocks of hundreds which, settling on a dead gum tree, would cover its silvery limbs in what seemed to be a thick blooming of white flowers; until, at the moment of alarm, the blossoms would re-form into birds and return screeching into the sky.

The Galahs, smaller cockatoos, had gray backs, white crests and fronts of the most delicate, intense dusty pink, like the center of a Bour-bon rose; so that a flock of them passing against the opaline horizon would seem to change color—pink flicking to gray and back to pink again —as it changed direction, uttering small grating cries like the creak of rusty hinges.

The exuberance of bird life around the harbor was balanced by the stillness and secrecy of the ground. Nothing about Australian animals was obvious. Many of them were camouflaged fossils, throwbacks that crept, slid, waddled or bounded through the dry brush. In them, the legends of antipodean inversion seemed to be made harmless flesh. Their remote ancestors had evolved in isolation ever since the Australian continent broke off from Antarctica, about 40 million years ago.[6]

One of these creatures, a small macropod called a wallaby, had already been shot and collected by Sir Joseph Banks far north of Sydney Harbor, as the *Endeavour* lay beached and holed among the coral mazes of the Great Barrier Reef in June 1770. It was skinned and taken to England, where it was stuffed by a London taxidermist and given to the great animal painter George Stubbs to have its portrait made. "Called by the natives *Kangooroo*," Captain Cook noted in his journal, it moved "by hoping or jumping 7 or 8 feet at each hop upon its hind legs only. . . . The skin is cover'd with a short hairy fur of a dark Mouse or Grey Colour. Excepting the head and ears which I thought something like a Hare's, it bears no sort of resemblance to any European animal I ever saw."[7] When Phillip arrived in Sydney Harbor, the one certain thing he knew about the language of the "Indians" was that they called this creature a kangaroo. But because their language bore no resemblance to that of the tribe Cook had encountered so far to the north, the Sydney Aborigines assumed that "kangaroo" was the white intruders' word for the ordinary familiar animal they themselves had always known as a *patagarang*.

Half a dozen kinds of patagarang lived around the harbor, nibbling its wiry grass and appearing silently, like fawn wraiths, among the guttered shelves of the fern-gullies.The silvery-coated Eastern Gray kangaroo, *Macropus giganteus*, moved in flocks of dozens; "the noise they make," a colonial diarist was to note, "is a faint bleat, querulous, but not easy to describe." Other species ranged down in size from the timid rock-wallabies to the tiny, ratlike Potoroo.

The kangaroos were not the only oddities of this landscape. Koalas clambered through the gum-tree branches or sprawled sedately in the comfortable forks munching their bunches of leaves. These were not the winsome, cuddly teddy bears of the Qantas commercial, but slow, irritable, aldermanic creatures with furry ears and a boot-heel nose, which ate two pounds of fresh gum leaves a day and, when captured, scratched furiously and drenched the offending hand with eucalyptus-scented piss. Indeed they were not bears at all (any more than the moon-spotted "native cat" was a cat, or the bandy-rumped Tasmanian Wolf a canine) but nocturnal marsupials with no clear relationship to any other animal, living or fossil. After sundown, their trees were filled with the thumping, scrabbling and chittering of other nocturnals—fat brushtailed possums, ringtails and sugar-gliders, which had wide furry airfoils slung between their fore and hind feet and parachuted from tree to tree in wobbly swoops. Like true Arcadians, these creatures lived by sucking sweet nectar from bush flowers.

The oldest and most bizarre of the mammals were, however, the platypus and the echidna. Both were exceedingly primitive, stuck at an intermediate point of evolution between reptiles and mammals. They were monotremes: the same orifice served them interchangeably for mating, excretion and egg-laying. The echidna, or spiny anteater, looked vaguely like a European hedgehog, but the resemblance was not even quill-deep: its elegant yellow-and-brown spines were actually a kind of fur, though of the most formalized sort. It laid eggs like a bird but carried them about in a pouch under its belly. It was very shortsighted but had an acute sense of smell and could sniff out the ants' odor of formic acid through yards of air or inches of sun-hardened earth. It had a beak rather than jaws—an open tube from which a whip of pink, sticky tongue almost as long as its body would shoot into the ants' nest. When threatened, the echidna would curl into a ball of bristles or put its head down and start to dig with its prodigiously strong claws, burying itself within moments.

The platypus, on the other hand, was an amphibian: the sole survivor of its prehistoric family, the Ornithorhynchidae or bird-beaked mammals. It had a bill and webbed feet like a duck, a tail like a beaver and exquisitely glossy, oil-rich fur. Like a tiny seal, it had a generous layer of fat under the skin, for it was too primitive to regulate its own body temperature. In a tunnel burrowed in the mud of a creek bank, the female platypus would lay a clutch of leathery, ancient-looking eggs and suckle her young when they hatched—not with teats, but through enlarged pores on her belly which she scratched until milk oozed forth. Most of a platypus's life had to be spent foraging on the streambed for worms and insects, since it ate rather more than its own weight in food a day and had a metabolic rate like a blast furnace. Hold one of these frantic little fossils (avoiding the hind legs, which carry a poison spur, like many "cute" things in Australia) and it seems to be all heart, pumping and quivering.

Wombats—lumbering, eighty-pound marsupials resembling squat, blunt-skulled bears—dug their meandering catacombs beneath the soil; bandicoots peeked from holes; the landscape was alive, but secretively so. Here in the Australian bush one needed to look, and look again, before glimpsing the gray koala camouflaged against the fleshy gray burl of its gum tree. The voices of the animals tended to be out of all proportion to their size. Just as space was drained of perspective by the random, flickering transparency of the trees, so it was hard to guess where sounds originated. The throbbing croak of the cicada on a branch ten feet away might seem to be coming from all around. It was hard to sneak up on these creatures of the harbor shores. The bush, baked tawny and bronze by the summer heat, its ground surface mantled in a crackling skin of dry gum leaves, grasses and fallen strips of eucalyptus bark, was like a stretched drum, a delicate resonator that informed every animal of each approach.

There was little sense of menace in this parliament of creatures. The only large meat-eating animal was the dingo, the "native dog" imported to Australia long ago by migrating Aborigines. Even the dragon of the bush, a carrion-eating monitor lizard known as a goanna, would rush up a tree when approached and cling there, its throat puffed out in soundless alarm, until the intruder went away. The only universal predator was man.

iii

A STATIC CULTURE, frozen by its immemorial primitivism, un-changed in an unchanging landscape—such until quite recently was, and for many people still is, the common idea of the Australian Aborigines. It grows from several roots: myths about the Noble Savage, misreadings of aboriginal technology, traditional racism and ignorance of Australian prehistory. It is, in fact, quite false; but in the experience of white city-dwellers there is little to contradict it. Nobody can guess how Sydney Harbor began to unfold itself to its white prisoners on January 26, 1788, just by subtracting the poultice of brick, steel and tar from its headlands, pulling down the Harbor Bridge and the Opera House and populating the beaches with black stick figures waving spears. The changes have been too radical for that. Yet the effort to perceive the landscape and its people as they were is worth making, for it bears on one of the chief myths of early colonial history as understood and taught up to about 1960. This was the idea, promulgated by the early settlers and inherited from the nineteenth century, that the First Fleet sailed into an "empty" continent, speckled with primitive animals and hardly less primitive men, so that the "fittest" inevitably triumphed. Thus the destruction of the Australian Aborigines was rationalized as natural law. "Nothing can stay the dying away of the Aboriginal race, which Providence has only allowed to hold the land until replaced by a finer race," remarked a settler in 1849.[8]

But the first white Australian settlers were so conspicuously unfit for survival in the new land that they lived on the edge of starvation in the midst of what seemed natural abundance to the Aborigines. They had practically no idea of what they could eat or how to get it. Most of the

First Fleet convicts had not moved ten miles from their place of birth and had never seen the sea before they were clapped in irons and thrust on the transports. They were as lost in Australia as an Aborigine would have been in a London "rookery." The tribesmen they encountered were so well adapted to their landscape that their standard of nutrition was probably higher than that of most Europeans in 1788. To the whites, convict and officer alike, Sydney Harbor was the end of the earth. But to the Aborigines it was the center. The landscape and its elusive resources, not yet named by the whites, stood between the two cultures, showing each group its utter unlikeness to the other.

At the time of white invasion, men had been living in Australia for at least 30,000 years. They had moved into the continent during the Pleistocene epoch. This migration happened at about the same time as the first wave of human migrations from Asia into the unpeopled expanse of North America, across the now sunken land-bridge between Russia and Alaska.

The first Australians also came from Asia. When they discovered Australia, the continent was perhaps a quarter larger than it now is. In the Pleistocene epoch the level of the Pacific was between 400 and 600 feet lower than it is today. One could walk from southern Australia into Tasmania, which was not yet an island. The Sahul Shelf, that shallow ledge of ocean floor whose waters separate Australia from New Guinea was dry land; Australia, New Guinea and possibly sections of the New Hebrides formed one landmass. By trial and error, accumulated over many human generations, it would then have been possible to get from Southeast Asia into Australia (via the Celebes and Borneo) across islands sprinkled on the sea like stepping-stones. Much of this voyage would have been done by eyeball navigation to coasts that the immigrants could have seen from their starting point; there would have been a few sea voyages of more than 50 miles, but not too many; but there was no direct route. In the words of the historian Geoffrey Blainey, "Australia was merely the chance terminus of a series of voyages and migrations."[9] But the moment when the first man stepped ashore from his frail chip of a canoe on the northwestern coast of Pleistocene Australia should rightly be seen as one of the hinges of human history: it was the first time *Homo sapiens* had ever colonized by sea.

Apart from their northern origin, no one knows who these Pleistocene colonists were or whence they emerged.[10] Whoever they were, they gradually spread south, east and west across the continent, killing giant kangaroos as they went, bringing with them their imported half-wild dogs, whose descendants are the dingoes. Their first campsites were drowned by the waters of the Timor Sea and the Gulf of Carpenteria, which rose so fast between 13,000 and 16,000 B.C. that the coast moved inland at a rate of three miles a year.[11] The oldest known northern camp-sites were pitched 22,000 years ago at Oenpelli, 150 miles east of Darwin.

But the southward march was under way long before that. By 30,000 B.C. there were well-established tribes eating crayfish and emu eggs beside the now arid basin of Lake Mungo, in southeastern Australia; they were perhaps the world's first people to practice cremation, and the pellets of ocher placed as offerings in a Mungo grave suggest that they had some idea of the survival of consciousness after death.[12] By about 20,000 B.C. the Aborigines had reached Sydney Harbor. Others were prizing flint nodules from the limestone walls of Koonalda Cave, under the Nullarbor Plain on the extreme southern rim of the continent. There, in the darkness, they scratched crude patterns on the walls that may be the first works of art ever made in the southern hemisphere—the merest graffiti, compared to the later achievements of aboriginal rock-painting, but clear evidence of some primal artistic intent. Two thousand years later, the Aborigines had left their shell-middens, flint chips, bone points and charcoal in nearly every habitable part of the continent. The colonization was achieved, and a membrane of human culture had been stretched over the vast terrain.

But it was exceedingly thin. When the First Fleet arrived, there were perhaps 300,000 Aborigines in the whole of Australia—a continental average of one person to ten square miles. The density of local populations, however, varied a great deal. Probably less than 20,000 people wandered in the 300,000-square-mile tract of dry limestone plain and saltbush desert between the Great Australian Bight and the Tropic of Capricorn, a place where even the crows are said to fly backwards to keep the dust out of their eyes. On the coast, where there was more food and a higher rainfall, the land could support more people. Phillip, after a few months on Sydney Harbor, reckoned that the areas of the Cumberland Plain he had explored sustained about 1,500 blacks; this rough guess yields a density of about 3 people per square mile.

The Australians divided themselves in tribes. They had no notion of private property, but they were intensely territorial, linked to the ancestral area by hunting customs and totemism. Hundreds of tribes existed at the time of white invasion—perhaps as many as 900, although the more likely figure is about 500. The tribe did not have a king, or a charismatic leader, or even a formal council. It was linked together by a common religion, by language and by an intricate web of family relationships; it had no writing, but instead a complex structure of spoken and sung myth whose arcana were gradually passed on by elders to the younger men. Geographical features could cause splits in tribal language. Thus in the area of Sydney, the ancestral territory of the Iora tribe—who roamed over about 700 square miles, from Pittwater to Botany Bay—was cut in half by Sydney Harbor itself; so that the "hordes" or tribal subgroups on the north and south sides of the harbor, the Cameragal and the Kadigal, spoke two distinct languages. For them, the harbor formed a linguistic chasm as wide as the English Channel.[13] In 1791, as white settlement was pushing out past Windsor and the Hawkesbury River, Governor Phillip was surprised to find on its banks

> people who made use of several words we could not understand, and it soon appear'd that they had a language different from that used by the natives we have hitherto been acquainted with. They did not call the Moon *Yan-re-dah* but *Con-do-in*, and they called the Penis *Bud-da*, which our natives call *Ga-diay*.[14]

These were the Daruk, who ranged over a territory of about 2,300 square miles from the coast north of Iora territory to the Katoomba–Blackheath area of the Blue Mountains in the south. The Daruk, the Iora and the Tarawal (whose territory began on the south shore of Botany Bay) were the three tribes with whom the white settlers of Australia first had to deal.

Watkin Tench (1758–1833), a young officer of marines on the transport *Charlotte*, was struck by the ease with which the tribes understood one another. He supposed that the Daruk language was only a dialect of Iora, "though each in speaking preferred its own [tongue]."[15] In fact, the variety of aboriginal language arose from the tight social structure of the tribes, their specified restricted territories, and their more-or-less fixed patterns of movement in relation to other tribal boundaries. These factors encouraged each tribe to keep its own language intact, while nomadism forced them to learn others. Compared to some inland tribes, who routinely exchanged goods (flint axes, baler shell ornaments, lumps of ocher for body painting and other local commodities) along trade routes as long as 1,000 miles, the Iora were provincial. They could not understand languages spoken 50 miles away. Their main diet was fish, and they had no reason to leave the coast. They held their territories—the Cameragal and the Walumedegal along the north shore of the harbor, the Boorogegal on Bradley Head, the Kadigal around what is now Circular Quay and the Botanical Gardens—as they had held them for centuries.

Their main food source was the sea. The women of the tribe twisted fishing lines from pounded bark fiber and made hooks from the turban shell. But since such hooks were brittle and the line weak, the Aborigines fished in pairs—a woman led the hooked fish in as gently as possible, while a man stood ready to spear the fish as soon as it got within range. At the ends of the fish-spears were three or four prongs of wallaby or bird bone, ground sharp and set in gum resin.

The Iora fished from canoes. These they made by cutting a long oval of bark from a suitable eucalypt and binding its ends together to make bow and stern. The old, scarred "canoe trees" were a common sight around the harbor a hundred years ago, but none remain today. The gunwale was reinforced with a pliable stick, sewn on with vegetable fiber. Shorter sticks, jammed athwartships, served as spreaders. The cracks and seams were then caulked with clay or gum resin. The Aborigines kept fire burning on a pat of wet clay on the bottom of the hull, so that they could grill and eat their fish at sea. Compared to an American Indian birch canoe, they were unstable craft and wretchedly crude, "by far the worst canoes I ever saw or heard of," in the view of William Bradley, who was first lieutenant on *Sirius*. They had neither outriggers nor sails (the Iora were ignorant of weaving); low in the water, they flexed with every ripple and leaked like sieves. Nevertheless, the Iora handled them skillfully. "I have seen them paddle through a a large surf," Bradley noted, "without oversetting or taking in more water than if rowing in smooth water." The frailty of these craft suited the Iora's nomadic way of life; they were easy to carry and just as easy to replace. A tribesman could slap one together in a day.[16]

The Iora also ate immense quantities of shellfish, mainly oysters, which were gathered by women. Middens of white shells lay at the entrances of scores of sandstone caves along the harbor shores. Bennelong Point, where the Sydney Opera House now stands, was first named Limeburners' Point by the colonists because it was mantled in a deposit of mollusc shells, built up over thousands of years of uninterrupted gorging.* Gathered again (this time by white convict women) and burned in a kiln, these shells provided the lime for Sydney's first mortar.

The Iora were not wholly dependent on the sea for their diet. They also hunted on land, though rarely with boomerangs. Boomerangs have to fly without obstruction and so were weapons for open grassland and desert, not for the sclerophyll forests where the Iora lived. Probably their role in providing food for the Sydney blacks was insignificant. Rather,

---

* Bennelong was an Iora tribesman, the first black to learn English, drink rum, wear clothes and eat the invaders' strange food. He was rewarded for his curiosity with the friendship of Governor Phillip—and a small brick hut, about 12 feet square, in which he lived on the end of what is now Bennelong Point. "Love and war," a colonial diarist noted, "were his favorite pursuits." He went to England with Phillip in 1792 and was much feted as an exotic Noble Savage, the first native Australian to be seen in London. But he lost most of his curiosity value after a year or two, and it was not until the end of 1795 that he returned to Sydney, with the newly appointed governor, John Hunter. By then he fitted neither his old tribal world nor the carceral microcosm of the whites, whose tolerance of the blacks had begun to disintegrate after Phillip's departure. Bennelong became increasingly sodden and pugnacious with rum, and died at the age of about 40 in 1813.

the staple hunting weapons were the spear, the stone axe and the fire-stick.[17]

The Ioras' hunting spears, unlike their fish-gigs, were one-pointed and tipped with a variety of materials—usually fire-hardened wood, but also bones and flints and sometimes a shark tooth. John White, a surgeon on board the transport *Charlotte,* noted that a skilled hunter-warrior threw his spear with formidable accuracy and power, "thirty or forty yards with an unerring precision," although throws of twice that length were recorded. They were flung with a spear-thrower or *woomera,* a stick with a peg in one end that fitted the butt of the spear and acted as an extension of the hunter's arm, like the thong of a sling. With this equipment, a small group of hunters could bring down anything from a bandicoot to an emu. They knocked birds out of the trees with stones or trapped them by dexterity and yogic self-control: "A native will in the heat of the sun lay down asleep, holding a bit of fish in his hand; the bird seeing the bait, seizes on the fish, and the native then catches it."[18]

By any standards, the Aborigines were technologically weak but manually adept. They had not invented the bow-and-arrow, but they had exquisite skill as stalkers, trackers and mimics. A competent hunter needs to be able to read every displacement of a leaf or scuffed print in the dust. He must freeze in mid-step and stand unblinking on one leg for half an hour, waiting for a goanna to work up the courage to come all the way out of its log. He must know how to pick up a blacksnake by the tail and crack its head off, as one cracks a whip. He must climb like a cat, shinnying up the gum trees to raid the wild bees' honey or chop some befuddled nocturnal possum from its hole with a stone axe. Above all, the hunter needed to know every detail of animal life in his territory —migratory patterns, feeding habits, nesting, shelter, mating. Only thus could a small nomadic group survive.

The same was true in the vegetable kingdom, which was the province of women. Like all other known Australian tribes, the Iora forced a rigid sexual division of labor between male hunters and female gatherers. Colonists in the 1790s do not say much about Iora plant-gathering, perhaps because the work of men, even of low savages, seemed more interesting than that of women; thus, one cannot judge the importance plant food had in the Iora diet. We can deduce from the available evidence, however, that the Iora had no conception of agriculture. They neither sowed nor reaped; they appear to have wrought no changes on the face of the country. They were seen as culturally static primitives lightly wandering in an ecologically static landscape, which seemed to eliminate any claims they might have had to prior ownership. To some eighteenth- and nineteenth-century eyes, this invalidated them as human beings.

However, the crude aboriginal technology did wreak changes on the landscape and fauna, for it included fire. Everywhere the tribes went, they carried firesticks and burned many square miles of bushland. They set fire to hollow trees and clubbed the possums and lizards as they scrambled out; they incinerated swathes of bush to drive terrified marsupials onto the waiting spears.

Bushfire and drought are the traditional nightmares of bush life. A bushfire driven by a high wind through dry summer forest is an appalling spectacle: a wreathing cliff of flame moving forward at thirty miles an hour, igniting treetop after treetop like a chain of magnesium flares. Bushfire is the natural enemy of property. But the black Australians had no property and did not hesitate to burn off a few square miles of territory just to catch a dozen goannas and marsupial rats, at the cost of destroying all slow-moving animals within that area.

Fire, to the Iora, was shelter. That was part of the necessary logic of their life, since to survive at all the small knots of family groups that made up the tribe had to range easily and rapidly over a wide area, feeding as they went; and that made the idea of solid, permanent dwellings inconceivable. To them, the hearth was of far greater significance than the home. A firestick made the hearth portable. But they had never had to invent a portable house (i.e., a tent). They were far more backward than any Bedouin or Plains Indian. They used what they could find: the sandstone caves of the harbor shores, with sheets of bark propped up to form crude "humpies." "Their ignorance of building," remarked John Hunter, second captain on *Sirius*,

> is very amply compensated for by the kindness of nature in the remarkable softness of the rocks, which encompass the sea coast . . . They are constantly crumbling away . . . and this continual decay leaves caves of considerable dimensions: some I have seen that would lodge forty or fifty people, and, in a case of necessity, we should think ourselves not badly lodged [in one] for a night.[19]

He was putting the cart before the horse: It was not that the Iora lived in caves because they could not build huts, but rather that they chose not to build huts because they had caves. Another colonial observer grasped why the natives had no architecture a European could recognize:

> . . . Those who build the bark huts are very few compared to the whole. Generally speaking, they prefer the ready made habitations they find in the rocks, which perfectly accords with the roving manner in which they live, for they never stay long in one situation, and as they travel in tribes together, even making the bark huts would engage them more time than they would be happy on one spot.[20]

Caves and bark humpies are drafty places and it gets cold on the harbor at night. The Iora therefore slept huddled together close to their ever-smoldering campfires, and accidental burns were common. The debris of possum skins, fishbones and wallaby guts scattered around the entrance brought swarms of flies and insects, for the tribal "hygiene" of the nomads consisted simply of walking away from their rubbish and excreta (an ancient habit that would have catastrophic results for their marginal descendants, detribalized and trapped in their ghetto shacks on the fringes of white communities a generation or two later). Wherever they went they were plagued by mosquitoes, against which they employed the deterrent of fish oil: "It is by no means uncommon to see the entrails of fish frying upon their heads in the sun, till the oil runs over their face and body. This unguent is deemed by them of so much importance, that children even of two years old are taught the use of it."[21] Since the Iora never washed, they spent their lives coated with a mixture of rancid fish oil, animal grease, ocher, beach sand, dust and sweat. They were filthy and funky in the extreme. But their stamina and muscular development were superb, and, because there was no sugar (except for the rare treat of wild honey) and little starch in their diet, they had excellent teeth—unlike the white invaders.

No property, no money or any other visible medium of exchange; no surplus or means of storing it, hence not even the barest rudiment of the idea of capital; no outside trade, no farming, no domestic animals except half-wild camp dingoes; no houses, clothes, pottery or metal; no division between leisure and labor, only a ceaseless grubbing and chasing for subsistence foods. Certainly the Iora failed most of the conventional tests of white Georgian culture. They did not even appear to have the social divisions that had been observed in other tribal societies such as those in America or Tahiti. Where were the aboriginal kings, their nobles, their priests, their slaves? They did not exist. Although elders enjoyed special respect as the bearers of accumulated tribal myth and lore, they had no special authority over their juniors, once those juniors had reached manhood and been fully initiated; and the idea of hereditary castes was inconceivable to the Aborigines, who lived in a state approaching that of primitive communism. But if the Aborigines lacked firm hierarchical instincts, what was to be respected in their society? What, in short, was "noble" about these "savages"? The Tahitians could be seen as the last survivors of the classical Golden Age; with their fine canoes and intricate ornaments, strict rankings and plentiful supply of free coconuts, they clearly had superfluity, the paradisiacal ancestor of property, as well as strong class instincts to back it up.

Australia was no place for such Ovidian sentiments. The Tahitians might live like prelapsarian beings, illiterate Athenians; compared to them, the Iora were Spartans. They exemplified "hard" primitivism, and the name Phillip gave to a spot in Sydney Harbor alluded to this: "Their confidence and manly behavior," he reported to Lord Sydney, "made me give the name of Manly Cove to this place."[22] Iora boys, like young Spartans at play, practiced incessantly with their spears and woomeras. They believed implicitly in the power of their weapons, and a touching passage in Surgeon John White's *Journal* describes how one of them reacted when he demonstrated his pistol:

> He then, by signs and gestures, seemed to ask if the pistol would make a hole through him, and on being made sensible that it would, he showed not the smallest sign of fear; on the contrary he endeavoured . . . to impress us with an idea of the superiority of his own arms, which he applied to his breast, and by staggering and a show of falling seemed to wish us to understand that the force and effect of them was mortal and not to be resisted.[23]

Skirmishing with other clans, or with foreign tribes along the frontier between tribal territories, was an inevitable fact of nomadic life. In this the Iora were probably no less bellicose than other southeastern Australian tribes, despite the often merely symbolic nature of their encounters. They had no "specialist" army. They recognized no distinction between fighters and civilians, or between hunter and warrior. Moreover, the idea that they were intrinsically violent—"savage" in behavior, as well as in looks and economy—seemed to be borne out by the harsh relationships that obtained within their clans, especially in their treatment of women.

That hoary standby of cartoonists, the Stone Age marriage, in which the grunting Neanderthal bashes the fur-clad girl with his club and drags her off to his cave, began with classical satyrs and medieval legends of forest-dwelling Wild Men. But it was certainly amplified by the first accounts of aboriginal courtship. In a plate in the pseudonymous Barrington's *History of New South Wales*, 1802, it appears for the first time in its perfect form: the muscular savage, club in hand, lugging his unconscious victim through the scrub on her back. "Their conduct to women makes them considerably inferior to the brute creation," the author sternly and titillatingly observes:

> In obtaining a female partner the first step they take, romantic as it may seem, is to fix on some female of a tribe at enmity with their own. . . . The monster then stupefies her with blows, which he inflicts with his club, on her head, back, neck, and indeed every part of her body, then snatching up one of her arms, he drags her, streaming with blood from her wounds, through the woods, over stones, rocks, hills and logs, with all the violence and determination of a savage, till he reaches his tribe.[24]

Obviously, the real matrimonial arrangements of the Iora were less lurid than this. Armed rape as a by-product of tribal warfare was not unknown among the Aborigines, but no tribe that had to depend entirely on border raids for its supply of women could have lasted very long. Besides, what would have been the point? There were enough Iora women for the Iora men. However, the unalterable fact of their tribal life was that women had no rights at all and could choose nothing. A girl was usually given away as soon as she was born. She was the absolute property of her kin until marriage, whereupon she became the equally helpless possession of her husband. The idea of a marriage based on romantic love was as culturally absurd to the Iora as it was to most Europeans. The purpose of betrothal was not, however, to amalgamate property, as in European custom, but to strengthen existing kinship bonds by means of reciprocal favors. It did not change a woman's status much. Both before and after, she was merely a root-grubbing, shell-gathering chattel, whose social assets were wiry arms, prehensile toes and a vagina.

As a mark of hospitality, wives were lent to visitors whom the Iora tribesmen wanted to honor. Warriors, before setting out on a revenge raid against some other aboriginal group, would swap their women as an expression of brotherhood. If a tribal group was about to be attacked and knew where its enemies were, it would sometimes send out a party of women in their direction; the attackers would then show that they were open to a peaceful solution by copulating with them. But if the women came back untouched, it was a signal that there was no choice but battle. A night's exchange of wives usually capped a truce between tribes. On these occasions most kinship laws except the most sacred incest taboos were suspended. Finally, at the great ceremonies or *corroborrees*, which involved hours of chant and ecstatic dancing and were meant to reinforce the tribe's identity by merging all individual egos in one communal mass, orgiastic sex played a part. However, since these affairs were rarely seen, sketchily described and never understood by the early colonists, it is impossible to say how large or how strictly prescribed a part it was.[25] If a woman showed the least reluctance to be used for any of these purposes, if she seemed lazy or gave her lord and master any other cause for dissatisfaction, she would be furiously beaten or even speared.

Fertility, the usual protection of women in settled agricultural societies, was a poor shield. A surplus of children would have impeded the Ioras' nomadic life. On the march, each woman had to carry her infant offspring as well as food and implements. She could only manage one child in arms. That child was always weaned late; it fed from the breast until it was three or more years old, since there were no cows or goats in Australia to give substitute milk. Without their mother's milk, the roughness of the adult diet would have starved them, as there was no way to make a thongy gobbet of barely singed wallaby meat digestible to a teething infant.

To get rid of surplus children, the Iora, like all other Australian tribes, routinely induced abortions by giving the pregnant women herbal medicines or, when these failed, by thumping their bellies. If these measures failed, they killed the unwanted child at birth. Deformed children were smothered or strangled. If a mother died in childbirth, or while nursing a child in arms, the infant would be burned with her after the father crushed its head with a large stone.

This ruthless weeding-out of the helpless at one end of life also took place at the other. The Iora respected their old men as repositories of tribal wisdom and religious knowledge, but the tribe would not hamper its mobility, essential to nomadic survival, by keeping the old and infirm alive after their teeth had gone and their joints had seized up.

It was a harsh code; but it had enabled the Aborigines to survive for millennia without either extending their technology or depleting their resources. It still worked as of January 1788, although it had not the slightest chance of surviving white invasion. The most puzzling question for the whites, however, was why these people should display such a marked sense of territory while having no apparent cult of private property. What was it that bound them to the land? The colonial diarists tried as best they could, hampered by the opacity of a language they could not understand, to discover signs of a developed religion among the blacks, but they found very little to report. "We have not been able to discover," wrote Captain Hunter, "that they have any thing like an object of adoration; neither the sun, moon nor stars seem to take up, or occupy more of their attention, than they do that of any other of the animals [sic] which inhabit this immense country."[26] Certainly they had few of the external signs of religious belief: no temples or altars or priests, no venerated images set up in public places, no evidence of sacrifice or (apart from the corroborrees) of communal prayer. In all this they differed from the Tahitians and the Maori, who were settled agricultural peoples. The Iora were not: they carried their conception of the sacred, of mythic time and ancestral origins with them as they walked. These were embodied in the landscape; every hill and valley, each kind of animal and tree, had its place in a systematic but unwritten whole. Take away this territory and they were deprived, not of "property" (an abstract idea that could be satisfied with another piece of land) but of their embodied history, their locus of myth, their "dreaming." There was no possible way in which the accumulated tissue of symbolic and spiritual usage represented by tribal territory could be gathered up and conferred on another tract of land by an act of will. To deprive the Aborigines of their territory, therefore, was to condemn them to spiritual death—a destruction of their past, their future and their opportunities of transcendence. But none of them could have imagined this, as they had never before been invaded. And so they must have stood, in curiosity and apprehension but without real fear, watching from the headlands as the enormous canoes with their sails like stained clouds moved up the harbor to Sydney Cove, and the anchors splashed, and the outcasts of Mother England were disgorged upon this ancestral territory to build their own prison.

A Horse Foaled by an Acorn

i

M OST EDUCATED PEOPLE have felt twinges of nostalgia for Georgian England.

We are tied to the Georgian past through artifacts that we would still like to use, given the chance. The town houses, squares, villas, gardens, paintings, silver and side tables seem to represent an "essence" of the eighteenth century, transcending "mere" politics. Since they present an uncommonly coherent image of elegance, common sense and clarity, we are apt to suppose that English society did too. But argument from design to society, like the syllogism that ascends from the particular to the general, usually goes awry. "We shall learn," wrote one typical English exponent of this approach, "from the architecture and furniture and all other things . . . that nearly everybody in the eighteenth century looked forward to a continuation and an agreeable expansion of gracious fashions."[1]

"Nearly everybody"—that, until quite recently, was the conventional picture. A passing reference to violence, dirt and gin; a nod in the direction of the scaffold; a highwayman or two, a drunken judge, and some whores for local color; but the rest is all curricles and fanlights. Modern squalor is squalid but Georgian squalor is "Hogarthian," an art form in itself.

Yet most Englishmen and Englishwomen did not live under such roofs, sit on such chairs or eat with such forks. They did not read Johnson or Pope, for most of them could not read. Antiques say little about the English poor, that vast and as yet unorganized social mass—Samuel Johnson's "rabble," Edmund Burke's "swinish multitude"—from whose discontents in the nineteenth century the English working class would shape itself. The Georgian London a modern visitor imagines was not their city. There were two such Londons, their separation symbolized by the cleavage that took place as the rich moved their residences westward

from Covent Garden between 1700 and 1750, as the speculators ran up
their noble squares and crescents—an absolute gulf between the new
West End and the old, rotting East End of the city.

West London had grown rationally. Its streets and squares were
planned; property was secured by long leases and enforced standards of
building. East London had not. It was a warren of shacks, decaying tenements, and brand-new hovels run up on short leases by jerry-builders
restrained by no local ordinances. Georgian residential solidity stopped
at the lower fringe of the middle class. The "rookeries" of the poor
formed a labyrinth speckled with picturesque names: Turnmill Street,
Cow Cross, Chick Lane, Black Boy Alley, Saffron Hill, the Spittle. West
of the old City of London, the worst slum areas in the mid-eighteenth
century lay around Covent Garden, St. Giles, Holborn and the older parts
of Westminster. To the east, they spread through Blackfriars and beyond
the Tower, by the Lower Pool and Limehouse Reach: Wapping, Shadwell,
Limehouse, Ratcliffe Highway, the Jewish ghettos of Stepney and White-
chapel on the north side of the Thames, the brick canyons of Southwark
with its seven prisons on the south bank. Their courts and alleys were
dark, tangled, narrow and choked with offal. Because men had to live
near their work, tenements stood cheek by jowl with slaughterhouses
and tanneries. London was judged the greatest city in the world, but also
the worst smelling. Sewers still ran into open drains; the largest of these,
until it was finally covered in 1765, was the Fleet Ditch. Armies of rats
rose from the tenement cellars to go foraging in daylight.

The living were so crowded that there was scarcely room to bury the
dead. Around St. Martin's, St. James's and St. Giles-in-the-Fields, there
were large open pits filled with the rotting cadavers of paupers whose
friends could get them no better burial; they were called "Poor's Holes"
and remained a London commonplace until the 1790s.

Within the rookeries, distinctions of class were seen. Their cellars
were rented at 9d. or 1s. a week* to the most miserable tenants—rag-
pickers, bonegatherers or the swelling crowd of Irish casual laborers
driven across St. George's Channel by famine, rural collapse and the lure
of the Big City. Thirty people might be found in a cellar. Before 1800 an
artisan might expect to find a "cheap" furnished room in London for 2s.
6d. a week, and most London workers lived in such places with no rights
of tenancy.

To speak of an eighteenth-century "working class" as though it were
a homogeneous entity, united by class-consciousness and solidarity, is

---

* In English currency, d. stands for pence (one penny used to be equivalent to ¹⁄₂₄₀ of a
pound; it is now ¹⁄₁₀₀ of a pound); s. stands for shilling (one shilling is equivalent to ¹⁄₂₀
pound, or 12 pence).

both anachronistic and abstract. It is a projection of the twentieth century onto the eighteenth.

Loyalties ran between workers in the same trade but rarely between workers as such. The variety of trades and work underwrote the complexity of this other London. It contained a huge range of occupations, and a passion for close divisions of social standing held for workers as well as for gentry. They too had their pecking orders and were bound by them. At the upper end of income and comfort, just below the independent shopkeepers, were the skilled artisans in luxury trades, regularly employed: upholsterers and joiners, watch-finishers, coach-painters or lens-grinders. At the lower end were occupations now not only lost but barely recorded: that of the "Pure-finders," for instance, old women who collected dog-turds which they sold to tanneries for a few pence a bucket (the excrement was used as a siccative in dressing fine bookbinding leather). In between lay hundreds of occupations, seasonal or regular. None of them enjoyed any protection, since trade unions and "combinations" were instantly suppressed. There were no wage guarantees, and sweated labor was usual.

Occupational diseases ran rampant. Sawyers went blind young, their conjunctival membranes destroyed by showers of sawdust—hence the difference of status between the "top-notcher," or man on top of the log in the sawpit, and his partner pulling down the saw below. Metalfounders who cast the slugs for Baskerville's elegant type died paralyzed with lead poisoning, and glassblowers' lungs collapsed from silicosis. Hairdressers were prone to lung disease through inhaling the mineral powder used to whiten wigs. The fate of tailors, unchanged until the invention of electric light, was described by one to Henry Mayhew:

> It is not the black clothes that are trying to the sight—black is the steadiest of all colours to work at; white and all bright colours makes the eyes water after looking at 'em for any long time; but of all colours scarlet, such as is used for regimentals, is the most blinding, it seems to burn the eyeballs, and makes them ache dreadful . . . everything seems all of a twitter, and to keep changing its tint. There's more military tailors blind than any others.[2]

Children went to work after their sixth birthday. The Industrial Revolution did not invent child labor, but it did expand and systematize the exploitation of the very young. The reign of George III saw a rising trade in orphans and pauper children, collected from the parish workhouses of London and Birmingham, who were shipped off in thousands to the new industrial centers of Derbyshire, Nottinghamshire and Lancashire. One London child-slave, Robert Blincoe, who was placed in the St. Pancras

Workhouse in 1796 at the age of four and sent off with eighty other abandoned children to the Lambert cotton mill outside Nottingham, gave testimony to a Parliamentary committee on child labor some forty years later:

Q. Do you have any children?—Three.

Q. Do you send them to factories?—No; I would rather have them transported. . . . I have seen the time when two hand-vices of a pound weight each, more or less, have been screwed to my ears, at Lytton mill in Derbyshire. These are the scars still remaining behind my ears. Then three or four of us have been hung at once on a cross-beam above the machinery, hanging by our hands, without shirts or stockings. Then we used to stand up, in a skip, without our shirts, and be beaten with straps or sticks; the skip was to prevent us from running away from the straps. . . . Then they used to tie up a 28-pounds weight, one or two at once, according to our size, to hang down our backs, with no shirt on.[3]

Doctors tended to side with their class allies, the factory-owners, and went on record again and again with their considered opinions that cotton lint, coal dust and phosphorus were harmless to the human lung, that fifteen hours at a machine in a room temperature of 85 degrees did not cause fatigue, that ten-year-olds could work a full night shift without risk of harm. Employers, naturally, resisted the very thought of reform. Some of them were cultivated men like Josiah Wedgwood, uncle to Charles Darwin and heir to his father's great pottery in Staffordshire, who employed 387 people—13 under ten years old, 103 between ten and eighteen—in such work as dipping ware in a glaze partly composed of lead oxide, a deadly poison which, as he admitted, made them "very subject to disease," though no more so than plumbers or painters. Yet "I have a strong opinion," Wedgwood told the Peel Committee in 1816, "that, from all I know at present of manufactories in general, and certainly from all I know of my own, we had better be left alone."[4]

Of all the testimony offered to the Royal Commissions on factory labor, there is perhaps none more chilling than the evidence of Joseph Badder, a children's overseer in a Leicester mill, to the Factory Commission of 1833. It has a prophetic ring: Here, the factory-induced dystopic visions of man as automaton that would run from Mary Shelley's *Frankenstein, or The Modern Prometheus* (1818) to Fritz Lang's *Metropolis* (1926) are made pitiably concrete:

I used to beat them. . . . I told them I was very sorry after I had done it, but I was forced to it. The masters expected me to do my work, and I could not do mine unless the children did theirs. Then I used to joke with them to keep up their spirits.

I have seen them fall asleep, and they have been performing their work with their hands until they were asleep, after the billy had stopped, when their work was over. I have stopped and looked at them for two minutes, going through the motions of piecening fast asleep, when there was really no work to do, and when they were really doing nothing.[5]

Such flat and distant voices confirm the rhetoric of William Blake: "Grace" is underwritten by constant, speechless suffering, and "culture" begins in the callused hands of exhausted children, weaving robotically in sleep, "going through the motions . . . when they were really doing nothing." For the first time in human history, the machine dictates the term of organic existence to its servants; the body becomes an inferior machine. If respectability was to be judged by people's endurance of such work, there is no surprise in the growth of crime. In a sense, the children of the mills were inoculated against the dread of punishment; "they appeared as complete prisoners as they would be in gaol," remarked one observer to the Peel Committee.[6]

But mill labor, at least, was regular and gave fairly steady employment. Not all workers in London had such a prospect. Home industries like weaving were prostrated by industrial competition. To be whipsawed between long work-hours and patches of unemployment was deeply demoralizing. As Francis Place found, it bred the familiar torpor of the laid-off:

I know not how to describe the sickening aversion which at times steals over the working man, and utterly disables him for a longer or shorter time from following his usual occupation, and compels him to *idleness.* I have felt it. I have been obliged to submit and run away from my work. This is the case with every workman I have known; and in such proportion as a man's case is hopeless will such fits occur and be of longer duration.[7]

A common solace was gin. After 1720 this white grain spirit flavored with crushed juniper berries became England's national stupefacient, the heroin of the eighteenth century (but worse, because its use was far wider). Brandy, port, claret and Madeira, the rich man's four tipples, were taxed on import and no workingman could afford them. But gin was made in England and cost next to nothing: "Drunk for a penny, dead drunk for twopence" meant what it said. Its consumption was eagerly promoted by the landed gentry, because England nearly always had a surplus of corn, which gin-distilling used up. Consequently there were no restrictions of any kind on making or selling the liquor until the Gin

Act of 1751, by which time London was said to have one gin-shop for every 120 citizens. By 1743 the laboring poor of England were consuming 8 million gallons of gin a year, and they presented a most squalid appearance: "Lazy, sotted and brutish by nature," a French visitor called them in 1777.[8] The contrast between the new, degraded "mob," sodden with gin, and the honest peasantry, merry with ale, was by now a commonplace with every moralist up to and including William Hogarth, who gave it memorable form in his engravings *Gin Lane* and *Beer Street*.

The "mob," as the urban proletariat was called, had become an object of terror and contempt, but little was known about it. It was seen as a malign fluid, a sort of magma that would burst through any crack in law and custom, quick to riot and easily inflamed to crime by rabble-rousers. This moral prejudice affected most efforts to find out about English crime and English poverty.

Thus Patrick Colquhoun, in his *Treatise on the Police of the Metropolis* (1797), made one of the first attempts to gauge the number of criminals in George III's London. He claimed that there were 115,000 people living off crime in the city—about one Londoner in eight, which constituted a "criminal class" in itself. But who were they, and what did they do? Colquhoun lumped thieves, muggers and forgers, who clearly were criminals, together with scavengers, bear-baiters and gypsies, who were not, or at least not clearly so. He estimated that there were 50,000 "harlots" in London—about 6 percent of its population—but, as Edward P. Thompson pointed out, "[Colquhoun's] prostitutes turn out, on closer inspection, to be 'lewd and immoral women', including 'the prodigious number among the lower classes who cohabit together without marriage' (and this at a time when divorce for women was an absolute impossibility)."[9] If the same criteria of whoredom were applied to London today, how many "harlots" would a modern Colquhoun find?

The fact that their superiors *thought* that such people were prostitutes is no guide: In social matters, Georgian Englishmen far preferred generalization to reportage, and there was no eighteenth-century Mayhew. A Spitalfields weaver, an Irish casual laborer and a Scottish ditch-digger might not even understand one another's speech, let alone share any aspirations; but seen from above they all belonged to the "mobbish class of persons." The "mob" was Georgian society's id—the sump of forbidden thoughts and proscribed actions, the locus of the raging will to survive. Amid the general fear of Jacobinism that swept England after the French Revolution, it would seem an even greater menace. Then, the issues of crime and of revolution became conflated, and so the rising crime-rate—or rather, the belief that it was rising—became a potent issue. Accordingly, the Georgian legislators fought back against a threat which they believed came from a whole class. The criminal became the dreaded *sans-culotte*'s cousin. Georgian fear of the "mob" led to Victorian belief in a "criminal class." Against both, the approved weapon was a form of legal terrorism.

ii

THE BELIEF in a swelling wave of crime was one of the great social facts of Georgian England. It shaped the laws, and the colonization of Australia was its partial result.

Sending criminals to the far Antipodes was like sending them from one disagreeably fabled land to another. The slum areas of London seemed a foreign country of crime, and in 1751 Henry Fielding reflected that

> had they been intended for the very purpose of concealment, they could hardly have been better contrived. Upon such a view, [London] appears as a fast wood or forest, in which a Thief may harbour with as great security, as wild beasts do in the deserts of Africa or Arabia.[10]

Crime was up in the countryside, too; "Our people have become what they never were before, cruel and inhuman."[11] The reasons, Fielding thought, were gin, gambling and the love of "luxury" that had caused men and women to reject their traditional stations, even among "the very dregs of the people." The helpless begged, while those "of more art and courage" stole. The innocent lived in a state of siege.

A quarter of a century later, things seemed no better. In 1775 Jonas Hanway indignantly exclaimed that

> I sup with my friend; I cannot return to my home, not even in my chariot, without danger of a pistol being clapt to my breast. I build an elegant villa, ten or twenty miles distant from the capital: I am obliged to provide an armed force to convey me thither, lest I should be attacked on the road with fire and ball.[12]

Two centuries later one can see broader reasons for this growth of crime. English society was violently changing, under the stresses of industrialization, the growth of towns, and a soaring birthrate. From 1700 to 1740, the population of England and Wales remained almost constant at about 6 million people. Then it started rising fast—so fast that between 1750 and 1770 the population of London doubled—and by 1851 it stood at 18 million. This meant that the median age of Englishmen kept dropping and the labor market was saturated with the young. No mechanisms existed for the effective relief of mass unemployment; it was not a problem England had ever before had to contend with on this scale. The Poor Laws had been written for a different England. Parish relief and the workhouse were the primitive devices of a pre-industrial society; now they were overwhelmed. But crime is, was and always will be a young man's trade, and English youth, rootless and urban, took to it with a will.

They found easy pickings, especially since Georgian England had none of the tools for catching criminals that the twentieth century takes for granted. Official crime records and registers of criminals were primitive, and there would be no fingerprinting until 1885. Artists made sketches, for popular consumption, of famous offenders like Dick Turpin or Jack Sheppard, but one could no more recognize a felon from such semi-devotional effigies than pick St. Paul from a crowd by consulting a Byzantine icon. Identification of wanted men had to be made from verbal descriptions in the police gazettes, circulated to mayors and magistrates after the early 1770s: "*Benjamin Bird*, a tall thin man, pale complexion, black hair tied, thick lips, the nail of the forefinger of his right hand is remarkably clumsy, comes from Coventry, and is charged with several forgeries, the last at Liverpool . . ." Sketchy as they were, such descriptions did produce some arrests, mainly in villages where people noticed strangers. Some officers of the law had long memories. Henry Fielding's sightless half-brother John, a magistrate known at Bow Street as the "Blind Beak," was said to be able to identify 3,000 different malefactors by their voices alone. But on the whole, it was easier for criminals to escape scot-free in the 1780s than it would ever be again.

There was one main reason for this: England had no effective, centralized police force and would not form one until Peel's Police Act of June 1829. Law and order on the street was left to the parishes and wards; hence those enfeebled butts of every street urchin, the "Charlies" or parish watchmen. There were about 2,000 of them in London in the late eighteenth century, "poor old decrepit people" as Fielding bluntly put it, charity cases who had cast themselves on the mercy of the parish because they no longer had the strength to do other work. From the parish, each Charley got a greatcoat with three capes, like a coachman's; a lantern, to light his tottering progress through the alleys; a wooden rattle to summon help; and a staff to defend himself. He would bang its butt rhythmically against the cobbles as he walked, to give thieves plenty of warning. Thus the embarrassment of a meeting between Law and Crime could be averted. He was easily bribed, with sixpence or a quart of gin. Charley's deterrent power was therefore slight.

In practice, the magistrates preferred an older way of catching suspects: a graduated scale of rewards for information. This reward system was the eighteenth century's chief way of detecting crime. It pressed private enterprise into service against its Other, the criminal. The pickings were large enough to support a whole subclass of informers, police narks and thief-takers. Suspects could bribe the informer not to lay information against them. Thus there was hardly a petty trade conducted in the London alleys whose members did not sell gin on the side, and few of them bothered to pay—or could afford—the price of a liquor license. Instead, they paid the nark £10 or so not to denounce them. If paid by the courts, informers could squeeze sap from every twig of the huge, ramifying tree of English criminal law. Nineteen separate offenses relating to the use of hackney coaches in London carried a reward of 50 shillings for informants; from there to the exalted levels of murder and grand larceny, each crime carried its reward.

One could grow prosperous by informing, but not rich. The larger profits went to a more daring and astute kind of professional, the thief-takers. In theory, the thief-taker was no mere informer. He tracked down criminals and, at his own risk, intrepidly brought them to court. He was the eighteenth-century ancestor of the private eye, a detective with no official standing and, of course, no police protection. No niceties about laws of evidence or suspects' rights governed the thief-takers' forays into the "alsatias" (criminal purlieus) of London. They had a vested interest in fostering crime, for it kept up the flow of rewards. By playing both ends against the middle, they invented a new pattern of English felonry, thus presenting the good Georgian citizenry with a new and extraordinarily threatening spectacle: organized crime. The archetype of the thief-taker had been Jonathan Wild (1683–1725).[13]

The perception of organized crime would not go away, and in time it became more and more frightening to property-owners. A single criminal could be singly met. The householder, armed with blunderbuss and paired horse-pistols, defended by locks, grilles, bells, man-traps and loyal servants, could drive him away. But a collective of thugs and thieves, a united "criminal class" working together in gangs—that was quite another matter. It was a largely fantastical notion, exaggerated and nourished by deep-rooted territorial instincts. Gangs certainly existed in Georgian England, but they were only responsible for a fraction of the deeds that the law defined as criminal. Crime was still a cottage industry, a jumble of individual acts of desperation. The failure of language—the tyranny of moral generalization over social inspection—fed the ruling class's belief that it was endangered from below.

iii

YET THE PEOPLE who had most to gain from a police force opposed its founding, tooth and nail. Despite the unrest that smoldered in England throughout the eighteenth century—the mobs at Tyburn, the Penlez riots of 1749, the Wilkite riots of the 1760s and the Gordon riots of 1780—there was no concerted Parliamentary move to set up a police force until the nineteenth century was a quarter gone. Georgian authorities preferred to rely on thief-takers for dealing with individuals, the Riot Act and the militia for dealing with groups. This was a source of wonder to foreigners, especially the French. "From sunset to dawn," wrote one such visitor in 1784, "the environs of London become the patrimony of brigands for twenty miles around," but the government did not improve the police because it was hampered by "clashes of interest" between people and King.[14] When the Duc de Levis asked his friends in 1814 why they had no *maréchaussée*—the rural police, the powers of arbitrary pursuit and arrest, that had all but stamped out brigandage in the French provinces—he was firmly told that "such an institution is not compatible with liberty."

There lay the nub. The English refused to create a regular police force because they had seen what lay across the Channel, where no Frenchman's home was his castle. "I had rather half-a-dozen peoples' throats be cut in the Ratcliffe Highway every three or four years," wrote one returned traveller, "than be subject to the domiciliary visits, spies and the rest of Fouche's contrivances."[15]

There were limits, of course, to this bluff libertarian attitude, and they showed up wherever the issue of class was involved. Those who opposed a police force did so from concern for the rights of property, not those of suspects. Modern precedents governing arrest and search, such as the *Miranda* decision, would have struck them as insanely favorable to the criminal. There was distress at the "tenderness" of the English legal system. "The regard shown to offenders falls little short of respect," complained Sir John Hawkins, a Middlesex magistrate of the 1760s.[16] Georgian justice may look fierce to us, but seen from Europe then it was lenient. The suspect had basic rights not recognized in France, Italy or Germany: He could not be tortured until he confessed; he could not be held indefinitely without bail or trial; and he was innocent until proven guilty. The liberalism of the English Common Law, compared to their own systems based on Roman and Canon Law, astonished European visitors. They noticed that, although it reduced the likelihood of an innocent man's conviction, it also made it easier for the guilty to escape.

The English knew this, too; hence the draconic laws they created to avenge their sense of a disturbed social order. Against the relative fairness of British trials, one must set the most striking aspect of Georgian law—the sheer scope of its capital statutes. If detection and arrest were feeble and trials tenderly fair, what punishment could keep men from crime? Only the extreme one: hanging without benefit of clergy. During the reigns of the first three Georges, law enacted death upon what seemed a limitless variety of human deeds, from infanticide to "impersonating an Egyptian" (posing as a gypsy). Between the enthronement of Charles II in 1660 and the middle of George IV's reign in 1819, 187 new capital statutes became law—nearly six times as many as had been enacted in the previous three hundred years. Nearly all were drafted to protect property, rather than human life; attempted murder was classed only as a "misdemeanor" until 1803. These grapeshot laws scattered death impartially. Why must forgers hang? Because the increase of paper transactions in eighteenth-century banking and business—checks, notes, bonds, shares, as distinct from concrete transfer of bags of gold—had made property of all sorts more vulnerable to forgery. Why was it death to "steal an heiress"? Because, like a queen bee swollen with jelly, an heiress was property incarnate; her abductor went to the gallows not for rape but for his theft of a family's accumulated goods and rights.

Some capital statutes were very broad. The most notorious of them was 9 Geo. I, c. 22, otherwise known as the Waltham Black Act. It had been drafted ostensibly to repress some minor agrarian uprisings in 1722–23 near Waltham Chase in Hampshire, where rural laborers, moving at night with blacked faces, had taken to poaching game and fish, burning hayricks and posting threatening letters on their landlords' gates. The act, passed by the Commons without a murmur of dissent, prescribed the gallows for over two hundred possible offenses in various permutations. One could be hanged for burning a house or a hut, a standing rick of corn, or an insignificant pile of straw; for poaching a rabbit, for breaking down "the head or mound" of a fishpond, or even cutting down an ornamental shrub; or for appearing on a high-road with a sooty face. As Sir Leon Radzinowicz remarked, "The Act constituted in itself a complete and extremely severe criminal code which indiscriminately punished with death a great many different offences, without taking into account either the personality of the offender or the particular circumstances of each offence."[17]

Such legislation was part of a general tendency in eighteenth-century England: the growth of the Rule of Law (as distinct from any particular statute) into a supreme ideology, a form of religion which, it has since been argued, began to replace the waning moral power of the Church of England.[18]

Like the Church, Law had its own diction and rituals and its own priests—bewigged men in scarlet and ermine. At the assizes, the judge's rolling sermons on vice and virtue, his reprobations, didactic asides and calls to repentance, were the secular equivalent of that pulpit eloquence which, in the seventeenth century, had shaken and fascinated those who thronged to hear the great preachers like John Donne or George Cokayne. Well into the nineteenth century, hanging verdicts continued to produce extremes of emotion, on both sides of the bench, that would be hard to match today. When two agricultural protestors named Peter Withers and James Lush were sentenced to death at the Salisbury assizes in 1831, a reporter from the *Dorset County Chronicle* described how

there were . . . no dry eyes in the crowded court. The tears of pity, of compassion, of regret, at the necessity of such severity were to be seen flowing and chasing one another down the cheeks not merely of the spectators, but of those who had long been accustomed to hear the last dreadful sentence which a human being has the power of passing on a fellow-creature in this world. [The judges] were frequently obliged to rest their faces on their extended hands, and even then the large drops were to be seen falling in quick succession. . . . Every one [of the prisoners] was in a state of dreadful agitation—some sobbing aloud and others with a pallid cheek . . . [After the death sentence] their mothers, their sisters, and their children clasped them in their arms with an agonizing grasp—the convicts . . . gave way, they wept like children . . . Nature had begun to play with every force, and the heart was broken.[19]

Why did the judges weep with the accused? Because both were bound —though not, of course, in equality of pain—to the law. This drama of immutable rules lay at the heart of the tremendous power that Law held over the English imagination. The judge simply surrendered to the imperative of the statutes, a course of action that absolved him of judicial murder, and that caused him to weep. His tears humbled him not before the men in the dock, which would have been unthinkable, but before the idea of Law itself. When the Royal Mercy intervened as it commonly did, transmuting the death penalty into exile on the other side of the world, the accused and their relatives could bless the intervening power of patronage while leaving the superior operations of Law unquestioned. The law was a disembodied entity, beyond class interest: the god in the codex. The judge was invested with its numen, as a priest was touched by sacerdotal power. But he could no more change the law than a clergyman could rewrite the Bible. All men were equal before the law, and none might evade its reach. It might demand the death of a poor ten-year-old boy, but noblemen could and did hang as well. The famous one was Lord Ferrers, who in a fit of paranoid suspicion blew his steward's brains out in 1760. Convicted and sentenced to hang, the peer made his journey to Tyburn in a landau drawn by six horses, wearing a white wedding-suit sumptuously encrusted with silver embroidery; thousands of people cheered him over the drop. This, as upholders of the Law's impartiality were given to stress, was equality indeed.

i v

NOTHING IN English criminal law seems more disgusting than public hanging. We are apt to think of it as the very saturnalia of death: a man or woman carted through the screaming mob that lined the road from Newgate to Tyburn, and then killed by a civil servant while more pockets were picked around the scaffold than the victim had picked in his life.[20]

Yet the official view of hanging was the very opposite. The Georgian lawmakers believed that public execution would reform those who saw it. A writer in 1772 recounted how parents would bring their children to a hanging and flog them afterward "that they might remember the example they had seen."[21] The scaffold was the altar of a ritual whose aim was to fill society with moral awe. This expiatory theater, solemn and fatal, deserved the widest audience.

To a well-anticipated hanging, if the victims were famous—a Jack Sheppard, a Lord Ferrers—twenty-five thousand people might come. Thirty thousand are said to have attended the execution of the twin brothers Perreau (for forgery) in 1776, and in 1767, eighty thousand people—or about one Londoner in ten—flocked to a hanging in Moorefields.[22] Against this may be set the extreme unreliability of Georgian statistics. Nevertheless, hanging was clearly the most popular mass spectacle in England; nothing could match the drawing-power of the gallows or its grip as a secular image.

Hence the importance of the ritual. On the eve of Tyburn Fair (one of the colloquial names for execution-day at Tyburn gallows), it began with a prayer intoned by the sexton of the parish church of Newgate prison, St. Sepulchre's, addressed to the occupants of its condemned hold, the Stone Room:

> You prisoners that lie within, who for wickedness and sin, after many mercies shown you, are now appointed to die tomorrow in the forenoon, give ear and understand that tomorrow morning the greatest bell of St. Sepulchre's shall toll for you in form and measure of a passing bell, as used to be tolled for those at the point of death, to the end that all godly people, hearing that bell and knowing that it is for your going and your deaths, may be stirred up heartily to pray to God . . .[23]

With the morning came the minatory prayers, the hoarse clanging bells and the procession westward along the busiest streets of London, from Newgate to Tyburn, the present site of Marble Arch. Each condemned man sat in the cart facing the rising sun, with a noose bound to his chest. At the gallow's foot, phrase by halting phrase, he had to recite Psalm 51, the "Hanging Psalm":

> Behold, I was brought forth in iniquity,
> and in sin did my mother conceive me.
>
> Behold, thou desirest truth in the inward being,
> therefore teach me wisdom in my secret heart.
> Purge me with hyssop, and I shall be clean;
> wash me, and I shall be whiter than snow.
> Fill me with joy and gladness;
> let the bones which thou hast broken rejoice.
> Hide thy face from my sins . . .

Sometimes he would append a conventional speech of repentance, known as the "dismal ditty." Then came the donning of the white shroud, an undignified and spectral garment like a coarse nightgown; the climb up the ladder; the choking drop.

But what did the lower classes think of this spectacle staged for their benefit? There is much to suggest that the panoply of Tyburn was not taken in a proper spirit by the "mobbish class of Persons." Hanging had two languages. The official one was elevated and abstract: A hanged man "paid the supreme penalty," "suffered the ultimate exaction of the Law," or was "launch'd into Eternity." But there was also a vast gallows argot, for, next to those hardy perennials sex, money and crime, nothing on the social horizon of the English poor produced more slang and cant than hanging. Not a word of it reflects the official solemnities. Terse in its irony, bitter in its defiant concreteness, it rejected the values of the Law and its makers.

A condemned man "died with cotton in his ears" because Cotton was the name of the praying sexton at Newgate. The hangman was Jack Ketch, the nubbing-cove, the crap merchant, the crapping cull, the switcher, the cramper, the sheriff's journeyman, the gaggler, the topping-cove, the roper or the scragger. Tyburn being in the parish of Paddington, execution-day was also known as Paddington Fair, the hood drawn over one's head on the scaffold was the Paddington spectacles, and in dying one danced the Paddington frisk.

Some hangmen bequeathed their names to the rite. In the 1770s a man would be "dempstered," and around 1785 the gallows briefly became the Gregorian tree, after a London hangman named Gregory Brandon. But its other names were legion. The Being a construction of three posts linked by cross-bars, the gallows was the three-legged mare, and to ascend it was to "climb three trees with a ladder"; being made of oak, it was the wooden mare, and to die on it was to "ride a horse foaled by an acorn." It was the morning drop, the trining-cheat, the nubbing-cheat, the scragging-post, or, in a laconic parody of the pastoral mode, "the deadly Nevergreen that bears the fruit all the year round." The noose was a horse's nightcap, a Tyburn tippet, a hempen casement or an anodyne necklace. Before the invention of the hinged trapdoor through which the victim dropped, he or she was "turned off" or "twisted" by the hangman who pulled the ladder away. To ascend it was "to go up the ladder to bed," "to take a leap in the dark." Some names for this death were bald: to stretch, to squeeze, to be jammed or frummagemed or haltered. Others referred to epidemic disease: "to die of a hempen quinsey or a hempen fever." "To be in a deadly suspense" predicts the nudging humor of the music hall, as does another elaborate Cockney locution for hanging: "to have a hearty choke [artichoke] and caper sauce for breakfast." The most chilling are the phrases that evoke the solitude and sterility of public death: "dance upon nothing," "take the earth bath," "shake a cloth in the wind," "go off at the fall of a leaf." Or, because of the noises and grimaces a strangling person makes: "to cry cockles," "to piss when you can't whistle," "to loll your tongue out at the company."[24]

This is not the language of the penitent thief. Its brusque, canting defiance reminds one that hanging meant one thing to the judges but another to the poor and the "mob." Samuel Johnson objected to the "fury of innovation" in the movement to abolish public hanging. "Executions are intended to draw spectators," the Rambler grumbled. "If they do not draw spectators, they do not answer to their purpose. The old method was most satisfactory to all parties; the public was gratified by a procession; the criminal was supported by it."[25]

The idea that condemned men could draw solace and support from the crowd at their hanging offends our deepest sense of propriety about death. It seems unspeakably grotesque. Nevertheless, they did. There are many accounts of young men setting forth in the Tyburn coach dressed like bridegrooms in new white suits emblematic of innocence, ribbons fluttering from their hats, posies in their white-gloved hands, cockily saluting a crowd that showered them, not with dead rats and cabbages, but with fruit and flowers in tribute to their passing. This was a common enough sight for Swift to take for granted:

As clever Tom Clinch, while the Rabble was bawling,
Rode stately through Holbourn to die in his Calling;
He stopt at the George for a bottle of Sack,

And Promis'd to pay for it when he came back.
His Waiscoat and Stockings, and Breeches were white,
His cap had a new Cherry Ribbon tied to it.
The Maids to the Doors and the Balconies ran,
And said, lack-a-day! he's a proper young Man.
But, as from the windows the Ladies he spied,
Like a Beau in a Box, he bow'd low on each Side.[26]

As early as 1701 a pamphleteer was complaining that the condemned rode to Tyburn in bright clothes "like Men that triumph," as though the journey of shame were the parade of a Caesar.[27] A man's bearing on the cart and at Tyburn was discussed like the form of a boxer at a prizefight. The phlegm of English malefactors was renowned in Europe, whose criminals tended to beg and blubber or become reduced to bovine passivity when confronted by their executioners. One admiring Italian felt that the English faced the gallows *come se andasse a Nozze . . . colla più soave indifferenza nel Mondo*, "as if going to be married, with the calmest indifference in the world."[28] The crowd wanted to see this and supported those who showed it. A "Tyburn blossom" must be an exemplary dandy, trim, gay and uncaring.

Hanging crowds were unruly. Hogarth's engraving *The Idle Prentice Executed at Tyburn* gives a powerful sense of them: the crush of jostling voyeurs, a trampled child, squabbling fruit-sellers, pamphleteers hawking the just-printed "Last Dying Speech and Confession"—a turgid mass of drunks, whores, cripples, gospellers, pikemen and building-workers from the new West End squares nearby, parting to make way for the fatal cart. Beside the scaffold rises a grandstand that belonged to a famous scalper, the Widow Proctor, who made £500 in one day selling seats for Lord Ferrers's hanging.

People also went to Tyburn to mourn, to reclaim the body of their friend or relative, to give the corpse its due dignity. They waited below the gallows to retrieve it in order to give it a proper burial and did not hesitate to fight the sheriff's officers for it. The law did not recognize the relatives' rights to a hanged corpse. It gave the body to the Royal College of Physicians for dissection, which heaped further ignominy on the dead. Thus there was a continuous record of brawls and riots at Tyburn and other English places of execution, as the "mob" battled with the surgeons' corpse-takers for possession of bodies. And, as Peter Linebaugh remarked,

When brickmakers came out to defend the bodies of two felons with several years' good standing in the trade against the surgeons, when bargemen came down from Reading to guard one of their own at a hanging, when the hackney coachmen rallied to keep the body of a fellow coach-man "from being carried off with Violence," or when the small cottagers and market people of Shoreditch surrounded the tumbril of Thomas Pinks their neighbour in the village, "declaring that they had no other Intention, but to take care of the Body for Christian burial," the evidence . . . shows the depth of the mutuality of the poor, their solidarity in the face of personal disaster.[29]

This solidarity, as Dr. Johnson perceived, gave support to the condemned. Public execution, meant to terrify the populace, enabled the "mob" to show its defiance of authority. How mulish, the scientific onlooker might say, to deny the science of medicine its rights of progress by way of the bodies of the poor! What anatomical Luddism! What counted, however, was that the laboring poor of England gave the rituals their own meaning, quite at odds with its official one.

At this distance, one cannot say whether public hanging did terrify people away from crime. Nor can anyone do so, until we can count crimes that were never committed. Probably some people in the Tyburn crowds did fear hanging more for having seen it. Despite (or, from another point of view, because of) the intimidating ferocity of the statutes, there were more than twice as many capital convictions in the London and Middlesex courts in the 1780s as there had been in the 1750s. This does not prove, however, that capital punishment failed to deter anyone. Population had grown, poverty was worse, and there might have been even more crime if some people were not frightened by the gallows.

But one fact is certain. As the eighteenth century went on, fewer people were actually hanged for capital crimes that they had been convicted of. In ten-year periods, the figures for London and Middlesex (the area of highest crime) are:[30]

DECADE	CAPITAL CONVICTIONS	EXECUTIONS	PERCENTAGE
1749–58	527	365	69.3
1759–68	372	206	55.4
1769–78	787	357	45.4
1779–88	1152	531	46.1
1789–98	770	191	24.8
1799–1808	804	126	15.7

Why did the English write their fatal laws and then not use them to the full? One answer is squeamishness: Judges and juries simply frustrated the hanging statutes out of decency. A judge would commute the death sentence on a suitably penitent felon, while juries (and sometimes even prosecutors) cheated the gallows by deliberately undervaluing stolen goods. Thus, hundreds of convictions were handed down every year for thefts of goods that juries valued at 39 shillings, not because that was their actual value, but because the law said that anyone who stole above 40 shillings in a house or on a highway must hang. However, there would not have been so many remissions if they had not been encouraged by an active intent to exercise mercy.[31]

George III took the exercise of the Royal Prerogative of Mercy (the King's power to override his courts and remit a sentence at will) very seriously. The Royal Mercy showed his subjects that their monarch cared about them. One besought it by letter, through the home secretary, enclosing whatever references and sub-petitions could be raised from clergymen and other respectable people, and it was quite often given. The laws were the stick, mercy the carrot. There was subtlety in maintaining the hanging laws but not automatically using them. If they had merely been repealed, the effect would not have been the same. For mercy to evoke gratitude, the ruler must be seen to *choose* mercy, so that each reprieve is a special case, to be paid for in gratitude and obedience, never taken as a right.[32]

Moreover, the Royal Mercy and judicial commutation of sentences kept the crossroads of England from being decorated with scores and scores of corpses—a sight that could have provoked general riots. But what could the courts do with the convicts? The less rope was used, the more jails were needed. Yet eighteenth-century England was short of jails.

v

THE ONES it had were old. They had changed little since the Middle Ages. Their archetype in London was Newgate, which began its career in the twelfth century as a city gatehouse strengthened to hold prisoners and ended after almost eight hundred years of service and four rebuildings, with demolition in 1903. Newgate's walls were of a Piranesian thickness, and there was virtually no way past its labyrinth of dark cells, subterranean corridors and iron bars as thick as a navvy's wrist. To escape from this accursed place—especially from its condemned cell, the Stone Room—was to achieve immediate celebrity in the London underworld. Newgate was called the "whit" or "wit," and all flash lads drank to its destruction. "The Wit be burnt," ran a common criminal toast, "the Flogging Cull [flogger] be damned, the Nubbing Chit [gallows] be curs'd." The debtor's section of Newgate was called "Tangier," because of the miseries suffered by English prisoners of Arab pirates on the Barbary Coast; its inmates, some abandoned by the outside world for ten years over a matter of a few shillings, were "tangerines."

Inside Newgate one simply rotted away, staring through the bars (or, as the phrase went, "polishing the King's iron with your eyebrows"). No work was done there. The central idea of the Victorian penitentiary, as proposed by Bentham and his Panopticon and first tried in Philadelphia —that prison should be a place of isolation, discipline and systematically graded punishment alleviated by precise injections of hope—was quite new and untried in the reign of George III. It affected neither the way judges thought about sentences, nor the manner in which prisons were run. The project of creating a captive society within the state, populated by convicts fed and housed at public expense and repaying an offended world (however nominally) with forced labor—in short, the idea of the penitentiary as it developed after 1820—would have struck the rules of Georgian England as utterly chimerical. Jails were simply lockups, and no one was "improved" by a spell in one. They were holes in which prisoners could be forgotten for a while. Their purpose was not reform, but terror and sublimation. But they were also meant to turn a profit.

About half the jails of England were privately owned and run. Chesterfield Jail belonged to the Duke of Portland, who sublet it to a keeper for 18 guineas a year. The Bishop of Ely owned a prison, the Bishop of Durham had the Durham County Jail, and Halifax Jail belonged to the Duke of Leeds. Their jailers were not State employees but small businessmen—malignant landlords—who made their profits by extorting money from prisoners. On entering the Bishop of Ely's lockup, a prisoner was chained down to the floor with a spiked collar riveted round his neck until he disgorged a fee for "easement of irons." Any jailer could load any prisoner with as many fetters as he pleased and charge for their removal one at a time. The "trade of chains" though often denounced as a national disgrace, survived well into the 1790s.

One paid for food, for drink—the prison tap room, dispensing gin, was a prime source of income for jailers—for bedding, water and even air. A well-off prisoner could live in some ease (although nothing could buy him immunity from typhus, the endemic disease of eighteenth-century prisons). For poorer men, the system was crushing. The entrance fee at Newgate was 3s., the weekly "rent" 2s. 6d., the charge for sharing a straw mattress with another prisoner 1s 6d a week. These sums sound small, but they often represented the full amount for which a debtor or thief had been clapped in prison, and there was little or no hope of earning them inside. "The prisoners have neither tools nor materials of any kind," wrote John Howard, the pioneer of penal reform, in the 1770s, but spend their time in sloth, profaneness and debauchery . . . Some keepers of these houses, who have represented to magistrates the wants of their prisoners, and desired for them necessary food, have been silenced with the inconsiderate words, *Let them work or starve.* When these gentlemen know the former is impossible, do they not by that sentence inevitably doom poor creatures to the latter?[33]

Howard travelled all over collecting material for his monumental report, *The State of the Prisons in England and Wales* (1777). He drew a detailed picture of this hidden world, of which the respectable and literate knew nothing—its crowding, darkness and scant rations, the cruel indifference of the Bench and the venal favoritism of wardens, the garnish and chummage and easement fees, the cell floors awash with sewage, the utter lack of medical care, the fatal epidemics. Even the air was unbreathable. Howard discovered that

my cloaths were in my first journeys so offensive, that in a post-chaise I could not bear the windows drawn up: and was therefore obliged to travel on horseback. The leaves of my memorandum-book were often so tainted, that I could not use it till after spreading it an hour or two before the fire: and even my antidote, a vial of vinegar, has after using it in a few prisons, become intolerably disagreeable.[34]

The idea that prisons could not reform criminals but were incubators of crime was the merest commonplace in the 1780s; everyone, magistrates included, took it for granted. There was no attempt to classify or segregate prisoners by age, sex or gravity of crime. Women were thrown in the same common ward as men, first offenders with hardened recidivists, inoffensive civil debtors with muggers, clerkly forgers with murderers, ten-year-old boys with homosexual rapists. All prisoners, authority thought, were united by the common fact of their malignant otherness. They had crime in common, and that was enough. There was no need for fine distinctions in the black hole.

The common simile for the prison was a monastery or seminary, a closed order of people who studied vice, not holiness—an appealing figure in its perfect inversion. To Henry Fielding in 1751, prisons were "no other than . . . seminaries of idleness, and common sewers of nastiness and disease."[35] Howard, echoing him, saw them as "seats and seminaries (as they have very properly been called) of idleness and every vice."[36] The line continued to Australia in the 1820s, where one finds Governor Thomas Brisbane complaining that "The Convict-Barracks of New South Wales remind me of the Monasteries of Spain. They contain a population of consumers who produce nothing."[37]

However, it was Dr. Johnson who most pithily set forth the vision of Georgian jails as anti-monasteries:

> The misery of gaols is not half their evil . . . In a prison the awe of publick eye is lost, and the power of the law is spent; there are few fears, there are no blushes. The lewd inflame the lewd, the audacious harden the audacious. Everyone fortifies himself as he can against his own sensibility, endeavours to practice on others the arts which are practised on himself, and gains the kindness of his associates by similitude of manners. Thus some sink amidst their misery, and others survive only to propagate villainy.[38]

Such passages indicate how far apart modern and Georgian penal ideas are. In practice, high-security prisons are still human zoos. But the liberal view is that a jail is a sad but necessary expedient, harsh but susceptible of reform, which, if decently run, can keep a criminal out of social circulation without making him or her much worse. No such opinions were held two hundred years ago. Then it was clear that prisons, before they are institutions, are *concentrations of criminals*: Their institutional definition began with the fact of criminality, not the hope of reform, and their essential nature was to degrade all their occupants by the relentless moral pressure of the group. The prison pickled the felon in evil, hardened him, perfused him with the hard salt of sin. Hence the loathing in which English jails were held by those who would never see the inside of one. They were the republics of a sublimated criminal class; they belonged to the antipodes of crime, not to the bright world of authority, which they represented only in a nominal way. In due course, this train of thought would provide the underlying logic of transportation to Australia. For transportation made sublimation literal: It conveyed evil to another world.

Howard's *The State of the Prisons* had an immediate effect on thought and the drafting of law. But practical reforms were slow in coming. The English authorities talked incessantly about the need for new jails, legislated for their urgent construction, but did not actually build them. Within two years of the publication of Howard's report, an act of 1779 called for two large prisons in London, designed along the lines Howard advocated, with provision for work, segregation of the sexes, and confinement in single cells rather than common wards. They were not even started. In 1786 the prime minister, William Pitt, wrote to William Wilberforce, the great liberal abolitionist who was pressing him for prison reform, that "the multitude of things depending, has made the Penitentiary House long in deciding upon. But I still think," he added vaguely, "a beginning will be made on it before the season for building is

over." Again, no beginning was made, but in the summer of 1788 Pitt
reassured Wilberforce that penitentiaries "shall not be forgotten."[39] Forgotten they were, because by then the Government could only see one
remedy for the increase of crime and the apparent ineffectiveness of
prisons: transportation "beyond the seas."

Transportation—forced exile, in plain English—had undeniable merits. It preserved the Royal Prerogative of Mercy, as the felon was left
alive. At the same time he was removed from the realm as completely,
if not as permanently, as any hanged man. Transportation got rid of the
prison as well as the prisoners. It supplied Britain with a large labor force,
consisting entirely of people who, having forfeited their rights, could be
sent to distant colonies of a growing Empire to work at jobs that no free
settler would do. Free-born Englishmen had always disliked the idea of
laboring bands of convicts engaged on public works at home. A bill of
1752 introducing public chain-gang labor as punishment for criminals
was rejected by the Lords partly because security was too great a problem
but mainly because the sight of chain gangs in public places was felt to
be degrading. How could onlookers distinguish such a punishment from
outright slavery? In the New World, there would be no such problem.

The germ of the transportation system lay in a law of 1597, 39 Eliz.
c. 4, "An Acte for Punyshment of Rogues, Vagabonds and Sturdy Beggars." In essence, it declared that obdurate idlers "shall . . . be banished
out of this Realm . . . and shall be conveyed to such parts beyond the seas
as shall be . . . assigned by the Privy Council." If a "Rogue so banished"
returned to England without permission, he would be hanged.

It was through this act that in the seventeenth century, convicts
under commuted death sentences were sent across the Atlantic to labor
on the plantations of the Virginia Company. Sir Thomas Dale, Marshal
of Virginia, took three hundred "disorderly persons" with him in 1611,
but they turned out so "profane and mutinous, . . . diseased and crazed
that not sixty of them may be employed."[40] Still, bad labor was better
than none in the New World; the Indians could not be enslaved, while
the English gentlemen of the Virginia Company had an extreme distaste
for manual work. Soon Dale was asking for two thousand more convicts.
"All offenders out of the common gaols condemned to die should be sent
for three years to the Colony; so do the Spaniards people the Indies."[41]
And from 1618 onward, a steady infusion of felons came to England's
embryo settlements in the New World, to Puritan Massachusetts as well
as to the tidewater settlements of the South. Most of them were common
criminals. Some were Scots and English prisoners-of-war taken by Cromwell at the battles of Dunbar (1650) and Worcester (1651); others—
mostly shipped to the sugar plantations of Jamaica and Barbados in the

1650s—were Irishmen who had been so unwise as to resist the invasion of the Lord Protector.

After 1717, transportation was stepped up and rendered fully official by a new act, 4 Geo. I, c. 11, which provided that minor offenders could be transported for seven years to America instead of being flogged and branded, while men on commuted capital sentences (recipients of the King's Mercy) might be sent for fourteen. English jailers did excellent business by selling these luckless colonists to shipping contractors, who in turn sold them (or, to be legally precise, the rights to their labor during their seven or fourteen years) to plantation-owners in the Caribbean and America. For the next sixty years, about 40,000 people suffered this thinly disguised form of slavery: 30,000 men and women from Great Britain, 10,000 from Ireland. This steady drainage of felons, averaging fewer than 700 people a year, kept the crowded jails of England from crisis.

But after 1775, the crisis could no longer be postponed. The American colonies rebelled. One result of the revolution was that the British could no longer send its convicts there. The American air filled with nobly turned resolutions against accepting criminals from England, for a new republic must not be polluted with the Crown's offal. This was cant, since the American economy was already heavily dependent on slavery. The real point was that the trade in black slaves had turned white convict labor into an economic irrelevance. On the eve of the American Revolution, 47,000 African slaves were arriving in America every year—more than English jails had sent across the Atlantic in the preceding half-century. Beside this labor force, the work of white indentured convicts was inconsequential; the Republic did not need it.

As soon as the American outlet was stopped up, English prisons began to overflow. At first, the Crown did nothing about this. The Americans would surrender sooner or later, and then the convict transports could ply the Atlantic again. In July 1783, only a month before Britain was forced to recognize the United States at Versailles, George III wrote to Lord North: "Undoubtedly the Americans cannot expect nor ever will receive any favour from Me, but the permitting them to obtain Men unworthy to remain in this Island I shall certainly consent to."[42]

So the English did not enlarge their prisons and in 1776 they found a compromise. The idea of forced convict labor on public works no longer seemed so tainted with slavery. It was dusted off and Lord North drew it up as 16 Geo. III, c. 43, known as the Hulks Act, a stopgap meant to last only until the American insurgents were crushed.

The Thames and the southern naval ports of England were dotted with hulks—old troop transports and men-o'-war, their masts and rigging gone, rotting at anchor, but still afloat and theoretically habitable. Convicts sentenced to be transported would now be kept on them until the government decided where to send them; this would relieve the bursting land prisons. Tactfully, the Hulks Act did not mention the revolt of the American colonists. It made a virtue of necessity by noting that transportation had deprived England of people "whose labour might be useful to the Community." These men would now be set "to Hard Labour . . . cleansing the River *Thames*." Thus the felons "might be reclaimed."

But the convicts jammed on the hulks were no more reclaimed than the Thames was cleansed. By 1790 their number was rising by about one thousand a year. Not only had the problem of security become acute, but typhus was by then endemic and the prospect of general infection terrified free citizens outside. The authorities would have done almost anything to get rid of the criminals their laws had created. Clearly, transportation must begin again—but to where? They chose the least imaginable spot on earth, which had been visited only once by white men. It was Australia, their new, vast, lonely possession, a useless continent at the rim of the world, whose eastern coast had been mapped by Captain Cook in 1770. From there, the convicts would never return. The names of Newgate and Tyburn, arch-symbols of the vengeance of property, were now joined by a third: Botany Bay.

3

The Geographical Unconscious

TO GRASP what exile to such a place meant, one must think of the size of the world in the late eighteenth century, so much vaster than it is today.

In the 1780s, most of the world was still unknown to Europeans. The outlines of all the continents but two, Australia and Antarctica, had been traced. In profile, it had today's shape, but immense blanks lay behind the coasts. North America was a populated eastern fringe tacked onto millions of square miles of wilderness. The interiors of South America, Asia and Africa were scarcely explored. No European had ever visited the high Himalaya, the fountains of the Nile or the poles; while the Pacific basin, to all except the most educated Englishmen in 1780, was the least imaginable of all.

The social strata from which the convicts would be drawn knew little about the remoter facts of geography. Perhaps seven Englishmen in ten still lived in the countryside; the urban population of England would not outnumber the rural until 1851. Fixed to the soil and its demands, such people did not travel; their world had a radius of ten miles or so. Because they did not read, news came to them erratically and no English newspaper, in any case, sold more than 7,000 copies.[1]

For most people, the Pacific remained as obscure and unimaginable after Captain James Cook's death as it had been before his birth, and as monstrous: an oceanic hell. Nevertheless there was a deposit of rumor and legend about it, a myth that filtered into popular culture. This was the idea of a Southern Continent, set in the antipodes. It was first raised by two late classical geographers, Pomponius Mela and Ptolemy. Symmetry, Pomponius Mela argued in A.D. 50, demanded such a continent. The northern continents must be balanced by an equal land mass below the equator. In this land, *terra australis incognita*, Pomponius placed the source of the Nile. Supported by the prestige of Ptolemy, the father of

Renaissance geography, this Southern Continent survived the flat-earth doctrines of the medieval scholars, and Marco Polo seemed to confirm it. The Venetian wanderer described how, coming home from the kingdom of Cathay, he had sailed south to "Chamba" (modern Vietnam) and thence southwest for 1,200 miles, to a place named Locac.

Locac was the Malay Peninsula, but an ambiguity in the text anchored it somewhere between the East Indies and the South Pole, far below the equator, thus turning it into the Southern Continent. As such, with its name corrupted to Luchach, Locach or Beach, it appeared in the maps of influential sixteenth-century cartographers such as Mercator and Ortelius. Without the colossal mass of Locac, Mercator wondered, what would stop the world toppling from its axis?

By the end of the sixteenth century, Locac was encysted with fable. To some, it was the golden country, filled with every kind of wealth—jewels, sandalwood, spices—and inhabited by angelic beings: an embellishment upon the myth of the Terrestrial Paradise. To others it was the land of deformity. Legends of the freaks and wonders of India had proliferated since Alexander the Great's Indian expedition (327–325 B.C.)—dog-headed men, basilisks, people whose faces grew on their chests or who had a single huge foot which, during siestas, shaded them from the equatorial sun. These creatures infested medieval books and Romanesque tympana; they were invoked in sermons, in glosses on the Bible, in romances and epics, and by Shakespeare.

It made sense, of a kind, to assume that the further south one went, the more grotesque life must become. What demonic freaks, what affronts to normality, might the Southern Continent not produce? And what trials for the mariner? Waterspouts, hurricanes, clouds of darkness at midday, ship-eating whales, islands that swam and had tusks—this imagined country was perhaps infernal, its landscape that of Hell itself. Within its inscrutable otherness, every fantasy could be contained; it was the geographical unconscious. So there was a deep, ironic resonance in the way the British, having brought the Pacific at last into the realm of European consciousness, having explored and mapped it, promptly demonized Australia once more by chaining their criminals on its innocent dry coast. It was to become the continent of sin.

ii

THE MAN WHO named the ocean *el mar Pacifico* and was the first to cross its stupendous expanse was the Portuguese captain Fernão de Magalhães or, as he is known to history, Ferdinand Magellan. During the entire voyage between Portugal and Guam, he glimpsed only two little uninhabited islands near the strait that now bears his name. *"Que de seu Rey mostrando se agrauado / Caminho ha de fazer nunca cuidado,"* wrote Camoëns in his praise: "Feeling affronted by his King, he took a route unimagined by others before."[2] Having opened the westward way to the Spice Islands with his epic voyage, Magellan was killed at Mactan in the Philippines in 1521.

Spanish explorers who followed him into the Pacific at the end of the sixteenth century were seeking the glory of God and a Southern Continent full of gold. Sailing out of Peru in 1567, blown by the Pacific trades across the low latitudes between 18° S. and the equator, Alvaro de Mendana brought his ships four-fifths of the way across the Pacific to an island group which—after King Solomon's fabled gold mines of Ophir— is still known as the Solomons. Perhaps these were the outer markers of the Southern Continent, perhaps not; half-mad with starvation, thirst and scurvy, Mendana and his conquistadors had to retreat. He tried again twenty-eight years later, in 1595, but the Solomons had vanished and no one would find them again for two centuries. They are at about 160° E. longitude; navigational instruments were so inaccurate that their estimated position varied by a full seventy-five degrees, between longitude 145° E. and 140° W.

Piloted by the young Portuguese Pedro Fernandez de Quiros, Mendana struggled on to the west, finding no continent, only scattered islands. His track lay too far north to encounter Australia. Seven months out of Peru, on the island of Santa Cruz, Mendana died. The great expedition, which was to have claimed *terra australis* in the name of Philip III, dissolved in a nightmare of violence and malaria, but de Quiros brought its demoralized survivors westward to Manila and then returned across the Pacific to Acapulco and safety.

This, one might think, would have put anyone off continent-hunting in the Pacific. It did not stop de Quiros. Somewhere to the west, on the blind blue eyeball of the world's greatest ocean, the Southern Continent must lie, and its discovery would be the climax both of Spanish imperialism and of the Church Militant's mission on earth. From Acapulco, de Quiros struggled back to Spain and thence to Rome, bombarding the Pope with letters about *terra australis* and its millions of innocent heathen souls, ripe for salvation. It took him two years to raise the money for three ships and three hundred men from Philip III. In December 1605, de Quiros sailed to find the continent.

He took a new track, further south than either Magellan or Mendana, well below the Tropic of Capricorn. He ran through the Tuamotu Archipelago, passed north of Samoa and, after five months at sea, saw land to the south and southeast—high mountains, their peaks veiled in clouds, retreating to the horizon. On May 3, 1606, de Quiros's fleet anchored in a bay. They had reached the New Hebrides group at 167° E., 15° S. De Quiros decided without any further evidence that this must be the southland and, fast succumbing to religious mania, named it *Austrialia del Espiritu Santo*,* created an order of nobility, distributed taffeta crosses for almost every man-jack on his fleet to wear, christened the stream that ran into the bay the Jordan, and announced in a prophetic ecstasy that the New Jerusalem would be built there among the coral reefs—which, in his feverishly optimistic mind, were already turning into quarries of porphyry and agate.

All this was an illusion, but de Quiros, convinced of its truth, sailed back to Mexico while Luis Vaez de Torres, the captain of his second ship, pressed on across the Pacific to Manila, passing just north of Australia between Cape York Peninsula and New Guinea through the strait that now bears his name. But he hugged the New Guinea coast and did not see the continent.

After eight years' struggle to raise another fleet, de Quiros died in 1614, his quest unfulfilled. There is some intriguing evidence, in the form of the so-called Dieppe Maps copied by spies from secret Portuguese charts and presented to the future Henri II in 1536 (one of which shows a Southern Continent strikingly similar in eastern profile to Australia's), that the northeast and east coasts of Australia had been found and charted before 1550 by a Portuguese fleet sailing south from the Spice Islands. If this voyage was made, it would have been illicit. Under the Treaty of Tordesillas (1494), Portugal and Spain had agreed to divide the Earth along the great diameter of 51° W. and 129° E. longitude. Thus, everything east of 129° W., which passes through Australia, became part of the Spanish imperium—including the east coast of Australia. Portugal had no rights of exploration there and could well have chosen to keep the results of such a voyage secret. However, the originals of the Dieppe Maps, along with any logs and documents that may have amplified them, were destroyed in the Lisbon earthquake in 1755. The only other relics of European contact with Australia before 1600 are two Portuguese brass cannon, datable around 1475–1525, found at Broome Bay in northwest Australia—evidence of another voyage, but this time on Portugal's side of the Tordesillas line.[3]

There had been Asian landings in the sixteenth century, but none resulted in colonization. They were made by Makassan traders from the island of Celebes, who ran down the northern monsoons in their slat-sailed praus to what is now Arnhem Land, on the north coast of the continent.[4] The goal of their 1,200-mile voyages was a sea slug, the tre-

---

* "Austrialia" was a reference to his King's Hapsburg blood ("Austria") and a pun on *tierra austral*, "the south land."

pang or *bêche-de-mer*. These creatures, which looked like withered penises when smoked and dried, were Indonesia's largest export to the Chinese, who esteemed them as an aphrodisiac. Thus, until the nineteenth century, Australia's sole contribution to the outside world was millions of sea slugs.

In 1605 the Dutch East India Company in Bantam sent a pinnace, the *Duyfken*, under Captain Willem Jansz, to see if New Guinea had gold and spices. The little boat entered the Torres Strait, turned south after coasting New Guinea for more than two hundred miles and found a cape that its skipper named Keerweer ("turn back"). The place was wilderness, and "wild, black, cruel savages" killed some of the crew. Jansz had found a northern promontory of Australia.

In 1616 another tessera was added to the edge of the puzzle by Dirck Hartog, an Amsterdam captain who reached the west Australian coast in his ship *Eendracht* and nailed up an engraved pewter dish as proof of his visit. In 1618 another vessel on the outward voyage to Java, the *Zeewulf*, glimpsed more coast to the north.

The next year, Frederick de Houtman, an outward-bound captain who steered further south from the Cape of Good Hope than most, landed on the west coast of Australia south of modern Perth. In time, more Dutch mariners offered their fragments of information: Jan Carstens in 1623, and Francis Pelsart in 1629. Clearly, the southland seemed to be worth exploring, with the expectation that it held more than sand, reefs and choleric savages. To that end, Anthony van Diemen, Governor-General of the Dutch East India Company, organized in 1642 a grand expedition that would map "the remaining unknown part of the terrestrial globe." Abel Tasman, its commander, was to sail from Batavia to Mauritius, drop south to latitude 54° S. and then sail east until he found the Southland.

He missed it completely. Tasman's two vessels, the *Heemskerck* and the *Zeehaen*, sailed right past Australia without once glimpsing its mainland; his course had been too far south. The only part of the country he touched was an island in the southwest which he guessed was mainland and named for his patron: Van Diemen's Land. Two centuries later, when that name had become so tarnished with stories of criminality and cruelty that respectable settlers would no longer endure it, the island was renamed Tasmania after its discoverer.

It looked poor and wild. No natives showed themselves, although notched trees and traces of cooking-fires were seen. There was little to remark. Tasman sailed east across what is now the Tasman Sea and discovered the west coast of New Zealand. Sailing on into the Pacific he discovered Tonga and Fiji as well, before returning to Batavia in June 1643. The voyage, as far as van Diemen and his merchant colleagues were concerned, was a fiasco. Tasman had found no people to trade with, no commodities to exploit. So they ordered Tasman out on a second voyage, to see if the north coast of Australia held anything worthwhile. Tasman sailed in 1644, but the only people he found on that coast were black, "naked beach-roving wretches, destitute even of rice . . . miserably poor, and in many places of a very bad disposition." There would be no trade. With this, the Dutch East India Company's interest in Australia languished.

The last seventeenth-century explorer to try the northwest coast of Australia was an English buccaneer, William Dampier, in 1688. He found nothing but the propertyless men of New Holland; his description of them is one of the minor classics of racism:

> The inhabitants of this country are the miserablest people in the World. The *Hodmadods* [Hottentots] of *Monomatapa*, though a nasty People, yet for Wealth are Gentlemen to these . . . and setting aside their humane shape, they differ but little from Brutes. They are tall, strait-bodied, and thin, with small long Limbs. They have great Heads, round Foreheads, and great Brows. Their Eye-lids are always half closed, to keep the Flies out of their Eyes . . . therefore they cannot see far . . .
>
> They are long-visaged, and of a very unpleasing aspect; having no one graceful feature in their faces.
>
> They have no houses, but lye in the open Air, without any covering; the Earth being their Bed, and the Heaven their Canopy . . . The Earth affords them no food at all. There is neither Herb, Pulse, nor any sort of Grain, for them to eat, that we saw; nor any sort of Bird or Beast that they can catch, having no instruments wherewithal to do so.
>
> I did not perceive that they did worship anything.[5]

Such was the Ignoble Savage, orphan of nature. Dampier's visit to the northwest coast produced no discoveries, but his book was popular in England and its notion of a Southern Continent—still a geographical hypothesis separate from New Holland—struck a responsive chord. The Spaniards and Dutch had failed in the Pacific; the eighteenth century would make it either a French or a British ocean.

So the direction of approach shifted again, and ships once more began probing the Pacific from the east, coming round the Horn or through the Straits of Magellan: Roggeveen in 1721, Byron in 1764, Wallis and Carteret in 1766, Bougainville in 1766 and 1769. They all sailed too far north in the trade winds to find the Australian coast; only Bougainville kept far enough south and would have discovered Queensland had he not been turned back by its coral rampart, the Great Barrier Reef, and gone north like the rest. They were all resolute men, but there were some problems courage alone could not beat. The first of these was scurvy.

This disease, caused by vitamin C deficiency, was the bane of every seaman. The victim weakened; his flesh puffed up and his joints were wracked with gouty pain; his teeth loosened while his gums swelled and turned black, so that he could not eat. Scurvy could kill most of a ship's company on a long voyage. The simple cure for it was fruit (especially lemons or oranges) and green vegetables. Captains did not know this; some had noticed that scurvy victims recovered in port on a green diet, but fruit and vegetables would not keep long at sea. In mid-Pacific, Magellan's crew had to eat a mixture of biscuit crumbs and rat droppings; then they ate the rats; at last they sucked and chewed the ship's leather chafing-gear in their desperate need for animal protein. Scurvy afflicted them so badly that to chew their rations, they had to keep slicing the swollen tissue of their gums away. From de Quiros in the sixteenth century to Bougainville in the eighteenth, none of the Pacific explorers suffered as badly from scurvy as Magellan and his crew.

Scurvy chilled the ambition of every voyage. Because they did not know the causes of the disease, they could not control it. In 1768–71, James Cook first beat scurvy on a long voyage by the regular issue of the proper anti-scorbutics. By then, it was known to be a dietary problem. Dr. James Lind, in 1753, had hit on the right cure: a daily dose of citrus juice. Yet neither Cook (who always worried about the health of his crew) nor the officers of the Admiralty's Victualling Board read Lind's treatise, and instead of citrus juice Cook tried other anti-scorbutics: sauerkraut, malt, and half a ton of "portable soup," made by boiling down meat broth into a gummy cake, the ancestor of the bouillon cube. In combination, these worked. Throughout the three-year voyage of the *Endeavour*, Cook did not lose a man from scurvy—a feat without precedent in the history of seafaring. Malt-juice and pickled cabbage put Europeans in Australia, as microchip circuitry would put Americans on the moon.

The other obstacle to Pacific exploration had been finding the longitude. Exploration means nothing unless you know your daily position, but to do this two coordinates are needed. The first is latitude, the measure of one's distance from the equator. The second is longitude, the distance between a fixed prime meridian (for British navigators, that of Greenwich) and the meridian of one's position. (A meridian is the shortest line drawn from the north to the south pole on the Earth's curved surface.) A ship's latitude was easy to figure and had been since antiquity. But without longitude, one could not determine one's position with any certainty. Mariners had to make do with guesswork, based on the ocean current, the wind and the speed of the ship. Mistakes of more than 2,000 miles were common on the early Pacific voyages, because accumulated longitude error could not be checked. In calculating the longitude of the

Philippines, Magellan's pilot was wrong by some 53 degrees—more than a seventh of the world's circumference.

The more they thought of Empire, the more the British realized the need for a longitude fixing method. As England began to challenge Dutch mercantile supremacy in the Far East, the more urgent this became. In 1714 the British government put up a prize of £20,000, a fortune, for anyone who could come up with a method by which a navigator could fix longitude at sea that would be correct within thirty miles at the end of a six-week open-water voyage.

By Cook's time, there were two systems of finding longitude. Both relied on the fact that as the earth spins, local time alters from place to place—thus, when it is noon in London, it is 7 a.m. in New York. The Earth rotates once a day; and as there are 24 hours in a day and 360 degrees of longitude around the equator, an hour's difference in time represented a shift of 15 degrees in longitude. So if one knew when and at what angle a given astronomical event would be seen at Greenwich, and observed it from, say, a spot in the Pacific at that same angle, the difference in hours multiplied by 15 would yield the longitude in degrees. This constant was the angle between the moon or sun and a fixed star, such as Polaris, and was known as "lunar distance." The English Astronomer Royal, Nevil Maskelyne, was the first man to publish a complete tabulation of future lunar distances in relation to Greenwich Mean Time; this was the famous Nautical Almanac, first issued in 1766. Armed with "Mister Masculine's Tables," along with some basic trigonometry and some well-made instruments, any captain could now find his longitude. That was the first method. The second was to carry Greenwich Mean Time on board ship, compare it with local time and multiply the difference by 15 as before. That was far quicker, but it required a chronometer, a clock more accurate and durable than any other. If it ran fast or slow, every minute it lost or gained would mean an error of longitude of nearly 20 miles on the equator. It had to stand up to salt, corrosion and the ceaseless pounding of a ship at sea. Such a chronometer was finally built in 1764 by the great John Harrison.

For his first Pacific voyage, Cook had no chronometer, preferring to rely on lunar distance calculations. But the *Endeavour* was well-equipped with other instruments, as measurement rather than discovery was the main purpose of her voyage. Her passengers were to observe from Tahiti the transit of Venus across the Sun's face. The importance of this celestial event was that, if accurately observed and recorded, it could help establish the earth's distance from the sun. The last time that Earth, Venus and the sun had come into line was in 1761; the silhouette of Venus on the solar disk was watched and timed by 120 observers scattered across the world from Russia to South Africa, but even so the readings had been fuzzy and the British wanted to improve them. From Tahiti, on the predicted date of June 3, 1769, the whole transit would be seen in daytime, in clear air.

After Cook completed this task, he could then pursue his explorations. The Admiralty wanted him either to find or to eliminate the Southern Continent. He must do this by dropping south of Tahiti, below the tracks of all previous Pacific navigators, to 40° S. latitude. He must then make a sweep westward, keeping between 35° and 40° S. until he either found the Southern Continent or reached "the Eastern side of the Land discover'd by Tasman and now called New Zeland."[6] One way or the other, a myth that had haunted exploration for centuries would be cleared up.

iii

ON AUGUST 25, 1768, the *Endeavour*—a converted Whitby collier, small and brawny, 106 feet long—set sail from Plymouth. Along with her crew, marines and officers, she had on board a number of civilians. The most important of them, from Greenwich's point of view, was the astronomer Charles Green. The rest made up a private scientific party: a brilliant, mercurial young amateur named Joseph Banks and the servants and specialists he had hired to accompany him. At twenty-five, Banks was well-educated (Eton, Oxford), well-connected, well-off (a rural fortune) and in the proper sense a dilettante: one who took an eclectic, educated pleasure in the world about him. His passion was botany, and his hero (whom he had not met) was the great Swedish botanist Carolus Linnaeus. On hearing of the expedition to Tahiti, Banks realized that this was his chance. To be the first botanist into the South Seas would make his reputation, for he would have the flora of a new world to himself. "Any blockhead can go to Italy," he is said to have told a friend who wondered when he would take his Grand Tour. "Mine shall be around the world." He would go with Cook. Friends in the Admiralty and the Royal Society arranged it. Banks went on board the *Endeavour* with a retinue consisting of two artists (one of them a young genius of botanical illustration, Sydney Parkinson), several servants, a secretary, two hounds, and another naturalist, the most affable, enthusiastic and learned of travelling companions, a favorite pupil of Linnaeus himself: Dr. Daniel Solander.

The *Endeavour* took almost eight months to reach Tahiti via Rio de Janeiro and Tierra del Fuego, dropping anchor in Matavai Bay in mid-

April 1769. The doings of Cook, Banks and the crew in this barely touched Eden must no more concern us here than the details of Cook's coastal exploration of New Zealand, as the Crown never considered either Tahiti or New Zealand as penal settlements.[7]

The transit of Venus was duly, though imperfectly, observed. Banks's crates and bottles were filling up with specimens, his artists' folios with sketches. Early in August they left Tahiti, taking with them a young Tahitian of exalted birth named Tupaia, whom Banks intended to bring back to London as the ultimate exotic pet, a live Noble Savage. Their search for the Southern Continent now began.

For months, beating west through the toppling green hills of the Pacific, they were misled by what Banks called "Our old enemy Cape fly away"—cloudbanks on the horizon. Then, on the afternoon of October 6, 1769, land lay before them. "All hands seem to agree," wrote Banks, viewing the low solid line to the west, "that this is certainly the continent we are in search of."[8]

It was not, and their track across the southern Pacific had nearly eliminated that continent. They had reached Poverty Bay on the east coast of the north island of New Zealand, and for the next four months Cook sailed the *Endeavour* around the coasts of both the north and the south islands, mapping every reef, cliff and indentation and, with caution, observing the habits of the brave and bellicose Maori: The Tahitians made love, but these men with faces rigidly tattooed like purple fingerprints made war. "I suppose," Banks jotted, "they live intirely on fish, dogs, and enemies."

At the end of March 1770 Cook was ready for the homeward voyage. The Southern Continent had proved "imaginary"; however, more than 2,400 miles of New Zealand's coastline were charted. He had fulfilled the Admiralty's brief and could shape his course for England.

He could return eastward around the Horn or westward via the Cape of Good Hope. The western route was unlikely to bring forth new discoveries. But March is the end of the Pacific summer and Cook did not want to commit his ship—battered and wormy as she was from two years' voyage—to the eastern route and the winter storms of Cape Horn. Cook had Tasman's charts, and he decided to try another way. Somewhere to the west, there must lie the east coast of New Holland. They would follow Tasman's track, in reverse, from New Zealand to Van Diemen's Land. Then they would find whether Van Diemen's Land was part of New Holland, or a separate island. If it was separate, they would find the coast of New Holland and sail north along it.

On March 31 they left New Zealand. Southerly gales rose and drove the *Endeavour* to latitude 38°, too far north to make Van Diemen's Land.

But on April 19 a new coast announced itself. Flat and sandy, most unlike the magnificent scenery of New Zealand, it lay dry on the gray horizon. Their landfall was at Cape Everard, in Victoria.

They coasted north, finding no harbor. But now and then they saw smoke rising from the scrubby headlands, so they knew that the place must be inhabited. To Banks, the landscape looked poor after Tahiti and New Zealand. "It resembled in my imagination the back of a lean Cow, covered in general with long hair, but nevertheless where her scraggy hip bones have stuck out further than they ought accidental rubbs and knocks have intirely bar'd them of their share of covering."⁹ On April 22, they saw some Australians on a beach. They looked black but it was hard to tell their real color. Exactly a week later, the first contact was made. Heading up from the south, Cook saw a wide bay and steered into it, sending the pinnace ahead to make soundings.

They saw bark canoes and in them blacks were fishing. The ship floated past these frail coracles. It was the largest artifact ever seen on the east coast of Australia, an object so huge, complex and unfamiliar as to defy the natives' understanding. The Tahitians had flocked out to meet her in their bird-winged outriggers, and the Maoris had greeted her with *hakas* and showers of stones; but the Australians took no notice. They displayed neither fear nor interest and went on fishing.

Only when they anchored and Cook, Banks, Solander and Tupaia—who, all hoped, might act as interpreter—approached the south shore of the bay in a longboat did the natives react. The sight of men in a small boat was comprehensible to them; it meant invasion. Most of the Aborigines fled into the trees, but two naked warriors stood their ground, brandished their spears and shouted in a quick, guttural tongue, not a syllable of it familiar to Tupaia. Cook and Banks pitched some trading-truck ashore—nails and beads, the visiting cards of the South Pacific. The blacks moved to attack, and Cook fired a musket-shot between them. One warrior ran back and grabbed a bundle of spears, while the other began shying rocks at the boat. Cook fired again, wounding one of them with small-shot, but still the man did not retreat; he merely picked up a bark shield.

It was time to land. A young midshipman named Isaac Smith was in the bow. Years later, after many promotions, Admiral Smith—the cousin of Cook's wife—would proudly tell how the greatest navigator in history hesitated before quitting the longboat, touched him on the shoulder and said, "Isaac, you shall land first." The lad sprang into the green, bottle-glass water as it prickled on the floury white sand, and waded ashore. Cook and the others followed, and the seal of distance and space that had protected the east coast of Australia since the Pleistocene epoch was broken. The colonization of the last continent had begun. The blacks threw their stone-tipped spears.

Cook fired a third shot. With an insolent lack of haste, the tribesmen retreated into the bush. The whites found some bark shelters near the beach from which the adult natives had fled, although in one humpy there were "four or five children with whome we left some strings of beeds &ca." What kind of people were these, who ran away and left their babies to the mercy of strangers? Nothing could win their confidence. "We could know but very little of their customs," Cook complained on May 6, a week after at anchor, "as we were never able to form any connections with them, they had not so much as touch'd the things we had left in their hutts." They seemed to have no curiosity, no sense of material possessions. "All they seem'd to want was for us to be gone." Tupaia, in particular, had a low but prophetic opinion of these elusive men and women of Australia. He was heard to remark that "they were *Taata Eno's* that is bad or poor people." The Polynesian phrase *taata ino* denoted the very lowest caste of Tahitians, the *titi*, who were used as human sacrifices.

Cook saw them differently, and in a famous passage in his journal he contradicted Dampier's view of them. "They may appear to some to be the most wretched people upon Earth," he remarked,

> but in reality they are far happier than we Europeans; being wholly unacquainted not only with the superfluous but the necessary Conveniencies so much sought after in Europe, they are happy in not knowing the use of them. They live in Tranquillity which is not disturb'd by the Inequality of Condition.[10]

These few days of sparse contact on the coast of New South Wales sealed the doom of the Aborigine. There was no chance that the Crown would ever try to plant a penal colony in New Zealand, for the Maori were a subtle, determined and ferocious race. These Australians, however, would give no trouble. They were ill-armed, backward, and timid; most of them ran at the sight of a white face; and they had no goods or property to defend. Besides, there were so few of them. All this the British authorities would presently learn from Joseph Banks, without whose evidence there might have been no convict colony in Australia.

The men of the *Endeavour* gave little thought to any of this as they explored that distant sheltered bay in the Pacific autumn of 1770. Banks and Solander were especially busy. The low, flat shores were full of plants and creatures unknown to European science. The animals were elusive —they found one kangaroo-turd, without seeing the 'roo—but there was a staggering quantity of "nondescript" (unclassified) plant life. Eventually, the young botanists were to bring back 30,000 specimens from their voyage, representing some 3,000 species of which 1,600 were wholly new to science. The harbor was full of fish, and on its shallow flats immense stingrays, *Dasyatis brevicaudatus*, were caught; Sydney Parkinson, Banks's botanical artist, commented that their guts tasted "not unlike stewed turtle." Cook decided to call the bay Stingray Harbor, but later he changed his mind. The place represented such a triumph for his young companions' science that, thinking of all the accumulated specimens and drawings in the *Endeavour*'s stern cabin, he fixed on the name Botany Bay. Its northern and southern heads went on the chart as Cape Banks and Point Solander.

They sailed and kept coasting north. They passed but did not enter a harbor fifteen miles north of Botany Bay, which Cook named Port Jackson, after the Secretary for the Admiralty. Their track up the immense eastern flank of Australia ran through twenty-eight degrees of latitude, more than two thousand miles from Botany Bay to the tip of Cape York. In the labyrinth of the Great Barrier Reef—Cook had unwittingly sailed into it like a fish into the funnel of a trap—the ship struck; a coral fang ripped through her sheathing and broke off, by the merest fluke stopping the hole until the ship could be kedged clear, beached and repaired. This brush with annihilation delayed them seven weeks at Endeavour Bay, giving Banks more time for botanizing. At last the mysterious kangaroo was seen, and two were shot; they tasted like tough venison. A seaman told Banks, to his amusement, about a ghastly monster he had spied, "about as large and much like a one gallon Kegg, as black as the Devil and had 2 horns on its head, it went but slowly but I dar'd not touch it." It was a flying fox. More Aborigines appeared, behaving in the fickle uncertain manner of people startled by an alien intrusion. They seemed as timid as those of Botany Bay. Apparently, the variations of culture and nature were small along this immense coast.

On August 21, 1770, the *Endeavour* rounded Cape York. From there, to the west, stretched a discovered sea crossed by Dutch ships. Cook, Banks, and Solander landed on a nubbin of rock now called Possession Island, hoisted a Union Jack and formally claimed the whole coast south of where they stood—down to 38° S., near their original landfall—as "New South Wales" in the name of George III. They fired three volleys, which were answered from the ship. The salute had to be given with small arms, for all the *Endeavour*'s cannon had been trundled overboard to lighten her when she lay holed on the Barrier Reef. In this modest way, by the slap of muskets echoing across a flat warm strait, Australia was added to the British Empire.

iv

AMID THE TUMULT of publicity that greeted the safe return of the
ship and her crew to England in July 1771, it was clear that only one
place ravished the public imagination: Tahiti, languid isle of the Golden
Age, Cytherea of the Pacific. New Zealand was next in order of interest,
while Australia ran a poor third. Naturally there was professional curiosity among scientists as to the plants and fauna of the new continent.
But no kangaroo, even when painted by George Stubbs, could possibly
compete with Tahitian princesses as an object of fantasy. There was
something, if not exactly dull, at least ungraspable about that flat hot
fringe of a blank continent, sown about with deadly reefs. Cultivated
opinion on the matter was symbolized in a portrait of Banks done in 1773
by Benjamin West, the rising young prodigy of America paying his homage to the even younger virtuoso of a world still newer, the Pacific. Banks
stands wrapped in a fine chief's cloak, pointing out a detail of the weave;
around him are trophies of his periplus—Tahitian ceremonial gear, a
carved paddle, a Maori *mere* (jade war-club). But the only thing that
might stand for New South Wales, and rather ambiguously at that, is an
open folio with Parkinson's drawing of a lily. The disappointing truth
about Australia was that once the legend of the Southern Continent had
been disproved and the facts about New Holland were known, there was
not much reason to go there.

In 1772 Cook boarded the *Resolution* and began his second voyage,
that epic navigation of the Antarctic Ocean which took him further
south than any human had ever been—to 71° S.—and which destroyed
the last vestiges of that legend. There was no habitable latitude where
such a continent could be, and "the greatest part of this Southern Continent (supposing there is one) must lay within the Polar Circle where
the sea is so pestered with ice, that the land is thereby inaccessible."
Cook's intuition of Antarctica was correct.

Thus eighteen years passed before another ship called at Botany Bay,
and for the first eight of those years the subject of Australia, as far as
George III's government was concerned, was forgotten. It was revived
after 1783, when Pitt the Younger became prime minister. The idea that
Australia might carry a British penal colony was raised by the revolt of
the American colonies, and by a crisis in England's hulks and jails. However, it is by now a common (though by no means general) opinion among
students of Australian history that the "grand design" of Botany Bay was
really strategic, hatched by Pitt's desire to deny France power over India
and the Far Eastern trade routes that were so vital to British interests in

the late eighteenth century. This vision of the embryo colony as a "strategic outlier" of England, not just an opportunistically chosen dump for its criminals, has become popular with Australians as our national bicentenary approaches. It lends dignity to our origins. "The rag and bone shop of Australia's beginning," wrote the main spokesman for this view, Alan Frost, "was perhaps not so foul as we have long supposed."[11] We shall see.

In 1779, the year Captain James Cook was killed by the Hawaiians at Karakakoa Bay, a House of Commons committee was set up to determine where convicts, if sentenced to transportation, could be sent now that America was closed to them. The place should be very distant but not a mere desert, for it was essential that a colony there be able to support itself. What about New Holland? The committee invited Joseph Banks, now a celebrity and soon to be knighted, to deliver his views. Nobody in England knew more about Australia. The great man, now thirty-four years old, spoke of Botany Bay and its naked cowardly savages. The climate was good, the soil was arable; he described the abundance of fish, pasture, fresh water and wood and set forth the opinion that a colony of felons could support itself within a year. Perhaps he actually believed this farrago of optimistic distortions; but though the committee was impressed, it made no decision. It heard other witnesses, who suggested transportation to Gibraltar or the west coast of Africa.

There was reason to be skeptical about such projects. The American transportation system had relied on free settlers who would buy indentured labor. The convicts were sold by middlemen and from the moment they stepped on American soil they ceased to cost England a penny; they were not a charge on the State.

Yet in Australia, these conditions would not apply. Thousands of men and women would be packed off, in ships that would bring back no cargo, to a place expected to produce no surplus. There were no free settlers to buy the indentured labor of the felons, and every item of their upkeep would be a dead charge on the government. Even granted the pervasive sense of a crisis in the criminal system and the widespread desire to solve it by expelling the "criminal classes" of England to some place "beyond the seas," the notion of setting a convict colony in a place as remote and ill-known as Australia was certainly bizarre. The argument for strategic colonization of Australia seems, at least on the face of it, to make the exercise more rational.

When William Pitt the Younger became its prime minister in 1783, England was half-bankrupted from war with France. Pitt believed it was essential to keep the French from gaining any influence over India and the trade routes of the Far East. The East's economic importance to Britain was growing. It had not approached the volume of Britain's Atlantic trade,[12] but its direction was clear: In the future, a great part of Britain's economic destiny would lie in the "East Indies," a vast swath of territory that ran from the Cape of Good Hope through India and Malaya to the coast of China and on into the Pacific.

The main instrument of British interests there had been the sprawling, corrupt East India Company, which had the closest relationships to government of any English business. For ten years, starting with Lord North's Regulating Act (1773), the government strove to curb and reform "John Company." With the passage of Pitt's India Act (1784), which partly nationalized control of the East India Company, the matter of India was at the front of all political argument, the responsibility not of the Company men but of the Crown and its ministers. Trade had brought territory, territory war, war an Empire. With this had come immense problems of security as well as trade. Not only did India have to be run, but the East as a whole—not excluding the Western Pacific—had to be kept open to British shipping, especially along the vital trade route from India to Canton. Eastern trade represented Britain's best hope of economic recovery from the setbacks of the early 1780s: her loss of North America, her costly war against the French, and her alienation from once friendly European states—notably, Holland.

For Holland was the key to strategic power in the East. The forts and harbors of the Dutch trading empire ran from Cape Town to the southwest Pacific. The Dutch monopoly of the Spice Islands was the oldest and toughest obstacle the East India company had to face. Yet the *military* weakness of this trading empire had been revealed after England declared war on Holland in 1780. The British began a series of inconclusive naval strikes against Dutch bases in the East. In March 1781 a British squadron bungled an attack on the "Gibraltar of Africa," the Cape of Good Hope, from which East India convoys sailing round the tip of Africa could be harassed by privateers. This backfired badly with the net result that the French, under Admiral de Suffren, reinforced the Dutch garrison at the Cape and held it to the end of the war. Another British fleet captured two lesser Dutch ports which had some strategic influence over the sea lanes to the Bay of Bengal: Negapatam (modern Negapattinam) on the southeast coast of India, and Trincomalee in Ceylon. Soon after, de Suffren retook Trincomalee.

The lesson Pitt drew from this distant, inconclusive sea war, after hostilities ceased, was that the combination of Dutch depots and French ships posed dangers for the British in India even though Holland was no longer a major sea power. There was a vacuum of naval power in the Far East, and the British had to fill it before the French did. In the postwar negotiations, Pitt tried very hard to reach friendly agreements with the Dutch on seaborne trade in the East Indies, while edging the French garrisons out of the Cape. He hoped (in the words of Sir James Harris, Pitt's minister at The Hague) "not only to separate the Interests of the Dutch East India Company from those of France, but to unite them with those of Great-Britain."[13] The fabric of England's Far Eastern trade was too delicate to permit anything but conciliation in dealing with the Dutch. If provoked again, they could join the French to drive England from the East Indies.

But though there was no doubt that the French wanted India, they lacked the military force to take it. After the peace of 1783, they made a series of diplomatic moves to weaken British influence there. In 1785 they struck a treaty with the Bey in Cairo to give them trading rights in Egypt, which was seen as a distant gambit to a possible invasion of India. They also formed a chartered trading company, the French East India Company of Calonne, to compete with Britain's East India Company. The peace settlement had called for a balance between British and French fleets in Indian seas—the understood figure was five warships each, none larger than 64 guns. There was some British concern (more from spies and diplomats than from naval men) when it appeared that the French East India Company was using decommissioned 64-gun cruisers, known as *flûtes*, as merchantmen. Their lower gun-decks had been removed, but in theory they could soon be re-armed. On the other hand, the French thought the massive and growing tonnage of British East India merchant fleets from the Cape to Canton could easily be converted to war, and they too were right. Despite the highly colored intelligence reports it got, there is no sign that Pitt's government saw the French *flûtes* as a grave threat.

Its main field of concern, in the problem of keeping the Indian trade routes open, was relations between the French and the Dutch. French postwar diplomacy concentrated on the majority faction in the Dutch government, the Patriot Party. At the end of 1785, France and Holland signed a treaty of defensive alliance. Early in 1786, the Patriots took control of the Dutch East India Company and, encouraged by their French allies, moved to put thousands more troops into the Cape and Trincomalee. The French also pressed the Patriots to take all military decisions about India and the Cape from the ailing hands of the Dutch East India Company. Sir James Harris gloomily reported to Pitt in March 1786 that France had told the Dutch Patriots "that a Rupture with England in Asia is not of a very distant Period—no Time should be lost in augmenting [British] Naval and Land Force in that Quarter of the World."[14]

The threat of such a "rupture," according to the strategic-outlier arguments of Australian historians like Frost and Blainey, led to Botany Bay. The reason lay in pines and flax.

In eighteenth-century strategy, pine trees and flax had the naval importance that oil and uranium hold today. All masts and spars were of pine, and flax was the raw stuff of ships' canvas; neither could be had in quantity in the Far East, although there was plenty of coir fiber for rigging. A first-rate ship of the line needed immense quantities of spar timber. The mainmast of a 74-gun first-rater was three feet thick at the base, and rose 108 feet from keelson to truck—a single tree, dead straight and flawlessly solid. Such a vessel needed some 22 masts and yards as well. No other timber would do. Only conifers made good masts, because of their natural straightness and because the pine resin cut down friction between the fibers in their grain. This second characteristic made the great sticks relatively supple, so that they could absorb the punishing stress of heavy-weather sailing.

No such spar timber grew in the British Isles or in India. It all had to come from Riga, on the Baltic coast of Russia. The flax for sails also came from Russia, and England spent half a million pounds a year importing it. The supply line from Riga to Portsmouth through Russian and Scandinavian territorial waters was 1,700 miles long and highly vulnerable to shifts of alliance between England, France and their northern neighbors. Even when these strategic materials reached England, they still had 10,000 miles to go before they could be of use to a British squadron in the Far East. Hence the anxiety of the British in September 1784, when France got from Sweden the right to put a naval depot on the island of Göteborg at the mouth of the Baltic; from there, French ships could harass the British timber-transports.

One reason for the French-British naval stalemate in Indian seas in 1782 was the drastic shortage of spar timber, all of which had to be shipped from Europe. "There was not anywhere in India, so much as a Spar fit to make a Jibb Boom for a 64 gun ship," Admiral Sir Edward Hughes reported in 1781, "nor any Timber to be had of a size to make an Anchor Stock for a Line of Battle Ship."[15]

Faced now by the prospect of a Far Eastern war (so the argument goes) Pitt's counsellors remembered Norfolk Island, a rock that Captain James Cook had discovered in the Pacific a thousand miles east of Botany Bay during his second voyage a decade earlier, in 1774. His track toward it had taken him past several islands on which pine trees grew, some trunks of which were the size of the foremast of his ship, the *Resolution*. Larger ones, he thought, might well grow on larger islands, and this would be a boon to navigators. As he noted in his log, "I know of no Island in the South Pacifick Ocean where a Ship could supply herself with a Mast or a Yard, was she everso much distress'd for want of one. . . . the discovery may be both useful and valuable." His guess proved right. The Norfolk Island pines grew to 3 feet in diameter and 180 feet in height. Better still, the island's cliffs and shoreline were densely covered with stands of flax, *Phormium tenax*, seemingly ideal for the manufacture of canvas.[16]

Samples of the flax were gathered and, back in England, test pieces of hawser, canvas and twine were made from them. The "New Zealand flax" proved to be exceptionally tough and durable. Surely it, and the pines, were to be seen as a strategic asset for the Indian ships? And—stretching the possibilities further—might not the coast of New South Wales provide an armed haven, a "strategic outlier," where warships could refit with this timber, sailcloth and cordage, protected by a garrison?

To some people then, and to later historians, this looked good on paper, but there is no hard evidence that it did so to William Pitt or his ministers. The first man to propose it was an American-born functionary, James Mario Matra (ca. 1745–1806), who had held minor administrative posts in London and diplomatic ones in Tenerife and Constantinople. Matra held no official position in England. He was one of the bit-players in the drama of Empire: a speculator petitioning for a commercial scheme that, he hoped, would give him a job. It is in this light that one must see his suggestion—the first on record—that pines and flax might afford a strategic reason for colonizing Australia. It was read because he, at least, had seen Botany Bay, having sailed as a midshipman under Cook on the *Endeavour*. He presented his idea in a letter to Lord North, who had briefly replaced Thomas Townshend, Viscount Sydney, as the home and colonial secretary in 1783. His memo was endorsed by Banks, whose name Matra invoked in flattering terms throughout.[17]

It did not involve convicts. To "atone for the loss of our American colonies," the loyalist Matra proposed a free settlement in New South Wales, a country that held out "the most enticing allurements to European adventurers." The settlers should be of two kinds: British peasants, and dispossessed Loyalists fleeing from America to find asylum. Matra was an apostle of prophylactic emigration; he wanted to export the British poor before they turned to crime. "Few of any country," he realistically observed, "will ever think of settling in any foreign part of the world from a restless mind and from *Romantick* views." Thus, he reasoned, the Australian colonists ought to be the newly poor, of whom there was no shortage, as the economic woes brought about by the American revolt had caused a serious rural depression in England by 1783.

Matra rhapsodized on what the colony might produce, with the help of Chinese slave labor: tea, silk, spices, tobacco, coffee. There would be trade with China, Japan, Korea and the Aleutians. Best of all there were the flax and the pines, material "of the greatest importance," "eminently useful to us as a naval Power." Through them, the blank coast of New Holland would acquire a very commanding influence in the policy of Europe. If a Colony from Britain was established in the large Tract of Country, & if we were at war with Holland or Spain, we might very powerfully annoy either State from our new Settlement. We might with a safe, & expeditious voyage, make Naval Incursions on Java, & the other Dutch Settlements, & we might with equal facility, invade the Coasts of Spanish America . . . This check which New South Wales would be in time of War on both those Powers, makes it a very important Object when we view it in the Chart of the World, with a Political Eye.[18]

Lord North ignored Matra's scheme, and a glance at the atlas will show why: These strategic promises were puffery. The "facility" with which Chile could be attacked from Sydney involved crossing the whole Pacific. The "safe and expeditious voyage" to Java was some 4,000 miles long, through ill-charted and reef-strewn seas, with a dangerous choke-point in the Torres Straits.

Lord Sydney replaced Lord North at the end of 1783. He faced a rising clamor over the problem of criminal confinement—the shamefully over-crowded hulks and prisons. As home and colonial secretary, he was pressed to come up with a plan for disposing of British convicts. Matra heard he was casting around for a place to send them, and so he quickly wrote convicts into his plan and re-submitted it to Sydney:

Give them a few acres of ground as soon as they arrive . . . in absolute property, with what assistance they may want to till them. Let it be here remarked that they cannot fly from the country, that they have no temp-tation to theft, and that they must work or starve.[19]

Meanwhile, the administration drafted a new bill authorizing the revival of transportation to places other than America, "to what Place or Places, Part or Parts beyond the seas" the Crown might think fit. This Transportation Act (24 Geo. III, c. 56) became law in August 1784. All that was lacking was a place to receive the felons. Lord Sydney passed Matra's idea of an Australian thief-colony along to Lord Howe, the first lord of the Admiralty, who curtly rejected it as impractical.[20] But another naval man liked it, Sir George Young (1732–1810), a future admiral who had served in Indian waters. He advised Pitt that Botany Bay would make a good base for British ships "should it be necessary to send any into the South Seas"; that it should be established by convict labor; and that Pacific flax could replace that of Russia. Like Matra, he fancied that every imaginable cash crop could be grown in New South Wales, "uniting in one territory almost all the productions of the known world." Although his plan was scarcely distinguishable from Matra's, Young proposed sending only 140 convicts a year.[21]

Another proposal for opening a strategic supply-base in Australia with convict labor came from John Call (1732–1801), a former colonel in the service of the East India company, whose specialty was military engineering. He pointed to "the declining if not . . . precarious state" of Britain's East Indies trade, and recommended a British base in either New South Wales or New Zealand, with Norfolk Island and its superior flax as a convict-worked source of naval supplies.[22]

Nothing suggests that Pitt gave this more than glancing attention, although his attorney general, Pepper Arden, liked the idea. The strategic argument was ridiculed in July 1785 by a man whose views carried more weight in official circles than Young's, Call's or Matra's: Alexander Dalrymple, hydrographer to the East India Company, who opposed plans to colonize Norfolk Island as a violation of the company's monopolistic charter. In a report to the Court of the company's directors, Dalrymple sharply pointed out that serviceable mast timber could be got in Borneo and Sumatra—Chinese and southeast Asian shipwrights, after all, had done without Riga pines for centuries—and that "the best cables in the world" were made from Eastern coir and a palm fiber called gummatty. Dalrymple thought there was every reason to grow Pacific flax in England, but none to bring "so bulky an article" from Norfolk Island—"The absurdity . . . is too great to merit any serious consideration." And he heaped scorn on the way promoters like Matra, Young and Call had tried to tailor the idea of a strategic thief-colony to fit whatever the British Government seemed to have on its mind: .

This project of a Settlement in that quarter has appeared in many Proteus-like forms, sometimes as a halfway house to China; again as a check upon the *Spaniards* at *Manila* and their *Acapulco* Trade; sometimes as a place for transported Convicts; then as a place of Asylum for American Refugees; and sometimes as an Emporium for supplying our Marine Yards with Hemp and Cordage, or for carrying on the Fur Trade on the N.W. Coast of America; just as the temper of ministers was supposed to be inclined to receive a favorable impression.[23]

But through the flurry of promotional schemes, more attractive to historians as documents today than they had ever been to Pitt's government at the time, the real problem continued to grow. The jail and hulk population swelled through the winter of 1784–85, and the task of finding a place for transported convicts became perceptibly more urgent. Provincial jails were filled to bursting and even Newgate, whose complete rebuilding by George Dance the Younger was finished in 1785, was already so overcrowded that three hundred convicts had to be taken from it and put in a hulk in Langston Harbor at Portsmouth. On April 20,

1785, as the pressure on Pitt's government mounted, a committee met to decide once and for all where to send the convicts. Its chairman was Lord Beauchamp.

The first proposal was the island of Lemane, 400 miles up the Gambia River in West Africa. It was put up by the governor of the Africa Company, a British slaving enterprise. "Notorious felons," he urged, could be sent there packed in British slavers; stranded on Lemane with natives all around and a guardship stationed downstream in the Gambia River to stop them fleeing to the coast, the prisoners could be left "entirely to themselves" without a garrison and permitted to elect their own disciplinary officers. Many would perish in this African grave, but the survivors would turn into planters.

The Beauchamp Committee, to its credit, saw through this lunatic scheme, and one of its members, Edmund Burke, spoke against it in the House of Commons. So Lemane was dropped, and the committee was left with two alternatives: Das Voltas Bay, by the mouth of the Orange River on the southwest coast of Africa, and Botany Bay. It closely questioned its witnesses on the cost of sending convicts to Botany Bay, and how to keep them alive and disciplined once they got there. Yet despite the arguments of Matra, Call and Young for a convict settlement in New South Wales, the vote went to Das Voltas Bay, for several reasons. Das Voltas Bay was more strategically located. Unlike Botany Bay, it sat plumb on the main sea route from Europe to the Far East and promised to be an excellent staging depot for naval supplies. A British garrison there could offset a French one in Cape Town. The country behind it was said to be fertile and could serve as a new home for American Loyalists, those displaced and slightly embarrassing reminders of England's vast failure in the New World. Besides, there were rumors of copper ore in the mountains, at a time when the British Navy had started coppering the bottoms of all its ships to increase their service life in distant seas.[24] With high hopes, the government dispatched a sloop to survey Das Voltas Bay in September 1785, but it came back with the news that the place was too dry and sterile to be settled.

That left Botany Bay as a mediocre second choice. Perhaps its putative access to flax and pines, as raw material to be obtained by convict labor, gave it the edge over other suggested places such as Gromarivire Bay, on the Caffre Coast east of Cape Town, or Madagascar or Tristan da Cunha. But the "strategic" arguments for Botany Bay do not seem to have impressed Pitt. References to them in his correspondence are few and vague. His concern was getting rid of convicts, for by the spring of 1786 he was under severe political pressure from independent MPs to enforce the sentence of transportation and get convicts out of hulks within their constituencies at Plymouth and Portsmouth. "Though I am not at this

Moment able to state to You the Place, to which any Number of the Convicts will be sent," he wrote placatingly to one of these Devon men, John Rolle, "I am able to assure You that Measures are taken for procuring the Quantity of Shipping necessary for conveying above a thousand of them. . . . [A]ll the Steps necessary for the removal of at least that Number, may be completed in about a Month."[25]

It took longer than that. No ship was sent to reconnoiter Botany Bay because, as Lord Sydney and his more able undersecretary Evan Nepean stressed, the hour was late and the British hulks and jails were facing an imminent breakdown. (In one hulk riot, in March 1786, eight prisoners were killed and thirty-six wounded.[26]) The Government did not have eighteen spare months to send a ship to New South Wales and back; and in any case the Beauchamp Committee trusted what Banks told them of its merits as a spot for convict settlement. Nepean and Sydney also appeared to believe Matra's claim (supported by Young) that New South Wales was not so very far from the strategic centers of the Far East: "a Months run from the Cape of Good Hope, five weeks from Madras, and the same from Canton; very near the Moluccas, & less than a Months Run from Batavia." These figures were absurdly low. It took the First Fleet two months to reach Botany Bay from the Cape, with the prevailing westerlies behind it. Returning against them, the run was more like three months. And no ship could reach Canton or Madras from New South Wales in five weeks.

Attractive though it may have looked on paper to the geographically naïve, the "strategic" argument of Matra, Young, Call and Banks for a convict-colony in New South Wales remained a chimera to which Pitt's government showed no attachment. The flax industry began weakly and was soon abandoned. No ship (except the *Buffalo*, a small colonial-built vessel) ever had a suit of sails woven from Norfolk Island flax or sailed under spars of Norfolk Island pine. Although the early colonial governors Arthur Phillip and Philip Gidley King did pursue the cultivation of the flax plant *Phormium tenax* on Norfolk Island, their home government's actions spoke louder than its instructions: It sent neither trained flax-dressers nor appropriate tools to the colony. (David Mackay is probably right in seeing King's enthusiasm for flax production as "a personal and colonial necessity, rather than a strategic one"[27]; he wanted to be remembered as the governor of an infant state, one with its own export economy, not just as the keeper of the human dump that New South Wales actually was.)

As for the direct strategic role of the colony, it was nugatory. Port Jackson was thousands of miles from England's areas of strategic interest and, in any case, the threat posed by French ships in the Far East dwindled to insignificance by the mid-1790s. The garrison sent to guard the convicts was too small and weak to resist a determined invader; not that it mattered, for no invaders were interested. In terms of military advantage, the English presence in Australia at most caused some ripples of apprehension in France and on the far side of the Pacific. In 1790 the Viceroy of Mexico thought there were "not enough forces in our South Seas and the Department of San Blas to counteract those which the English have at their Botany Bay." A visit to the half-starved, virtually shipless colony of Sydney would have put his mind at ease. Although Napoleon thought about invading New South Wales, he did not try, and the place played no role in the Napoleonic Wars.[28]

Thus, despite the talk about strategic advantage that was heard up to the dispatch of the First Fleet in 1787, the actual benefits of the new colony to England were only two: It was a sign of claim, a foothold on the new continent; and, in Evan Nepean's words, it absorbed "a Dreadful banditti." For all the hopes, New South Wales was too far out on the geopolitical periphery of the late eighteenth century to do much else.

In the summer of 1786, Pitt's Cabinet, having run out of alternatives, decided to found its penal colony at Botany Bay. Lord Sydney's announcement to the Lords of the Treasury (drafted by Evan Nepean) held a note of urgency: "The greatest danger is to be apprehended" of escape from the crowded hulks and jails, while "infectious distempers" threatened their inmates. Thus "measures should immediately be pursued" for getting the transportable convicts out of England. In round numbers, the first shipment should contain 600 of them (later 750), guarded by three companies of marines. Nepean estimated the cost of the equipment for founding the settlement in Australia at £29,300. Running it would cost the government £18,669 the first year, £15,449 the second and under £7,000 the third; after that, if all went to plan, it would be self-victualling.[29]

The proposal to colonize Botany Bay with convicts was formally drawn up (almost certainly by Nepean rather than Sydney) in an unsigned document titled "Heads of a Plan for effectually disposing of convicts" and was presented to the cabinet in August 1786. Its emphasis was clear: The proposed colony would serve as "a remedy for the evils likely to result from the late alarming and numerous increase of felons in this country, and more particularly in the metropolis." The secondary benefit of the region's raw materials was presented at the end of the document: "It may also be proper to attend to the possibility of procuring . . . masts and ships' timber for the use of our fleets in India, as the distance between the two countries is not greater than between Great Britain and America." The author's eulogies on Pacific flax repeated Matra's almost phrase for phrase.[30]

The cabinet gave its approval; and without further ado, the government chose a man to lead the expedition and govern the new colony. He was found on the navy's semi-retired list: a man of independent but modest means, living as a gentleman farmer at Lyndhurst in the New Forest of Hampshire. His name was Captain Arthur Phillip.

v

WHEN PHILLIP received his commission from George III on October 12, 1786, appointing him "Governor of our territory called New South Wales," he was one day past his forty-eighth birthday. To judge from the surviving portraits, he was slight in build, with a long nose, a slightly pendulous lower lip, a smooth pear of a skull, and liquid melancholy-looking eighteenth-century eyes. It is a face most unlike the square-boned visage of Cook; one could imagine it under a European peruke, perhaps belonging to a kapellmeister in some little Bavarian court. Phillip was half German. His father, Jakob Phillip, was a language teacher from Frankfurt, who emigrated to London and married a certain Elizabeth Breach.

Phillip first went to sea at the age of sixteen, in time for the start of the Seven Years' War against France. Three years later he was promoted to lieutenant, but when peace resumed in 1763, he retired early on half-pay at the age of twenty-five. He married, but the marriage was not a happy one and he was formally separated from his wife in 1769. They had no children. Rural life at Lyndhurst now palled on him, and by 1770 he was back on the active list. In 1774 he got leave to join the Portuguese Navy, then at war with Spain. As captain of a Portuguese ship, Phillip delivered 400 Portuguese convicts across the Atlantic to Brazil without losing a man—a feat that presumably convinced Lord Sydney of his fitness to govern a penal colony.

By 1778 he was back in the British Navy and in 1779 he received command of the fireship *Basilisk*. To be past forty with no better post was no triumph, but three years later he had risen to be master of a full ship of the line, the 64-gun *Europe*. Yet by 1784 he went back to his farm again, on half-pay.

The best reputation Phillip could have had, in view of this lackluster record, was that of a reliable, forthright and rather unimaginative man; solitary, perhaps; competent on ship and self-effacing on shore. Nobody could have mistaken him for a charismatic leader. He had no apparent political talents. But politicians were the last people the Crown needed in a remote penal settlement. If the colony were to survive at all, it must be run by chain of command, not consensus, led by an eminently practical man. Australia's remoteness would set free cruelty and madness in some British officers sent to guard convicts there. But power made Phillip equitable and level-headed, and he appears to have believed that at least some of his convicts could be reformed, provided they were isolated. "As I would not wish convicts to lay the foundations of an empire," he wrote,

> I think they should remain separated from the garrison, and other settlers that may come from Europe, and not allowed to mix with them, even after the 7 or 14 years for which they are transported may be expired. The laws of this country will, of course, be introduced in [New] South Wales, and there is one that I wish to take place from the moment his Majesty's forces take possession of the country: *That there can be no slavery in a free land, and consequently no slaves.*[31]

One could hardly compare Phillip's words with the clarion speech of a Jefferson or a Lafayette, but they were the only ones verging on the description of a social ideal that would be uttered in, or about, Australia for the rest of the eighteenth century. However, what Phillip was really talking about was *apartheid*. He had no "democratic" feelings toward the convicts, and his later gestures of apparent equality, such as cutting rations for free and bond impartially in times of crisis, indicated no special sympathy for them. He thought of the convicts essentially as slaves, by their own fallen nature if not in the strict terms of the law. In declaring that "there can be no slavery in a free land, and consequently no slaves," he was not suggesting that his new colony would *begin* free; he was pointing to a remote future in which it might *become* so, a time when the convict system would have withered away and New South Wales would be populated by free emigrants, English yeomen and planters.

On August 31, 1786, Lord Sydney told the Admiralty that the voyage was going ahead, and instructed it to commission the fleet. There were, in all, eleven vessels. Only two of them were naval warships—the flagship *Sirius* and the brig-rigged sloop *Supply*. The rest were converted merchantmen. The Navy Board chose three storeships—*Borrowdale* (272 tons), *Fishburn* (378 tons) and *Golden Grove* (331 tons)—and six transports: *Alexander* (452 tons), *Charlotte* (345 tons), *Friendship* (278 tons), *Lady Penrhyn* (338 tons), *Prince of Wales* (333 tons) and *Scarborough* (418 tons). Most of them were fairly new vessels; *Scarborough*, the oldest, had been launched in 1781. The terms of the charter contract were that all of these ships, except the naval vessels, would cost the Government 10 shillings per register ton per month. Assuming an eight months' passage out and the same back, the government would have to pay the contractors at least £20,900 for the hire of their ships, and that was the largest single expense of the First Fleet.

But they were all small vessels, and very overcrowded by modern standards of sea travel. The largest transport, the *Alexander*, was 114 feet long and 31 feet in beam. In all, the fleet had to carry almost 1,500 people —officers, seamen and marines, women, children, and convicts. That meant a close pack—less than 3 tons of ship per person embarked.[32] (The ration on a modern passenger liner is closer to 250 tons per person.) In an exasperated letter Phillip complained that his passengers, convicts and marines alike, "after taking off the tonnage for the provision of stores . . . have not one ton and a half per man."[33]

As the winter wore on, Phillip did what he could to call the authorities' attention to the lack of space. On January 11, 1787 he wrote to Nepean,

> I find that 184 men are put on board [*Alexander.*] . . . [T]here are amongst the men several unable to help themselves, and no kind of surgeons' instruments have been put on board that ship or any of the transports. . . . It will be very difficult to prevent the most fatal sickness among men so closely confined; on board that ship which is to receive 210 convicts there is not a space left . . . sufficiently large for 40 men to be in motion at the same time.[34]

No craft, then or later, was ever designed specifically to carry convicts; that would have cost the owner too much for too specialized a vessel. It became the practice to dump the bulkheads, sleeping-racks and iron grilles in Sydney before the ships sailed north to China for their cargoes of tea on the home run. The 'tween-deck plans of the First Fleet transports are lost, but the quarters were certainly very cramped for the marines and crew, let alone for the convicts: Four transportees lying in a space seven feet by six feet, the dimensions of a modern king-size bed, were the norm. There was little headroom; *Scarborough*, the second-largest transport, had only four feet, five inches, so that even a small woman had to stoop and a full-grown man had to bend double. Philip Gidley King, second lieutenant on *Sirius*, described the security, "which consists," he wrote in his journal,

> of very strong & thick Bulkheads, filled with nails & run across from side to side in ye tween decks abaft the Mainmast with loop holes to fire between the decks in case of irregularities. The hatches are well secured down by cross bars, bolts & locks & are likewise nailed down from deck to deck with oak stanchions. There is also a barricade of plank about 3 feet high, armed with pointed prongs of Iron on the upper deck, abaft the Mainmast, to prevent any connection between the Marines & Ships Company, with the Convicts. Centinels are placed at the different Hatchways

& a Guard always under arms on the Quarter Deck of each Transport in order to prevent any improper behaviour of the Convicts.[35]

The prisoners' quarters had no portholes or sidelights; such things were an innovation and perhaps a security hazard. The lower decks were as dark as the grave, as lanterns and candles were banned for fear of fire. The only fresh air the convicts got was from a windsail rigged to scoop a breeze down a hatchway. In a storm, when the hatches were battened down, there was no fresh air below. In calm weather, prisoners could exercise on deck.

By January 6, 1787, the first convicts were loaded from the Woolwich hulks, the men onto *Scarborough* and the women aboard *Lady Penrhyn*. But two months passed before all the convicts embarked and the eleven ships were mustered at anchor on the Motherbank outside Portsmouth harbor, and they would remain at anchor two months more. The late winter and spring of 1787 went by in a stream of blunders and delays. The bureaucrats of Whitehall naïvely supposed that the logistics of a six-week slave run across the Pacific could be applied to an eight-month passage to Australia—which, as Phillip kept stressing, they could not. His letters to Nepean and Sydney are full of the complaints of a practical sailor. Luckily, Nepean understood them; Sydney was too insulated or obtuse to do so.

To begin with, the fleet was undervictualled by its crooked contractor, Duncan Campbell. He had shortchanged the convicts with half a pound of rice instead of a pound of flour—"this will be very severely felt"—and supplying only enough bread to give each prisoner the pitiful ration of six ounces (two slices) a day.[36] Even worse, despite the lessons of Cook's voyages, there were no anti-scorbutics. Phillip knew it would be murder to sail without them, and his letters now grew very blunt:

> The contracts . . . were made before I ever saw the navy Board on this business. . . . I have repeatedly pointed out the consequences that must be expected of the men's being crowded on board such small ships, and from victualling the marines according to the contract which allows no flour. . . . this must be fatal to many, and the more so as no anti-scorbutics are allowed on board. . . . [I]n fact, my Lord, the garrison and the convicts are sent to the extremity of the globe as they would be sent to America—a six-weeks' passage.
>
> . . . I am prepared to meet difficulties, and I have only one fear—I fear, my Lord, that it may be said hereafter that the officer who took charge of the expedition should have known that it was more than probable he lost half the garrison and convicts, crowded and victualled in such a manner for so long a voyage. And the public . . . may impute to my ignorance or

inattention what I have never been consulted in, and which never coincided with my ideas.[37]

A stickler for detail, a true professional, Phillip knew that survival might depend on the humblest item of inventory and that he had to double-check them all. Why were only six scythes and five dozen razors provided? Could Nepean not see that they would need 560 pounds, not 200 pounds, of buckshot? How would the convict superintendents be paid? Where were the bolts of cloth against the inevitable day when, thousands of miles from Portsmouth, the convicts' clothes wore out? Phillip begged for fresh meat for the convicts, wine for the sick, fumigants, extra medicine. His masters moved with maddening slowness.

The work of the embarkation dragged on through late February and March. The convicts came rumbling down to the Plymouth and Portsmouth docks in heavy wagons, under guard, ironed together, shivering under the incessant rain. The pale, ragged, lousy prisoners, thin as wading birds from their jail diet, were herded on board and spent the next several months below; orders forbade them to exercise on deck until the flotilla was out of sight of land. The condition of the women provoked Phillip to a furious outburst:

> The situation in which the magistrates sent the women on board the *Lady Penrhyn*, stamps them with infamy—tho' almost naked, and so very filthy, that nothing but clothing them could have prevented them from perishing, and which could not be done in time to prevent a fever, which is still on board that ship, and where there are many venereal complaints, that must spread in spite of every precaution I may take hereafter.[38]

Who were these First Fleet convicts? It was once a cherished Australian belief that at least some of the people on the First Fleet were political exiles—rick-burners, trade-unionists, and the like. In fact, though victims of a savage penal code, they were not political prisoners. On the other hand, few of them were dangerous criminals. Not one person was shipped out in 1787 for murder or rape, although more than a hundred of them had been convicted of thefts (such as highway robbery) in which violence played some part. No woman on the First Fleet, legend to the contrary, had been transported for prostitution, as it was not a transportable offense. Many were treated as whores, and doubtless some were, although only two—Mary Allen and Ann Mather—had been described by their judges as "unfortunate girl" or "poor unhappy woman of the town."

In all, 736 convicts went on the First Fleet. Of these, we know the age or occupation, and sometimes both, of 330 people—127 women, 203 men.[39] They came from all over England, but most of them were Londoners. Their main categories of crime were as follows:

OFFENSE	NUMBER
Minor theft	431
"Privy theft," including breaking and entering	93
Highway robbery	71
Stealing cattle or sheep	44
Robbery with violence (mugging)	31
Grand larceny	9
Fencing (receiving stolen goods)	8
Swindling, impersonation	7
Forgery of documents, banknotes, etc.	4
Other	35
Total of known indictments	733

All these were crimes against property, some forced by a pitiful necessity. Elizabeth Beckford, the second oldest woman on the First Fleet, was seventy. Her crime, for which she got seven years' transportation, was to have stolen twelve pounds of Gloucester cheese. At the Stafford Assizes, a laborer named Thomas Hawell went down for seven years for "feloniously stealing one live hen to the value of 2d., and one dead hen to the value of 2d." Elizabeth Powley, twenty-two and unemployed, raided a kitchen in Norfolk, took a few shillings' worth of bacon, flour and raisins, with "twenty-four ounces Weight of Butter value 12d," and was sentenced to hang; but a reprieve came and to Australia she went, never to eat butter again. Hunger drove a West Indian named Thomas Chaddick into a kitchen garden where he "did pluck up, spoil and destroy, against the form of the statute" twelve cucumber plants; he, too, went to Australia, there to contemplate the exactness with which the god of property had measured out his black life in cucumbers.

Some purloined inedible trifles. William Rickson, a nineteen-year-old laborer, made off with a wooden box which proved to contain merely a piece of linen and five books. James Grace, an eleven-year-old, took ten yards of ribbon and a pair of silk stockings. William Francis stole a book entitled *A Summary Account of the Flourishing State of the Island of Tobago* from a London gentleman named Robert Melville. Fifteen-year-old John Wisehammer grabbed a packet of snuff from an apothecary's counter in Gloucester. They all went down for seven years.

There were, of course, less trivial crimes. Apprentices robbed their masters' stock. John Nicolls, a hairdresser's assistant, drew seven years' transportation for stealing goods worth £14 9s. 6d., enough to start his own barbershop: fifty-seven razors, sixty-two ivory combs, six bunches of human hair, soap, wig ribbon, pomade, scissors, hairnets and powder. A journeyman watchmaker mugged another watchmaker for a dozen silver watchcases; another stole a mass of parts, comprising 185 complete watch movements, barrels, fusees, arbors, verges and studs.

None of these acts were news when they happened. They were mere drops in a swollen torrent of eighteenth-century crime. The only exception was Thomas Gearing, who created a brief sensation in Oxford in 1786 by breaking into the chapel of Magdalen College and stealing some ecclesiastical plate. For this sacrilege, he was condemned to death, reprieved and then transported for life.

Judges were particularly severe on thieves who used violence and threats. In 1782 Thomas Josephs accosted a married woman on a London street, "putting her in fear" and seizing her handkerchief, worth 2 shillings. The sentence was death; after five years in jail he was embarked on *Scarborough*, to serve the Crown for seven years in New South Wales. All the cattle duffers and horse thieves on the First Fleet were under commuted death sentences.

The Beauchamp Committee had urged that the new colony consist of "young Convicts," and so it did. The convicts' average age was about twenty-seven years. Age distribution was much the same for either sex:

AGE (YRS.)	MEN	WOMEN
under 15	3	2
16–25	68	58
26–35	51	50
36–45	11	6
46–55	4	3
over 56	3	3
Total convicts of known age	140	122

The oldest female convict was Dorothy Handland, a dealer in rags and old clothes who was eighty-two years old in 1787. She had drawn seven years for perjury. In 1789, in a fit of befuddled despair, she was to hang herself from a gum tree at Sydney Cove, thus becoming Australia's first recorded suicide. The oldest male convict was a Shropshire man, Joseph Owen, who was somewhere between sixty and sixty-six. The youngest boy was John Hudson, a nine-year-old chimney sweep. He had stolen some clothes and a pistol. "One would wish to snatch such a boy, if one possibly could," the judge remarked, "from destruction, for he will only return to the same kind of life which he has led before." So little John Hudson was sent to Australia for seven years. The youngest girl was Elizabeth Hayward, a clogmaker aged thirteen, who had stolen a linen gown and a silk bonnet worth 7 shillings.

Classed by occupation, the First Fleet convicts were an anthology of country and town trades—but that did not guarantee their fitness as pioneers. The details of employment (or lack of it) for 190 men and 125 women have survived. Of the men, twenty-four (12 percent) were noted as unemployed. The largest occupation group was laborers, mostly rural —eighty-four men, or 44 percent of the total. From there the size of the professional groups dropped sharply:

TRADE	NO. OF PERSONS
Seamen	8
Carpenters, shipwrights and cabinetmakers	6
Shoemakers	5
Weavers	5
Watermen	4
Ivory turners	3
Brickmakers	2
Bricklayers, masons	2
Other trades	47

"Other trades" included three domestic servants, two leather-breeches makers, two tailors, two butchers, a jeweller, a baker and a silk-dyer. There was also one fisherman, a Cornishman named William Bryant. Of the women, fourteen (11 percent) were "unemployed," and some if not most of these may have been prostitutes. More than half the women were domestic servants. The rest were milliners, mantua-makers, oyster-sellers, glove-makers, shoe-binders—a spatter of trades that reflected the kind of jobs women in eighteenth-century England could expect to find, all of them fairly menial.

So it had a motley crew, this Noah's Ark of small-time criminality; and for all the trades represented aboard, it was absurdly ill-chosen for the task of colonizing New South Wales. The authorities had used no criteria of selection apart from youth, and that erratically. There was no choice by trade. The colony that would have to raise its own crops in unknown soil had only one professional gardener, and he was a raw youth of twenty. It would need tons of fish, but had only one fisherman. There were only two brickmakers, two bricklayers and a mason for all the houses that would need building; no sawyers were aboard, and only six carpenters. It had no flax-dressers or linen-weavers—proof of the government's indifference to the prospect of a "strategic" colony. This muddle and lack of foresight in the choice of convicts typified the planning, being one of many matters over which Captain Arthur Phillip had no control.

And there was one general class of crook not represented on the First Fleet: the successful ones. This was pointed out a few years later in a mordant ballad entitled *Botany Bay: A New Song* (1790):

> Let us drink a good health to our schemers above,
> Who at length have contriv'd from this land to remove
> Thieves, robbers and villains, they'll send 'em away,
> To become a new people at Botany Bay.

> Some men say they have talents and trades to get bread,
> Yet they spunge on mankind to be cloathed and fed,
> They'll spend all they get, and turn night into day—
> Now I'd have all such sots sent to Botany Bay.

> There's gay powder'd coxcombs and proud dressy fops,
> Who with very small fortunes set up in great shops,
> They'll run into debt with design ne'er to pay,
> They should all be transported to Botany Bay. . . .

> There's nightwalking strumpets who swarm in each street,
> Proclaiming their calling to each man they meet:
> They become such a pest that without more delay,
> Those corrupters of youth should be sent to the Bay.

> There's monopolizers who add to their store,
> By cruel oppression and squeezing the poor,
> There's butchers and farmers get rich in that way,
> But I'd have all such rogues sent to Botany Bay. . . .

> You lecherous whore-masters who practice vile arts,
> To ruin young virgins and break parents' hearts,
> Or from the fond husband the wife lead astray—
> Let such debauch'd stallions be sent to the Bay.

> There's whores, pimps and bastards, a large costly crew,
> Maintain'd by the sweat of a labouring few,
> They should have no commission, place, pension or pay,
> Such locusts should all go to Botany Bay.

> The hulks and the jails had some thousands in store,
> But out of the jails are ten thousand times more,
> Who live by fraud, cheating, vile tricks and foul play,
> And should all be sent over to Botany Bay.

> Now should any take umbrage at what I have writ,
> Or find here a bonnet or cap that will fit,
> To such I have only this one word to say:
> They are welcome to wear it in Botany Bay.[40]

In March 1787, with two months to sailing date, typhus broke out in the ships anchored on the Motherbank outside Portsmouth. The crammed decks of *Alexander* incubated it; by April 15, eleven of its prisoners had died, and the rest were hastily disembarked. Enlisted men fumigated the ship, scrubbed her with creosote (the navy's all-purpose disinfectant and pesticide) and swabbed the convict quarters with quicklime. Even so, five more men died on *Alexander* before she sailed. One woman convict died of "jail fever" on *Lady Penrhyn*, but luckily the disease did not spread through the squadron.

This outbreak of fever provoked a flood of rumors on shore. The expedition to Botany Bay had piqued the curiosity of the public from the moment it was announced. It had been furiously lampooned and defended by pamphleteers. "What is the Punishment intended to be inflicted?" cried Alexander Dalrymple, the official of the East India Company who was an unsparing critic of penal colonies in the South Seas:

> Not to make the Felons undergo *servitude* for the *benefit of others*, was the Case in America; but to place them, as their own Masters, in a temperate Climate, where they have *every object* of *comfort* or *Ambition* before them! and although it might be going too far to suppose, This will *incite men* to become *Convicts*, that they may be *comfortably* provided for; yet surely it cannot *deter* men, inclined to commit Theft and Robbery, to know that, in case they are detected and convicted, all that will happen to them is that they will be sent, at the Publick Expense, to a good Country and Temperate Climate, where they will be their own masters![41]

In the same vein but more facetiously, ballads had described the southern arcadia, free of death and taxes, where the lucky felons were going:

> They go to an Island to take special charge,
> Much warmer than Britain, and ten times as large:
> No customs-house duty, no freightage to pay,
> And tax-free they'll live when in Botany Bay.[42]

A theatrical producer commissioned an opera entitled *Botany Bay*, which opened at the Royal Circus in London in April and closed the night before the fleet sailed.

The typhus outbreak was played up by the newspapers, which had one good effect: At last Duncan Campbell, the contractor, was forced to issue the fresh beef and vegetables Phillip wanted for the convicts and marines. The marines also complained that they would not be issued liquor in New South Wales, "without which . . . we cannot expect to survive the hardships"[43]—and three days later Nepean guaranteed them a three-year issue of rum and wine. However, the womens' clothes had still not arrived, and neither had the small-arms supplies for the marines. "We have neither musquet balls nor paper for musquet cartridges, nor have we any armourers' tools," Phillip complained—and it had to be kept a dead secret all the way across the Atlantic, for fear of a convict mutiny.[44]

Nevertheless, on the evening of May 12, Phillip ordered his flagship *Sirius* to weigh anchor. The signal flags fluttered, but nothing happened; the merchant seamen in some of the transports refused point-blank to go aloft. Lieutenant King went to investigate. It turned out that the seamen —who were not under military command, being the crew of chartered commercial vessels—were on strike against the ships' owners, who owed them seven months' back pay. The owners, skinflints all, hoped to force their crews to buy "necessaries" from ships' stores on credit at inflated prices during the long voyage; the sailors naturally wished to equip themselves cheaper and better, for cash, in Portsmouth. Their complaints were sorted out, after a fashion, and at three in the morning of Sunday, May 13, before the first cold gristle of pre-dawn light had spread upon the sea, the First Fleet weighed anchor and shaped its course in a rising wind for Tenerife.

vi

THE CONVICTS were "humble, submissive and regular" on this first leg of the voyage, Watkin Tench wrote with relief. They had been told "in the most pointed terms that any attempt . . . to force their escape should be punished with instant death." Escape, however, was unlikely, as they were chained, in shock and atrociously seasick. Through the long rolling weeks at anchorage on the Motherbank, the literate prisoners had written letters to their families and friends ashore, and Tench had had the "tiresome and disagreeable" duty of acting as censor. "Their constant language," he noted, "was an apprehension of the impracticability of returning home, the dread of a sickly passage, and the fearful prospect of a distant and barbarous country." He dismissed their laments as "doubtless an artifice to awaken compassion."[45]

There was nothing artificial about them. None of the convicts could have had any idea of their destination. Before them yawned a terrifying void of time and space. They were going on the longest voyage ever attempted by so large a group of people. If they had been told they were off to the moon, the sense of loss, deracination and fear could hardly have been worse—at least one could see the moon from England, which could not be said for Botany Bay.

The convicts, of course, were not the only ones who felt their lives cut in half. As the flotilla sailed from Portsmouth, a young second officer of marines, not long married, began his diary:

> 5 o'clock in the morning. The Sirius made the signal for the whole fleet to get under way. O Gracious God send that we may put into Plymouth or Torbay on our way down Channel that I may see my dear and fond affectionate Alicia and our sweet son before I leave them for this long absence. O Almighty God hear my prayer and grant me this request . . . what makes me so happy this day is it because that I am in hoppes the fleet will put into Plymth. O my fond heart lay still for you may be disappointed I trust in God you will not.

But Plymouth fell astern, and Ralph Clark's journal for May 14 bears the anguished scrawl, "Oh my God all my hoppes are over of seeing my beloved wife and son."[46]

The run to Tenerife passed almost without incident. The weather was fine and, once out of sight of land, the convicts were allowed on deck to exercise. On June 3 the fleet made its anchorage in the port of Santa Cruz, under the high conical peak of Tenerife.

The officers and crewmen had a week to stretch their legs on land, while the ships took on fresh water, pumpkins, onions, indifferent and costly meat and Canary wine. Phillip and twenty of his chief officers were lavishly entertained by the Sicilian-born governor of the Canaries. One night, a convict named John Power escaped from *Alexander* by shinnying down her anchor hawser. He swam quietly astern, scrambled into a dinghy, cut its painter and drifted on the current across the bay to a Dutch East Indiaman. Its crew would not take him on board; so Power rowed to a small island in the lee of the fleet, where he beached the boat, rested up for the night (his plan being to row thirty miles to the Grand Canary) and was captured by a search party the next morning. But Power's was the only such venture, and on June 10 the fleet set sail for Rio de Janeiro.

At first, Phillip's track looks remarkably indirect: Why cross the Atlantic twice to get to Australia? In fact, his course from Portsmouth to the Cape of Good Hope via the Canaries and Rio made the best of prevailing winds and currents. Boosted south-southwest by the Canary Current and the northeast trade winds, a ship would pass the Cape Verde Islands and sail south until it entered the equatorial doldrums in the Atlantic Narrows. Once through that zone of calms and fluky winds it could pick up the southbound Brazil Current, getting a good slant on the southeast trades to reach Rio and drop further south into the zone of the westerlies, around 30°S. Then it had a straight run downwind to Cape Town.[47]

The fleet raised the Cape Verde Islands on June 18. Adverse winds prevented the ships from anchoring at Port Praia on São Tiago, and on they sailed. Now the weather became intolerably hot and humid, and as the fleet entered the tropics waves of vermin crept out of each vessel's woodwork, up from the bilges—rats, bedbugs, lice, cockroaches, fleas. Officers and convicts alike were tormented by them and fought back as best they could with "frequent explosions of gunpowder, lighting fires between decks, and a liberal use of that admirable antiseptic, oil of tar."[48]

The bilges were foul in all of the ships. Even those whose guts have heaved at the whiff from the boat's head at sea can have little idea of the anguish of eighteenth-century bilge stink: a fermenting, sloshing broth of sea water mixed with urine, puke, dung, rotting food, dead rats and the hundred other attars of the Great Age of Sail. On *Alexander*, another batch of convicts fell sick from the bilge effluents,

> which had by some means or other risen to so great a height, that the pannels of the cabin, and the buttons on the back of the officers, were turned nearly black, by the noxious effluvia. When the hatches were taken off, the stench was so powerful that it was scarcely possible to stand over them.[49]

When tropical rainstorms whipped the fleet, the convicts—who had no change of dry clothes—could not exercise on deck. They stayed below under battened hatches, and conditions in their steaming, stinking holds were extreme. "The weather was now so immoderately hot," noted John White, surgeon on *Charlotte*, "that the female convicts, perfectly overcome with it, frequently fainted away, and these faintings generally terminated in fits." At night, some of them rutted like stoats. "Notwithstanding the enervating effects of the atmospheric heat," White recorded with some amazement,

> so predominant was the warmth of their constitutions, or the depravity of their hearts, that the hatches . . . could not be suffered to lay off, during the night, without a promiscuous intercourse immediately taking place between them and the seamen and marines . . . [T]he desire of the women to be with the men was so uncontrollable that neither shame (but indeed of this they had long lost sight) nor the fear of punishment could deter them from making their way through the bulkheads to the apartments assigned to the seamen.[50]

It sounds like bedlam, and probably it was. The marines on the four female transports—*Charlotte, Lady Penrhyn, Prince of Wales* and *Friendship*—could buy a woman with a pannikin of rum from their daily rations, and from then on the drunkenness of some female convicts would become another problem for Captain Phillip.

When the women got unruly, they were ironed and sometimes flogged. One prisoner on *Friendship*, Elizabeth Dudgeon (7 years for stealing £9 19s. 6d. in London), was especially troublesome. She spent the first nine days of the Tenerife–Rio run in irons for fighting, and on release she was found carousing in the seamen's quarters. Back into irons she went, but a few days later she rashly gave a guard officer, Captain James Meredith, a tongue-lashing. He had her triced up to a grating and flogged, to the pleasure of Lieutenant Ralph Clark: "The corporal did not play with her, but laid it home, which I was very glad to see . . . she has long been fishing for it, which she has at last got to her heart's content."[51]

Once the fleet reached the doldrums, Phillip rationed water to three pints a day. But by mid-July the ships picked up the southeast trades, the sails cracked and bellied, and down to Rio they rolled, *Lady Penrhyn* lagging and wallowing, nimble little *Supply* herding up the slow transports until, on August 5, the whole fleet was snugged down in Rio harbor.

It stayed there a month. There was much to be done: watering and cleaning ship, buying stores and making repairs. Sixteen people had died since England—ten on one boat, the mephitic *Alexander*—and there were eighty-one on the sicklist. By eighteenth-century standards, things could have been much worse. Phillip busied himself with stores. He could not get the small-arms supplies he needed in Rio—Portuguese armorers' tools did not fit English guns—but he obtained 10,000 musketballs from the local arsenal. The clothing of the women convicts was already disintegrating, and to replace it Phillip parsimoniously bought 100 sacks of tapioca (which would substitute, in a pinch, for flour), the sacks of which "being of strong Russia [burlap] will be used hereafter in cloathing the convicts, many of whom are nearly naked."[52] He bought seeds and laid in supplies of the local beef, which was excellent, and of the local firewater or *aguardiente*, which was not. "That [Brazilians] have not learnt the art of making palatable rum," Watkin Tench morosely noted many hangovers later, "the English troops in New South Wales can bear testimony."

The Viceroy, who had known Phillip in the days of his mercenary service for Portugal, entertained him and his men generously and gave them carte blanche to go wherever they pleased, unescorted. They promenaded contentedly about, admiring the macaws and toucans, gorging themselves on limes, lemons and oranges, and ogling the "lusty" girls of Rio whose long hair, once unbraided, trailed two inches on the floor when they walked barefoot. They envied the Portuguese their police, but their English souls were affronted by Rio's tropical Catholicism.

The convicts, of course, saw none of this. They were kept below deck. But some of them had been up to their old tricks on the long Atlantic run. John White found that a convict named Thomas Barrett had "with great ingenuity" started a forgers' ring, making quarter-dollars out of old buckles and pewter spoons:

> The impression, milling, character . . . was so inimitably executed that had their metal been a little better, the fraud, I am convinced, would have passed undetected . . . How they could effect it at all, is a matter of the most inexpressible surprise to me; as they were never suffered to come near a fire; and a centinel was constantly placed over their hatchway, which . . . rendered it impossible for either fire or fused metal to be conveyed to their apartments. Besides, hardly ten minutes ever elapsed, without an officer going down among them. The adroitness, therefore, with which they must have managed, in order to complete a business that required so complicated a process, gave me a high opinion of their ingenuity, cunning, caution and address.[53]

Barrett was lightly punished, but James Baker, a marine who had tried to pass off one of the forged coins on shore, got 200 lashes. As a rule, the floggings inflicted on the marines were far worse than anything the convicts got. The inequality of punishment would turn out to be a great source of friction between marines and convicts later.

Other tensions were felt not long after the fleet left Rio on September 3 for its drop south and its long run before the westerlies to Cape Town. In the confined space of a ship, irritations grow and all raw spots chafe. Some of the officers took to drink, traded insults in the mess and cursed their hangovers. One could find relief from the bickering on deck, watching the frigate birds and pintadoes, trolling a line for fish and admiring the hungry grace of albacore tearing into the schools of flying fish as they burst, like scattering chainshot, from the heaving indigo rollers. Luckily the fleet had a quick crossing. By mid-October they were at Cape Town, the tip of Africa, the extreme point of European penetration into the southern hemisphere.

The fleet spent a month in Cape Town. The main task was to stock up on plants, seeds and livestock for the colony in New South Wales. This Phillip did, with much hard bargaining against phlegmatic Dutch tightwads. He also tried to build up the convicts' strength for the last, most difficult leg of the voyage, by giving them fresh beef and mutton, soft bread and as many vegetables as they could eat, every day.[54] His officers hated Cape Town—the Dutch, the Kaffirs, the heat, the dust.

Nevertheless it was the last civilized place, the last repository of recognizable European values, that the men and women of the First Fleet would see for years; and the thought must have lain heavily on them when at last the tars stood to the capstans and the anchor-cables rose dripping through their hawser-holes. This was the end of Europe. Before them stretched the awesome, lonely void of the Indian and Southern Oceans, and beyond that lay nothing they could imagine.

The modern traveller, gazing down on the wrinkles of the earth's waters from an armchair six miles up, has no conception of the forbidding grandeur of the sea into which the First Fleet now moved. Its waves are the largest of any of the world's oceans, and from the deck of a boat they are overwhelming: tottering hills of indigo and malachite glass, veined in their transparencies with braids of opaque white water, their spumy crests running level with the ship's cross-trees. The inexorable rhythm of their passage numbs the brain, first with fear and then with repetition.

The fleet transports labored now, clawing up the swells and staggering down into the troughs. They were loaded down with new supplies, including some five hundred animals mooing, clucking and bleating frantically in their improvised pens. The convict quarters were more crowded than ever, because room had to be made for the future colony's livestock (and its bales of food)—two Africander bulls, three cows, three horses, forty-four sheep, thirty-two hogs, poultry of all sorts, and such animals as the officers had managed to cram on board for their private stock. All the women convicts had been moved off *Friendship* and redistributed among the other three female transports; their place was taken by sheep which, Ralph Clark opined, would be "much more agreeable shipmates." Arthur Bowes Smythe, the surgeon on the women's transport *Lady Penrhyn*, felt the same way. "I believe few Marines or Soldiers going out on a foreign Service under Government were ever better, if so well provided for as these Convicts are," he remarked, but

> I wish I cd. with truth add that the behaviour of the Convicts merited such extream indulgence—but I believe I may venture to say there was never a more abandon'd set of wretches collected in one place at any period than are now to be met with in this Ship. . . . The greater part of them are so totally abandon'd and callous'd to all sense of shame & even common decency that it frequently becomes indispensably necessary to inflict Corporal punishment upon them. . . . [E]very day furnishes proofs of their being more harden'd in their Wickedness—nor do I conceive it possible in their present situation to adopt any plan to induce them to behave like rational or even human Beings. . . . Nor can their matchless Hippocracy be equalled except by their base Ingratitude.[55]

As the vessels slipped further down the map, below the fortieth south parallel, under the southern coast of Australia and toward Van Diemen's Land, the gales stayed favorable and the weather "dark, wet and gloomy." Gannets and terns circled the ships. Whales were sighted, and often the wandering albatross, *Diomedea exsulans*, would materialize out of the spindrift, white from white, and wheel silently about the plunging masts on its fourteen-foot wings before vanishing into a rainsquall. Waves broke green over the decks, dumping tons of freezing water down the companionways and sluicing the marines and the shivering, half-clothed convicts out of their bunks. Coming north around Van Diemen's Land on January 10, 1788, they ran into a violent thundersquall that split the *Golden Grove*'s topsails and carried away *Prince of Wales*'s main yard; the women on *Lady Penrhyn* "were so terrified that most of them were down on their knees at prayers, and in less than one hour after it had abated they were uttering the most horrid oaths and imprecations that could proceed out of the mouths of such abandoned prostitutes as they are."[56]

Surgeon John White on *Charlotte* had a revelation of how far from the company of European man they had all come. Flocks of "large oceanous birds" flew about the ship, and the marines amused themselves by shooting at them; but the seabirds showed no alarm "either at the report, or at the balls . . . [for] they had never been harassed with firearms before."[57]

On the evening of January 19, *Sirius* and the transports sighted the coast of mainland Australia. By ten the next morning they were all anchored in Botany Bay. "To see all the ships safe in their destined port," White wrote with commendable restraint, "without ever having, by any accident, been one hour separated; and all the people in as good health as could be expected or hoped for, after so long a voyage, was a sight truly pleasing, and at which every heart must rejoice."[58]

It had been one of the great sea voyages in English history. Captain Arthur Phillip, the middle-aged nonentity, had brought them across more than fifteen thousand miles of ocean without losing a ship. The entire run had taken 252 days. A total of forty-eight people had died—forty convicts, five convicts' children, one marine's wife, one marine's child and a marine. Given the rigors of the voyage and the primitive medical knowledge of the day, the crammed ships and the lack of anti-scorbutics, the poor planning and the bad equipment, it was a tiny death rate—a little over 3 per cent. The sea had spared them; now, they must survive on the unknown land.

4

The Starvation Years

i

PHILLIP AND HIS OFFICERS soon realized that there could be no settlement at Botany Bay.

Everything they had been told about it, even the testimony of Cook's log, was wrong. They had expected grassland with deep black soil and well-spaced trees, where crops could be planted without clearing; an ample source of building-stone; a protected anchorage.[1]

But what Captain Phillip saw from the deck as his ship rounded Point Solander and hauled into Botany Bay on Friday, January 18, 1788, was a flat heath of paperbark scrub and gray-green eucalypts, stretching featurelessly away under the grinding white light of that Australian summer. The dry buzzing monotony of the landscape did not match Cook's account. The bay was open and unprotected, and the Pacific rollers gave it a violent, persistent swell; the water was shallow, the holding-ground poor.

Supply anchored in the north of the bay, so that she could plainly be seen by ships in the offing. Phillip and some officers, including Lieutenant Philip Gidley King, hoisted out the boats in the afternoon and went looking for water. They made tentative contact with the Aborigines, giving them beads and mirrors. These "trembling" savages, King thought, "seemed quite astonished at the figure we cut in being cloathed. I think it is very easy to conceive the ridiculous figure we must appear to these poor creatures, who were perfectly naked."[2]

Over the next two days all the rest of the fleet arrived in Botany Bay. The Aborigines began to assemble in greater numbers on the rock-strewn spits and white beaches. As *Sirius* sailed past Point Solander, Captain John Hunter watched them flourish their spears at her and cry "*Warra, warra!*" These words, the first recorded ones spoken by a black to a white in Australia, meant "Go away!"

But the intruders did not go away. Issuing from the ships, they tramped about in their scarlet tunics, looking for water, entangling themselves in scrub and branches. Formal threats were exchanged. With guttural yells of *warra, warra!* one tribesman "threw his spear wide of us to shew how far they could do execution"; it flew forty yards and stuck quivering in the earth. Another black flung his spear straight at them. A marine answered with a blank cartridge, "when they all ran off with great precipitation."

But before long the Aborigines were accepting presents from Phillip. They swarmed around the boats, plucking at the whites' clothes and shouting with amazement and pleasure whenever anyone lifted his hat. The general bonhomie was such that the blacks

> ran up to the man who had thrown the lance & made very significant signs of their displeasure at his conduct by pointing all their lances at him & looking at us, intimating that they only waited our orders to kill him. However, we made signs for them to desist & made the culprit a present of some beads & c[a 3]

Soon the Englishmen ran out of beads and ribbon, but the hesitant contacts went on through the afternoon as more tribesmen gathered on the beach. King gave two Aborigines a taste of wine, which they spat out. Names for things were exchanged. But the great enigma, for the Aborigines, was the sex of the whites. They poked at the marines' breeches. Finally King ordered one of his men to satisfy their curiosity. The embarrassed marine fumbled at his fly, and the first white cock was flashed on an Australian beach. "They made a great shout of admiration," King wrote,

> and pointing to the shore . . . we saw a great number of Women and Girls, with infant children on their shoulders, make their appearance on the beach—all *in puris naturalibus*, not so much as a fig-leaf. Those natives who were around the boats made signs for us to go to them & made us understand their persons were at our service. However, I declined.[4]

Instead, he produced his handkerchief and tied it on one of the women "where Eve did the Fig Leaf; the natives then set up another very great shout."

Thus the acquaintance of black and white on the shores of Botany Bay grew. There was no violence; the convicts were still cooped up in the transports, and the officers and seamen were under strict orders from Governor Phillip (as the commodore now officially became, on landing in New South Wales) not to molest the natives in any way. Of course, they could not be ordered to like them. "Altogether a most stupid insensible set of beings," concluded Surgeon Arthur Bowes Smyth, after dilating on their "miserable wigwams" and fishy stink.[5] The blacks, in turn, were consumed with curiosity about the whites. One even scalded his fingers trying to swipe a fish from a cookpot on the beach, for, being totally ignorant of pottery (let alone iron), he had never seen water boiled in a container before. Surgeon White demonstrated his pistol to a group of Aborigines, shooting a hole in a bark shield at several paces. It produced consternation, and to calm them White whistled "the air of *Malbrooke*, which they appeared highly charmed with, and imitated him with equal pleasure and readiness." It was the first sign of the astounding powers of mimicry that the Australian Aborigines would show the whites in years to come.[6]

This was all very well, but it was not what the First Fleet had come for, and the colonists had a colony to make. "If we are obliged to settle here," wrote Lieutenant Ralph Clark after five days in Botany Bay, "there will not a soul be alive in the course of a year." In the meantime, Phillip had left with Hunter and some marines to explore Port Jackson, a few miles to the north. Its opening had been seen, named but not visited by Cook as he sailed by it in 1770. Phillip returned with the news that this place was a paradise compared to Botany Bay: a harbor with many branching arms in which ships could find shelter from any wind, with plenty of fresh water and fertile soil. He ordered the fleet to make ready for sea again.

But the next morning they were thunderstruck to see, far out on the cloudy horizon, two large and obviously European ships trying to beat in to shore against a stiff breeze. If coincidence, this was incredible; if not, menacing. Were they Dutch men-o'-war, sent to attack the fleet? In the evening the strange ships vanished in the haze, still tacking impotently against the shore wind. Phillip left for Port Jackson the next morning. Whoever the intruders were, he must beat them to the new harbor; to lose that would mean losing the whole expedition.

It was a prudent move, but he need not have worried. The ships were *La Boussole* and *L'Astrolabe*, commanded by the French explorer Jean-François de la Pérouse, two and a half years out of Brest on a voyage of Pacific discovery. La Pérouse had been as startled to see an English squadron as Phillip had been to see his, but, as he noted in his log, "All Europeans are countrymen at such a distance from home." When he dropped his hook in Botany Bay on the morning of January 26, La Pérouse was fairly cordially received by Hunter, who was in a blinding hurry to get the rest of the fleet to Port Jackson. He politely told La Pérouse that he could give him any assistance he wanted—except, of course, for food, stores, sails, ammunition or anything else he needed.

After lunch, *Sirius* got the fleet under way. There was a light south-

southeast breeze, which made it as hard for the ships to get out of port as it had been for La Pérouse to get in. The departing English now gave the French a spectacular show of fumbling. *Friendship* rammed *Prince of Wales*, losing her jib boom. *Charlotte* nearly ran on the rocks, clawed off and cannoned into *Friendship*. *Lady Penrhyn* just avoided ramming her amidships. The blue Pacific air darkened with nautical oaths. However, by 3 p.m. the transports had cleared Botany Bay and were working north; four hours later, while the pinkish-gray glow of evening began to fume delicately upward from the long flat inland horizon, they rounded South Head and stood in for Port Jackson or, as it would presently be called, Sydney Harbor.

ii

''WE ... HAD the satisfaction of finding the finest harbour in the world, in which a thousand sail of the line may ride with the most perfect security.''[7] Phillip's jubilant words to Lord Sydney suggest that he was already looking beyond the convict colony to the day when this harbor would become a strategic outpost for England, filled with the white-sailed emblems of a dominated Pacific. The chosen anchorage had a small stream of fresh water flowing into a sheltered bay, where ships could ride close to the shore in deep water. To honor the man who had sent them there, Phillip called it Sydney Cove.

Pink eucalypts grew thickly along its rock shores, and Phillip marvelled at how stoutly they flourished in mere cracks of the rock, drawing nourishment from the thinnest soil. The work gangs stumbled and cursed among the ferns as the ground heaved beneath their legs, and "the confusion," David Collins noted, "will not be wondered at when it is considered that each man stepped from the boat literally into a wood."[8] Over the next few days, some military order began to emerge. "Business now sat on every brow," Watkin Tench reported,

and the scene, to an indifferent spectator, at leisure to contemplate it, would have been highly picturesque and amusing. In one place, a party cutting down the woods; a second, setting up a blacksmith's forge; a third, dragging along a load of stones or provisions; here an officer pitching his marquee, with a detachment of troops parading on one side of him, and a cook's fire blazing up on the other.[9]

The marines had to watch for runaways. Within a few days some of the prisoners had escaped and struggled through the bush as far as Botany Bay, where La Pérouse's ships still lay at anchor. They gave the French commander "trouble and embarrassment"[10] by begging him to take them on board, but he dismissed them with threats and sent them back to Sydney Cove, where they were flogged. In fact, they had been lucky not to be taken on board. On March 10, 1788, after a six-week sojourn at Botany Bay, La Pérouse sailed off into the Pacific and was never heard from again. It took the French thirty years to establish that his ships were wrecked with the loss of all hands on Vanikoro in the New Hebrides.

The presence of the French boats warned Phillip that he must quickly colonize Norfolk Island. It would be a disaster to lose its pines and flax to France; and La Pérouse told him that he had already been there, although the surf prevented him landing.[11] So Phillip dispatched *Supply* to Norfolk Island, with twenty-two people on board under the command of *Sirius*'s second lieutenant, Philip Gidley King. They had six months' rations and were told to start sowing crops and retting flax immediately. Norfolk Island would be more fertile than the sandy dirt of Sydney Cove, at which the convicts were now scratching.

They had no ploughs or draft animals; it was all hack-and-peck hoe cultivation, and they sowed the first corn on a patch half a mile east of the stream, where the Botanical Gardens of Sydney now stand. Some of the trees they felled were giants, red gums more than twenty-five feet around the trunk, whose root systems had to be dug out and grubbed from the stony earth—an exhausting labor for men whose muscles had gone to suet after months at sea. Some officers had to sleep ashore. "I never slept worse, my dear wife, than I did last night," the homesick Lieutenant Clark wrote in his journal, "what with the hard cold ground, spiders, ants and every vermin you can think of was crawling over me."[12]

A fortnight passed before enough tents and huts were ready for the female convicts. On February 6 their disembarkation began, and all through the day the longboats plied between the transports and the cove, carrying their freight of women. Those who had decent clothes had put on all their finery: "Some few among them," noted Bowes Smyth, heartily glad to have them off his ship, "might be said to be well dressed." The last of them landed by six in the evening. It was a squally day, and thunderheads were piled up in livid cliffs above the Pacific; as dusk fell, the weather burst. Tents blew away; within minutes the whole encampment was a rain-lashed bog. The women floundered to and fro, draggled as muddy chickens under a pump, pursued by male convicts intent on raping them. One lightning bolt split a tree in the middle of the camp and killed several sheep and a pig beneath it. Meanwhile, most of the sailors on *Lady Penrhyn* applied to her master, Captain William Sever, for an extra ration of rum "to make merry with upon the women quitting the ship." Out came the pannikins, down went the rum, and before long the drunken tars went off to join the convicts in pursuit of the women, so that, Bowes remarked, "it is beyond my abilities to give a just description of the scene of debauchery and riot that ensued during the night." It was the first bush party in Australia, with "some swearing, others quarrelling, others singing—not in the least regarding the tempest, tho' so violent that the thunder shook the ship exceeding anything I ever before had a conception of." And as the couples rutted between the rocks, guts burning from the harsh Brazilian *aguardiente*, their clothes slimy with red clay, the sexual history of colonial Australia may fairly be said to have begun.[13]

Its political history began the next day. Late in the morning, as the sun stood up above the treetops and the drenched ground steamed, the marine band summoned all the colonists on shore to hear the Governor's Commission read. Phillip stood at a folding table, with his senior colonial officers—Robert Ross the lieutenant-governor, David Collins the judge-advocate, Reverend Richard Johnson the clergyman and John White the surgeon—ranked next to him. Two leather cases on the table held George III's seal and the documents commissioning the colony. With a rattle of drums and a small needling of fifes, the convicts were herded together in a circle around the gentlemen and officers; the soldiers formed a ring outside them. The convicts were ordered to squat. The soldiers remained standing with loaded muskets. This simple choreography summed up the main transactions of power.

Collins read the Royal Instructions giving Phillip, as Governor, the power to administer oaths, appoint officers, convene criminal and civil court and emancipate prisoners—the customary imperial boilerplate. He could raise armies, execute martial law and build "such and so many forts and platforms castles cities boroughs towns and fortifications as you shall judge necessary," a clause that must have deepened the hungover prisoners' gloom as Collins recited it.[14]

Phillip now harangued the convicts. He would stand no repetition of the last night's orgy, and any prisoners who tried to get into the women's tents would be shot. Cattle-duffers and chicken thieves would be hanged, without exceptions. Breeding stock was infinitely precious to the colony. Having watched the felons at work, "he was persuaded nothing but severity would have any effect upon them, to induce them to behave properly in future." If they did not work, they would not eat. Up to now only one man in three had been working; discipline would fix that, and discipline they would have. Their task, apart from clearing and hoeing the soil, would be building houses: first for the officers, then for the marines and lastly for themselves. *God Save the King!* The marines fired three volleys and marched the convicts off. Phillip and his officers sat down to a lunch of cold mutton, chatting sociably amid the stuttering whir of the cicadas. Alas, the meat proved to be crawling with maggots, although the sheep had only been butchered the night before. "Nothing will keep 24 hours in this country, I find," Lieutenant Clark morosely noted.

Now the hard work began, and it soon became clear that the colonists were wretchedly equipped for it. Not only was there a dearth of skilled labor, but tools were short and, Phillip complained, "the worst that ever was seen."[15] The only good building timber came from the cabbage-tree palms that grew in profusion around the stream at Sydney Cove. They were straight, easy to work and had little natural taper. All were cut down within a year. The huts they became might have been drawn by a child—boxes about 9 by 12 feet, with a hipped roof and two windows like eyes on either side of a doorway, the archetypal cottage-as-face. Their construction was equally simple. Walls were framed with 6-inch-square timber posts, set directly in the ground; vertical studs went between these, three feet apart. Between the roughly rabbeted studs, the carpenters inserted horizontal lengths of sapling whose ends were tapered to fit grooves. The walls, at this stage, looked like crude washboards. Then they were daubed (roughly sealed) on both sides with mud. This method of construction was used in every peasant community in England and Ireland; it was called "wattle-and-daub." Because, in Sydney, the horizontal wall slats were cut from mimosa saplings, that golden tree of the Australian summer has been known as a "wattle" ever since.[16]

The usual roof was reed thatch, gathered from the tidal marshes of Rushcutters' Bay. It harbored colonies of bugs and spiders, and it leaked. Presently it would be replaced by shingles. But when the winter rains came, the mud washed out of the walls. What the colony needed was brick, and before long some suitable clay was found. One convict, James Bloodworth, had been a brickmaker in England and took charge of manufacture. Convicts ground clay with water in natural depressions in the sandstone, using a log for a pestle; then, in barelegged teams, they squelched and trod it into a homogeneous pug. The bricks were molded, racked, dried and fired. They shrank unequally, and nobody could build level courses with them. For mortar, the only source of lime was burned oyster shells, laboriously gathered by convict women. That supplied just enough for a permanent Government House, a two-storied brick building with a tiled roof, stone quoins and real glass windowpanes—the first true piece of Georgian architecture in Australia, "composed of the common and Attic orders, with a pediment in front," wrote Thomas Watling, "simple, and without any other embellishment whatever." All other buildings had to be constructed without mortar and instead were made with a mixture of sheeps' hair and mud. The rain soon washed it out. No ruins of the earliest convict buildings, therefore, have survived at Sydney Cove.[17]

There was even, one may guess, a psychological reason for the poverty of building. Architecture signifies permanence; it announces the desire to stay. No other officers shared Phillip's dream of a colony of free immigrant settlers. To the convicts, all talk of a national future, or indeed a nation, was a joke. If your one dream was to escape from this Georgian shantytown, why build for the future? "Every person," wrote Lieutenant-Governor Ross, "who came out with a design of remaining in this country were [sic] now most earnestly wishing to get away from it."[18] This was the motif of life over the next decade in Sydney, until the Rum Corps gentry—grasping, ruthless and nepotistic, but resolved to make a life for themselves in New South Wales—perceived what there was to be gained and how the gains could be consolidated through the use of slave labor.

Since the First Fleet officers did not expect to stay, their diaries emphasized the exotic, the unique: animals, plants and Aborigines. They wrote very little about the convicts themselves, who had been sent there to be forgotten. Their work, infractions and punishments were all duly logged; but of the convicts as people, the records say little. What did the first man hanged in Sydney, a seventeen-year-old lad of "most vile character" named Thomas Barrett, really mean to say when, stammering and trembling and seeming "very much shocked," he announced at the foot of the ladder that "he had led a very wicked life"? How much "wickedness" could a boy compress into that small span from his birth to the fatal act of stealing some butter, dried peas and salt pork at Sydney Cove?[19]

The Australian blacks interested the First Fleet officers much more, and no account of the new thief-colony in the antipodes could be complete without a chapter or two on its "Indians." Spartan in bearing, they had a general appeal to men whose education reposed on neoclassical foundations. They were not as attractive as the Tahitians, and they seemed less like that fiction of the liberal European mind, the Noble Savage. They exemplified "hard" as against "soft" primitivism. But certainly the colonists did not wish to exterminate or enslave them, and they seemed at first to pose no threat.

Nevertheless, they were destroyed. Cholera and influenza germs from the ships began the work. By 1789 black corpses were a common sight, huddled in the salt grasses and decomposing in the creamy uterine hollows of the sandstone. These epidemics were not meant to happen; the days of arsenic and the infected trading-blanket were still far off. Governor Phillip's instructions as to blacks were quite clear: He must "conciliate their affections, enjoining all our subjects to live in amity and kindness with them," and punish anyone who harmed them. Common sense dictated that: why add tribal warfare to the problems of the colony?[20]

If at first the officers of the fleet saw the Aborigines through a scrim of Arcadian stereotypes and Rousseauist fancies, this pleasant delusion did not last long. The proper denizens of Arcadia were nymphs, but those of Port Jackson were unlike the welcoming girls of Tahiti. Young aboriginal women provoked mild longings in George Worgan, the surgeon on *Sirius*. "I can assure you," he wrote,

> there is in some of them a Proportion, a Softness, a roundness and Plumpness in their limbs and bodies ... that would excite tender & amorous Sensations, even in the frigid Breast of a Philosopher,
>
> > Would stop a Druid in his Pious Course,
> > Nor could Philosophy resist their Force.[21]

Their virtue, or at least their relative immunity to rape, was nonetheless secured by their dirtiness, repellent even by the norms of Georgian hygiene. "What with the stinking Fish-Oil," Worgan complained,

> with which they seem to besmear their Bodies, & this mixed with the Soot which is collected on their Skins from continually setting over the Fires, and then in addition to those sweet Odours, the constant appearance of the Excrementitious Matter of the Nose which is collected on the upper pouting Lip, in rich Clusters of dry Bubbles, and is kept up by fresh Drippings; I say, from all these personal Graces & Embellishments, every Inclination for an Affair of Gallantry, as well as every idea of fond endearing Intercourse, which the nakedness of these Damssels might excite one to, is banished.[22]

In the same way Lieutenant Daniel Southwell, mate on *Sirius*, dreamed of Palladian villas on the shores and islands of "this extraordinary harbour"—"charm'g seats, superb buildings, the grand ruins of stately edifices ... 'Tis greatly to be wished these appearances were not as delusive as in reality they are."[23]

This was a common complaint. The land was not what it seemed. It looked fertile and lovely, but it proved arid, reluctant, incomprehensible. "Here, a romantic rocky craggy Precipice, over which a little purling Stream makes a Cascade. There, a soft, vivid-green, shady Lawn attracts your eye. Such are the prepossessing Appearances which the country that forms PORT JACKSON presents. . . . [H]appy were it for the Colony, if these appearances were not so delusive."[24] The most vivid complaint about the scenic treachery of Sydney Harbor came from a Scots convict, young Thomas Watling of Dumfries, transported for forging guinea notes on the Bank of Scotland, who arrived on the *Royal Admiral* in 1792 at the age of thirty. He was a landscape painter, and as the first European artist to live in Australia he soon found how hard it was to depict the sights of Sydney Cove within the conventions of the journeyman picturesque that had formed his training. To be sure, Australia presented itself to the artist or naturalist as "a country of enchantments," with "numberless beauties" and "Elysian scenery."[25] But Arcadia is underwritten only by leisure and surplus, and the infant colony had neither. Soon Watling found the place offered no respite. The earth was sandy, swampy or full of rocks; fertile topsoil only existed in pockets, and every yard of ground was impenetrably tangled with brush. There were no streams of any size, or lakes or even ponds, and rain simply ran off the meager soil into bogs. Away from the harbor, the bush crushed the eye with its monotony. "The landscape painter," wrote poor blistered Watling, "may in vain seek here for that beauty which arises from happy-opposed offscapes" (meaning the beauty of romantic contrast, à la Salvator Rosa). Close up, the country matched the harshness of the penal regime, and Watling lamented

> the sterility and miserable state of *N. S. Wales*. It will be long before ever it can even support itself.—Still that country so famed for charity and liberality of sentiment will I doubt no persevere to continue it.—When I have seen so much wanton cruelty practised on board the *English* hulks, on poor wretches, without the least colour of justice, what may I not reasonably infer?—*French* Bastille, nor *Spanish* Inquisition, could not centre more of horrors.[26]

Most of all, the young Scot resented being treated worse than the Aborigine, a "barbarian *New-Hollander*":

> Many of these savages are allowed what is termed a freeman's ratio of provisions for their idleness. They are bedecked at times with dress which they make away with [at] the first opportunity, preferring the originality of naked nature; and they are treated with the most singular tenderness. This you will suppose is not more than laudable; but is there one spark of humanity exhibited to poor wretches, who are at least denominated Christians? No, they are frequently denied the common necessaries of life!—wrought to death under the oppressive heat of a burning sun; or barbarously afflicted with often little-merited secondary punishment— this may be *philosophy*, according to the calculation of our rigid dictators; but I think it is the falsest species of it I have ever known or heard of.[27]

Undoubtedly most of the other convicts felt the same way, although they could not write it down. For eight months and 15,000 miles they had seen nothing except the pitching ocean horizons, the darkness of their prison hold and sometimes a curve of foreign bay. Now they stumbled ashore in a land of inversions where it was high summer in January, where trees kept their leaves but shed their bark, where squat brown birds roared with laughter and thin stinking blacks, painted like panto- mime skeletons, mocked them with their freedom. The blacks were an extension of the prison, its outer defense. Take to the bush and they would spear you; they were on the officers' side, just as the officers were on theirs.

In convict eyes, the tribesmen had only one use: they made tools and weapons and left them lying in the open, unattended, so that they could be stolen and sold to the free sailors who took them back to England as souvenirs. The loss of these fish-spears and clubs "must have been attended with many inconveniences to the owners . . . [as] they were the only means whereby they obtained or could procure their daily subsistence."[28]

And so relations between convict and tribesman began badly and soon got worse. In May 1788, a convict who worked on the government farm to the east of the freshwater stream—known by then as the Tank Stream, because the whites had been scraping storage sinks out of the soft rock on its verge—was speared dead in the bush. A week later, two convicts on thatch-cutting detail were found speared and mangled, "the head of one beaten to a jelly." It was supposed, a seaman noted, "to have been thro' revenge for taking away one of their canoes."[29] The killers had melted back into their tribe and it was useless to pursue them. "Not- withstanding all our presents," wrote a woman convict from Port Jack- son in November 1788, "the savages still continue to do us all the injury they can, which makes the soldiers' duty very hard, and much dissatis- faction among the officers. I know not how many of our people have been killed."[30]

Revenge was easier dreamed of than exacted, as Phillip forbade puni- tive expeditions. The officers and marines, with their muskets, were theoretically better-armed than the Iora—but the tribesman could throw four spears in the time it took to reload a flintlock. The convicts were not armed at all, and so their efforts at revenge were futile. In March 1789, sixteen of them set off with clubs to beat up the "Indians" for injuring one of their friends; the Iora ambushed them, killing one and wounding seven. Not only did Phillip refuse to order a retaliatory attack on the blacks, but he had the eight unharmed survivors flogged with 150 lashes each and placed in leg irons for a year.

Such actions rankled. In the eyes of the British Government, the status of Australian Aborigines in 1788 was higher than it would be for another 150 years, for they had (in theory) the full legal status and so, in law if not in fact, they were superior to the convicts. The convicts re- sented this most bitterly. Galled by exile, the lowest of the low, they

desperately needed to believe in a class inferior to themselves. The Aborigines answered that need. Australian racism began with the convicts,
although it did not stay confined to them for long; it was the first Australian trait to percolate upward from the lower class.

But if the convicts hated the blacks, the military detested both—and
for similar reasons. When Phillip summarily punished the steward of
a marine officer with 50 lashes for giving a convict a gallon of rum
in exchange for a pet possum, Arthur Bowes Smyth railed against the
governor:

> ... This Government (if a Government it can be called) is a scene of
> anarchy and confusion; an evident discontent prevails among the differ-
> ent officers throughout the settlement. The marines and sailors are pun-
> ished with the utmost severity for the most trivial offences, whilst the
> convicts are pardoned (or at least punished in a very slight manner) for
> crimes of the blackest die. I do not even except stealing, which the Gov-
> ernor himself . . . assured them would be punished capitally. What may
> be the result of such a very inconsistent and partial mode of acting, time
> (and I may venture to say a very short time) will shew.[31]

To the marines, Phillip's even-handedness was bias. In the famine years
of the early settlement convicts were hanged for stealing food—but so,
in March 1789, were six marine privates. Why, marines grumbled, should
the convicts be flogged with a lighter cat-o'-nine-tails than the dreadful
"military cat" used on servicemen? Why should marines and soldiers get
the same ration as prisoners? Pinpricks, like the cancellation of a rum
allowance to the marines' wives, became inflammations. Most of all,
they resented doing duty as convict supervisors. They had not enlisted
as jail wardens, and they felt (not unreasonably) that the government's
failure to send civilians to keep the work gangs in order was one more
proof of its incompetence and indifference.

So they hated the place, hated the convicts for bringing them there
and despised the Aborigines into the bargain. "I do not scruple to pronounce," wrote the marine major whom Phillip had made lieutenant-
governor, Robert Ross,

> that in the whole world there is not a worse country. All that is contig-
> uous to us is so very barren and forbidding that it may with truth be said
> that *here nature is reversed;* and if not so, she is nearly worn out. . . . If
> the minister has a true and just description given him of it he will surely
> not think of sending any more people here.[32]

Ross—"without exception the most disagreeable commanding officer I
ever knew," in the opinion of one of his subordinates—was a choleric,

whining martinet who hated Phillip and the colony equally. He would stop at nothing to cast Phillip in a bad light. But most of the colonists, marine or convict, shared his gloom about the future of New South Wales.

iii

THE HATEFUL equalizer was hunger. This first democratic experience in Australia spared no one. It made most of the colonists stupid and some crazy, playing havoc with morale and producing endless displays of petty tyranny.

The First Fleet carried enough food to keep its passengers alive for two years in Australia. The rations issued to sailors, marines and officers each week were:

Beef	4 lb.	Hardtack	7 lb.
Pork	2 lb.	Cheese	12 oz.
Dried peas	2 pints	Butter	6 oz.
Oatmeal	3 pints	Vinegar	½ pint

The male convicts got one-third less, while female convicts got two-thirds of the male ration, or slightly less than half the naval standard. On paper, this was not a bad allowance. In practice it meant scurvy, and the meat was mostly bone and gristle.

At Table Bay in South Africa, their last port of call before Australia, some officers had bought livestock for themselves. When these were added to the animals Phillip had bought for the government herd, the colony's total stock came to 2 bulls and 5 cows, 29 sheep, 19 goats, 74 hogs and sows, 18 turkeys, 35 ducks, 35 geese and 209 chickens. There were also 5 rabbits. All these creatures were guarded with reverential care. As Phillip had put it to the convicts, the life of a breeding animal was worth a man's. In August 1788, when a sheep fattened for the officers' dinner on the Prince of Wales's birthday vanished from its pen, Phillip offered full emancipation to anyone who informed on the thief. None would. Gorgon, the colony's prize Africander bull, and four of his five cows strayed into the scrub and were lost. Sheep died from bloat, while dingoes and convicts kept poaching the hens.

All ranks ate the same monotonous diet of salt meat and leathery johnnycakes baked on a shovel. Thus, food could not symbolize the proper social demarcation between bond and free. "Our allowance is very scanty," wrote James Campbell, captain of marines on Lady Penrhyn,

I know not why, or whither it was so intended by administration that the only difference between the allowance of provisions served to the officer & served to the convict, be only half a pint (per day) of vile Rio spirits, so offensive both in taste & smell that he must be fond of drinking indeed that can use it—but such is the fact.[33]

Phillip knew that the survival of the colony had to preclude all comforts of status. With surplus food, the officers would start to become aristocracy—but not yet. They all lived for five years on the bleak edge of starvation. The first crops failed and the whole harvest of the second planting—a meager forty bushels—had to be saved for seed. In 1788 the convicts had no draft animals; no plough would be used in Australia until 1803.

Only a third of the prisoners could work—320 men out of the 966 victualled from public stores. More than 50 convicts were too feeble from age and incurable illness to work at all, and many others—slum-raised, utterly ignorant of farming—"would starve if left to themselves."[34] The ideal of each man feeding himself was a mockery in New South Wales.

Some officers had their own vegetable gardens, tended by convicts. The kitchen garden for the public stores was planted, for security, on an island 300 yards out in the harbor; there, it was fairly safe from the prisoners and marines who, desperate for green food, would pull turnip-tops and gobble the leaves before the turnip had grown. But the yield from Garden Island, as it was named, was still poor—just enough for the sick in the hospital tents. The officers guarded their private plots zealously but unsuccessfully. Thus when Lieutenant Clark, who had the use of another islet in the harbor (still known as Clark Island), went to look at his onion bed in February 1790, he found "some Boat had landed since I had been there last and taken away the greatest part . . . It is impossible for any body to attempt to raise any Garden stuff here, before it comes to perfection they will steal it."[35]

The colonists found few plants they could eat, and little game. They gathered wild spinach and a liquorice-flavored creeper, *Smilax glycophylla*, which they called "sweet tea." A few officers had brought their fowling pieces, but it seemed unwise to use up the colony's limited stock of gunpowder.

The only reliable source of fresh protein, therefore, was fish. There was some prejudice against it. The ration was 10 pounds of fish issued in place of 2½ pounds of salt beef. King remarked, "If there were more convicts here, they would not submit to having their salt rations stopped where a quantity of fish were caught by them."[36] In Sydney the "Roast Beef of Old England"—even salted and half-rotten—was more prized than any fish.

By October 1788, Phillip still had no idea if relief ships were on their way, and there was only enough food in store to last, if strictly rationed, one more year. Given the eerily long time-lag between England and Sydney, he had to decide. He cut 1 pound from the weekly flour ration and sent his largest vessel, *Sirius*, to Cape Town to buy supplies.

Her captain, John Hunter, gambled on taking a longer but faster route, sailing around Cape Horn before the westerlies. Speed was all-important, for his sailors were sickening from scurvy and hunger. *Sirius* reached Cape Town in three months, instead of the five the western route against the prevailing winds would likely have taken. Hunter loaded, refitted and brought her back to Sydney Cove, laden with wheat, barley and flour, by May 1789. There had been no news of relief ships in Cape Town. But the 56 tons of new flour would last the colony four months, and the seed would plant the allotments around Sydney and at the new farms inland at Rose Hill.

By now, most agricultural hope centered on the governor's farm at Rose Hill, or Parramatta as the blacks called it, where the soil was deep and rich and the fields ran down to a navigable river. By the end of 1789, this farm had produced Australia's first agricultural marvel, a 26-pound cabbage; but it was still a long way from keeping the whole settlement in greens. In fact, in the year to come, the idea of progress shrunk to a mockery, for 1789 brought no ships, and as 1790 crept by, the little settlement inexorably sank into the torpor and despair of slow starvation. "God help us. If some ships dont arrive, I dont know what will," Ralph Clark scrawled in his diary, and Watkin Tench described the mood that now descended over Sydney Cove:

> Famine . . . was approaching with giant strides, and gloom and dejection overspread every countenance. Men abandoned themselves to the most desponding reflections, and adopted the most extravagant conjectures.
>
> Still we were on the tiptoe of expectation. If thunder broke at a distance, or a fowling-piece of louder than ordinary report resounded in the woods, *"a gun from a ship"* was echoed on every side, and nothing but hurry and agitation prevailed.[37]

Lieutenant Southwell wrote how his eyes, in the evening, had sometimes been deceived "with some fantastic little cloud, which . . . for a little time has deceived impatient imagination into the momentary idea that 'twas a vessel altering her sail or position while steering in for the haven."[38]

Supplies were running so low that Phillip decided to take another gamble. He dispatched 281 people—more than a third of the convicts in the colony, guarded by half the battalion of marines—to Norfolk Island in the *Sirius*, which would then sail on to Canton to load up with desperately needed provisions. The convicts and their guards, Phillip reasoned, would stand a better chance on Norfolk Island, with its fertile soil and abundant fish. The marines disliked the idea—which, as a bonus, enabled Phillip to get rid of his obstreperous bête noire, Major Ross—but they had no choice, and *Sirius* sailed with her tender, *Supply*, in March 1790. The Sydney colonists now had no means of communication with the outside world. "The little society that was in the place was broken up," wrote David Collins, "and every man seemed left to brood in solitary silence over the dreary prospect before him."[39]

On April 1, Phillip cut the rations "without distinction" to 4 pounds of flour, 2½ pounds of salt pork and 1½ pounds of rice per week. This was just enough to sustain life but not enough to work on, and so he humanely reduced the convicts' hours of work to six per day, so that each man could cultivate a private vegetable patch in the afternoon.

Then, on April 5, *Supply* appeared off South Head. She was alone. As her launch cast off and made for the shore of Sydney Cove, Tench saw her captain "make an extraordinary motion with his hand, which too plainly indicated that something disastrous had happened; and I could not help turning to the Governor . . . and saying, 'Sir, prepare yourself for bad news.' "[40]

The news was catastrophic. *Sirius* had struck a reef at Norfolk Island and was a total wreck. All the ships' crew and company, including the convicts, were saved. But both settlements, at Sydney and Norfolk Island, were now cut off from the world and—except for one 170-ton brig —from one another. Both were failing fast, for Norfolk Island was just as badly off as Sydney.

iv

TWO YEARS BEFORE, when Philip Gidley King and his party of twenty-two colonists glimpsed, from the pitching deck of *Supply*, the island that would eventually become the worst place in the English-speaking world, what they had seen was not inviting.

Magnificent in scenery, Norfolk Island was also a natural prison, harborless, cliff-bound and girdled with reefs on which the long Pacific swells broke with a ragged, monotonous booming. King had to wait five days in the lee before he could lead a scouting party ashore. They landed at Anson Bay on March 4, 1788. The high pines grew right to the cliff face; King guessed the tallest of them was 160 feet.[41] Their trunks were wreathed in vines. The ship's surgeon got lost in this maze and spent the night in the forest. In the dark, where phosphorescent fungi gleamed beneath the Gothic vaults of cabbage-trees, he heard nibbling and thought he was surrounded by rabbits. The rabbits were rats.

King found a passage through the reef at Sydney Bay (modern Kingston) and landed the convicts and supplies on March 6. They raised the Union Jack on a sapling. "I took possession of the isle, drinking 'His Majesty,' 'The Queen,' 'Prince of Wales,' 'Governor Phillip' and 'Success to the Colony.' " The ragged chorus of English voices was sucked away by the Pacific air, swallowed in the blue immensity behind the wall of dark pines. Two days later, *Supply* made sail for the Australian coast, a thousand miles away.

The first crops perished from wind and salt. Rats ate the vegetables; then came cutworms, black caterpillars and bright, screaming, seed-eating Norfolk Island Parrots. The wreck of the *Sirius* meant new mouths to feed. In March 1790, Norfolk Island had 425 people (200 convicts), but by November 1791 with new arrivals from Sydney, it had 959 (748 convicts). Thereafter, until the first settlement was abandoned in 1806, the population would remain fairly steady at about a thousand people, with one guard to every seven prisoners.

Despite the rich, deep soil, they had, by March 1790, only about fifty acres of land under the hoe. The reef swarmed with red snapper, but the colonists' two boats—a cutter and a leaky dinghy—could not always brave the pounding surf. What saved all their lives was the mutton-bird, *Pterodroma melanopus*, which flocked in immense numbers on Mount Pitt, the island's highest hill. Its flanks were riddled with their nesting tunnels. The mutton-birds arrived on Norfolk Island early in March and stayed until the end of August—almost the length of the Pacific winter. "They are very fine eating, very fat and firm," wrote Ralph Clark in August 1790, "and I think (though no Connoisseur) as good as any I ever eat." The Bird of Providence—as the officers called it; the convicts more laconically dubbed it a Pittite—tasted oily and fishy, somewhere between a penguin and a chicken. The birds had never seen men before, and their abundance struck Clark as Biblical:

> They generally hovered about the Mount for an hour before they came down, which was as thick as a shower of hail, this account will make the old story of Moses in the Wilderness (Exodus xvi.13) be a little more believ'd, respecting the shower of Quails, everyone here owes their existence to the Mount Pit Birds.[42]

Once grounded, they were encumbered by their long planing wings, like albatrosses. As quartermaster of public stores, Clark kept a daily tally: More than 170,000 of them were massacred in one three-month span, April to July 1790, an average of nearly four birds per person per day. Some convicts went to brutal lengths to get their eggs:

They catch the birds and them that have no eggs they let go again and them that are with Egg they cut the Egg out of them and then let the poor Bird fly again which is one of the cruelest things which I think I ever heard. I hope that some of them will be caught at this cruel work for the sake of making an example of them.[43]

Naturally the Birds of Providence could not survive this slaughter. By 1796 they were thinning out, and eight years later they were almost gone. By 1830, no more was heard of *Pterodroma melanopus* on Norfolk Island.

Meanwhile, the arduous work of clearing and building went on. Hungry men work slowly, so less ground is cleared; which means small crops and more hunger. There was little time or energy left over for the crops the island was meant to produce, pines and flax.

The Norfolk Island pines, however, like the rest of antipodean nature, were deceptive. They turned out to be useless for anything but huts and firewood. Their wood was not resilient enough for spars. It was short-grained, wanting in resin, more like beech than Norway pine; it snapped like a carrot.

That left the flax plant. *Phormium tenax*, Phillip had optimistically reported to Lord Sydney at the end of 1788, "will supply the settlers with rope and canvas, as well as a considerable part of their cloathing, when they can dress it properly."[44] But the Admiralty had sent no flax workers with the First Fleet. Phillip's sanguine vision of settlers and convicts wearing homespun linen whilst dispatching argosies of sailcloth to England quickly faded. He besought London to send a flax dresser, but it took two years for this expert (a convict superintendent named Andrew Hume) to reach Norfolk Island. In 1791 Hume managed to produce for the Admiralty a couple of square yards of rough Norfolk Island linen—perhaps among the costliest textiles ever woven by man.

Meanwhile, King had an idea. He remembered Banks telling him about the linen woven by the Maoris in New Zealand. Plainly, he needed a Maori; and about a year later, a ship did manage to kidnap two wildly struggling and resentful tribesmen from the Bay of Islands in New Zealand and get them to Norfolk Island. One was a young chief named Woodoo; the other, Tooke, was a priest's son; both were twenty-four years old and neither had the slightest idea of how to prepare flax, for such menial work was done by women. So Tooke and Woodoo moped haughtily about the settlement, gazing out to sea from the headlands where "almost every evening at the close of day [they] lament their separation by crying or singing a song expressive of their grief, which is at times very affecting." After six months' exile on Norfolk, King returned them to New Zealand.[45]

Meanwhile, by trial and error, flax production went on. At its peak, the convict workers (mainly women) were turning out some 100 yards of coarse canvas a month. At that pace, however, it would have taken two years to make the sailcloth for one first-rate ship. Gradually, the project wore down and lapsed. By 1800, the hopes that began with Matra's descants on the flax plant and Cook's enthusiasm for the pines were proven a total delusion. The place would produce nothing for England; it would never pay for itself. Its colonists sank, as on the mainland, into a demoralized torpor.

v

As soon as he heard of the wreck of the *Sirius*, Governor Phillip had inventory taken of the stores at Sydney. It showed that they had only a few months' grace left, so he cut the rations again. These sad morsels— a third of what they should have been—were doled out daily, to groups of seven people, so that the convicts could not bolt a whole week's ration at once. Some women prostituted themselves for a few handfuls of weevily flour or a hunk of gristle. Most of the men on the work gangs were already as naked as the Aborigines, having traded off their clothes for food. There was no question of the convicts' helping one another; Sydney Cove had only distilled the dog-eat-dog misery of the English slums. When one elderly prisoner fell down and died in the food queue in May 1790, Collins's autopsy showed his stomach was quite empty. He had lost or sold his cooking utensils, and instead of helping him out, his fellow prisoners had demanded a cut of his ration before they would share their cookpot, so that he starved.

Phillip reluctantly stepped up the punishments for food theft, which were already draconic but no longer deterred the starving. In 1790 one man got 300 lashes and 6 months in chains for stealing 20 ounces of potatoes, and another drew 1,000 lashes for taking 3 pounds of the precious tubers. After such treatment, a man would be incapacitated, literally skinned alive. Huge rewards (in food, the only currency that mattered, for there was no money circulating in this jail) were offered to convicts who helped catch food thieves. Thus in May 1790, convict Thomas Yarsley received 60 pounds of flour for catching a man stealing garden vegetables. Such inducements, Watkin Tench remarked, were "more tempting than the ore of Peru or Potosi."[46]

Hunger, fear, exhaustion and the pervasive sense of abandonment— these destroyed whatever scraps of morale may have been left among the convicts. One of their few surviving letters, from an unknown woman, speaks of "our disconsolate situation in this solitary waste of the creation

. . . not to be imagined by any stranger" and revealingly noted, "In short, everyone is so taken up with their own misfortunes that they have no pity to bestow on others." No wonder that by April 1790 the settlement chaplain, Reverend Richard Johnson, was lamenting the convicts' apathy to the Divine Word. "Little apparent fruit yet among the Convicts, &c., Oh that they were wise—but alas! nothing seems to alarm or allure them."[47]

The guards were as apathetic as the convicts. They grew peevish; they could not make up their minds on simple matters; they hallucinated. Lieutenant Southwell felt the torpor of starvation: "I confess myself incompetent . . . being perplexed with a variety of conjectures, but able to conclude nothing."[48] Conversation, friendship and curiosity faltered and died, having nothing to sustain them. The spirit of inquiry about the new environment, which had filled several officers' journals in the first year of settlement, now dwindled; there are only about half as many observations on flora, fauna and "Indians" for 1789–90 as for 1788. Monotony reigned. The classes were now at a simmering distrust of one another, wrote an anonymous male convict lamenting their "Crusoe-like adventures":

> We fear the troops, and they are not contented with seeing those who live better than themselves, nor with us who live worse. . . . [W]e have had so many disappointments about arrivals, &c., that the sullen reserve of superiority has only increased our apprehensions; and some of the most ignorant have no other idea than that they are to be left by the troops and the shipping to perish by themselves![49]

The signs of status were vanishing. All uniforms were threadbare or ragged. Most of the marines were barefoot; drill, rituals, spit-and-polish were gone. "Nothing more ludicrous can be conceived," wrote Watkin Tench, "than the expedients of substituting, shifting and patching, which ingenuity devised, to eke out wretchedness and preserve the remains of decency."[50]

The marines resented Phillip's order that equal rations be issued to convicts and guards. When the governor turned over his private stock of flour—more than 300 pounds—to the public store, Collins wrote that the gesture "did him immortal honor, in this season of general distress" —as indeed it did.[51] But the marines did not agree. If clothes and rations could not symbolize rank, then actions would; and one may be sure that every curse, kick and blow the marines rained on the exhausted "crawlers" was meant as a reinforcement of superiority, not just an incitement to work. The convict artist Thomas Watling, transported for forgery, summed it up:

Instances of oppression, and mean-souled despotism, are so glaring and frequent, as to banish every hope of generosity and urbanity from such as I am:—for unless we can flatter and cajole the vices and follies of our superiors, with the most abominable servility, nothing is to be expected —and even this conduct, very often . . . meets with its just reward— neglect and contempt.[52]

To construct a sense of power from the meager social resources of the colony, the top dog had to be capricious—otherwise, the underdog's servility might be taken as a contract. Watling could neither dignify himself by rebelling, nor protect himself by truckling. This proved utterly demoralizing for genteel convicts who still clung to the belief that they were not "common" criminals. To them, servility—the very condition they had tried to escape with their pathetic embezzlements and forgeries —was indeed "abominable."

By grit, example and stubborn evenhandedness in the face of hopeless prisoners and near-mutinous marines, Phillip pulled his wretched settlement through these months of crisis. "We shall not starve," he wrote, "though seven-eighths of the colony deserves nothing better; the present want will be done away by the first ship that arrives."[53]

That long-awaited sail was glimpsed on June 3, 1790, a rainy, blustering day. Watkin Tench realized it when he saw, through the doorway of his hovel, "women with children in their arms running to and fro with distracted looks, congratulating each other, and kissing their infants with the most passionate and extravagant looks of fondness." The ship was *Lady Juliana*, eleven months out of Plymouth, carrying the first news from home the colonists had received in almost three years:

"Letters! Letters!" was the cry. They were produced, and torn open in trembling agitation. News burst on us like meridian splendour on a blind man. We were overwhelmed with it: public, private, general, and particular. Nor was it until some days had elapsed, that we were able to methodise it, or reduce it into form.[54]

They learned, for the first time, of George III's attack of porphyria, of the trial of Warren Hastings, of George Washington's inauguration as the first president of the United States. Most amazing of all—and, given their social situation, most ominous—they learned of the French Revolution, "that wonderful and unexpected event," as Tench called it.

They also learned why no stores had arrived. The *Guardian*, laden with two years' worth of food and stores, had struck an iceberg and limped into Cape Town, where she was abandoned. But for that she would have reached Sydney in early March, thus preventing the loss of

Sirius. All her stores were lost. *Lady Juliana* had brought some flour, but it also brought more useless mouths in the form of 222 women convicts. At least they were in good health. Not so the other prisoners on the Second Fleet. More than a thousand had embarked, but a quarter of them died at sea, and half were landed helplessly ill at Sydney Cove from the three remaining ships, *Neptune, Surprize* and (making her second voyage to Australia) *Scarborough.* Some died from the brutality of the ships' masters, others because they had been too sick to sail.* The authorities in England had simply used the Second Fleet to rid the hulks and prisons of invalids, dispatching them into oblivion. "The sending out of the disordered and helpless," Phillip wrote angrily to his superiors in London,

> clears the gaols and may ease the parishes from which they are sent; but
> ... it is obvious that the settlement, instead of being a colony which will
> support itself, will, if this practice is continued, remain for years a bur-
> then to the mother-country.[55]

Before his letter reached London, however, the Third Fleet was on its way, carrying 1,864 convicts. One man in ten died, and the survivors were landed in 1791 "so emaciated, so worn away," in Phillip's words, that they were utterly unfit to work—more helpless parasites to drag the colony down.

So the ships had come, but brought little change. David Collins wrote to his father and summed up his plight:

> I find that I am spending the Prime of my Life at the farthest part of the
> World, without Credit, without ... Profit, secluded from my Family, ...
> my Connexions, from the World, under constant Apprehensions of being
> starved ... All these Considerations induce me ... to embrace the first
> Opportunity that offers of escaping from a Country that is nothing better
> than a Place of banishment for the Outcasts of Society.[56]

In fact, the marines would soon be relieved. The Second Fleet brought two companies of the New South Wales Corps, a new unit tailored for service in Australia. The corps' officers knew they had to do the administrative work, such as jury duty, that Major Ross and his men objected to; and its enlisted men would guard convicts as well as fight the French —the latter a remote possibility. As soldiers, the Botany Bay Rangers (as they came to be nicknamed) were poor stuff even by the current low standards of the British Army. Most of them were scum, and they found service in New South Wales the best alternative to beggary or crime. Few of the officers were better than the men.[57]

---

* For the voyage of the Second Fleet, see chapter 5.

But the impact of the New South Wales Corps on life in early New South Wales was to be out of all proportion to its quality as a force. Between 1791 and 1808 the corps was de facto—if not quite de jure—the most powerful single internal influence on the colony, producing its first ruling clans and even, in 1808, overthrowing the governor.

The arrival of the Second and Third Fleets proved one thing: However bad the colony's prospects were, at least it had not been abandoned by England. From now on, sails would continue to be seen off the Heads. Some were convict ships, others supply vessels, and yet others were the first harbingers of trade in that remote ocean: sealers, whalers, and merchantmen drawn to the infant colony by the hugely inflated prices the colonists would pay for ordinary goods—3,000 to 4,000 percent on "every little Article of Comfort or Convenience," Collins noted.[58]

So by the end of 1791 there were signs that Sydney might support itself—although not, as Phillip stressed in his reports to England, on convict labor alone. The prisoners had no incentive to work. They were not so much rebellious as flaccid: "Neither kindness nor severity have any effect, and tho' I can say the convicts in general behave well, there are many who dread punishment less than they fear labour." The only hope, Phillip insisted, was a colony "formed by farmers and emigrants who have been used to labour, and who reap the fruits of their own industry."[59]

But no such sturdy free yeomanry would come to New South Wales. In fact, only twenty free settlers would migrate there before 1800. So Phillip resolved to see if the more deserving and sober Emancipists—convicts whose term of punishment had expired but who wanted to stay on and make a new life in Australia—could be made into yeomen. He would grant them land and the use of tools. If their farms prospered they would "take themselves off the store," becoming independent of government rations and eventually selling their surplus crops back to the colonial government stores. Such men might set an example and show that transportation could reform.

The first convict to succeed as an independent farmer was Richard Phillimore, who by January 1791 was growing enough grain on Norfolk Island to support himself and two workers. But the father of Australian agriculture, the first man to grub a living from the more stubborn earth of the mainland, was James Ruse, to whom Phillip gave one cleared acre and some raw bush at Parramatta. Ruse had been a farmer in Cornwall. Having no animal manure, he burned off the timber on his little acre and dug in the ashes, which were rich in potash. Lacking ploughhorse and plough, he hoed the ground thoroughly—"not like the Government farms, just scratched over, but properly done," he proudly told Watkin Tench—and turned the sod over, so that the grass and weeds composted into the soil; then, just before sowing, he turned the earth again. By late summer (February 1791), his wheat and maize were up and he jubilantly told Phillip that he could keep himself in food. By December 1791 he took his wife and child "off the store" as well.

As a reward, Phillip deeded him thirty acres at Parramatta—the first land grant ever made in Australia. The place was named Experiment Farm. By 1819 Ruse had two hundred acres to his name, and although he lost it all by rum or ill luck and ended his days working as overseer for another farmer, the lines carved on his gravestone are full of an understandably biblical pride that shines through the home-made spelling:

> My Mother Reread Me Tenderley
> With me She Took Much Paines
> And when I arived in This Coelney
> I sowd the Forst Grain and Now
> With My Hevenly Father I hope
> For Ever To Remain.

By the end of 1792 all the economic hopes of the colony were centered on Parramatta. No one now struggled with the thin soil of Sydney, and the Tank Stream was a "morass," so damaged by the settlers that ships could no longer get water from it. But at Parramatta, the farms were slowly extending their frail patchwork into the ancient gray-green chaos of the bush. By October 1792 Phillip had given land grants around Parramatta and the nearby district of Toongabbie to sixty-six people, of whom fifty-three were time-expired convicts. But there were not many men like Ruse among them. Skilled, hardworking Emancipists could save money to pay their way back to England or could work their passage as seamen and carpenters: "Thus will the best people always be carried away," Phillip ruefully noted.[60] Four years after landing, most prisoners still could not support themselves and were worked like cattle. An old lag who arrived with the Third Fleet, Henry Hale, gave a vivid picture of labor at Toongabbie:

> For nine months there I was on five ounces of flour a day; when weighed out, barely four. . . . In those days we were yoked to draw timber, twenty-five in gang. The sticks were six feet long; six men abreast. We held the stick behind us, and dragged with our hands. One man . . . was put to the drag; it soon did for him. He began on a Thursday and died on a Saturday, as he was dragging a load down Constitution-hill. . . . Men used to carry trees on their shoulders. How they used to die![61]

At Toongabbie, "All the necessary conveniences of life they are strangers to, and suffer everything they could dread. . . . [I]t was not uncommon for

seven or eight to die in one day, and very often while at work." No
wonder that the convicts pilfered like ants. Despite a long drought in
1791, the harvest had produced nearly 5,000 bushels of wheat, of which
no less than 1,500 bushels—30 percent of the year's crop—vanished
somewhere between the fields and the granary.[62]

Yet at the end of 1792, a thousand public acres and 516 private were
under cultivation, and more than four thousand acres had been set aside
for future farming. This, Phillip thought, would be done by Emancipists
and members of the New South Wales Corps, all of whom would have
the use of convict labor to help them. Such was the germ of the assignment system, the modified form of slavery on which Australia's early
economy would be built.

By now, according to the meticulous bookkeeping of the Colonial
Office, the colony of New South Wales—four small red patches, representing Sydney Cove, Norfolk Island, Parramatta and Toongabbie—had
cost the government of George III 67,194 pounds, 15 shillings and four-
pence three-farthings, or about 3.35 million pounds in modern money.[63]

What had the Crown got in exchange? Not much, in strategic terms;
the hope of supplying England's East Indian fleet with spars and canvas
from Norfolk Island had failed miserably. On the other hand, the fact
that the Australian coast had been not only claimed but occupied, however feebly, meant that the French would find it harder to press their
territorial claims in the South Pacific. Given the broad nature of the
balance of power between England and France—whereby France dominated the continent of Europe, while England, global in its reach, ruled
the waves—there was at least a hypothetical strategic role for this colony
in the primitive terms of eighteenth-century geopolitics.

As for the convicts, William Pitt's Tory government claimed to be
not displeased by the results. Some critics wanted to know why the
felons were not being used on public works in England, as they were in
France or Germany; degraded though these creatures may be, their argument went, convict labor had some value, and it was wasted in Australia.
Pitt brushed these objections aside in his toplofty way, saying—quite
untruthfully—that the main expenses of the colony were a thing of the
past, that it was or would shortly become self-supporting and that transportation was by far the cheapest way of getting rid of felons.[64]

So the colony would go on; but it went on without Governor Arthur
Phillip. On December 10, 1792, accompanied by his two aboriginal
friends, or specimens, Bennelong and Yemmerawannie, he boarded the
storeship *Atlantic* and sailed down the harbor for the last time. He longed
for England. Twenty-two years later, retired, bored, an admiral of the
Blue living on a pension, still in touch (though desultorily now) with the
affairs of the colony he had fathered, he died in Bath.

vi

AS THE LAST decade of the eighteenth century went by, the British Government still thought of Australia and its convict colony in maritime terms. Its settlements were a port and an island; it faced outward to the sea, not inward to the land. It was a base (albeit a feeble one) for trade, refitting and defense, not for internal expansion. The first four governors of New South Wales were all naval officers: Captain Phillip, Captain Hunter, Lieutenant King and Captain William Bligh (of the *Bounty*).[65] The convict colony was, in London's view, a land-based hulk the size of a continent.

But after 1792 it became self-supporting, and that was the work of landsmen—the officers of the New South Wales Corps and their friends. For nearly three years between Phillip's departure in December 1792 and Hunter's return in September 1795, the colony was in effect run for the New South Wales Corps by its principal officers, Francis Grose and William Paterson. They set the pattern of private management and slave labor that created the wealth of Australia's first elite.

Francis Grose (1758?–1814) had fought against the American rebels in the War of Independence. Badly wounded and invalided home to England, he got back to full service pay by helping to raise and recruit the New South Wales Corps. As its commandant, and as lieutenant-governor of New South Wales, Grose took over when Phillip sailed. He promptly set about putting most civil affairs in military hands. He replaced magistrates with corps officers and appointed a thrusting young Scottish lieutenant, John Macarthur, as regimental paymaster and inspector of public works—posts that gave him leverage by controlling the supply of convict labor.

Grose did not forget his own rank and file. He cancelled Phillip's policy of equal rations for all and gave the troops more food than the convicts. He also let it be known that any member of the New South Wales Corps could have twenty-five acres of free land for the asking. But his crucial decision for the future of Australian farming was to offer 100-acre land grants to corps officers—along with ten convicts, free of charge and maintained at government expense, to work each one. The corps officers, Grose reported to London, were "the only description of settlers on whom reliance can be placed. . . . [T]heir exertions are really astonishing. . . . I shall encourage their pursuit as much as is in my power."[66]

Under Grose, officers had the economic edge on civilians; they could raise capital by borrowing against their regimental pay, and as a junta they seized a monopoly on most consumer goods arriving in Sydney

Harbor. The chief of these was rum, the social anesthetic and real currency of early New South Wales. Colonial Sydney was a drunken society, from top to bottom. Men and women drank with a desperate, addicted, quarrelsome single-mindedness. Every drop of their tipple had to be imported.

Early in 1793 an American trading vessel, the *Hope,* arrived with 7,500 gallons of rum in her cargo. The goods and stores she carried were badly needed, and the *Hope*'s hard-nosed skipper not only demanded grossly inflated prices for them but insisted that not a nail, a sack of flour or a yard of cloth would leave his ship unless the colony bought all his rum first. Rather than suffer this gouging, the New South Wales Corps' officers decided to pass it on. They formed a ring to buy the *Hope*'s cargo without competition. John Macarthur, as regimental paymaster, fixed the necessary IOUs against the regiment's funds in England.

This impromptu deal was hugely profitable, and the monopoly of the Rum Corps (as the regiment was presently nicknamed) soon pervaded the colony's economic life. For years to come, most of the cargo that came to Sydney passed through the hands of the corps and its favored satellites, among whom were several ex-convicts. Much of it was invested in land. Emancipated convicts and free settlers had an equal right to farm. At the beginning of 1794, twenty-two grants of land had been made along the rich plains of the Hawkesbury River, northwest of Sydney. Within a few months there were 70 settlers there, and a year later 400; these included 54 ex-convicts with their dependents. But by 1800, only 8 of those 54 still had farms there—and the Hawkesbury flats were the best farming land within reach of Sydney. In all, out of 274 settlers on granted land in New South Wales in 1795—the great majority, 251 of them, being ex-convicts—only 89 were still farming their own land in 1800.[67]

There were natural reasons for this: flood, fire, drought—the undying, malignant totems of Australian farming. There were cultural ones, too, since so many of the Emancipist farmers were utter novices, not experienced men like James Ruse. But this early tendency to consolidation—which reversed itself in the Emancipists' favor after 1800[68]—was certainly helped by the officers' money and access to credit, and by the rum itself. An officer could pick the best land for his grant; he could get the most skilled convicts, the "mechanics" and former agricultural laborers, to work it; he paid for his tools, seed and stock a mere fraction of what Emancipist farmers, due to the Rum Corps monopoly on imports, paid him; and if an ex-convict farmer started wasting his life with booze, some Rum Corps officer would always appear and buy him out.

"The changes we have undergone since the departure of Governor Phillip," wrote John Macarthur as early as 1793, are so great and extraordinary that to recite them all might create some suspicion of their truth. From a state of desponding poverty and threatened famine that this settlement should be raised to its present aspect in so short a time is barely credible. As for myself, I have a farm containing nearly 250 acres. . . . [O]f this year's produce I have sold £400 worth, and I have now remaining in my granaries upwards of 1,800 bushels of corn.[69]

By 1799, New South Wales Corps officers owned 32 percent of the cattle in Australia, 40 percent of the goats, 59 percent of the horses, and 77 percent of the sheep. Grasping, haughty, jealous of their privileges and prerogatives, Macarthur and his friends were on top and meant to stay there; and the official governors who followed Grose and Paterson—Hunter, King, and Bligh—had the utmost difficulty controlling them. They were so powerful, in fact, that on January 26, 1808, the twentieth anniversary of white settlement, they staged a coup d'etat by rebelling against Governor Bligh, deposing him and running New South Wales as a military junta for two years. For this remarkable mutiny, none of the officers was hanged or even seriously punished.

Their junta mentality fostered two assumptions. The first was that none of them—especially not John Macarthur, who organized the rebellion from a prison cell where Bligh had put him—believed that naval governors were ever on their side. The second was that convicts were there to be used, not reformed. Both caused a rapid hardening of attitudes against convicts, the *lumpenproletariat* of New South Wales. The New South Wales Corps stiffly resisted any effort to criticize, or even inspect, its treatment of the convicts. The emblematic form of this attitude would show itself on Norfolk Island.

vii

THE *ATLANTIC*, before taking Phillip away in 1792, had stopped at Norfolk Island on its outward voyage with supplies for its desperate colonists. Those crewmen and marines who went ashore were struck by how bad, under the hand of King, the place had become for its prisoners. When they got to Sydney they talked about it, and a marine named John Easty noted in his diary how "that Iland which was recond the most flourishing of any Iland in the World all most"

now turns out to be A Pore Mersable [miserable] Place and all manners of Cruelties an opresion uesed by the Governor floging and beeting the people to Death that its better for the pore unhappy Creatures to be hanged allmost then to come under the command of such Tyrants and the Govner

[King] behaves more like a mad man than a man in trus[t]ed with the
Goverment of an Iland . . . Belonging to Great Britain.[70]

King had gone back to England for a brief recuperative spell after the
wreck of the Sirius in March 1790, but he returned to Norfolk Island in
November 1791, newly married to his cousin, Anna Coombe. He had
been promoted to lieutenant-governor of the island and would be its
commandant for five years.

The Norfolk Island prisoners were now guarded by the Botany Bay
Rangers. The corps rank and file made no effort to keep their distance
from the convicts. They became "very intimate with the convicts, living
in their huts, eating, drinking and gambling with them, and perpetually
enticing the women to leave the men they were married to."[71] There
was friction. Emancipated convicts complained that the soldiers were
seducing their wives; and one of these convicts, Dring, the island's
coxswain, beat up a soldier who had repeatedly cuckolded him. King
fined the aggrieved husband twenty shillings, which, he hoped, "would
convince the soldier that he was not to be insulted with impunity." It
did no such thing; the soldiers felt Dring should have been flogged. During Christmas of 1793, four soldiers were seen heading with a torch for
Dring's farm, intent on burning his corn. When a civilian farmer tried to
stop them, one man jabbed the torch full in his face, "which bruised and
burnt him very much."

Even King could not tolerate this. He had the soldier arrested. That
evening, two other soldiers got bludgeons and went after Dring. He was
found half dead, covered with blood and cuts. His assailants were court-
martialled and one of them, Private Downey, was sentenced to receive
100 lashes and to give Dring a conciliatory present: a gallon of rum. At
this, to King's amazement, Dring and a few other Emancipists begged
him to forgive the soldiers: They were terrified of reprisals by the corps.
They got their wish, on the condition—as King strictly ordered—that
the Emancipists and the soldiers should all sit down and drink the gallon
of rum together.

Here one might expect the rancor to simmer down, but it did not.
Bored, bitter and pugnacious, the redcoats (which they were in name
only: King was to report that by night you could not tell from a man's
dress whether he was a soldier, a settler or a convict) kept stalking about,
picking fights, muttering darkly against King—whom they despised as a
naval officer, an outsider to the corps—and plotting mutiny. In January
1794, King learned from a convict informer that the soldiers had taken
an oath "not to suffer any of their comrades to be punished for an offence
against a convict any more"; they would rise, kill Dring, and put all the
prisoners to death.[72]

Quelling this, King realized, would be "a very delicate affair"; one did not lightly disarm, on mere suspicion, a whole detachment of soldiers who owed their allegiance to a governor, himself their commanding officer, only two weeks' sail away on the Australian mainland. Nevertheless, King managed to disarm and arrest the ten suspected mutineers. He hastily formed a civil militia, consisting of forty-four free settlers, all former seamen and marines (no Emancipist, of course, could be trusted with a gun). By a remarkable fluke, a colonial schooner—the first vessel they had seen in nine months—arrived at Norfolk Island two days later, with dispatches from Sydney. The mutineers were shipped to the mainland for trial.

After they reached Sydney Cove, Grose read King's long report on the incident and was apoplectic with rage. His old wounds, inflicted almost twenty years before by the musket-balls of the American militia, were hurting him badly in the unrelenting summer heat of 1793–94; and now he learned that his naval subordinate had actually armed a civilian militia on Norfolk Island. This was subversion. Grose picked up his pen. "No provocation that a soldier can give," he wrote to King, "is ever to be admitted as an excuse for the convicts striking a soldier." No soldier could be tried by a civil judge or magistrate, or even put in the custody of a civilian constable. Most important of all, these constables "are to understand that they are not on any pretence whatever to stop or seize a soldier, *although he should be detected in an unlawful act.*"[73]

This remarkable letter was a charter of immunity for the New South Wales Corps. For Grose, the word *convict* meant both felons under sentence and Emancipists. Since the number of free emigrants was negligible, "convict" in Grose's eyes included virtually every civilian in the colony. Thus, the civil establishment could no longer touch the military, but the soldiers could do as they pleased, subject only to the restraint of a court-martial conducted by their own officers. Fortunately, King stood his ground against his intemperate governor. He sent his own explanations to the secretary of state in London; they were accepted, and Grose had to withdraw and apologize.

But when King himself became governor, succeeding the aged Captain Hunter in 1800, he installed a tiger from the Rum Corps as commandant of Norfolk Island. He was Major Joseph Foveaux (1765–1846), in whose regime the military contempt for convicts would approach the level of mania.[74]

There is no record of who Joseph Foveaux's parents were, but his father is said to have been a French cook in the employ of the Earl of Upper Ossory at Ampthill Park, in Bedfordshire. His mother's name is not recorded. Someone evidently took the trouble (and spent the money) to give him an education and steer him into a regiment, and his rapid promotion within the New South Wales Corps—from captain in 1791 to major in 1796, a most unusual leap for a young man on minor routine duty in an insignificant outpost—suggests a powerful male patron in the background.

From his letters, one can glean little of Foveaux's tastes and interests except a passion for military correctness. But he seems to have had the mentality of many a later camp commandant; Norfolk Island liberated him, enabling his sadism, which had been restrained by the more public sphere of the mainland, to overflow far from courts and judges, thinly disguised as "necessary rigor."

Arriving there late in 1800, he found morale had sagged badly in the four years since King had left. The flax manufactory still survived, but it produced nothing exportable. Skilled labor was short, and most buildings were tumbledown. The grindstones were worn out, the saws rusted, and the master carpenter had been suspended for laziness and impertinence. The settlement swarmed with bastard children, some two hundred of them, rather more than a fifth of the total island population, all illiterate and wild. The schoolmaster was in jail for debt and the lone missionary seemed "very unfit for a minister." Clearly, there was much to do.[75]

Foveaux did not go into detail about his own methods. They survive in an account by his head jailer, a transported highwayman named Robert Jones (alias Robert Buckey, alias George Abrahams), who had got a conditional pardon in or around 1795 from Governor Hunter at King's instigation but had chosen to stay on Norfolk Island.[76]

"Major Foveaux," Jones remarked, "was one of them hard and determined men who believe in the lash more than the Bible." Foveaux was determined to leave solid stone buildings behind him: a jail, a barracks, staff houses. A day's convict work was breaking five cartloads of stone per man. When the picks and hammers broke, for they were of poor quality, their users were severely flogged. The hours were long and the food bad ("the Pork . . . was so soft that you could put your finger through it, and always rotten"). Prisoners turned out before dawn and, rain or shine, had to put their straw palliasses outside their cells; when it rained, the convicts returning from labor were

turned into their Cells in their wet state with no means of drying their clothes, such were my orders from the Governor; and did any one of them make a complaint they were immediately sent to the triangles and ordered 25 lashes. Any further complaint was an additional 50.[77]

The fate of the refractory convict on Norfolk Island was one of prolonged and hideous torture:

The flogger was a County of Clare man a very powerful man and [he] took great pleasure in inflicting as much bodily punishment as possible, using such expressions as "Another half pound, mate, off the beggar's ribs." His face and clothes usually presented an appearance of a mincemeat chopper, being covered in flesh from the victim's body. Major Foveaux delighted in such an exhibition and would show his satisfaction by smiling as an encouragement to the flogger. He would sometimes order the victim to be brought before him with these words: *Hulloa* you damn'd scoundrel how do you like it? and order him to put on his coat and immediately go to his work.[78]

One prisoner named Joseph Mansbury had been flogged so often—some 2,000 lashes in three years—that his back appeared

quite bare of flesh, and his collarer [sic] bones were exposed looking very much like two Ivory Polished horns. It was with some difficulty that we could find another place to flog him. Tony [Chandler, the overseer] suggested to me that we had better [do it on] the soles of his feet next time.[79]

A sentence of 200 lashes was called a "feeler"; one did not forget it. All the medical treatment the convict received was a bucket of sea water on his back, an operation known as "getting salty back." "Many were relieved by death from this treatment," Jones wrote. "It would be impossible to detail the torture received . . . [from] the commandant, his servants and overseers. One of the favourite . . . punishments was to make the leg irons more small each month so that they would pinch the flesh." There was also a black isolation cell, and a water pit below the ground where prisoners would be locked, alone, naked, and unable to sleep for fear of drowning, for forty-eight hours at a spell.

There were only two ways out of "the old hell," as convict slang called the place. One was death; the other—as at Macquarie Harbor and Moreton Bay in decades to come—was by committing an offense that justified sending the convict to Sydney for trial. "Many murders," Jones wrote, "most of them were committed for the purpose of getting to Sydney, it being their only way of seeing heaven [convict slang for the mainland] again." Some men, including a convict named Thomas Carpenter whom Jones seems to have befriended, simply expired under the preliminary flogging:

His 250 killed him, died of heart-failure they said. God forgive them, and him too. For he was well liked on the Island. But feeling that he was ill, and thinking that his end was near, he struck his officer, with the hope that he would see his friends (in Sydney) once more, he did so but it was his last time. Considering the purpose for which these poor devils obtain

justice their lot is all the worse for the manner in which they chose to
obtain it.[80]

Foveaux's main obstacle on Norfolk Island was its deputy judge-
advocate, a dim but decent ex-Etonian lawyer named Thomas Hibbins
(1762–1816), who had got the post through the patronage of an old school
friend, the Earl of Morton. Hibbins was neither ambitious nor gifted (if
he had been, he would hardly have considered such a post), but he did
have a certain compassion for the convicts. Since it was his task to
interpret the civil and criminal law there—and to decide which cases
should be tried in Sydney, there being no criminal court on Norfolk
Island—he was often in conflict with Foveaux, who saw him as a felon-
loving drunk.

For his part, Hibbins seems to have made no secret of his dislike of
the commandant and his methods—methods that Foveaux himself delicately described as "vigorous if not exactly conformable to law." These
had to do with Irish political prisoners, originally transported to Sydney
for their part in the rebellion of 1798 and then, after appalling floggings
of up to 1,000 lashes each for their supposed complicity in a rising that
never took place at Parramatta in 1800, sent to Norfolk Island for life.

The Irish gave signs of mutiny almost as soon as they arrived. Most
of the convicts already on Norfolk Island were Irish, too; and the insurgents from Sydney, with their tales of the '98, must have catalyzed them.
On the morning of December 14, 1800, an Irish convict named Henry
Grady (whose crime was rape, not sedition) appeared at Foveaux's quarters "apparently in much agitation." There would be a rising that night,
he blurted; a hundred pikes were already made. Foveaux sent a soldier to
look for the pikes, and he found them just where Grady said they were—
long, fire-hardened sticks, not tipped with iron, but indubitably weapons
of a sort. The ringleaders, Grady claimed, were two "politicals"; John
Wolloghan, twenty-four years old, of Munster, and Peter McClean, forty,
of Ulster. Wolloghan had been in charge of making the pikes, and Mc-
Clean had recruited the rebels and given them their oath to kill the
English officers and guards.

Foveaux put the two under close arrest and called in Thomas Hibbins,
the judge-advocate. Hibbins opined that the men could not be tried for
their lives by a panel of officers; and moreover, as there were no statute
books on Norfolk Island, he did not know how an indictment could be
framed against them. Enraged by this "pedantry," Foveaux convened his
officers to discuss "the fatal consequences that were likely to ensue if
such daring & wicked designs were not checked in their earliest appearance." There was no hesitation; the officers, as terrified of mutiny as

Foveaux, unanimously agreed to hang Wolloghan and McClean summarily and without trial. They strung them up that night, by the light of flambeaux. Grady, the informer, got a free pardon. "Encouragement to such people," Foveaux wrote to King, "is ever well bestowed."[81]

At a perfunctory inquiry some months later, Foveaux was exonerated; in fact, his dispatch in hanging the Irish drew praise, not only from King but from Lord Hobart, the secretary of state for the colonies, and in 1802 he was promoted to lieutenant-colonel. He summed up his own views on the matter in a note to Lord Portland:

> The nature of this Place is so widely different from any other part of the World, the prisoners sent here, are of the worse Character & in general only those who have committed some fresh crime since their transportation to Port Jackson, in short most of them are a disgrace to human Nature. . . . [a]fter considering these circumstances, the very little support I receive from the Judge-Advocate and the situation of this Island, your grace will (I am persuaded) perceive that different Examples however vigorous if not exactly conformable to Law are on occasions indispensably necessary.[82]

Hibbins's objections counted for nothing. If the Irish in Ireland needed martial law to keep them in order, why should their dregs in Australia be protected by civil statutes? The military must not be hampered with niceties. What it most feared was an alliance against this weak and remote English colony between United Irish prisoners and a French naval force. Thus, one finds Robert Jones, Foveaux's jailer, quoting a fragment of some official address by his commandant—"His Majesty King George has been pleased to grant to all his subjects complete protection, in out of the way places . . ." Then he scribbles, "What a mockery to issue such a piece of information to chained convicts. Protection when we were the greatest enemy—as my orders were to murder all the prisoners under my care should any foreign nation bear down upon us. Protection be dam'd."[83]

He was looking back to a moment in 1804, when a convoy of China traders escorted by a French warship, *L'Athenienne*, appeared off Norfolk Island. The garrison mistook them for an invasion fleet and prepared to do battle. Redcoats were sent scouring about for broken rum bottles, and the island's two corroded six-pounders were crammed "with these fragments of glass, which (the Commandant swore) would cut the French to pieces." Foveaux was not there. He had sailed for England two months before, leaving the island under the command of Captain John Piper. But he had also left standing orders about the Irish with his civilian staff, headed by Jones. Thus, when the ships were sighted, Jones and his chief constable Edward Kimberley herded some sixty-five Irish convicts into the settlement jail, barred the doors, closed the windows so that they could not signal to the French and then piled up masses of Norfolk Island pine brushwood around the walls on a hastily constructed scaffold, thus turning the whole building into a pyre for living men. "The soldiers," Jones wrote, "were to set fire to the prison upon the signal from me." If any of the "politicals" escaped being burned alive, they were to be shot. Captain Piper, who was supervising the cannon several miles away, knew nothing of these preparations for a mass burning of the Irish; and providentially, since the ships sailed on, the prisoners escaped the incineration Foveaux had prepared for them.

No record of Foveaux's sadism, or of the torments he and his men visited on women at Norfolk Island, found its way into the official reports, although it is hard to believe that Governor King had no inkling of what his lieutenant-governor was up to. Foveaux censored all letters. "No person," Jones noted, "was allowed to write any information about the place or the work done here, they were only to write in reference to the state of our good conduct and friends." Norfolk Island was a sealed universe and its reputation among the mainland convicts existed only by word of mouth; you could not officially threaten with what did not officially exist. In a society where the line between convictry and freedom was always being crossed—by emancipation or by reconviction— the stories of the convict subculture spread quickly through the lower class, but their rulers did nothing about them.

They felt no need to. Civil law was sketchy; England had not equipped its colony with a normal judicial framework and would not do so until after 1810. The general attitude was that one did not need full civil courts in a jail. Not one judge-advocate appointed by England in these early years was properly trained. The first, David Collins, was a marine officer with no prior experience of the law. The next in office, Richard Dore (1749–1800), was a blundering and cantankerous incompetent, much given to petty graft. His successor, Richard Atkins, was even worse: The drunken fifth son of a baronet, he had run through his legacy, bought and then sold a military commission and skipped from England in order to elude his creditors. Arriving in the colony in 1791, Atkins managed, by assiduous name-dropping and currying of favor with the officials (especially with Governor Hunter), to get himself appointed judge-advocate. His professional conduct was enough to disgust the next governor, Bligh, who called him "the ridicule of the community: sentences of death have been pronounced in moments of intoxication; his determination is weak, his opinion floating and infirm; his knowledge of the law is insignificant and subservient to private inclination." The measure of his detachment from the interests of the military may perhaps be gauged from the fact that the wife of this pathetic drunk ("She wears the breeches completely," noted the convict John Grant, who lived for a time in their household) raised two of the six bastard children whom Major George Johnston of the New South Wales Corps had sired on various women.[84]

Such men could not defy the junta. The corps, therefore, was virtually immune from civil law; and military law was exercised by its own officers to protect the interests of their own group. One sees why a Foveaux could flog and kill without restraint on Norfolk Island and yet have no word breathed against him by his brother officers. The question of the "rights" of convicts was barely worth raising in New South Wales between the departure of Arthur Phillip in 1792 and the arrival of Governor Lachlan Macquarie in 1810.

By then, the English colony in Australia had spread and solidified. It was no longer a tiny outpost, racked with hunger and scurvy, clinging to the edge of the continent. Sydney was a fortified town and the country behind it, the Cumberland Plain, was fast becoming a patchwork of cleared, productive fields, self-sufficient and worked with varying degrees of efficiency by convict slave labor. The hoped-for economic importance of Norfolk Island had not materialized. But it had been bound up with the idea that New South Wales was a naval outpost, and that was beginning to change. In the early 1800s, a few last efforts were made to utilize the pines and flax that had been the colony's naval raison d'être.[85]

Thus in 1802, the government tried the experiment of sending forth to Australia a few batches of convicts in Royal Navy vessels; and rather than waste space on the return voyage—for Navy ships, unlike the contracted ones that carried most of the convicts out, could not fill up with Oriental trade goods on the return run—the Admiralty sent with them drawings for major frame timbers of three classes of ships, to be cut and rough-shaped in New South Wales and brought back to England. The order was partly filled by King, but the practice lapsed. In 1805, King also had a small naval vessel, the *Buffalo*, rigged with a suit of sails woven from Norfolk Island flax by the women convicts in the Female Factory at Parramatta. She was the only ship to sail under such canvas. Up to 1810, sporadic efforts continued to be made to supply the Royal Navy with Australian timber.[86] But they were never more than a footnote to the main economic life of the colony, which was shifting decisively to agriculture—to the land and its owners, rather than the sea and its captains. So Norfolk Island, with its dark pinnacles and stands of now strategically useless pines, was allowed to fall into decay. By March 1810, its population had sunk to 117 people, and one of Lachlan Macquarie's first actions in assuming his governorship of New South Wales was to recall the mild officer who had succeeded Foveaux as commandant, Captain

Piper, and order the abandonment of the island. "The impolicy of the original settlement," the colonial secretary, Lord Liverpool, had told him, "has been fully demonstrated."[87]

In 1813, the breaking-up began. The frame huts were torn down and burnt (the nails frugally saved), the stone houses demolished, and every last animal except a few pigs that got away was slaughtered, skinned, butchered and packed down in casks of brine. There must be nothing left to catch the eye of a passing ship, no base from which another settlement could be made. They even left behind a dozen dogs to run wild and breed into a hunting pack to discourage visitors from landing. The last salvage from the settlement was loaded into the brig *Kangaroo* in February 1814, and when she sailed, the island was as empty as it had been before the arrival of Cook. It would stay so for a decade; the new abode of misery was Van Diemen's Land, far in the south.

viii

THE ENGLISH invasion of Van Diemen's Land was by higher imperial standards a muddled and squalid affair. It produced no setpiece battles, no benevolent occupation, no heroes, profits or cultural loot. It merely opened another pit within the antipodean darkness, a small hole in the world about the size of Ireland, which would in due time swallow more than 65,000 men and women convicts—four out of every ten people transported to Australia. How many Tasmanian Aborigines died while the invading whites readied this cavity is not known, because no one knew how many there were to begin with. Probably not very many: The best guess at present is 3,000 to 4,000 people, hunting and gathering in small bands of 30 to 80—a population density roughly equal to that of the Aborigines of coastal New South Wales.[88]

But die they did—shot like kangaroos and poisoned like dogs, ravaged by European diseases and addictions, hunted by laymen and pestered by missionaries, "brought in" from their ancestral territories to languish in camps. It took less than seventy-five years of white settlement to wipe out most of the people who had occupied Tasmania for some thirty thousand years; it was the only true genocide in English colonial history. By the standards of Pol Pot, let alone Josef Stalin or Adolf Hitler, this was a small slaughter. But not to the Tasmanian Aborigines.

Between convict and black, much blood is mingled in the soil of this green, lovely, lugubrious island—so much, in fact, that parts of it seem to be emblematic spots, places where ordinary nature is permanently corrupted by the leaching of history, a salt that nothing can extract from the earth. Except that, in Tasmania, it is hard at first to sense the violence of the implanted culture. Its relics are so modest: an earnestly detailed stone bridge spanning the river at Ross, overseen by a convict mason who once worked for Beau Nash; the squat, authoritarian Doric columns of a Hobart government building. Yet when the first white invaders reached the shores of the Derwent River, the idea that they would last long was much in doubt.

Van Diemen's Land had been occupied to forestall the French who, to the alarm of New South Wales's tarpaulin Governor King,[89] had been nosing about in the ill-charted waters of southeastern Australia. Bass Strait, which separates Van Diemen's Land from the mainland, was discovered in 1797–98. Its weather was bad and its waters were strewn with islands whose vast colonies of wildlife would support the future seal trade of Australia, but which were a peril to ships—King Island to the west, the Furneaux group in the east, and a nasty prickle of rocks and reefs athwart the strait. But to go through the Bass Strait, avoiding the long southern route below Van Diemen's Land, clipped weeks off the passage from England to Sydney.

The strategic importance of this sea lane was obvious, and King strongly felt there had to be a settlement to secure it. In January 1802 Lieutenant John Murray, surveying the southern coast in the *Lady Nelson*, discovered a great bay on the mainland near the head of the strait, which in due course was named Port Phillip Bay: the harbor of modern Melbourne.

The following April, another coastal explorer, Matthew Flinders, was working eastward along the coast when he ran into two westbound French ships at an anchorage near the present site of Adelaide, which he named Encounter Bay. They were *Le Géographe* and *Le Naturaliste*, on a cartographic mission for the French Navy under Captain Nicolas Baudin. Baudin's expedition seems to have had no direct military purpose, despite the Napoleonic Wars. Like Flinders, he was trying to find out whether the western part of Australia was all of a piece with its eastern, British-occupied flank, New South Wales. He had spent more than a month mapping the southern coast of Van Diemen's Land and had bestowed a number of French names on his rough charts of Terre Napoléon, as he called the south coast of mainland Australia. Baudin and his exhausted, sick crew put into Sydney Harbor in June 1802; he stayed there for several months refitting, and he showed Governor King his survey charts.

King thought he smelled a rat. The mere presence of French ships in these waters was bad enough, but French names tacked on the British coast—albeit an unoccupied, unclaimed one—were worse. The idea of having to share this continent with "Boney," no matter how large it might be, was intolerable. And when Baudin sailed south again, King was sure he was going to start claiming territory and hoisting the *tricolore*.

King had already urged London to occupy Port Phillip as soon as possible. Now he sent an armed schooner to shadow Baudin. (It caught up with him at King Island in Bass Strait, where Baudin handed over some escaped convicts who had stowed away in his ship in Sydney.) Since Baudin had been snooping around the D'Entrecasteaux Channel, while intrepid American whalers from the far side of the Pacific had already penetrated the calving grounds of the black whales there and in Storm Bay at the mouth of the Derwent River—thus threatening to seize the fisheries that should have been a British monopoly—King decided to put a settlement on the Derwent.

In August 1803 a little party of forty-nine souls, made up of free settlers and Rum Corps men with twenty-one male and three female convicts, sailed from Port Jackson. Their leader was a twenty-three-year-old lieutenant from Devon, John Bowen (1780–1827), just arrived in the colony on the convict transport *Glatton*, whom King promoted to the rank of commander in the belief that it would impress foreign sea captains. Armed with minute instructions from King, Bowen sailed up the Derwent estuary and pitched his camp, complete with a pair of 12-pound carronades, at a spot on its eastern shore which he named Risdon. It had a stream of fresh water and a splendid view of the snowy brow of Mount Wellington, but little else to recommend it. Its soil was poor; it was whipped by gales blowing from the 4,000-foot mountain; and the stream itself went dry when the weather did—a familiar event in Australian colonization.

Meanwhile, King's pleas for a settlement at Port Phillip Bay, protecting Bass Strait from the questing French, had reached London. England's response was to send a ship to colonize the bay. She was HMS *Calcutta*, a vessel of the Royal Navy, bearing 308 convicts with a smattering of their wives and children (who were allowed to go out with their husbands as indentured servants), guarded by marines. The expedition was under the command of David Collins, the marine officer who, having served as the first judge-advocate of Phillip's settlement at Port Jackson, had returned to England and written one of the first and best books on the infant colony, his two-volume *Account of the English Colony in New South Wales*, 1798–1802. It earned him a public name as an expert on matters Australian, and on the strength of his eight years' service in Sydney the government asked him to go back as lieutenant-governor of the new colony at Port Phillip. Harassed by his debts—a situation aggravated by a bureaucratic hitch in his emoluments as a marine officer—Collins accepted. As soon as his appointment became known in London, he found himself pursued by Jeremy Bentham, who had just published *Panopticon Versus New South Wales*. This was a lengthy diatribe against the policy of transportation whose aim was to persuade Lord Pelham to build penitentiaries instead; the model Bentham put forth was his Panopticon, with its circular plan and central watchtower, affording continuous totalitarian inspection of the caged prisoners, which had become his obsessive project. Bentham even wrote to Collins urging him to build a Panopticon in New South Wales, and the two men dined together twice. "I have given him a copy of the Panopticon book," Bentham reported to his brother, adding that Collins had asked him for "a Draught [sketch] of the Panopticon Plan. . . . I said, I hoped I might—with the book and a little *nous*, he might be able to do without the draught; [but] the *nous*, I fear, is lacking." Despite Bentham's unjustifiably low view of Collins's intelligence, he kept lobbying: "Are you serious in your intention of building a prison, and moreover of building it on the central inspection principle?" Just before sailing, Collins brushed him politely off. "I have been lately so occupied . . . as to prevent my waiting on you to receive the Hints for my pursuing the *Panopticon System*, which you were so good as to prepare for me. Be assured that my Prison shall if possible be a circular one." Of course, no Panopticon would rise by the shores of Port Phillip Bay. The *Calcutta*, escorted by the transport *Ocean*, sailed in April 1803.[90]

The fleet reached Port Phillip in October. The bay proved a miserable disappointment, as bad (or almost) as Botany Bay had seemed to the men of the First Fleet fifteen years before: sandy sterile ground, little water, a persistent hot northerly wind, swarms of biting flies, and great difficulties of access by sea because of the adverse tidal currents. After six months at sea, all hands were yearning for dry land again, but their enthusiasm soon waned. In "Canvas Town," their encampment on the sand dunes, the shade temperature in Collins's tent was 102°, and in the sun it reached 132°. It seemed a "barbarous country," the surveyor George Prideaux Harris wrote to his brother after three months there: nothing but sand, with no water and so few animals that, for meat, he had once been reduced to eating a swan's carcass fit only for a dunghill. The one recompense was the lobsters, so plentiful that the convicts could catch five hundred in an evening. "Never, surely, was a more barren land," wrote one prisoner, the counterfeiter James Grove, to his friends in faraway England. "I thought it unlikely to answer to any good purpose."[91]

Everyone else thought so, too. After a couple of weeks camped on the sand hills, the marines were muttering and grumbling their way toward mutiny, and to set an example Collins had a couple of insubordinate privates savagely flogged, one with 700 lashes. Some convicts tried to escape. A former army officer named Lee, transported for forgery, who seemed "quite a pedant, eternally quoting passages from the Greek and Latin authors," wrote some scurrilous lampoons on Collins which circulated among the tents; he was found out and bolted into the bush, never to be seen again, taking the lieutenant-governor's fowling piece with him. Groups of four or five men would vanish into the dunes, heading (as they thought) for China.* [92]

So there was general relief when dispatches arrived from Governor King in Sydney authorizing Collins to abandon Port Phillip and move his settlement down to the Derwent, to join Bowen's tiny band. But King also instructed Collins to take a look at Port Dalrymple, at the mouth of the Tamar River on the northern coast of Van Diemen's Land (the site of modern Launceston) and see if an outpost could be put there to guard the fisheries of Bass Strait from American whalers and sealers. Collins reported that it could not, or not yet, as the river entrance was difficult, and the local blacks seemed very aggressive. [93]

In any case, the strength of his party was low. So many men were sick that he could not mount enough sentinels; if one more officer went ill, he would not even find the quorum for a court martial. So the prudent course was to join forces with Bowen on the Derwent. A settlement, Collins felt, would be better on the Derwent than on the Tamar: "Its position at the Southern Extremity of Van Dieman's Land gives it an Advantage over every Harbour yet discovered in the Straits . . . [A]s a Port of Shelter to Ships from Europe, America or India, either for Whaling or other speculation, it will be greatly resorted to." [94]

So Port Phillip was abandoned. When the settlers reached the Derwent, Collins relieved Bowen of his command and moved the settlement from Risdon to the western shore of the estuary. In a sketch from about 1805, one sees the embryo town of Hobart, named after the secretary of state for the colonies who was the patron of Collins's expedition. It is a little straggle of tents and huts, with Government House—hardly more than a cottage—on Battery Point, and the huts of the surveyor-general, the surgeon and the chaplain ranged alongside it; casks are stacked up on the dock island, and an ensign flutters from its mast in front of the public store, while the whole scene is dominated by the brooding wall of Mount Wellington, capped with snow. In 1805 it must have looked very frail and ephemeral. But in the green valley folds that ran down to the water, in the copses and meadows that (seen through half-closed eyes) reminded young Bowen of a nobleman's park, there was at least some reminiscence of the England that most of the colonists would never see again. Nostalgia could cling to this Tasmanian landscape.

---

* For the peculiar phenomenon of the "China Travellers," see chapter 7.

Yet life by the Derwent was hard for all the colonists at first, bond or free. The isolation, torpor and semi-starvation of early Sydney repeated themselves in Van Diemen's Land. "With no ships visiting us," recalled Collins's second-in-command, Lieutenant Edward Lord,

> the whole settlement was called upon to endure hardships of no ordinary kind. The Governor himself, the officers, and the entire settlement for eighteen months, were without bread, vegetables, tea, sugar, wine, spirits, or beer, or any substitute, except the precarious supply of the wild game of the country.[95]

Memories of this starvation time died hard. Thirty years later a Hobart woman recounted what she had known as a child in the first settlement: coming off the ship and sleeping under a wet blanket, then in the hollow trunk of a tree; being "treated kindly" by curious, not yet persecuted Aborigines, in whose care white infants were sometimes left by their parents; living on "Botany Bay Greens" (boiled seaweed scraped off the rocks), and even wolfing down the "crap" (cindery residue) of whale blubber, shovelled overboard from the roaring try-pots of American whalers in Storm Bay and washed up on the beaches. The same oily gobbets were used to feed the colony's precious pigs, contaminating the taste of their flesh.[96]

By the winter of 1805 the convicts were down to a ration of 2 pounds 10 ounces of salt pork and 4 pounds of bread a week, a ration that in normal times would scarcely last two days. By 1806 the colony was starving to death. Collins had hoped that supplies would come from Sydney. But in March 1806 the farms along the Hawkesbury River, on which the food supply of Sydney depended, were devastated by flood. The water covered 36,000 acres and destroyed all the standing crops, along with the farmers' tools, livestock and seed reserves. What remained was not enough for Sydney and Parramatta; and for Hobart, there was nothing. Two years later things had improved a little in Hobart—but not much. "Bring with you as much Flour and Wheat as possible," wrote an early political transportee to Van Diemen's Land, the Irish schoolmaster William Maum, to a friend who was about to move to Hobart Town in 1808,

> and a sufficiency of corn for whatever Stock you may bring down, bring down about 12 good young Ewes, four or five Sows in pig (if possible) as there are no Boars here—as much poultry as you can get off . . . bring with you Hoes and all other Tools as they are here remarkably scarce. . . . [t]he houses in general are of Lath & plaister and immoderately dear . . . [t]he Gov' here has it not in his power to fulfil the intentions of Gov', as he has

neither Tradesmen nor Labourers, and nothing in the Stores. . . . Fowls
here are of the utmost consequence, their Value being beyond Money.[97]

There was very little of the fellow-feeling that makes privation bear-
able. Shortages on this Georgian frontier bred stony, grasping men, who
robbed one another like jackals snarling over a carcass and cheated the
government blind whenever they could. The clerks who ran the government stores were so deep in collusion with the farmers who sold them
their produce that a newly appointed chief clerk of the Hobart commissariat declared, in 1816, that not one document or account could be found
in its records.[98]

Between the vulpine rapacity of the settlers and the short commons
of government, the Derwent colony—along with the smaller one set up
in October 1804 at Port Dalrymple on the Tamar, under Lieutenant-
Colonel Paterson, to fix an English foothold on Bass Strait—might well
have perished. What saved them both was that inoffensive marsupial,
the kangaroo.

Kangaroos were plentiful in the bush of Van Diemen's Land—much
more so than they had ever been around Sydney. Every able-bodied man
who could use a gun went hunting them, for kangaroo flesh, not bread,
was the staff of life. Collins tried to keep the market under strict control.
Hunters were obliged to sell the meat to the commissariat store. To
convicts and others "on the store," it was issued free; the usual ration
was 8 pounds a week. To settlers living "on their own hands," its price
fluctuated between 6d. and 1s. 6d. a pound. In one six-month period the
settlers ate 15,000 pounds of dressed meat from haunches and tails, representing a slaughter of perhaps a thousand 'roos.[99]

This reliance on hunting brought prompt social results, all of them
bad. It installed the gun, rather than the plough, as the totem of survival
in Van Diemen's Land. It favored a mood of opportunism, of social im-
providence. Small settlers tended to neglect the long-range pursuits of
farming and instead concentrated on killing whatever they could. Before
long, the kangaroos around Hobart were hunted out, and men and dogs
had to push further into the bush, competing against the Aborigines for
game. Thus, the pattern of ambush and murder between white and black
began; it would end, in a few decades, with the near-extermination of the
Tasmanian Aborigines. Hunger had put guns in the hands of convicts—
and this had never been allowed to happen in New South Wales. It soon
created a fringe class of armed, uncontrollable bushmen, most of whom
regarded Aborigines as vermin. They would go out for days at a stretch
with their "mates" and their kangaroo-dogs (half-wild mongrel lurchers,
with jaws like mantraps) and bring back whatever they could corner and
kill. Very soon these mountain men of Van Diemen's Land shed what-

ever vestiges of obedience they might have felt to the System. They became the first bushrangers (see chapter 7). They kept the guns, stole their masters' dogs and stayed in the bush. Earlier absconders from Sydney and Parramatta had died because they were not armed, but not these kangarooers. When Hobart and Port Dalrymple were tiny and the outlying farms few, they could be controlled to some degree, if only because they had to sell most of their kangaroo meat directly to the government before getting more ammunition. But as settlement pushed outward, farmer and assigned servants started buying the meat and skins directly from the outlaws. And since few settlers had any scruples about cheating their neighbors as long as they were not seen at it, they also "received" the mutton the kangarooers stole from other sheep runs and kept on the good side of the hunters by giving them ammunition, tea and rum. As the stock of sheep and cattle in the colony grew, so the demand for kangaroo meat dropped. But everyone needed kangaroo skins, for shoes, hats, bags, jackets and pants; and in between killing 'roos, the hunters moved to sheep stealing. They could do this with impunity, unless a settler caught them in the act and shot them. The redcoats could not catch them; they did not know the bush.

So in theory, the founding years of Van Diemen's Land displayed a rigidly patterned Georgian fabric of rank and power which, in practice, did not survive inspection. It was a façade. The official barriers between military and civilian, bond and free were breached in a score of ways by hunger, shortages, the rub of proximity, the ferocity of the good and the occasional decency of the criminal. "They call it the end of the world—and for vice it is truly so, for here wickedness flourishes unchecked."[100] So did boredom, a great equalizer. Technique of any kind was rare, technology feeble, and "cultivation" in any but the most rudimentary sense scarcely existed at all. When he wanted some conversation to take his mind off the miseries of his post, Lieutenant-Governor Collins, "a literary and excellent man," had to turn to the forger James Grove and his family, "passing with him under his roof many no doubt intellectual hours."[101] In return, Grove designed Collins a house; and when the lieutenant-governor died in 1810 of a heart attack at the early age of 54, worn out by the strain of keeping his precarious little colony alive, it was Grove, "his eyes suffused with tears the whole time," who cut and planed the yellow Huon pine boards for his double coffin, helped place the corpse in it, engraved the silver memorial plate and screwed down the lid. Five weeks later, heartbroken at the loss of the friend and patron who had returned him to respectability on this far edge of the world, Grove himself died. "As sensible, ingenious a man as I ever met with, & highly esteemed and respected by the Gov' & every officer in the settlement, for his uniform and excellent character"—such had been the judg-

ment of the surveyor Harris on this convict.[102] He was buried near
Collins. The friendship of these men was perhaps emblematic, suggesting at its most benevolent, and thus uncommon, level the interdepen-
dence between prisoners and masters. Wherever new settlements were
made, whatever fields were broken, English settlement in Australia
rested on its convicts. As Mary Gilmore would write in 1918 of the
prisoners who built Australia:

> I was the convict
> Sent to hell,
> To make in the desert
> The living well:
>
> I split the rock;
> I felled the tree—
> The nation was
> Because of me.[103]

We must now look more closely at these reluctant pioneers.

5

The Voyage

i

"I T IS THEREFORE ordered and adjudged by this Court, that you be transported upon the seas, beyond the seas, to such place as His Majesty, by the advice of His Privy Council, shall think fit to direct and appoint, for the term of your natural life." Or seven years, or fourteen —in any case, the shock of sentencing was dreadful. In law, seven years' banishment meant what it said; but what man could be certain of returning to England at the end of it? For many people, the sentence of transportation—whatever its announced length—must have seemed like a one-way trip over the edge of the world.

A man could bear it with dignity in the dock, but despair followed soon after. Anguish shows in the few surviving letters, like this one from a Lancashire weaver named Thomas Holden, who in the course of struggling for his rights as an early trade-unionist was convicted in 1812 of "administering an illegal oath" to one Isaac Crompton in Bolton, Lancashire. It seems probable that Holden was a Luddite. He was also happily married. "Dear Wife," he wrote from a cell in Lancaster Castle,

Its with sorrow that I have to acquaint you that I this day receiv'd my Tryal and has receiv'd the hard sentance of Seven Years Transportation beyond the seas. . . . If I was for any Time in prison I would try and content myself but to be sent from my Native Country perhaps never to see it again distresses me beyond comprehension and will Terminate with my life. . . . [T]o part with my dear Wife & Child, Parents and Friends, to be no more, cut off in the Bloom of my Youth without doing the least wrong to any person on earth—O my hard fate, may God have mercy on me. . . . Your affec. Husband until Death.[1]

In April 1831 Peter Withers, the "Swing" protestor from Wiltshire, wrote from the convict ship *Proteus* at Spithead to his wife Mary Ann:

My Dear Wife belive me my Hark is almost broken to think I must lave
you behind. O my dear what shall I do i am all Most destracted at the
thoughts of parting from you whom I do love so dear. Believe me My Dear
it Cuts me even to the hart and my dear Wife there is a ship Come into
Portsmouth harber to take us to New Southweals.

Inconceivable distances loom before Withers, who has never even been
as far from home as London; and he tries to explain them, to normalize
them by promising a fidelity that will annihilate separation:

it is about 4 months sail to that country But we shall stop at several
cuntreys before we gets there for fresh water I expects you will eare from
me in the course of 9 months. . . . you may depend upon My keeping
Myselfe from all other Woman for i shall Never Let No other run into my
mind for tis onely you My Dear that can Ease me of my Desire. It is not
Laving Auld england that grives me it is laving my dear and loving Wife
and Children, May God be Mersyful to me.[2]

In December 1831 Richard Dillingham, a convict in the hulks at
Woolwich, awaiting transportation, writes less tragically to the girl who
had borne him a son out of wedlock, "my ever adorable Betsey Faine."
He casts it in the form of the sweet doggerel rhymes one could buy
inscribed on favors at a market fair:

Dearest Betsey the first of human kind the thoughts of you will ever ease
my mind for though we at a distance are I hope that God will be your
leading star—

> The first is B a letter bright
> Which plenty doth afear,
> The next is F in all women slight,
> The surname of my dearest dear. Adieu.[3]

Tossing on his iron cot in the lockup, a convict would obsessively
recall his life and its mistakes. So John Ward, sentenced to 10 years'
transportation in 1841 for theft:

A miserable object in truth, all my feelings and passions now rushed upon
mc at once. Remorse for an instant filled my breast with abandoned
thoughts of plunging deeper into the depravity of heart, to which I had
fallen a victim. . . . The many enemies there was to contend with all stood
in dark array before my burning imagination.

Ward thinks, with bitter irony, of some lines of affectionate rhyme he
once sent to his sweetheart:

Had I possessed candour enough to marry the girl, I sincerely believe I should have been one of the happiest of men!—but!—It occurred to my memory the words I wrote to Rose! some years before this, on a particular occasion—

> Far beyond the seas
> Unpittied I'll remove,
> And rather cease to live
> E'er I will cease to love!

But I did not, at that time, ever dream of putting these words into practice, much less of being sent as a poor convict.[4]

Many prisoners hoped their wives would go into Australian exile with them, although few actually did; it was hard to get passage out there, and tickets were far beyond the means of a worker's wife. "I hope you will strain your utmost to keep my Company," Thomas Holden wrote to his wife Molly as he was leaving for the hulks, "and not let mee go without you for with your company I don't mind where I go nor what I suffer, if I have your Company to chear my allmost Broken Hart." And later, from the hulk: "My sorrow is greatly Encreased by parting with you, what Comfort can I enjoy when we are separate. . . . I could wish to know if you think you Could rise money to pay your passage & go with me."[5] She did not go. Neither did Mary Ann, Peter Withers's wife, despite his heart-wringing pleas:

> We [h]ears we shall get our freedom in that Country, but if I gets my freedom evenso i am shure I shall Never be happy except I can have the Pleshur of ending my days with you and my dear Children, for I dont think a man ever loved a woman so well as I love you.
>
> My Dear I hope you will go to the gentlemen for they to pay your Passage over to me when I send for you. How happy I shall be to eare that you are a-coming after me. . . . Do you think I shall sent for you except i can get a Cumfortable place for you, do you think that I wants to get you into Troble, do you think as I want to punish my dear Children? No my dear but if I can get a cumfortsable place should you not like to follow your dear Husband who Lovs you so dear?[6]

There was no reply, and two years later Withers was writing to his brothers from Van Diemen's Land: "I have sent 2 letters to My Wife an Cant get heny Answer from her Wich Causeth Me a great deal of unhapyness for i think she have quite forgotten me an I think she is got Marred to some other Man, if she is pray send me Word." But there was still no word from her, and eleven years would pass before Mary Ann wrote in distress to her husband in Van Diemen's Land, asking to be reconciled.

She received the news that Peter had married again (there was no question of divorce for the lower classes; one simply relied on the inaccessibility of records and married bigamously) to a "staidy vertus Woman":

> I have no Property of my own but my Wife have Property wich she will have in the course of two years and then we have agreed to help you an the Children if God spares our lives.
>
> I know that for to eare that I am married is a hard trial for you to bear, but it is no good to tell you a Lye.
>
> I sent a great maney Leters before I took a Wife; so not earing from you, I being a young man, I thought it would be Proper thing to look [for] a partner which would be a Comfort to me in my Bondage. I sent for you to Come out to this country when I came first and if you had you would have got me out of Bondag for nothing, for a wife could get a release for her husband. So we must not think about Coming together again.[7]

Poor repentant Mary kept trying. The last news of her is a curt form letter from the colonial secretary's office in Whitehall dated August 1847, telling her that he "was living on the 30 Septr. 1846" but that "no further information can be given respecting him." There must have been many variations on this small colonial drama.

The Privy Council records contain hundreds of letters from wives asking to go into Australian exile with their husbands. Generally the authorities would not allow this, unless the convict had earned his ticket-of-leave and shown that he could support a family in Australia.* Permission was only rarely given for a wife to accompany her man on the transport vessel. An intense pathos rises from some of these letters, written in the neat hand of a local curate or the labored scrawl of the petitioner herself. From Rochester in Kent, Deborah Taylor, whose husband James has been transported for life for stealing a lamb, encloses, for Peel's perusal, a document infinitely precious to her: his letter exhorting her to join him in Australia. She beseeches Peel "most humbly and fervently"

> that I may be sent out with my Remaining Children a boy 10 years of age and a girl 6 years, having buried two since my Application. My husband it will be seen by the enclosed letter is very anxious to be sent out. . . . I humbly hope that I may be favored with the return of my poor husband's letter should I not be successful, pray God I may find favor.[8]

It seems she did get the letter back (at least it is not in the file) but her application was denied. "Usual answer," Peel's secretary minuted on the back of her petition, as on so many others.

---

* The ticket-of-leave system is discussed on pages 307–308.

The determination of some of these women was heroic; they yearned for their men and they would not accept the common fate of abandonment. Jane Eastwood, the thirty-year-old wife of a transported Manchester bootmaker, told Peel in April 1830 that her husband "has written several letters to me from Sidney Island [sic] requesting me to apply to Government in order to be sent out there to him. . . . I am determined to go out to my Husband even at the risk of my life." She implored the home secretary to "Put it in my power of becoming happy, by uniting me again to the Best of Husbands":

> Prevent me from the shame of casting myself & Child upon the Parish for Relief . . . as work is not only scarce but so ill paid for that it is utterly out of my Power to gain a living for myself & Child, and I have no other thing to depend upon except what I can earn by my needle in dress and stay making.[9]

She cannot wait for more letters, across the vast antipodean time lag; she will pay her own fare with whatever she has. "I know not how to get over the time until word come back from him, about 9 months at least. I would rather sell my household furniture which will amount to about six or eight Pounds, this sum I will most willingly give to Government to lessen their expenses of sending me out to Sidney, provided they would be graciously pleased to send me by the first Ship." She knows her skills, joined to his, will keep them without government support once she is there. "I myself have been thoroughly bred to the Dressmaking business, and have wrought for years at the Umbrella Business, I can also bind Shoes & boots and can render him every assistance. . . . [T]here can scarcely remain a doubt that we would at all become a burden upon this Colony but rather a gain to them."[10] This time the government listened, and to Australia she went.

Local clergy, with their charitable concerns, would endorse such petitions. Thus in 1819 Charles Isherwood, the curate of Brotherton, collected signatures from ten colleagues on behalf of Elizabeth Rhodes, asking that she and her two small children "may be permitted to accompany her unfortunate husband to his place of Exile." Sometimes whole groups, or part of an entire community, would intervene. "A man by the name of Mitchel has lately had the sentence of 21 yrs. transportation passed on him," wrote a Stirling magistrate, Robert Downie, to Peel's office. "The Stirling people are most anxious that he should be allowed to carry his wife and 3 children with him. Does Government ever allow of such shipments?" Parishioners would write, promising to raise a local subscription for a wife to join her husband; they offered clothes, food and bedding for her passage.[11]

Husbands and lovers were also sons, and in an age when family ties across the generations were the very mortar of society the misery felt by the parents of a transported man—and the shame he felt for them—could be unbearable. Convicts' letters to their parents were filled with promises of self-amendment. "I can assure you that since I have been here i have had plenty of leisure time to reflect on my past misconduct," a weaver named Richard Boothman writes to his father in Lancashire, "and I can assure you most sincerely that if it pleases God to bestow my Liberty upon me once more, that my life will be one series of amendment, and I trust that i shall yet be able to close your eyes in peace and comfort and render the downhill part of your life happy." [12] From his "unhappy situation" in York Castle, awaiting transfer to the hulks, Richard Taylor tells his father, "i wish i had taken your Advice. . . . I listen to my fellow Prisoners till my heart goes as Cold as Clay." But no letter comes from his father, and Taylor, fearing that he has been spurned and forgotten, writes in agitation to his "Dear unkles":

> You must let him now I ham very well and he must think as little about me as he can for i ham quite innesent and I hope god will be mersful to me an I shall see you all agane but if not I must live for a beter world. For my part I [am] determined to lead a godley life. [13]

He invokes the future, trying to shore up the spirits of his parents. He writes from York in May 1840—this time with better spelling, through the medium of a scribe—that "the prayers of a sincere heart are as acceptable to God from the dreary Prison as from the splendid Palace. What a blessing that assurance is to a poor unfortunate mortal in my hapless condition." He promises reunion:

> When I have lived out my ten years in a far distant land how happy I shall be to return to my native home, and with how much more delight will I return home if God shall spare my dear Father until that time, that we may once more meet in the flesh, and convene together about heavenly things—why, my dear Parent, if he spare us both to enjoy that Happiness, it will be like a foretaste of Heaven itself. [14]

Such utterances were sincere but they hardly masked the deeper fear that transportation would sunder the family forever. Richard Boothman beseeches his father "not to forget me to my brother-in-law" and other relatives, "and tell them that I should like to see them before my leaving here, *as it may be for the last time.*" On leaving for the hulks in June 1841, he complains of being cast off by his kin: "I think it rather strange that you have not attended to my request but I certainly should have been glad to see some of my Friends before I left here, but alas now it is too late." For every brave assertion that the writer will come back ("Dear Father I hope that you will not fret and Greeve And make yourself uncomfortable . . . I hope in a short time I shall see you again"), there are many expressions of despair. "My spiritts is low with thinking how I am sent from my Natiff Contrey, and I am inisent," Thomas Holden writes in June 1812. "Dear mother I do not think of seeing you in this world any more." [15]

That transportation inflicted social and filial death was a common theme of ballads and it occasionally percolated upward into literature: One finds George Crabbe, for instance, alluding to it in "The Borough" by evoking a pathetic still life meant as a *vanitas:*

> On swinging shelf are things incongruous stored,—
> Scraps of their food, the cards and cribbage-board,—
> With pipes and pouches, while on peg below
> Hang a lost member's fiddle and his bow;
> That still remind them how he'd dance and play
> Ere cast untimely to the Convicts' Bay. [16]

Some convicts clung to the hope of a last-minute pardon, usually in vain. The prerogative of the Royal Mercy was often extended to those sentenced to hang, especially if their crimes were political (more especially still, if they were committed after the death of Castlereagh in 1822 and seemed to represent a wave of popular opinion). Thus in 1831, at the height of agitation for reform, Peter Withers and his fellow protestor James Lush were snatched from the gallows on the very eve of their execution by a mass petition addressed to the king through the Home Office. However, once the machinery of transportation had begun to turn, one could not jump free. Yet English life was so enlaced with patronage, with lines of favor and gratitude running throughout the strata of the social pyramid from navvy to duke, that prisoners and their families would seize any chance of mitigation after sentencing. In 1798 a gentleman named C. M. Waller writes to his acquaintance in Sydney, the Irish dynast and assistant surgeon for the colony, D'Arcy Wentworth. He intercedes for an "Unfortunate young Man, who has been cast for Transportation, for the trifling sum of Half a Crown":

> His situation is so much more to be pittied as he not only bore a universal good Character [but] was the whole supporter of a Sickely old Father & a Aged Mother, who is now standing Wheeping before me, & laments the

loss of a Son. . . . [T]he only favour she begs of you, Sir, is, that you will be so obliging as to render him any service which is in your power, that his Situation may be more comfortable.[17]

Thomas Holden, on the eve of his sailing in 1812, was still imploring his wife "to go to Mr Fletcher & Mr Watkin [and] tell them that I still Protest my inosentse"; while at sea, despite the "great deal of truble and difficklty to get to Right a letter," he hopes "you will keep sending up Pertisions to Government to get me off or to get my Sentence mitigated." In 1841 Richard Boothman wrote that "if a little trouble was taken by my friends . . . it might be of very great service to me. . . . [I]f ever I needed help I do now."[18] The convict and his family had to find as many character references among the respectable—landowners, local magistrates, merchants, clergy—as they could raise. Through a scribe with an educated hand, a woman wrote to the home secretary's office from Salisbury in 1819:

> I beg to inform you that Silas Harris, a transport on board the *Laurel* at Portsmouth, is my Husband & has left 6 children to lament his Loss, who are at present in the greatest distress, a Gentleman has promised me he would lay my case, together with my helpless Family, before Lord Sidmouth praying me to interfere for his Releasement, Should you think that his Character annex'd would be of Service I should feel myself Thankful.[19]

It was by no means unusual for the victim of the crime to petition on the prisoner's behalf, once he or she had realized the terrible fate that lay in store for the convict in Australia and his abandoned family in England. Many Englishmen and Englishwomen were disturbed by the disproportion between crime and punishment and did not want to carry on their consciences the stigma of destroying a whole family over some relatively trivial possession, especially when it had been stolen in time of general need. William Tidman, a farmer at St. Albans, had lost some sacks of wheat to an agricultural laborer named Thomas Tate, "now lying at Wolledge [Woolwich] under sentence of Transportation for seven years." He asked Viscount Sidmouth to remit Tate's sentence on behalf of his wife and four small children, "as I freely forgive him myself." In the same vein, Mrs. Lycot, wife of "a gentleman of considerable landed property," wrote in May 1819 to the local magistrate in Minchin Hampton, Sir George Paul, begging clemency for Thomas Barker, an itinerant vendor of rabbit skins who had been sentenced to transportation for buying some silverware that a servant had stolen from her house. She asked for the sentence to be withdrawn, "in consequence of [Barker's] age which is 57, and the improbability that he and his wife would ever meet again, which being in poor circumstances would render her situation one of great distress." In forwarding her letter to Lord Sidmouth, the magistrate noted that "the man is already in the Hulk, it will not do to send him back to *our* Penitentiary, in which there are already *three* prisoners confined where there should be *one*." Revealingly, he added: "These are times when the current of public opinion seems to disarm the law of *all* its terrors!" And so Barker left for the Fatal Shore, leaving his wife to fend for herself.[20]

Occasionally a husband and wife would be convicted together and find themselves both sentenced to transportation. The fear of being exiled to different parts of the world would produce its own petitions. From Carlton Jail in Edinburgh, in 1830, Helen Guild begged not to be separated from her husband of six years, "to crave your sanction that he and I may be sent abroad to some place as near each other as we may with propriety be sent. Altho' it has been our lot to meet with this visitation from both the laws of God & man . . . your sanction would be receiv'd with more sincere pleasure than even my liberation."[21]

The hope of remission through influence, then, was a constant theme. So was the terror of losing touch. Men on the edge of transportation, about to slip off the social map into the void of the antipodes, were apt to construe every postal delay as a sign of rejection, like poor Thomas Holden writing to his mother:

> Nothing in this life gives me such uneasiness as not hearing from you. . . . I have not received a letter but one and that was from my wife since i receiv'd my Tryal, surely you have not forgot me so soon, let me know if there is any hopes of my time being shortened. . . . I will expect to see you if not it will break my Heart that I may take my last farewell of you as I never shall think of seeing you after I leave.[22]

But whether the letters and visitors came or not, the day of transfer to the hulks or the transport inevitably did. Holden was carted from Lancaster Castle, via London, to board the hulk *Portland* in Langston Harbor, where he would work a daily ten-hour shift in the shipyards while awaiting his final departure five months later. The journey, he reported, "has been very wett and uncomfortable and I have been eight days and nights without having my cloaths off my back, so dear wife I will leave you to judge what state I am in at present." Most transportees were neglected and many brutalized on this stage of their journey. The parliamentarian Henry Bennett, in an indignant booklet addressed to the home secretary in 1819, wrote of convicts on the road to the hulks: "Among them were several children all heavily fettered, ragged and sickly. . . . The women too are brought up ironed together on the tops of coaches." Hundreds of them went down from London "in an open caravan, exposed to the inclemency of the weather, to the gaze of the idle and the taunts and mockeries of the cruel, thus exciting . . . the shame and indignation of all those who feel what punishment ought to be." John Ward, in 1841, went down to the Portsmouth hulks from Northampton Jail in a coach, leg-shackled to six other prisoners, treating them to gin and ale whenever the Black Maria stopped at a coaching-inn to change horses, "which seemed to shorten the night's fatigue, and lessen our uneasiness." But though he was well-clothed, his fellow prisoners "had scarcely clothing . . . to cover their nakedness, and could only raise 18 pence amongst them."[23]

ii

THE SIGHT OF the hulks at Portsmouth, Deptford or Woolwich was deservedly famous. They lay anchored in files on the gray heaving water, bow to stern, a rookery of sea-isolated crime. As the longboat bearing its prisoners drew near, the bulbous oak walls of these pensioned-off warships rose sheer out of the sea, patched and queered with excrescences, deckhouses, platforms, lean-tos sticking at all angles from the original hull. They had the look of slum tenements, with lines of bedding strung out to air between the stumps of the masts, and the gunports barred with iron lattices. They wallowed to the slap of the waves, and dark fleeces of weed streamed in the current from the rotting waterlines. Some were French warships captured in battle, but most were obsolete first-raters that had once borne a hundred guns for England; now all that remained of their pride was a battered figurehead and the rusty chains, each link half the size of a man, that held them to their last anchorage. They were like floating Piranesi ruins, cramped and wet inside, dark and vile-smelling.

The reception never changed. The new convicts were mustered on the quarterdeck and ordered to give their money to the captain for safe-keeping. The old hulk hands would descend on the new like locusts:

> When a party of men comes down . . . it is the hay-day for those who have
> grown old in the service . . . [The novice is] asked by those around you "if
>   if—if" twenty things at once, and at the same time "copping" (stealing)
> as it is called every little article, such as combs, knives, braces or thread
> and needles &c, you have been allowed by the Captain to keep, out of the
> few things you have had the luck to bring on board with you.[24]

Mansfield Silverthorpe, an impecunious young actor who, having trod the boards in the 1830s as Iago, Edgar, the Ghost in *Hamlet*, Eugene

Aram, and Bernard in *Guy Mannering*, stole a trunk from a Scottish officer and was sentenced to transportation, went in irons down the river to Woolwich on a public steamer, still in his frilly shirt and long tumbling locks. He found that, on the *Ganymede* hulk,

> I was soon metamorphosed into a very different looking Animal, my long hair underwent the operation of clipping by the *Barbarous Barber*, I was then soaked in a cold bath & afterwards was arrayed in the Uniform of the Hulks. When the Quartermaster took our clothes from us I observed he thrust a knife through each article, and they are then considered to be the property of the Queen; however, when he came to Mine (which were of the best quality) he omitted this act, and as my new Shirt scraped me very much I asked him to let me wear the one I had brought down; but he threatened to flog me for what he called my *impudence*, and told me all my clothes would be burned. Next week I was not at all surprised to see my own Hat and Satin Scarf adorning his goodly person, and my Coat & Trowsers that of the Captain's son, a young man about my own size.[25]

Usually the captain had a deal with an old-clothes merchant: "An old Jew paid us several visits, for the purpose of buying up all the ordinary clothes of the men, and no matter how new a suit might be it was either a matter of take half-a-crown or throw it away." In exchange, a prisoner got shirts "like coarse wrapping," canvas trousers, a gray jacket and shoes that slopped or bit, "to remedy which you must give a couple of white loaves, a week's allowance, to one of your shipmates to change for his and so get a good fit."[26]

Every kind of graft and corruption flourished in the hulks. George Lee, sentenced to fourteen years' transportation for having a forged banknote, wrote in January 1803 from his captivity on a hulk in Langston Harbor to denounce "the bad Police and the injudicious Government so prevalent in places of this kind, making them in reality seminaries not of penitence and reform . . . but of every vice which degrades human nature below the ferocious brute." Of the 440 prisoners on his hulk, about half were "what they call Johnny Raws, i.e., country bumpkins in whose composition there is more of the fool than the rogue," who were relentlessly preyed on and cheated by all officers from the captain down. Only the chaplain and surgeon, he thought, were honest. "Owing to the impositions on all hands by Contractors, Agents, Victuallers and Captains, nine at a time out of Four Hundred have lain dead on the shore, the pictures of raggedness, filth & starvation."[27]

A 14-pound iron was riveted to the felon's right ankle—a practical discouragement to swimmers. Some were more heavily ironed, for no discernible reason: Bennett in 1817 saw a "very little boy 13 years of age" miserably creeping about the hulk *Leviathan* in double fetters, while adult men wore single ones; presumably the child had not been able to pay the warder's bribe for "easement of irons," and an example was made of him. (Months later, when the weight was removed for the voyage, the prisoner's right leg would jerk up uncontrollably as he walked.) After a felon was put in irons, he was ready to go to work in the government dockyards. He was taken off the hulk at dawn and rowed back to it at dusk. Chained convicts working for the Royal Navy at Portsmouth, Deptford or Woolwich were a sight for tourists; gawking at them satisfied some of the impulses that had been denied the British public when English madhouses stopped letting them in to jeer at the lunatics. The chain gangs presented a moral spectacle, good not only for adults but for naughty children as well. Being stared at amplified the convicts' shame, especially since many of them had chosen to embrace their social death, cutting off all contact with friends and family. James Grove, soon to sail for Van Diemen's Land, wrote to a friend in 1803 that "I purposely delayed writing to you at Portsmouth, in order to avoid the continuance of your notice of me. . . . I shrank from being noticed by the world." Mansfield Silverthorpe was glad to be in a coal gang; it rendered him black and unrecognizable, a toiling absence whom not even his mother would have known.[28] John Mortlock, a young Cambridge graduate and army officer who was soon to sail for Norfolk Island, glimpsed in the crowd of onlookers a fellow student from Cambridge, the son of a banker:

> I shrank within myself, but need not have been alarmed, for his eye passed unconsciously over the group of smudged, cadaverous-looking wretches, one of whom a few weeks before had cheered him riding in winner of the steeple-chase at Bythorn.[29]

The idea that such public labor did anything but degrade the prisoners was, as Bennett pointed out, absurd: "Among men who are condemned to labor in public, exposed to the gaze and criticism of all around them, self-debasement and the loss of personal pride . . . are not instruments to work moral reform." He claimed that within a few months the prisoner's expression changed to "a furious cast of countenance, expressive of bad passions and suppressed rage. . . . This dreadful look is to be seen universally in the Presidii of Naples and Spain, in the Galleys of France, and the Hulks of England."[30]

The food was adequate if one got one's whole ration, but that did not always happen. There were three meat days a week, on which the convicts were issued an "institutional pound" (14 ounces) of fresh raw meat. But as it passed down the line to the convict, first the steward took his cut, then the cook, then the inspectors, then the boat's crew who rowed the food ashore, and lastly the dock overseer; at the end, the convict was lucky to receive 4 ounces, clapped on "a pound of stuff named bread."

When the "new chums" went to their cells, they lay down in darkness and foul air. John Mortlock, on board the hulk *Leviathan* in Portsmouth—an old 90-gunner from Nelson's Trafalgar fleet, jammed with 600 convicts rendered "tame as rabbits" by starvation and discipline—was reminded of a verse in Lamentations 4: "They that were brought up in scarlet embrace dunghills." They also had to put up with the damp, since to make life harder for the prisoners it was often the custom on hulks to sluice the upper decks with sea water instead of holystoning them with sand. And then there were the endless practical jokes the "old hands" played on the new, starting with lessons in how to tie up a hammock with running knots so that, when a man turned into it, he crashed to the deck in a tangle of canvas.[31]

Discipline was a foretaste of what the convicts were to expect on the "Bay side," as Australia was called. The great emblem of desire and repression in hulk life, more than sex or food or (in some cases) even freedom itself, was tobacco. Possession of tobacco was severely punished, but the nicotine addict would go through any degradation to get his "quid." Silverthorpe noted how this cycle of addiction and flogging broke prisoners down: "They grow indifferent . . . they go on from bad to worse until they have shaken off all moral restraint." He described how this befell a quiet, harmless man named John Woolley, one of his hulkmates on the *Ganymede.* Woolley's nicotine addiction was such that

> he had been flogged and put in the Black Hole a dozen times but it was no use: "I cannot help it, sir," he would say to the Captain. "Then I will cut the flesh off your back," the Captain would reply, and indeed the Boatswain used to do his utmost, for stepping back a couple of Paces he would bound forward with his arm uplifted, take a jump and come down with the whole weight of his Body upon the unfortunate victim, at every Blow making a noise similar to a paviour when paving the streets. At length the poor fellow (as I often heard him say) became *weary of his life.* He found that his blameless conduct in every other respect could not save him from the consequences of this trifling breech of discipline . . . and from being one of the best he became the worst character in the Yard. When I left it, he was in the Black Hole for having bitten off the first joint of the finger of Mr. Gosling the Quartermaster, who had put it in his mouth to see if he could detect any Tobacco.[32]

Each prisoner's life was governed by a maze of rules, interpreted at the whim of the hulk's quartermaster. "Sometimes my Iron was too dirty.—at other times too bright.—At one time my Hat was not properly poised on my head.—At another my neckerchief was not tied according to the rules of the Establishment." These gave endless scope for extracting bribes, large and small, from prisoners or their families. Three gold sovereigns bought Silverthorpe a transfer from coal-heaving to easier labor for three months. The naval clerks would slip a name in or out of the "Bay drafts"—the lists of who was to be shipped to Australia—for a bribe that ranged between one and six pounds. Though prisoners could not carry money, the hulks (like all prisons) supported a labyrinthine and complicated underground economy, with convict bankers, moneylenders and even lobbyists. "A man that can get money on board, he can buy anything he wishes. . . . There are so many stratagems of the convenience, and so many schemes of barter and trade, that it would be tedious to particularize." Even the doctors were on the take, Mortlock found; when a hulk prisoner died, his corpse would sometimes be sold for £5 or £6 to the dissectors' agents who haunted the docks, instead of being buried on the cemetery mudbank in the Portsmouth estuary known as Rats' Castle. And die they did, in numbers, because the naval doctors saw no harm in bleeding a sick prisoner a pint too much. Then the coffin would be rowed to Rat's Castle, where a chaplain intoned his brief exequies over a box full of stones and sand. Thus, few prisoners looked forward to a spell in the hospital hulk.[33]

But nearly all lived, and for them the day came eventually: Cast for transportation, they filed on board the Bay ship. Her sailing was always preceded by a flurry of requests for money, clothing, tobacco, combs, mementos; sometimes a convict's family could get a trifle to him, but more usually not, for if they had money to spare, who would have turned thief? Some who had been "mechanics" or skilled craftsmen in their previous life brought their tools, against the day when they would win their emancipation and work for themselves again. When relatives came to say goodbye, pathetic scenes ensued. John Ward remembered how his mother "was ill able to support herself under such trying circumstances; we exchanged but few words; for grief choked her utterance, and shame kept me silent."[34] John Nicol, steward on the women's transport *Lady Juliana* fifty years earlier, described the reactions of the parents of a young convict, Sarah Dorset, who had been "ruined" by a London rake and then, like thousands of other girls, driven into prostitution and "taken up as a disorderly girl":

> The father, with a trembling step, mounted the ship's side; but we were forced to leave the mother on board. I took them down to my berth, and went for Sarah Dorset; when I brought her, the father said, in a choking voice, "My lost child!" and turned his back, covering his face with his hands; the mother, sobbing, threw her hands around her. Poor Sarah

fainted and fell at their feet; at length she recovered, and in the most heart-rending accents implored their pardon.[35]

Some women had been subjected to terrible psychic cruelty, and would not soon recover:

> A woman was sent up from Carlisle on the top of one of the coaches. . . . [S]he had been brought to bed of a child while in prison, which she was then suckling,—the child was torn from her breast, and deposited, probably to perish, in the parish poor-house: in this state of bodily pain and mental distraction she was brought to Newgate . . . and was then sent out to Botany Bay. . . . I saw her on board, and she could not speak of her child without an agony of tears.[36]

There can hardly have been a soul among the 162,000 men and women transported to Australia who did not feel, as the transport weighed anchor and began the long voyage to its unimaginable destination, the sentiments that Simon Taylor tried to express in stumbling verse to his father:

> The distant shore of England strikes from Sight
> and all shores seem dark that once was pure and Bright,
> But now a convict dooms me for a time
> To suffer hardships in a forein clime
> Farewell a long farewell to my own my native Land
> O would to God that i was free upon thy Strugling Strand.[37]

iii

WE NOW TURN to the mechanics of transportation. How did Britain get its outcasts to Australia? Like everything else in the System, the method was made up over the years. Its changes had direct consequences for the prisoners, affecting their health, their state of mind, and their chances of survival.

Between 1787, when the First Fleet sailed, and 1868, when the last convict transport *Hougoumont* deposited its load of Irish Fenians in Western Australia, the Crown sent 825 shiploads of prisoners from England and Ireland, an average loading of about 200 convicts per ship. This exodus began feebly: By the end of 1800 only 42 ships had gone to Australia. It continued to be weak and irregular for another fifteen years, because England was too hard-pressed in her war against France to expand her empire with Pacific thief-colonies. There was no year from 1801 to 1813 in which more than five convict transports anchored in Sydney, and not until 1814 would as many as a thousand convicts arrive in a single year.

Then, after 1815, the flood began. Its climactic period was 1831–35, in which no less than 133 vessels brought 26,731 convicts to Australia. The peak year was 1833: 36 ships and 6,779 prisoners, some 4,000 to New South Wales and the rest to Van Diemen's Land. With this practice, the system of transportation, which had begun uncertainly and with great loss of life, became smooth-running. It was not only efficient and profitable (to the contracting shipowners), but quite safe, at least by the standards of nineteenth-century ocean travel. Nobody, however, could say it was pleasant.

The First Fleet had been entirely fitted out and provisioned by the commissioners of the navy; it had been a government affair from start to finish, although the vessels had been chartered through a shipbroker at a flat 10 shillings per ton. The results, as we have seen, were muddled and potentially disastrous, but they were better than what might have happened with private contract. In the long run, though, the navy did not want to be saddled with continuous responsibility for a system of human trash-disposal. Once the guidelines were laid down, every convict transport that sailed from England or Ireland after 1788 was fitted and victualled by private contract. It was said to be cheaper, and certainly it was easier, since it relieved the government of the letting and supervision of dozens of subcontracts. And why should firms of proven respectability not make a fair profit from ridding England of its thieves and scum? The only people the arrangement did not suit were the convicts themselves, since the contract system guaranteed their miseries and, often, their deaths.[38]

By the end of the eighteenth century, as experience of the peculiar problems of shipping prisoners halfway around the world grew and was added to Britain's knowledge of sending armies on long voyages and landing them in fighting shape, the private contractor faced an imposing list of government demands. From the number of lifeboats to the size of rations, all was laid down, along with the exact responsibilities to convicts borne by captain, surgeon and officers.

The rules would reduce (but never eliminate) suffering and death on board. People at sea always suffered and died, whether they were prisoners or not. During the Napoleonic Wars the British Navy simply assumed that one sailor in thirty would die of disease or accident at sea, apart from casualties in battle; one man in six was always ill. Even among free emigrants to America in the mid-nineteenth century, a much shorter crossing than the Australian voyage—one in thirty died.[39]

By the standards of the time, then, the convicts did not do so badly once the system for getting them out to Australia was working smoothly. This happened after 1815, when the average death rate per voyage for male convicts in any five-year period varied between 1 in 85 and (by the end of transportation, in 1868) 1 in 180. At the peak of the System, the average death rate from illness on board was slightly more than 1 percent.[40]

But before 1815 it was much larger, and in the 1790s, when the System was finding its sea legs, it was huge. The defects of the contract system appeared with the Second Fleet, which sailed from Portsmouth in January 1790. Apart from *Lady Juliana*, it consisted of only three transports: *Surprize, Neptune* and *Scarborough*. They were contracted from Camden, Calvert & King, whose agent on board was Thomas Shapcote. It undertook to transport, clothe and feed the convicts for a flat, inclusive fee of £17 7s. 6d. per head, whether they landed alive or not.

The voyage of the Second Fleet turned out to be the worst in the whole history of penal transportation. Out of 254 convicts on *Surprize*, 36 died at sea; out of 499 on *Neptune*, 158 died; and on *Scarborough*, which had finished her voyage in the First Fleet without losing a single life, 73 people perished out of 253. In sum, out of 1,006 prisoners who sailed from Portsmouth, 267 died at sea and at least another 150 after landing.

Camden, Calvert & King had been slaving contractors, and they had equipped the fleet with slave shackles designed for Africans on the infamous "Middle Passage"—not the chains and basils (ankle irons) that, cruel though they were, allowed a man's legs some range of movement, but short rigid bolts between the ankles, about nine inches long, that incapacitated them. As William Hill, a second captain in the New South Wales Corps who sailed on *Surprize*, indignantly reported, "it was impossible for them to move but at the risk of both their legs being broken."[41] *Surprize* was an old ship, and in a heavy sea the water sluiced through her. The starving prisoners lay chilled to the bone on soaked bedding, unexercised, crusted with salt, shit and vomit, festering with scurvy and boils. One convict, Thomas Milburn, would later describe the voyage in a letter to his parents, later printed as a broadsheet in England:

> [We were] chained two and two together and confined in the hold during the whole course of our long voyage. . . . [W]e were scarcely allowed a sufficient quantity of victuals to keep us alive, and scarcely any water; for my own part I could have eaten three or four of our allowances, and you know very well that I was never a great eater. . . . [W]hen any of our comrades that were chained to us died, we kept it a secret as long as we could for the smell of the dead body, in order to get their allowance of provision, and many a time have I been glad to eat the poultice that was

put to my leg for perfect hunger. I was chained to Humphrey Davies who died when we were about half way, and I lay beside his corpse about a week and got his allowance.[42]

The horrors of the slave trade, Hill thought, were "merciful" beside this. He railed against the "villainy, oppression and shameful peculation" of Donald Traill, master of *Neptune*, and Nicholas Anstis of *Scarborough*. Traill was a demented sadist and Anstis not much better. But their interests coincided with the contractors', as Hill indignantly noted:

> The more they can withhold from the unhappy wretches, the more provisions they have to dispose of on a foreign market, and the earlier in the voyage they die the longer they can draw the deceased's allowance to themselves; for I fear few of them are honest enough to make a just return of the dates of their deaths to their employers.[43]

And in fact, when the Second Fleet reached Sydney and disgorged its cargo of the dead, the dying and the sick, the first thing Anstis and Traill did was to open a market on shore, selling the left-over food and clothing to the half-starved pioneers of the First Fleet.

The colony's Anglican chaplain, Reverend Richard Johnson, counted the sick: 269 people on *Neptune* were incapacitated—which meant that, out of her 499 prisoners embarked, only 72 landed in fair health. The figures for *Scarborough* and *Surprize* were a little less terrible. Johnson braved the 'tween-decks stench of *Surprize*, but he could not face going below in *Neptune*. Mewing and groaning, scarcely able to gesture or roll over, monstrously infested with vermin (Johnson estimated that one man had ten thousand lice swarming on his body) the convicts were slung overboard

> as they would sling a cask, a box, or anything of that nature. Upon their being brought up to the open air some fainted, some died upon deck, and others in the boat before they reached the shore. When come on shore, many were not able to walk, to stand or to stir themselves in the least, hence they were led by others. Some creeped upon their hands and knees, and some were carried on the backs of others.

Among the survivors who landed, all fellow-feeling was extinguished by the ferocity of their repression. Johnson was horrified to see that

> When any of them were near dying, and had something given to them as bread or lillie-pie (flour and water boiled together) . . . the person next to him would catch the bread, &c., out of his hand and, with an oath, say he was going to die, and therefore it would be of no service to him. No sooner

would the breath be out of their bodies than others would watch them and strip them entirely naked. Instead of alleviating the distresses of each other, the weakest were sure to go to the wall. In the night-time, which at this time [June, the Australian winter] is very cold, where they had nothing but grass to lay on and a blanket amongst the four of them, he that was the strongest of the four would take the whole blanket to himself and leave the rest quite naked.[44]

While this was going on at Sydney Cove in 1790, the Lords of the Committee of Council were busy submitting the proposed Great Seal of New South Wales to their King. Its obverse depicted "Convicts landed at Botany-Bay; their fetters taken off and received by Industry sitting on a Bale of Goods with her attributes, the distaff, bee-hive, pickaxe and spade, pointing to oxen ploughing, the rising habitations, and a church on a hill at the distance, with a fort for their defence," and the Virgilian motto *Sic fortis Etruria crevit*, "Thus Etruria grew strong."[45]

When the news of the Second Fleet reached England, through Phillip's dispatches and Hill's letters, there was a small official flap. Neither the government nor the public had expected so much death and misery, but memories were short and the victims, after all, were convicts. Nothing could be done about the wretched contractor's agent, Thomas Shapcote, for—in the only Second Fleet death that tasted of justice—he had died soon after sailing from Cape Town. Although a strict inquiry was promised, it was never carried out. Voluminous evidence was taken at the Guildhall in London. But Captain Traill had prudently absconded and no one could find him until 1792; whereupon he and his ship's mate were brought to trial for murdering a single convict. Both were acquitted and not prosecuted again. Three years later Traill was given a senior post at Cape Town. Anstis went scot-free, and the grim firm of Camden, Calvert & King was never indicted. In fact, it had already contracted with the government to prepare and victual the Third Fleet, which sailed in 1791. Once again its ships were old, crowded and barely seaworthy; there were inadequate medical supplies, and the treatment of prisoners was disgustingly abusive. The second mate of the *Queen*, whose duty it was to issue rations to the 150-odd men and women prisoners on board, used short weights to serve out 60 pounds of beef instead of the regulation 132 pounds at a sitting.[46] Conditions were such that 576 Third Fleet convicts needed medical attention when they got to Sydney. But out of a total of 1,869 men and 172 women embarked, only 173 men and 9 women died on the passage—a gross death rate of slightly under 9 percent, or one-third the death rate of the Second Fleet. After that, the government gave no more contracts to Camden, Calvert & King.

Nervous of publicizing the defects of transportation, it held no public inquiry either. But some improvements were made. The government put

restrictions on "these low-lifed barbarous masters, to keep them honest."
It set up deferred payments—so much per convict embarked, the rest
(usually about 25 percent) when he or she landed in decent health. Masters and surgeons had to get a certificate by the governor when they
arrived in Sydney, rating their performance; if this paper commended
their "Assiduity and Humanity," there would be a bonus from the transport committee when they got back to England.[47]

Some captains were beyond such inducements. In 1798 the contractors of the transport *Hillsborough* were to get a bonus of £4 10s. 6d. for
every convict landed alive, over and above the £18 per head paid on
embarkation. But her master, William Hingston, starved the prisoners,
kept them so heavily chained that they could not walk on deck and kept
them below in double irons at night. Typhus also raged through the
vessel soon after she left Langston Harbor, and one convict in three died.
No action was taken against Hingston.[48]

The commissioners tried but usually failed to stop contractors filling
their ships with goods to be sold in Sydney at huge markups. However,
they put a naval surgeon aboard each vessel who was answerable to them
and not the contractors; his job was to supervise convict health, correct
the abusive conduct of the ships' officers and keep an eye on lax or
incompetent contractors' surgeons. No mere medical officer could tell a
master what to do on his own ship. Still, their presence was felt. The
first transport to sail under this arrangement was the *Royal Admiral* in
May 1792, followed in 1793 by three more shiploads of English and Irish
prisoners. All had supervisors on board, and out of 670 prisoners only 14
died.[49]

The moral was clear, but by 1795 the Napoleonic Wars had begun and
England had no naval surgeons (and few ships) to spare for Botany Bay.
In the next twenty years only one privately contracted transport sailed
with a naval surgeon on board. Between 1792 and 1800, eighteen convict
ships went to Australia from Britain. The first six (from 1792 to 1794) all
had supervising agents. Their death rate was one man in 55, one woman
in 45. Of the next six ships, only two carried naval agents or surgeons,
and their death rate was one man in 19 and one woman in 68. The last
group of six had no naval supervision of any kind, and one man in 6 died,
and one woman in 34.[50]

Most of the dead were Irish convicts. Many had been sent out for
political offenses and they were especially ill-treated because the captains feared mutiny. Thus on *Britannia*, which sailed from Cork late in
1796 with 144 male and 44 female Irish on board, the master Thomas
Dennott went on a sadistic rampage. He had a supposed ringleader, William Trimball, flogged until he gave a list of 31 names of convicts who

had allegedly taken an oath to mutiny. He then had the ship searched for weapons; the guards found home-made saws, half-a-dozen improvised knives, some lengths of hoop iron and a pair of scissors. This was enough. One convict, James Brannon, received the appalling total of 800 lashes on two successive days, the second session with pieces of fresh horse-skin braided to the cat-o'-nine-tails. "Damn your eyes, this will open your carcase," Dennott bellowed at him, and it did, although he took several days to die. In all, Dennott meted out 7,900 lashes to the suspects and killed six of them. The surgeon, a half-mad incompetent named Augustus Beyer, refused to dress their wounds and, being terrified of Captain Dennott, would not supervise the floggings; he cowered in his cabin, listening to the whistling lash and the screams of the Irish. A poor female convict named Jenny Blake tried to commit suicide, for which Dennott cropped her hair, slashed her repeatedly across the face and neck with a cane and had her double-ironed.[51] The government held an inquiry into the conduct of Dennott and Beyer but took no action against either. It found Dennott had "bordered on too great a degree of severity" and Beyer had been "negligent." However, neither sailed on a transport ship again.

Although this nightmarish voyage was an exception, it would be some years before Irish convicts were decently treated. Sir Jerome Fitzpatrick, a frequent agitator for reform on the hulks and in the transports, was able to get the rigid slave leg-bolts struck off prisoners on two vessels waiting to sail from Cork in 1801, *Hercules* and her sister ship *Atlas*; they were replaced by lighter chain-fetters, "preferable as well in the Political as the Humane sense." but he was appalled by the treatment meted out to convicts waiting for transportation in the hulks, both in Ireland and in England. "Prisoners are sent to the Hulks . . . infirm and diseased, completely Blind, crippled and so advanced in Age that no sort of profit can be made from their labour . . . [They] cannot in justice to the cause of Humanity or to the profit of the Colony be sent to *New South Wales*."[52] Writing to Lord Pelham in 1801, he described

> their bad and filthy bedding; some not having half the covering of their bodies; the privation of the nutritious part of their diet, by scumming the Fat off their Brooths; the defect of their Cloathing in the most intense cold; the indiscriminate application of their Labour . . . with complete and painful *Testicular Ruptures* hanging towards their knees—without Trusses, yet in common yoked in the Carts; the asthmatic and swelled or ulcerated legg'd subjects equally employed; the tender and painful-eyed at Lime Burning;—on the whole I seldom could discover a rational system in respect either to a profit arising from their labor, or the exercise of reason & humanity in its application.[53]

After *Hercules* sailed from Cork late in 1801, the convicts mutinied. Fourteen were shot out of hand and thirty more died from disease and exhaustion, a death rate of one in four. Conditions on *Atlas* were even worse; sixty-five died on the voyage, largely because they had to make way for 2,166 gallons of rum, which her master, Captain Brooks, planned to sell in Sydney. Governor King very properly refused to let him land it, but Brooks was never punished. He captained several more convict voyages and died, a respectable old salt, as a justice of the peace in Sydney.

It was hard to bring these men to book. To prosecute a cruel or corrupt master in England, the Crown would have had to ship convicts back as witnesses; the alternative was a trial in Australia, which would entail giving a New South Wales court criminal jurisdiction over visiting English ships' captains. In either case, a lot of public money would be spent on a trial, and no one wanted that. Only once were convicts returned to England to testify against a captain. This was in 1817, and on the orders of the relatively liberal, pro-Emancipist governor Lachlan Macquarie, who wanted to arraign the master and officers of the *Chapman* for killing three and wounding twenty-two unarmed convicts with fusillades of gunfire after rumors of a possible mutiny. Although Macquarie did not expect convictions (and did not get them: all were acquitted) he hoped the case might "protect the persons of the convicts in future on their passage from the cruelties and violence to which they have heretofore been exposed." All he got was a stiff rebuke from the government.[54]

Fitzpatrick summed up the convicts' predicament in a letter to Pelham's secretary. "I entreat you again and again to impress [on Pelham] the Idea that in these days of venality, of selfishness and design, you are not to expect just reports to be made by Persons . . . immediately connected with those who have concern with either the Prison or the Contract Departments," he wrote. One must not expect

> that the Doctor will ever state his own neglect or mismanagement of his patients, or that Keepers will state the exercise of cruelties . . . that those who supply Diet or Cloathing should . . . report these Matters, other than of good Quality, or that the General Managers should criminate the persons who may deserve it but are more or less within their own Appointments.[55]

After 1815, however, hell-ships were few; conditions improved on convict transports because of a further change in supervision. Naval doctors had learned more about their craft from the Napoleonic Wars, although military medicine was still a hideously primitive business by modern standards. The man who did most for Australia-bound convicts was William Redfern (1774?–1833), a transported convict himself, and the most skilled and popular surgeon in Sydney. Redfern was family doctor to Governor Macquarie. As such, the "father of Australian medicine" was ideally placed to reform the System. Macquarie ordered him to investigate conditions on three calamitously bad ships that arrived in 1814, *Surry*, *Three Bees* and *General Hewitt*. Redfern's report was the turning point, for it impressed not only Macquarie but the authorities in England. He stressed the need for ventilation, swabbing, clean heads, disinfection with lime and "oil of tar," fumigation and exercise. He also insisted that naval surgeons go in every ship as both medical officers and government agents, "as Officers with full power to exercise their Judgment, without being liable to the Control of the Masters of the Transports."[56]

The benefits of this plan showed as soon as it was adopted. After 1815, the volume of convict shipping to Australia more than trebled— 78 ships carrying 13,221 souls from 1816 to 1820, as compared to 23 carrying 3,847 in the preceding five years. From 1811 to 1815, the gross average death rate on the voyage had been 1 in 31. After Redfern's plan went into force it plummeted to 1 in 122. Thereafter it seldom rose above 1 in 100, and never beyond 1 in 85.[57]

Besides, the voyage was now faster and the vessels roomier, although these are very relative terms. No modern traveller can really imagine the tedium and social friction of this voyage. Down the map the transports dropped, sometimes escorted by naval convoys bound for Africa or India. But soon each was on its own in the blue immensity, a socially infected speck flying the red-and-white "whip" (pennant) that proclaimed the convict vessel. Its route would depend on its supplies of food and water. The First Fleet took 252 days to reach Botany Bay, spending nearly ten weeks in ports along the way. It had to carry several years' supplies of provisions, and so the rations for the voyage had to be constantly replenished. But by 1810 the ships no longer needed to carry everything for the convicts' future survival; and by 1820 most captains sailed to Rio and then "ran down their easting" straight to the southern coast of Australia, either dropping their convicts at Hobart or sailing north to Sydney. Sometimes they went out non-stop. By the 1830s, most transports did the passage in less than 110 days, but only four vessels took less than 100: *Eliza I* in 1820, *Guildford* in 1822, *Norfolk* in 1829 and *Emma Eugenia*, the fastest of all, with a 95-day passage, in 1838.

No ship was ever custom-built to be a convict transport. They were all (except for a few naval vessels) converted merchant ships, fitted out with the necessary berths and security devices.[58] The prisoners' berths were usually ranged in two rows, each double-height (a berth above and one below) against the hull, with a walkway down the center. Peter Cunningham, who made five voyages to Australia as surgeon-superintendent on convict transports (and lost only three of the 747 convicts under his care), noted that "ample space" was four convicts in a wooden berth six feet square. There was rarely as much as six feet of headroom, and the only air came from the hatchways, which were kept closed with thick grilles and heavily padlocked. Hence ventilation was always poor; and even though the naval surgeons urged masters to fit wind-sails over the hatches, these primitive airscoops failed to work just when air was most needed—as the ship lay becalmed in the suffocating heat of the doldrums. The Irish "political" John Boyle O'Reilly, transported to Western Australia with other Fenians in 1868 in the *Hougoumont*, the last of all the convict transports, described the miseries of its hold:

> The air was stifling . . . [T]here was no draught through the barred hatches. The sun above them was blazing hot. The pitch dropped from the seams, and burnt their flesh as it fell. There was only one word spoken or thought—one yearning idea in every mind—water. . . . Two pints of water a day were served out to each convict—a quart of putrid and blood-warm liquid. It was a woeful sight to see the thirsty souls devour this allowance.[59]

In bad weather everyone suffered, but the convicts worst of all. George Prideaux Harris, who sailed with David Collins's expedition to colonize Port Phillip Bay in 1803, wrote that after leaving Rio,

> we were constantly meeting with squalls of wind, rain, lightning and heavy rolling seas, so that for many days we could not sit at table, but were obliged to hold fast to boxes &c. on the floor & had all our crockery ware almost broken to pieces, besides shipping many seas into the Cabin and living in a state of Darkness from the Cabin windows being stopped up by the deadlights.—I never was so melancholy in my life before.—Not a single comfort either for the body or the mind—the provisions, infamous—the water, stinking—our livestock destroyed by the cold & wet, and every person with a gloomy countenance.[60]

The security had to be formidable. Captain Alfred Tetens, a German master who spent many years traversing the Pacific, took a shipload of 300 convicts on the *Norwood* to Fremantle in the last phase of transportation in 1861. Her 'tween-decks were "enclosed in a shotproof wall of heavy timbers," and

> the main and forward hatchways were furnished with three-inch iron bars; through the small door remaining, only one person at a time could squeeze with some difficulty. . . . [A] barricade was erected across the width of the ship on deck behind the mainmast. This also had a narrow door. A watch of ten soldiers with loaded guns was stationed night and

day at the rear of the quarterdeck. Four cannon loaded with grapeshot were aimed forward and a multitude of weapons were piled here. This gave the whole warlike picture an imposing aspect that had a calming effect not only on the prisoners but on their warders as well.[61]

The prisoners' food was coarse but sufficient, except for the lack of greens. Its staple was still brined beef, known to passengers as "salt horse"—which, no doubt, some of it was. An officer of the 50th Regiment, John Gorman, sailing to Australia on the transport *Minden* in 1851, wrote down the words of a sailor's verse about it:

> Salt horse! Salt horse! What brought you here?
> I have been carrying turf for many a year
> From Limerick going to Ballyhack
> I fell down and broke my back.
> Cut up was I for sailors' use,
> Now even they do me despise—
> They turn me over and they Damn my Eyes.[62]

Peter Cunningham adjudged the rations "both good and abundant," about two-thirds of the standard navy allowance. The convict Mellish, sailing to Australia at about the same time (the early 1820s), found

> not much reason to find fault; on Sundays, plum pudding with suet in it, about a pound to each man, likewise a pound of beef; Monday, pork (a pound with peas in it); Tuesday, beef and rice; Wednesday, same as Sunday; Thursday, same as Monday; Friday, beef and rice and pudding; Saturday, pork only.[63]

Against scurvy, the convicts got lime juice, sugar and vinegar. For a bonus, they received a nightly half-pint of port wine to keep their spirits up. This was considered a great luxury and on some ships, like the *Woodbridge* when she sailed in 1840 with the convict diarist Charles Cozens on board, its distribution was a ritual:

> for the purpose of exercising the men, and as preventive to disease, each man entered at one door on the quarter-deck, *danced* to the cask, drank his allowance, and then danced off again, round by the opposite doorway. . . . [T]he steps, as various as the performers, formed altogether a most amusing "ballet."[64]

The prisoners' irons were struck off when the ship was in blue water, though their bunks usually carried chains and basils so that the refractory could be fettered down in an emergency. The surgeon-superintendent got the convicts on deck for fresh air and exercise as often as possible. They holystoned the decks, swabbed and scrubbed and laundered, and took as much menial work off the crew's shoulders as discipline would allow. They could not carry knives—all eating-irons except spoons were issued with each meal and collected after it—but they could get needles, and bones from "salt horse." So they passed the long weeks making scrimshaw, "manufacturing seals, toothpicks, tobacco-stoppers, and other ornaments out of bones; and likewise a few ingenious and experienced ones, in making rings, brooches &c. out of common buttons, at which they were very expert."[65]

They fished, trolling hooks with strips of canvas greased with fat. Bonitos would grab them and be hauled like silvery finned melons, shuddering and tail-tapping, into the scuppers; they were eagerly eaten, as were the sharks, the ominous "sea-lawyers" that followed patiently at the vessel's stern. These "were pronounced excellent; the most trifling change of circumstance in so long and wearisome a voyage being greedily grasped at and joyfully entertained." Now and then sailors would catch albatrosses with baited hook and a sounding-line, drag them screaming on board, slaughter them, and skin them, there being a market for their stuffed carcasses.[66]

The convicts' efforts to amuse themselves were noted by various surgeons and free passengers. They danced and (when in irons) managed a clinking beat with their chains. On Christmas Day, one ship's carpenter observed, "the greatest joviality prevailed among the Convicts, who celebrated the anniversary of the Christian era by the execution (in a masterly style) of an abundance of vocal music in the shape of glees, trios, duets &c., probably the result of their double allowance of wine."[67]

They gambled for anything from tobacco to clothes, and if no one had cards they would dismember Bibles and prayer-books to make them, as a clergyman found to his distress on a transport in 1819. Sometimes they staged amateur plays, or held mock trials on deck—cathartic parodies in which the "judge," robed in a patchwork quilt with a swab combed over his head for a wig, his face made up with red-lead, chalk and stovebacking, would volley denunciations at the cowering "prisoner."

The big ceremony of the voyage was always the Crossing of the Line, a boisterous rite of passage in which Neptune would come aboard and initiate those who had never crossed the equator before. Fearsome in swab-wig and iron trident, shells and dried starfish entangled in his oakum beard, sewn into the flayed skin of a dolphin and stinking to heaven under the vertical sun, the sea-god would bear down on the neophytes flanked by grinning Jack-tar "mermaids" holding buckets of soap and gunk. The initiates were clipped with scissors and lathered with a mop, "shaved" and then ducked in a tub of seawater. No wonder the tradition has since been much attenuated by mass tourism. "Neptune was on board for two nights shaving the soldiers & People," Lieutenant William Coke reported to his father from the transport *Regalia* in 1826,

> he was a sulky Old Fellow & covered his new born sons over with Tar from head to foot, each night after having finished shaving he & his Constables came into my cabin to know if I was pleased with the Lenity he had treated my men, but His Majesty was such a drunkard that he & his Constables drank three gallons of my Whiskey & made my head ache terribly by obliging me to drink raw spirits with him.[68]

By the 1820s discipline ran smoothly, almost automatically, in most ships. Captains kept a vigilant eye on their human cargo, and rumors of mutiny brought down summary punishment—though not, as a rule, with the flagellatory orgies staged on early hell-ships like the *Britannia*. Four dozen lashes was usually enough; the convict would be triced to a grating, and the ceremony of his pain watched by the mustered prisoners and the ship's company. Minor offenders were ironed, or put in a cramping-box for a few hours.

Dreams of mutiny, however, were rarely absent. Lieutenant Coke mentioned that the Irish prisoners he was guarding on *Regalia* "had formed a scheme to seize & carry the ship to South America. I and my men were all to have been murdered. The Doctor, Captain & sailors were to have been saved . . . [I]t was lucky they did not attempt it or else they would have been most of them shot, and had any of the Soldiers been killed the rest would have been so enraged they would have murdered every convict on board."[69]

If there was a rising, the ship's master had to act fast and shrewdly, like Captain Tetens facing rebels on the *Norwood*:

> Hardly had I told the nearest soldiers what was going on when with revolvers cocked, I stormed into the midst of the startled gang. In spite of the stinging wound which the ringleader gave my arm with some sharp instrument, I did not let go [of him]. I kept both hands around the criminal's neck so that he had no little trouble in breathing. . . . I should not have shot him except in the greatest need, so as not to make the others needlessly embittered.[70]

But such mutiny attempts were few. The *Norwood*'s was fomented by a group of "former captains and pilots who scuttled their ships," but no ordinary convicts could navigate. Generally they would remain passive and mutter threats, rather than go up against overwhelming odds of firepower. In the whole period of transportation (1788–1868), more than eight hundred outward voyages produced only one successful mutiny—

on a female transport, the *Lady Shore*, in 1797. The insurgents were not female convicts, but their guard—a detachment of the New South Wales Corps who rose "in the name of the French Republic," seized the ship without much bloodshed, sailed her to Montevideo and were eventually accepted by France as political refugees, after they had disposed of the bewildered women prisoners as servants to Spanish colonial ladies of quality.

A captain who treated his prisoners well—as Tetens did, by making the regulations "markedly more lenient" and having long individual chats with his charges so that they could unburden their minds—was certain to be shown gratitude and even affection. At the end of the voyage "the exiles prepared a surprise for me which I remember today with deep emotion. . . . [H]atred and bitterness seemed to have vanished." Before they filed ashore the prisoners lined themselves up in ordered ranks, clasped Tetens's hand one by one, "all looking very serious," and presented him with a letter of thanks signed by 270 out of 300 men:

> HONORED SIR!
> It is our deep regret that we are not able to give you a greater proof of our thankfulness and respect. We can only ask you to receive our sincere thanks for the kindness, generosity and liberal treatment which you have always shown us on the long voyage to Western Australia. To this earnest request we add the sincere wish that Heaven may grant you every earthly joy, that you may succeed in all your future enterprises, and while we must follow our unknown fate in an inhospitable land far from home and family, may the hand of the Almighty protect you and bring you back to a happy home.[71]

However, the usual representative of humanity was the surgeon-superintendent, who was not only a healer but the closest thing to an ombudsman the convicts had. Most captains were not like Tetens; they were not sadists by nature, but they were tough unlettered men risen from the foc's'le in the harsh school of the sea, and they placed scant value on convict comfort. On a ship with no surgeon-superintendent, Thomas Holden (the political exile from Bolton) complained in 1812 that "we have been three weeks without Clean Shorts and we asked the Captain for Shorts and he said they could not be Durty yet, and I wear Irons on both legs . . . Dear honored Father and Mother if you cannot do nothing for me and very soon I am sure you will never see me alive again."[72] That, in essence, was what the surgeon-superintendent was on board to prevent, and when he did so, showing a constant level of "firmness alleviated by compassion," the convicts trusted him.

The surgeon's logs had to be kept in duplicate and turned in at the end of the voyage. The duller reading they make, the better the voyage for the prisoners. The log of Surgeon-Superintendent John Smith on the *Clyde*, carrying 215 men from Ireland to Sydney in 1838, is typical. It is a record of cleaning and scraping, sprinkling chloride of lime by the water-closets, supervising the laundry, lancing abscesses; blankets become lousy and are soaked all night in the urine-tubs in the hope of killing the accursed insects; the coarse trousers give some convicts "excoriations of the scrotum and thigh"; prisoners squabble and are put in the cramping-box, a lad whispers about mutiny and spends the night handcuffed on deck; the soldiers and their women fight like Kilkenny cats—"a more undisciplined, quarrelsome, noisy set have seldom come together, yet the behavior of the Prisoners is quiet and orderly with little exception." Surgeon Smith dispenses advice, purges, blisters and bleedings; he buries the dead (but very few men die); and there is a note of quiet gratification at the end, when *Clyde* warps into Sydney Cove and an official from the colonial secretary's office asks the customary question of the mustered prisoners: Is there any complaint about the Surgeon? "No, no, God bless him, was the universal cry."[73]

Individual convicts also poured forth their gratitude and hoped that Surgeon Smith would commend them to the authorities in Sydney, as in this letter from a middle-aged man of some education, Bernard Murray, protesting his innocence:

> Money turned the scales of Justice and unfortunate Murray was cast—yes Sir, cast out of Society, and banished from his home—his friends & his Country—but in you, Sir, I have found the tender & feeling Gentleman, —you have done more to meliorate my unhappy condition than I, in any manner, deserved,—you knew nothing of me, I was a stranger, but your humanity for an injured man—now nearly in the decline of his life—Sir, your masterly and very impressive discourse delivered to us last Sunday week, will be long remembered and, please God, strictly followed by me. Altho' a convict, Sir, I hope to bring my grey hair unsullied by Crime to the Grave.—Should you, Sir, still think of recommending me here to notice—rest assured, Kind Sir, that sobriety, steadiness & honesty with the strictest attention will not be wanting on my part.[74]

A good surgeon-superintendent represented whatever was best in the System; he might not be a great doctor, but his decency made him exceptional in the netherworld of transportation. Once ashore, few convicts could expect as much fair play. The society into which they now came, as they were mustered at the side of Sydney Cove or the Hobart dock, feeling the beaten clay heave beneath their feet after those months at sea, was more punitive in its conventions, more capricious in its workings: a lottery, whose winners went on to found Australia but whose losers were no better off than slaves.

6

Who Were the Convicts?

i

IT IS A QUARTER-CENTURY since the Australian in London risked hearing languid sneers directed at his criminal ancestry. This colonial vestige was already dying a generation ago. Nevertheless, it was part of English attitudes to Australians before 1960, and especially before World War II. When it appeared, it would send upper-middle-class Australians into paroxysms of social embarrassment. None wanted to have convict ancestors, and few could be perfectly sure that some felon did not perch like a crow in their family tree. Fifty years ago, convict ancestry was a stain to be hidden.

Working people in Australia saw their convict past differently. Growing up free and reaching for social trust, children born in the colony— the Currency, to use the common colonial term, many of whom had convict ancestry—might be obsessed with respectability. But memories lived on as social myths, particularly among the Irish, who never forgot what treatment their convict forbears received on the Fatal Shore. As we shall see, the System inadvertently produced Australia's first folk-heroes, the bushrangers, most of them escaped prisoners. The basic class division of early colonial Australia—guards versus prisoners—lived on as a metaphor of future disputes there. It was something to think about at the Trades Union meeting, and on the picket lines. It provided a scheme of historical oppression. The Good Squire, the Benevolent Landowner, the Paternal Peer, all those figures of property who rise to modify the simple picture of early nineteenth-century labor relations in England—and who did in fact exist—were not features of the mythic Australian landscape. Instead, there were the harsh overseer, the treacherous "special," the flinty officer, the brute with the whip; and under them, the suffering convict.

From these twin pressures to forget and to mythologize arose the popular Australian stereotype of convict identity. It says that convicts were innocent victims of unjust laws, torn from their families and flung into exile on the world's periphery for offenses that would hardly earn a fine today. They poached rabbits or stole bread to feed their starving offspring—and they had to, because their rulers had so brutally mismanaged England that they could no longer survive as honest yeomen in a collapsing rural economy. Crushed between economic forces they could not understand and laws they had not written, they were the people Thomas Gray apostrophized in "Elegy Written in a Country Churchyard" (1750) and Oliver Goldsmith in "The Deserted Village" (1770).

The stereotype insists that the human fodder of transportation sprang from the root of British decency, the yeoman in the rural village. This would be given allegorical form by William Blake, whose vision of industrial desolation mingled with accounts he had heard of the Pacific thief-colony, the "Horrible rock far in the south," where "my sons, exiled from my breast, pass to & fro before me," and

> The Corn is turn'd to thistles & the apples into poison,
> The birds of song to murderous crows . . .[1]

The commonest tag in Australian ideas about the convicts' class identity came from Gray's "Elegy," where, musing on the decent obscurity of the village dead, the poet evoked a yeoman resisting the power of the enclosing landowner: "Some village-Hampden that with dauntless breast / The little tyrant of his fields withstood." Hence, wrote J. L. and B. Hammond in 1913 in their influential study *The Village Laborer, 1760–1832*, "the village Hampdens of that generation sleep by the shores of Botany Bay." From there it was only a step to the full form of the myth, stated more than sixty years ago in the rhetorical question of an Australian historian, Arnold Wood: "Is it not clearly a fact that the atrocious criminals remained in England, while their victims, innocent and manly, founded the Australian democracy?"[2]

It was no fact, but a stout and consoling fiction. The innocence of convicts as a class (if not their manliness) was first exposed to criticism by Manning Clark in the 1950s and finally demolished with statistical analysis by L. L. Robson in 1965.[3] Basing his work on a "random" sampling of one name in twenty in the Home Office Papers in the London Public Record Office, which list the names, ages, places of trial and crimes of about 150,000 of the transportees, Robson was able to show that, far from being first offenders, one-half to two-thirds of the convicts carried previous convictions. Eight in ten were thieves, and only a minuscule fraction could be classed as political offenders. Most were city-dwellers, not villagers or peasants. Nearly all were propertyless laborers rather than smallholders. Three-quarters were single, and their average age was about 26. The idea of the convict that one might extract from the earliest transportation indents—an old woman who stole cheese, a mere child, a harmless wigmaker's 'prentice or a sensitive Scottish painter like Thomas Watling—is very far from the whole truth about the majority of convicts who came later.

The ferocity and scope of eighteenth-century capital statutes created, as we have seen, an extraordinary range of hanging crimes. The erratic mercy of the courts could, and did, transmute such sentences to exile in Australia. Hence, many early convicts, up to the end of the Napoleonic Wars, went on board the "Bay ships" for small, often ridiculously slight, offenses. But after 1815, the general tendency (to which, of course there were thousands of exceptions) was to reserve transportation for less trivial crimes. By 1818, the first stirrings of postwar legal reform were felt in England. A parliamentary committee urged that some kinds of theft (though by no means all) should be punished by transportation, not death, and that forgery should cease to be a capital offense. Sir Robert Peel's attempts to reform and consolidate the criminal statutes in the 1820s did have a gradual effect on men in the dock. And as the number of hanging crimes shrunk, so the volume of "transportable" offenses grew.

There was no third choice, for England had no penitentiary system, could not keep her felons at home and would not be forced to do so until the Prison Acts of 1835 and 1839. Consequently, each liberalization of the law helped to increase the flow of convicts to Australia. Only extreme Tories saw the period 1820 to 1840 as a time of "reckless" liberalization of the criminal law. But a sense of humanity did creep forward. By 1837, hanging was mainly restricted to cases of murder, while crime after crime—forgery, cattle-theft, housebreaking—was relegated to the less terrible and magical status of a "transportable" offense. Slowly, the English authorities acknowledged the mistakes and fantasies that had led their predecessors to fetishize the death penalty. But the real rise of transportation began, not with the law itself, but with its new enforcers: the "peelers," the English police, established by Sir Robert Peel in 1827. A police force meant a huge rise, not in gross crime, but in successful arrests and convictions. Likewise, the abandonment of transportation was not caused by any fall in crime, but by three other factors: the growing moral and political opposition to the System among English reformers in the 1830s, the growth of an alternative English penitentiary system and the Australians' own opposition to a continuous dumping of fresh criminals on what, after 50 years of settlement, they had come to view as their soil.

A graph of transportation to Australia would run fairly flat (though uphill) from 1788 to 1816, then climb more steeply, shoot to a peak in the mid-1830s and then flatten again. After 1850, the English prison and penitentiary system could hold nearly all the criminals the courts could convict. Transportation to New South Wales finished in 1840; to Van Diemen's Land, in 1853; and by 1868, when the last convict ship from England discharged its Irish prisoners on the other side of the continent, in Western Australia, transportation was part unpleasant memory and part unhealed wound.

Thus we can roughly distinguish four phases of transportation. The first—"primitive" transportation, as it were—runs from 1787 to 1810. It began, as we have seen, as an attempt to clear the English hulks and jails and to post a British strategic presence in the Pacific. It involved relatively few convicts: in round figures, about 9,300 men and 2,500 women from England and Ireland (no more than 7 percent of the total number who would eventually be transported). They started coming out at a rate of about 1,000 people per year; but this fell by half when the Napoleonic Wars began in 1793 because convicts were needed for dockyard labor. Some were press-ganged into the Navy, or even dragged into the uniformed rabble of the British Army. England could not spare the ships to transport them "beyond the seas" to Australia.

The second stage belongs to the two decades between 1811 and 1830. Around 1811, the transportation rate began to rise again. The accumulation in jails and hulks had cleared, but the government felt that, having set up its criminal waste-disposal system, it should keep using it. The sharp rise in this second phase came after 1815, when the wars ended and England was struck by a succession of internal crises. Its population was increasing out of hand; between 1801 and 1841 it nearly doubled, from 10.1 to 18.1 million, and its fastest *rate* of growth in this period was in the decade 1811–20. Workers were pincered between falling wages and rising prices; the mechanization of hand trades created runaway unemployment; and the inexorable spread of enclosure was driving people from the country to the slum. Hence the crime wave which so troubled England's rulers after the war, and which prepared Parliament to accept Peel's novelty, a police force. Once the police existed, the supply of felons rose. So there was a great pressure driving the convicts onto the transports—and a corresponding suction at the other end of their journey, Australia, where the growth of the pastoral industry after 1815 created a ravenous demand for convict labor. From 1811 to 1820, some 15,400 male and 2,000 female convicts sailed out from England and Ireland. From 1821 to 1830, the corresponding round figures were 28,700 men and 4,100 women. So in this second phase, about 50,200 people—some

31 percent of the total number of transportees—went to Australia. By 1830, the System was mature and working at the full stretch of its efficiency.

In the third stage, 1831 to 1840, the System peaked and began its decline. In those years, 43,500 male and 7,700 female convicts sailed for Australia—a total of 51,200 people, more than the previous two decades' decantation on the Fatal Shore. The most active year was 1833, when 6,779 prisoners of both sexes were shipped to Sydney and Van Diemen's Land. By then, transportation had been accepted by most respectable Englishmen as the best of all answers to crime; the idea of the penitentiary was still a Benthamite hypothesis in England, although it was being tested by the novelty-loving Americans across the Atlantic. Nevertheless, the English Prison Acts were passed in that decade, and they distantly signalled the end of transportation. By the late 1830s, a strong current of opinion, fed by anti-slavery sentiment, was running against Botany Bay. English liberals were hearing more about the System and were shocked by what they heard, especially when the sensational and tendentious Molesworth report was published in 1838. Meanwhile, native-born Australians had come to hate the stigma of convictry—and the competition from assigned convict labor. In 1840, all transportation to New South Wales ceased.

This prepared the fourth and last stage of transportation. After 1840, convicts were of diminishing use as pioneers, and even their value as slave labor was falling. England kept sending them to Van Diemen's Land; by 1847, only 3.2 percent of the population of New South Wales were convicts under sentence, as against 34.4 percent in Van Diemen's Land.[4] From 1841 to 1850, some 26,000 convicts were poured into Van Diemen's Land, a number that soon jammed the System and led to its administrative breakdown. Transportation to Van Diemen's Land was not abolished until 1853. In 1850 the embryo colony of Western Australia announced, with naïvely eager opportunism, that it would like some convicts too—there being little enough to attract free labor, in those pre-mineral days, to a place cut off from Sydney by 3,000 miles of desert and bush. In response, the System produced one last dribble: 9,700 felons, shipped there from Great Britain over a period of eight years, finishing with a group of Irish Fenians. By 1868, transportation was all over, except for the social and psychic results. These were considerable, for a young country does not serve as the pad on which England drew its sketches for the immense Gulags of the twentieth century without acquiring a few marks and scars.

ii

THERE WERE NO "fashions" in English crime. Poverty begets theft, monotonously and predictably. Year after year the same proportion held: about four-fifths of all transportation was for "offences against property." Of the male convicts in L. L. Robson's survey, 34 percent were transported for unspecified larcenies; 15 percent for burglary or housebreaking; 13 percent for stealing domestic or farm animals (as distinct from poaching wild game, which accounted for less than three people in a thousand); and 6 percent for "theft of wearing apparel"—a reminder of how ill-clothed the English poor were in the days before cheap, mass-produced clothing. Only a little more than 3 percent of the male convicts went down for "offences against the person," which ranged from assault, rape, kidnapping and a few statistically negligible sodomy convictions to manslaughter and murder. A meager 4 percent were under sentence for "offences of a public nature," which embraced an assortment of acts thought to undermine the rights or prestige of the Realm—mainly "coining and uttering" bad money (2 percent) followed by another 1.5 percent convicted of treason, conspiracy to riot or membership in trade unions or Irish secret societies like the Whiteboys and Ribbon Men. A few people were sent to Australia for bigamy, smuggling and perjury.[5]

Seven men in ten were tried in England, mainly at assizes and quarter sessions in London and six chief counties: Lancashire, Yorkshire, Warwickshire, Surrey, Gloucestershire and Kent. These areas were home to four transportees in every ten. About one convict in five was tried in Ireland, most of them in Dublin.[6]

Men outnumbered women six to one. Over the whole transportation period, only 24,960 women were sent out, half to New South Wales and half to Van Diemen's Land. Probably 60 percent of the male English convicts had previous convictions, and 35 percent are known to have been charged with as many as four earlier offenses before they "napped a winder" and "went to the Bay." With women it was the same: A little more than two in ten had certainly never been convicted before, but the probable ratio of second-offenders or worse was about 60 percent.[7]

Set against the popular Australian belief that the "typical" convict was an innocent creature who had sinned once and been savagely punished for it, these figures speak for themselves. They do not, of course, tell the whole story. The English criminal law was without a doubt as savagely repressive as it was inefficient. But a code's badness does not necessarily acquit its victims—even though law reflects the interests and ideology of those who frame it.

The System swelled in the 1830s because its administrative machinery had improved—that is, more criminals were caught and processed. This did not imply a catastrophic increase in crime, even though there was no end of talk about "crime waves." Rather, because it was working so much better, it was able to gratify the social desires of respectable Britons much more readily. It answered a deep desire for sublimation and generalization. Few people want to take direct responsibility for hanging; understandably, they prefer abstractions— "course of justice," "debt to society," "exemplary punishment"—to the concrete fact of a terrified stranger choking and pissing at the end of a rope. Likewise, the idea that flogging reforms the criminal was an abstraction. The realities of the lash were only apparent where the cat-o'-nine-tails met the skin. Neither the man inside the skin nor the other wielding the cat was apt to think that an act of reformation was taking place. What happened was crude ritual, a magical act akin to the scourging-out of devils. All punishment seeks to reduce its objects to abstractions, so that they may be filled with a new content, invested with the values of good social conduct. But the main use of prison, from the viewpoint of the respectable, is simply to isolate and neutralize the criminal. Australia met this requirement perfectly. Since it was not a building but a continent, it could receive a whole class, with room to spare. And it was a class, not just an aggregation of individual criminals, that the English authorities thought they saw.

For in the 1830s a new language of class had begun to take hold in England. The older Georgian vocabulary of social difference spoke of "order," "degree" and "rank," implying society stabilized by "vertical dependence," its social strata linked by bonds of common interest and patronage. The new one, by contrast, was a language of division, not merely distinction. "Class" implied sharp demarcations and possible oppositions; the hierarchies of the old order may have seemed "natural" and conventional (at least to those on top), but relations of one class to another were adversary, contractual and based on the negotiation of opposed interests rather than a commonly recognized system of duties. The very idea of "class" implied a society, and a world, in change.

We are used to thinking of the language of class as the language of the working class—perhaps, as Gertrude Himmelfarb suggested, "because social history has generally been written by labor historians and socialists."[8] But the language of class in the 1830s was mostly invented and used by a middle class trying to describe the social complications that surrounded it, and it did not resemble the scheme of a two-class society—proletariat versus bourgeoisie—that Engels would later invent. Instead of a working class, they spoke of working *classes*: an idea that reeks of atomization and false consciousness in Marxist nostrils, but which in the 1830s seemed to recognize the variety of interests among working people. Even Chartists and other radicals usually spoke of a singular "middle class" and plural "working classes" or "working people."[9] Meanwhile, the English middle classes had achieved a state of "class consciousness"—meaning an awareness of their identity, desires and hopes—long before the workers. In the 1830s, it was they, not the Left of the future, who owned the rights on the definitions of "class," which they always took to be plural.

One of these, the authorities felt, lay in crime. Criminals did not need to name themselves as a class—to show class-consciousness—before law-abiding citizens felt entitled to call them a "criminal class." There was a crucial line between the "deserving" (frugal, hardworking, stoic) and the "undeserving" (lazy, improvident) poor, and crime certainly arose from the ranks of the "undeserving." "I am anxious," declared Henry Mayhew, "that the public should no longer confound the honest, independent working men with the vagrant beggars and pilferers of this country; and that they should see that the one class is as respectable and worthy, as the other is degraded and vicious."[10]

The idea of a criminal class, as understood by the English in the 1830s, meant that a distinct social group "produced" crime, as hatters produced hats or miners coal. It was part mob, part tribe and part guild, and it led a subterranean existence below and between the lower social structures of England. The criminal class had its own argot, its hierarchies, its accumulated technical wisdom. It preserved and amplified the craft of crime, passing it on from master to apprentice. This idea emerged from the late-eighteenth-century perception that crime in England had risen so fast that Authority must deal with an orchestration, not just an accumulation, of criminal acts. The spectacular career of Jonathan Wild promoted a vision of "generals" of crime—criminal masterminds—leading "armies" of thugs. This proved a durable fantasy. It lasted right through the nineteenth century and culminated in the image of the pre-Mafia super-criminal—Arthur Conan Doyle's Moriarty.

Stabs were made at guessing the size of this class. Patrick Colquhoun figured in 1797 that there were 50,000 whores and 10,000 thieves in London, along with more specialized citizens of the demimonde (Mudlarks, Bludgeon Men, Scufflehunters and dozens of other types) who brought the criminal total to some 115,000, more than 12 percent of the city's population.[11] He was guessing, of course, and his figures were ridiculed even then. The crime statistics assembled by the early Victorians were "harder," more voluminous, but still misleading—for criminal statistics have little to tell us about crime and criminals in the nineteenth century. *

The data of the early nineteenth century are further clouded by the prejudices of those who interpreted them at the time.[12] Around 1800, the "mob" was seen, with every reason, as dangerous. It was fuel for the same revolutionary fire that had destroyed the monarchy on the other side of the Channel. Propertied Englishmen were obsessed with Jacobinism. In their eyes, it justified every resurgence of repression, inhibited every effort at reform, and deeply unsettled the poise with which they had hitherto contemplated the lower classes. It also lent a pervasive if unconscious tinge to all guesses about the nature and composition of the "mob." Their fear of the political threat translated itself into repeated exaggerations of criminal nature. Thus, it was all too easy to assign criminal propensities to the marginal, the outcast, the rag-and-boner—in short, to those who might be seen as English *sans-culottes*. For that large tract where the unpropertied survived, where tricks of subsistence had to be invented from day to day, where the cunning, the illicit and the illegal blended into one another without fine distinction, they had only one name: the criminal class.

Their tendency to invest the struggling and the low with an aura of criminality was sometimes amplified by Evangelical Methodism. If the lower orders were not frugal, humble, hardworking and devout, if they clung unrepentantly to their rum, rutting and fairs, the randy humor and coarse songs and all the other amusements that make life at the bottom of the heap intermittently tolerable, then they were on the Devil's side, not God's.

The fear of crime itself cast an exaggerated solidity on "the distinct body of thieves, whose life and business is to follow up *a determined warfare against the constituted authorities*" and who "may be known almost by their very gait in the streets from other persons."[13] Was all crime as professional as such sentinels believed? Probably only a minority of thieves ran in gangs. Many thefts were spontaneous, desperate and often bungled efforts to relieve want and hunger. Crimes of violence were

* The inherent difficulty may readily be seen if one thinks of a modern equivalent: How many cocaine-dealers are there in Manhattan? Despite the public preoccupation with drugs, despite immense publicity given to the production, distribution and consumption of cocaine, its physiological and psychological effects, its social imagery, its power as a status symbol and sexual stimulant, despite the relative social visibility of the dealers who sell it and its cachet as a "respectable" drug, nobody really knows. Nor is it known, despite spectacular guesses from police and government, how much money the cocaine trade in New York is worth a year. The number of convictions bears only the sketchiest relation to the number of criminal transactions. Yet here we have a crime which is thought, by many Americans, not to be criminal at all, involving a product they regularly use and dealers they often meet face-to-face. Project this back 150 years, into a different culture, and one sees the impossibility of guessing the size of the English "criminal class" in transportation days.

not always premeditated. There was a wide gray area between the "occasional" criminal, stealing a rabbit or a coat, and the hard-core professional whose strategies were evoked by the idea of a criminal class. The latter were taken to be permanently degraded, "members of a sort of criminal *race*," as Sydney Smith's *Edinburgh Review* expressively put it; the former, not. Although hard-core criminals did not drift into respectability, the respectable drifted into crime. For the official English morality of the early nineteenth century was far more absolutist than ours. Today's orthodoxy is to look for the environmental excuse and to seek the roots of crime in nurture, not nature—that is, outside the criminal's power of choice. One hundred and fifty years ago it was assumed that men and women *chose* a life of crime. The way to this life was seen— and its image was reinforced by the immense power of official and church imagery—as a sequence of irrevocable steps leading downward, the easy road to Hell. This accorded with the basic conservative tenet, that people are not "naturally" wise or good: We must be restrained by law, and frightened by punishment.

Such ideas, however, were in themselves a harshly coercive part of the social environment and may have caused many people to give up the struggle—to let go, to be what society said they would become, and accept the only milieu that would not rebuke them: crime. The son of a well-off country grocer, caught stealing apples over a neighbor's wall, might get a small fine and a heavy thrashing from his father and so, chastened, go on to respectability. The son of an Irish casual worker in a London slum, caught breaking a window, might experience no such change in the House of Correction. All people, but especially the young, tend to become what society says they are.

Belief in a "criminal class" was self-fulfilling in other ways too— mainly because it made rehabilitation so difficult. Once off the edge, it was not easy to find another respectable job. Records were better in 1830 than in 1770, and they could be checked by any prospective employer.

Many observers realized that crime does not appear in a social vacuum. From 1800 onward, a large literature—at first Evangelical in tone and rising at last to the power of Dickens's encyclopedic vision of the city as ultimate social and moral compressor—sought to describe the causes of crime: poverty, lack of work, dislocation, vile housing, addiction, the death of hope. But the official inquiries into crime, drunkenness, prisons and transportation that were held between 1815 and 1840 tended to confirm the same view of crime: that its class nature mattered more than its causes. The criminal class, in the view of one writer in 1854, "constitutes a new estate, in utter estrangement from all the rest."[14]

But how threatening was it? And was there not hope for the respectable in its estrangement and apparent cohesiveness? The difference between the "criminal classes" of London and the *classes dangereuses* of Paris was that the English were not as dangerous; events like the Gordon Riots in London were the exception, not the rule. England had no tradition of riot and revolt abetted by outpourings of aggression from the criminal classes, whereas the French were used to such explosions from the "vile mob," as the French minister Adolphe Thiers called it in 1850, that had brought "every Republic down in ruin."[15] But, despite the inflamed rhetoric of some Tory extremists, there had never been any alliance, natural or otherwise, between English criminals and English radicals—indeed, the latter took care to exclude the former from their ranks, always stressing their own respectability as workingmen.

But if English crime, unlike French, seemed to present no political threat to the state as such, it certainly menaced its citizens—chiefly the laboring poor. The "criminal class" threatened middle-class property, but what most worried the authorities was the moral contagion it offered to workers and their impressionable children. They had tried to remove the bad apples from the lower classes before they could contaminate the good. The New Poor Law had tried to separate the independent laboring poor from the paupers; the ragged-schools tried to keep the offspring of the lowest and most depraved paupers apart from the "respectable."[16] Transportation sought to remove, once and for all, the source of contamination from the otherwise decent bosom of the lower classes, and ship it "beyond the seas" to a place from which it could not easily return. There it would stay, providing slave labor for colonial development and undergoing such mutations toward respectability as whips and chains might induce. The main point was not what happened to it *there*, but that it would no longer be *here*.

The final aim of the transportation system, then, was less to punish individual crimes than to uproot an enemy class from the British social fabric. Here lay its peculiar modernity; its prediction of the vaster, more efficient techniques of class destruction that would be perfected, a century later, in Russia. However, it failed. Transportation did not stop crime in England or even slow it down. The "criminal class" was not eliminated by transportation, and could not be, because transportation did not deal with the causes of crime. And before we leave the generalizations that led authorities to their ideas about the "criminal class," we should consider a voice from inside it. Written by the wife of a thief bound early for the Fatal Shore, it recounts in bare language the descent into a crime of desperation that must have been traced by thousands of convicts, in an England without pity for the "undeserving poor."

Isaac Nelson, clerk, has been sentenced to seven years' transportation at the Stafford Assizes in 1789. He is now in chains at Portsmouth, cast for transportation on the Second Fleet. His crime was stealing "a Quantity of plated goods" (silver) from a former employer in Birmingham, Matthew Boulton, whom he had served "with the uttermost fidelity" for three years. After quitting Boulton's service, he had come to London and worked for several employers (all of whom signed the letter as character witnesses). Nelson's wife—only the initial of her Christian name, *S*, appears on the letter—begs to assure the authorities she is petitioning that her husband, after losing his last job with a Piccadilly optician,

> from that time was so unfortunate as to be Destitute of all kind of Imployment for upwards of Twelve Months in which Time we were redused to the uttermost Distress possible. Myself afflicted with Illness the whole time and in want of the Common Necessaries of life through a Long and Sevear Winter, and my Husband, the only one I had to look up to get Support, Deprived of the means to gain subsistence, and in this Deploreable Situation to Heap Up the Measure of our Misfortunes, I was Delivered of a Male Infant, who died in a few days from want of proper nourishment, My Self being in so weak a Condishion as not to be able to afford it any assistance.
>
> Think, most gracious Sir, the Feelings of a Husband who tenderley loved a Wife and had allways been used to afford a comfortable Subsistence, to see her in such a Situation, without the Possibility of releaving her Wants, and humbly hope the Gates of Mercy will not be shut against him.

Isaac Nelson went back to Birmingham and got a job at Boulton's for six weeks at 10s. 6d. a week, which was garnished to repay his coach fare and an employer's advance. His wife in London was still destitute and frantic, and so "in a fitt of distraction" he stole the silverware, which was recovered later. Mrs. Nelson goes on to beg the home secretary that

> You will in Humanity to a poor unfortunate man be pleased to Interview with His Majesty to grant him His Most Gracious Pardon or . . . [that] he will mitigate his Sentence, by allowing him to stay the time of his sentence in England, or allow Your Petitioner the favour to accompany her husband in his exile, that she may be able to afford him some Consolation amidst his Afflictions as his long confinement joined to his other Trobles, being of a weak Constitution, has brought him into a deep Consumption that has nearly reduced him to the Grave.[17]

The "Infinite Mercy and Goodness" of George III did not extend so far and Isaac Nelson sailed for Australia on the terrible Second Fleet.

Such lives confirm the truth of E. P. Thompson's bitter remark: The

worst offense against property was to have none. We do not know, and
never will, how many Isaac Nelsons figured in the "criminal classes." At
the same time, rising somewhat on the scale of culpability, people were
transported for offenses that the law condemned but their communities
tended to condone. Some popular codes stood at a sharp angle to law.
Thus youths made heroes of highwaymen, and whole communities in
Cornwall and Devonshire not only engaged in wrecking but claimed
a traditional right to plunder ships.[18] In smuggling communities along
the Sussex coast, people used every shift to avoid the excise on rum and
tea, despite the threat of transportation and the gallows. Poaching
was another offense that few countrymen, if any, thought wrong, for
the poaching laws were among the most corrupt of all English
statutes; in sum, they forbade a man to kill a wild animal, even on his
own land, unless he could show an income of £100 a year from a
freehold estate. Since a laborer in 1830 might expect to make between
£10 and £20 a year, the poaching laws were a constant theater of class
conflict.

The popular legend of transportation in Australia still insists that
there were many convict poachers, but there were not. The number of
men transported for poaching was infinitesimal, about the same as those
sent out for buggering sheep or boys; those poachers who did get sent to
Australia were usually convicted for resisting arrest or assaulting a
gamekeeper, not just for the pheasant in the pocket. It was very hard to
find witnesses in village communities. Nevertheless, the fact that authorities pursued country people for such morally insignificant crimes—
and were quick to identify them with the "dissolute and idle" rather
than the "working" peasantry—shows that there was as wide and ill-
recognized a gray area between harmless offense and real crime (like
sheep or cattle stealing, acts condemned by all villagers) in the country
as in the town.

iii

THERE IS NO doubt that many Britons made their living, wholly or in
part, from crime. At trial and again on the boat, prisoners had to give
their trade or occupation; the two largest categories among the transported were "farm workers" (20 percent) and "laborers" (19 percent). The
prisoners did not always use these descriptions themselves; they were
more blunt about what they really did for a living. Peter Cunningham,
remembering his first voyage to Australia as surgeon-superintendent of
convicts on the transport *Recovery* in 1819, described how a seaman he
had ordered to list the trades of the prisoners on board

came to me in a doubtful mood, scratching his head and observing, "When I ask what their *trades* are, all the answer I can get from three-fourths of them is, 'a thief, a thief'; shall I put them down as *labourers*, sir?"[19]

Although we cannot speak of a "criminal class" with the same confidence as early Victorians did, there certainly was a subculture of crime in the British Isles, in London most of all. It expressed itself in common interests, cant language, specialization, loyalties. Its main character, to the journalist's eye, was the fantastic range of "trades" it contained, as though the Industrial Revolution, breeding an ever-expanding range of products and specialists to make them, had brought forth an equal army of specialists to steal them. The arch-reporter of the underworld, Henry Mayhew, tabulated at least a hundred subspecies of London criminal by their argot names; a small fraction of his list runs as follows:

2. "Sneaksmen" or those who plunder by means of stealth.
[a.] Those who purloin goods, provisions, money, clothes, old metal, &c:
    i. "Drag Sneaks," or those who steal goods or luggage from carts or coaches.
    ii. "Snoozers," or those who sleep at railway hotels, and decamp with some passenger's luggage . . .
    iii. "Star-Glazers," or those who cut the panes out of shopwindows.
    iv. "Till Friskers," or those who empty tills of their contents during the absence of shopmen.
    v. "Sawney-Hunters," or those who go purloining bacon from cheese-mongers' shop windows.
    vi. "Noisy-Racket Men," or those who steal china and glass from outside of china-shops.
    vii. "Area Sneaks," or those who steal from houses by going down the area steps.
    viii. "Dead Lurkers," or those who steal coats and umbrellas from passages at dusk, or on Sunday afternoons.
    ix. "Snow Gatherers," or those who steal clean clothes off the hedges.
    x. "Skinners," or women who entice children and sailors to go with them and then strip them of their clothes.
    xi. "Bluey-Hunters," or those who purloin lead from the tops of houses.
    xii. "Cat and Kitten Hunters," or those who purloin pewter quart and pint pots from the top of area railings.[20]

And so on. Argot, like all technical jargon, set its users apart. English criminal slang was impenetrable to the "straight" ear. It described actions that did not exist in respectable society, high or low, but were known to "the family"—all those who lived "upon the cross." A *running-rumbler*, around 1800, "gets a large grinding-stone, which he rolls along the pavement; the passengers hearing the rumble, get out of the way, for fear of its running against them, or over their toes; in this critical moment some of the gang give you the *rum-hustle*, or pick your pocket."[21] *Amusers* or *puzzlers* would throw handfuls of street filth in a victim's eyes and run away while their accomplice picked his pockets. A horse-thief was a *prigger of prancers* or a *pradnapper*; a coiner, a *bit-smasher*, a *bit-cull* or a *benefeaker*. To clip coins and keep the gold-dust was to *sweat* them or to be *in the diminishing way*. If one stole loaves from a baker's basket, one was said to be *pricking in the wicker for a dolphin*. There seemed to be no substance that could not be stolen: The *black-spice racket* consisted of stealing bags of soot from sweeps, and the word *buff* for skin gave rise to *buffer*—a man who killed dogs by running a sharp wire into their hearts and then sold their pelts to glovers. There was even a market for *curls*, or human teeth; they were used by some dentists to replace the lost molars of the living.

These were low trades. But a man *whose means are two pops and a galloper* had real status as a mounted highwayman with a pair of pistols, fearless as Turpin in bailing up *rattling-coves*, or coachmen. Forgers *drew the King's picture* in Georgian days or, in Victorian ones, *dummied the old woman's ticket*. A shoplifter practiced the *fam lay*, sometimes palming a ring from a jeweler's counter "by means of a little Ale held in a Spoon over the fire, by which the Palm being daub'd, any light thing sticks to it."[22] His female equivalent would *cant the dobbin* (steal rolls of ribbon) from haberdashers.

Of all the myriad kinds of thief—"the sons of St. Peter, with every finger a fish-hook"—the most dexterous were the *files* and *buzz-gloaks*, or pickpockets. Dickens's description of Fagin's school for boy thieves in *Oliver Twist* was no fantasy. Larger schools (whose ten-year-old initiates were known as *erriffs*, a straight word for young canaries, or *academy buzz-nappers*) were a favorite topic of London journalists. They taught the arts of *fogle-hunting* (drawing out handkerchiefs), *bung-diving* (taking purses), *speaking to the tattler* (lifting a watch, with its *onions*, or seals) and *chiving the froe* (cutting off a woman's pockets with a razor). A pupil with no talent for this was scorned as a *purple dromedary*. A skilled, coordinated adept became a *boman prig* (from the French "beau," fine) with *rum daddles* (expert hands). Out he would go, with a *bulker*, or accomplice, whose role was to jostle the mark, to do fieldwork among the crowds in Piccadilly, the sauntering dandies in Vauxhall Gardens, or the milling crush in Drury Lane during the *breaking-up of the spell*, as theater interval was called. It was under such circumstances that George Barrington, an Irish pickpocket of high vanity and considerable skill, was caught picking the pocket of the Russian Prince Orlov during an operatic first night at Covent Garden; he was transported, and ended up as a "decayed macaroni" at Parramatta with 110 acres farmed for him by lesser convicts. Barrington's celebrity was such that a number of books, none of which he wrote, were published under his name, including an early "history" of New South Wales.[23]

One could not, of course, enter the milieu of crime just by learning its argot. It took work to build up a name. There was nothing unlikely about the words Dickens put into the mouth of young Charley Bates, as he sees his *beau idéal* the Artful Dodger facing transportation for pinching a mere snuffbox. "Oh, why didn't he rob some rich old gentleman of all his walables, and go out *as* a gentleman, and not like a common prig, without no honour nor glory! . . . How will he stand in the Newgate Calendar? P'raps not be there at all." "See what a pride they take in their profession," Fagin crows.[24]

No classless society has ever existed or ever will. Every group has bottom and top dogs. The hostile glare of the decent did not prevent men and women "on the cross" from constructing pecking orders whose minuteness and punctilio were almost worthy of Versailles. From the lowest thief to the highest member of the "Swell Mob," all was graded; the criminal milieu was a meritocracy with strong tribal overtones. The pyramid of crime was a buried, inverted reflection of the pyramid of respectability, and those who lived where the two met—beggars and charity cases, with neither the skill to work nor the gumption to steal—were despised by both. Thus, Mayhew noted that a poor boy might be "partly forced to steal for his character." One's criminal record was an index of rank. At a party in a thieves' kitchen Mayhew found that

> the announcements in reply to the questions as to the number of times that any of them had been in prison were received with great applause, which became more and more boisterous as the number of punishments increased. When it was announced that one, though only nineteen years of age, had been in prison as many as twenty-nine times, the clapping of hands . . . lasted for several minutes, and the whole of the boys rose to look at the distinguished individual. Some chalked on their hats . . . the sum of the several times they had been in gaol.[25]

One had to start young, but inexperience gets caught. The young thief was eager to prove himself, rash, and hence an easy target for the police, even before fingerprints. After 1815 it was quite rare for a first-time thief to be sentenced to transportation, but the number of thefts committed by habitual criminals meant that further convictions, and Botany Bay, were bound to follow.

Illustrators depicted the "criminal type" as a mask of low cunning, stunted but alert. In fact there was no difference between the look of English criminals and that of the working class from which they came. Against the jargon of "criminal types" and the pseudo-scientific babble of the phrenologists one must balance the description of cotton-mill workers offered by Peter Gaskell in 1833:

> An uglier set of men and women . . . it would be impossible to congregate in a smaller compass. Their complexion is shallow and pallid—with a peculiar flatness of feature, caused by the want of a proper quantity of adipose substance to cushion out the cheeks. Their stature low—the average height being five feet six inches. Their limbs slender, and playing badly and ungracefully. A very general bowing of the legs.[26]

The convicts' height was not always recorded, but they tended to be short. Thus a giant poster published in Hobart in 1850, listing 465 escaped convicts at large (cumulative over 20 years) puts more than 80 percent of the men below 5 feet 8 inches, with the largest group, some 15 percent, only 5 feet 3 inches tall. Compared to most modern Australians of Irish or English descent, these men were runts, and the difference was one of diet.

They shared other traits with *lumpen* workers, chiefly a loathing of authority. The "criminal classes" of England were apolitical; on that, all observers agreed. They played no role whatsoever in the radical disturbances of the day. Tribal loyalties could be fanatically strong among them, and they stuck together against the peeler, the beak and the pink chaplain in his "cackle tub," as the prison pulpit was known. "The more you value your number one, the more careful you must be of mine. . . . [A] regard for number one holds us all together, and must do so, unless we would all go to pieces in company." Fagin's words sum up an ethos of loyalty among thieves, a clannishness much like Sicilian *omertà*.

This contemptuous resistance to everyone and everything outside one's small group was one of the roots of Australian mateship. But no convict ever felt that all convicts were his brothers. They would often trample and oppress one another, behaving with the utmost cynicism and cruelty toward weaker prisoners. And often they would not. There was no hard-and-fast rule of "convict solidarity." From authority's point of view, the London "sneaksman" had something in common with the Northumbrian cattle rustler—both had broken the law. But the two men, who knew nothing of one another's background and barely had a language in common, would feel no bond at all. Even when people were transported from the same place for the same offense, they did not always stick by one another. "I hope you will not mind what you may hear from anyone that writes to Boulton saying how good anyone have been to me," wrote the young protestor Thomas Holden, transported with other Luddites in 1812, to his parents. "I in all my illness have Receiv'd no favour from any one of they that come from Boulton, but far the other way."[27]

Most were irreligious too—except, obviously, the Irish—since the reformed man or woman devoted to Methodist "enthusiasm" and the Evangelical meeting was the last person apt to be transported. Chaplains on transport vessels and tractarians visiting the hulks felt like missionaries among hostile white heathens. They bewailed the hard-heartedness of the convicts, their imperviousness to the Word, their cynicism about prayer, their inability to imagine God, Heaven or Hell. They were "abandoned," "profligate," "irreclaimable." They respected neither God or man but truckled shamelessly to both when expediency whispered.

Mateship, fatalism, contempt for do-gooders and God-botherers, harsh humor, opportunism, survivors' disdain for introspection, and an attitude to authority in which private resentment mingled with ostensible resignation—such was the meager baggage of values the convicts brought with them to Australia. They also brought, if men, the phallocracy of the tavern and ken, and, if women, a kind of tough passivity, a way of seeing life without expectations. What they bequeathed to their native-born Australian offspring, the Currency of the colony (as distinct from the Sterling, or English-born free settlers), was summed up by the Australian poet James McAuley in the 1950s as

> a futile heart within a fair periphery.
> The women are hard-eyed, kindly, with nothing inside them:
> The men are independent but you could not call them free.

iv

ONLY A FEW convicts were sent out for political offenses. Yet transportation was an important feature in the machinery of English state repression. The right to send political offenders to Botany Bay was jealously wielded by the British Government. English interests did not want to make martyrs of radicals—and there were obvious constitutional problems attached to hanging a Dissenting clergyman for owning a copy of Tom Paine. But transportation got rid of the dissenter without making a hero of him on the scaffold. He slipped off the map into a distant limbo, where his voice fell dead at his feet. There was nothing for his ideas to engage, if he were an intellectual; no machines to break or ricks to burn, if a laborer. He could preach sedition to the thieves and cockatoos, or to the wind. Nobody would care.

The first political agitators were transported to Australia early in the life of the System. They were convicted in Edinburgh and were known as the "Scottish Martyrs."

In the early 1790s, "reforming" English intellectuals flirted with Jacobinism. To enable such parsons, lawyers and pamphleteers to make contact with like-minded workers, discussion groups known as "Corresponding Societies" were formed. Their officers called themselves "Jacobins" but were, in fact, reforming constitutionalists, who wanted to recall Britain's laborers and artisans to a sense of their ancient rights. It was to this audience that Paine's *Rights of Man* sold most of its million copies in Britain. Tories, thinking of Jacobinism in terms of the guillotine and the September Massacres, viewed the Corresponding Societies with horror and set out to break them up.

They would have liked to stage a crushing trial of some English Jacobins in England, but they could not be sure a jury would convict them. So their blow against the Corresponding Societies was struck in Scotland, where juries were easily rigged. It fell on a young, blue-eyed Scottish lawyer named Thomas Muir (1765–1799), vice-president of a Jacobin discussion group in Glasgow. Muir was an ardent constitutionalist whose offense was to advocate yearly elections of Parliament and a broadening of the Scottish franchise. He stood trial for sedition in Edinburgh in 1793, and every juror was handpicked from the rolls of a Scottish Tory organization known as the Life-and-Fortune Men, the equivalent of the Loyal Orange societies in Ireland.[28]

The main charge against Muir was that he had lent out radical tracts, among them a copy of Paine's *Rights of Man*. Muir admitted the charge but claimed he could not receive a fair trial from the packed jury. The judge—Robert Macqueen, Lord Braxfield, Lord Justice Clerk of Scotland —brushed that aside, as he had been told to do. He was a coarse cunning old drunk whose remarks during this trial won long notoriety. (When one of the Jacobins pointed out that Christ himself had been a reformer, Braxfield chuckled and snorted: "Muckle he made o' that—*He* was hanget.") From such a man, Muir was unlikely to escape, whatever his forensic skills.

Braxfield's instructions to the jury could hardly have been clearer: It was axiomatic that the British Constitution could not be improved. Muir had been telling "ignorant country people" that it must be changed to secure their liberty—"which, if it had not been for him, they would never have thought was in danger." And what right did the "rabble" have to representation? None, for they had no property. "A government in this country should be just like a corporation," the judge declared,

made up of the landed interest, which alone has the right to be represented. As for a rabble, who have nothing but personal property, what
hold has the nation of them? They may pack up all their property on their
backs, and leave the country in the twinkling of an eye; but landed property cannot be removed.[29]

The jury quickly and unanimously found Thomas Muir guilty and he
was sentenced to 14 years' transportation.

A few months later another "radical" clergyman was tried in Perth,
for circulating a "seditious" pamphlet questioning Britain's motives in
her war against France and helping a Dundee weaver publish an "Address
to the People" on the subject of parliamentary reform. This was Thomas
Fyshe Palmer (1747–1802), no Scot but an Englishman, a Unitarian minister and fellow of Queen's College, Cambridge, who had spent the past
ten years preaching as a humble pastor in Dundee. He got 7 years' transportation.

These sentences caused apprehension in England, and not only among
Jacobins. A group of moderate constitutionalists, headed by Lord Lauder-
dale, complained about them to the home secretary, Henry Dundas.[30]
They asked Parliament to overturn the verdict on Muir and Palmer.
Dundas would hear none of that. He wanted to press on and see if English
radicals who did not live in Scotland could be arrested and tried there,
and his chance came in October 1793, when the National Convention of
British reformers met in Edinburgh.

Its two London delegates were middle-class dissenters, Joseph Gerrald
(1760–1796) and Maurice Margarot (1745–1815). The Edinburgh sheriff's
deputies worked hard to break up the other assemblies at which they
spoke. William Skirving (d. 1796), the Scottish secretary of the convention, was arrested at home and his papers impounded. Gerrald and Margarot were dragged out of bed in the dead of night, later to be released on
bail. Braxfield's court tried Skirving for sedition and sentenced him to 14
years' transportation. Gerrald, temporarily free, went back to London and
"as an Englishman in whose person the sacred rights of his country have
been violated" publicly challenged Dundas to confess that he had insti-
gated the night arrests.[31] He was ignored. His friends urged him to jump
bail and flee to Republican America. But Gerrald refused to abandon
his comrades, whose trials were now taking place in Edinburgh.
Margarot was sentenced to 14 years' transportation. Gerrald's turn
came a month later, and Lord Braxfield gave him 14 years. Both judge
and prisoner knew that this was a death sentence, for Gerrald had
tuberculosis.

Palmer, Muir, Skirving and Margarot were shipped to Australia along
with eighty-three less celebrated convicts in the transport *Surprize* in

February 1794. Gerrald followed a year later. On the voyage, Maurice Margarot seems to have had a nervous breakdown, and he denounced his comrades to the captain as parties to a mutiny plot. The indignant "Martyrs" spent the last five months of the voyage in the brig, on short rations. No wonder Muir wrote to a friend in London after their arrival to announce that "Palmer, Skirving and myself live in the utmost harmony. From our society, Maurice Margarot is expelled."[32]

In fact, despite their lamentations, Sydney did not treat them harshly. They did no forced work, wore no chains, and never tasted the cat-o'-nine-tails. Palmer and Muir got land grants and even managed to turn a profit in the rum trade. The government only wanted them neutralized. But they needed watching and the acting governor, Francis Grose, promised Palmer "every indulgence," provided that he "avoid on all occasions a recital of those Politicks which have produced in you the miseries a man of your feelings and abilities must at this time undergo."[33] Although Skirving was granted a hundred acres and Gerrald was bought a house on Sydney Harbor, the "Martyrs" felt the hostility of the Rum Corps—"they have kept us poor," said Palmer, though he may only have been complaining about the difficulty of getting into the rum trade himself. Political discussion was out—"they are all aristocrats here from ignorance, and being out of the way or desire of knowledge."[34]

Transportation did not destroy the political beliefs of the Scottish Martyrs. But it cooled their ardor, and one sees this reflected in "The Telegraph: A Consolatory Epistle," a lengthy poem Thomas Muir addressed to his fellow reformer Henry Erskine in Scotland. It opens with the depressing landscape of exile, "Where sullen *Convicts* drag the clanking chain / and Desolation covers all the plain." Here, Muir reflects that he is still a Jacobin and that

> The best and noblest privilege in Hell
> For souls like ours is, Nobly to rebell,
> To raise the standard of revolt and try
> The happy fruits of lov'd Democracy.
> The sacred right of Insurrection there
> May drive old Satan from his regal chair
> And the same honest means may raise perchance
> A *France* in *Hell*, that raised a *Hell* in *France*.

But doubts arise. Does not revolution wreck the constitutional principles they all stand for? (Muir was so much a moderate that he even went to Paris to plead with the real Jacobins for the life of Louis XVI.) Brooding on the dangers of the mob, he devised a new metaphor of revolution; thus, an Australian bushfire makes its first appearance in English poetry, as a symbol of political passions ignited by ignorance. He had seen aboriginal hunters setting fire to the scrub:

> Some naked Savage on the distant shore
> With rapid step advancing to the view
> Reminds me, Henry, of my friends and you:
> Of those dear friends who join with heart & hand
> To spread the flame of Freedom round the land,
> And restless labour, anxious to inspire
> Each sluggish bosom with the sacred Fire.—
>
> To clear the forest's dark impervious maze
> The half-starv'd Indian lights a hasty blaze
> Then lifts the Torch, and rushing o'er the Strand
> High o'er his head he waves the flaming Brand
> From Bush to Bush with rapid steps he flies
> Till the whole forest blazes to the skies.
>
> Often, 'tis true, this deed of Madness done
> He mourns the mischief which his hand begun,
> When the red torrent rushing o'er the plain
> No art can stop, no human power restrain,
> Till from a Rock he sees with wild amaze
> His Wife & Children perish in the Blaze.
>
> Stop Henry stop! and cautiously enquire
> If you can quench as you enflame the fire:
> Think on the Savage in my simple tale
> Who fires a Province, for a scanty Meal.[35]

The coarse intellectual clay of Sydney was not for their shaping. They tried to catechize some prisoners but got little response. Then Thomas Muir, with extraordinary daring, contrived to escape. Early in 1796 he managed to contact the skipper of an American fur-trading vessel, the *Otter*, provisioning in Sydney Harbor. As soon as the ship sailed, Muir stole a rowboat and hauled out through the Heads, at night; the Yankees picked him up a few miles offshore. Months later, when the *Otter* reached Alaskan waters, Muir learned that a Royal Navy ship had been seen in the area. Fearing capture, he transferred to a cruising Spanish gunboat, which took him south to Monterey in Spanish California.

From Monterey he made his way to the Caribbean, via Mexico City and Vera Cruz. He reached Cuba by the end of the year, hoping to work his way north on a ship to Philadelphia. But by then war had broken out between England and Spain, and the Spanish colonial *jefe* put Muir in the Havana prison for several months. At last he was shipped out, not to America but to Spain, on a frigate bound for Cadiz. Near the end of her voyage she was attacked by a British naval squadron, and an exploding shell mutilated Muir's face and destroyed his left eye; he was so badly wounded that the British officers, on learning he was aboard, could not recognize him. So unhappy Muir was put ashore in a prison-hospital in Cadiz. But after several months, word of his arrival reached the French, and as an English Republican he had friends in Paris. Talleyrand negotiated his release and brought him to Paris in December 1797 as a guest of the Directory. There he remained, a gradually fading celebrity, occasionally consulted on plans to invade England; he wrote an account of his exile and wanderings around the globe which, although it was eagerly read and discussed in manuscript, never saw publication and is now lost. Muir died at Chantilly, in lamentable poverty, on January 26, 1799— precisely eleven years after the convict settlement at Sydney Cove, the antithesis of all his republican ideals, had been founded. His grave is not known.

Two of the other Scottish Martyrs did not outlive him long, though they had no idea what had happened to Muir. Joseph Gerrald, the mild consumptive scholar, died of tuberculosis in March 1796; William Skirving followed him three days later. Both were buried in Sydney, and Skirving received the epitaph "A seditionist, but a man of good moral character."

Thomas Palmer finished his sentence in Australia, and went into the shipbuilding trade while he was serving it. He and his close friend John Boston—another "avowed Jacobin," who had voluntarily come with his wife on the long voyage to Sydney to keep Palmer company—had little experience of business, but they possessed a singular advantage: the only encyclopedia in the colony. With it, they taught themselves to make beer. Then they learned how to make soap. Next they looked up "ship" and, after some trial and error, contrived to build a somewhat cranky but adequate small vessel for trading stores to Norfolk Island. It was followed by a 30-ton sloop, the *Martha*. Finally Palmer bought and refitted *El Plumier*, a decrepit Spanish warship, and tried to sail her to England via the East Indies. Near Guam, a remote Spanish outpost in the Marianas east of the Philippines, her rotten hull opened. The survivors of the voyage, Palmer included, were detained in jail by the Spaniards. Palmer died there of cholera in June 1802. The Spanish priests, hearing of his radical opinions, refused his body Christian burial; and so the most civilized and liberal-souled gentleman to breathe Australian air in early colonial days was buried among pirates in a common grave on the beach, until an American captain (himself a man of reforming opinions) took the trouble in 1804 to retrieve Palmer's body and bring it back to burial in a Boston church.

The only Scottish Jacobin who stayed on in Australia was the erratic

Maurice Margarot, who managed to lead a shadowy, ill-documented life as a double agent between the various colonial cliques. He seems to have reported to Governor Hunter on the financial doings and political discontents of the New South Wales Corps Officers; and some evidence suggests that he kept both Grose, Hunter's predecessor, and King, Hunter's successor, informed on the conversations of his own former friends the Jacobins. King believed he plotted rebellion with the Irish convicts in 1801 and again in 1804, but he also feared that Margarot was reporting on him to the Colonial Office in London. In 1810, after seventeen years' Australian exile, Margarot struggled back to England. He died in London five years later, wretchedly poor, and politically broken, disliked and distrusted by the friends of his former radical associates.

Transportation had dealt effectively with the Scottish Jacobins. It would continue to do so with representatives of nearly every English protest movement, industrial upheaval and agrarian revolt for the next half-century. But first, it would deal with the Irish.

v

AUSTRALIA WAS the official Siberia for Irish dissidents at the turn of the century. Their presence there caused the System acute strain and insecurity. Rebellious Irishmen, known as "United Irish" and "Defenders," had been sent out in dribs and drabs during the 1790s. But between 1800 and 1805 their influx began in earnest, swollen by political exiles transported for their role in the rebellion of 1798, when Ireland tried unsuccessfully to ally with France in revolt against England.

Some of these men had been formally tried and sentenced to transportation. Others—most prominent among them was "General" Joseph Holt (1756–1826), the leader of the 1798 United Irish rebellion in County Wicklow—had surrendered under the promise of amnesty given by Lord Cornwallis and agreed to be exiled without trial rather than rot in prison. Others still had been bundled onto the convict transports without any form of trial; in 1797, the undersecretary in Dublin had been advised from England that "a light punishment for rebellion will excite revenge, not terror. . . . [Y]ou should transport all prisoners in the gaols and give full power to the generals."[36]

The Irish, on arriving in Australia, were treated as a special class. As bearers of Jacobin contagion, as ideologically and physically dangerous traitors, they were oppressed with special vigilance and unusually hard punishments. They formed Australia's first white minority. From the outset, the Irish in Australia saw themselves as a doubly colonized people.

The colonization of Ireland—the absolute ascendancy of Gall over Gael—had been going on since the twelfth century, when the first English Pope, Adrian IV, encouraged his fellow Anglo-Norman, King Henry II, to invade Ireland and "proclaim the truths of the Christian religion to a rude and ignorant people." When the English knights landed and started hewing their red way through the Gaelic resistance, Ireland had been Christian for seven hundred years. It took nearly a century to impose the Anglo-Norman feudal system on the Irish clans, but by the end of the thirteenth century it was done. The puppet Dublin parliament, owing its loyalty to the English crown, would last seven hundred years and only be dissolved by the Act of Union with England in 1801.

Throughout those seven centuries, no Irish Catholic could expect justice from its laws. As they tightened, so the rights of Irishmen dwindled; and by the end of the eighteenth century these "penal laws" reached into every cranny of the Catholic majority's life. Under them, Catholics were legislated down to helotry. They divided Ireland, as Edmund Burke remarked in 1792,

> into two distinct bodies, without common interest, sympathy or connection. One . . . was to possess all the franchises, all the property, all the education; the other was to be composed of drawers of water and cutters of turf for them. Are we to be surprised when by the efforts of so much violence in conquest . . . we had reduced them to a mob?

Under the Popery Laws, no Catholic could sit in Parliament, on the bench or in a jury; none could vote, teach or hold an army commission. They were disabled in property law, which was rewritten to break up Catholic estates and consolidate Protestant ones. Protestant estates could be left intact to eldest sons, but Catholic ones had to be split between all the children. Thus Catholic landowning families degenerated into sharecropping ones within a generation or two.

These laws cut across all class barriers. They beat the Catholic peasantry "into the clay," as the phrase went, but they also gagged and paralyzed the Catholic landowner, the intellectual, the entrepreneur. Thus, they unified the Irish Catholics more strongly than softer laws could ever have done and voided the question of a class struggle within the Catholic ranks. Hence the fervor with which working Irishmen supported middle-class leaders like Tone and O'Connell. This breadth of disaffection meant that Irish political prisoners transported to Australia ranged across a wide social spectrum, from peasant to lawyer. In March 1800, Governor Hunter was complaining that far too many of the Irish convicts were "bred up in gentle life," and successive governors of New South Wales viewed the Specials, or educated Irish convicts, with extreme wariness; they might "contaminate" the rank and file with their ideas.

The expression of middle-class dissent from English colonial rule was the Society of United Irishmen, formed in 1791, an alliance of Dublin Catholics with Presbyterian merchants from Belfast, Down and Antrim. Its Ulster Protestant members had risen above their sectarian squabbles with the Catholic majority; they saw that English laws—especially, the crippling trade embargoes on Irish linen exports to America—oppressed them too. A free Irish Republic, they felt, was in the interest of all who made money from Irish resources and Irish labor; but what they needed was an alliance that cut across Irish religious divisions, taking its stand on Tom Paine and the *Rights of Man*.

The United Irish movement spread quite rapidly among the poor. Nobody could call the Irish peasantry of the 1790s politically educated, but it had a great deal to be angry about. It bitterly resented enclosure and tithing, the bailiffs with their writs of eviction, the landlord's bullies with their dogs and shillelaghs. The English looked to the priests to keep the peasants subdued, but the clergy did so, not out of any love for the English, but from a Christian dislike of violence and a fear of what the military could do to their parishioners.

The seeds of rebellion were already there. Before the birth of the Society of United Irishmen was formed, protest movements had risen from the peasantry and been punished by prison, exile and the gallows. The Whiteboys or Levellers, peasant gangs who toppled the new enclosure-fences around old commons, appeared in Tipperary in 1761. In 1772 the Presbyterian Hearts of Steel tried to oppose rack-renting in the Ulster counties. The Rightboys, formed to protest enclosure in Kerry in 1775, were Catholic.

Such country dissidents could not work together. In Ulster, whose population was roughly half Catholic and half Protestant, the Catholic Defenders and the Protestant Peep-o'-Day Boys fought pitched battles, to the amusement of their landlords. The achievement of Wolfe Tone and the twenty-seven other Protestants who founded the Society of United Irishmen was to merge the factions in one common goal of reform, a "cordial union," an Irish nation-state. The English were quick to strike at these nationalist subversives. The first convict ship to carry known political prisoners from Ireland to Australia was the *Marquis Cornwallis*, which sailed from Cove in August 1795 with 168 male and 73 female prisoners. Of the men, "several . . . were known by the name of Defenders, and the whole were of the very worst description."[37] The Irish began to plot mutiny as soon as the ship sailed, and when informers disclosed the plan to the captain he had more than forty men summarily flogged. Two Irish soldiers who had abetted the mutineers, Sergeant Ellis and Private Gaffney of the New South Wales Corps, were flogged and ironed to one another with handcuffs, thumbscrews and rigid slave leg-bolts. Ellis died after nine days; the captain then unshackled Gaffney from his corpse and ironed him to one of the Defenders, leaving them bolted together for the remaining five months of the voyage.

The Defenders continued to give trouble after they arrived in Australia. "Turbulent and worthless creatures," Governor Hunter called them in 1796, promising to watch them "narrowly." He had had to build new log-house jails "since it has been found necessary to send to this country such horrid characters as the people call'd *Irish Defenders*, who, I confess . . . I wish had either been sent to the coast of Africa, or some place as fit for them."[38]

There was good reason for their unrest, beyond the normal sufferings of transportation. Most of the Irish convicts already in the colony, who had come out on transports from Cork between 1791 and 1793, were doing seven years on ordinary criminal charges. But their records had not been sent with them, so no one knew how long they had to serve in Australia or when they were eligible for the tickets-of-leave that were usually given after four years' good conduct on a seven-year sentence. In one case, it took eighteen years for the lists of a shipload of political prisoners (*Anne*, 1801) to catch up. "The manner in which the convicts are sent from Ireland is so extremely careless and irregular," Hunter complained, "that it must be felt by these people as a particular hardship." No wonder that the radical Defenders off the *Cornwallis* found a ready ear among "non-political" Irish convicts who were already in New South Wales.[39]

It was taken for granted that all Irishmen were "wild" and "lawless"; and the authorities in Sydney, who had enough difficulty with the relatively tractable English prisoners, were never glad to see them. When the *Marquis Cornwallis* arrived, Judge-Advocate David Collins cast a cold eye on "Defenders, desperate and ripe for any scheme from which danger and destruction might come." The Irish women were just as bad; they had plotted "the preparing of pulverised glass to mix with the flour of which the seamen were to make their puddings. What an importation!" Half-Irish himself, Collins despised the Irish prisoners: "They do not deserve the appellation of men."[40]

Tension in Sydney between the chafed Irish and the English authorities became worse when the *Britannia* arrived in May 1797. This hell-ship, one of the worst in transportation history, arrived with 134 men and 43 women, mostly Defenders and other agrarian rebels. Within a few months, they had persuaded other Irishmen to escape inland. Sixty of them were caught and flogged; two were hanged. Others tried again, and were flogged too, since in view of their "obstinacy and ignorance . . . I conceived that there could be no better argument than a severe corporal punishment."[41]

By the middle of 1798, there were 653 Irish convicts in New South Wales, of whom some 265 were political prisoners.[42] None of them knew what had happened in Ireland since they had been sent into exile. During the year 1796, the Defenders had secretly begun to merge with the United Irishmen, and Wolfe Tone had gone to France to persuade its revolutionary government to send an invasion fleet to Ireland. Once it came, he believed, the Irish middle class and peasantry would rise together. The French landing at Bantry Bay in 1796 was a fiasco, however, and the English Tories unleashed a storm of reprisals, setting Orange against Green, Protestant against Catholic.

The time was ripe for an alliance of Catholic and Protestant under the United Irish banner. In 1797 martial law was declared in Ulster, and William Orr, a Protestant United Irishman who would be transported without trial to Australia on the *Friendship* in 1800, greeted this as a sign. "All ground of jealousy between us and the Catholics is now done away," he declared.

> [The English] have denied us reform and them emancipation. They have oppressed them with penal laws and us with military ones. . . . [T]here is nothing surer than that Irishmen of every denomination must stand or fall together.[43]

The colony had reached its flashpoint, and late in May 1798 the United Irish, who proved to have a better military organization than the English had ever dreamed, rose in rebellion. The fighting began in Kildare and flared from county to county. By July, all Ireland lay under martial law. The first victories of the rebels—at Three Rocks and Tubberneering, Wexford and Oulart—were soon converted into heroic legend by the "treason songs," to be sung in many an Australian humpy and rum shop throughout the next century; but in the end, musket was bound to prevail against pike. The momentum of the '98 rebellion was soon lost. Lord Cornwallis, the lord lieutenant of Ireland, wrote a heartsick letter to a colleague in England, asking him to judge how far worse the horrors of martial law became when that law was enforced by Irishmen, "heated with passion and revenge," guilty of "numberless murders . . . without any process or examination whatever":

> The yeomanry are in the style of the Loyalists of America, only much more numerous and powerful, and a thousand times more ferocious. These men have saved the country, but they now take the lead in rapine and murder. The feeble outrages . . . which are still committed by the rebels, serve to keep up the sanguinary disposition on our side. . . . [T]he conversation, even at my table, where you may suppose I do all I can to

prevent it, always turns on hanging, shooting, burning, etc., and if a priest
has been put to death, the greatest joy is expressed by the whole company.
So much for Ireland, and my wretched situation.[44]

Such were the memories transplanted to Australia on the next convict ships full of Irish Defenders. Those sentenced to transportation in
the wake of the '98 rebellion had left a gutted country behind them,
devastated by fire, bayonet and the portable wheeled gallows, where
whole counties looked like "the carcase of a goose, standing up." So the
authorities could be a little more lenient. If every United Irishman had
been indicted for treason, they could all have been hanged—but the
jurors would still have had to go home to their villages and live among
those who knew the accused. Juries avoided capital convictions, and, an
Omagh magistrate reported, "All the United Irish who were in on trea-
sonable practices are only indicted for a lesser offence, so as to come
under transportation; for that reason no objection lay against Jurors."[45]

This practice makes it hard to distinguish, on the face of recorded
charges, between "political" and "social" rebels—if, indeed, such a distinction in time of revolution makes much sense. Many of the prisoners
who went to Australia on charges related to property damage or assault
were probably, in their own eyes, as much political prisoners as Joseph
Holt, the farmer who rose to lead the Wicklow insurgents after some
Protestant militia burned his house in May 1798.

When nine ships appeared from the Pacific with the condemned men
and women of the '98 rebellion on board, they brought the worst load of
bitterness the System had yet seen. Of the 1,067 people on board, 775
were at a conservative estimate political exiles.[46] They presented a new
problem. As a jail for passive English felons, Sydney in 1800 was fairly
secure. But how to handle the Irish? In 1798 Hunter had already begged
for fewer rebels: "The infant state of this colony will not admit of it
being filled up with the very worst of characters."[47] The great fear was
another rebellion. "The *Minerva* arrived about a month ago with the first
cargo of rebels," Elizabeth Paterson, wife of the lieutenant-governor,
wrote to her uncle. "They have already begun to concert schemes—I fear
they will be a troublesome lot—I cannot say I like the place near so well
as I did before."[48]

The ship contained not only Irish rank and file but also some lesser
leaders who had been named in the Banishment and Fugitive Acts: Joseph Holt, and a medical doctor from Cork named Bryan O'Connor; two
seditious teachers, William Maum and Farrel Cuffe; a Kildare priest,
James Harold; and a Protestant clergyman, Henry Fulton. Literate and
thinking men like these were bound to be a nuisance, or even a real
danger, in British eyes; presently Governor King would inveigh against

Maum, who had written "pipes" (seditious pasquinades) against him. "His principles and conduct have changed as little as the others, nor can time and place have any Effect on such depraved characters. . . . [We] may treat such Incendiaries with Contempt."[49] Yet Governor Hunter had taken pity on them at first. They were softhanded and "bred up in genteel life," he told Portland:

> We can scarcely divest ourselves of the common feelings of humanity so far as to send a physician, a formerly respectable sheriff of a county, a Roman Catholic priest, or a Protestant clergyman and family to the grubbing hoe or the timber carriage.[50]

Yet this restraint did not survive the rumors of Irish conspiracy. In September 1800 they grew loud, and Hunter set up a court of inquiry to look into them. The Irish, informers said, had made iron pikes on secret forges and hidden them around Toongabbie and Parramatta, ready for the rising of the "Croppies" (as Irish peasants, being sharecroppers, were called). There were signs, tokens and passwords. "A ship is in sight." "What ship?" "A store-ship." But after a week's interrogation, the court had nothing but rumors, and certainly no pikes. Nevertheless, it found that "seditious meetings" had been held, "tending to excite a Spirit of Discontent which was fast ripening to a serious Revolt." Five "ringleaders" were to get 500 lashes each, and the Catholic priest, Father Harold, must watch their torment "as a peculiar Mark of Infamy and Disgrace." Then, along with "General" Holt and a dozen other suspects, they would all be sent to Norfolk Island, "where the baneful Influence of their Example cannot be experienced."[51]

Hunter might not have carried this out. But as the convicts' bad luck had it, his term of office finished on September 28 and his successor, Philip Gidley King, endorsed the court's suggestions. Meanwhile the Reverend Samuel Marsden was making his own inquiries among the Irish at Parramatta.

Marsden (1764–1838), a grasping Evangelical missionary with heavy shoulders and the face of a petulant ox, had sailed to New South Wales in 1793 as the protégé of William Wilberforce, who recommended him as assistant to the chaplain of the colony. Once there, the protégé showed few of his patron's instincts to mercy, but focused his considerable energies on getting land, breeding sturdy Suffolk sheep, preaching hellfire sermons and (as magistrate at Parramatta) subjecting convicts to draconic punishment—hence his nickname, "The Flogging Parson." Marsden soon became the chief Anglican clergyman in New South Wales, and his hatred for the Irish Catholic convicts knew no bounds. It spilled into his sermons, pervaded his table talk and was set down at length in a ranting memo to his church superiors in London which, for bigotry, rivals William Dampier's thoughts on the Australian blacks:

> The number of Catholic Convicts is very great . . . and these in general composed of the lowest Class of the Irish nation; who are the most wild, ignorant and savage Race that were ever favoured with the light of Civilization; men that have been familiar with . . . every horrid Crime from their Infancy. Their minds being destitute of every Principle of Religion & Morality render them capable of perpetrating the most nefarious Acts in cool Blood. As they never appear to reflect upon Consequences; but to be . . . always alive to Rebellion and Mischief, they are very dangerous members of Society. No Confidence whatever can be placed in them. . . . They are extremely superstitious, artful and treacherous, which renders it impossible for the most watchful & active Government to discover their real Intentions. . . . [If Catholicism were] tolerated they would assemble together from every Quarter, not so much from a desire of celebrating Mass, as to recite the Miseries and Injustice of their Banishment, the Hardships they suffer, and to enflame one another's Minds with some wild Scheme of Revenge.[52]

Marsden was set on finding the pikes, and his belief in conspiracy was confirmed by such vague observations as this from Hester Stroud, an illiterate prisoner off the *Sugar Cane:* "From what she saw of the Irishmen being in small parties in the Camp at Toongabby and by their walking about together and talking very earnestly in Irish, deponent verily believes they were intent on something improper."[53] Gaelic, of course, was their native tongue and many spoke nothing else. But Marsden was so certain they were hiding something that he resolved to have some of them "punished very severely" until they talked. Joseph Holt—who, as a voluntary transportee, could not so easily be tortured—was brought up to Toongabbie to watch the lord's representative in Australia, the Flogging Parson, at work. In his description of Marsden's interrogations under the blue indifferent Australian sky one sees the heroic determination to resist the tyrant that some of these Irish felt and paid for, as their spines were slowly opened to the air and the blowflies. The first one up was Maurice Fitzgerald, a middle-aged farmer from Cork, transported for life on the *Minerva* and now sentenced to 300 lashes.

> The place they flogged them their arms pulled around a large tree and their breasts squeezed against the trunk so the men had no power to cringe. . . . There was two floggers, Richard Rice and John Johnson the Hangman from Sydney. Rice was a left-handed man and Johnson was right-handed, so they stood at each side, and I never saw two threshers in a barn move their strokes more handier than those two man-killers did.

The moment they began I turned my face round towards the other side and one of the constables came and desir'd me to turn and look on. I put my right hand in my pocket and pulled out my pen-knife, and swore I [would] rip him from the navel to the chin. They all gathered round me and would have ill used me . . . [but] they were obliged to walk off. I could compare them to a pack of hounds at the death of a hare, all yelping.

I was to leeward of the floggers. . . . I was two perches from them. The flesh and skin blew in my face as it shook off the cats. Fitzgerald received his 300 lashes. Doctor Mason—I will never forget him—he used to go feel his pulse, and he smiled, and said: "This man will tire you before he will fail—Go on." . . . During the time [Fitzgerald] was getting his punishment he never gave so much as a word—only one, and that was saying, "Don't strike me on the neck, flog me fair."

When he was let loose, two of the constables went and took hold of him by the arms to keep him in the cart. I was standing by. [H]e said to them, "Let me go." He struck both of them with his elbows in the pit of the stomach and knocked them both down, and then stepped in the cart. I heard Dr. Mason say that man had strength enough to bear 200 more.

Next was tied up Paddy Galvin, a young boy about 20 years of age. He was ordered to get 300 lashes. He got one hundred on the back, and you could see his backbone between his shoulder blades. Then the Doctor ordered him to get another hundred on his bottom. He got it, and then his haunches were in such a jelly that the Doctor ordered him to be flogged on the calves of his legs. He got one hundred there and as much as a whimper he never gave. They asked him if he would tell where the pikes were hid. He said he did not know, and would not tell. "You may as well hang me now," he said, "for you never will get any music from me so." They put him in the cart and sent him to the Hospital.[54]

The frustrated Marsden reported to Governor King that "I am sure [Galvin] will die before he reveals anything."* King ordered a second court of inquiry, which concluded (once again) that although there was no evidence, things looked suspicious; so the "several atrocious offenders" on whom suspicion fell should be flogged again and sent to life exile on Norfolk Island, with "the strictest discipline to reduce them to due obedience, subordination and order." Thus, the Irish suspects were shipped off to the tender mercies of Major Foveaux.[55]

None of this assuaged the fears of the free colonists, who remained— as Elizabeth Paterson wrote to a friend in October 1800—in "an uncomfortable state of anxiety . . . [at] the late importations of United Irishmen. . . . Our military force is now very little in comparison with the number of Irish now in the Colony, and that little much divided. Much trouble

---

* Both lived; Galvin received a free pardon from the compassionate Governor Macquarie in 1810, Fitzgerald in 1812.

may befall us, before any succours can arrive. . . . [O]ther ships with the same description of people are now on their voyage to this place."[56]

At Sydney Cove, the ships kept coming. The *Anne*, in 1801, brought "137 of the most desperate and diabolical characters . . . together with a Catholic priest of the most notorious, seditious and rebellious principles," wrote King, "which makes the numbers of . . . United Irishmen amount to 600, ready and waiting an opportunity to put their diabolical plans in action."[57] Anxiety was running so high that people could not even farm properly; the infant colony was glutted by "violent Republicans" and imperilled by no less than three Irish priests, the most recent of whom, Father Peter O'Neil, had been transported untried after being tortured for information in a Dublin jail, with 275 lashes on his back. (Father O'Neil was later pardoned and returned to Dublin at the end of 1802, much shaken by his experiences in Sydney and Norfolk Island.) King felt it was a breach of security to have priests in the colony. The Irish interpreted this as one more violation of their rights to Mass and the Sacraments. They petitioned King once, twice and again to let Father Dixon, transported on *Friendship* in early 1800, say Mass for them. King thought Dixon's conduct had been "exemplary," and so perhaps he would not inflame his flock with seditious notions. The governor weighed the matter. "An artful priest may lead [Irishmen] to every action that is either good or bad." But more than 25 percent of the convicts in New South Wales were now Irish, and their religious impulses must have some vent. To the disgust of Samuel Marsden, King permitted Father Dixon to say mass once a month, "under stipulated restrictions"—meaning police surveillance. The first Mass and the first Catholic marriage in Australia were celebrated in Sydney on Sunday, May 15, 1803.[58]

Meanwhile the Irish had convinced themselves that the masters of convict ships had been under orders to starve and murder them by neglect on the outward voyage. They had reason to think so. When the *Hercules* arrived from Cork in 1802 it showed a 37 percent death rate; on *Atlas II*, 65 of 181 Irish convicts died. King found this "a situation shocking to humanity," but it was pointless to try and persuade the Irish that it was unintentional.[59]

The surprising fact is not that the Irish eventually rose but that they took so long before doing it. It was not until 1804 that rebellion broke out, and it did not last long, for it was badly planned. In his dying confession to Samuel Marsden, one of the rebel leaders, William Johnston, said that the Irish had been talking about a rising all through February 1804 but had fixed no date for it. The idea was to take the relatively ill-guarded and remote settlement of Castle Hill, seize what weapons they could, link up with Irish convicts in Parramatta and then march all together on Sydney. A password was fixed ("St. Peter"). But because of poor communication between the settlements, the attempt was ill-coordinated and, worse, there was an informer: an Irishman named Keogh, who had been thatching a Hawkesbury farmhouse when a fellow convict approached him with word that the rising was planned for the 4th or 5th of March. Keogh took this news to the Parramatta barracks, and before long all the guards in Sydney and Parramatta were counting their ammunition.

On Sunday, March 4, a Protestant chaplain named Hassall preached to the "desperate characters" at Castle Hill, but only a fraction of the two hundred convicts there came to hear him, "from which circumstance I thought that some alarm would take place." The Reverend Hassall guessed right, for the Irish rose at Castle Hill at seven that evening. They set fire to a house to announce their revolt and then ran from cottage to cottage, grabbing what arms they could find—mostly scythes and axes, but a few muskets as well. A convict stonemason, Philip Cunningham, hopped up on a stump and harangued his mates—"He sang out, Now my Boys, Liberty or Death"—and away they marched in the dusk to Parramatta, singing their treason songs. On the way some of them burst into the cottage of Duggin, the hated government flogger at Castle Hill, and beat him up. They also found a full keg of rum and, fortified, they split into parties and spent the night looting farms and exhorting other Irish assigned men to join them. Inspired by the rum and the headier intoxication of their liberty, they saw the roof beams of the burning sheds knuckle under, black against gold-vermilion, into the heart of the fire, while trails of sparks wreathed upward into the lavender darkness and the Irish voices joined a capella in the rebel anthem of '98, "The Croppy Boy":

> It was early, early in the spring
> The birds did whistle and sweetly sing
> Changing their notes from tree to tree,
> And the song they sang was Old Ireland free.
>
> It was early, early in the night,
> The yeoman cavalry gave me a fright,
> The yeoman cavalry was my downfall,
> And taken was I by Lord Cornwall.

As the commotion gathered in the dark and the news of the rebellion filtered into Parramatta from the outlying farms, a cry ran from house to house: "The Croppies are coming!" The Reverend Marsden, with his wife and Mrs. Elizabeth Macarthur, prudently scrambled into a boat and started floating down the Parramatta River toward Sydney. Drums beat, fowling pieces were loaded with ball and the little garrison kept anxious watch. The glow of burning sheds and shanties was seen in the distance. But meanwhile, a horseman had reached Sydney with news of the Castle Hill rising. Governor King learned about it by midnight, only five hours after it began, and he immediately had a detachment of four officers and fifty-two privates of the New South Wales Corps mustered out of barracks.[60]

One is apt to think of the Rum Corps as a rabble of incompetents, but they performed well enough that night. Commanded by Major George Johnston, they set off at 1:30 a.m. and achieved a forced march from Sydney to Parramatta by dawn, with full equipment and musket. The town was intact when they arrived, and after a swig of water and a bite of biscuit Major Johnston split his detachment into two sections, sending one toward Castle Hill and leading the other at double time along the road to Toongabbie. But the Irish were not there either. They had moved on toward the banks of the Hawkesbury River, and Johnston and his men had to chase them for another ten miles.

The "croppies" made their stand, such as it was, on a knoll which later became known as Vinegar Hill, after the site of a famous rebel battle in Wexford six years before. They had been wandering about and drinking all night, and the first rush of excitement had long since dissipated. Sheepish and confused, they did not know what to do when the "lobster-backs" in their sweat-soaked red tunics fanned out at the bottom of the hill and Major Johnston (accompanied by his adjutant and, on foot, the Catholic priest Father Dixon, who wanted to negotiate a truce without bloodshed if he could) rode forward to meet them. The Irish leaders Phillip Cunningham and William Johnston stepped out. Major Johnston said he wanted to parley. Cunningham told him to come into the rebel ranks, "which I refused, observing to them that I was within pistol-shot and that it was in their power to kill me, and that their captains must have very little spirit if they would not come forward to speak to me."[61]

At this, Cunningham and Johnston naïvely supposed the major had come in a spirit of truce. They walked up to his horse, Cunningham protesting that his men would not surrender, "that he would have Death or Liberty." Major Johnston and his trooper promptly drew their pistols and clapped them to the rebel leaders' heads, forcing them back into the ranks of the government soldiers. Then Major Johnston gave the order to fire.

The scene is fairly well rendered by an illustration of the time. Cunningham, hat in one hand and sword in the other, cries, "Death or Liberty, Major!" while Johnston, pointing his horse-pistol, retorts, "You Scoundrel, I'll liberate you!" "Croppies lie down!" the trooper barks at the rebel Johnston, who replies, "We are all ruined." In the far distance, Father Dixon exhorts the rebels to "lay down your arms, my deluded

Countrymen." A redcoat in the foreground slashes a rebel across the scalp, crying, "Thou rebel dog," while the Irishman utters (in comic accent) a woebegone "Oh Jasus." And in the middle ground, the line of serried redcoats is firing its volley as the motley Irish on the hill spout blood, stagger and fall.

In this way, fewer than thirty Botany Bay Rangers put 266 insurgents to flight within minutes. Untrained, poorly led and lightly armed with one musket for every ten men, the Irish caved in. "I never saw more zeal and activity than what has been displayed by the officers and men of the detachment for destroying or securing the runaways," Major Johnston reported with evident relish to King.[62]

They strung up Cunningham, who had been badly wounded in the melee, from the stair of the Government Store in Parramatta—no need for trial. For the next few days, under martial law, the redcoats scoured the bush and farms, bringing all the croppies in. On March 8, King convened a court-martial to try the ringleaders: John Brannon, John Burke, George Harrington, Charles Hill, Timothy Hogan, Samuel Humes, William Johnston, Bryan McCormack, John Neale and John Place. There were no courtroom heroics and the trial was brief. Seven of the ten pleaded that they had been "forced" to join the rebellion. Only William Johnston admitted all charges and threw himself on the mercy of the court. Most of them were sentenced to hang in chains, as a special mark of infamy; the only ones not hanged were Burke and McCormack. The executions were carried out at Parramatta (Hill, Humes and Place), Castle Hill (Johnston, Neale and Harrington) and Sydney (Brannon and Hogan). In this way, the greatest example could be wrung from the hangings; everyone, in all three settlements, had a chance to see what the deluded Irish slogan of "death or liberty" really meant. For months to come, the rotting bodies would dangle in their rough iron frames: "Butcher'd by Scores in New Wales / Dead Men—by me—shall tell sad tales," wrote John Grant, the first exile to write verse in Australia, and explained how on his trips around Parramatta

the Path . . . rises suddenly to an Eminence, from where—Alas! how often!—as I glanced down at the little valley before me, through which I had to pass—the *sight* and *smell* of a man called Johnston (hanged there in chains from a high Tree for his part in the Rebellion last March)—would often halt my steps, hold my Gaze, and in fact bring the tears flowing from my Eyes! . . . [T]he excellent character of that man, added not a little to the Shock.—Several spectacles of this kind were exhibited, until the arrival of Mrs. Kent from India in the Buffalo with her Husband, when . . . she obtained, by her entreaties, an order from Governor King for the burial of all these Martyrs who were hanging in the Sacred Cause of Liberty.[63]

Other United Irishmen were flogged nearly to death and sent to the mouth of the Hunter River, north of Sydney, to hew coal in a recently discovered seam, on a diet scarcely above starvation. As for the "less culpable" Irish, King had them worked in widely separated chain gangs on the rim of the little colony, where they were driven mercilessly "with no other intermission than the time allowed for their meals and the Sabbath."[64]

So ended the only concerted uprising of convicts ever to take place on the Australian mainland. With it, the prospects of a Jacobin rebellion were extinguished. The System had learned some valuable lessons from it—for instance, the basic strategy that political agitators should never be left long in one place or with the same company. "Altho' there are some violent perturbators in this Colony," King remarked a year later, "however, by their being occasionally removed from one Settlement to another, there is no present cause for apprehension." The croppies would murmur and grumble and distill poteen from maize, but they would never rise again.[65]

The English kept sending Irish political prisoners to New South Wales. From 1815 to 1840, the Irish countryside was in a state of more-or-less continuous civil war. At least 1,200 land-and-tithe protestors—probably many more, since not all political offenders were described as such in the ships' indents after 1816—were shipped to New South Wales. They called themselves Caravats and Carders, Whiteboys, Rightboys, Hearts of Steel and Ribbon Men. The most dangerous, from the English point of view, were the Whiteboys, who pretended to be a trade-union association for the protection of Irish peasants, but were in fact enforcers and assassins, the ancestors of today's Provisional IRA, who took on the dirty work of crushing knees, gouging eyes and burning houses that more squeamish Republicans would not touch. In the early 1830s, the Whiteboys were thought to have killed, maimed and otherwise discouraged two-thirds of the English informers in Ireland.

But neither they nor any other Irish rebels transported after the 1804 rising at Castle Hill would pose much of a threat to the System, simply because they were dispersed in an expanding colony. Settlers pushed westward from Parramatta across the Blue Mountains and into the fertile Bathurst plains beyond. They went southwest to Berrima and Bowral, and eventually down to the wide sheep plains of the high Monaro. They colonized the Hunter River Valley, inland from Newcastle. All this new property was worked by convict servants, assigned men and women. Scattered in threes and fours through the immense bush, living in outback isolation, political prisoners had no social resonance: They were neutralized by geography as much as by law.

Yet the story of English oppression and Irish resistance did not evap-

The other side of Georgian elegance, as seen by William Hogarth. Top: The Idle 'Prentice, doomed to hang, repents in the tumbril as the mob surges around Tyburn Tree (1749). Above: The proletariat ruined by addiction to spirits, in *Gin Lane*, 1750–51. (*The Bettmann Archive*)

OPPOSITE ABOVE: A Georgian satirist views the convicts' departure in the 1790s, as two flash lads bid adieu to their battered doxies and an official grimly points to the "Bay ship" waiting at anchor. Anonymous, *Farewell to Black-Eyed Sue and Sweet Poll of Plymouth*. (*National Library of Australia, Canberra*) OPPOSITE BELOW: Thomas Rowlandson, *Convicts Embarking for Botany Bay*, c. 1787–88. In the background, an alternative to transportation: a gibbet, with felons hanging in chains. (*National Library of Australia, Canberra*) ABOVE: Punishment by public labor on maritime projects: hulk prisoners working on the Thames at Woolwich in 1777. On the left, muscle-powered dredgers cleaning the river bottom; in the foreground, convicts laboring to construct a breakwater. Their prison hulk is anchored in midstream. (*National Library of Australia, Canberra*) RIGHT: Captain Arthur Phillip, the *Pater Patriae* of Australians, Commodore of the First Fleet and Governor of New South Wales, holding the sketch of a fort to be erected in the new colony. Portrait by Francis Wheatley, 1787. (*Mitchell Library and Dixson Collections, Sydney*) BELOW RIGHT: An idealized allegory of the infant colony: *Hope Encouraging Art and Labour, under the Influence of Peace*, a medal made from the clay of Sydney Cove by Josiah Wedgwood. (*Mitchell Library and Dixson Collections, Sydney*)

The *Sirius,* flagship of the First Fleet, rides at anchor in Sydney Cove with her tender, the *Supply*—and, to the despair of the colonists, is wrecked on the reef at Norfolk Island, a thousand miles away. Watercolors by George Raper (1768?–1797), midshipman on *Sirius.* (*British Museum of Natural History, London*)

The embryo of a city, its barracks and houses built by convict labor in the quarter-century since the arrival of Europeans. John Eyre, *A North-East View of the Town of Sydney . . . Taken from the West Side of Bennelong's Point*, 1812. (*Mitchell Library and Dixson Collections, Sydney*)

Conflict begins between blacks and whites on the harbor shores, as Iora tribesmen make ready to spear a convict. "Port Jackson Painter," *The Hunted Rushcutter*, c. 1790. (*British Museum of Natural History, London*)

The Noble Savage: At the first moment of contact between Cook's expedition and the Aborigines of Botany Bay, two warriors oppose the landing. They are commemorated in the poses of antique statuary by the botanical artist on Joseph Bank's scientific team. T. Chambers after Sydney Parkinson, *Two of the Natives of New Holland advancing to Combat*, 1773. (*Mitchell Library and Dixson Collections, Sydney*)

Further developments of the Aborigine in European eyes. ABOVE: The "Barbarian New-Hollander" as Domestic Savage, rude in family customs, depicted by a Scots convict artist: Thomas Watling, *A Groupe on the North Shore of Port Jackson*, c. 1794. (*British Museum of Natural History, London*) RIGHT: The Comic Savage, after twenty-five more years of white occupation: R. Browne, *Long Jack*, 1819. (*Mitchell Library and Dixson Collections, Sydney*)

OPPOSITE ABOVE: The hills of Norfolk Island, seen by a convict artist. Note the many stumps; the virgin forest of Norfolk Island pine was receding by the end of the first settlement. John Eyre, *A View of Queensborough on Norfolk Island*, c. 1812. (*Mitchell Library and Dixson Collections, Sydney*) OPPOSITE BELOW: The jail complex at Kingston on Norfolk Island, falling into decay by the 1870s, seen from the flank of Telegraph Hill. The remains of the Pentagonal Prison can be seen within the security wall of the compound. (*National Library of Australia, Canberra*) RIGHT: Major Foveaux's jailer remembers discipline on Norfolk Island in the 1800s: *The Flogging of Charles Maher*, watercolor in Robert Jones's "Recollections." "The flogging of Charles Maher almost brought about a mutiny. His back was quite bare of skin and flesh. Poor wretch, he received 250 lashes and on receiving 200 Kimberley refused to count, meaning that the punishment was enough." (*Mitchell Library and Dixson Collections, Sydney*) BELOW: The beginnings of Hobart Town on the Derwent River in Van Diemen's Land, with the bulk of Mount Wellington rising behind. Pen sketch, perhaps by the surveyor George Prideaux Harris, 1804. (*National Library of Australia, Canberra, Rex Nan Kivell Collection*)

The Flogging of Charles Maher

1. Gov.t House
2. Chaplains
3. D.t Surveyor Gen.t
4. Surgeon
5. Commissary
6. Printing Office
7. Guard House
8. Hospital
9. 2 Assistant Surgeons
10. Commissary Cottage
11. Blacksmiths &c
12. Hunter Island Slaughter
13. Jetty
14. Magazine
15. Barracks
16. Table Mou
18. G.P.H. Cotta
19. Rivulet
Capt. Haddens Cotting

"They lay anchored in files on the gray heaving water, bow to stern, a rookery of sea-isolated crime." The hulks—decommissioned naval ships used as prisons—were an essential part of convict management in the early years of transportation. ABOVE: Louis Garnery, *Portsmouth Harbour with Prison Hulks*, c. 1820. RIGHT: G. Cooke after S. Prout, *Convict Hulk at Deptford*, 1826. (*National Library of Australia, Canberra, Rex Nan Kivell Collection*)

Rebellion and escape. ABOVE: The 1804 Irish rising at Castle Hill near Parramatta, recorded by an anonymous artist. "Death or Liberty, Major," exclaims the leader of the revolt, and Major Johnson, in command of the "Botany Bay Rangers," replies, "You scoundrel, I'll liberate you." (*National Library of Australia, Canberra*) LEFT: "The Flogging Parson," the Reverend Samuel Marsden (1764–1838), Evangelical chaplain, missionary, sheepbreeder and implacable scourge of the Irish convicts. (*Mitchell Library and Dixson Collections, Sydney*)

The convict Popjoy and Morgan, building the coracle which they used to obtain rescue for the castaways. Lieut. Carew (lamenting), with wife and children. From the w.cut by the artist convict Wm. B. Gould, printed in The Hobart Town Courier, 12, Sept., 1829.

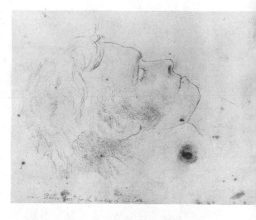

ABOVE: The castaways of the brig *Cyprus:* a woodcut by the convict artist William Gould, printed in 1829, shows Lieutenant Carew lamenting on the hostile shores of Macquarie Harbor, while two loyal convicts, Popjoy and Morgan, helped by Mrs. Carew, build a coracle for their survival. (*Mitchell Library and Dixson Collections, Sydney*) RIGHT: A pencil drawing of the Irish cannibal and absconder Alexander Pearce, made in the Hobart morgue after his hanging, from Thomas Bock's "Sketches of Australian Bushrangers," 1823. (*Mitchell Library and Dixson Collections, Sydney*)

OPPOSITE ABOVE: James Taylor, *The Entrance of Port Jackson and Port of Sydney Town*, 1821. Note the convict gang quarrying sandstone at left, the relaxed New South Wales Corps officers in the foreground and the tame kangaroo. (*Mitchell Library and Dixson Collections, Sydney*) OPPOSITE BELOW: The Great Perturbator and the Patriot-Chief: John Macarthur, the New South Wales Corps officer who created a pastoral dynasty and was leader of the Exclusives; and Governor Lachlan Macquarie (1762–1824), the veteran soldier who ruled New South Wales from 1810 to 1821, striving to bring Emancipists into the colonial power structure. (*Mitchell Library and Dixson Collections, Sydney*) BELOW: Georgian architecture comes to Sydney: the hospital in Macquarie Street, designed by Governor Macquarie and his wife with the help of a pattern book, and financed by rum. (*Mitchell Library and Dixson Collections, Sydney*)

OVERLEAF ABOVE: In a watercolor by Augustus Earle, c. 1819, an overseer shows the new Female Factory at Parramatta, designed by Macquarie's convict architect Francis Greenway, to two of its future inmates. (*National Library of Australia, Canberra*) OVERLEAF BELOW: Lieutenant Ralph Clark of the First Fleet and his "dear picture" of his wife, Betsy Alicia Clark, "surely an angel and not a woman," his idealized contrast to the "damned bitches of convict women" he had been sent to guard. (*Mitchell Library and Dixson Collections, Sydney*)

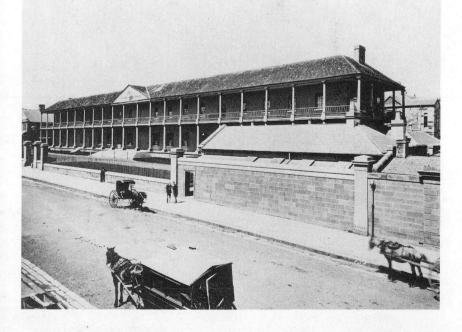

orate in Australia. On the contrary: It survived most tenaciously as one of the primary images of working-class culture, flourishing long after the System itself had receded from memory. The Irish stuck to one another. They were clannish and had long memories: "much hatred, little room." They always felt they were being punished, not for their crimes, but for being Irish. In Australia, as in Ireland, each act of oppression contributed to a common fund of memory; fact might waver into legend, but the essential content did not change. By the 1880s, when the Protestant majority in Australia had all but sublimated the "hated stain" of convictry, the Irish still kept the memory of the System alive. Naturally, they also fostered the ennobling delusion that most Irish convicts had been sent to the Fatal Shore for political offenses, as though there had been no common thieves, muggers or rapists among the 30,000 men and 9,000 women who had been transported directly from Ireland. Of course, the numbers contradict the myth. Probably no more than 20 percent of the Irish transportees could have been called social or political rebels (except by those, if they still exist, who imagine that all crimes against property are political statements). And the hard core—those transported between 1793 and 1840 for political crimes (as distinct from actions related to riot, such as assault or destruction of property, which were usually treated as common felonies)—numbered less than 1,500.[66] Nevertheless, the legacy of sectarianism in Australian politics, the sense of a community divided between English Protestant "haves" and Irish Catholic "have-nots," began with them and influenced the patterns of power in Australian life for another 150 years.

vi

THIS DID NOT HAPPEN with English political dissidents. But between 1800 and 1850, at the most conservative estimate, about 1,800 people were transported to Australia from England for political "crimes." Among them were representatives of nearly every protest movement known to the British Government, so that Australia received samples (if not big influxes) of most working-class movements. Frame-breaking Luddites were sent out in 1812–13, and food rioters from East Anglia in 1816. Fourteen members of the betrayed Pentridge Rising near Nottingham were exiled in 1817, and five dazed fanatics from the Cato Street Conspiracy—which had absurdly hoped to set off a general insurrection of English workers by assassinating Lord Sidmouth's cabinet as its members sat down to dinner—came in 1820. Radical weavers from Scotland in 1820 and from Yorkshire in 1821, rioters from Bristol in 1831 and Wales in 1835; Swing rioters and machine-breakers in the early 1830s, the Tolpuddle Martyrs in 1834, more than 100 Chartists between 1839 and 1848—all went to Australia. So did "politicals" from other countries. From 1828 to 1838, the Supreme Court at the Cape transported each year 30 to 40 members of what it called "the excitable classes"—South African blacks* who, although they seem to have had no political ideas, were believed to have transgressed the racial supremacist laws of the Cape colony; there, transportation was another threat to keep the Hottentots and Bushmen in line.[67]

In Canada in 1837 and 1838, there were two risings against the Tory legislature, the Anglican Church and their seeming unbreakable power over law and land: one by "Lower Canada" (Quebec) militants, the other in "Upper Canada" (Ontario) by English-speaking Canadians backed by some Americans from south of the border. Both these insurrections of tradesmen and farmers were put down by the British Army, and 153 Canadian *patriotes* were transported to Australia.[68]

Of course, the number of Englishmen transported was only a minuscule fraction of those indicted for protest offenses. But the government, especially up to 1830, did not want to transport every English protestor; it wanted to demonstrate its weapons of repression while keeping intact, as far as possible, its reputation for "mercy," which it could sustain by not pressing for extreme penalties in court.

Never had there been deeper unrest among the common people of England than between 1810 and 1845; hopelessness, poverty and resentment were endemic to postwar Britain, and they expressed themselves in a rising sense of class crisis that traced the graph of England's economic malaise. The climax of this tension, between 1830 and 1845, saw more than 10 percent of the working population of England classified as paupers, thrown by the Poor Laws on the meager charity of the parish. Working people believed, with reason, that their government cared nothing for them; and manufacturers complained that official economic policy was strangling growth. Eric Hobsbawm pointed out that "in the post-Napoleonic decades the figures of the balance of payments show us the extraordinary spectacle of the only industrial economy in the world and the only serious exporter of manufactured goods unable to maintain an export surplus in its commodity trade."[69] But for this, men were losing

---

* These were not the first black convicts to arrive in Australia; in the 1790s a small number of blacks, usually servants or slaves who had been brought to London from the West Indies and then been transported for theft, made their appearance in Sydney. One, a First Fleet convict nicknamed Black Caesar, had become Australia's first bushranger by "eloping" into the scrub in 1789 with a stolen gun and making one-man raids on tents and vegetable gardens; when this "mere animal," as David Collins referred to him, was captured, he proved "so indifferent about meeting death, that he declared in confinement that if he should be hanged, he would create a laugh before he was turned off, by playing some trick upon the executioner."

the only jobs they could do. The bitterness of the silk-weaver thrown out of work by machinery came, not solely from his own poverty, but from the sense that a whole tradition of craftwork was being thrust into oblivion by inferior products. This despair was reinforced by the anomie of city life; the Machine, with its demand for new concentrations of labor in new places, was creating a society of people who no longer knew who they were or where they came from.

Such dissatisfactions ran so deep that governments from Pitt's to Sidmouth's invented a demonology to explain them: "Our" common people would never feel this if left to their natural inclinations; hence, they have been wrought upon by foreign agents, the French; thus, all protest is tinged with treason. From the 1790s to the 1820s, the government found itself increasingly hampered by the apparatus of spies and agents it had set up to penetrate movements of working-class dissent. It was drowning in spurious information, distracted by the phantom of insurrection. This made it easier for it to ignore or misunderstand the clear import of demands for reform. It helps explain the often remarkable disproportion between the mild deeds of political protestors and the vindictiveness with which the social death of transportation was inflicted on them. It may also suggest why so many English political transportees, unlike their Irish counterparts, seem to have shed their "radical" attributes once they decided to stay on as Emancipists and enjoy the high wages that free skilled labor could command in Australia. They had been protesting against want, not foreign occupation; and in Australia, want could be relieved.

The heyday of political transportation from England was the 1830s. The 1820s were by no means peaceful, although corn prices were lower, the hated Lord Castlereagh had been succeeded by the more moderate George Canning, and workers, especially industrial workers, seemed better off. This did not apply in the country, however. To William Cobbett —who had just returned from his American exile carrying the bones of Tom Paine in a box and had set out on the long journey on horseback through the shires that was to give him the material for *Rural Rides*— the once-sturdy countryfolk of England were "villeins" and "serfs." He railed against Abolitionists like Wilberforce who, he claimed, cared more for the condition of African slaves in the colonies than for the fate of English workers at home. Most rural workers were below the poverty line at a shilling a day or less; some earned only three shillings a week. But the Tory politicians of the day saw the problem in terms of one hypnotic ideology: that of Malthus, who taught that it was futile to spend any money on poor relief, since it would only encourage the poor to breed and thus make the problem worse. If left to survive or starve, the poor would find their "natural" level. And since the out-of-work did not, by definition, generate wealth, their survival was not an issue for the government.

Aggravated by a slump in the economy and a rise in staple prices toward the end of the 1820s, such was the background to the political unrest that after 1830 landed the largest single group of protestors in Australia. Most of them were tried and convicted in the southern counties, where farm wages were lowest; and their crime was complicity in what came to be known as "The Last Laborers' Revolt." The figurehead around whom they rallied was a fictional leader to whom custom gave the name of Captain Swing: a bogeyman to the propertied, in whose name threatening letters were tacked on gateposts and shoved under front doors in the dead of night. These were known as "Swing letters" and the disturbances they promised were "Swing riots."

Captain Swing stood for several issues. He expressed grievances against the loss of common land by the policy of enclosure. He protested against high wheat prices. The Corn Laws, framed to help English farmers by keeping cheap European wheat off the market, naturally worked against the poor in times of shortage; and by 1830 many farm laborers were deprived of their white bread. Efforts to feed them potatoes were indignantly rejected. The English worker believed his bread and cheese set him several cuts above the porridge-eating Scot or the root-grubbing Irish croppie. The loaf of wheat bread was, to him, a natural right, and the fact that landlords and gentry ignored such traditions did not make them unreal.[70] The protestor's weapon was fire: a match at the base of a hayrick.

The other issue behind the Swing riots was mechanization. The impact of steam-driven farm machinery on unskilled rural labor was disastrous. One threshing-machine, rented out and hauled from farm to farm, could put a hundred men out of seasonal work. The economist today sees this as the natural result of technology; the farmworker in 1830 saw it as a cruel denial of his natural right to work. Both are right, one in the historical perspective, the other in the immediate world of need. So, like the Luddities before them, the Swing rioters went for the machines, breaking the rollers, holing the boilers, jamming the gears with crowbars.

Most Swing threats were inspired by rural grievances. Thus on January 20, 1831, an eighteen-year-old solicitor's clerk named Thomas Cook, from Whitchurch in Shropshire, wrote a letter to a local cabinetmaker and auctioneer named William Churton:

> We men of determination, firm, resolute, and undeviating, are now without scruple and determined that your property shall not be of long duration, nor yet your existence—property which has been got through roguery.

Roguery Churton has been your practice since first you were established in life, but no longer shall it be continued.

Mark, therefore, the time is at hand when your blood shall atone for your rash and untoward acts. We shall waylay your body, and bring your family to total subversion, which you know you are well deserving. . . . PS, we give you this previous note in order that you may prepare for that awful and sad end.

SIGNED: Men determined to right the oppressed. Agents to Swing. London.[71]

Why make such threats to a provincial cabinetmaker? Because, although Churton was not a landowner, he had helped put out fires. During 1830–31 there were no less than sixteen acts of arson—rickburning and barnburning—in the vicinity of Whitchurch, which seems to have been a hotbed of rural political dissent. Churton was among the "respectables" who had called for more police protection and harsher punishment for incendiarists. So Thomas Cook was convicted at the Shrewsbury Assizes in March 1831 and sentenced to fourteen years in Australia, where in due course he would write his invaluable account of the System, *The Exile's Lamentations.*

Compared to Ireland thirty years before, the rioting of 1830–31 was mild; in any case, it was directed against property, not people. But it spread rapidly across the southern counties, where rural wages were about one-third the national average. Men marched, burned ricks and broke machines in Kent and Surrey, Shropshire and Lincolnshire, Berkshire, Wiltshire, Hampshire, Essex, Oxfordshire, Dorset and Norfolk. These "curiously indecisive and unbloodthirsty mobs"[72] were harshly met by Lord Grey's new Whig government. It offered the enormous reward of £500 for the capture and conviction of arsonists and machinebreakers, and it sent army detachments and locally organized posses against them. Some counties raised their own squads of mounted yeomanry to ride down the protestors. Lord Melbourne enjoined all magistrates to maintain "a firm Resistance to all demands."

To frighten protestors, the Whig government now began an orgy of prosecution. Nearly 2,000 insurgents were tried in 34 counties. Of these, 252 were sentenced to death but, in the usual way of showing the Royal Mercy, only 19 of them were actually hanged and the rest had their sentences commuted to prison or transportation. In this roundup, 481 Swing followers were shipped out to Australia, for terms of seven or fourteen years.[73]

Most of them were older than the normal run of transported felons— an average of twenty-nine years among those sent to Van Diemen's Land, as against the convict average of just under twenty-six years. More than half of them were married men. Many of them had letters of commendation from former employers, and not a few were skilled craftsmen or "mechanics," the most desirable kind of assigned servant in Australia. This puzzled the magistrates: What could a millwright, a carpenter or a blacksmith have to fear from the threshing-machines? But these skilled and settled people could read; they knew they had allies in Cobbett and Tom Paine, and they were often the first villagers to speak of rights and to raise discontent among their less skilled and literate neighbors. The case of one Hampshire radical, William Winkworth, a shoemaker who read Cobbett aloud to a circle of "bumpkins" on Saturday nights, should be multiplied by many hundreds to grasp its social import.[74] Now their lives were shattered, their hopes gone, their families riven as the transport ships bore them away.

Not one of them seems to have sustained any overt kind of political activity in Australia. In fact the surviving letters from transported protestors of 1830–31—Richard Dillingham and Peter Withers in Van Diemen's Land—sketch a scene of resignation amid relative plenty. The 1830s were prosperous years on that green, fertile island, and the demand for skilled labor was high. Dillingham had been transported as a rioter, but he seems to have had few political opinions and no connection with organized protest; he found Van Diemen's Land to be a veritable Land of Cockaigne. In 1836 he was assigned as a market-gardener to David Lambe, a mild decent settler who had held the post of colonial architect early in Sir George Arthur's regime. He was "very comfortably settled," he told his parents through a scribe, less than a mile from Hobart:

> As to my living I find it better than ever I expected thank God. I want for nothing in that respect. As for tea and sugar I could almost swim in it. I am allowed 2 pound of sugar and ¼ pound of tea per week and plenty of tobacco and good white bread and sometimes beef sometimes mutton sometimes pork. This I have every day. Plenty of fruit puddings in the season of all sorts and I have two suits of Cloths a year and three pairs of shoes in a year.[75]

Peter Withers, from Wiltshire, adds to the picture: "I have got a very good place," he told his brother in 1833,

> all the Bondage I am under is to Answer my Name Every Sunday before I goes to church, so you must not think that I am made a slave of, for I am not, it is quite the Reverse of it. And I have got a good Master and Mistress, I have got plenty to eat and drink as good as ever a gentleman in this country [has], so all the Punishment I have in this Country is the

thoughts of leaving my friends, My wife and My Dear Dear Children, but I lives in hopes of seeing Old England again.[76]

Assignment, as we will see, was a lottery; Withers and Dillingham drew good masters, whereas Thomas Cook in New South Wales suffered under a bad one. "I want for nothing but my liberty," Dillingham remarked, "but though I am thus situated it is not the same with all that come as prisoners." Clearly, however, the System made no effort to persecute English politicals *as a group*, as it had done to the Irish earlier. Individual masters might give ex-rioters a hard time because they feared unrest on their own farms, but this was uncommon. Generally, the English protestors, skilled family men with a stubborn sense of their own worth, worked out their sentences and lived on as Emancipists in Australia. Significantly fewer of them than of the ordinary criminal population committed second offenses. They had paid long and bitterly for their beliefs. As Peter Withers wrote, "16 years, that is a grate While." They were not ideologues or professional agitators, but laborers and craftsmen jealous of what they believed to be their ancient rights as Englishmen. Above all, they needed to work, and the stigma of "politics" was hard to shake: Australian squatters and settlers were even more conservative than the English squirearchy whose manners and customs they were learning to ape. "You are one of the Dorchester machine-breakers, but you are caught at last!" were the first words James Brine, one of the Tolpuddle Martyrs, heard from his new master on the Hunter River in New South Wales.

Thus most English protestors lived quietly on in Australia, doing the work England had denied them. They had no marked effect on the future politics of their new country. In England, nothing could stop the trade-union movement in the long run. But in the short run, transportation certainly worked as a tactic of repression. It knocked the fight out of its victims. At home, in the villages, it held up a frightening example to workers who had little means of knowing what had really happened to the transported men, since letters back from the Fatal Shore were rare. In Australia, it turned the protester into a political eunuch without making a martyr of him. The wives of transported men, widowed and yet not widowed, taught their sons to avoid the ways of the dissenter; some of them were asked to do so quite specifically by their husbands. In 1835 a former non-commissioned officer, who had taken part in Swing activity and was transported for political insurrection to Van Diemen's Land (where he forged a deed and was re-transported to Norfolk Island), gave the Quaker missionaries James Backhouse and George Washington Walker a letter to take home to his wife. "You and I have lived for a long

time without God in our hearts," he admonished her. But in bondage he
had come to see that his sufferings were meant "to bring me to a sense
of my own depravity and wickedness."

> You will make our children read, and get off, the above Scripture passages.
> *Never let them read any political works. Keep their minds from being
> entangled with political men, and their productions.* This, you will not
> need to be told, has been the prelude to all my present misery.[77]

Probably this fairly represents the usual feelings of transported ex-
protestors. Budding radicalism withered in the antipodes, unless—as
with the Irish—it had close bonds and ancient national grievances to
prop and feed it. In convict Australia, repression won in politics, as in
the rest of life.

Bolters and Bushrangers

i

MOST PRISONERS of the System acquiesced in their fate. They waited out their time, knowing that longer and worse constraint—the triangle, the iron gang, Norfolk Island—would be the price of rebellion. But in any carceral society, there is always a spark of genius for escape. The worse the odds, the more hope escape gives others.

In Australia it was easy to escape. The hard thing was to survive. The odds against surviving were high, but hundreds of convicts made their bets. Some confronted Australia's external wall, the sea: They stowed away, or hijacked ships, or built their own rafts, or stole a longboat. Others took to the land, even less charted than the sea. At first these runaways were called "banditti" (evoking ragged, romantic figures among dark caverns); more colloquially, "bolters." In time, the skulking escapee became that primal figure of popular Australian culture, the bushranger—enemy of flogger, trap and magistrate, the poor man's violent friend, the emblem of freedom in a chained society.

At first, from the 1790s to early 1800s, most of the runaways went inland. After a brief exhilaration they either died or wandered, broken, back to the settlement, "so squalid and lean," David Collins remarked, "the very crows would have declined their carcasses." There were reports that fifty skeletons, picked white by dingoes and birds, could be seen on a day's march to Botany Bay.

The most persistent absconders were the Irish, who in their ignorance had constructed a Paradise myth to alleviate their antipodean Purgatory. They kept sneaking out of the settlement in the belief, as one of them put it to Watkin Tench,

> that at a considerable distance to the northward existed a large river, which separated this country from the back part of China; and that when

it should be crossed (which was practicable) they would find themselves among a copper-coloured people, who would receive and treat them kindly.[1]

The fantasy of escape to China was one of the obsessive images of early transportation. Yellow girls and tea, opium and silk, queer-looking blue bridges and willows just like the ones on plates; and surcease from the hoe, the iron, the roasting sunlight and the dumb ache of hunger. For this, not a few of the "deluded Irish" died of fatigue, thirst or the spears of blacks. Their crow-pecked remains, with a rag of government slops and a rusty basil still around them, would be found in the bush between Parramatta and Pittwater.

The first large group of "Chinese travellers," as they came to be derisively known, took off from Rose Hill in November 1791—twenty men and one woman, Irish convicts off the *Queen*. They separated, blundered about in the bush for days, and in their starving bewilderment were easily recaptured (although three of them were so sure they had nearly reached China that they soon ran away again, and died). In time, the China myth was joined by another fancy, reported by Collins with his usual disapproval of the croppies who held it: "In addition to their natural vicious propensities, they conceived an opinion that there was a colony of white people, which had been discovered in this country, situated to the SW of the settlement, from which it was distant between three and four hundred miles." This other Shangri-la, where no work ever needed to be done, sustained some hope for a time.[2]

In 1798 the Irish were still running away to China, as many as sixty people at a time. Since none of them had a compass (and few possessed any idea of how to use it even if they had had one), they went out armed with a magical facsimile consisting of a circle crudely sketched on paper or bark with the cardinal points but no needle.

In 1803, King reported that fifteen "infatuated" Irish had made a run to China from Castle Hill; they were out for four days "committing every possible enormity except Murder" (one blew half a constable's face away with a musket, but he lived). The court sentenced them all to death, but King only hanged two. He then fixed the punishment for bolting at five hundred lashes, plus double chains for the remainder of the sentence. He expressed the hope that "the Convicts at Large will be assured that their ridiculous plans of leaving public labor to go into the Mountains, to China, &c., can only end in their immediate detection and punishment."[3]

As the settlement slowly moved outward and tracks were made through the raw bush, even the blindest optimist could see that the convict skeletons that kept turning up must mean something. The will to walk to Peking guttered out as it became clear that the logical escape route from this continental prison was not the land but the sea.

The sea route produced one epic escape in the early 1790s whose notoriety blossomed in London, reached back to Botany Bay and gave heart to would-be absconders for years to come. It was led by a woman, Mary Bryant (b. 1765)—"the Girl from Botany Bay," as the English press later dubbed her—who, with her two small children, her husband William Bryant, and seven other convicts, managed to sail a stolen boat all the way north from Sydney to Timor, a distance of 3,250 miles in just under ten weeks. As a nautical achievement, this compared with William Bligh's six-week voyage in a longboat from Tahiti to Timor with the "loyalists" of the *Bounty* in 1789. No one since James Cook in the *Endeavour*, twenty-one years before, had sailed all the way up the eastern coast of Australia, through the treacherous Barrier Reef, and lived to tell about it.[4]

Mary Bryant, née Broad, was a sailor's daughter from the little port of Fowey, in Cornwall. She had been transported for seven years for stealing a cloak. She went with the First Fleet, on the transport *Charlotte*. Before the fleet reached Cape Town, Mary Bryant gave birth to a girl and named her Charlotte, after the ship. Soon after the fleet reached Port Jackson, Mary Broad married one of the male convicts, who fathered her second child, Emanuel, born in April 1790. He, too, was Cornish and had come out on *Charlotte*. He was a thirty-one-year-old fisherman named William Bryant. Like many another Cornishman who kept a boat on that wild and indented coast, Bryant was a smuggler as well as a sailor, and in 1784 he had been convicted of resisting arrest at the hands of excise officers. He had already spent three years in the hulks when the First Fleet sailed, and his full seven-year sentence still loomed before him.

A fisherman was just what the half-starved colony needed. Governor Phillip put Bryant in charge of the boats that hauled the fishing nets every day in the harbor. But the black-market opportunities were too good for a Cornish smuggler to resist. He was caught selling some of his fish on the sly, instead of delivering them all to the Government Store; for this, he got one hundred lashes. If he had not set his heart on it before, Bryant was now determined to escape. At worst, he would rather drown quickly at sea than starve inch by inch on land. He had access to the boats but had no weapons, tools, navigational instruments, charts or food.

In October 1790 an East Indies trader, the *Waaksamheyd*, lumbered into Port Jackson heavily freighted with stores from Djakarta. Her Dutch captain, Detmer Smit, felt no obligations to the English convict system. He listened to William Bryant and was persuaded to part with a compass, a quadrant, muskets, food and even a chart of the waters between Sydney

and Timor. Bryant hid this precious stuff in rolls of bark under the floor-
boards of his hut and began assembling a crew. He picked his time carefully. In March 1791 the *Supply* was dispatched to Norfolk Island. At the
end of the month, *Waaksamheyd*, having sold the last of her cargo and
finished her repairs, also set sail. Now there were no ships left in Port
Jackson—nothing that could overtake an escaping boat. On the night of
March 28, in the dark of the moon, the Bryants, their two children and
seven other convicts scrambled into the governor's own six-oar cutter.
In nervous silence, holding their breaths every time the oar-blades kissed
the dark water, they rowed out into the harbor, past the little island of
Pinchgut, heading east to the gate of the Pacific. The lookout on South
Head did not see the cutter as it crept by in the night. They turned north
toward New Guinea.

Their escape caused consternation next morning. The officers could
hardly believe that although most of the men who had escaped had "connections" with female convicts in the settlement, not one woman had
breathed a word about the long-laid escape plan. "They were too faithful
to those they lived with to reveal it," observed David Collins. One of the
men, a spare-time cabinetmaker named James Cox who had been transported for life on the First Fleet for stealing 12 yards of lace and a pair of
stockings, left a note on his workbench for his lover Sarah Young. It was
a plain, fond letter, "conjuring her to give over the pursuit of the vices
which, he told her, prevailed in the settlement, leaving to her what little
property he did not take with him, and assigning as a reason for his flight
the severity of his situation, being transported for life, without the prospect of any mitigation, or hope of ever quitting the country."[5]

By no means all the guards were unsympathetic to the escape. "They
got Clear off," wrote a marine private, John Easty, in his diary,

> but its a very Desperate attempt, to go in an open boat for a run of about
> 16 or 17 hundred Leags and in pertucalar for a Woman and 2 small Chil-
> dren the eldest not above 3 years of age—but the thoughts of Liberty from
> such a place as this is Enoufh to induce any Convicts to try all Skeemes
> to obtain it, as they are the same as Slaves all the time they are in this
> Country.[6]

At first the going was easy. At their landings they found edible palms
whose hearts they chopped out, "a Varse Quantity of Fish which [was] of
a great Refreshment to us," and natives either friendly or timid. But then
the rain poured and the seas rose; for five continuous weeks, they were
soaked to the skin and rarely able to light a cooking fire. On the long
stretch of surf-bound coast between Port Macquarie and Brisbane they
were driven out to sea by an adverse wind, and "making no harbour or

Creek for nere three weeks we were much distress'd for water and food."
There was a brief respite for them in "White Bay being in Latt^d 27°"
probably Moreton Bay. But on leaving it, they were blown out to sea
again, helpless before

> a heavy Gale of Wind and Current, expecting every Moment to go to the
> Bottom; next morn^g saw no Land, the sea running Mountains high . . .
> thinking every Moment to be the last, the sea Coming in so heavy upon
> us every now and then that two Hands was obliged to keep Bailing out
> and it rained very hard all that night . . . [We] cou'd make no Land [the
> next] Day—I will leave you to Consider what distress we must be in, the
> Woman and the two little Babies was in a bad condition, everything being
> so Wet that we Cou'd by no means light a Fire, we had nothing to Eat
> except a little raw rice.[7]

After several days of this ordeal they were blown ashore, half-dead,
on one of the desert islands of the Barrier Reef. On its circling coral they
found turtles, one of which furnished "a Noble Meal this Night."
They butchered a dozen and made jerky of their meat. Thus victualled,
they made the coast again and kept creeping north, stopping for water
wherever they could get ashore, caulking the cutter—whose seams were
loosened by the incessant pounding of the ocean—with soap and turtle-
fat, fighting skirmishes with hostile blacks. Food was short all the way,
but they were all still alive when they turned the point of Cape York
Peninsula, the northernmost tip of Australia, and found themselves in
the Arafura Sea with a clear run—pursued, part of the way, by stout
cannibals in mat-sailed canoes—of five hundred miles of open water to
Arnhem Land, and another five hundred to Timor. They reached Koepang
in Timor on June 5 and passed themselves off to the local Dutch governor
as survivors of a shipwreck on the Australian coast. In new clothes, with
full bellies, they settled down to wait for a ship back to England. But
after a couple of months, by Martin's account, Bryant for some unexplained reason told the truth to the Dutch governor. Perhaps he got
drunk:

> Wm Bryant had words with his wife, went and informed against himself
> Wife and children and all of us, [upon] which we was immediately taken
> Prisoners and was put into the Castle we was strictly examined.

The governor now put them in detention. In mid-September, some
more shipwrecked Englishmen appeared from the sea at Koepang: Captain Edward Edwards, who had been chasing the *Bounty* mutineers in
the frigate *Pandora*. He had captured some of them at Tahiti but lost his

ship on a reef south of New Guinea; in the pinnace, longboat and two yawls, he and 120 survivors had escaped the wreck and made their way across the Arafura Sea to Timor. Now Edwards took the Bryants and their comrades prisoner; they were clapped in irons, put on board the *Rembang*, a Dutch East Indiaman, and shipped to Batavia. In that mephitic port, both William Bryant and his little son Emanuel died of fever just before Christmas 1791.

The survivors were shipped back to the Cape. Three of the men died at sea. At the Cape, Mary Bryant, her daughter and the remaining four convicts—James Martin, William Allen, James Brown and Nathaniel Lucas—were put on board the *Gorgon*, the man-o'-war which was carrying the marine detachment (just replaced by the newly formed New South Wales Corps) back from Australia to London. "We was well known by all of the marine officers which was all Glad that we had not perished at sea," Martin noted. That he did not exaggerate this is shown by the remarks of Captain Watkin Tench, of the Royal Marines, who had known the Bryants and Martin on the outward voyage of the First Fleet ("always distinguished for good behavior") and now, seeing them on board the *Gorgon*, could not suppress his esteem for them. "I confess that I never looked at these people," he wrote, "without pity and astonishment. They had miscarried in a heroic struggle for liberty; after having combated every hardship, and conquered every difficulty . . . I could not but reflect with admiration, at the strange combination of circumstances which had again brought us together, to baffle human foresight, and confound human speculation."[8]

Mary Bryant's sufferings were not over yet. On May 5, her three-year-old Charlotte died and was buried at sea. When she reached London and was committed to Newgate as an escaped felon, all she could look forward to was another transport ship, more irons and a second voyage to Botany Bay. But Mary Bryant soon acquired friends. Word got out about that indomitable curiosity, "the Girl from Botany Bay," who had so far overcome the inherent weakness of her sex to make this epic voyage through cannibals, coral, fever-isles and mountainous seas, from the edge of the chart back to England and civilization. Surely a just government could not send this bereaved heroine and her companions back to the thief-colony? So thought James Boswell, for one; and this kind-hearted writer pressed Dundas, the home secretary, and Evan Nepean, the undersecretary of state, with letters urging clemency and pardon for her. In May 1793, Mary Bryant received an unconditional pardon. Boswell then settled an annuity of £10 on her, and back she went to Cornwall. In November 1793 her four companions were pardoned, too; one of them promptly, if unexpectedly, enlisted in the New South Wales Corps and set sail again for Botany Bay.[9]

Boswell's interest in Mary Bryant was such that his friends, used to his amatory divings among the lower classes, joked that Botany Bay had given him a new mistress. One of them, William Parsons, penned a "Heroic Epistle from Mary Broad in Cornwall to James Boswell, Esq., in London." Mary languishes in her new, Cornish exile, pining for the Apollo of Auchinleck:

> Was it for this I braved the ocean's roar,
> And plied those thousand leagues the lab'ring oar?
> Oh, rather had I stayed, the willing prey
> Of grief and famine in the direful bay!
> Or perished, whelmed in the Atlantic tide!
> Or, home returned, in air suspended died!

Instead, she dreams of being united with her Boswell in the ultimate transport of bliss, their *liebestod* on the scaffold at Tyburn—a new thrill for her, and even for him:

> Great in our lives, and in our deaths as great,
> Embracing and embraced, we'll meet our fate:
> A happy pair, whom in supreme delight
> One love, one cord, one joy, one death unite!
> Let crowds behold with tender sympathy
> Love's true sublime in our last agony!
> First let our weight the trembling scaffold bear
> Till we consummate the last bliss in air.[10]

But despite the elegantly turned prurience of his friends, there is nothing to suggest that Boswell's interest in Mary Bryant—who faded from the newspapers and from history, on her return to Cornwall—was inspired by anything but compassion. His only souvenir of her (apart from some receipts for the annuity) was a packet of dried Australian "sweet tea" leaves, which she had held on to through thick and thin and given to him as a curiosity; they now repose in the archives of Yale University, very far from Botany Bay.

ii

AFTER THE BRYANTS made their escape from Sydney, security there had to be tightened. Collins, in April 1791, described the new arrangements: a sentinel at night on each wharf at Sydney Cove, and no boats allowed to leave the cove without direct spoken word from the officer of the guard, who also had to have a written list of all personnel, convict or free, allowed to use the fishing skiffs after sunset. Sydney Harbor was the gate to this little police-state and it had to be kept locked. In the beginning, with few ships coming and going, this was easy. But as traffic increased, the loophole widened. The Bryants' escape gave absconders new heart. "The lenity and compassion expressed in England [for them]," Hunter grumbled, "I fear may have contributed to encourage similar attempts now. Had those people been sent back and tried in this country for taking away the boat . . . we should not have any schemes of that kind projected now."[11]

American whaling captains out of Nantucket and Sag Harbor, who cared not a spit for English penal policies, let convicts stow away when they needed new crewmen. Some English transports, turned back into trading vessels for the homeward voyage, also let convicts on board—no less than thirty absconders were flushed from the transport *Hillsborough* as she made ready to leave Sydney in 1799. Even the French captain Nicolas Baudin, while mapping the southern coast of Australia in 1802–3, found eight convict stowaways on board; he cast them ashore on King Island in the Bass Strait, without holding out much hope of their survival.[12]

There were natural sympathies between convicts and sailors, for some tyrannous captains treated tars little better than prisoners. Crewmen would sometimes stow prisoners away in crannies that were unknown even to their officers. Before a ship sailed from Sydney or Hobart, the constables would swarm through her, banging on casks and prodding bales and sacks with their bayonets. Watchers on shore would see white smoke pouring from the ship's ports and ventilators, a sign that sulphur bombs had been ignited to smoke the stowaways out of their hiding places like rabbits from a warren. In 1814 a search of the trader *Earl Spencer* produced twenty-eight escapees, some concealed in barrels of flour and cheese and one wrapped up in a spare jib in the sail-locker. When the *Harriet*, a merchant ship out of Sydney, was found to have brought sixteen escaped convicts to the Cape even though she had been "diligently Searched" before sailing in December 1817, Governor Lachlan Macquarie complained to Lord Bathurst that

> it is scarcely possible to find these Runaways, when the Sailors are in league with them and Connive at their Concealment on board, few ships leaving this Port without Carrying off some Convicts of both Sexes in the same way . . . [T]he Convicts, who have been the Shortest Time in the Colony, are always those who are the Most Anxious to make their Escape from it.[13]

In 1826 a memo to George Arthur, lieutenant-governor of Van Diemen's Land, outlined some of the security problems in Hobart. The seal

trade in Bass Strait was mainly carried on by runaways working for mainland businessmen, most of whom were Emancipists themselves. Arthur's correspondent lamented

> the facility with which a Prisoner gets conveyed away from the Colony
> in the boats and small Vessels employed in Sealing . . . They soon find
> Employment in the Straits, become sharers in Plunder, and finally get
> away to New Zealand, or some other more distant Country.[14]

Arthur clamped such strict port regulations on Hobart that not even
a mouse, one would have thought, could get through them. Every ship in
the Derwent River had to have a 24-hour officer watch, or else face severe
and automatic fines. All vessels leaving were "searched and smoked"—
fumigated with sulphur to drive stowaways out. For every convict found
on board a vessel, each officer and seaman was fined a month's wages, to
be paid in full by the captain before the ship could sail. Informers were
exempt from this, and any informer got half the total fine from the ship's
crew if a convict were found on board, the search-party receiving the
other half. Since any seaman who informed in this way—and ended up
with his shipmate's wages—would face an unusually short and unpleasant life after his vessel cleared the D'Entrecasteaux Channel, Arthur's
regulations permitted the informer to "have his discharge from the ship
should he require it," unless he had actually brought the absconders on
board himself.[15]

By 1820, Hobart was the main port for whaling and sealing, and Sydney the same for island trading in sandalwood, pearlshell, bêche-de-mer
and New Zealand spar timber, throughout the South Pacific. Each had to
be both a jail and a port of call—an awkward contradiction. In stowing
away, most convicts merely exchanged one kind of imprisonment for
another. It was a fine arrangement for the ship's masters because, once
on board, the convict could not return to land—not, at any rate, to New
South Wales or Van Diemen's Land—without risking the gallows. He
was shanghaied, and there was no romance in this cramped world of the
fo'c'sle and the skinning-knife. Yet it was better than the chain gang. By
the 1830s the southern bays and refuges, from the Bay of Islands in New
Zealand (a veritable rookery of absconders) to the Recherche Archipelago
on the west coast of Australia, were littered with grim little communities and patriarchal clans of convicts.

On other trading vessels, they ranged even farther afield. The sandalwood trade littered the central Pacific with escaped convicts. For a short
time, between about 1812 and 1816, American ships had been kept out
of the Pacific by the British-American War. This gave the Sydney traders,
merchants like William Campbell and Simeon Lord, a near-monopoly on

the cutting of sandalwood, the rare and sweetly aromatic timber for which there was an enormous market among the Chinese. It grew on mid-Pacific islands, most profusely in the Marquesas and the Tuamotus. Between 1811 and 1821, colonial trading vessels out of Sydney, such as Campbell's diplomatically named *Governor Macquarie*, brought back perhaps a quarter of the total sandalwood harvest of the Marquesas. On the islands, the wood was not so much gathered as plundered. If a captain ran short of trading goods to exchange for sandalwood, he would steal them from one island to sell to another, as John Martin, master of the *Queen Charlotte*, stole canoes from Tahuata to sell in Nuku Hiva in 1815.

No law restrained these captains, and only their own violence—the lash, the battened hatch, the duck's-foot pistol with its splayed barrels that could blast a fan of slugs down on a companionway and make a shambles of mutineers—could restrain their crews. They would find space on board for any escaping convict. But it was a one-way trip: Such absconders would be cast ashore three thousand miles from Sydney to fend for themselves as beachcombers. Sometimes a captain would be genuinely surprised by their presence on board. Thomas Hammond, master of the Pacific trader *Endeavour*, did not know he had five escaped convicts until they came blinking from their holes in the 'tween-decks on the way to New Zealand. He wanted to put them ashore there, but the magistrate in the Bay of Islands refused to let them land unless Hammond left six months' provisions for them, so he sailed on and dumped them on the beach of Hiva Oa in the Marquesas.[16]

It is not known how many escaped convicts ended up as beachcombers on the sandalwood islands. Hundreds of them must have been scattered in remote parts of the Pacific. "Strangers in their new societies and scandals to their old," they contributed their own violence and opportunism, incubated and hardened by the System, to the ruin of the island cultures. By 1850 there was no part of the Pacific where the name of Botany Bay did not carry a sour infected reek—the breath of England, gone carious in double exile.

It was much harder for convicts to steal a boat for themselves than to stow away on someone else's; but that did not prevent some from trying. Most attempts to escape from Australia on stolen or secretly built craft failed. The Bryants' escape became legendary precisely because it was unique. More typical by far was the escape in September 1790 of a party of five life-sentence convicts off the Second Fleet. They stole a punt from Rose Hill, poled it down the Parramatta River to Sydney Harbor, stole a "very small and weak" skiff from the look-out station at South Head and set out for Tahiti with a week's food, three iron pots, some bedding and no compass. Naturally, no trace of them was ever found. One desperate man tried to get away from Major Foveaux's atrocious reign on Norfolk Island, around 1800, by stealing a door, cutting two leg-holes in it, and paddling out over the Kingston reef in the hope of somehow floating a thousand miles to the Australian mainland. In secret, men constructed skiffs out of green eucalyptus wood, which opened and sank; risked being skinned by the cat-o'-nine-tails to hide precious iron nails in their mouths, armpits, anuses; stole twine and needles to sew coracles out of kangaroo skin. Thomas Cook, author of *The Exile's Lamentations*, spent weeks working by moonlight in relays with four accomplices, building a boat hidden in the bush of Norfolk Island:

> Many sleepless hours did I experience in silent meditation on the schemes of Escape. All consideration of the long and perilous voyage of 1000 miles in a precarious Boat over the watery deep without either chart or compass was waived by the thought of my afflicted Parents, and the impossibility of my ever more seeing them in this world. . . . Blessed and sweet Liberty, that I had been doomed to forfeit in a place of unparalleled torture & sin, now appeared to me in all its grandeur. Those who I held dear now appeared in my dreams as transported by joy at my presence. But Alas! How visionary my calculations! A clue was gained to the boat by some means then to me unknown.[17]

The skiff, nearly finished, was found and destroyed. Such projects could not be kept secret, especially in the confines of Norfolk Island.

Sometimes, though not often, a group of convicts would manage to pirate a full-size ship. In 1797 the *Cumberland*, a Sydney-built smack, the "largest and best boat in the colony," according to Governor Hunter, was seized by an Irish convict crew on a routine trip delivering stores from Sydney to the Hawkesbury River; she went north and was never seen again, although Hunter sent a rowboat laden with armed men after her for sixty blistering miles.[18]

Late one Sunday night in May 1808, as the brig *Harrington* was riding quietly at anchor in Farm Cove in Sydney Harbor under the very windows of the Pacific trader William Campbell, her owner, a "body of desperadoes"—some fifty convicts—silently came alongside in boats and swarmed over her rail. Her chief officer awoke staring down the bore of a pistol held by the ringleader, Robert Stewart; other convicts stole forward and pinioned the crew. They cut the ship's anchor-cables and used the rowboats to tow her down the harbor to the Heads, and by dawn they were well out to sea. Stewart put the officers and crew over the side, into the boats. It took them eight hours to row back to Sydney, and by then the *Harrington* was over the horizon. It was thought that she would never be seen again—she had just been fully provisioned for a voyage to

Fiji—but three months later she ran on a reef in the South China Sea and was taken by a Manila-bound British frigate, the *Phoenix*. Robert Stewart and other ringleaders were shipped back to Sydney and hanged.[19]

Despite a widespread belief among the free that convicts who pirated boats wrought orgies of vengeance on their unhappy crews and passengers, the absconders usually showed pity and moderation. In 1826 the brig *Wellington* was seized by the sixty-six convicts it was taking to Norfolk Island. They killed nobody and, having carried the ship, solicitously treated the minor flesh wounds, cuts and bruises some of the guards had suffered. Having shaped their course for New Zealand, the convicts set up a "Council of Seven" to keep order on board and especially to punish any mutineers who tried to dishonor the escape by brutalizing their former guards. Such people were to be put back in irons and then dropped ashore in New Zealand, "instead of proceeding with us to our ultimate destination." One of the convicts was actually found guilty of "attempting a revolt and mutiny" by urging his fellow prisoners to revenge and was sentenced to spend the rest of the run to New Zealand in irons day and night on deck. The new masters of the *Wellington* kept a log of these respectable proceedings, parts of which sound cozy, almost domestic:

> This being Christmas Day, and the only deficiency we have at present found on the part of government, was in not supplying us with plums; issued an order, if any individual on board had any plums they must be given up for all hands; plums were procured, four geese killed, together with three sheep, spent a very comfortable day, moderately indulging ourselves with some gin and brandy.[20]

The *Wellington* and its escapees were recaptured by a whaler in New Zealand, and this log told in their favor at their trial. When their merciful conduct was revealed—and confirmed by the ship's guards and crew— there was a swell of public sympathy for them, and out of twenty-three men condemned to hang, only five were actually executed.

The prisoners who seized the brig *Cyprus* in 1828 were less fortunate, although their escapade became as celebrated in convict lore as the Bryants'. By the early 1830s they had become the subject of one of the "treason songs" or proscribed convict ballads. The men of *Cyprus*, reconvicted in Van Diemen's Land for "little trifling offences," were being taken from Hobart to the penal station of Macquarie Harbor, "that place of tyranny":

> Down Hobart Town streets we were gathered, on the *Cyprus* brig conveyed,
> Our topsails they were hoisted, boys, our anchor it was weighed,

The wind it blew a nor'-nor'-west, and on we steered straightway,
Till we brought her to an anchorage in a place called Recherche Bay.

The facts do not match the song at all points. Far from being guilty of
minor offenses, most of the thirty-one convicts going to Macquarie Harbor on the *Cyprus* had been convicted of capital crimes but had had their
sentences commuted. The most intrepid of them was a former sailor,
William Swallow. Swallow was a veritable Houdini. In 1810 he had hijacked a schooner in Port Jackson and been sent to Van Diemen's Land
as his secondary punishment. The ship that took him there, the *Deveron*,
was disabled in a storm and Swallow, "remarking that his own life was
of little moment," volunteered to go aloft and cut away a slatting tangle
of broken spars and rigging. It seems that the *Deveron*'s sailors were so
grateful for his courage in saving the ship that, as soon as Swallow was
landed in Hobart, they smuggled him back on board. Thus he escaped,
and got all the way west across the ocean to Rio, where he was captured
again by the British authorities. Once more he got free and stowed away
on a London-bound boat. But he was finally recognized in London, arrested and shipped out again to Van Diemen's Land. Such was the man
who, "confined within a dismal hole" with his fellow convicts as the
Cyprus rode at anchor near the southern tip of Van Diemen's Land,
decided to make a last bid

> To take possession of that brig or else die every man:
> The plan it being approv'd upon, we soon retired to rest,
> And early next morning, boys, we put them to the test.
>
> Up steps bold Jack Muldeamon, his comrades three more—
> We soon disarmed the sentry and left him in his gore:
> "Liberty, O liberty! It's liberty we crave—
> Surrender up your arms, my boys, or the sea shall be your grave!"

After a rush, a scuffle and some shooting, the convicts overpowered
the guard and carried the ship. They put the officer-in-charge, Lieutenant
Carew, over the side along with his wife, the soldiers and thirteen convicts who had not joined the mutiny. The *Cyprus* was heavily laden with
stores for Macquarie Harbor, enough to sustain 400 men for six months,
but the convicts gave the forty-five castaways a stingy ration—a live
sheep, some salt beef, a bag of biscuits and 30 pounds of flour, with no
weapons and no boat:

> First we landed the soldiers, the captain and his crew,
> We gave three cheers for Liberty, and soon bid them adieu:

William Swallow he was chosen our commander for to be—
We gave three cheers for Liberty, and boldly put to sea.
Lay on your golden trumpets, boys, and sound their cheerful note!
The *Cyprus* brig's on the ocean, boys, by Justice does she float!

After prolonged sufferings from exposure and starvation, living on a handful of raw mussels and a quarter-biscuit a day, the castaways eventually got back to Hobart. They might not have done so without a convict named Popjoy, who framed up a 12-foot coracle out of mimosa branches, covered it with hammock canvas (sewn by Mrs. Carew, who had a needle) and waterproofed it with soap and resin. Popjoy and Carew sailed this fragile shell twenty miles to Partridge Island, where they were saved by a passing ship.*

In the meantime, the *Cyprus* and her pirates were well away. Swallow shaped his course for Tahiti, and then turned north for Japan, where he and his crew landed some time in 1829; seven of the convicts jumped ship there. Several months later, Swallow and three of his mates appeared in a skiff off the Chinese trading port of Whampoa. They had abandoned the *Cyprus*. Swallow presented himself to officials in Canton as Captain Waldron of the ship *Edward*, set on fire and sunk at sea by the Japanese. In this way, Swallow and his mates wangled a free passage home to England. Unfortunately, soon after they sailed, other survivors of the *Cyprus* turned up in Canton and Swallow's story began to unravel. Eventually, Swallow and his mates were arrested in England, and were identified by Popjoy, who, by a bizarre stroke of colonial ill-luck, had returned to London after receiving a free pardon for helping save the castaways at Recherche Bay. But Popjoy insisted that Swallow had been forced by his fellow absconders to navigate the ship, and the court believed him. So, although Swallow's companions were hanged, he was not. For the third time, he was forced to go on board a transport and make the long, lugubrious journey to Australia. It was his last. As soon as he arrived in Hobart, he was shipped to Macquarie Harbor—and this time there was no escape. William Swallow eventually died of tuberculosis in the penal colony of Port Arthur, to which he had been transferred when Macquarie Harbor was closed down in 1834. Unfortunately, he never wrote a memoir of his adventures.[21]

But one later absconder did: James Porter, a twenty-six-year-old Londoner who helped his convict companions, ex-sailors among them, to hijack the brig *Frederick* from the slipway where they had built her for the government at Macquarie Harbor in 1833, just as the settlement was

---

* The rescue of the survivors of the *Cyprus*, and Popjoy's construction of the coracle, was adapted by Marcus Clarke in *His Natural Life*.

being abandoned. This caused much embarrassment, not least because the vessel had been named after one of Lieutenant-Governor Arthur's seven sons. They cast the guards and crew ashore (all survived) and with remarkable skill and courage sailed clear across the Pacific to the coast of Chile, where they abandoned her to sink and took to the longboat. Reaching Valdivia, they came before its Chilean governor, who assumed that they were pirates, not innocent shipwrecked sailors, and promised to shoot them. Porter saved their skins with a stirring speech (as recorded years later, by himself):

> "Avast there! We as sailors shipwrecked and in distress expected when we made this port to have been treated in a Christian-like manner, not as though we were dogs! Is this the way you would have treated us in 1818 when the British Tars were fighting for your independence, and bleeding in your cause against the old Spaniards? If we were pirates do you suppose we should be so weak as to cringe to your tyranny? Never! I also wish you to understand that if we are shot England will know of it and will be revenged . . . [S]hould you put your threat into execution we will teach you Patriots how to die."[22]

Impressed by this magnificent bluff, the governor let them stay unmolested, and asked his superiors in Santiago to issue them with residence permits. Porter and his companions now settled down to a picaresque life among the ladies and knife-wielders of Chile. But the governor was replaced soon afterward, and his successor—suspicious that Porter and his shipmates were, in fact, escaped convicts—alerted a passing British frigate, HMS *Blond*. Thus they were taken again, first back to England, and then on a second transport ship to Van Diemen's Land. On the weary voyage south, Porter was falsely denounced as a mutineer by two of his former shipmates, Charles Lyon and William Cheshire, who hoped to curry favor with the captain and escape hanging for piracy when, as seemed inevitable, they were recognized in Hobart. "Knowing my innocence I stood nearly petrified," he recounted:

> I was seized by the soldiers and seamen, lashed to a grating (and to that degree until the blood hoosed from the parts where the lashings went round different parts of my person) and a lump of a black-fellow flogged me across the lines and every other part of my body until my head sank on my breast. As for the quantity of lashes I cannot say, for I would not give them the satisfaction to scringe to it, until nature gave way through exhaustion.

Then he and his mate William Shires were chained below, bleeding and infected, hands manacled behind their backs, in a steaming rat's-hole and were given no more than quarter-rations of water and food for three weeks, until they presented "the appearance of anatomies [i.e., skeletons] more than living beings." "I craved for death," Porter noted, but on recovering the use of his arms he wrote a pathetic verse on a scrounged leaf of paper:

> How wretched is an Exile's state of mind
> When not one gleam of hope on earth remain,
> Through grief worn down, with servile chains confined,
> And not one friend to soothe his heartfelt pain.
>
> Too true I know that man was made to mourn,
> A heavy portion's fallen to my lot
> With anguish full my aching heart is torn
> Far from my friends, by all the world forgot.
>
> The feathered race with splendid plumage gay
> Extent their throats with a discordant sound,
> With Liberty they spring from spray to spray,
> While I a wretched Exile gaze around.
>
> Farewell my sister, Aged Aunts dear,
> Ere long my glass of life will cease to run,
> In silence drop a sympathetic tear
> For your Unhappy, Exiled, Long-Lost Son.
>
> O cease, my troubled aching Heart, to beat,
> Since happiness so far from thee has fled!
> Haste, haste unto your silent cold retreat
> In clay-cold earth to mingle with the Dead.

But Porter was not to die; or not yet. He survived the voyage and landed in Hobart in March 1837, where he was instantly recognized as one of the pirates of the *Frederick*. He was tried and convicted of piracy, despite his ingenious argument in defense: As the vessel had not been formally commissioned by the government—"it was canvas, rope, boarding and trenails, put together shipwise—yet it was not a legal ship: the seizure might be theft, but not piracy." Luckily for him, "the bloodthirsty Arthur" had left Van Diemen's Land five months earlier, "and had not the colony been under the Government of the humane Sir John Franklin I should not now have been alive to have given this small Narrative." So Porter and Shires did not hang. They ended up on Norfolk Island, where Porter was able to write his memoirs under the kindly eye of Captain Alexander Maconochie.

These were the last men to escape from Macquarie Harbor, but they were by no means the first. Ever since 1821, when Lieutenant-Governor

Sorell had pitched this dreaded prison settlement on the isolated west coast of Van Diemen's Land, convicts had been trying to get away from it, mostly on foot. In 1822 and 1823, one man in ten disappeared. In 1824, the rate rose to nearly one in seven. They went inland, trying to reach the settled and farmed districts to the east, and most of them died. In the long list of Macquarie Harbor absconders for the first six years of settlement, only eight carry a brief remark like "Reported to have reached the cultivated part of the island: this requires confirmation." The rest is a gray official litany, punctuated by sparks of saturnine humor. Timothy Crawley, Richard Morris, John Newton, June 2, 1824: "Seized the soldiers' boat, provicions, fire-arms &c., and supposed to have perished in their way across the interior. The boat was afterwards found moored to a Stump, and written upon her stern, with chalk, 'to be Sold.' " But the usual requiem was "Supposed to have perished in the woods."²³

Only one man escaped from Macquarie Harbor twice. His name was Alexander Pearce (1790–1824), a little, pockmarked, blue-eyed Irishman from County Monaghan who had been transported for seven years at the Armagh Assizes in 1819, for stealing six pairs of shoes.²⁴ He had arrived in Van Diemen's Land in 1820, and as an assigned servant he gave continuous trouble to his masters by running away, stealing and getting drunk. He soon learned enough bush skills to "stay out" for three months at a stretch with some other absconders. Flogging did not impress him. Eventually, in 1822, he was sent to Macquarie Harbor for forging a two-pound money order and absconding from service. On September 20, 1822, Pearce seized an open boat from Kelly's Basin on Macquarie Harbor, where he had been working in a sawpit gang. Seven other convicts piled into the craft with him. Two of them had already tried to escape from Van Diemen's Land by stealing a schooner moored in the Derwent estuary: Matthew Travers, an Irishman under life sentence of transportation, and Robert Greenhill, a sailor from Middlesex. For that failed escape, they had been sent to Macquarie Harbor. The others were an ex-soldier, William Dalton (perjury in Gibraltar, fourteen years); a highway robber, Thomas Bodenham; William Kennelly, alias Bill Cornelius, transported for seven years and re-sentenced to Macquarie Harbor for an escape attempt; John Mather, a young Scottish baker, working a seven-year sentence and then sent to Macquarie Harbor for forging a £15 money order; and a man called "Little Brown," whose Christian name is unknown and who cannot, due to the commonness of his surname, be identified.

Flogged with the adrenaline of escape, the eight men rowed across the harbor, ran the boat ashore, smashed its bottom with a stolen axe, and set out on foot. At first they made good time through the dank maze of the shore forest, lugging their axes and their meager rations. They spent the night on the slopes of Mount Sorell, not daring to light a fire, and

struck east the next morning toward the Derwent River, where they
planned to steal a schooner, sail it downstream past Hobart and out into
Storm Bay and so "proceed home," 14,000 miles to England. The first leg
of their route lay across the Darwin Plateau, keeping to the north of the
Gordon River.[25]

Before them, although they did not know it, lay some of the worst
country in Australia. Even today, bushwalkers rarely venture into the
mountains between Macquarie Harbor and the inland plains: fold after
fold, scarp on scarp, with giant trees growing to a hundred feet from clefts
in the steep rock where, clambering along rotted limbs or floundering
through the entangling ferns and creepers, one cannot possibly move in
a straight line. The convicts struggled along in a gray, dripping twilight
from dawn to dusk, with one man beating the scrub in front "to make
the road." At night, like exhausted troglodytes, afraid of winds and shadows, they lit a fire in the cleft of a rock and huddled around it to sleep as
best they could. Within a week, the weather turned to gales and sleet
and their little store of tinder was soaked. Then they finished the last of
their rations. Hungry, cold and failing, the band struggled for another
two days through "a very rough country . . . in a very weak state for want
of provisions."

But now the fugitives were straggling. "Little Brown . . . was the
worst walker of any; he always fell behind, and then kept cooing [sic] so
that we said we would leave him behind if he could not keep up better."[26]
No man felt able to gather all the wood for a fire. In the feeble hysteria
of exhaustion, they began to squabble about who should do it; in the end,
each convict scraped together enough twigs for himself and eight little
fires were lit. Kennelly made what might or might not have been meant
as a joke. "I am so weak," he said to Pearce and Greenhill, "that I could
eat a piece of a man."

They thought about that all night, and "in the morning," Pearce's
narrative goes on,

> there were four of us for a feast. Bob Greenhill was the first who intro-
> duced it, and said he had seen the like done before, and that it eat much
> like a little pork.

John Mather protested. It would be murder, he said; and useless, too,
since they might not be able to choke the flesh down. Greenhill overrode
him:

> "I will warrant you," said Greenhill, "I will well do it first myself and eat
> the first of it; but you must all lend a hand, so that you may all be equal

in the crime." We then consulted who should fall. Greenhill said, "Dalton; as he volunteered to be a flogger, we will kill him."

In these flat declarative outlines, the scene might come from an Elizabethan revenge-tragedy: the conclave, the ritual to overcome the great taboo, the literary diction, the avenging choice of the flogger as victim. Indeed, it may be too pat; Dalton was never a flogger at Macquarie Harbor, and other "literary" touches in the narrative may come from the amanuensis to whom Pearce eventually dictated his story. But in any case, Dalton was killed. He fell sound asleep at about three in the morning, and Greenhill's axe

> struck him on the head, and he never spoke a word after . . . Matthew Travers with a knife also came and cut his throat, and bled him; we then dragged him to a distance, and cut off his clothes, and tore out his inside, and cut off his head; then Matthew Travers and Greenhill put his heart and liver on the fire and eat it before it was right warm; they asked the rest would they have any, but they would not have any that night.

But the next morning, hunger won. They had been without food for four days. Dalton's flesh was carved and doled out into seven roughly equal portions, and the band got moving again.

Brown was walking slower and slower; he must have reflected as he limped along that he, the weakest, would be next. Kennelly, too, was afraid for his life. And so the two of them fell back, and silently disappeared in the forest mazes of the Engineer Range, hoping to get back to Macquarie Harbor. Realizing that their story "would hang us all," the others tried to catch them but failed. On October 12, Brown and Kennelly were found half-dead from exposure on the shore of Macquarie Harbor, still with pieces of human flesh in their pockets. Brown died in the prison hospital on October 15, and Kennelly four days later.

Now five convicts were left. They reached the Franklin River, swollen with rain, and spent two days trying to cross it; Pearce, Greenhill and Mather went across first and dragged the other two over with the help of a long pole. Mather was crippled with dysentery and the others "were scarcely able to move, for we were so cold and wet." But they struggled on across the Deception Range and then the Surveyor Range after that, and on October 15 they saw below them a fine open valley, probably the Loddon Plains. Here, in the long grass by a creek, thoughts of fresh food rose again. It was Bodenham's turn to die. As he slept, Greenhill split his skull. Ten years later, the first official explorer to reach the Loddon Plains, a surveyor, would find human bones in this valley.[27]

Four men were left, and they kept marching. By about October 22, they had apparently reached the first line of the Western Tiers and before them lay "a very fine country," full of "many kangaroos and emus, and game of all kinds"; but they had no hunting weapons, and the frustration of starving while watching the mobs of shy gray marsupials bounding invulnerably past must have been overpowering. "We then said to ourselves," Pearce declared, "that we would all die together before anything should happen."

But Greenhill had no intention of dying together with anyone, and Mather was very apprehensive. He and Pearce "went to one side, and Mather said, Pearce, let us go on by ourselves; you see what kind of a cove Greenhill is; he would kill his father before he would fast one day." But on that open button-grass moor, which may have been the King William Plains, they could not have lost Greenhill. Since he carried the only axe they had left, he could not be killed; and none of the famished men could hobble faster than the rest. Thus bound together, they went on; and around the last week in October (from here, the chronology of Pearce's accounts grows hazier), they stopped by a little creek and lit a fire to boil the last of Bodenham, "which scarcely kept the Faculties in Motion."[28]

Mather could not eat his share. He had gathered some fern roots, which he boiled and wolfed down, but

he found it would not rest on his stomach (no wonder) for such a Mess It could not be expected would ever digest in any Mortal whatever, which occasioned him to vomit to ease his Stomach & while in the act of discharging it from his Chest, Greenhill still showing his spontaneous habit of bloodshed seized the Axe & crept behind him gave him a blow on the head.

It did not kill Mather. He jumped up and grappled with Greenhill, wresting the axe from him. Pearce and Travers managed, for a time, to calm the two men down. But Mather was doomed, and that night the four men made camp around a fire "in a very pensive and melancholy mood." Greenhill and Travers, bosom friends, were determined to eat Mather next; Pearce, without telling Mather, was secretly on their side. He walked a little way from the fire and looked back: "I saw Travers and Greenhill collaring him." The team was at work again, and Pearce made no effort to save poor John Mather, who now made ready to die a Christian death, very far from England.

They told him they would give him half an hour to pray for himself, which was agreed to; he then gave the Prayer-book to me, and laid down his head, and Greenhill took the axe and killed him. We then stopped two days in this place.

The three men kept heading east, but Travers was sinking. He had been bitten on the foot by a snake and could no longer walk. Terrified that his two companions would eat him, he begged them to leave him to die and go on with what remained of Mather, which might be rations enough to carry them to a settlement. Greenhill refused to abandon him. He and Pearce stayed with the delirious Travers for five days, tending him. Travers lapsed in and out of his fever, "in great agitation for fear that they would dispose of him. . . . [T]he unfortunate Man all this time had but little or no sleep."[29]

They half-dragged, half-carried Travers for several days more. But it was no use:

> [Greenhill and Pearce] began to Comment on the impossibility of ever being able to keep *Traviss* up with them for their strength was so nearly exhausted it was impossible for them to think of making any Settlement unless they left him. . . . It would be folly for them to leave him, for his flesh would answer as well for Subsistence as the others.

Travers awoke and, through his haze of pain, heard them talking.

> In the greatest agony [he] requested them in the most affecting manner not to delay themselves any longer, for it was morally impossible for him to attempt Travelling any more & therefore it would be useless for them to attempt to take him with them. . . . The Remonstrances of *Traviss* strengthened the designs of his companions.[30]

They killed Travers with the axe. The victim "only stretched himself in his agony, and then expired."

Now they were two. But for the kangaroos, the terrain through which Pearce and Greenhill were now walking was not unlike England: undulating fields of grass sprinkled with little copses, a mild and fruitful landscape ringed with hills, all golden in the early summer light.

> Greenhill began to fret, and said he would never get to any port with his life. I kept up my spirits all along, and thought we must shortly come to some inhabited parts of the country, from the very great length we had travelled.

But there could be no doubt that one would sooner or later eat the other. Greenhill had the axe, and the two men walked at a fixed distance apart. When Pearce stopped, so did Greenhill. When one squatted, so did the other. There was no question of sleep. "I watched Greenhill for two nights, for I thought he eyed me more than usual." One imagines them: a small fire of eucalyptus branches in the immense cave of the southern

night, beneath the drift and icy prickle of unfamiliar stars; the secret
bush noises beyond the outer ring of firelight—rustle of grass, flutter and
croaking of nocturnal birds—all sharpened and magnified by fear, with
the two men fixedly watching one another across the fire. One night
Pearce became convinced of Greenhill's "bad disposition as to me." He
waited, and near dawn his adversary fell asleep. "I run up, and took the
axe from under his head, and struck him with it, and killed him. I then
took part of his arm and thigh, and went on for several days."

Pearce was now utterly alone. "I then took a piece of a leather belt,"
he notes laconically, "and was going to hang myself; but I took another
notion not to do it." He walked on a little further and blundered into his
first stroke of good luck since Macquarie Harbor: a deserted aboriginal
campsite. The blacks had seen him coming and had fled, leaving pieces
of game scattered around their still-lit cooking-fires.

Pearce settled down and gorged himself on the first non-human meat
he had tasted in nearly seven weeks. It gave him strength to keep going
for several days until, from a hilltop, he glimpsed the landmark that
signalled his arrival in the farmed country of the Derwent Valley: Table
Mountain, a hill just south of Lake Crescent. Below him lay the Ouse, a
large tributary stream of the Derwent.

Two days later, following the river down, Pearce came on a flock of
sheep. He managed to grab and dismember a lamb. As he was devouring
its raw flesh, a convict shepherd emerged from the bush "and said he
would shoot me if I did not stop immediately."

The shepherd's name was McGuire, and he soon realized that he
knew the blood-boltered little goblin he had at gunpoint. Before his banishment to Macquarie Harbor, Pearce had worked on a sheep run nearby.
McGuire "carried the remains of the lamb, and took me with him into
his hut, and made meat ready for me, where I stopped for three days, and
he gave me all attendance." He would not turn a fellow Irishman in to
the authorities, and for several weeks more Pearce hid in the huts of
McGuire and other Irish convict shepherds. Then he fell in with a pair of
bushrangers, Davis and Churton, who armed him; and they skulked
about in the bush together for two more months. But his new companions had a £10 reward on their heads, and convict solidarity—never a
dependable bond—could not hold up forever against that. On January 11,
1823, near the town of Jericho, the three of them were arrested by soldiers
of the 48th Regiment acting on the word of informers and were brought
down to Hobart in chains.

Churton and Davis were tried and hanged, an automatic punishment
for bushrangers. While in jail, Pearce confessed the whole story of his
escape—cannibalism and all—to the acting magistrate, the Reverend
Robert Knopwood. It was transcribed and sealed, and not a word of it was

believed. The authorities assumed—in the manner of the Cretan paradox —that since all convicts were liars, this one could only be covering for his "mates," who must still be alive and at large. This grotesque tall story could only be the invention of a felon's debased mind. There were no living witnesses to that nightmare trek from Macquarie Harbor to the Derwent, and no *corpus delicti*. And so Pearce was not executed; instead, they sent him back to Macquarie Harbor, where he arrived in February 1823.

He became, of course, a celebrity among the convicts. He was living proof that a man could get out of Macquarie Harbor, and only he kept the secret of how to do it. One newly arrived convict, a young laborer named Thomas Cox, kept begging to come along the next time. Finally, Pearce gave in to Cox's whispered entreaties; but he would not try the eastern route again. Instead, he decided to try and go north to Port Dalrymple—once again, through totally unexplored territory, but perhaps not as bad as the Western Tiers. On November 16, 1823, the two men absconded.[31]

They did not get far. On November 21, a lookout on Sarah Island saw a plume of smoke rising from a distant beach. The fire was also seen by a convict transport, the *Waterloo*, as it made sail for Hell's Gates. The ship lowered a boat, and the shore guard dispatched a launch. Before dark, the exhaused Pearce was back in the settlement where he told the commandant that he had killed Cox two days before and had been eating him since. By way of proof, he produced a piece of human flesh weighing about half a pound. Next morning he led a search-party to the bank of a stream, where Cox's body lay "in a dreadfully mangled state," according to one official report,

> being cut right through the middle, the head off, the privates torn off, all the flesh off the calves of the legs, back of the thighs and loins, also off the thick part of the arms, which the inhuman wretch declared was the most delicious food.[32]

Probably Pearce killed Cox in rage, not gluttony; his own account rings true, despite its apparent gratuitousness:

> We travelled on several days without food, except the tops of trees and shrubs, until we came upon King's River. I asked Cox if he could swim; he replied he could not; I remarked that had I been aware of it he should not have been my companion. . . . [T]he arrangement for crossing the river created words, and I killed Cox with the axe. . . . I swam the river with the intention of keeping the coast around [to] Port Dalrymple; my heart failed me, and I resolved to return.[33]

The authorities did the only thing they could. Pearce was shipped straight down to Hobart on the *Waterloo*, tried and hanged. When he was dead, a local artist, Thomas Bock, drew his likeness. The court had ordered that, as its ultimate brand of infamy, Pearce should be "disjointed" after death—delivered to the anatomizing surgeons. This was done, and Mr. Crockett, the head doctor in the Hobart Colonial Hospital, made a souvenir of the cannibal's head. He skinned it and scraped the flesh away, plucked out the eyes and the brain, and boiled the skull clean. Thirty years later, the relic was given to an American phrenologist, Dr. Samuel Morton, who was busy assembling his collection of skulls and shrunken heads, more than a thousand specimens, known as "The American Golgotha." It went into a glass cabinet in the Academy of Natural Sciences in Philadelphia, where it may still be seen, a yellowed label pasted across the blackened ivory bone, recording its small role in the taxonomy of an extinct scientific fad.

iii

IN EARLY New South Wales, up to 1825, the escaped convict was a bogey, a nuisance, an embarrassment to the seamless image of Authority —but rarely more. In Van Diemen's Land, however, he became a social force.

We have seen in Chapter 5 how the Tasmanian bushrangers began as convict kangaroo hunters who stayed out in the bush and formed gangs. Until the mid-1820s, the government had little chance of catching them, as it had few soldiers and none were skilled bushmen. No squad of stumbling "lobsters" could take these bandits. In the wild lovely terrain of Van Diemen's Land, riven by gorges and precipices, that was like trying to pluck quicksilver from a carpet with one's fingers.

Besides, some settlers had a vested interest in protecting them. As the populace's food supplies grew more secure and its dependence on kangaroo meat declined (although the need for the skins remained, as they were the main source of leather), the banditti took to sheep stealing. They would sell the mutton to free farmers for sugar, flour, tea and gunpowder, and vanish into the wild again. They stole from big farmers and sold to small "bent" ones, and with this began the Robin Hood reputation (wholly undeserved in nine cases out of ten) of the Australian bushranger. Sometimes assigned convicts would bring food to bushrangers in hiding, and by 1815 there was an efficient network of bandits' spies in Van Diemen's Land—one bushranger boasted from his mountain fastness that he had the Hobart newspapers in his hand within five hours after they came off the press. These exasperating alliances were forged from a shared hatred for the System.

Convicting the bushrangers was a worse headache than catching them. Sheep-stealing was a capital crime. Any convict charged with a second and potentially capital offense had to be tried in Sydney. But without witnesses there could be no case, and Sydney was so far north that the settler would have to abandon his farm for several months to go there at his own expense and testify against a sheep-duffer. Few could afford to. Edward Lord (1781–1859), the Welsh marine officer who in 1803 built the first private house in Hobart, was the most powerful man in the early settlement next to Collins—and next to nobody, its largest stock-owner, an arrogant land-grabbing troublemaker who burned all the Government House papers when Collins died in 1810 in order to cover his business tracks—and even he could not get legal redress against the bandits, who made off with five hundred head of his stock every year.[34]

These cave-dwelling satyrs of the penal system resist all romanticization. They were hardly worth dignifying with the name of *banditti*. As John West put it, with some asperity:

> The Italian robber tinged his adventure with romance; the Spanish bandit was often a soldier, and a partisan; but the wandering thieves of Tasmania were no less uncouth than violent—hateful for their debasement, as well as terrible for their cruelty.[35]

They had long ratty hair, thick beards, roughly sewn garments and moccasins of kangaroo hide, a pistol stuck in a rope belt, a stolen musket, a polecat's stench. When on raids, they blacked their faces with charcoal. Most of them would kill a man as soon as a kangaroo. Some joked about this. One of the earliest "gangs" in Van Diemen's Land consisted of only three men: two Irishmen named Scanlan and Brown and an Englishman named Richard Lemon, who had gone on "the out and out" from Hobart and roamed the bush in the area of Oyster Bay. Lemon did not like Brown and Scanlan talking in Gaelic, of which he understood not a word. One morning when Brown was out hunting 'roos, Lemon crept up on Scanlan at the campfire, put a pistol to the back of his head and pulled the trigger. He then strung up the corpse by the heels on a gum tree, as if he were hanging a "boomer" (big kangaroo) for skinning. "Now, Brown," he laconically observed when his partner returned, "as there are only two of us, we shall understand one another better for the future." The two of them ranged the bush for two more years, murdering four whites and an uncounted number of blacks, until some convict bounty-hunters took them prisoner. They shot Lemon dead and forced Brown, at gunpoint, to hack off his mate's head and carry it back to Hobart in a bag. Their reward was an invitation to Government House (leaving their bag outside, presumably) and a free pardon.[36]

By 1814 there were so many bushrangers at large, and the authorities in Hobart could do so little about them, that Lachlan Macquarie decided to save Lieutenant-Governor Thomas Davey's face with a proclamation. It offered amnesty to any bushranger who turned himself in by December 1, 1814. But it was so ambiguously drafted that it offered six months' grace to bushrangers to commit with impunity any crime they wanted, short of murder, before that date. Robbery, rapine and mayhem multiplied at once. When the deadline for amnesty came, few bushrangers had surrendered and the colonists were frantic. They were sure the convict population (then 1,900 souls) was ready to rise and join the bushrangers, consigning Van Diemen's Land to anarchy. So the flustered Davey reacted like the soldier he was: He hoisted the red flag in Hobart and proclaimed martial law. He then imposed a strict curfew, revoked all tickets-of-leave, forbade the sale of kangaroo skins and ordered that all kangaroo-dogs should be shot on sight, thus hoping to destroy the bushrangers' means of support. And as a court-martial could hang anyone without reference to the criminal court in Sydney, Davey strung up as many bandits as he could catch, gibbeting their corpses in chains on a little island off the Hobart docks until they stank too much even for the wheeling, scavenging birds.[37]

But although these summary proceedings (which exasperated Macquarie when he found out about them) somewhat damped the progress of banditry in Van Diemen's Land, there were bushrangers Davey's troops could not catch. The most conspicuous one was a twenty-seven-year-old seaman from Yorkshire named Michael Howe. Twice a deserter —from the merchant marine and from the army—Howe had finally come to grief on a charge of highway robbery and been transported for seven years. He arrived in Van Diemen's Land in 1812 and absconded almost at once. By 1814, he and a fellow convict named Whitehead had brought together a roving gang of twenty-eight bushrangers, terrorizing settlers in the region of New Norfolk, on the Derwent. Their favorite targets were landowners with a reputation for treating convicts badly. One of these, an especially hated "flogging magistrate" named Adolarius William Humphrey, who lived at Pittwater, some thirty miles from Hobart, lost hundreds of his Saxon merinos to them. Howe had struck when he was away; the bandits burnt Humphrey's corn, terrified the servants and then trashed the house in a paroxysm of rage after finding two pairs of leg irons.[38]

Howe left a wide and furious swath across Van Diemen's Land. His comrade, Whitehead, was captured near Launceston. Howe became sole leader, recruiting new members to replace some who had cast themselves on the mercy of Davey's amnesty, and continued to pillage across an area of some five hundred square miles, from Launceston in the north to homesteads not far from Hobart in the south. He always stressed, in his rambling chats with the "slaves" on the farms he plundered, that he was like Dick Turpin, robbing the rich and helping the poor. Many of them believed him, and so he acquired a network of informers among assigned convicts and small farmers and was able to hear about troop movements almost as soon as they began.

Howe was a natural leader, endowed with immense vitality and a gift for organization. The gang was under quasi-naval discipline, and each member had to swear an oath of obedience on a prayer book. He had the gloomy charisma of the paranoid. He kept a kangaroo-skin diary in which he inscribed his bad dreams in blood. It also contained lists of the flowers he had known as a boy in Yorkshire, for Howe was passionately interested in botany and planned to adorn his mountain hideout with an instructive garden. He believed that Fate had singled him out as the convicts' instrument of revenge on the hated System. He had the gall to style himself "Lieutenant-Governor of the Woods," in contrast to the lieutenant-governor in Hobart. He was so sure of his safety that in 1816 he sent Davey a haughty letter, thinking the lieutenant-governor would negotiate a general pardon for him and his gang if they would "come in." Howe thought Davey was stalling until informers betrayed him.

> We have thought proper to write these Lines to you—As We have been Kept in the Dark so long—and We find it is only to Keep us Quiet until By some Means or other you think you Can Get us Betrayed. But We will Stand it no Longer. We are now Determined to have A full and satisfactory [answer?] Either for or against us, As we are determined to be Kept No longer In Ignorance, for we think ourselves Greatly Ingured By the Country at Large.

Howe ironized on Davey's fear that his gang was growing into a guerrilla army: "I have not the least Doubt but you are Glad that those new Hands [are] joining us—We are Glad Also." God was on the bushranger's side, "and He who Preserved us from your Plotts in Publick will Likewise Preserve Us from them in secret." So let Davey send word back within ten days: "Answer either for or Against us . . . clap on it the King's Seal —and Your Signature"; and let the redcoats not sneak along behind, for "We [are] As Much Inclined to take Life As you are in your Hearts; We could destroy All the partyes you can send out. . . . You Must not think to Catch Old Birds with Chaff." This singular missive, only one of several Howe sent to Davey and his successor William Sorell, was written in blood and signed by ten other bushrangers.[39]

Davey would not cooperate. "The Power of Pardoning Capital Offences," he replied to Howe, "rests solely with the Governor in Chief,
but no application for favor can avail those, who are in the daily Commission of the greatest outrages." Thus the war of cops and robbers went
on, with the robbers generally winning, through the end of Davey's administration and the arrival of the next lieutenant-governor, Colonel
William Sorell, in 1817.

In that year, Michael Howe's luck began to run out. He had acquired
a devoted aboriginal "wife," Black Mary. (Such liaisons, which usually
began with abduction and rape, were of course invaluable to all bushrangers, as they could learn a host of survival tricks from a friendly black.)
One day, the couple was ambushed by soldiers. Howe ran, and Black
Mary, who was many months pregnant, could not keep up with him. In
an exchange of shots, one of Howe's bullets struck her. The soldiers,
anxious to cultivate Howe's image as a monster, claimed afterward that
he had shot her in cold blood to stop her from talking. Howe insisted it
was an accident, and probably it was. But the jilted Black Mary, left
painfully wounded on the ground by her lover, wanted revenge—and she
sought it, after she had recovered from the bullet and given birth, by
volunteering to track him down. Even with her superb skills to guide
them, the soldiers could not catch up with him; but Howe felt the law
was closing in on him and tried to negotiate with Sorell. The new lieutenant-governor of the town offered the "Lieutenant-Governor of the
Woods" a conditional pardon for all of his crimes except murder and a
strong recommendation for clemency on the murder charge itself, if he
would turn his gang-mates in. Howe began to testify, naming a surprising
number of "respectable" settlers as receivers of stolen stock and goods.
One of these, to the potential embarrassment of the law-abiding, was
Hobart's resident man of God, the Reverend Robert Knopwood. Sorell
began an investigation of Knopwood's relations with the bushrangers;
he may have been on to something, because one night all of the transcribed evidence mysteriously vanished.

The promised pardon never came. Howe got jittery at the delay, and
in September 1817 he fled back into the bush. Without his gang, which
in his absence had fallen apart into little pillaging groups, he had to go
deep into the mountain valleys of the upper Shannon near the aptly
named peaks of Barren Tier and Rat's Castle, "a dreary solitude of cloud-
land," as one chronicler put it, "the rocky home of hermit eagles." From
time to time he would waylay farmers—who were very remote and unprotected, for the Great Lake area was the extreme limit of settlement in
Van Diemen's Land—and extort food and ammunition from them, with
horrible threats. In September 1818 he barely escaped from an ex-convict
bounty hunter named John McGill, who had found him with the help of

Muskitoo, an aboriginal blacktracker imported from Sydney. A month later, two white men named Worrall and Pugh cornered him at his hut on the Shannon. Worrall and Howe faced one another, with pistols levelled, at fifteen yards. "He stared at me with astonishment," Worrall testified later, "and . . . I was a little astonished at him, for he was covered with patches of kangaroo skin and wore a black beard . . . [A] curious pair we looked. After a moment's pause he cried out, 'Black beard against grey beard for a million!' and fired"—but missed. Worrall shot him down and Pugh battered his brains out with his gun-butt. They cut off the bushranger's head and carried it back to Hobart Town, where Sorell put in on public view, spiked to a base.

If Howe's short violent career had proven one thing, it was the embarrassing volatility of imposed social order on the colonial frontier. Neither Howe nor his gang could possibly have stayed at large for more than three years without the sympathy, and sometimes the active collaboration, of assigned servants, ex-convicts and even free settlers out for profit. An Australian type was being cast—the bushranger as popular hero. Although Howe was gone, his emulators lived on, mocking the law and causing great anxiety to the government. These desperadoes threatened—as Sir John Wylde, Macquarie's deputy judge-advocate, warned after a judicial circuit of the island in 1821—to break down "the sense of Restraint and Coercion, which may be urged to keep the Prisoners of the Crown, so comparatively numerous here, in proper awe and subjugation."[40]

For by that year, 53 percent of the entire population of Van Diemen's Land were convicts under sentence, and "a Spirit of Insurrection" was on the judge's mind. Dozens of bushrangers were out around Hobart; fifteen or twenty had run away from their masters or from the government punishment gangs at Launceston and seven or eight had broken out of Hobart Jail itself. The amount of theft, cattle-rustling, sheep-stealing and general predacity "forbade," Wylde urged in his creaking syntax, "as illusory almost, the Hope that a renewed extension of Mercy to them would influence an amelioration of Principle." Translated, this meant, "Hang as many as you can."[41]

They did. Macquarie, visiting Van Diemen's Land with Wylde, conferred with Sorell and made sure that plenty of rope was used against the "depraved Wretches, . . . cruel and savage Depredators" then in custody awaiting trial. A circuit court convened in Launceston, and nine out of thirteen bushrangers swung. In Hobart, out of twenty-six awaiting their fate, ten were hanged. "Now that these dreadful examples have been made," Macquarie wrote to London, "I am enabled to report that there is every reasonable prospect of the Bush-Ranging System being completely at an End, most probably for many Years to come."[42]

He was wrong. Bushranging continued with unabated vigor after 1821, still with the clandestine support of the convict population. The next "Dick Turpin" to win fame in Van Diemen's Land was Matthew Brady (1799–1826), a Manchester boy sentenced by the Salford Assizes in 1820 to seven years' exile on the Fatal Shore for stealing a basket with some bacon, butter and rice. Wild with resentment, he tried again and again to abscond and was pushed down from assignment to the chain gang and finally to the penal nadir: Macquarie Harbor. In the first four years of his transportation he took 350 lashes.[43]

In June 1824, Brady and thirteen other convicts escaped from Macquarie Harbor in a whaleboat. Before the end of the month they reached the Derwent, came ashore, robbed a settler of his guns and provisions and began to range the bush. They quickly found themselves famous. Colonel George Arthur, the new lieutenant-governor of Van Diemen's Land, papered the gum trees with proclamations calling "in the most earnest manner" on all settlers to join in the hunt for the Brady gang, and to order their Crown servants to pass on whatever information they heard. It was futile, for the convicts would rather join Brady than rat on him. Convict servants hid Brady and his men in barns, fed them and showed them where the master's guns were kept. Arthur next appealed to baser motives by posting rewards: first £10 per head for each member of the growing Brady gang—which by now was rumored to be one hundred strong—then £25. If a convict gave information that led to the arrest of one of these bandits, he would get his ticket-of-leave. If he caught the bushranger himself, he got a conditional pardon. The only result was a notice pinned to the door of the Royal Oak Inn at Cross Marsh a week later:

> It has caused Matthew Brady much concern that such a person known as Sir George Arthur is at large. Twenty gallons of rum will be given to any person that can deliver his person to me.

There was no question that the lad was flash. He was chivalrous, too, in his way. Brady would never harm a woman or let any of his gang do so. When his partner McCabe threatened to rape a settler's wife, Brady shot him through the hand, flogged him mercilessly and threw him out of the gang; Arthur's police caught McCabe ten days later, and hanged him. A psychopath named Mark Jeffries, a government executioner and flogger who had absconded and was known as "The Monster," had captured a settler's wife while he was on the run but was irked by the squalling of her newborn baby. He picked it up by the legs and smashed its head against a gum tree. Later he was caught and jailed for trial in Launceston. When Brady heard about this he had to be argued out of leading his gang in a frontal assault on the Launceston lockup, freeing all the prisoners, dragging Jeffries out and flogging him to death.

Knowing that his protection was other convicts, Brady took care not to harm assigned servants in the homesteads he robbed; but in case they "gave music" to the police later, he forced them to drink their masters' whiskey until they were too fuddled to remember what his men had said, or which way they had gone. At least one luckless teetotaller died from this; and others, due to the vile quality of colonial spirits, became very sick.

The Brady gang fought like Tasmanian devils when cornered, with skill and coolness, shooting their way past many police ambushes. They had no compunction about revenging themselves on people who they believed were their oppressors—especially "flogging magistrates"—but they would also treat their captives fairly if such people had once been fair to them. Thus they made a prisoner of John Barnes, a colonial surgeon, while ransacking a magistrate's house at Coal River:

> One of them men who stopped me . . . had been punished a few days before by order of the magistrate, upon some trifling complaint of his master; the man was not in very good health . . . and I took him down before the whole of the flagellation had been inflicted, and requested that the magistrate would pardon him the rest; he recollected the circumstance with a little gratitude, or probably I might have been more severely handled.[44]

They took his watch but gave him back his lancet-case, "telling me that that might be of service to them by and by."

But Lieutenant-Governor Arthur was a tirelessly methodical man, and he wore Brady down. With a reorganized police force and more soldiers from the 40th Regiment under his command, he picked off the gang members in running skirmishes, one by one. He offered irresistible rewards—300 guineas or 300 acres of land free of quit-rent to the man who brought Brady in; or, for convicts, a full unconditional pardon and free passage to England. He sent rank-and-file field police convicts out wearing fetters, to infiltrate the remnants of Brady's gang with a story of having escaped from the chain gang. Betrayed and outflanked, Brady was shot in the leg in a skirmish near Paterson's Plains outside Launceston. He got away but was captured a few days later, limping and exhausted, by a settler named John Batman (the future founder of Melbourne).

They put Matthew Brady in Launceston Jail and a few days later loaded him with chains and brought him down to Hobart—accompanied, to his disgust, by the man he most despised in the world, the infant-killer Mark Jeffries. Before his trial and hanging, Brady was feted as a popular hero. Dozens of petitions for clemency arrived at Government House. Women shed tears for the "likely lad," the "poor colonial boy," who had shown such consideration to their sex. His cell was filled every day with visitors bringing baskets of flowers, fan letters, fruit and fresh-baked cakes. If his fate had been decided by vote, he would have gone free. But the judge was determined to make a solemn and awful example of him. On May 4, 1826, Brady received his last Communion and mounted the scaffold above a sea of colonial faces, contorted in grief or cheering him over the drop; only his enemies were silent. The government could not expunge his name from popular memory: A 4,000-foot peak in the Western Tiers, which frowns directly down on Arthur's Lake below, is still known as Brady's Lookout, and there is a Brady's Lake out past Tungatinah power station on the Lyell Highway—whereas Mike Howe is remembered in less noble geographical detail, a gully near Lawrenny and a marsh east of Table Mountain.

Matthew Brady was by no means the last Tasmanian bushranger, or even the last to acquire a popular aura (that man was Martin Cash, an Irish *picaro* who absconded no less than four times from Port Arthur in the early 1840s and lived to a ripe age as a farmer near Glenorchy). But he was the last politically significant bandit, the last menacing avatar of a convict counterculture in Van Diemen's Land that soon withered under the patient, systematic totalitarianism of Sir George Arthur. After Brady's death, no roaming bushranger would be able to impede, or even threaten, the progress of Tasmanian settlement. Nor would any of them threaten a *jacquerie*, the convicts' revolt that had figured in the nightmares of Australian settlers and governors since the Irish rose at Toongabbie in 1804. Van Diemen's Land was a small island, soon filled up, and the pattern of ownership and intensive grazing that dominated it by the mid-1830s disposed of the bushrangers' environment. They could no longer strike from virgin wilderness to prosperous farm or town in a day's walk, or even a day's ride. They were left without cover, like foxes in a bare field; whereas 700 miles north on the mainland, in the wide expanses of New South Wales that lay back from the coast, the bandits continued to pillage and present their threats to the law, reminding convicts and awakening the fears of their masters that chains were made to be broken.

iv

IT WAS ON the mainland, after 1825, that the popular myth of the Australian bushranger took its final form in story and folksong. Repressed in Van Diemen's Land by Lieutenant-Governor Arthur—significantly, there seem to be no bushranger ballads of Tasmanian origin—it sprang up like an irritant weed in New South Wales. Bushranging became a social problem there later than in Van Diemen's Land, because Sydney and Parramatta had never had to rely on convict kangaroo-hunters for their early survival. Not until the colony broke out of the narrow coastal plains and expanded over the mountains to Bathurst (giving plenty of scope for outlaws to hide in the gorges and caves of the Blue Mountains, now within striking distance of new trunk roads and farms) did bushranging start to flourish. And the supply of new bushrangers was guaranteed by Governor Ralph Darling's crackdown in convict discipline. Most of them came from the dreaded iron gangs working on the "Great West Road" across the Blue Mountains and on the "Great North Road," surveyed in 1825 and completed in 1831, which ran through 170 miles of rough sterile gorges and linked Sydney to the burgeoning farm districts of Maitland and the Hunter River Valley. The local names for spots along this road were eloquent: "Hungry Flat," "Dennis's Dog-Kennel," "No-Grass Valley," "Devil's Backbone." As the iron gangs of Darling's administration wore their way through the mountain sandstone, cutting the roads foot by anguished foot, there was no shortage of men who would rather take to the bush at any risk than spend another day "condemned to live in slavery, and wear the convict chain."

For ten years the roads and semi-settled districts of New South Wales, west to Parramatta and Bathurst, north to the Hunter River, were pestered by bushranging convicts who struck singly or in small gangs. There was nothing romantic about them. A few were pathetic harmless men who ran away from chain gang or master because, like a Bathurst absconder named Charles Jubey, they were "so harassed and torn about" by cruel discipline that they became "weary of life." Many were mere thugs: muggers, chicken-stealers and occasional rapists. Small farmers were their victims, not the "rich," and their crimes were brutal when not petty. Some tended, not without reason, to be paranoically suspicious: Daniel "Mad Dog" Morgan (ca. 1830–1865), one of the second wave of bushrangers who terrorized Victoria and New South Wales after the convict period, was so afraid of poison that he would accept no food from the settlers he robbed except hard-boiled eggs.

When caught, the mainland bushrangers did not comport themselves like Robin Hood either. Their speeches from the dock or at the gallows' foot were apt to be primitive. In 1834, Dr. Robert Wardell, barrister and former editor of the colony's chief newspaper, *The Australian*, was riding the river boundary of his 2,500-acre estate at Petersham, near Sydney. Outside a humpy, he surprised three escaped convicts, whose leader, an iron gang absconder named John Jenkins, took aim with a stolen rifle and shot him dead. Jenkins and his adult accomplice, a runaway assigned servant named Thomas Tattersdale, were tried on the evidence of the third prisoner, a terrified boy called Emanuel Brace. At the verdict of guilty, the judge uttered his ritual question: Did either have anything to say before sentence of death was passed? Jenkins did:

> Throwing himself into a threatening and unbecoming attitude, [he] remarked, that he had not had a fair trial, a bloody old woman had been palmed upon him for Counsel; he did not care a bugger for dying, or a damn for anyone in court; and that he would as soon shoot every bloody bugger in court . . . [He made] a violent attack on Tattersdale, and struck him two tremendous blows in the face, which knocked him down in the dock . . . The Judge sat in mute astonishment. . . . [I]t took a dozen constables to secure and handcuff him.[45]

Not until 1839 would the traveller be able to speak with confidence of "bushrangers, a *sub-genus* in the order *banditti*, which, happily, can no longer exist, except in places inaccessible to the mounted police."[46] These mounted police, whose sole task was tracking and capturing bushrangers, began in 1825 as a small force of dragoons (whence, "goons") under Governor Brisbane, drawn from infantry regiments in Sydney—2 officers and 13 troopers, operating mainly around Parramatta. Darling increased it until by 1839 it had swollen to 9 officers, a sergeant-major, 156 non-commissioned officers and enlisted men, with 136 horses—not a large net to throw over so large a territory, but often an effective one. The "horse-police" or "traps" (mounted police) like Sir George Arthur's constabulary in Van Diemen's Land, were disliked only a little less than the bushrangers themselves. They were apt to use violence when dealing with small Emancipist settlers whom they routinely suspected of harboring bushrangers out of criminal sympathy. Free workers hated them, because of the "pass system" enforced under Darling's emergency Bushranging Act of 1830 (11 Geo. IV, c. 10), whereby any man in the colony who could not produce his ticket-of-leave and travel pass on demand could be clapped in jail until he could prove he was *not* an escaped convict. Despite its unpopularity, the Bushranging Act was renewed under Governor Bourke in 1832, and again in 1834. Although Bourke's gubernatorial instincts were more liberal than Darling's, he persuaded himself that it was worth offending the spirit of British law with such an act: "I believe . . . it would occasion very great dissatisfaction among the free People of the Colony to deprive them of the protection which this law affords," he told London in 1832.[47]

Furthermore, because Governor Darling had followed Sir George Arthur's lead in setting up government rewards for information against bushrangers, the colony was a morass of denunciation and spying. In this way the lower classes came to feel victimized by the bushranger laws, and this created a wave of sympathy toward the bushrangers themselves.

Much as the "free objects" (as convicts and ex-convicts sardonically called emigrant settlers in Australia) might detest the bushrangers, it was not easy to stamp out every vestige of fellow-feeling between men who had undergone the government lash. Alexander Harris, while working in the 1820s as a cedar-cutter on the coastal slopes of the Illawarra, noted that bushrangers would freely join the loggers' jamborees around the rum keg on deserted beaches and he compared the sight of their boisterous revelry to "a pirate's isle." No one would denounce them to Darling's dragoons (who seldom dared to penetrate those deep coastal forests), partly from fear of reprisals but mainly "because, having mostly been prisoners themselves, it was a point of honour among the sawyers to help them as much as they could."[48]

By the late 1820s, such sympathies had already crystallized into folk ballads—none of whose texts, unfortunately, survive. To be the hero of a song offered a snatch of immortality to the convict, as the surgeon Peter Cunningham speculated in *Two Years in New South Wales* (1827):

> The vanity of being talked of, I verily believe, leads many foolish fellows to join in this kind of life—songs being made about their exploits by their sympathising brethren. . . . It is the boast of many of them, that their names will live in the remembrance of the colony long after their exit from among us to some penal settlement, either in this world or the next; Riley, the captain of the Hunter's River banditti, vaunting that he should be long spoken of (whatever his fate may be) in fear by his enemies, and in admiration by his friends!

The year Cunningham published this, the prototype of Australian convict-ballad heroes began his desperate colonial career. His ballad, the first surviving one about a bushranger, opens in fine style:

> Come all you gallant bushrangers who gallop on the plain,
> Who scorn to live in slavery and wear the convict chain,
> Attention pay to what I say, and value it if you do—
> I shall relate the matchless fate of bold Jack Donohoe!

"Bold Jack" was a short, freckled, blond-haired, blue-eyed Irishman named John Donohoe (1806–1830), sentenced to life transportation in Dublin in 1823. On arrival in 1825, Donohoe had been assigned in the usual way (to John Pagan, a settler of Parramatta). He had misbehaved and spent time in a road gang; then he returned to assigned service under a Parramatta surgeon, Major West. The ballad, with a reasonable minimum of exaggeration, takes up the story:

> He'd scarcely served twelve months in chains upon the Australian shore,
> When he took to the highway as he had done before:
> He went with Jacky Underwood, and Webber and Walmsley too,
> These were the true companions of bold Jack Donohoe.
>
> Bold Donohoe was taken for a notorious crime,
> And sentenced to be hanged upon the gallows-tree so high—
> But when they brought him to Sydney Gaol he left them in the stew,
> For when they came to call the roll, they missed Jack Donohoe.

The "notorious crime" was committed in December 1827: Donohoe "went out" with two Irish confederates named Kilroy and Smith, holding up the bullock-drays that plied between farm and market on the Windsor Road—a kind of highway robbery which, because of the lumbering slowness of its target, did not demand a horse. The three men were soon caught, and in March 1828 they were sentenced to hang. Kilroy and Smith duly swung, but Donohoe made a break for freedom between the court and the condemned cell and fled. Before long he had assembled a small gang of other Irish and English absconders. They stole horses from settlers and, for the next eighteen months, to the discomfiture and occasional terror of the law-abiding, ranged across a wide swath of territory beyond the Blue Mountains, from Bathurst south to Yass and the Illawarra, close to Sydney and Parramatta, and north almost to the Hunter River. Hardly a week passed without a stickup, and in the bush where goods of any kind were hard to come by, Donohoe easily got rid of the swag. After his death, police searches (directed by a gang member named Walmsley, who turned informer to save his neck) showed that no less than thirty small settlers had received stolen goods from him.

> As Donohoe made his escape, to the bush he went straightway,
> The people they were all afraid to travel by night or day—
> For every day in the newspapers they brought out something new,
> Concerning that bold bushranger they called Jack Donohoe!

This verse commemorates what would become a frequent gripe of Australian authorities—that the press, in its lurid pennycatching, works against the government by making heroes out of criminals. With Ralph Darling as governor there was more point to this, for the Sydney papers took any chance they could get to make him look like a fool. In Van Diemen's Land, the colonial press pointedly observed, Lieutenant-Governor Arthur took the field himself in pursuit of bushrangers and stamped them out; but in New South Wales, Governor Darling sat in Government House, while "with a mounted police and a police establishment, *which if not effective is not for want of expense,* and a strong garrison of armed soldiery, the bushranging gentry seem to carry on their pranks almost without molestation." Donohoe and his mates even displayed a raffish elegance of dress and "a remarkably clean appearance," their leader sporting "black hat, superfine blue cloth coat lined with silk surtout fashion, plaited shirt (good quality), laced boots." Not only were they Pimpernels, the *Australian* sardonically implied, but they were not as bad as they were painted:

> *Donohoe,* the notorious bushranger, whose name is a terror in some parts of the country, though we fancy he has more credit given to him for outrages than he is deserving of, is said to have been seen by a party well acquainted with his person, in Sydney, enjoying, not more than a couple of days ago . . . a ginger-beer bottle.[49]

The price on Donohoe's head rose from £20 to £100, and Darling sent more police and volunteers into the field to refute the myth—which had spread beyond "the ignorant and tainted portion of the population"—that the fierce little Dubliner had a charmed life. They caught up with him at Bringelly, near Campbelltown outside Sydney.

> As he and his companions rode out one afternoon,
> Not thinking that the pangs of death would overtake them soon,
> To their surprise the Horse-Police rode smartly into view,
> And in double-quick time they did advance to take Jack Donohoe.
>
> "Oh Donohoe, oh Donohoe, throw down your carabine,
> Or do you intend to fight us all? And will you not resign?"
> "To surrender to such cowardly dogs is a thing I never would do—
> Today I'll fight with all my might!" cried bold Jack Donohoe.
>
> "It never shall be said of me that Donohoe the brave
> Could surrender to a policeman or become an Englishman's slave—
> I'd rather roam these hills so wild like a dingo or kangaroo
> Than work one hour for Government," cried bold Jack Donohoe.
>
> The Sergeant and the Corporal they did their men divide,
> Some fired at him from behind, and some from every side,
> The Sergeant and the Corporal they both fired at him too,
> And a rifle-bullet pierced the heart of bold Jack Donohoe.
>
> Nine rounds he fired and nine men shot before the fatal ball
> That pierced his heart and made him smart and caused him for to fall—
> And as he closed his mournful eyes, he bade the world adieu,
> Crying "Convicts all, pray for the soul of bold Jack Donohoe!"

The song embellishes, as ballads do. Donohoe did not kill nine "traps" with nine shots (or even six with six, as variants of the ballad have it) and his only recorded utterance at the moment of battle was a stream of oaths, inviting the effing buggers to come and get their bloody guts blown out, or something to that effect; he was not shot in the heart, but in the head, by a trooper named Muggleston—and so forth. Ballads are not history. Nevertheless, they do give us some sense of the penumbra of received opinion that surrounds historical events, even small ones like the killing of a flash, cursing little Mick by a squad of mounted police among the gum trees on one hot September afternoon in 1830. In death, Donohoe became more than the meager sum of his parts in life. At one end of the social scale, one finds Darling's surveyor-general Thomas Mitchell (later Sir Thomas, distinguished Australian explorer and translator of Luis de Camoëns's epic *Os Lusiades* from the Portuguese) visiting the Sydney morgue to view Donohoe's corpse and drawing his portrait, beneath which he quoted a couplet from Byron:

> No matter; I have bared my brow
> Fair in Death's face—before—and now.

At the other end of the scale, there was the Sydney shopkeeper who within a week or two of Bold Jack's death produced a line of clay pipes in the form of his head, complete with the bullet-hole in the temple. They were snapped up as devotional effigies—ceramic ballads, as it were. If Donohoe had been a sadist, a rapist or a baby-killer like Mark Jeffries in Van Diemen's Land, the outpouring of popular emotion that coalesced in the Donohoe ballads would not have occurred. But Australians admired flashness; most of them disliked Governor Darling and took great glee in seeing his authority ridiculed by this elusive bushranger. They—or, at any rate, the Emancipist and convict majority—felt that Donohoe posed no threat to them. He was a figure of fantasy, game as a spurred cock, a projection of that once-subjected, silent part of their own lives into vengeful freedom, thrown against the neutral gray screen of the bush. The legends of his freedom relieved Australians' dissatisfaction with the conformity of their own lives, and this has been the root of the cult of dead bushrangers ever since. Moreover, he was Irish, and the ballads make a point of this to commemorate the hatred of Irish convict for English guard. "It never shall be said of me that Donohoe the brave / Could surrender to a policeman or become an Englishman's slave."

Thirty years ago, the Australian historian Russel Ward noted the differences between "Bold Jack Donohoe" and earlier ballads like "Van Diemen's Land." They bespeak a big shift of attitude. The earlier ones accept the System in the name of English values, while later ballads oppose it in the name of Irish values that become Australian.[50]

"Van Diemen's Land" is a cautionary song directed to an English audience at home—"for if you knew my miseries," one version of it enjoins, "you'd never poach again." The call to repentance was a convention of the English ballads (without it, they could hardly have been printed and distributed in England). It stresses that convicts are the victims of a harsh fate that they cannot change for themselves. "May youth take warning e'er it is too late," begins one lengthy excursus in cautionary doggerel, "A Solemn Advice to All Young Men," attributed to a convict named James Kevel or Revel, returned from a fourteen-year sentence in 1823, but more likely written by some London ballad-monger, and continuing

> Lest they should share my hard unhappy fate.
> To see so many dying with hunger, pain and grief,
> And buried like dogs because they prov'd a thief.
> May all young men with speed their lives amend
> And take my advice as one that is their friend,
>
> For tho' so slight of it you may make here,
> Hard will be your lot if you are once sent there.

Such verses do not question either the order of the classes or the validity of English laws, whereas the Donohoe ballad explicitly does. Hence the ill-documented distinction, in the eyes of Australian authorities in convict days, between ordinary ballads and "treason songs," which (tradition insists) could not legally be sung, although there seems to be no local law that explicitly banned them. The voice of rebellion, defiantly inveighing against floggers and tyrants, is plainly heard in other ballads that invoke the name of Donohoe, such as the last four verses of "Jim Jones":

> For night and day the irons clang, and like poor galley-slaves
> We toil and toil, and when we die must fill dishonoured graves.
>
> But bye-and-bye I'll break my chains: into the bush I'll go,
> And join the brave bushrangers there—Jack Donohoo and Co—
>
> And some dark night when everything is silent in the town,
> I'll kill the tyrants one and all, and shoot the floggers down,
>
> I'll give the Law a little shock: remember what I say—
> They'll yet regret they sent Jim Jones in chains to Botany Bay.

And so, as the only New South Wales bushranger thrown into such high relief in the convict era, Donohoe became a general, idealized image of bushranging itself and survived long after the System had passed away.

He kept popping up with the same initials but different names: Jack Dowling, Jack Duggan, and—in the most famous of all bushranging ballads—Jim Doolan, the "Wild Colonial Boy": still Irish, still "agin the system," though it had shed its capital *S* sometime after the convict era ended. There used to be as many ways of singing "The Wild Colonial Boy" as there were pianos in Australian parlors. The most piercing one this writer has heard was not recorded: It was sung by a fat, seamed old Sydney prostitute, buoyed up by a few too many glasses of sweet port, in a pub on the Woollomooloo docks late one night in 1958—not in the rollicking front-room way of men, but as the off-key dirge of a mother grieving for her dead son:

> 'Tis of a wild Colonial boy, Jim Doolan was his name,
> Of poor but honest parents he was born in Castlemaine,
> He was his father's only hope, his mother's pride and joy,
> And so dearly did his parents love the Wild Colonial Boy.
>
> He was scarcely sixteen years of age when he left his father's home,
> And through Australia's sunny clime bushranging he did roam.
> He robbed the wealthy squatters, their stock he did destroy,
> A terror to Australia was the Wild Colonial Boy.
>
> In eighteen hundred and sixty-two he started his wild career,
> With a heart that knew no danger, no foeman did he fear.
> He bailed up the Beechworth Royal Mail Coach, and robbed Judge Macoboy,
> Who trembled and gave up his gold to the Wild Colonial Boy.
>
> He bade the Judge good morning, and told him to beware,
> He'd never robbed a poor man, or one who acted square,
> But a Judge who'd rob a mother of her only pride and joy,
> That Judge was worse of an outlaw than the Wild Colonial Boy.
>
> As Jim rode out one morning the mountain-side along,
> A-listening to the kookaburra's pleasant laughing song,
> He spied three mounted troopers, Kelly, Davis and Fitzroy,
> All riding forth to capture him, the Wild Colonial Boy.
>
> "Surrender now, Jim Doolan, you see there's three to one—
> Surrender in the Queen's name, you daring highwayman."
> Jim pulled his pistol from his belt and he waved the little toy,
> "I'll fight but not surrender," cried the Wild Colonial Boy.
>
> He fired at Trooper Kelly, and brought him to the ground,
> But turning round to Davis he received his mortal wound.
> All shattered through the jaw he lay, still firing at Fitzroy,
> And that's the way they captured him, the Wild Colonial Boy.

The second big difference between the Donohoe variant ballads and the earlier cautionary songs written for English consumption lies in what they imply about Australian nature and space. Until about 1830 the transportation ballads and broadsides present the bush as sterile and hostile, its fauna (except for the kangaroo, which no one could dislike) as eerie when not disgusting. The Fatal Shore is a desert full of snakes and cannibals, insufferably strange, the world upside down. "Our cots were fenced with fire, to slumber when we can, / To drive away wolves and tigers come by Van Diemen's Land." So goes the complaint in the ballad "Van Diemen's Land," faithfully mirroring the penal intentions of the colony, where nature was destined to punish. Space and the bush imprisoned it.

And so the absconder, by making the bush his new home, renamed it with the sign of freedom. On its blankness, he could inscribe what could not be read in spaces already colonized and subject to the laws and penal imagery of England. "As Donohoe made his escape, to the bush he went straightway." The bush is the citadel of the nay-sayer, the rebel: hence the poignancy, to Irish-Australian ears, of the chorus of "Wild Colonial Boy":

> O come along, me hearties, and we'll roam the mountains high—
> Together we will plunder, together we will die.
> We'll wander over valleys and we'll gallop over plains,
> And we'll scorn to live in slavery, bound down by iron chains.

The bushranger is the first figure in the low undergrowth of Australian literature to be identified with the bush animals: " 'I'd rather roam these hills so wild like a dingo or kangaroo / Than work one hour for Government,' cried bold Jack Donohoe." And the identification of bushranger with national landscape would persist until the railroads put an end to bushranging itself, with the destruction of the Kelly gang and the capture of their leader Ned at Glenrowan in 1880. By taking to the bush, the convict left England and entered Australia. Popular sentiment would praise him for this transvaluation of the landscape (though at a safe distance, of course) for another hundred and fifty years.

8

Bunters, Mollies and Sable Brethren

i

OF THE PEOPLE transported to the antipodes between 1788 and 1852, about twenty-four thousand were women: one person in seven. Many Australians still think their Founding Mothers were whores. Undoubtedly some were prostitutes in the real sense of the word —that is, they survived by selling their sexual services, casually or regularly, without sentimental attachments. A commonly quoted figure, though a somewhat impressionistic one, is one woman in five.[1] When a woman at her trial described herself as a prostitute—"on the town" was the usual phrase—one can assume that she was telling the truth. In the mouths of Authority, the word "prostitute" was less a job description than a general term of abuse.

What is quite certain, however, is that no women were actually transported for whoring, because it was never a transportable offense. The vast majority of female convicts, more than 80 percent, were sent out for theft, usually of a fairly petty sort. Crimes of violence figured low among them, as one might expect—about 1 percent.[2] Sentences of more than seven years were exceedingly rare. None of this, given the severity of the English laws, suggests at the outset a very high degree of moral profligacy.

And yet there was rarely a comment on colonial society, scarcely a passage of evidence to the various Select Committees on Transportation, hardly a tract or a diary or a letter home, that missed the chance to describe the degeneracy, incorrigibility and worthlessness of women convicts in Australia. Military officers believed this, and so did doctors, judges, parsons, governors and, of course, their respectable wives. Convict men might in the end redeem themselves through work and penance, but women almost never. It was as though women convicts had passed the ordinary bounds of class and become a fiction, not far from pornography: crude raucous Eve, sucking rum and mothering bastards in the exterior darkness, inviting contempt rather than pity from her social superiors, rape rather than help from men.

Australian historians once swallowed this stereotype whole. "Even if these contemporaries exaggerated," wrote A. G. L. Shaw, "the picture [that women convicts] presented is a singularly unattractive one!"[3] Some later feminist historians, led by Anne Summers and Miriam Dixson, have striven to retain the picture while dismantling the biases, arguing that many or even most convict women became whores but that their fate was foisted on them by a tyrannous male power structure. The most influential statement of the case was made by Anne Summers:

> It was deemed necessary by both the local and the British authorities to have a supply of whores to keep the men, both convict and free, quiescent. The Whore stereotype was devised as a calculated sexist means of social control and then . . . characterised as being the fault of the women who were damned by it.[4]

The classic double-bind, in short. The problem is the quality of the contemporary opinions on which the Whore stereotype, accepted by Reverend Samuel Marsden and feminist historians alike (though for very different motives), was based.

The British Government did not send women to Australia to keep men "quiescent" in any political sense; the lash could do that. But the presence of women, considered as carrot rather than stick, did have its uses in social control. Eve the Whore would keep Adam the Rogue from turning homosexual, an important consideration: William Pitt would underwrite a colony of thieves, but not one of perverts. The government did not, of course, announce in so many words that female convicts were sent to Australia as breeding-stock and sexual conveniences. Indeed, the original plan of settlement drawn up by Lord Sydney in 1786 spoke of enslaving women for this purpose

> from the Friendly Islands, New Caledonia, Etc., which are contiguous thereto, and from whence any number may be procured without difficulty; and without a sufficient proportion of that sex it is well-known that it would be impossible to preserve the settlement from gross irregularities and disorders.[5]

Arthur Phillip rejected this idea, of course, for kidnapped Tahitian women would only "pine away in misery." He asked for more women convicts to be sent out, not for their labor but because he wanted the felons to marry one another and so raise a native-born yeomanry—the genetic equivalent of his hope for an economic base of agriculture run by small-farming Emancipists. He offered rewards of land or free time (an extra day a week for raising their own crops for sale or barter) to convicts who married. Some of these hastily legitimized unions proved bigamous, since a number of the newlyweds were, in fact, already married but had left their husbands or wives behind them in England. From a "respectable" viewpoint, this policy seemed a farce, and the matrimonial rush only a scramble for gubernatorial favors.[6]

The Scottish forger Thomas Watling, himself a convict, sniffed that "little I think could reasonably have been expected from the coupling of *whore* and *rogue* together." "Prostitution" and "concubinage" flourished in early colonial Sydney, as marriage did not. On this, the respectable convict, the respectable officer and the respectable cleric all agreed, because their terms of judgment were exactly the same. "There is scarcely a man without his mistress," Watling complained, adding with sublime ignorance of the sexual habits of English working people that "the high class first exhibit it; the low, to do them justice, faithfully copy it." The officers, being officers, got first pick of the women; and a female convict soon learned that her best chance of survival in New South Wales was to give herself over to the "protection" of some dominant male. In a tone of resentful irony, Watling advised "ladies of easy virtue" to get transported if they possibly could:

> They may rest assured, that they will meet with every indulgence from the humane officers and sailors in the passage; and after running the gauntlet there, will, notwithstanding, be certain of coming upon immediate keeping at their arrival. . . . Be she ever so despicable in person or manners, here she may depend that she will dress and live better and easier than ever she did in the prior part of her prostitution.[7]

Watling's prejudices were genteel. He believed he was writing as a "respectable" person (forgers always did) and his opinion of women convicts exactly reflected the attitudes of the middle class from which he had fallen. Respectable people in London—let alone in the chilly latitudes of John Knox, north of the Scottish border—saw little moral difference between prostitution and cohabitation. Patrick Colquhoun, as we have seen, included the female half of all unmarried couples in his attempts to guess the number of "prostitutes" in the "criminal class" of London. Before long the word "prostitute" came to be used of anyone promiscuous, paid or not. Eventually the distinction was so worn down by the weight of moral disapproval bearing upon the lower classes from the middle classes that Henry Mayhew, that indefatigable reporter, could claim that "prostitution . . . does not consist solely in promiscuous intercourse, for she who confines her favors to one may still be a prostitute," even if her motives were "voluptuous" and not mercenary. In short, the moral vocabulary of the English middle classes enabled the free in Australia to speak of "prostitution" among convicts when they meant any extramarital relationship. And as neither the penal system nor pioneer life favored marriage (official policy always encouraged it, but such encouragement was more than offset by the general poverty of small settlers and the uncertain, bush-wandering nature of an Emancipist worker's life), the respectable saw "prostitution" everywhere, even in sturdy matches that had lasted years out of wedlock and produced broods of children.[8] As the historian Michael Sturma points out, the idea that convicts shared the same ideas about sexual behavior as their superiors is very dubious:

> Working-class mores [in England] differed markedly from those of the upper and middle classes. . . . [A]mong the British working-class, cohabitation was prevalent. It is highly unlikely that working-class men, and in particular male convicts, considered the women convicts to be in some way sexually immoral. . . . The stereotype of women convicts as prostitutes emerged from . . . an ignorance of working-class habits.[9]

One notorious result of such thinking was the "Female Register" drawn up by the Reverend Samuel Marsden in 1806, an inspired piece of creative bigotry in which every woman in the colony, except for a few widows, was classified as either "married" or "concubine." By Marsden's count, there were 395 of the former and 1,035 of the latter. The only kind of marriage he recognized was one performed by a Church of England clergyman—ideally, himself. It followed that all Catholic and Jewish women who married within the form of their religion were automatically listed as "concubines," as were all common-law wives whose relationship with their men, however durable, went unsanctified by Anglican rite. One such woman, Mary Marshall, had lived with her "husband" Robert Sidaway for eighteen years but was listed as a "concubine." Sarah Bellamy had lived for sixteen years with the colony's master-builder, James Bloodworth or Bloodsworth, the bricklayer who was transported on the First Fleet and supervised the erection of Sydney's first permanent buildings, and had borne him seven children. No relationship could have been more respectable, devoted or tenacious than theirs. It ended in 1804 with Bloodworth's death from pneumonia. In gratitude for his services to the infant colony, Governor King buried him with military honors. Nevertheless, Sarah Bellamy went down on Marsden's list as "concubine," along with a twelve-year-old girl and a sixty-four-year-old widow. Yet when it reached London, this absurdly pharisaical document was read and apparently believed by Lord Castlereagh and William Wilberforce, and it became an authoritative text on colonial morality. As the historian Portia Robinson comments:

> That few women were legally married did not necessarily imply that the conduct of the remainder made New South Wales "a sink of infamy." It simply meant that the standards of morality and the definitions of marriage familiar to the women concerned did not agree with those imposed on society by Samuel Marsden. Contemporaries accepted his conclusions as to the nature of the women of Botany Bay and modern historians have continued to perpetuate this view.[10]

Marsden was not alone in his prejudices; and as people are named, so they will be treated. While one may doubt that the British Government set out to create special forms of humiliation and degradation for women in Australia, there is no doubt that the whore-stereotype, accepted by the upper layers of a rigid little colonial society, wielded immense power. Indeed, it would remain, though gradually fading, as part of the design of Australian sexual politics for a century after transportation was abolished. The attitudes behind the stereotype can be seen clearly in the private journal of Ralph Clark (?–1794), marine officer on the *Friendship* in the First Fleet.

When Lieutenant Clark sailed for Australia in 1787 he left behind his wife Betsy Alicia Trevan, a pretty Devon girl from a landed family, and their chubby firstborn son, Ralph Stuart Clark, aged not quite two. As the First Fleet rolled southward, Clark was tortured by remorse and nostalgia. Was a promotion worth this sundering? Betsy Alicia fills the journal as he pours forth his grief in ink, trying to conjure up the family he might not see again:

> Dear good woman I did not know thy worth . . . Alicia, my friend, my dear wife, and beautiful little engaging son, Oh sweet boy, what would your father give for a kiss of your mother and you, oh I think I hear him cry Papa, Papa, as I am taking my hat to go out, dear sweet sound, music to my poor ears, the only happiness that I have is the kissing of my Betsy's dear picture and my little boy's hair that she sent. I would not part with them for a Captain's commission.[11]

Clark devises a small ritual with the "dear picture," a miniature under a hinged glass lid. Each morning, Monday to Saturday, he kisses the glass. On Sundays he raises the tiny oval pane to kiss "my dear Alicia's picture out of the case," the image symbolically laid bare, a little closer to flesh. This act is both a denuding and a prayer, as to the effigy of a female saint. Holiness and sexuality are intertwined through the knot of marriage. Sometimes his dreams of Alicia are sexual ("Dreamt last night of seeing my dear beloved Alicia in bed and I pulled her towards me"), but usually they reflect his guilt at leaving her and his fear of losing her. He cannot quite make sense of his dreams, but they seem ominous; he is unhappy

> from dreaming that my Alicia took a dead louse from herself and gave it to me, oh unlucky dream, for I have often heard her say that dreaming of lice was a certain sign of sickness.[12]

Alicia is the fixed star of well-being in Clark's emotional universe. Her name summons up what he left behind: security, fidelity, licit sexual delight, social continuity, maternal tenderness. The conventional form in which he phrased these feelings belies their intensity. He never meant to publish his journal; he was not a writer but a miserably homesick young marine trying to set down his deepest emotional engagements in a language of sensibility derived from the genteel culture of the day:

> Read the remainder of the *Tragedy of Douglas* this day, oh it is a sweet play. . . . [W]hat are the emotions in the breast of Lady Randolph when she sees the features and shape of her lost and stained husband Douglas in that of young Norval, little does she know, fond mother, that it is her long lost son . . . but still I cannot think that she loved as my Betsy, my virtuous Alicia does.[13]

To say that Ralph Clark idealized his wife would understate his feelings: She monopolized his image of women. If another woman misbehaved, her violence or immorality became a slur on Alicia, suggesting to him on some less-than-conscious level that she too might fall from grace. Hence the vindictive contrast Clark drew between Alicia and the female convicts over whom he was placed in authority. He was being punished for their sins by losing his adored wife. "I could never have thought that there were so many abandoned wenches in England, they are ten thousand times worse than the men Convicts, and I am afraid we will have a great deal more trouble with them," he wrote while they were still in the English Channel. In July, when four of *Friendship*'s sailors were found at it with four female convicts in the 'tween-decks, the captain had the men flogged; but, Clark added, "if I had been the Commander I would have flogged the four whores also."[14] The Whore was typically foulmouthed:

> Elizabeth Barber one of the Convict women abused the doctor in a most terrible manner and said that he wanted to f—— her and called him all the names she could think of. . . . She began to abuse Capt. Merideth in a much worse manner, and said she was no more a whore than his

wife. . . . In all the course of my days I never heard such expressions come from the mouth of a human being. . . . She desired Merideth to come and kiss her Cunt for he was nothing but a lousy rascal as were we all. I wish to God she was out of the ship, I would rather have a hundred more men than have a single woman.[15]

The gulf between such "damned bitches of convict women" and distant Betsy, "surely an angel and not a woman," is absolute, and his hatred of the debased lower orders for taking him away from his wife leads to fantasies and dreams of violence. "If they were to lose anything of mine that I gave them to wash I would cut them in pieces," he writes of women doing laundry duty on board; and later he dreams that "I was going down to Tregadock to take leave of [the family] before I went to Botany, but was assaulted by a great mob, whom I was obliged to handle rather roughly with my sword." Three years later, suffering the rigors of Norfolk Island duty after the wreck of the *Sirius*, he pens a brutally dismissive epitaph on the first person to die a natural death there, a convict woman named Ann Farmer: "She was better than half dead before they sent her from England, by all accounts she was a most wicked woman having been the occasion of more than twenty men and women coming to untimely ends, but she is now gone where she will be rewarded according to her merits." Soon he was wishing death on other women convicts as well. "I wish the Almighty would be so kind to us as to take a few of them, for we could do much better without them at present."[16]

Clark got away eventually and was briefly reunited with his Betsy Alicia in June 1792. After that, his diary ceases before he could see his ideal again. In December 1792, he returned to service in the war against France. Early in 1794 Betsy Alicia died in childbirth, and the child was stillborn. A few months later, Clark's darling boy, Ralph, then a nine-year-old midshipman, died of yellow fever on board ship in the Caribbean, during a fight with a French ship. Clark was on board, too, and was killed in battle the same day. However, that was not quite the end of Clark's line, for at the time of his death he had a three-year-old daughter, whom he scarcely knew. She had been born to a convict woman, Mary Branham, on Norfolk Island in July 1791. At Clark's insistence, she had been christened Alicia. There is no reference to her mother in his journal.

ii

THE WOMEN in the First Fleet were picked haphazardly, ranging from old crones to mere children. There was more system on the next female transport, *Lady Juliana*, which brought young women of "marriageable" age, "the colony at that time being in great want of women." A few of them were hardened professional criminals, like Mrs. Barnsley, a shoplifter who boasted that her family had been swindlers and highwaymen for a hundred years; her brother, a highwayman, often visited her on board before the fleet sailed, "as well-dressed and genteel in his appearance as any gentleman." At the other end of the scale was a meek little creature who bore a curiously strong resemblance to the prime minister, William Pitt, and was thought by all on board to be his bastard daughter.

Some wept and stormed, some tried to escape, and others spent the weeks before sailing hidden in corners, pale with shock and shame, their eyes red with incessant weeping; a young Scottish girl died of a broken heart before the ship left the Thames. Most of them were so demoralized by their "ruin"—the cycle of poverty, pregnancy and survival by theft or prostitution that formed the plot of a thousand melodramas and ballads simply because it was one of the commonest things that could happen to a girl—that John Nicol, a Scottish steward on the *Lady Juliana*, thought they were actually glad to be on board. "When I inquired their reason," he recalled,

> they answered, "How much more preferable is our present situation to what it has been since we commenced our vicious habits? . . . Banishment is a blessing to us. Have we not been banished for a long time, and yet in our native land, the most dreadful of all situations? We dared not go to our relations, whom we had disgraced. Other people would shut their doors in our faces. We were as if a plague were upon us, hated and shunned."[17]

Such sentiments, whatever their literary garnish, remind one how the morale of female convicts, never very strong, must have broken down on the way to Australia. London or Botany Bay: both poles of the world were, to many, equally alien and empty of hope. "Harmless unfortunate creatures," Nicol called them, "the victims of the basest seduction . . . a troublesome cargo, yet not dangerous or very mischievous, as I may say more noise than danger."

As soon as the Second Fleet was at sea, the seamen of *Lady Juliana* began to pair off with their cargo, thus starting the almost invariable pattern of later voyages. Doubtless some of the tars felt like pashas, lording it over a seaborne seraglio. Yet Nicol's phrase is significant: "Every man on board took a wife from among the convicts, they nothing loath." Offensive as such pairings were to later middle-class morality they were simply taken for granted among workers in villages, in ports and in London itself. Certainly Nicol did not regard his "wife," Sarah

Whitlam, transported to Australia for seven years for stealing a cloak, as a whore. He remembered her with respect and tenderness as

> a girl of a modest reserved turn, as kind and true a creature as ever lived; I courted her for a week and upwards, and would have married her on the spot, had there been a clergyman on board. . . . I had fixed my fancy on her from the moment I knocked the rivet out of her irons upon the anvil, and as firmly resolved to bring her back to England, when her time was out, my lawful wife.[18]

He could not get her released, however, and he sailed back to England alone, leaving Sarah Whitlam and their son, born on shipboard, in Sydney.

One may doubt, however, that all sailors showed convict women as much respect as Nicol claimed he showed his Sarah. Lord Auckland, the chairman of the 1812 Select Committee on Transportation, visited a brig loaded with women convicts that lay in the Thames in the summer of 1812 (well after the committee's work was done) to question its skipper "as to the means of preventing improper intercourse between the sailors and the women." The captain told him that

> every sailor was allowed to have one woman to cohabit with him during the voyage.—Had information of this practice been laid before the Committee . . . it would have been marked with the strongest reprobation as likely to lead some and confirm others of these unfortunate women in habits of prostitution and disorder.[19]

Clearly, such "unfortunates" were not being sent to Australia to drain England of some social purulence. Even if they all had been prostitutes, their banishment would have made no difference to English crime; but it would mean a great deal to an infant colony troubled by sexual starvation. The policy was reflected in the the age of transported women— "marriageable age," as the 1812 Select Committee on Transportation was told:

> Q. To what ages are women limited? —We generally confine it, as near as possible, to about 24 and not more than 45. . . . [T]hey are very young that go out, from London in particular.[20]

"A lonely woman is a poor thing in a Country where there are so many villains," wrote one of the officers of the female transport *Britannia* in 1798.[21] When a ship bearing women anchored in Sydney Cove, its upper deck became a slave-market, as randy colonists came swarming over the bulwarks, grinning and ogling and chumming up to the captain with a bottle of rum, while the female convicts—washed for the occasion and dressed in the remnants of their English finery—were mustered before them, trying as hard as they could "to set themselves off to the best advantage." Military officers got the first pick, then non-commissioned officers, then privates, and lastly such ex-convict settlers as seemed "respectable" enough to obtain the governor's permission to keep a female servant. (Such permission was a very great favor before Macquarie's day; and it was stingily given, as an unusual reward, by the governors after Phillip: Grose, Paterson, Hunter, King and Bligh.) According to one former convict, not all the women assigned to officers were made their mistresses (some men, after all, were married and had brought their wives). In fact, "there were several women who were rather taken by the officers as prostitutes than as servants"; [22] most of the convict women in the colony cohabited with men and the fitful attempts to curb this did not really apply to officers. Thus, Bligh had forbidden women to be "taken off the store, without being married, unless it was as servant to an officer." Bligh himself declared, bluntly enough, that "it was impossible to prevent prostitution" (but here he clearly means cohabitation), "and therefore there was no necessity for any regulations respecting it . . . [S]ettlers wanted female servants, and pitched upon particular women for whom they applied, who perhaps cohabited together; these things could never be prevented." [23]

Some witnesses found this spectacle morally barbarous, "rendering the whole Colony little better than an extensive Brothel," [24] but the governors were slow to discourage it because it got the women—whose labor was not much use—"off the store," so that they did not have to be fed and supported at government expense. It petered out during Macquarie's administration, after some harsh injunctions from London. [25]

It was the sense of helplessness, above all, that ground the women prisoners down. Reflecting on the regular shipboard slave market, "a Custom that reflects the highest Disgrace upon the British Government in that Colony," one observer noted that all the women were not equally "depraved" on arrival; but they were driven down by "Jealousy Vexation & want." "All have not run to the same Excesses of Iniquity; some occasionally are found better disposed, and perhaps their number would be much increased if they were not, on their first arrival, promiscuously thrown into such difficulties and temptations." [26]

Since the liaisons were free of legal ties, a settler could simply throw a convict woman out when he was tired of her. This caused a troublesome floating population of whores and unattached "disorderly women" to accumulate around Sydney Cove, whose westerly arm, "The Rocks," soon acquired a well-deserved name as the rowdiest and most dangerous thieves' kitchen in the colony. As early as 1793, these women were offending all who met them, including a Spanish lieutenant who stopped in Sydney on an exploration vessel, the *Atrevida:* They made "continuous seductive advances" to his crewmen, slipped them Mickey Finns, robbed them blind, and were so "degraded by vice, or rather greed" that the notorious dock-women of Tenerife paled in memory beside them.[27] In 1802 Michael Hayes, an Irishman from Wexford who had been transported as a political prisoner for his part in the abortive Irish uprising of 1798, wrote to his sister Mary pleading with her not to come out and join him. He warned her of

> the distress that generally accompany [sic] unprotected Females coming to this distant part of the world. . . . Even were you with me your life would be a solitary one, [unless] you were to asociate with Prostitutes. In this country there is Eleven Hundred women I cannot count Twenty out of that number to be virtuous. The remainder support themselves through the means of Ludeness. . . . This way of life was sanctioned by the Governors, from the first Landing to this day.[28]

Hayes also mentioned the punishments, similar to the barbarous treatment of adulteresses in Puritan societies, visited on convict women who could not, due to their weaker constitutions and the relative mercy of the governor, be flogged as severely as men:

> They are so accustomed to their lude way of life that the most severe punishments will not restrain them. I have been witness to some flogged at the Tryangle, more led through the Town [with] a rope round their waist held by the common Executioner, and a label on their necks denoting the crime. The mode of punishment mostly adopted now is mostly shaving their heads and Ducking, and afterwards [they are] sent up to Hard Labour with the men.[29]

Women who had money or evidence of property were usually given their ticket-of-leave on arrival—at least up to the early 1820s and the departure of Macquarie. So were married women joining their husbands in Sydney; if the husband was a convict, he too would generally get his ticket, "as affording greater facilities of support." A female convict could also secure her ticket-of-leave on the dock if she had a special recommendation from the captain or surgeon of the transport ship—an arrangement that gave the ship's officers a great deal of sexual leverage, although most refrained from using it.[30]

All the others—those pregnant or with children born on shipboard, the rejects from the "market," the poor, the ugly, the mad, the old, the wizened—were sent to the Female Factory in Parramatta. They travelled by barge, along the long crinkling silver arm of Sydney Harbor, up the

Parramatta River: a stately progress through that wild and exquisite land-scape between banks lined with ancient eucalypts, where sudden green clouds of budgerigars whirled over the water and the white cockatoos flapped, shrieking like colonies of lost souls, from tree to tree. If the wind set fair, the trip took all day, but sometimes it used up the night as well; then they had to bed down at one of the ramshackle inns, mere huts with straw in back, along the river. The innkeepers—not jolly publicans, but hard-eyed ex-convicts who had got their little corner of the rum trade—plied them with liquor until they were stupefied and then robbed them of their small possessions. The barge constable did nothing to protect them.[31]

What greeted them the next day, as they floundered blearily into Parramatta, was a scene of disgusting squalor. The Female Factory was a loft above a jail, some sixty feet by twenty. This loft was filthy and its floor could not, in any case, be washed, since its boards had warped so much that water went straight through the cracks onto the heads of prisoners in the cells below. The roof leaked, the privies stank, and the kitchen was just a fireplace. Here, the women were expected to card and spin wool into yarn, and from the yarn weave the coarse "Parramatta cloth" from which convicts' winter clothes were made. Those who had not managed to bring their bedding from the transport ship had to sleep on piles of scungy raw wool, full of ticks and dags; the government did not give mattresses or blankets to Parramatta women.[32]

The Factory had room for only a third of the women prisoners. The rest had to lodge on whatever terms they could get with the local settlers. The cost of "lodging and fire" was usually about four shillings a week, a sum which most women could only raise by "buttock-and-twang." Their main clientele consisted of the male convicts, who had no money either and had either to steal it or work for it in their own time after they had done their "government task" for the day. Most preferred the former; and so, one irritated colonist pointed out, more than £1,560 was stolen every year in Parramatta to pay the "whores." Macquarie reported that almost any night one could see up to three hundred convicts of both sexes roaming the town "at full liberty."[33] And the Reverend Samuel Marsden complained that

> there is not a bushel of wheat or maize in the farmer's barn, nor a sheep in his fold, nor a hog in his stye—nor even a potatoe, turnip or cabbage in his garden—but what he is likely to be robbed of every night . . . to supply the wants of these abandoned women, to whom the men can gain access at all times of the night.[34]

Meanwhile the superintendent of the Female Factory did nothing for his prisoners except give them their rations and reassure the government that all was quiet among the women. One of these incumbents, an oily Emancipist named Durie, went so far as to admit in 1811, after a testy memo from Macquarie, that he had let women sleep outside the Factory; but now he had abolished "this indulgence" and in future they will all sleep inside the Factory walls. Actually, it had no "walls," except the ones that held up its roof, and convicts of both sexes came and went as they pleased.[35]

In 1819 Macquarie had his ex-convict architect Francis Greenway design a new Female Factory, a pretty three-story Georgian structure complete with clock, cupola and security wall. But the social conditions inside it were still imperfect. Thomas Reid, surgeon on the female transport *Morley*, visited his former charges there early in 1821 and found it hard to describe their "miserable state." They gathered around him, weeping incoherently, and he learned that when they had arrived there the previous evening they had been surrounded by hordes of idle fellows, convicts . . . provided with bottles of spirits . . . for the purpose of forming a banquet *according to custom*, which they assured themselves of enjoying without interruption, as a prelude to excesses which decency forbids to mention."[36]

In the new Factory, the women were sorted into three classes: "general," "merit" and "crime." The "crime" class of incorrigibles wore no badge, but their hair was cropped, as a mark of disgrace. The "merit" class was made up of those who had sustained six months' good behavior. The "general" class was by far the largest, and it resembled a nursing-hospital, being mainly composed of unlucky girls who had been sent back to the Factory when they got pregnant on assigned service. They were not compelled to reveal the father's name, and when asked they usually said he was the Reverend Samuel Marsden.

The Female Factory was the colony's main marriage-market, and settlers took themselves to Parramatta to find a "Factory lass" (the Australian equivalent of the mail-order bride). All it took was a written permit from Marsden, written notice to the matron and enough phlegm to endure the teasing and taunts of the women. "It requires the face of a Turk to come on such an open and acknowledged errand." A bizarre scene: The women lined up in their coarse flannel dresses, some scowling and others hopefully primping; the "Coelebs" or bachelor, often an elderly and tongue-tied "stringybark" from the back country, hesitating his way along the rank; the matron reeling off the women's characters and records. "After uttering the awkward 'yes,' " recalled one witness to this colonial mating ritual in the 1820s,

the bride-elect flies around to her pals, bidding hasty adieus, and the bridegroom leads her out. "I'll give you three months before you're returned!" cries one, and "It's a *bargain* you've got, old stringy-bark!" cries another. Hubbub and confusion mark the exit of the couple. . . . The clothes of the convict are returned to her, and dressed again like a free woman she hies with her suitor of an hour to the church. Government gives her a "ticket of leave" as a dower, and she steps into her husband's carriage to go to his farm.[37]

These unions were not guaranteed to last. The "Factory lasses," one ex-convict thought, only wanted to get back to Sydney and "dress themselves up and go to the flash houses, and at night to the dancing houses, then they are happy":

I have known . . . very nice young women as you could wish to see, actually marry an old man, as ragged as possible, and perhaps he lives 20 or 30 miles up in the country, and no house within 5 or 6 miles of him, right up in the bush, where you can see nothing but the trees; but there is a policy in that, this man is a free man, and when they are married it makes her free, then after she has stop'd a day or two she will make some excuse which a woman is never at a loss for, to come down to Sydney; she will get what money she can of him (the Old Fool!) but she don't return again.[38]

Punishments for the "crime" class at the Parramatta Factory—and at its no less disagreeable southern cousin, the Female Factory in Hobart, which was built in 1827 and was so overcrowded that it stank like the hold of a slave ship—were not as severe as for the men. By the 1820s, female convicts in New South Wales could no longer be seen hauling big baskets of earth for bridge construction; nor, as a rule, did "refractory" women have to wear spiked iron collars, or be whipped to the beat of a drum. However, a treadmill was put in the Parramatta Female Factory in 1823, and in 1837 another was installed in Hobart; women condemned to it suffered "a very horrible pain in the loins."[39] And there was punishment by humiliation, whose most hated form was shaving the woman's head. This could produce rebellions, as the superintendent of the Hobart Factory found in 1827 when he told the assigned convict Ann Bruin that she was to be shorn for spending a night away from her master's house:

She screamed most violently, and swore that no one should cut off her hair. . . . She then entered my Sitting Room screaming, swearing, and jumping about the Room as if bereft of her senses. She had a pair of Scissors in her hand and commenced cutting off her own hair. . . . Coming before the window of my Sitting Room [she] thrust her clenched fist

through three panes of glass in succession. . . . With a Bucket [she] broke
some more panes of glass and the Bottom Sash of the Window Frame.[40]

Naturally, this was seen as the action of a crazed termagant, not the
protest of a woman whose physical rights were brutally transgressed.
There were several riots and near-breakouts at both factories, including one in 1827 when the soldiers had to be brought in because the
"Amazonian banditti" stood together, "declaring that, if one suffered,
all should suffer." In 1829 the women in the Hobart Factory tried to
burn the whole place down with "Parcels of fire" thrown through their
ventilation-hatches.[41]

iii

"WHORE" AND "PROSTITUTE," then, were bandied about to
serve the moral views of middle-class ideology; and neither the male nor
the female convicts thought it disgraceful, or even wrong, to live together
out of wedlock. However, female convicts in Australia were all to greater
or lesser degrees oppressed *as women*—as members of an inferior sex.
The sexism of English society was brought to Australia and then amplified by penal conditions. A convict woman needed unusual strength of
character not to be crushed by its assumptions. Language itself confirmed
her degradation. and some sense of this may be gleaned from the slang
and cant words applied to women in Georgian times—a brusque, stinging
argot of appropriation and dismissal.

A woman was a *bat*, a *crack*, a *bunter*, a *case fro, cattle*, a *mort*, a
burick, or a *convenient*. If she had a regular man, she was his *natural* or
peculiar. If married, she was an *autem mott;* if blonde, a *bleached mott;*
if a very young prostitute, almost a child, a *kinchin mott;* if beautiful, a
rum blowen, a *ewe*, a *flash piece of mutton*. If she had gonorrhea, she
was a *queer mort*. This language was the lower millstone; the upper was
the pompous moral phraseology of the Establishment, the good flogging
Christians. Ground between the two, a woman would need unusual reserves of tenacity and self-esteem to resist the pressure of the stereotype.
The pervasive belief in their whorishness and worthlessness must have
struck deep into the souls of these women. The double-bind to which
they were condemned was piercingly illustrated by the remark of one
Scottish settler, Peter Murdoch (who had more than 6,000 acres in Van
Diemen's Land and had helped set up the penal station on Maria Island),
to the 1838 Select Committee in London. "They are generally so bad,"
he said, "that the settlers have no heart to treat them well."[42]

The brutalization of women in the colony had gone on so long that it was virtually a social reflex by the end of the 1830s. The first full account of it was given by Robert Jones, Major Foveaux's chief jailer on Norfolk Island in the early 1800s, who thought the lot of the women prisoners there "must surely have been greater than the male convicts. . . . Several have not recovered yet from their treatment at the hands of the Major." Passages in Jones's memoir show how absolute the chattel status of women was. "Ted Kimberley chief constable considered the convicts of Norfolk Island no better than heathens unfit to grace the earth. Women were in his estimation born for the convenience of men. He was a bright intelligent Irishman."[43] Jones's sentiments are echoed in a fragmentary letter from a free settler on Norfolk Island, an ex-missionary turned trader named James Mitchell. "Surely no common mortal could demand treatment so brutal," he wrote around 1815.

> Heaven give their weary footsteps their aching hearts to a better place of rest for here there is none. During governorship of Major Foveaux convicts both male and female were held as slaves. Poor female convicts were treated shamefully. Governor King being mainly responsible.[44]

The rituals of courtship on Norfolk Island were, to put it mildly, brusque. We see the "bright intelligent" Kimberley pursuing a married convict woman named Mary Ginders with an axe, shouting that "if she did not come and live with him he would report her to the Major and have her placed in the cells." Major Foveaux got the woman of his choice, Ann Sherwin, away from one of his subordinate officers by throwing him in jail on a trumped-up charge "so that," claimed the Irish rebel leader Joseph Holt, a Norfolk prisoner at the time, "the poor fellow, seeing the danger he was in, thought it better to save his life, and lose his wife, than to lose both."[45] (At least their union lasted: Foveaux married Ann Sherwin in England in 1815.)

In such a moral environment, although male convicts had some rights (however attenuated), the women had none except the right to be fed; they had to fend for themselves against both guards and male prisoners. "England for white slaves, why were they sent here," Jones scribbled in one of his outbursts of delayed guilt, while reflecting on the fate of three women sent to Norfolk Island for the "crime" of abortion,

> for crimes that required pity more than punishment. Heaven forbid [sic] England if that is her way of populating her hellholes. What would our noble persons think of our virgin settlements and their white slaves. In every case the women treated as slaves, good stock to trade with and a convict having the good chance to possess one did not want much encouragement to do so.[46]

Thus the women were prisoners of prisoners. The price of a young, good-looking girl, fresh off the ship from Sydney, was "often as high as ten pounds." The island's bellman or beadle, Potter by name, had acquired the right to sell them. The same woman might be sold several times during her Norfolk Island sentence, with Potter "in most cases reselling them for a gallon or two of rum until they were in such a Condition as to be of little or no further use." The sales would be held in an old store where the women had to strip naked and "race around the room" while Potter kept up a running commentary on their "respective values."

The regular social pleasure of Norfolk Island under Foveaux, however, was the Thursday evening dance in the soldiers' barracks where, Jones wrote,

> all the women would join in the dances of the Mermaids, each one being naked with numbers painted on their backs so as to be recognized by their admirers who would clap their hands on seeing their favorite perform some grotesque action . . . with the assistance of a gallon or two of Rum. Such amusements were the talk of the soldiers for days before and after the performance.[47]

Such dances commonly took place in London brothels, where they were known in flash-talk as "ballum rancums." In these scenes, with the drunken, lurching bodies of women numbered like sides of beef, we see the epitome of sexual politics in early Australia. Women had to adapt as best they could; the system of sexual exploitation provoked competition among them, and they would fight like cats to stay in with the guards. Mary Ginders, the chief constable's woman, was "the leader of all the dances in the barrack Room and was well liked among the soldiers"; when Bridget Chandler, another convict woman, challenged her as favorite, Ginders broke her arm. James Mitchell, despite his moral disapproval of Norfolk Island promiscuity, gave up his missionary work and acquired a mistress, rather to Jones's envy,

> a beautiful young woman named Liza McCann who was as cunning as himself, who could drink more rum than most of the Hardened Soldiers, and took every opportunity to make herself disagreeable to the other females who would never dare venture within her store. Her greatest pride was to be clothed in silk and a bonnet with feathers.[48]

Women on the mainland or in Van Diemen's Land were rarely flogged, but such punishment was common on Norfolk Island and, indeed, appears to have been Major Foveaux's special treat. "To be remembered by all there," Mitchell alleged, "was his love for watching women in their agony while receiving a punishment on the Triangle. . . . [I]t was usual for [him] to remit a part of the sentence on condition that they would expose their nakedness it being considered part of the punishment. And poor wretches were only too glad to save their flesh and pain."[49] With his pistol in one hand and cutlass in the other, Foveaux would muster the male convicts in a semicircle; the naked woman was compelled to walk past them before she was trussed up to the triangle and the "skinner" or "backscratcher" (Norfolk Island cant for the flogger) went to work. The usual sentences were 25 lashes, the "Botany Bay dozen," but they could go as high as 250. The last Norfolk Island woman to be flogged on Foveaux's orders, in 1804, received such a sentence, but the flogger was squeamish about it; he said he was sick and Kimberley had to take the cat-o'-nine-tails, "upon which," as Jones described it, "[he] cried out that he did not flog women. This reply made the Major furious. He then asked one of the soldiers, Mick Kelly by name, to take the tails and go on with the punishment, which he immediately proceeded to perform in such a manner that not one mark was left on her back. This made the Major so wild that he ordered the woman to be placed in the dark cells for a fortnight."[50]

This was the man whom Ellis Bent, Macquarie's deputy judge-advocate, found "attentive and obliging." Foveaux's amusements may suggest how much of the true nature of the British regime in early Australia lies hidden under the smooth language of administration. Crimes die with their witnesses, and so, no doubt, did most of the crimes against women in the early colony. Yet there is no lack of evidence that women continued to be treated as a doubly colonized class throughout the life of the penal system. Almost four decades later, the fate of women excited the horror and contempt of François-Maurice Lepailleur, one of the fifty-eight Canadian *patriotes* who had been transported for political rebellion against the English colonial authorities in "Lower Canada" (Quebec). Arriving in 1840, these Canadian exiles were confined on a penal farm in the forest at Longbottom, halfway between Sydney and Parramatta. All of them, and especially Lepailleur (who was able to keep a journal in secret), were disgusted by the way the local free men, Emancipists, guards and police treated their women. "A farce," Lepailleur called the New South Wales police force. "Drunks and scum."[51] At night, the huts around the stockade would resound with the shrieks of women being thrashed. The forest warden at Longbottom, a man named Rose, tied his wife to a post and gave her 50 lashes with a government cat-o'-nine-tails; another settler, a Portuguese, stabbed his wife and hung her on a gum tree, with complete impunity. Not surprisingly, most of the women Lepailleur encountered in his Australian exile were alcoholic sluts, broken down by abuse, wife-beating and rum:

> During the afternoon a drunken woman, just come from the factory at Parramatta, began to abuse the woman who lives in the small cabin in front of the gate. After she had sworn a lot, cursed and blasphemed, . . . [she] turned her back to us, lifted up all her clothes and showed us her bum, saying that she had a "Black Hole" there and slapping her belly like the wretch she was. Nothing more vile than that tribe; animals are more decent than they. I would say much more but it would dirty my little journal to go on. It is incredible to see so many drunken women in this country. The roads are full of women drunkards.[52]

Thus it would seem that some prisoners—especially those who, like Lepailleur, believed themselves to be the respectable victims of tyranny and hence a cut above the "real" criminals—had exactly the same contempt for convict women as the free witnesses who discoursed so unanimously on their evils to the Molesworth Committee in 1838. "More irreformable than the male convicts," opined Bishop Ullathorne, declaring that "when a woman is bad, she is generally very bad." "I do not believe that one woman in a thousand has the moral energy to resist the temptation [to promiscuity]," Peter Murdoch testified.

Religious authorities and social workers claimed that convict women, in and out of the Female Factory, responded eagerly to any gesture of compassion or attention. But such assertions were rarely unbiased. The Roman Catholic prelate William Ullathorne (1806–1889), who had been appointed vicar-apostolic for New South Wales in 1834, never missed an opportunity to assert the success (and hence the necessity) of Catholic missionary work among the convicts. He had brought out a large contingent of Catholic clergy to Australia in 1838, including the first nuns ever seen in the colony—five Irish Sisters of Charity. Ullathorne described how these devoted women would go and visit the prisoners of the Female Factory at Parramatta five evenings a week. About a third of the factory women, he said, were Catholics, and most of them were desperate to pour their hearts out to a friendly ear. "It was sometimes difficult to prevent these poor creatures from making complete confession to the nuns. They wanted to unburden their minds, and said they would as soon speak to a nun as to a priest. The reverence with which the Sisters were regarded by all these women was quite remarkable, and the influence they exercised told . . . throughout the Colony."[53] If one has difficulty swallowing this, it can only be because Ullathorne's sentimental picture of women convicts begging to be shriven flies in the face of most other evidence about them; there is not much reason to suppose that they were any less tough or any more pathetic than their male equivalents—which is not, of course, to say that they were the degenerate creatures some authorities made them out to be. Clearly, it was in Ullathorne's interest to increase the Catholic clergy in Australia, and his testimony on the moral iniquities of transportation must be seen in that light.

Yet some were certainly grateful for a kindly ear. The prison reformer Caroline Anley visited the factory in 1834 and met two "young and extremely pretty" women who, while drunk and in a desperate outburst of temper, had attacked their tyrannous master—a Captain Charles Waldron of the 39th Regiment—and killed him. For once, popular sentiment intervened (and none of the other assigned convicts would give evidence against them), so that their death sentence was commuted to three years. Nevertheless they were regarded inside the factory as incorrigible demonesses, and Caroline Anley was the first prison visitor ever to ask for their side of the story. "If I had always been kindly treated," one of them told Anley, through the first tears she had shed since her conviction, "I wouldn't be as I am."[54]

Life in the factory—whether in New South Wales or in Van Diemen's Land—was a vegetative misery for all who led it. The minds of the women convicts rotted through lack of anything to do, although most of them preferred this stagnant leisure, punctuated by bouts of inefficient taskwork at the hand-loom, to being "treated like dogs and worked like horses" by some abusive master. The steadily growing population of freemen and colonial-born Australians objected to the Female Factories on more pragmatic grounds. By cloistering women in a colony short of females, it slowed down the birthrate. Their main mouthpiece, *The Australian,* editorialized at length on this in 1825, defending traditional "colonial marriage"—living together out of wedlock—as a great civilizer of the bush, a styptic against "dissoluteness and crime":

> How many parties are living to this day together by virtue of no other bond? How many . . . are there who, after conducting themselves in an exemplary manner in that state of "resemblance to marriage," have been made *honest women,* and who, but for the forming of this species of obligation, would have been vagrants in the streets? How many by mutual industry have rendered miserable hovels comfortable homes? How many families have sprung up where nothing but a wilderness would have been seen? Had this order of things continued, even in this objectionable shape, many a vagabond, who had been lost to Society, might have been reclaimed; might have become a decent Settler. . . . But we live in an age,

when it is fashionable to assume a demureness of manner, an extraordinary degree of godliness, and lay claim to an uncommon share of holy endowment.[55]

Here spoke the voice of rough-and-ready sense; but it was not one that penal officials, imprisoned by their own moral stereotypes of convict evil and female whoredom, were disposed to believe. The barrier of class thinking—of judging the social behavior of working-class convicts in terms of the desiderata of the English and colonial middle classes—was too strong for that; and ecclesiastical witnesses, from Quaker missionaries to Catholics like Ullathorne, were never slow to produce the bogey of convict sexual depravity when they needed to raise funds and muster support for their own evangelical programs in Australia. It was also, as many pages of the Molesworth Committee's evidence record, an incomparably useful weapon for Abolitionists. To show the vileness of the System they had to emphasize its power to degrade. Hence the additional emphasis, in the English reformers' decade of the 1830s, on something even less discussable: convict homosexuality.

iv

ONE WOULD naturally suppose that, in a remote colony whose proportion of men to women varied between 4 to 1 in the city and 20 to 1 in the bush, homosexuality would have flourished. So it did, especially on the chain gangs and in the outer penal settlements; but it did not leave much official evidence behind.

This was not only because sodomy was a capital crime. In the eyes of the law, sodomy deserved death; but in the eyes of social custom, especially the customs of English and Irish working people, it was more than ordinarily loathsome—"the crime whose name cannot be uttered," the phrase that Oscar Wilde would later soften into "the Love that dare not speak its name." Arthur Phillip, the first governor, was not by the ordinary standards of his time and calling a harsh man; indeed, he generally acted with humane decency. "I doubt if the fear of death ever prevented a man of no principle from committing a bad action," he noted before the First Fleet sailed. But in his code there were two exceptions: murder and sodomy. "For either of these crimes I would wish to confine the criminal until an opportunity offered of delivering him to the natives of New Zealand, and let them eat him. The dread of this will operate much stronger than the fear of death." Thus the sodomite, "violent against Nature," would be erased from society, denied even the small social niche that burial affords. This draconic idea was not carried out, or even mentioned again—there were no spare ships to ferry the "madge culls," "mollies" and "fluters," as homosexuals were known in Georgian cant, across the Tasman Sea to enrich the Maori diet.[56]

Buggery, it has been said, is to prisons what money is to middle-class society. It was as utterly pervasive in the world of hulks and penal settlement as it is in modern penitentiaries. "The horrible crime of sodomy," reported the convict George Lee from the *Portland,* a hulk in Langston Harbor, in 1803, "rages so shamefully throughout that the Surgeon and myself have been more than once threatened with assassination for straining to put a stop to it. . . . [It] is in no way discountenanced by those in command." Jeremy Bentham claimed that prisoners entering the Woolwich hulks were raped as a matter of course: "An initiation of this sort stands in the place of garnish and is exacted with equal rigour. . . . [A]s the Mayor of Portsmouth, Sir John Carter . . . very sensibly observes, *such things ever must be.*"[57]

Not until 1796 was anyone in Australia charged with a homosexual offense. This pioneer was Francis Wilkinson, accused (but acquitted) of buggering a sixty-year-old settler named Joseph Pearce. The first forty years of the colony provide scattered mentions of homosexual acts, routinely listed in the magistrates' bench-books and remarked on, in a general way, by lay and church authorities.[58] Nothing in the reports of the Select Committees on convict establishments and transportation for 1798 or 1812 can be construed as a reference to homosexuality. But after 1830, the documents are full of references to it—for that was the decade in which the movement to abolish transportation, dormant since the protestations of Jeremy Bentham, began to gather steam. Abolitionists like Lord John Russell and Sir William Molesworth wanted to show that transportation to Australia depraved most of its victims and reformed none of them. Proponents of transportation—especially the wealthy Australian landowners, who stood to lose their assigned labor if convictry was abolished—did not want convict homosexuality discussed; but its opponents did. Mentioning the unmentionable would complete the picture of Australia sketched by William Ullathorne as a polity of fallen souls whose "otherness" was all the worse because they were white, not black. "The eye of God," Ullathorne feelingly declared,

> looks down upon a people such as, since the deluge, has not been. Where they marry in haste, without affection; where each one lives to his senses alone. A community without the feelings of community; whose men are very wicked, whose women are very shameless, and whose children are very irreverent. . . . The naked savage, who wanders through those endless forests, knew of nothing monstrous in crime, except cannibalism, until England schooled him in horrors through her prisoners. The removal of such a plague from the earth concerns the whole human race.[59]

When speaking of sodomy, Bishop Ullathorne's eloquence became sublime and cloudy. He spoke to the Molesworth Committee of "crimes that, dare I describe them, would make your blood to freeze, and your hair to rise erect in horror upon the pale flesh." But he, like all the Abolitionists, offered more impressions than figures. We do not know (and probably never will) how widespread homosexuality was in penal Australia.

An example of the difficulty occurs in the minutes of evidence of the 1832 Select Committee on Secondary Punishments. John Stephen, a former judge in New South Wales, related how in the first trial he had attended in Australia four or five Norfolk Island prisoners were sentenced to death. "They thanked the Judge for having ordered them to die: stating, that they lived in such a state of horrid misery, witnessing the most horrid crime known to human nature, committed in numberless cases from morning to night, that they preferred death." In the course of another trial, Stephen testified, a witness had mentioned "50 or 60 cases [of sodomy] occurring in a day" on Norfolk Island, a sexual epidemic which "made men so perfectly miserable, that many preferred death to living in that penal settlement." Since the total convict population of Norfolk Island at the time was about 600, this argues an impressive priapic energy on the prisoners' part, perhaps caused by the sea air. Yet in the same report there is the testimony of the Crown botanist, Allan Cunningham, who spent four months on Norfolk Island in the same year, 1830. Were the convicts in a state "of the most horrible degradation"? "Not that I heard of," said Cunningham, dismissing the idea of Norfolk Island as a sea-girt Sodom, which he thought had been cooked up by the "radical" press, particularly the "most scurrilous paper" in the colony, the *Monitor*, ever critical of Governor Darling. The crime of sodomy, he thought, "might have been committed once or twice in the course of ten years, but I do not believe it was common."[60]

Once a decade or sixty times a day? Inflated though Stephen's guess may have been, Cunningham's was clearly absurd; but both were, in fact, produced by the same reflex. Because the act was unspeakable, it must not be inspected; easier to deny its existence, or else to believe any horror story about it. All that is known about Norfolk Island, however, suggests that Stephen's guess was not far off the mark, especially by the mid-1840s under Major Childs, when the muddle of laxity and brutality there had reached its absolute nadir.

Obviously, most lovers were not caught; hence, statistics on sodomy from the penal period are of little use, as they were based only on court indictments. Homosexual acts in penal Australia were done in secret, and prisoners seldom swore out complaints against other prisoners for performing them. Consequently few "sodomists" were arraigned, let alone convicted. Over the period 1829–35, in New South Wales and Van Diemen's Land, only twenty-four men were tried for "unnatural offences." Twelve were convicted and sentenced—four capitally, though only one (in 1834) was actually hanged. Five drew hard labor in irons on the chain gang, and three were re-transported to Norfolk Island or Moreton Bay.[61]

Why so few convictions? Ernest Augustus Slade, who had been superintendent of the convict barracks at Hyde Park in Sydney from 1833 to 1834 (his resignation was forced by sexual scandal, though over a woman), testified that "among [the lower] class of convicts sodomy is as common as any other crime." It was an ineradicable part of jail culture. But only about one case in thirty could be proven. Molested youths lodged complaints but then prevaricated in court; and other evidence tended to be vague, since "shirtlifters" were rarely caught in the act of buggery. "If you had it proved," Slade told the Molesworth Committee in 1838, "that men were found with their breeches down in secluded spots, and they stated that they had gone there to ease themselves, and upon examination it was found that they had not done so, what could have occurred?" But no jury would convict on such grounds. Out in the bush, the dreaded act became more obscure still, as there was nobody to watch the assigned convicts. Bishop Ullathorne believed that sodomy was less frequent among the shepherds, who tended to live alone, than among stockmen, "a much more dissolute set" who practiced "a great deal of that crime" and even taught it to the formerly innocent Aborigines. And if the Man from Snowy River's convict forebear was not content with the brusque embraces of Jacky-Jacky, there were always sheep. "As a juryman," one witness told the committee, "I have had opportunities of hearing many trials for unnatural offences, with animals particularly. . . . I think they are much more common than in any other country inhabited by the English." "That is, among the convicts?" interjected one committee member. "Yes," said the witness, dispelling the thought of the colonial gentry practicing abominations on their own merinos.[62]

The testimony given to the Molesworth Committee suggests a demimonde not quantified by the statistics of the time. Homosexuality was the norm in the Hyde Park barracks in Sydney, where new arrivals were decanted from the ships, old lags thrown together with young boys. As in all systems of confinement since prisons began, lads became "punks" (passive homosexuals) to get the protection of a dominant man; they went by girls' names, Kitty, Nancy or Bet. Few of them had any homosexual experience before they got to Australia, according to Ullathorne —and his testimony was more than guesswork, since as a priest he had heard thousands of prison confessions and had to struggle with his conscience as he testified, generalizing so as not to violate the seal of the confessional. As one bewildered youth exclaimed to him, "Such things no one knows in Ireland."[63]

The only account of penal homosexuality in Australia by a convict was set down by the Swing letter-writer from Shropshire, Thomas Cook, in his memoir of the System in the 1830s, *The Exile's Lamentations*. His contact with it began when he was sent to labor in the road gangs in the Blue Mountains, cutting the Great Western Road through raw bush and sandstone at Honeysuckle Flat. "It was now," he wrote, "that my miseries commenced," although he would not press their "nauseous details" on the reader:

> I was yet in the dark of the horrible propensity which the coarse and brutish language of my Gangmates in calamity, coupled with their assignations one towards the other, shortly told me the greater part of them had imbibed. So far advanced were these wretched men in depravity, that they appeared to have entirely lost the feelings of men, and to have imbibed those that would render them execrable to all mankind.[64]

For warmth, men bedded two or three together, a custom which "appeared to me altogether objectionable"; and before long, Cook was so broken down by labor and lack of sleep that a medical officer transferred him to another gang working closer to Sydney, at Mount Victoria. But at night, the same fumbling and rooting went on there; the only difference was that there the gangers "were less public in their demonstrations of brutal regard." Naïvely, Cook tried to remonstrate with a ganger who took a fancy to him. "Extraordinary as it may appear," he wrote indignantly,

> it is not the less true, that an appeal to their better feelings was the certain cause of insult and derision, which they would copiously inflict on their less depraved fellow Prisoner; and if he nevertheless persisted in publicly deprecating their horrid propensities, he would be struck, kicked and otherwise abused.[65]

There was no appeal to authority, because all the overseers on the mountain road gangs were convicts, and most of them, according to Cook, were homosexuals. "Woe unto that man who had the courage to pass a remark at all disrespectful of the despicable objects of their horrible ambition! He would be selected as a Lamb for the Slaughter!" If crossed, they could send a man to be summarily "lacerated at the Triangles" at the courthouse at Mount Wallawarang.

With his virtue stubbornly intact, Cook labored in the Mount Victoria gang for several months before losing his temper with an importunate homosexual, whom he thrashed "rather unmercifully." For this, he was sentenced to a year in irons on the road at No. 2 Stockade, whose overseers were the worst of all—"without exception, the most overbearing and depraved Villains it were possible to find in the mountain district," Cook wrote, his abstract figures of moral obloquy creaking under the strain:

> The only regard they had to classification, was evidently that which to all *natural* beings, bespoke their own abominations,—or, in other words, the most execrable portion of their men found no difficulty in ingra:iating themselves into favor, by the coarseness of their language, and the open demonstrations of Pleasure with which they give effect to their horrible propensities, in their Overseers' hearing.[66]

At the stockade, convicts could sometimes bribe their way out of a flogging with money or tobacco, but the only other way was to "come out" as a homosexual and so mollify the overseers. A circle of sexual tyranny sustained itself because, according to Cook, the overseers on the iron gangs were chosen from the working hands on unshackled gangs, like those at Honeysuckle Flat and Mount Victoria. They were recommended by those gangs' overseers, so that like chose like; an overseer's sexual favorites could be rewarded with a ration of power on the iron gangs, enforcing "Starvation, Flogging and insupportable Labour" upon any resistant "straights." Cook declared that in his time on the road gangs, he had only known two overseers who were not homosexual.[67]

Although Cook, like most Englishmen of his day, thought homosexuality disgusting in itself, his deeper objection to its role in the penal world was that it multiplied the injustices of power. It represented an abusive control over the will of others, often involving rape. If this carceral society of the 1830s was anything like prisons today, we must recognize that many of the sexual episodes Cook witnessed were not lovemaking but acts of sadistic humiliation, in which sexuality was merely the instrument of a deeper violence—the strong breaking the weak down into a punk, a molly, a gobbling queen. Nothing in Cook's background prepared him for such transactions, and so he went down through the circles of the System—from the road gangs to Port Macquarie, from Port Macquarie to Norfolk Island—in amazement and outrage. He described, in language that can scarcely bear to encompass its subject, how sexual contact in prison tends to be metabolized into relationships of power.

Cook thought that the System nurtured sodomy—that it flourished in Australia as nowhere else. He believed that there was little homosexuality in English jails and hulks, but that inversion, in the sexual sense as well as the geographical, ruled the antipodes; and that cruelty was the seed of "the practice which was engendered at the Penal Settlements of Old where they were tortured by Tyrants in a manner that tended to brutalize all Nature." If "nature"—which, for Cook, included the idea of "natural law" or justice—is perverted by tyranny, then other realms, including the sexual, will be warped as well. Reflecting on this years later, in the relative peace and security of Alexander Maconochie's administration on Norfolk Island, Cook speculated that the System meant to *encourage* sodomy, using the perpetual threat of rape or humiliation as one of the automatic punishments for the unwitting convict. In this he was wrong, but one can understand why he thought it. Until Maconochie took over Norfolk Island in 1840, not one commandant in the System had shown the least concern for the rehabilitation of his prisoners. They acted purely as agents of repression, as guardians of the pit. And if the men in the pit had ways of degrading one another, why trouble to stop them? So Cook, writing in the early 1840s, makes his climactic outcry against the "Old System" of the 1830s:

> No prospect being afforded them of a woman's Love,—without hope of Heaven or fear of Hell; their already darkened reason became more clouded. Their lax morals gave way and they indulged with apparent delight in every filthy and unnatural propensity. None but a mind capable of powerful reasoning, into which early moral habits had been instilled, or a heart filled with early affection could prevent a being falling into the lowest depths of infamy, never more to rise to the rank of man. . . . [I]t would be better to introduce the *Dracon Laws* than revert to the *Old System.*[68]

Between Cook's objurgations one glimpses the workings of homosexual society among the prisoners. Clearly, there was a good deal of solidarity:

> Several individuals were punished for the heinous offence, and although it may appear incredible it is nevertheless true that these wretches were generally viewed with feelings of sympathy and those who had brought such cases forward were looked upon with contempt, and very few would afterwards associate with them.[69]

Cook also hints at the strength of attachments between prison lovers on Norfolk Island, a fact confirmed by the disapproving testimony of Thomas Arnold, the deputy-assistant commissary on Norfolk Island, to the Molesworth Committee: "Actually, incredible as it may appear, feelings of jealousy are exhibited by those depraved wretches, if they see the boy or young man with whom they carry on this abominable intercourse speak to another person." Eight years later an official report by Robert

Pringle Stuart, a convict department magistrate in Norfolk, described how convicts called themselves "man and wife," that there were probably 150 such couples, not counting more casual attachments, and that they could not bear to be separated: "The natural course of affection is quite distracted, and these parties manifest as much eager earnestness for the society of each other as members of the opposite sex." Bishop Ullathorne, visiting Norfolk Island in 1835–36, heard at second hand (from a Protestant clergyman, who had been told it by a prisoner under sentence of death) that "two-thirds of the island were implicated" in homosexual activity. He thought the same proportion obtained at Moreton Bay and other penal stations.[70]

Certainly there was no decline in sexual coercion on Norfolk Island, except perhaps between 1839 and 1843, the time of Maconochie's brief adminstration. By the mid-1840s it had grown even worse, largely because there was no effort to sort out the hardened criminals from the new arrivals. "Youths are seized upon, and become the victims of hoary and unnatural villains," reported Thomas Naylor, chaplain on Norfolk Island from 1841 to 1845:

> With these scoundrels the English farm labourer, the tempted and fallen mechanic, the suspected but innocent victims of perjury or mistake, are indiscriminately herded. With them are mixed Chinamen from Hong Kong, the aborigines of New Holland, West Indian Blacks, Greeks, Caffres, and Malays; soldiers for desertion; idiots, madmen, pig-stealers and pickpockets. In the open day the weak are bullied and robbed by the stronger. At night the sleeping-wards are very cess-pools of unheard-of vices. I cannot find sober words enough to express the enormity of this evil. . . . I watched the process of degradation. I saw very boys seized upon and lost; I saw decent and respectable men, nay gentlemen . . . thrown among the vilest ruffians, to be tormented by their bestialities.[71]

In no less heated terms, Robert Pringle Stuart reported to his superiors in Van Diemen's Land in 1846 that Norfolk Island under the lax, vacillating sway of Major Childs had become a citadel of sodomy:

> How can anything else be expected? Here are 800 men immured from 6 o'clock in the evening until sunrise . . . without lights, without visitation by the officers. Atrocities of the most shocking, odious character are there perpetrated, and that unnatural crime is indulged in to excess; the young have no chance of escaping from abuse, and even forcible violation is resorted to. To resist can hardly be expected, in a situation so utterly removed from, and lamentably destitute of, protection. A terrorism is sternly and resolutely maintained, to revenge not merely exposure but even complaint.[72]

Convict homosexuality seemed, from Stuart's perspective, to be the quintessential form of convict evil. Other reformers and officials, staring timorously into the pit that England had created and whose very bottom was Norfolk Island, agreed. The danger seemed to be that this "contagion" would spread unchecked like an epidemic disease from the island to the mainland of Australia, so that, as Stuart put it, "in future years a moral stain of the deepest dye may be impressed, perhaps immovably, on its people, and thus become attached to the name of Englishmen."[73] This fear cannot have been felt by Stuart alone. The portions of his report that had to do with convict homosexuality were censored from its published form; but it is hardly possible that news and rumors of such doings on Norfolk Island and other penal stations, over the years, did not leak out into the colony and contribute to the atmosphere of nameless evil, of unutterable degradation, that surrounded the idea of convictry in the ears of its respectable citizens. This inevitably fostered more repressive attitudes toward all homosexuals in Australia. Their sexual preference was doubly damned: first, because it was a crime under law, and second, because it was mainly committed by those who were convicts already.

There could have been no better breeding ground for the ferocious bigotry with which Australians of all classes, long after the abandonment of Norfolk Island and of the System itself, perceived the homosexual. And this in turn seemed like an act of cleansing—for homosexuality was one of the mute, stark, subliminal elements in the "convict stain" whose removal, from 1840 onward, so preoccupied Australian nationalists.

v

THE THIRD "minority" in penal Australia was not, in round figures, a minority at all, for until about 1845 there were probably more Aborigines scattered across the continent than whites clustered around its coastal settlements. But aboriginal groups were always small and scattered, whereas the white groups (except on the rim of pastoral settlement) tended to be larger and denser. On the shores of Sydney Harbor, whites outnumbered blacks from the moment the First Fleet arrived; no black could ever have seen so many people before. One is apt to think of Sydney and its outlying penal settlements, from Hobart and Launceston in the south to Moreton Bay in the north, as small and weak. So they were, but to the Aborigines they looked large, strange and imposing, and the malign gravitational field they emitted would destroy their culture.

The fate of the Australian blacks was intimately connected to the System. A frontier society based on slave labor, run by the threat of extreme violence and laced with rigid social divisions was not likely to treat the Aborigines compassionately or even fairly. Nor did it. There was a great gap between policy and practice. The Royal instructions to every governor of Australia, from Arthur Phillip in 1788 to Thomas Brisbane in 1822, always repeated the same themes. The Aborigines must not be molested. Anyone who "wantonly" killed them, or gave them "any unnecessary interruption in the exercise of their several occupations", must be punished. The aim in racial relations was "amity and kindness."[74] The idea of converting them to Christianity would not be embodied in official policy until Brisbane's successor as governor, Ralph Darling, came in 1825. Yet, even though white settlement began with no *policy* of racist persecution, the coming of the whites was an unmitigated disaster for everyone with a black skin.

The legal status of Aborigines—and of their "claims," as white officials interestingly put it, to the territory they had occupied for some eighteen millennia before the arrival of the whites—seemed almost insoluble to the whites. Everywhere else in the historical experience of the British Empire, colonies had been planted where the "natives" and "Indians" understood and defended the idea of property. In Virginia as in Africa, in New Zealand as in the East Indies, British colonists encountered cultures of farming people who had houses, villages and plots of cultivated land. These proofs of prior ownership might be violated by the whites (and often were); but they could not be denied or ignored. Even Charles II's instructions to the Council of Foreign Plantations on the conduct of the English colony in Virginia had recognized that as the new settlement would "border upon" the lands of the Indians, their territory had to be respected, for "peace is not to be expected without . . . justice to them."[75]

But the Aborigines were hunter-gatherers who roamed over the land without marking out boundaries or making fixed settlements. They had no idea of farming or stock-raising. They saved nothing, lived entirely in the present and were, in the whites' eyes, so ignorant of property as to be little more than intelligent animals "whose only superiority above the brute," as one visiting naval surgeon put it, "consisted in their use of the spear, their extreme ferocity and their employing fire in the cookery of their food." The whites were not the only ones to think so; when a Maori named Tipahee visited Sydney with his son around 1800 at the behest of Governor King, both warriors formed "the most contemptible opinion" of the Aborigines' nakedness, weak technology, poor comforts and "trifling mode of warfare."[76]

Macquarie hoped they could be brought from their "rambling Naked state" and made into farmers. In 1815 he tried to put sixteen aboriginal men on a small farm on Sydney Harbor, complete with huts and a boat. They lost the boat, ignored the huts and wandered off into the bush.[77]

From then on, it was assumed that "native labor" was useless. Hence, the rights normally assigned to colonized native workers within the Empire were not extended to Aborigines. The early colony was so overwhelmingly dependent on the slave labor of white convicts that the effort of training nomadic blacks even for the most menial work was not worthwhile. The convicts might be scum, but they had an economic value. The blacks clearly had none; therefore, they were less than scum. The decay of fringe-dwelling blacks on the edge of white urban culture —the remnants of the Iora, Gammeraigal and Daruk—was inexorable and all-pervasive; to sympathetic onlookers it seemed a plague, and to racist ones a bestial joke. Stupefied with the cheapest grade of rum, racked with every new disease from tuberculosis to syphilis, begging and babbling in the flash-talk and gutter argot of the convicts, they were caricatures of misery. Even their traditions of authority had been parodied by the whites, who insisted on giving some elders patronizing identity cards in the form of crescent-shaped copper plates, with their rank as "chief" engraved on them in English. And yet, as the Russian explorer Captain Bellingshausen noted of some Sydney Aborigines in 1820,

> The natives remember very well their former independence. Some expressed their claims to certain places, asserting that they belonged to their ancestors. . . . Despite all the compensation offered to them [!], a spark of vengeance still smoulders in their hearts.[78]

The tribes further out were better off, but only for a short time. They, too, were about to lose their land. Where did their title to it lie? Only in their own collective memory and oral traditions, to which the whites paid no attention. They seemed to drift across the territory in little ragged groups, never staying long in one place, appearing from the forest and vanishing back into it. They carried what they owned and killed the infants they could not carry. The complex and ancient ideas about territory that were embedded in aboriginal thought—ideas that had to do more with land as the "property" of mythic ancestors than with material ownership in the here and now—were completely unfamiliar to the whites and would have been opaque to them even without the barrier of language. The Aborigines had no visible political framework, and certainly they were not united as a people with common interests: There were perhaps five hundred languages and dialects spoken by the aboriginal tribes of early colonial Australia. Moreover, they lived in an almost continuous state of tribal warfare, aggravated by the kind of random contact made inevitable by nomadic life. One Australian historian cautiously ventured that the aboriginal death rate from these bloody encounters—rarely involving more than fifty men on each side—lay between 1 person in 270 and 1 in 150, a death rate "not exceeded in any nation of Europe during any of the last three centuries."[79] If these strange people showed so little solidarity among themselves, what common rights would their invaders assign them? In practice, almost none. The government simply declared all Australian land to be Crown land; and the idea that Aborigines might have some territorial rights by virtue of prior occupation was settled to the entire satisfaction of the whites by a New South Wales court decision in 1836, which declared that the Aborigines were too few and too ill-organized to be considered "free and independent tribes" who owned the land they lived on.[80] Even the humanitarians could salve their consciences by reflecting that the Aborigines were, after all, nomads—and to a nomad, one tract of land is "as good as" another. This absurd misreading of nomadic life meant that Aborigines could be driven without compunction out of their ancestral territory and into new conflicts, not only with the whites, but with other tribes.

At the same time, the Aborigines were classified as British subjects; indeed, the early governors wanted to see them converted to Christianity and farming so that they could be absorbed, socially if not genetically, into the lower class of the colony—an idea loathed and resisted by every white, no matter what his class. The first policies about clashes between settlers and Aborigines were therefore most equivocal. In 1802, after nearly seven years of undeclared warfare against the Daruk tribe on the Hawkesbury River—guerrilla raids by blacks, punitive torture and killings by settlers—Governor King saw fit to remind the colonists that the killing of natives "will be punished with the utmost severity of the Law," but that "the Settler is not to suffer his property to be invaded, or his existence endangered by them." Thus, he would commute the hanging of five colonists who had killed two blacks on the Hawkesbury River two years before. In 1805, King's judge-advocate opined that, since the Aborigines had no grasp of such basics of English law as evidence, guilt or oaths, they could neither be prosecuted nor sworn as witnesses, for either would be "a mockery of judicial proceedings." And so the best course would be to "pursue and inflict such punishment as they may merit," without the formalities of a trial. A settler would have had to be blind or a saint not to see the point, and from then on the miseries of dispossession began.[81]

They were brought to full spate over the next thirty years by the Australian wool industry and its insatiable appetite for land. They would go on far beyond the end of the penal system itself. Between 1800 and 1830, the settled stations pushed inexorably outward: south to Goulburn and the high Monaro plains, west across the Blue Mountains to the golden grasslands that stretched around Bathurst and Mudgee, and north to the valley of the Hunter River. At every contact with the Aborigines, the pattern would be much the same: a collision between a white culture of private property and a black one of "primitive communism" in which no resources, land least of all, were privately owned. Sometimes the blacks would move on. Usually they attacked, launching a small guerrilla war until enough of their warriors had been cut down by the settlers' firearms to render the tribe helpless. If their resistance was strong enough, martial law could be declared against them: In 1824 the stockholders around Bathurst persuaded Governor Brisbane to send soldiers in to "pacify" the blacks in their area. Brisbane, who a few years before had been impressing missionaries with his liberal expressions of concern for the Aborigine ("If something is not done for these poor, distressed creatures, they will become extinct: the race of them will perish from absolute want!" he told a Wesleyan),[82] dispatched his troopers and native police, and the death toll was not tallied.

Until lately, historians have not paid enough attention to the fierceness with which Australian aboriginal clans fought the European invaders for possession of their land. "The other side of the frontier"—to use the title Henry Reynolds gave to his study of this subject—showed a pattern of tenacious and often well-organized resistance, ranging from massed frontal attacks through guerrilla warfare to the carefully plotted tracking and revenge-murder of individual Europeans for known crimes against tribespeople. The Aborigines' tactical superiority was generally, if reluctantly, admitted by whites. Aborigines stole guns and learned how to use them; they made devastating attacks on sheep and cattle, harassed miners, killed horses and burned homesteads, thus undercutting the economic basis of many areas of white settlement.[83]

This resistance did not always begin at once. Aborigines—at least in the early colonial years, before awareness of European rapacity became general among them—seemed to have no idea of dispossession. As Reynolds pointed out, "While conflict was ubiquitous in traditional societies, territorial conquest was virtually unknown. . . . If blacks often did not react to the initial invasion of their country it was because they were not aware it had taken place. They certainly did not believe that their land had suddenly ceased to belong to them and they to their land. The mere presence of Europeans, no matter how threatening, could not uproot certainties so deeply implanted in Aboriginal custom and consciousness."[84] Many tribes were convinced of the ignorance and weakness of the whites—at first. It was not the coming of the Europeans that provoked resistance, but their unrelenting seizure of all rights and uses of the land.

In some districts the Aborigines' resistance lasted as long as ten years, but they were fated not to win. European technology was against them, and so was the breakdown of their hunting environment caused by the introduction of stock. Pasturage altered the environment and began to obliterate the old material bases of aboriginal life. Sheep and cattle drove out kangaroos and other game. Fences blocked ancient routes and runs. The forests were cut back. Familiar plants died out. And always, everywhere on the expanding limits of settlement, the Aborigine was seen as a mere native pest, like a dingo or kangaroo. He was a *myall*, a *murky*, a *boong* or (in a phrase that precisely expressed the whites' belief in his inevitable passing) a *dark cloud*. He could be killed without hesitation— and, given the remoteness of the outer settlements and the thinness and inherent racism of the police force, without much chance of detection and punishment. "They may be destroyed by their fellows, and what is worse, may be shot wholesale by Europeans, and yet the arm of the law has no power to punish unless the evidence of a white person can be procured."[85] One observer heard "a large proprietor of sheep and cattle" maintain "that there was no more harm in shooting a native, than in shooting a dog"; and another

> narrated, as a good thing, that he had been one of a party who had pursued the blacks, in consequence of cattle having been rushed by them, and he was sure they shot upwards of a hundred. . . . [H]e maintained that there was nothing wrong in it, that it was preposterous to suppose they had souls.[86]

The death toll of this long frontier war is a matter of informed guesswork rather than hard fact. Probably between 2,000 and 2,500 European settlers were killed, and upwards of 20,000 Aborigines.[87]

The emblematic massacre in New South Wales occurred in 1838 on the property of Henry Dangar, at a place called Myall Creek near the Gwydir River. It was meant as a reprisal for stock-theft and "cattle-rushing" or stampeding, which stockmen resented because it thinned the animals through panic and so reduced their salable weight.

The station-hands had no idea who the actual culprits were, but they found an inoffensive encampment of Aborigines some forty miles from the site and attacked them. A dozen armed stockmen, led by a white who had kept company with the little tribe for the previous three weeks, rounded up twenty-eight unarmed men, women and children, roped them together, drove them to a killing-ground nearby, and slaughtered them all with muskets and cutlasses. Then they chopped some up and mutilated others, and burned the corpses on a pyre. But as it happened, there was a white witness among the killers who turned informer against the other eleven. Although the jury in their first trial acquitted them all, a second trial produced verdicts of guilty for seven of them, who were hanged; four went free. The case was politically explosive. Probably it would never have come to court at all had Governor George Gipps not intervened directly. As no treaties with the Aborigines existed, Gipps concluded that they "had never been in possession of any Code of Laws intelligible to a Civilized People," but he maintained that "in putting the Law into Force against the Aborigines, the utmost degree of Mercy and forebearance should be exercised." Settlers had exterminated thousands of Aborigines before, but none had swung for it. So acute was the resentment of this sentimental interference with the code of the frontier that some graziers, led by a magistrate, even raised a defense fund for the murderers. Although the Myall Creek massacre caused a passing revulsion of public conscience, it did nothing to stop the majority of those who believed the Australian version of Manifest Destiny—that "it is in the order of nature that, as civilization advances, savage nations must be exterminated" and that the safety of explorers and settlers should not "be sacrificed out of deference to . . . political and humbugging maniacs who write and prate of matters of which they knew nothing whatever."[88]

The best way to deal with the "sable brethren" was "by the discriminating application of firearms." Ten days after Myall Creek (the news of which, however, had not yet leaked out), a correspondent in another Sydney paper, piqued by Gipps's "softness" in not sending a punitive military force against the blacks in the Hunter Valley, urged that

> if, by one decisive step, the Aborigines are shown their own weakness, and convinced that it is useless for them to contend with Europeans, they will submit and cease their outrages, and much bloodshed may be spared. . . . [U]nless prompt measures are adopted, these dusky "lords of the soil" will fairly drive the pale faces from their territories.[89]

The people who most craved this Final Solution were the convicts. It was not thought surprising that, of the twelve white murderers at Myall Creek, only one (the witness) was born in the colony and all the rest were either convicts or ex-convicts; or that, of the eleven, not one would inform on his fellows. Convicts' hatred of Aborigines was a well-established tradition by then.

In Chapter 4, we saw how the first conflicts between black and white in the colony began with the convicts, who stole the Aborigines' weapons to sell as souvenirs, transgressed their territory while trying to escape and hated the blacks not only for their freedom but for the conciliatory treatment the officers, acting on instructions, gave them. If a convict stole a chicken, he would be flogged; if a tribesman did the same, he would go scot-free. Such things rankled, particularly as the blacks soon came to be seen as a wild extension of the jail of infinite space: To escape into the bush was to risk almost certain death from either starvation or the blacks' waddies and spears. Thus the conviction grew among the convicts that the Aborigines, if not exactly in league with their hated jailers, were on their side; and this was confirmed when, in the penal stations of Newcastle and Moreton Bay in the 1820s, the guards took to rewarding Aborigines who captured escaped prisoners, beat them bloody and dragged them in. By the 1830s, the systematic use of blacktrackers —Aborigines who, at the behest of the hunting police, used their superb skills at following a man through the bush—had confirmed the convicts' picture of the Aborigine as a skilled, treacherous enemy. If not an enemy, he was merely subhuman—a spindly nomadic wretch, Nature's dull orphan. "The natiffs of this Country they are Blacks," a typical convict description goes, "and they go naked just as they came into the world, and they live on Ruts of trees and snails or aney other Creeping thing, Women and Children goes all naked alike."[90] Every underdog needs a dog below him so he can feel canine. That, in the convicts' eyes, was all the Aborigines were good for. The cruelty of the authorities toward whites was stored up as blind resentment in the convict *lumpenproletariat*, and discharged—though not always as efficiently as at Myall Creek and other sites of massacre—upon the blacks.

For their part, the Aborigines seem to have despised the convicts, whom they saw laboring under conditions which their own pride would never have accepted, treated like the defeated members of some enemy tribe, as in a sense they were: driven, harried, kicked, flogged, scorned and occasionally killed. "No good—all same like croppy," some tribesmen said when offered some left-over convict slops, "croppy" being the disdainful term for an Irish convict. In 1837 a missionary was surprised to find that Aborigines who had accepted a gift of winter dresses and cloaks painstakingly sewn from blankets had unpicked all the stitches and turned them back into blankets, because they thought them "Irish cloaks"—"our natives commonly attach some idea of inferiority to what is Irish and Ireland."[91]

Without records from the blacks' side, one can only guess what the structure of the System contributed to their opinion of whites; but their behavior showed that if they were to take sides, however briefly or opportunistically, it might as well be with the esteemed warriors—the men in red coats who dispensed the power, the tobacco, the blankets. The idea that the despised black might have had some "natural" sympathy with the oppressed convict is the flimsiest sentiment. Across the cultural chasm that separated them, no such alliances were possible and none were ever made, except for a few escaped convicts who successfully "went native" and adapted to tribal life.[92]

Convicts did not stop despising and fearing Aborigines after they had served out their sentences, received their pardons and become free men.

On the contrary: Because "settled" land near the towns was always taken, the newly emancipated settler with little or no capital—and no government subsidies beyond a grant of raw bushland—was more likely to put up his slab hut on the very fringes of white occupation. This brought him and his family into contact with fresh tribal groups who would begin, all over again, the pattern of black resistance and "treachery," answered by white retaliation and murder. In this way life on an expanding frontier ensured that convict attitudes toward Aborigines were carried and transmitted from generation to generation, from bond parents to free children. When one free farmer in the 1840s remonstrated with a hutkeeper—a former convict and soldier—for shooting an unarmed Aborigine, "he looked on me as a sort of dangerous lunatic for troubling myself about the lives of a few Blacks, which he evidently thought he had a perfect right to dispose of as he chose, so long as he did not get into trouble." Let missionaries and city-dwellers prattle humanely about the blacks—they did not have to deal with them, or defend their huts and runs against them. They did not know how shiftless, feckless and dangerous they could be. In some parts of Australia, as any traveller can verify for himself, this attitude has never died.

With convicts, the hatred was greater because the fear was more pervasive. An emigrant free settler was likely to have good weapons. An Emancipist, newly pardoned by the governor, might be able to get hold of an old musket or a rusty horse-pistol. More likely he would set off with nothing but cutlass and axe. Even with a gun, a man was at a disadvantage against Aborigines with spears, especially in close bush; he could not load and fire fast enough, and in any case few convicts had the kind of military training or sporting experience that would have turned them into good shots. And when the fire-sticks were clattering on the roof of the hut, and its slab walls began to smolder, there was no colonial cavalry to come galloping over the hill. The cavalry was a long way off—in America, in fact. Thus the typical form of frontier skirmish was ambush and small, indiscriminate massacre, along the lines of the atrocity at Myall Creek. Whites laid for blacks and shot them in the back. Blacks crept into the hut and crushed the skulls of a settler and his woman with their waddies. "The normal condition of inland life was an armed, watchful, wary, nervous calm," slow in tempo but punctuated by sunny explosions of horror that soon settled again on the indifferent skin of the land.[93]

Other factors helped worsen this long, bitter contact with men brutalized by the convict system. The remnants of aboriginal groups, their strength and numbers blasted away by the settlers' guns, gave in to a marginal life as "station blacks" living on handouts and irregular work, like tracking stray cattle. Men who had sweated out years as assigned slave laborers were not averse to seeing blacks worse degraded. Ill from epidemic disease, blacks would sometimes "come in" to a settlement begging for medicine and be given sheep-drench, as befitted their animal status, and the crude veterinary medicines killed them. The one thing they could usually sell to Europeans was their women, and this led to debilitating outbreaks of venereal disease as well as further loosening of their vestigial tribal structure, through the birth of half-caste bastards. Missionaries often complained that the "lower-class whites"—former convicts and their descendants—deliberately undermined their efforts to educate and convert the fringe-dwelling Aborigines. Sewing-bees and Bible readings had no chance against rum and prostitution. And the politician who wanted to get and keep some popularity with the majority of white settlers had to deride government and missionary aid as the meddling of soft busybodies. Thus William Charles Wentworth, in bygone years the tribune of the ex-convicts but now widely known as "the lord of the lash and the triangle," was reported as saying in a speech to the Australian Legislative Council in 1844:

> He could not see if the whites in this colony were to go out into the land and possess it, that the Government had much to do with them. No doubt there would be battles between the settlers and the border tribes; but they might be settled without the aid of the Government. The civilized people had come in and the savage must go back. They must go on progressing until their dominancy was established, and therefore he could think that no measure was wise or merciful to the blacks which clothed them with a degree of seeming protection, which their position would not allow them to maintain. . . . It was not the policy of a wise Government to attempt the perpetuation of the aboriginal race of New South Wales. . . . They must give way before the arms, aye! even the diseases of civilized nations—they must give way before they attain the power of those nations.[94]

For the original Australians, then, the arrival of the convicts was a catastrophe. Perhaps they might have suffered less if New South Wales had been colonized by free emigrants who were, at least notionally, less brutal; who had a less obvious investment in kicking a subject class. The more opportunistic the settlers were, the more their sense of being poor white trash demanded relief, the more they spoke of civilization and racial superiority, reflecting that even their diseases facilitated Destiny's plan for the blacks. It was a thin, embittered comfort; but it was one of very few the System offered its white subjects, at the end of their own deracination.

9

The Government Stroke

NOBODY ON SHORE in Sydney was blasé about the arrival of a
convict transport. For the people who crammed the bobbing flotilla of rowboats around the ship as she warped in, it meant news
from home or even the glimpse of a familiar face, pallid from life below
the hatches. But for the settlers, it meant a small gush of the most
precious commodity in Australia: labor. Every convict faced the same
social prospects. He or she served the Crown or, on the Crown's behalf,
some private person, for a given span of years. Then came a pardon or a
ticket-of-leave, either of which permitted him to sell his labor freely and
choose his place of work. What this came down to, in the common view
of English critics of transportation—most of whom had not been to Australia and had no first-hand knowledge of the convict system—was that
the Crown used them as slaves until they were judged fit to become
peasants.

An equation between convictry and slavery was the invariable trope
used to attack the System. Some key figures in the convict administration also used it—such as George Arthur, the Tory lieutenant-governor
of Van Diemen's Land from 1824 to 1836—but it was most commonly
heard from Abolitionists, in a lengthy succession that began with Jeremy
Bentham and William Wilberforce and continued to William Molesworth
and Lord Russell in the late 1830s. It lasted, therefore, for fifty years and
remained (at least as a figure of speech) largely unquestioned in English
liberal circles. But was it correct? Were convicts, in fact, slaves? And
could the matter of their rights—or lack of them—rightly be brought
under the great moral umbrella of the English Abolitionist movement,
which had at such vast cost and effort extirpated black slavery from the
British Empire and, by the 1830s, was busy trying to suppress the tenacious institution of slavery among the Africans and Arabs themselves?
English liberal reformers were sure it could. Today, one is less sure.[1]

In theory, the social contract of slavery is simple, rigid and one-sided. It is pure power in action, rampant will. The master *owns* the slave: his work, his time, his person. Slaves are bought and sold; they are property. Their rights begin and end with their status as chattels. They do not have the right to negotiate, to set the tempo or length of their work, to organize collectively or to protest. Incentives are unknown in the theoretical world of slavery (though not, as the experience of slave societies always shows, in its real world). Slavery is permanent and it perpetuates itself from generation to generation; slave parents beget slave children. When slaves are freed, it is an indulgence—or a revolution.

None of these conditions applied to the convicts Britain exiled to Australia. Each served a fixed term of punishment and then became free. None was a chattel, the property of a master. All of them, within limits, had the right to sell some portion of their labor on the free market. Harsh and rigorous as their social world often was, it was enlaced by concepts of right and law, not of simple ownership. They could appear as witnesses in court, bring suits in civil law, and write petitions to the governor, which were given full and usually prompt consideration. Their masters did not have the right to flog them; such punishments could only be inflicted by the sentence of a magistrate, or, in later years, two magistrates. A convict could bring a master to court for ill-treatment. Often, when they had served their terms, convicts were given land and assigned convicts to work it. Their children were born free. They could not vote; but neither could anyone else in New South Wales until after 1840. If this was slavery, as its critics insisted, it was not of a kind recognizable in Barbados or Atlanta, let alone in ancient Athens, Rome or Luxor.

It had its own name: the assignment system. Most convicts were "assigned"—lent out, as laborers, by the government—to private settlers. A few, perhaps one in ten, were kept by the government to labor on public works, digging ditches and tunnels, building jails, courthouses, stores and breakwaters, making roads through the bush. Thus the "government man"—a favorite euphemism in a society where the word "convict" was rarely used—could serve the Crown directly and pay back his debt to English society. Government labor was thought the worse punishment. But assignment was the staff of colonial life for the first fifty years of European settlement. It shaped the colony and molded its social institutions; and it was one—if not quite *the*—main reason why emigrants went there at all.

Penal Australia was too distant, weird and tainted to attract many free immigrants from the working class. However, its government hoped to bring in "opulent" settlers, men of capital who would spend it in the colony, with offers of free land and free labor. In its unexplored vastness, the colony was glutted with land, and the government gave it away.

Prime grazing country less than a hundred miles from Sydney could still be had for 2 shillings an acre in the 1830s.

Because it was far scarcer, skilled free labor was much more valuable than land. It could name its own price. When the green and hopeful colonist brought his free servant to Australia with him, the servant often deserted:

> My own man, who had served me for eight years in England . . . never reached my new abode. About a month after our arrival I missed him one morning. Before night I received a letter, by which he informed me that he had taken a grant of land near Hunter's River, and that he "hoped we parted friends." He is now one of the most consequential persons in the Colony, has grown enormously fat, feeds upon greasy dainties, drinks oceans of bottled porter and port wine, damns the Governor, and swears by all his gods, Jupiter, Jingo and Old Harry, that this colony must soon be independent.[2]

Cheap land and free grants meant that anyone with hard hands and a strong back could become his own boss. They also meant that the only stable source of labor, whatever its defects, came from the assignment system. Thus, assignment was as important to colonial Australia as black slavery was to the antebellum South, and both had practical disadvantages in common.

Black slave labor was rarely as efficient as the paid work of the free. Its unproductiveness was rooted in the effect of slavery on men's souls, for "bondage forced the Negro to give his labor grudgingly and badly, and his poor work habits retarded . . . the general level of productivity."[3] Most slaves were employed, not on Tara-like plantations, but in groups of one to ten on modest-sized farms.

Slavery suits the production line, where each worker does a rigidly set task over and over again, with no variation. It also suits the rural ancestor of a production line, the *latifundium* with a huge labor force. But on a small farm the worker must turn his hand to many tasks, and here the drawbacks of slave labor—lack of skills, absence of initiative— bit deep. Slavery is inherently static. No slave ever came up with a new farm tool or a better way of using an old one.

These drawbacks were just what a pioneer society did not need. But because the assignment system was more open and flexible than slavery, because it left some room for the initiative of the individual convict (if not in working for the master, then "on his own time"), it tended to be more innovative in its deployment of skills. Only in the outer penal settlements like Moreton Bay, Macquarie Harbor or Norfolk Island were the rigid, punitive inefficiencies of formal prison labor sustained, with men instead of animals dragging carts, and the hoe used instead of the plough. The economy of the mainland was more dynamic and, as John Hirst pointed out, "One of the colony's claims to fame ought to be that it was a forced labor economy which developed a staple industry [wool] in which the forced laborers—the convict shepherds—worked alone."[4]

Still, the convicts had an irreducible unit of labor. They called it the "Government stroke." Doing it kept you out of the hands of the flogger; you were seen to be working, but that was all. Colonial Australia progressed slowly because of its shortage of capital, its solitudes and distances, its small population, and because jails are inherently conservative. But its worst problem was a labor force with so few incentives to work.

The mediocrity of convict labor drove free workers' wages up. "Not the slightest dependence can be placed on convict labor as a permanent source of wealth."[5] But this was untrue. What was true was that being the master of assigned convicts did not give anyone the seigneurial confidence of the slave-owner, because the government could take them back. No farmer "had a property in" his convict servants. They were not part of his capital.

Nor would any master see them as morally neutral creatures, like black slaves. Convicts, by definition, were criminals; they had to be watched closely and kept in rigorous submission. The farther away from the city the master was, the harsher his vigilance tended to become, unless he was an ex-convict himself and treated his assigned man "softly"—an indulgence that, colonial conservatives believed, only led to disorder.

Yet the fact that convict labor produced less than the work of free men did not mean it was unproductive; indeed, fortunes were raised on it. Convicts did not represent capital, like slaves, but their work produced the same effect as the expenditure of capital. "The operation of the penal system has altered the face of the country where it has been set down," remarked the author of an emigrant's handbook published in 1851, "just as manure may have altered the character of a field." It could not produce extravagant surpluses, but it could and did offer the well-organized settler a solid prosperity. Nobody could visit Camden Park in the 1830s, the proud seat of the Macarthur family, with its 60,000 acres and its elegant Regency house by John Verge, without seeing what the System could do. And here was a "typical" large 800-acre farm in Van Diemen's Land in the 1840s:

> The house is of stone, large, and commodious. The farm-buildings are ample in extent, and built of stone, with solid roofs. The implements are all of the best kind, and kept in perfect order. The livestock . . . consists

of 30 cart-horses, 50 working bullocks, 100 pigs, 20 brood mares, 1,000 head of horned cattle, and 25,000 fine-wooled sheep. In this single establishment, by one master, 70 labourers have been employed at the same time. They were nearly all convicts. Nothing of the sort could have existed in this island if convicts had not been transmitted hither, and assigned, on their landing, to settlers authorized to make slaves of them.[6]

This idyll was more common on the small, fertile island of Van Diemen's Land than in the sprawling backblocks of New South Wales. Because it favored standardized work, and because men of influence could get the skilled servants (leaving the lumpen for the lumpen), assignment worked better for the large farmer than for the dirt-farming "dungaree settler." But in either case, it held several compelling merits from the viewpoint of the government.

First, it was cheap. It got convicts "off the stores" and, by shifting the cost of their food and keep to private citizens, it saved the British Government thousands of pounds a year.

Second, it induced well-to-do free settlers to think of emigrating to Australia. Where else in the world could "settlers of responsibility and Capital" assure themselves a free supply of labor? The authorities in New South Wales and their friends in England were apt to emphasize that advantage. The first capitalist-farmer to emigrate was a friend of Joseph Banks named Gregory Blaxland, a prosperous landowner from Kent who had sold most of his English property to invest in Australia, arriving in 1805. The authorities, realizing that here (at last) was the first settler of unimpeachable respectability, showered him with favors. On instructions from Castlereagh, Governor King gave him 4,000 acres of land "in perpetuity . . . in a situation of his own Chusing" and forty convicts to work them with. All were fed and clothed by the Crown for the first eighteen months of their assignment to Blaxland, at a total cost of £1,300, which is more than £50,000 in today's money.[7] Clearly, both the Crown and the colonial government were very anxious to have solid settlers. But in those years, few came out.

The assignment system had a third merit: social control. It dispersed convicts all over New South Wales and Van Diemen's Land, instead of concentrating them in potentially rebellious groups and gangs. It could also control settlers through patronage. The government could punish a settler by denying him convicts, or reward another by assigning them. This damped the political dissensions of free settlers, just as the convicts could be kept in line by the threat of the lash and the promise of eventual freedom. It was a power wielded with special vigor in Van Diemen's Land between 1824 and 1836, under Lieutenant-Governor Arthur—where, according to the wealthy settler George Meredith, a potential master's access to convict labor depended "not upon [his] wants, but upon the construction the Governor may be pleased to put upon the political sentiments and conduct of the applicant." Arthur's favoritism was such that in 1832 half the skilled artisan convicts in Van Diemen's Land were assigned to one-tenth of the settlers, mostly his own clique of officials.[8] The price of irking a governor might be to lose one's servants a week later, for "what the Settler is now allowed by the law to enjoy is a mere *indulgence*, a temporary, revocable loan of services."[9]

Convict assignment in Australia differed, in law, from its earlier form in America. Many respectable Americans railed at the influx of felons, which they thought polluted their society. "In what can Britain show a more Sovereign contempt for us," wrote an irate Virginian in 1751, "than by emptying their Jails into our settlements; unless they would likewise empty their Jakes on our tables!" But the fact was that most farmers and merchants in Maryland or Virginia, when offered a chance of convict labor, grabbed it—and paid handsomely for it. The American colonist owned his indentured servants. He had paid for their transportation across the Atlantic, and he expected to be safeguarded against financial loss if they were set free by some "unforeseen exercise of the Royal Mercy." Convicts were capital, like slaves, and had been freely traded as such since the early seventeenth century. "Our principall wealth consisteth in servants," wrote the Virginia settler John Pory in 1619. Under the transportation acts of the seventeenth and early eighteenth centuries, therefore, the Crown was bound to pay a convict's owner should it remit his sentence. Such a release was unlikely but possible.[10]

In any case, Virginia and Maryland were not penal colonies, but free ones that used felon slaves. In Australia, which had been settled as a jail, no free settler ever paid for a convict's passage from England; and that, in the official view, disposed of the settler's claim to a right of property in the convict's labor. All such rights belonged to the government. Nevertheless, disputes over the "right" of settlers to sell or reassign their convicts kept raising colonial hackles for decades.[11]

ii

IN THE FIRST years of the colony, under Governor Phillip, convicts worked only for the government, which also had a monopoly on all the crops grown; these went into a communal store and were rationed out to the colonists. The first stage of the assignment system, which lasted until 1800, was a refinement of this. The government gave convict labor, clothed and victualled at government expense, to free settlers. But the crops they raised could only be bought by the government, at fixed prices.

The government store became the sole market. In 1790 there were 38 such "assigned" convicts in New South Wales, working on private farms. By 1800 there were 356, and by December 1825 there were 10,800.

As the memory of the "famine years" receded and the economy of the colony grew and diversified, the government store gave up trying to hold its monopoly on farm produce. As it no longer controlled the market, it did not want to pay for the upkeep of assigned convicts either. Hence, by a General Order issued in October 1800, Governor King changed the system. In this second stage of assignment, the masters had to feed, clothe and shelter their servants. The government would advance them food and clothing out of its own stores, to be repaid at the year's end; a full year's rations for one convict cost about £13 13s.[12]

This not only stimulated farming; it got convicts "off the stores," so that they cost the government nothing. From 1800 to 1806, Governor King tried very hard to cut the routine costs of convict administration. Part of his strategy was to alter the rules of assignment again. After 1804, any settler who took a convict "off the stores" signed an indenture to keep him for at least twelve months.[13] The master must maintain his man on exactly the same terms of work, food and clothing as the felons in government employ. If a settler could not support the convict and had to discharge him, he must pay the government a shilling for every day of the unexpired year, a fine that few smallholders could readily afford.

In return, the convict worked the same hours as the government exacted: ten hours Monday to Friday, and six on Saturday, giving a fifty-six-hour week—not a brutal schedule, by any means. But every prisoner, whether he worked for the government or a settler, had to do his "task" of work. Labor by task rather than time followed the logic of having an unwilling convict work force. It had been excessively difficult to keep the hands at work all day; and the early settlement had no full-time guards except the military, who resented being used as jail overseers. Hence, very early, Phillip adopted the system of fixing an amount of product rather than a span of time as the daily norm, and convicts would work at their own rates, although at first, Collins complained, "they preferred passing in idleness the hours that might have been so profitably spent."[14] Task-work had an association with skilled labor in England; it suggested a higher status than mere toil. In this way, labor negotiations were installed in the fledgling penal colony almost from its birth—not what one would expect in a jail, still less in a "slave society." In 1800, Governor King fixed some typical task-rates: In one week, a male convict must fell an acre of forest timber, or split 500 five-foot palings, or thresh 18 bushels of wheat.

In the "famine years," convicts had been let off work at three in the afternoon so that they could raise their own produce. This dispensation became the custom, and it survived for both private and government workers after the shortages had passed. Convicts soon came to be paid wages for out-of-hours labor. They could sell this overtime anywhere, if the master did not want to pay for it. Some items in the 1808 code of labor prices were: 10s. for felling an acre of trees, £1 4s. per acre for "breaking up new ground," 6d. a bushel for pulling and husking corn, and so forth. If a convict always worked the whole day for his master, not just the ten standard government hours, his surplus time entitled him to a shilling a day, or about £18 a year. He might also get occasional bonuses of rum. "Mechanics" or skilled craftsmen—blacksmiths, shoemakers, tailors—could get much more on their own time, sometimes £4 to £5 a week.[15]

How well did the convict's right to earn overtime, which was part of the essence of the assignment system for some twenty years after 1804, translate into spending power? Certainly, worse than one would suppose. Successive governors fixed the price of overtime convict labor, but the colony had no money supply. England had not sent money there, for one did not need cash circulating in a jail. Not until 1812 would the Crown dispatch a supply of silver coin to Australia; £10,000, which, as the Select Committee on Transportation had gloomily predicted, was sucked out of the colony by its unfavorable balance of trade. Not even Macquarie's creation of the "Holey Dollar"—a mutilated Spanish coin of Charles III, whose center or "dump" was punched out and given a value of 1s. 3d., the "ring" being worth 5 shillings—could keep coinage in the colony.[16]

As a result, the first twenty-five years of economic life were a crazy quilt of barter, IOUs and sliding coinage—guineas, johannas, guilders, mohurs, rupees, Spanish dollars and ducats, left in the colony by visiting ships. At one point in 1800, even the English copper penny was declared to be worth twopence. Official prices were given in sterling but the only notes with full sterling value equal to their face value were of two kinds: government bills of exchange on the British treasury, and paymaster's notes issued to the officers of the New South Wales Corps, which were consolidated as bills on the regimental treasury in England.

Of the two, the Rum Corps notes were much preferred, although the government could enforce the use of its own paper in settlement of debts up to £300. Rum Corps paper carried premiums of as much as 25 percent against copper cash, let alone personal IOUs, which no one trusted and whose use as circulating currency was finally proscribed by Governor Bligh.[17]

The convicts got the worst of these economic arrangements, of course. Their paid labor was mercilessly exploited by the means of payment, which was mainly in kind, at the prices of goods fixed by the free settlers. Sometimes they would be forced to take imported goods they

did not need at all: white cotton dress stockings, for instance, or "sheeps'
rumps" (lambskins) imported from Cape Town. In the heyday of the Rum
Corps, sugar was 7s. a pound, tea 6s. an ounce, and spirits 20s. a bottle.
King had known rum to go as high as £8 a gallon.[18]

Even when a convict could get cash wages, he received them not in
sterling but in the depreciated "currency" of the colony. In 1814, some
little while after Governor Macquarie had begun to deflate the exorbitant
prices of the 1800s, the convict weaver Thomas Holden wrote to his
parents in Bolton,

> Dear Mother, things in this Country is very dear, mens hats is too pounds
> too shillings and stockings ten shillings per pair and shoes 16 shillings
> per pair. sugar 3 shillings per pound and butter 7 shillings per pound . . .
> although the Prices is so high we are very glad to get [them] at any price.[19]

As an assigned man, Holden added, he was earning £20 a year in "currency," but that was only worth £12 in English money. In general, by
1820, the assigned man was paid in kind for overtime work at prices 40
to 70 percent above wholesale cash prices, and 25 to 35 percent over
retail. He could (and some did) appeal against this gouging to a magistrate, but magistrates, being settlers themselves, "must naturally feel an
interest in support of charges that have the effect of diminishing the
price of labour to themselves as well as to others." They always favored
paying convicts in store goods rather than money.[20]

The most sought-after commodity of all was rum, a word which stood
for spirits of all kinds—arrack, *aguardiente*, poteen, moonshine—but
which meant, especially, imported liquor from Bengal. In this little community (less than 5,000 people in 1799; about 7,000 in 1805; just over
20,000 by 1817), nearly all the men and most of the women were addicted
to alcohol. In Australia, especially between 1790 and 1820, rum became
an overriding social obsession. Families were wrecked by it, ambitions
destroyed, an iron chain of dependency forged. Many colonists drank
with an oblivion-haunted thirst, determined to blot out the harsh tenor
of their lives. In the heyday of the rum monopoly, William Bligh recalled,

> the thirst after spirits was so very strong that [the settlers] sacrificed every
> thing to the purchase of them, and the prices were raised by that monop-
> oly to so high a degree that it was the ruin of many of those poor people.[21]

Governor Bligh, who was firmly sympathetic to the plight and interests of struggling small farmers and sometimes supported them against
the Rum Corps officers, saw rum as an instrument of debilitation that

helped an elite maintain its power, even as it was debauching the quality of labor. Settlers would leave their farms and come forty miles into Sydney, a four days' round trip, to pick up a gallon of spirits, "in doing which they spent ten times more than it was worth, and lost their time in agriculture."

It may be that the reproofs of lower-class colonial boozing that came from the upper colonial crust should be treated with caution, like the pronouncements of Marsden and others on convict sexuality. If everyone had been drunk, the colony could not have survived. And yet there is little room for doubt about the hold rum had on the embryo society of New South Wales; and its evangelical pastors, first Richard Johnson and then Samuel Marsden, were powerless to stop it.

Because most convicts would rather be paid in rum than anything else, it gave great leverage to the wealthy landowner, who could secure any amount of overtime labor with a broached barrel. "You may get more ground worked for a little spirits than you can for anything else, and that I fancy is the reason of labour being so high," declared John "Little Jack" Palmer, Captain Phillip's former purser on the First Fleet who had risen to be the official banker and contractor to the early settlement. When Major George Johnston of the New South Wales Corps received a grant of 2,000 acres from Governor King as his official reward for crushing the Irish rebellion of 1804, he "used to barter spirits to pay the labourers for clearing our grounds," although it was not always easy to get the governor's permission to buy as many barrels of liquid incentive as he wanted.[22]

Naturally, the prudent master would find a balance between the quantity of liquor served out as a special indulgence to his men and the amount of work he needed done the next day. At Camden Park, the Macarthurs made it a rule to give steady workers a bonus in Cape wine. Colonial Australia showed little interest in beer or ale. It was rum that could make or break a man's prosperity, and although civil and military officers controlled the rum trade by getting first access to incoming cargo and selling the liquor at an initial markup of 500 percent, every small businessman tried to dabble in it, while judges, lawyers, surgeons, ministers and missionaries all got into the trade.

Long after the Rum Corps was recalled to England in 1810, the fledgling economies of New South Wales and Van Diemen's Land—particularly as they affected convicts—remained tied to a kind of rum standard. Quality hardly mattered. Real Jamaica rum, landed at 6 shillings a gallon, reached the small settlers land convicts at £2 to £4; but it was the first victim of the efforts of King and Bligh between 1800 and 1810 to fix rum prices, since their standards abolished the shippers' profit margin and sometimes sent the boats away at a loss. Bringing spirits from England became "a losing trade," but there was liquor from Bengal, half the price at 10 shillings a gallon. Cheap Bengali rum, even with restrictions, was the most profitable kind and it did incalculable social damage, from the bottom of the colony to the top.[23]

The civil establishment bore its quota of fuddled incompetents, from Richard Atkins (1745–1802), Governor King's deputy judge-advocate, to William Gore (1765–1845), acquaintance of Palmerston and the provost-marshal of New South Wales under Bligh, who became (in the words of a later governor) "so totally abandoned to drinking that I fear He is for ever lost to Society."[24] This sad, detested creature was transported to the penal settlement at Newcastle for shooting a trespassing soldier of the 48th Regiment, and he died at the age of eighty, penniless and disgraced, his body left for several years unburied along with his wife's beneath a heap of palings on his farm. The Sydney suburb of Gore Hill bears his name.

The convicts were even less able to stay off the rum, since their need for oblivion was worse. "Intemperance is the greatest curse we have on our land," wrote a convict named John Broxup, claiming that booze caused "three-thirds [sic] of the crimes that are committed." If a young assigned man managed to live soberly it was a cause for congratulation, to be mentioned in letters home: "Your son Richard I can say is very steady for though liquor is very cheap"—it is 1832 and the price of rum has dropped to 2 shillings a pint—"and he have the means and opportunity of getting it he never gets more than do him good," a convict scribe added to a letter home from Richard Dillingham, a convict in Van Diemen's Land.[25]

But most convicts would have found an anthem in the "Rum Song," supposedly of penal days:

> Cut yer name across me backbone,
>   Stretch me skin across a drum,
> Iron me up to Pinchgut Island
>   From today till Kingdom Come!
> I will eat your Norfolk Dumpling
>   Like a juicy Spanish plum,
> Even dance the Newgate hornpipe,
>   If you'll only give me rum!*

---

* It is not certain whether this canting, defiant ditty, quoted in Russel Ward, *Australia Since the Coming of Man* (Sydney, 1965), was written before or after 1830. It is not, however, an English music-hall song like the spurious jingle "Botany Bay," ca. 1880. "Pinchgut Island," or plain "Pinchgut," was a bare knob of rock in Sydney Harbor, now occupied by Fort Denison, where recalcitrant convicts were sometimes chained in semi-starvation. The "Norfolk Dumpling" was 100 lashes, and the "Newgate hornpipe" the hanged man's twitching in air.

Some authorities thought that the only solution was prohibition, which Governor Thomas Brisbane tried to enforce on Newcastle and the Hunter River Valley settlers in 1824. Ships entering Newcastle Harbor had to be placed under bond whether they carried liquor or not, because the mere sight of a possibly rum-laden boat caused "confusion and wild uproar."[26]

The English authorities had transported Gin Lane to Australia, and the harsh conditions of colonial life made for heavy drinking. Yet the relationship between drink, wages and work had long been ingrained in England. Benjamin Franklin, for instance, had been astonished to see that his fellow printers in London drank three-quarters of a gallon of strong ale every day at work, supplied against their wages, while the habit of paying workers and craftsmen on Saturday nights from a table in a public-house—thus assuring that all but the teetotaller would drink a hole in his salary before he got home—did not die out in London until the 1820s. Certainly, few convicts were likely to feel that their rights were under attack if their masters part-paid them in rum, and none complained about it.[27]

iii

THE MAN WHO cleaned up this system was Lachlan Macquarie (1762–1824), the last British proconsul sent to run New South Wales as a military autocracy. In guts, moral vigor and paternal evenhandedness, as well as in his bouts of self-righteousness and bull-headed vanity, Macquarie was a fine early example of that breed of Scottish administrators who kept the engine-room of Empire working throughout the nineteenth century. The son of a Hebridean tenant farmer, related through his mother to the Highland laird Maclaine of Lochbay, he was to become the laird of New South Wales, ruling his anomalous fief from January 1810 to December 1821—the longest tenure of any Australian governor.

Macquarie had risen through the British Army as a career officer, serving with increasing distinction for nearly twenty years in India and the Middle East. By his fortieth year he was a thoroughly seasoned Empire hand: a good organizer, resentful of critics, used to prompt obedience, socially rather creaky but shrewd about the needs of those who fell under his power—an "awkward, rusticated, Jungle-Wallah," in his own words, ramrod-like in port and bearing, with a bony jaw and eyes as hard as cairngorms.

But he was not too awkward to look after his career. In 1807 Macquarie transferred to a new regiment, the 73rd Highlanders. He then learned that it was being sent to New South Wales to clean up the chaos left in the wake of the Rum Corps's 1808 rebellion against Governor Bligh. Its commander would be the colonial governor, since the mutiny against Bligh had shown that a naval governor could not necessarily depend on the army's allegiance. But the commanding officer of the 73rd did not want to go, so Macquarie started lobbying for the post. In 1809 Lord Castlereagh confirmed his appointment as governor of New South Wales. With his wife and his regiment, he sailed for Sydney in May 1809, and was sworn in there on the first day of 1810.

Macquarie's orders were to arrest the leaders of the Rum Rebellion—John Macarthur and the corps's naïvely seditious second-in-command, Major George Johnston, who had arrested Bligh and taken charge of the colony—and to send them back to England for trial. But they had sailed for England already, to take their case before the government. Bligh himself came back to Sydney from his exile in Van Diemen's Land a fortnight after Macquarie's arrival, raging against the rebels in his foul "tarpaulin" lingo. Macquarie ignored him; he, not Bligh, was governor now. Bligh sailed back to England soon after and never saw the blood he wanted, for Johnston was cashiered, not hanged, and Macarthur, "the great perturbator," returned to New South Wales in 1814, his wings clipped (though not for long) by an order to stay out of public affairs.

Macquarie cancelled all the civilian and military appointments and revoked all the pardons, leases and land grants made in Sydney between January 26, 1808, the day of the Rum Rebellion, and his own arrival. He reinstated all dismissed officers and got rid of Macarthur's drunken stooge of a judge-advocate, Richard Atkins, replacing him with Ellis Bent (1783–1815), the first decently trained professional lawyer to hold office in Australia, who had come out with him on the same ship from England. Firmly seated now, all reins in his hand, Macquarie began the inchmeal conversion of a jail into a colony.

It was not an easy task. He could not, for instance, abolish the social addiction to rum by an act of will. The Rum Corps was gone but the thirst remained. However, as the farms spread, and free settlers seeped in and emancipated convicts got their land grants and businesses other than farming grew on the coast—mainly whaling and sealing—so the economy of New South Wales diversified and could no longer be ruled by a primitive cartel. The rum monopolists' day would therefore have ended anyway, but Macquarie hastened it by a series of enactments against drinking: Public-houses were to shut on Sundays and there was, instead, mandatory church parade for convicts; the number of licensed houses was sharply cut; a stiff duty went on imported spirits in the hope of pricing drunkenness out of existence. This last measure failed, as it was bound to do; despite Macquarie's brisk reports of moral improvement, it only caused more colonists than ever to drink themselves into debt.

His attitudes to convicts mattered more than his war on appetite. He rejected the idea that convict labor was a pool from which officers and a few favored settlers could enrich themselves. Convicts were there to be punished but rehabilitated through work. Macquarie saw that Emancipists so outnumbered emigrant settlers that Australia was bound to be an Emancipists' country, its political reality shaped by them and their descendants. If emancipated convicts were not given back their rights as citizens, New South Wales would become as riddled with false dreams of aristocracy as the American South.

Emancipation pointed a convict back into respectable society, which must receive him. With the flurry of capital letters that usually signalled his moral enthusiasms, Macquarie told Castlereagh that emancipation was "the greatest Inducement that Can be held out to the Reformation of the Manners of the Inhabitants. . . . [W]hen United with Rectitude and long tried Good Conduct, [it] should lead a man back to that Rank in Society which he had forfeited and do away, as far as the Case will admit, with All Retrospect of former Bad Conduct."[28] And for the emancipated to grasp the normal responsibilities of citizenhood, they must be shown that they had rights while they were still in the larval stage of convict serfdom. Macquarie's respect for the potential of convicts was noble. Yet it led to his political ruin at the hands of the "Merinos" and their allies in England, who believed in unrelenting exploitation of the convicts; and he died a broken man, obsessed with his detractors and their myriad calumnies.

But that lay in the future. What Sydney saw, at the beginning, was the vigorous administrator in his late forties, for whose attention no matter was too trivial. Whenever a convict transport disgorged its cargo in Sydney, Governor Macquarie was there to meet it. A convict remembered the ceremony that greeted the disembarked prisoners:

> The Governor, Superintender, and Doctor, &c., comes; the Governor addresses them, by saying what a fine fruiteful country they are come to, and what he will do for them if there conduct merits it; likewise tells them if they find themselves anyways dessatesfied with there employer, to go (immediately) to the madjestrate of the district, and he will see him righted.[29]

All convicts were initiated to Australia with this fatherly speech from the governor. By telling the new arrivals "what he will do for them," Macquarie made it plain that the channels of patronage were as much in operation here as the chains of the law. No matter who their master was, they would always be working for the government.

At first Macquarie complained of the shortage of labor and asked the government for more convicts. But for the first five years of his rule, not enough ships could be spared from the war against Napoleon to send them out. So he was faced with a ticklish balance. He would assign men and women to free settlers as far as it was necessary; he had no bias against the farmer and his need for labor. But he felt convict labor was best used in government service, where Authority could judge its incentives nicely and measure the reformation of each person instead of depending on second-hand reports from masters.

It would be better for the colony, too. For Macquarie was appalled by the shoddy look of Sydney: an unplanned straggle of shacks "in most ruinous decay," perched on the rim of the shining, amethyst, many-lobed harbor. The judge-advocate's residence was a "perfect pigstye," and the convict barracks at Sydney and Parramatta were beyond mere disgust. There was no proper hospital. The churches were huts—a fact particularly repugnant to Macquarie, who believed religious practice would reform his sinners. The town streets were dusty tracks in summer and ditches after a rain, and no sewers existed. Beyond the town's perimeter, the roads (except for the toll road to Parramatta) could scarcely be negotiated by a cart.

With a mixture of naïveté, zeal and creative drive, Macquarie set out to turn this hodgepodge into a Georgian city. His architectural education was necessarily slight, but he had seen the work of Nash, Soane and Wood, and believed their idiom was the correct one for the architecture of Empire. About the technicalities of building he knew nothing, but the taste of his time had rubbed off on him, as it was bound to do on any intelligent proconsul with firmly elitist values. Elizabeth Macquarie, his wife, had brought an album of building and town designs with her. It became the source-book for Macquarie's plans of urban renewal.

He started writing codes that specified the minimum floor area of houses and width of streets in Sydney. There would be no more hovels on Crown leases. These were the first such regulations in Australia. He laid out what is still the central grid of Sydney, and in five settlements along the Hawkesbury River he ordered that the core sites should be reserved for the court, the schoolhouse and the church, and that all houses must have their plans filed with the district constable.[30]

When he turned from rulebooks to real buildings, Macquarie faced more obstacles. The British Government wanted him to cut costs. That meant no "extravagances," no structures except of a strictly military or penal kind—and even they should be humble. It refused to send him an architect. But Macquarie had emergency powers, and felt he could define "emergencies" broadly enough to stifle long-range criticism with *faits accomplis*. So he tricked his way around the British Government's ban on building. His first effort was probably designed with his wife. It was a new hospital, a handsome three-block affair with wide verandas (which came, not from English Regency architecture, but from Macquarie's observations in India). It was by far the largest structure ever built in the colony. He financed it with rum, as the New South Wales Government, 150 years later, would part-finance its colossally expensive Opera House with lotteries. He gave its building contractors a trading monopoly on 45,000 gallons of spirits, from which the government drew a duty of 3 shillings a gallon; the £6,750 this generated was to be kicked back to the contractors as their fee, off the books. These arrangements did not work out, and bitter accusations of graft and cheating flew in all directions, but the "Rum Hospital," as it was inevitably nicknamed, got finished. Two of its three blocks survive today: jerry-built in parts, due to the greed of the contractors, but the first presentable Georgian public building in Australia.

It was followed by others. Lacking a free settler who was an architect, Macquarie found a convict of that profession: Francis Howard Greenway (1777–1837). The descendant of generations of West Country builders and stonemasons, Greenway was a trained architect—a pupil of Nash— but a poor businessman. Practicing in Bristol, he went bankrupt, forged a contract and received a death sentence which, as usual by then, was commuted to fourteen years' transportation. When Macquarie found out about Greenway's arrival in 1814, he grew cautiously interested. Given his modest talents and lack of savoir-faire in dealing with clients, Greenway might never have landed important commissions in England. But in Australia he was John Soane, he was Beau Nash—he might as well have been Gianlorenzo Bernini, for all the competition he had. Macquarie put him in charge of designing and building all government works, beginning in 1816.[31]

Over the next six years, Greenway turned out for Macquarie a series of buildings, uneven in quality, the best of which utterly transformed the architectural standards of the fledgling colony. The main ones were two convict barracks, the Female Factory in Parramatta (1819) and—his secular masterpiece—the Hyde Park Barracks for men in Sydney (1819), together with several churches, notably St. Matthew's in Windsor (1817–20) and St. James' in Sydney (1820–24). The Female Factory kept at least some women off the Parramatta streets, although it was never large enough. The Hyde Park Barracks—which, like the General Hospital, Macquarie began without permission from London—he believed was an unqualified success. It was designed to house all convicts working for the government in Sydney. Because the 800 convicts placed in it could no longer plead that they needed the income from their "own-time" work to pay for the lodgings the government had formerly not provided, moving them in there was a ticklish business: The Hyde Park Barracks had to provide all kinds of inducements, from extra rations to weekends off, in return for Macquarie's wholesale appropriation of the convicts' time. The extra surveillance it afforded seemed to affect them for the better, or so Macquarie thought. In 1820 he told Bathurst that "not a tenth part of the former Night Robberies and Burglaries [are] being now committed, since the Convicts have been lodged in the New Barracks." It held 800 felons, rather less than a third of the convict population of Sydney.[32]

Such projects demanded skilled labor from bricklayers, masons, tilers, blacksmiths, glaziers and joiners. These "mechanics," the riffraff of the immense body of craft on which the architectural achievements of England had been raised, were always in short supply and rarely much good. The government picked them out as soon as they arrived. When a ship anchored, the superintendent of convicts made a roll of names and trades, skimming off the men whom the government wanted for public works. Since most arriving felons had already learned that a skilled man's life was apt to be easier in private assignment than in government labor, this always produced a little ballet of lies on shipboard, with wheelwrights and coopers professing to be common ditch-diggers or hayseeds. From 1814 to 1820, the government took 1,587 (or 65 percent) of the 2,418 "mechanics" arriving in Australia, and 3,000 (or 32 percent) of the laborers—the peak year in its demand for the skilled being 1819, at the height of Macquarie's building schemes, when it took 80 percent of the artisans. Naturally, this policy irked the free settlers who needed artisans themselves.[33]

Besides skilled labor, there was an equally great need for unskilled. From 1814 to 1820, the government took over some 4,600 of the 7,200 convicts arriving in Australia, for it needed worker ants. In technological terms, Macquarie's Australia was more backward than Cromwell's England. There was as yet no steam power; draft animals were few; and there were no streams near Sydney reliable enough to turn watermills. So every hole was dug, every log sawn, every rock quarried and every ton of rubble moved by that least efficient of engines, the human body, toiling in gangs. Macquarie's plans demanded roads.

For by 1813 the colony was beginning to feel crowded. Along the Hawkesbury River and on the rich flats of Parramatta, every inch of land had been leased and granted. Settlers had pushed southwest to Stonequarry (modern Picton and Bowral) and the poor dry belt of the Bargo Brush. But the great barrier lay to the west—the line of mountains that could be seen, low on the horizon, from Sydney. The Blue Mountains, as they were named after their color, were an ever-present proof of the "impenetrability," the "hostility," of the continent to whose rim the colonists clung. Nobody had got across them—not in twenty-five years. Even the Aborigines said they were impassable. Some convicts who tried to cross them, thinking China lay beyond, died of hunger in their immense labyrinth of sandstone, where bellbirds chimed and long filaments of water fell, wreathing, from distant cliffs.

Then in 1813 three prosperous settlers, Gregory Blaxland, William Lawson and W. C. Wentworth, set out to look for a way over the divide. They took convict servants, dogs and horses; and after three weeks' exhausting struggle they found themselves looking down on a golden vista which, like other explorers in America, they compared to Arcadia and the land of Canaan. From the summit of what is now Mount Blaxland they saw, rolling like the sea, "Enough grass to support the stock of this colony for thirty years." There would never be a shortage of pasture again; but there had to be a permanent way to get to it. In 1815 Macquarie made a journey of inspection along their trail, bestowing names on its grander views: "The Prince Regent's Glen," "Black Heath," "Pitt's Amphitheatre." To record the picturesque splendors of this gateway to Goshen, he even took an artist, John Lewin, with his party. Surveyors followed; and Macquarie, determined to have "a good practicable Cart Road made with the least practicable Delay" from Parramatta to the other side of the Blue Mountains, chose sixty convicts "who had been a Certain Time in the Colony and who were also considered well-behaved Men, and entitled . . . to some Indulgence." He told them they would get conditional pardons for their "Arduous Labours" if they finished the road —126 miles of it—in six months. They did it and were set free. This meant cutting about 1,200 yards of road per day and building more than a dozen wooden bridges along the way from Emu Island to the Macquarie River—a feat that showed what prisoners could do if they had better incentives than the lash. There was only one major problem with this road: Parts of it, especially the descent of Mount York, were so steep that loaded bullock-carts had to go down with big logs hitched to them as brakes; and the ascent could only be made if the cart were dragged up in stages, by a chain run through iron ringbolts in the rock face harnessed to a second bullock team pulling downhill. The Western Road, as Macquarie pointed out to Bathurst (for whom its destination was diplomatically named), would have taken three years to finish by contracted free labor or the "Government stroke" of unmotivated prisoners, instead of six months.[34]

It was also the first public work in Australia to be praised in verse. For Macquarie had appointed a convict poet-laureate: Michael Massey Robinson (1744–1826), a graduate of Oxford and former lawyer who had tried to blackmail a London ironmonger by threatening to publish a scurrilous verse about him, and was transported for life. It was his task, each year, to recite a birthday ode at Government House in Sydney. These first frail pipings of the formal Australian muse included a paean to the Western Road across "yon Blue Mountains, with tremendous brow,"

> Behold, where Industry's encourag'd hand
> Hath chang'd the lurid Aspect of the Land;
> With Verdure cloathed the solitary Hills,
> And pour'd fresh Currents from the limpid Rills;
> Has shed o'er darken'd Glades a social Light,
> And BOUNDLESS REGIONS OPEN TO OUR SIGHT![35]

One can almost see Marquarie, stiff in his gold braid, nodding with approval to the march of his assigned iambics. For his vanity matched his energy. He loved, as the colony expanded, to name new places after himself, a harmless habit much satirized after (not before) he left the colony. " 'Twas said of Greece two thousand years ago," wrote another Scot, the Presbyterian minister John Dunmore Lang, who had arrived in Sydney in 1823, the year after Macquarie sailed,

> That every stone i' the land had got a name,
> Of New South Wales too, men will say that too,
> But every stone there seems to get the same.
> "Macquarie" for a name is all *the go;*
> The old Scotch Governor was fond of fame,
> Macquarie Street, Place, Port, Fort, Town, Lake, River;
> "Lachlan Macquarie, Esquire, Governor," for ever![36]

Nevertheless, Macquarie's commitment to public works rather than private assignment paid its dividends by giving the colony a civic armature. Its critics in London and New South Wales harped on how much it cost the Crown to have so many convicts working for the government, for during Macquarie's term of office, 1810–1821, the colony cost England about £3 million, which seemed a great deal for a place that sent no goods back to England and functioned in a merely negative way, as a social *oubliette.* But in 1810 it took £100 a year to transport a man and maintain him "on the stores," whereas by the time Macquarie's public-works policy was fully under way—between 1816 and 1821—the cost was down to less than £30 a year.[37]

The gross cost of the transportation system had certainly risen: £579,000 for 1810–12, £717,000 for 1816–18, £1,125,000 for 1819–21.

This worried the British Government and disposed Lord Bathurst to listen to critics who believed that convicts should work only, or mainly, for private enterprise—and especially for free emigrant settlers, whose numbers had increased from about four hundred in 1810 to nearly two thousand men, women and children by 1820.[38]

Such was the pressure that in 1819 Bathurst sent a commissioner of inquiry, John Thomas Bigge, to look into Macquarie's administration. Bigge, a diligent, intensely snobbish Tory lawyer who thought convicts were scum and unhesitatingly sided with the emigrants against the small farmers and Emancipists, fell out with Macquarie and in with the Macarthurs, and his eventual report was a litany of extravagance—a political disaster for Macquarie.

And yet Macquarie's policies were, if anything, frugal. What had driven the gross cost up was numbers—the flood of convicts that came after 1815 with the end of the Napoleonic Wars. England now had more crime and more ships to bear it away; and Macquarie, who had begged for more convicts, had not bargained for so many. The white population of New South Wales and Van Diemen's Land almost doubled between 1812 and 1817, going from 12,471 to 20,379. Most of these were convicts; in 1818 there were so few free settlers—and the ones along the Hawkesbury River had been so battered by a disastrous flood in 1817—that hardly one convict in eight could be assigned. "In the meantime I have no alternative but to employ large Gangs of them on the Government Public Works," Macquarie protested.[39]

By 1821, his last year in office, Macquarie had a total of 4,001 convicts working for the government—more than twice the number (1,853) that would be doing government labor under his successor, Sir Thomas Brisbane, in 1825.[40] And he had cut down the treasury bill expenditure for each convict per year from £60 in 1810 to less than £15.

The most parsimonious Scot could hardly have done better, but the British Government counted grosses, not averages, and did not like Macquarie's reputed kindness to convicts. Before Bigge sailed, Bathurst told him unequivocally that Australia must be "rendered an Object of real Terror" and that this must outweigh all questions of the economic or social growth of Australia as a colony.[41] Since Macquarie's policy was based on his belief that the social growth of Australia really mattered, and it could not grow unless some quilting of liberality softened the iron framework of its repressive laws, this idea of Australia as a theater of horror acted out for a distant audience was not to his moral taste. In the end, he was seen as too extravagant because his own government sent him more convicts than the colony could absorb—and too lenient because he, alone among the early governors of New South Wales, really thought about the rights of these prisoners.

iv

THE QUESTION of rights under the assignment system was, in fact, more delicate than it looked. The convicts were not slaves under the law, but British citizens whose enforced task, in Australia, was to work their way back to freedom through expiation. Certain rights were guaranteed them—to food, to shelter, to protection from summary punishment by masters. Others accrued to them by custom, such as the right to sell what one made or did on one's "own time." From the Crown's point of view, all convicts were legally dead under civil law from their arrival in Australia to their emancipation. They could neither sue nor be sued, nor could they testify in court as witnesses. In the colony, these restrictions were simply overlooked—they had to be, since no society composed mainly of present or former convicts, most of whom had businesses to run, debts to recover and wrongs to right, could function otherwise. But the rights to a convict's work were vested in the government, which owned his labor until his sentence was served or remitted.

This put the assigned servant in an odd relationship to his or her master. Government would only get between them to protect its own rights. The government strictly monitored a master's treatment of his assigned servants because each master was its agent in the scheme of punishment. The assignment system was not just a way of using the labor of people whose crimes had already been expiated by transportation. Assigned labor was their punishment—hence, the government had the right to control its conditions and to step in when a master became too hard or too soft. The strictest emphasis on this was laid in Van Diemen's Land under the rule of Sir George Arthur, but it was the ground rule of the System everywhere in Australia.

The axiom that the settler, in accepting a convict servant, was acting on behalf of the government caused resentment. No settler, for instance, could take it on himself to punish a convict; for that, the felon had to be tried before a magistrate. When the settler was himself a magistrate he could not flog his own men; they had a right to their day in court. Likewise, if a convict felt ill-treated, he could complain to a magistrate. In this way, the government meant to protect its rights in its prisoners' labor. But neither master nor servant was always willing to grasp that the rules were meant to safeguard the government's interests before their own.

Although the government took the skilled workers for its own projects and gave the dross of the labor force to settlers, it was a common practice under early governing officials such as Grose, Paterson and Hunter to give favored insiders a share of the first pick. Maurice Margarot thought "only the greatest ruffians" were assigned to the ordinary settlers, for "it is not in the interest of officers that settlers should get forward."[42]

A wealthy and established landowner could usually expect to get the convicts he needed. One finds Robert Townson (1763–1827), a scholarly friend of Joseph Banks who had published works on botany and mineralogy before taking up land grants in New South Wales, writing in 1822 to ask the government for "three men from the first ships" for his model estate, Varro Ville, near Minto. He made a request for "Shepherds, Gardeners, & Ploughmen—But *English or Scotchmen*, having already an undue proportion of *Irish*. The last three were Irish of no use—one was a runaway Soldier Lad—& another a Dublin Grocer's errand boy."[43]

The law could also be bent. New settlers were meant to get servants first, so they could get started on the land. The liberal Whig governor Richard Bourke (1831–37) wanted to make sure that convicts were assigned in proportion to the amount of land a master held. Unfortunately, the law did not care whether their land was freehold or leasehold, cleared or raw bush; hence the loophole, not closed until after 1835. A large farmer could issue dummy leases of land to his own dependents and get up to eight assigned servants on each lease, "whilst persons who were more scrupulous as to the means they employed could get none." He could also pad his application by claiming that acres of bush were actually worked land that needed assigned labor.[44]

The cure for these and other abuses lay in tighter bureaucratic control over assignment. Governor Darling set up a board to which all applications for servants had to be sent; he told its members to favor settlers with a good record and to turn down applications from men with a record of cruelty or excessive lenience. Unfortunately, much of the paperwork in processing applications for assigned servants was done by convict clerks, who rarely refused a bribe. Nevertheless the successive administrations of Darling and Bourke did much to make assignment more "objective." But it could not guarantee the quality of a convict's labor.

Throughout the life of the System, the average "dungaree settler" was likely to end up with an unskilled, resentful cuckoo of a convict who had been born and raised in a city and could not tell a hoe from a shovel. Only one convict in five had been an agricultural worker. But incompetents could neither be fired, like free workers, nor sent back to the government. This arrangement, Governor Richard Bourke remarked in 1832, was "for the most part very Unsatisfactory":

The Convict generally does as little as he can. . . . Much of his time is passed on the road going to or returning from Hospital, or to a Justice to complain of his master's treatment, or to answer the Master's charges against him for negligence, drunkenness or insubordination. Many also are unsuited to labour of any sort.[45]

By then, the cavalier habits of some settlers with their assigned convicts had already been causing some concern in England. A farmer saddled with an incompetent convict would swap him off with another settler or abandon him in town. The inconvenience and waste of time in haling a convict before a magistrate's court, which might be three days' journey from the farm, discouraged complaint through legal channels; so the incompetent assigned man would simply be dumped on the road or left in town, to beg or survive as best he could. The authorities had no choice but to put these outcasts in jail, on a skimpy allowance of bread and water, until they were either reassigned or put in a government work gang.[46]

It was demoralizing for them and irksome for the government; but in New South Wales, at least, there seemed to be no way of stopping it. Ten years after Bigge described the problem in his report, it was still perplexing the Crown. By 1831, there were about 13,400 assigned servants scattered around New South Wales, and keeping track of them was becoming a clerical nightmare. So although convicts could not, of course, be legally sold by one master to another, Governor Bourke compromised: Now they could be reassigned without the cumbersome business of recalling them to Sydney, endorsing their papers and sending them out into the remote bush again. All one needed was a formal permission to transfer, which "indeed is Seldom refused . . . as it is not only a convenience . . . but it saves expense."[47]

Masters who were caught transferring servants without permission would be blacklisted from getting assigned men again. But neither Bourke nor his predecessors could get rid of the common assumption among landowners that, whatever the Crown might *say* about its ownership of convict labor, the *fact* was that convicts were slaves, and masters should be left to treat them as such. Farmers without servants believed they had a right to them. "Every man, who cannot obtain Land or Convict Servants as he wishes, thinks no doubt he has a right to complain of the Governor's injustice," wrote Governor Darling in 1831.[48]

Nor were such feelings without legal support. Sir Francis Forbes, the first chief justice of the Supreme Court of New South Wales, thought masters did have a right to the labor of their assigned servants. He based this on seventeenth-century American precedents. The settlers wanted to believe him, but the Crown refused, pointing out that in America the settler paid for the convict's passage, which gave him this right—but not in Australia.

Even Forbes's position looked mild compared to the one adopted, a few years later, by William Charles Wentworth, who had become a power in the colony (see Chapter 10) by agitating for the rights of Emancipists. In 1839 Wentworth actually proposed that assignment should be cancelled altogether and that convicts be sold outright to the highest bidder. Worse still, he wanted to institute group punishments of assigned convicts. If one man on a property committed a crime, all the other servants should be penalized by an automatic extension of their sentence unless they informed on him. This, Wentworth thought, would reduce the main inconvenience settlers had to put up with from their assigned men—the difficulty of getting them to "tell" on one another.[49]

The convicts, on the other hand, believed they had rights, and that these arose from the fact that they worked. A man was a convict from sunrise to afternoon, but overtime was his to sell. The more skilled he was, the harder he could bargain with his master. In this way, some masters were gradually forced to make concessions, even within the unequal class relations of the colony.

What were these rights? Some were conventional: food, clothing, health care. The government enforced strict standards for the first two and was by no means indifferent to the third. By the 1830s, masters were obliged to pay a shilling a day, up to thirty days, toward the keep of an assigned man in hospital—hardly a lavish allowance, but the cause of much grumbling among settlers.[50]

Before 1830, the master had to give each assigned man a wage of £10 a year, which paid for his clothes and bedding. In 1831 Governor Darling changed this by ruling that the master must issue the blankets, palliasses, and clothes directly, instead of wages. The workers' diet was rough and monotonous. "They can make a meal from what would not be looked at in England," wrote the convict John Broxup. In 1823 a settler in Van Diemen's Land, Gilbert Robertson, was accused of feeding his men on dead magpies. But on most farms the servants ate what the masters ate.[51]

A master might give his convicts tea, sugar, milk or a bit of the rank, locally grown colonial tobacco as an "indulgence," a little reward for good work. But custom might turn the master's indulgence into the convict's right or claim. This tended to happen especially after the 1820s, when Macquarie's successors—Governors Brisbane and Darling—did away with wages and "own time" rights for assigned servants. They were replaced by an informal system of incentives and rewards, "indulgences" under the law but essential to the efficient ordering of a property. At the master's discretion, men could be favored with easy jobs or punished with hard ones; they could be given work that would teach them trade skills, or sent to the most routine tasks of common labor. "Luxuries" like tea, sugar and soap, a half-pint of rum or dinner in the homestead kitchen, were prized as signs of status and regarded as forms of payment, replacing the wages and overtime that Brisbane and Darling cancelled. Some men certainly felt they had a right to tea, sugar and tobacco, and they vociferously told their masters so. When William Larissey, a convict at Port Macquarie in 1836, was told his sugar and tea were stopped, he seized his master by the neck. "Damn my bloody limbs and bones," he shouted, "if I don't have the worth of that tea and sugar out of you." He paid for this outburst with twelve months in the iron gang.[52]

Not all convicts were as defiant as this, but the bench books of the magistrates' courts show many cases of men brought up for "insolent" behavior in disputes with their masters over rations and clothing. Sometimes—though much more rarely—a convict would bring his master to court. In 1833, in the district of Scone north of Sydney, there were 210 charges by masters or overseers against assigned convicts, and only six charges by convicts against masters—all of which, however, were upheld by the magistrates. They involved matters like rotten meat and insufficient shelter; one convict, Simon Lewis, assigned to an absentee station-owner, was found to have had no blanket or mattress from him in four years.[53]

Very occasionally, convicts would band together to bargain in defense of what they perceived as their rights. But it was more common to "go slow" (after sizing the master up), either for the pleasure of inconveniencing him or in the hope of being transferred. Thus, finding he was in bond to "a hard hearted wreach" in Van Diemen's Land, the convict George Taylor "began to only do that part of my work which I thought proper and soon aforded my Master an opertunity of takeing me to a magistrate, this was repeated two or three times [but] I found I could not get from him by this means."[54]

Although it was by no means impossible, or always difficult, for an assigned man, once before the magistrate, to justify his insolence or violence by proving his master had provoked him, not a few convicts took their legal rights at face value and brought their masters to court for ill-treatment. The usual complaints were stoppage of rations and physical violence. Thus, in 1829 the convict James Davis, assigned in New South Wales to Mr. David Hayes, "maketh Oath and saith . . . I swear I have had no Rations since Friday last excepting part of a Loaf; a Two-Pound Loaf was shared among five of us." He was backed by four other convicts and won. In the same year, Thomas Argent, assigned to a Sydney butcher named William Merritt, was ordered to wash Merritt's gig with warm water and then go to Parramatta to take delivery of some livestock. "Argent said he was weak and faint with hunger, having received nothing to eat since Friday, and that he would not go. . . . Mr. Merritt jumped up and gripped him by the breast with one hand, and struck him twice with the other, and dragged him out of the hut, and then took up a paling and threatened to beat his brains out." Argent, terrified, said he would put himself in police custody, at which Merritt mounted his horse and tried to run him down.[55]

Argent's reward for getting Merritt into court was to be reassigned to another and better master. The government had no interest in assigning convicts to brutes, but some masters seemed unable to grasp that their servants were, in the ordinary sense, human. Such was the case with a Mrs. Ramus of Hamilton, Van Diemen's Land, whose assigned man, George Willey, had in 1833 been sentenced to twenty-five lashes for insolence. The punishment was to be inflicted in the local jail, and Willey had words with Mrs. Ramus's brother over his right to take rations there when he was flogged. At this point, the Hamilton magistrate reported,

> Mrs. Ramus' brother ordered his hands to be tied behind him with a piece of hide rope, a heavy bullock chain to be put around his waist which was attached to another chain and yoked to a pair of bullocks, he himself following on horseback with a loaded gun. In this state the man was brought to my house, a distance of 5 miles, when I immediately ordered him to be set at liberty.[56]

An order followed, depriving Mrs. Ramus of all her assigned servants. Losing one's convicts in this way was more of a risk in Van Diemen's Land in the 1830s, because of Arthur's evenhanded strictness. But a cruel settler in New South Wales could be stripped of his servants, especially if his social connections were poor.

The most vivid disagreements over the matter of rights were caused by the ticket-of-leave system. There were only three ways in which the law might release a man from bondage. The first, though the rarest, was an absolute pardon from the governor, which restored him to all rights including that of returning to England. The second was a conditional pardon, which gave the transported person citizenship within the colony but no right of return to England. The third was the ticket-of-leave. The convict who had been given a ticket-of-leave no longer had to work as an assigned man for a master. He was also free from the claims of forced government labor. He could spend the rest of his sentence working for himself, wherever he pleased, as long as he stayed within the colony. He was, as the phrase went, "on his own hands," in contrast to the assigned man who was merely said to be "off the store." The ticket lasted only a year and had to be renewed, and it could be revoked at any time. It was an effective way of fostering conformity and self-help while keeping the convict on a leash.

Ticket-of-leave men could be denounced by anyone, and thus they lived in some uncertainty. As an editorial in the *Sydney Gazette* put it,

> A ticket-of-leave is the most tender kind of liberty that can be conceived; it is liberty in one sense, and non-liberty in another. . . . Under the present system, a ticket-of-leave exempts a man from the service of one master, while upon the other hand he becomes the slave of hundreds of others. From the Magistrate, down to the meanest constable in the district, a ticket-of-leave holder is continually kept the subject of apprehension.[57]

One lost one's ticket, Governor King proclaimed in 1804, by being idle, or insolent to "any officer, soldier or Constable," or charging too much for out-of-hours work. But fragile as it was, the ticket-of-leave was craved by every convict in the colony and regarded by most of them as a natural right, a goal that one struggled toward and was entitled to. It played an immense role in the moral economy of colonial life. The worst thing a master could do to a convict servant was to keep him from getting his ticket-of-leave.

The less scrupulous settlers sometimes tried to do this. More convicts were always coming in one end of the System from the transports than were going out the other, as "ticket-of-leavers" or Emancipists. Thus, from January 1826 to December 1828, 6,032 male convicts arrived in Australia, while 4,140 men were added to the free population by the expiry of sentence or the granting of tickets-of-leave.[58]

But this did not reduce the demand for assigned labor, because so many of the newly freed men became farmers themselves and needed working hands. "Since convict labour has become so exceedingly valuable as it now is," Governor Gipps reported to the secretary for war and the colonies in 1838,

> it is a matter of very frequent complaint that Masters prevent their Servants from getting Tickets of Leave from an unwillingness to lose their labour; and that they even cause (in some cases) their men to be punished, for the sake of retaining their services . . . [E]ach punishment which an assigned man receives, puts him back a year in getting his Ticket. I am willing to hope that the cases are but few.[59]

They were probably more common than Gipps was "willing to hope," and they had been going on for nearly forty years before the government cast an official eye on them. The prisoner Thomas Cook described the fate of one convict, assigned to "a very oppressive and miserable-hearted man" at White Rock in New South Wales during the early 1830s. Originally sentenced to 14 years' transportation,

> he had toiled hard and so fared for the space of 5 years and 9 months of
> that term, without a charge being preferred against him; but as he approached his probationary period of servitude (6 years) entitling him to a
> Ticket of Leave . . . his master, to benefit himself by the Blood and Sweat
> of a hard-toiling Slave, preferred a charge of insolence and threatening
> language against him.

That meant a magistrate's sentence of 50 lashes, and a year's delay on
the ticket-of-leave. When the year was almost gone,

> his cruel Master, unmoved by compassion or gratitude, again brought him
> before the Bench, and charged him again with disrespectful conduct upon
> which he was again sentenced 50 lashes. Thus was this pitiable object
> despairing of obtaining a moment's liberty until the death of his master
> or the termination of his sentence. He was nearly stupid from hard toil
> and cruel treatment.[60]

A master might goad an assigned man to insolence or violence, simply by battering him with insults. The *Sydney Gazette* in 1826 complained about "the all too prevalent custom"

> of casting an unhappy fellow creature's life and character into his teeth,
> and by this means leaving the man either passively to suffer under such a
> gross outrage . . . or to resent it by insubordinate language and conduct,
> whereby he becomes subject to . . . 50 lashes! for the magistrates . . .
> generally feel it imperative to lean on the side of power.[61]

District benches close to Sydney were apt to treat convicts fairly and
well, partly because their magistrates were more in the public eye. The
Stonequarry bench, run by a settler from New York named Henry Antill,
who had married the daughter of an Emancipist and settled down to
become the largest landowner in the modern district of Picton, had a
name for decency, and Antill was by no means the only even-handed
magistrate in New South Wales.

But the further outback a farm was, the more opportunity it held for
tyranny and the more likelihood there was of collusion between settlers
and magistrates. George Loveless, another Tolpuddle Martyr, believed
from his own experiences that no one could "form a just impression of
the System" unless he had been assigned in such remote places:

> One magistrate will bring his men to be tried before a neighbour magistrate, and it is a frequent practice for the master to pay a private visit to

the magistrate, and say he is going to bring such a man or men before
him, and wishes that such or such particular punishment may be dealt
out. On the arrival of the men . . . the magistrate enquires what they have
to say in answer to this charge, and frequently, if they attempt to answer,
he interrupts them, saying "I will not believe a word you have to say, and
I shall sentence you to receive so many lashes."[62]

While it is true that the masters won most cases in which they
brought their servants to court for disobedience or insolence, one cannot
simply assume that this was due to collusions of class between masters
and magistrates. As Hirst observed, the magistrates "were superior men
both in wealth and education and were free from personal ties or obligations to the middling and small masters. How better to demonstrate their
superior status than by carefully examining the complaint of a convict
against a small farmer and perhaps reproaching the master or even taking
his servant from him?"[63] The area of offense that magistrates always
paid attention to was summary punishment by master of man, and here
the claims of convicts often succeeded—partly because the physical evidence, the wounds and weals, spoke clearly in court. But a servant in the
settled areas had a better chance of access to a magistrate's court than
one in the outback, where lodging a complaint might entail a walk of
fifty miles or more—and require permission from the master to leave the
property for several days.

We cannot know how many assigned men were unjustly denied their
tickets-of-leave. Presumably the settlers minimized the number and the
convicts exaggerated it. What is not in doubt is the gulf that separated
the settler's from the convict's view of the ticket-of-leave—one calling
it (as the government declared it to be) an "indulgence," the other always
claiming it as a right. Thomas Cook, for instance, wrote of servitude
"entitling" the convict at White Rock to his ticket. The extreme opposite view on this was held by Chief Justice Francis Forbes, who thought
no convict had a right to a ticket while on assigned service to a private
settler. Luckily for the convicts, Forbes could not persuade the government of this.

Their belief in a right to a ticket did not mean the prisoners were
deluded. Rights emerge by bargaining between the powerful and the relatively powerless; they are not simply "granted," for if they were, there
would be none. Rights are solidified claims, sanctioned by usage and
expectation. When convicts spoke of wider rights than their simple, mechanical entitlement to food and shelter, they were speaking from their
inherited expectations as laborers—that masters should behave with fairness and circumspection, and that the law should offer some formal
protection to their own interests. In short, they expected the moral and

legal economy of the traditional English labor market to apply in the continental prison that was Australia. And that economy did not exclude the common English practice by which free workers, adults as well as apprentices, were bonded to their masters and suffered severe penalties, ranging from fines to ostracism, if they broke away. In this respect, at least, assignment was not as totally foreign to English labor relations as one might assume.

Some were cruelly disappointed. "The extent to which tyranny was formerly carried on with regard to assigned servants throughout the Colony," wrote one ex-convict, Charles Cozens, "is almost incredible." But sometimes the accounts of the same convict establishment, seen through different eyes, contradict one another like black and white. The Abolitionist J. D. Lang, who was certainly no friend of the assignment system, praised the way Governor Darling's private secretary, Colonel Henry Dumaresq (1792–1838) ran St. Heliers, his 13,000-acre estate near Muswellbrook in New South Wales: "one of the best regulated estates in the colony . . . rewards, not punishments . . . the men are sober, industrious and contented." To a visiting Quaker named James Backhouse, St. Heliers also seemed a model of convict management, and the future explorer Edward J. Eyre, a man of unquestionable decency and candor, thought it "the best-ordered, best-managed station on the Hunter." Yet in 1850, one of Lang's co-Abolitionists, John Goodwin, protested that his praises were only true of "the time of the late Mr. Whiteman's superintendence" of St. Heliers (after 1830) and that the previous superintendent, Mr. Scott, had been "a demon incarnate":

> He was in the habit of putting handcuffs, and leg-irons on them, and throwing them into a dungeon on that estate, where they remained generally for three days without either meat or drink. . . . [H]e did not trouble to take his men to court; but sentenced them for the most trivial offence, and just as his caprice dictated, to carry logs of wood on their shoulders, on his own verandah, and under his eye, for two to twelve hours; these logs weighed from 50 to 100 lbs. He never went out without a brace of loaded pistols and a belt-full of handcuffs. . . . Captain Dumaresque [sic], "that nice gentleman," has to my own knowledge drawn as much blood from the flogged backs of his assigned men, as would make him to swim in human gore.[64]

James Brine, one of the Tolpuddle Martyrs transported to Australia for trade-union activity in 1834, was assigned to a magistrate named Robert Scott at Glindon on the Hunter River. Scott set Brine to digging postholes, even though his bare feet were so cut and sore that he could not put them to the spade. Eventually Brine "got a piece of an iron hoop and wrapped it round my foot to tread upon," but for six months (the regulation period between issues) Scott would give him no shoes, clothes or bedding. Stricken by a severe cold after spending seventeen days up to his chest in a creek, washing sheep, Brine begged for a blanket and got a homily instead.

> "No," said he, "I will give you nothing until you are due for it. What would your masters in England have had to cover them if you had not been sent here? I understand it was your intention to have murdered, burnt and destroyed every thing before you, and you are sent over here to be severely punished, and no mercy shall be shown you. If you ask me for any thing before the six months is expired, I will flog you as often as I like. . . . You d—d convict!—don't you know that not even the hair on your head is your own?"[65]

E. J. Eyre, who found it "a most revolting sight to see the scarred and bleeding backs of human beings—convicts tho' they were," was impressed by the docility with which accused servants would trek unguarded to the split-slab outback courthouse. It was "singular," he wrote,

> that men said to be the most worthless of their kind and the most reckless ruffians should thus quietly march a distance of 5, 10, 20 or even 60 miles, knowing that at the end of their journey there was a moral certainty of being severely flogged; yet the instances of their absconding or failing to appear at Court were comparatively rare. Some of the men would almost willingly undergo punishment for the sake of a few days' wandering about in idleness and gossiping with the various persons they passed on the road.[66]

Some masters began as liberals and ended as martinets. One such man was "the Laird of Shoalhaven," a Scottish settler from Fife named Alexander Berry, who traversed almost the whole period of transportation, having arrived in Sydney in 1808 and died, aged 102 and worth 40,000 acres, in 1873. At first he was against flogging:

> It is silly to object to any man because he is a rogue, when they all come here for their crimes. All I care about is having able-bodied men—for the rest, no matter if they have been born and bred in Hell. With quiet, peaceable and humane measures, I will make the most refractory see that it is in their interest to behave well. . . . [T]o turn in men for flogging because they behave ill is utterly childish.[67]

"Childish," of course, because it showed a dependence on higher authority—the unwieldy power of the Bench—and so made the master lose face before his servants. But two years later, Berry was calling for irons and cat-o'-nine-tails: "We have been teasing ourselves to death," he wrote to his partner Edward Wollstonecraft, "in endeavouring to render ungrateful and irreclaimable profligates more comfortable than they have ever been in their lives."[68]

But a contented convict plainly worked better than a hungry, rebellious one. To that end, as John Macarthur's son James sensibly told the Select Committee on Transportation in 1837, it was best "where a man behaves well, to make him forget, if possible, that he is a convict." One of the first treatises on Australian farming (1826) advised settlers that "the belly is far more vulnerable and sensitive than the back." Use firmness and circumspection, the carrot not the stick; stay away from magistrates, because constant appeals to the formal powers of higher authority will diminish your own. Set up wages and a scale of rewards which will seem "a very great boon" and whose withdrawal will be "much more effectual . . . than the lash of the flogger." On one hand, do not get familiar with the convicts or give them the idea that their work is indispensable; on the other, a master must never forget "that they are men who, however degraded, still have the same feelings and passions as himself." The right stance is balanced paternalism, the instinctive attitude of the English squire when dealing with his laborers. For that was how the English workingman expected his employer to behave; the code of the country gentleman underwrote the modest, customary rights of his workers. Kindness, firmness and distance—with these, boasted a new settler with ten assigned men on the Yass Plains in 1835, "as Burns says, 'I labour them completely,' and have them in hand, bless your heart, as tame as 'pet foxes.' . . . I never had occasion to give a single lash."[69]

Most "government men" in bush service were, if not content with their fate, realistic about it. They knew that rebelliousness, insolence or conspicuous foot-dragging would probably extend their sentences and delay their tickets-of-leave for years—and knew as well, from experience, how pervasive and efficient the "pass system" was in preventing long escapes. (Every convict, when off his master's property for any time or for any reason, had to carry and show on demand a written pass that stated his name, where he had started from, where he was going and the precise number of days or even hours he was to be on the road.) So they behaved "admirably as a class," Edward J. Eyre observed after he took up land near Queanbeyan on the Molonglo Plains near the present site of Canberra in 1834, and became "most excellent, careful, industrious, trustworthy servants." Even the worst of them, though they might rob a passing visitor or a new assigned man, "would rarely plunder their own masters" and could be trusted anywhere:

> I have constantly known two convicts sent down to Sydney quite by themselves, a distance of 200 miles in a dray full of wool drawn by oxen, and having, after depositing their wool at the merchants', to bring back a load of . . . clothing, flour, tea, sugar, tobacco and other groceries—luxuries for the master, and even wines, beer and spirits, and yet tho' this journey involved an absence of five or six weeks during which the men were tempted constantly by the presence of so much property and the facility of appropriating it, the instances were very rare in which any plundering took place or loss ensued.[70]

And trust built reform. The posting of sanctioned rural relationships on the far soil of Australia mattered greatly to convicts and always evoked their gratitude. Everything else was strange—the bouncing animals, the upside-down stars, the resentful blacks and the nine agonizing claws of the cat-o'-nine-tails—but this was blessedly familiar. Besides, the man assigned to a decent master in the country districts in the 1830s was, as Eyre pointed out, "in a better position than half the honest laborers of England. No wonder then that convicts behaved well, and from being useful members of the community gained both the respect of others and learned to respect themselves."

The feeling was sometimes reflected in convict songs, or folk songs about convictry. In one of the versions of "Van Diemen's Land," a ballad circulated in the late 1820s, the narrator is at first horrified to see

> . . . my fellow sufferers,
> I'm sure I can't tell how,
> Some chained to a harrow
> And some unto a plough.
>
> No shoes nor stockings had they on,
> No hats had they to wear,
> Leather breeches and linen drawers;
> Their feet and heads were bare.
> They drove about in two and two
> Like horses in a team,
> The driver he stood over them
> With his malacca cane.

Such was the fate of the "government man." But then:

> As we marched into Hobart Town
> Without no more delay
> A gentleman farmer took me,
> His game-keeper for to be:
> I keep my occupation,

My master loves me well,
My joys are out of measure
I'm sure no tongue could tell.

Assigned convicts and their relatives often expressed their gratitude
to the good master. Thomas Holden, the Bolton weaver transported for
political protest, is assigned to a decent master, writes home about his
good luck, and in 1814 hears from his parents, "We are led to believe that
the man you are liveing with is a *gentleman*, we beg to say to him we
are very grateful that he hath so far condescended to take you into his
service." His wife, who with other wives of radical weavers has unsuccessfully petitioned the Prince Regent to be allowed to join their men in
Australia—"Let your situation in Life be prosperity or adversity it Woud
give me great satisfaction to share the Toil with you, but wether it will
Ever be our lot to meet at NS Wales or not I cannot tell"—reinforces his
gratitude:

> It gives us all the greatest pleasure to say [you have found] a friend . . .
> [W]e think it our Duty to say as he hath placed so much confidence in
> you we make not the least doubt but you will study to merit his Future
> Trust or Favors he may Chuse to bestow on you.[71]

This, from the point of view of authority, was an ideal penal relationship. But it depended on a steady market, as John Bigge pointed out: Only
constant production would keep felons too busy and tired for sin and
achieve "that stimulus to exertions that supersedes the necessity of coercion." And if there was not the proper class distance between master and
man, all was apt to be lost. Bigge frostily noted that Emancipist settlers
did not like to have a servant punished:

> This feeling is . . . attributable to a sympathy with that condition which
> was once their own, and is not corrected until they acquire property.[72]

Many settlers who had been convicts did, in fact, spare the lash. Samuel
Terry, the "Botany Bay Rothschild," was said never to have had a man
flogged; and Governor Bourke thought assigned men would rather work
for a newly freed Emancipist: "A Convict . . . prefers their coarse fare to
being better fed and Cloathed with a more opulent Master and less liberty."[73] Colonial conservatives were doggedly opposed to this. Their
views were mirrored in Bigge's report, which argued that convicts should
be assigned preferentially to "opulent" rural settlers. Giving them to
small Emancipists, the poor white trash of New South Wales, was "very
pernicious."[74]

Convicts who found benevolent masters far preferred their assigned life to the miseries they had known in England. When they could write home, they stressed their comforts, reassured their families and begged them not to fret. "When this you see, remember me, and banish all trouble away from thee," runs a little jingle in a letter from William Vincent, convict at Parramatta, to his family in Sussex in 1829. "Some people thought they had put me in [a] great deal [of] trouble, which they would, some of them, be glad to be as well as me; and I hope you are, mother, for I live at the Governor's table, along with the other servants." Two years later he is made an overseer, the much-coveted "bludger's job," and he jubilantly reports that "I have not worked one day since I have been in the country, so I am not hurt with work." But Vincent was not an assigned man. An experienced farmer, he had been grabbed for government service as soon as he landed, "for there is but a few in the country knows much about cultivation." He even urged his brothers to emigrate: "If I came free in this country, I could get 90£ a year to look after land." [75]

The sense of opportunity was a common theme. "Dear brother," wrote the rural protestor Peter Withers in 1833,

> I hav got a very good place all the Bondeg i am under is to Answer My [Name] Every Sunday before I goes to church so you Mit not think that I am made a Slave of, for I am not, it is quite the Reverse of it. And i have got a good Master and Mistress i have got Plenty to eate and drink as good as ever a gentleman . . . so all the Punishement I have in this Country is the thoughts of leaving My frends My Wife and My Dear Dear Children . . . [T]ell Samuel never to get trannsported for i knows Very Well he will not Like to Lave his Mother 16 thousand miles behind him. [76]

After this mild bit of child-scaring, the testimonials: "I think you would make your forting [fortune] in about 6 years, dear Brother," Withers adds. "I should like to see you and your famly Com to this Country if you could get to com, for it Whould be Well for your Children after you are dead, for this is a very Plentiful Contrey, pervisions is very Cheap and Labour is dear, this is the Plesents [pleasantest] Country that ever I saw." In the same way, Richard Dillingham, a ploughman from Flitwick in Bedfordshire who had been transported for life in 1831 for theft, is assigned to a colonial architect named David Lamb in Van Diemen's Land and, after a few years, assures his parents that "I am now very comfortably situated . . . [A]s to my living I find it better than ever I expected thank God. . . . I am doing much better than many labouring men in England." [77]

One must read such praises in context: Vincent, Withers and Dil-

lingham were all farm workers who had known the dreadful privations
of the agricultural collapse whose nadir came in the 1830s, when England
went closer to general agrarian revolt and "levelling" than it had been
since the days of Wat Tyler. After such miseries, the cheap food and high
wages in Australia must have seemed wonderful; in the words of such
convicts, the idea of Australia as the paradise of a working man finds its
first voice among workers. But the word about opportunities in Australia
spread quite rapidly, and by 1830 the Privy Council archives contained
many such petitions as this one, from Thomas Jones, a convict languish-
ing on the *York* hulk:

> Having made Frequent applications to leave the country . . . having served
> four years and upwards . . . my friends having deserted me and my char-
> acter lost, I dread to think of my situation when I obtain my liberty as no
> one will employ me; I have no resource left. . . . [H]ave the kindness to
> send me by the first ship that goes to New South Wales, I doubt not that
> I shall redeem that character that I have lost.[78]

Eight years before, Bigge had warned in his report that the shortness
of sentences—for most, a "mere" seven years—combined with the
ticket-of-leave system and the high labor market to disturb the penal
framework. A seven-year sentence was "too short" for convict laborers;
it gave them premature thoughts of becoming settlers and made them
less cautious, obedient and respectful. Thus by 1820, convicts were becoming uppity, or so Bigge thought, and "the prospect afforded by transportation to New South Wales is more one of emigration than of
punishment."[79] This became a common criticism of the System in the
1830s. In 1833 the Archbishop of Dublin, Richard Whately, a fervent
abolitionist, wrote that Australian felons

> are carried to a country whose climate is delightful, producing in abun-
> dance all the necessaries and most of the luxuries of life;—that they have
> a certainty of maintenance . . . are better fed, clothed and lodged, than (by
> *honest* means) they ever were before; [can get] all the luxuries they are
> most addicted to . . . are permitted, even before the expiration of their
> term, to become settlers on a fertile farm . . . [I]t certainly does not look
> like a very terrific punishment.[80]

When Thomas Potter Macqueen, an English magistrate who was the
absentee landlord of 10,000 acres in Australia granted him in 1823 by
Governor Brisbane, echoed this by remarking that assigned convicts in
New South Wales were better off than farmworkers in Bedfordshire, a
pseudonymous Australian settler fiercely disputed it:

The work in this new country is of the most laborious description:—
cutting down trees, the wood of which is of such hardness that English-
made tools break like glass before the strokes of the woodman; making
these trees into fires, and attending them, with the thermometer usually
ranging in the middle of the day from 80 to 100 deg. for eight months in
the year; grubbing up the stumps by the roots, the difficulty of which
would appall an English woodman; splitting his hard wood into posts and
rails, and erecting them into fences. . . . In what, then, does the superior
condition of the convict consist? Is it in a slavery more profound than
that of the West African negro?[81]

Farm work in Australia was always hard; and probably the toughest
of all jobs, in terms of the psychic tolls it could exact on a man, was a
shepherd's. As merino cross-breeds became the basis of Australian prosperity, more and more assigned men were sent to a lonely life in the
bush, tending sheep. They lived on the perimeter of remote properties;
and even places near Bathurst or in the Hunter River Valley were still
virgin bush in the 1830s, not much tamer than the "real" outback, 300
miles inland. A shepherd stood a high chance of being the first white
person to bear the revenge of Aborigines who had been evicted from their
hunting-grounds by the outward push of white settlement. When blacks
could not mount a frontal attack on a station homestead, they could
easily pick off a lone shepherd with their silent spears, especially since
assigned men are not armed. Even if local Aborigines had no special
grievance against the farmer, they loved mutton anyway and would kill
to get it. The assigned shepherd therefore lived in constant fear of death.

His flock could be as few as 200 or as many as 3,000 sheep. The work
sounds simple: All he had to do was drive the sheep out in search of
pasture each day, keep an eye on strays, and bring them back at night.
But he was rarely mounted and often had no dogs. Moreover, pasturage
was not as common in New South Wales before 1850 as it is today.
Millions of rolling acres were covered in box, a middle-sized eucalypt of
no commercial value, whose thirsty roots pulled every drop of surface
moisture out of the soil and prevented the growth of grass. The solution,
which later farmers resorted to with excessive zeal, was ringbarking.
This killed the box without using up extra labor in felling it and grubbing
out the stumps. Grass then sprouted in abundance on these spectral
landscapes of gesticulating, claw-white dead trees. But in the convict era,
ringbarking was not much used, and the shepherd had to cover much
more ground to find enough grass for his sheep. If he got lost, or if he lost
some of the flock, he would have to stay out for days until he rounded
them up again and struggled back to the out-station, although his master
would only give him a day's rations when he set out, to discourage him
from abandoning the flock and bolting.

The loneliness of a shepherd's life was increased by the medical need to keep flocks (and hence their keepers) away from one another. Besides dingoes, the terror of a pastoralist was a highly infectious ovine disease called the Scab which, as Eyre found from bitter experience, ruined the wool, checked breeding and was practically incurable:

> A single act of neglect or inattention on the shepherd's part might in a moment blast the prospects of his employer—and what more natural than that such acts should occur—the shepherd anxious to have a gossip would drive his flock as near to the boundaries of his run as possible—the shepherd of the infected flock would do the same, and while the two men were talking the two flocks would intermingle and the dreaded mischief be done.[82]

It was not unknown for a resentful convict to avenge himself on his master by deliberately infecting his stock.

In mallee scrub, patches of which could extend for miles—there was one district shared between northern Victoria and southern New South Wales that still covered 10,000 square miles in the 1880s—sheep were bound to get lost. The tough bushes of *Eucalyptus dumosa* were too high for a man to see across, even from horseback. In such a labyrinth, with dingoes howling in the middle distance—mallee was known as "dingo scrub" because it sheltered the wild dog that shepherds most feared—the assigned man was likely to go "cranky," as colonial slang termed the harmlessly mad. As stations got larger, all the grass near the homestead was needed for stock-horses and working bullocks. The shepherd had to mind the flocks on runs three, five or ten miles out; instead of coming back to the homestead each night, he would have to sleep out in the bush.

John Standfield, one of the Tolpuddle Martyrs, described what this did in 1834 to his father, Thomas Standfield, who was in his fifties and had been assigned to a farmer named Nowlan near Maitland, some 150 miles from Sydney. Three weeks after being sent to this out-station, he was

> a dreadful spectacle, covered in sores from head to foot, and as weak and helpless as a child. . . . [H]e pointed to the place where he slept, called a "watch-box." After my father had been out in the bush from sunrise to sunset, he had then to retire for repose to the watch-box, 6 feet by 18 inches, with a small bed and one blanket, where he could lie and gaze upon the starry heavens, and where the wind blew in at one end and out of the other, with nothing to ward off the pitiless storm—such were the comforts of the watch-box. Besides this he had to walk four miles for his rations, which journeys he was compelled to perform by night.[83]

The Tolpuddle men (and a few other "politicals" in Australia) seem
to have had especially harsh treatment from their masters. But even at
the best of times, life in the outback could have a hallucinatory strange-
ness for men fresh from England. One visitor to the Maitland area in the
1830s noted that convict quarters in the bush were like a cross between
a zoo and an Irish cabin, with

> a multitude of noisy parrots, intended for sale; pet kangaroos and opos-
> sums, and a variety of kangaroo dogs, greyhounds, and sheep-dogs; on the
> fire was a huge boiler filled with the flesh of a kangaroo, and close by
> were suspended the hind-quarters of another of these animals; in one
> corner was a large pan of milk; in another, a number of skins partially
> dried; while, a few feet from the ground, were the filthy bed-places or
> cribs of the people themselves.

Inside it all was fug and cockatoo-shit, dried sweat and blowflies and the
stink of hides. Outside, the landscape could be apocalyptic, vast; it was
like standing on the edge of one world and looking into another:

> The extreme silence that prevails here almost exceeds what the imagina-
> tion can conceive. . . . One would imagine that a residence in such a lone
> place would be liable to cause a change of some consequence in the minds
> and habits of any person; and it would be an interesting point to ascertain
> the effect on the convict stock-keepers, who, for weeks together, can have
> no opportunity of conversing with a white man, except their sole compan-
> ion; for there are always two to a hut.

And it did affect them. It promoted the pair-bonding, the feeling of
reliance on one's "mate," that would lie forever at the heart of masculine
social behavior in Australia. Because there were no white women in the
bush, it meant—as some authorities grudgingly acknowledged, by the
end of the 1830s—that "mateship" found its expression in homosexuality. Most important, in the eyes of some observers, was the fact that life
in the bush reformed the socially useless criminal by teaching him skills
and giving him time to reflect, with the bonus of exposure to "sublime"
landscape. Here was Wordsworth applied to penology—the nineteenth-
century belief that Nature, as the unaltered fingerprint of its Creator,
could serve as a moral text for the betterment of fallen man. The convict
becomes a hermit, cleansing his soul in the desert:

> This monotonous and solitary life has the effect of giving a new direction
> to the ideas of the moral patient, superior to any other which the most
> profound metaphysician could have invented. Solitude and idleness in a
> cell either subdue and subvert the mind entirely, by causing madness and

suicide, or they generate a hardihood and a caution which enable the criminal to pursue his career with greater chances of profit; while the combination of *pastoral occupation* with solitude, offers the fairest chance of success, by weaning and forcing him from his ancient habits.

The future Poet Laureate, Robert Southey, while still at Oxford in 1794, had drawn much the same picture of the moral benefits of Australian wilderness on the repentant sinner in his *Botany-Bay Eclogues*:

> Welcome ye wild plains
> Unbroken by the plough, undelv'd by hand
> Of patient rustic; where for lowing herds
> And for the music of the bleating flocks,
> Alone is heard the kangaroo's sad note
> Deepening in distance. Welcome ye rude climes,
> The realm of Nature! for as yet unknown
> The crimes and comforts of luxurious life,
> Nature benignly gives to all enough,
> Denies to all a superfluity . . .
> On these wild shores Repentance' saviour hand
> Shall probe my secret soul, shall cleanse my wounds,
> And fit the faithful penitent for Heaven.

The bassoon-like sound of the distant 'roo, one feels, must have made the journey worthwhile.

Probably about one-fifth of the masters in Van Diemen's Land and New South Wales were genuinely interested in reforming their assigned servants, and two-fifths more "encouraged the convicts for their own interests." The latter might treat their assigned servants like farm equipment, but at least they would teach them skills and keep them away from bad company. Out in the bush, there were no booze-shops, whores, or criminal cabals. There, convicts led "a healthy useful life of labor, well clothed and well fed, with the prospect of attaining their freedom," Eyre wrote. "Transportation of convicts to a healthy country and the assignment of them to settlers . . . is . . . the true means of reforming the criminals themselves."[84]

Masters and government authorities generally believed that it was far harder for an assigned convict to "go straight" in a butcher's shop or wearing servant's livery in Sydney. The city was the condenser of vice; in the bush, there were more routines and less company, and the master's life shared more of the hardships of the servant's than in town. In Sydney or Hobart, the *bon bourgeois'* need to demarcate his life from the felon's led to exaggerated rituals of class superiority, which promoted the feeling that convicts could not be reformed at all. But the issue of class loomed large in penal Australia—a society traversed by confusingly rapid movements of individual status, where tides of men and women were constantly flowing from servitude into citizenhood and responsibility, from bitter poverty to new-found wealth. By the 1830s, Australia was as class-obsessed a society as any in the world.

Gentlemen of New South Wales

i

T HE VISITOR from England, arriving in Sydney in the 1820s, saw a bright prospect from the deck of his ship: Across the glittering blue of the harbor, under the immense clarity of the southern sky, a neat-looking town of freestone or whitewashed cottages with shady verandas, their gardens marked off from one another and from the still-encircling bush with paling fences or clipped geranium hedges, their kitchen-yards "teeming with culinary delicacies." And yet, as the naval surgeon Peter Cunningham noted in his memoir of New South Wales life, the sense of domestic familiarity dissipated as soon as he stepped ashore, among the English faces and not-quite-English accents, the caged cockatoos and rosellas shrieking among the overflowing fruit stalls, and the silent caged men:

> The government gangs of convicts . . . marching backwards and from their work in single military file, and the solitary ones straggling here and there, with their white woollen Parramatta frocks and trowsers, or gray and yellow jackets with duck overalls (the different styles of dress denoting the oldness or newness of their arrival), all daubed over with broad arrows, P.B.'s, C.B.'s, and various numerals in black, white and red; with perhaps the chain-gang straddling sulkily by in their jingling leg-chains, —tell a tale too plain to be misunderstood.[1]

Inequality did not stop with the public gangs. In penal Australia, the question of class was all-pervasive and pathological. Distance had made it so. Tiny as it was (about 7,500 people in 1807; 10,500 in 1812; 24,000 in 1820; and 36,598 at the time of the first census in November 1828), the colony was gnawed by isolation and boredom, plagued by foolish vendettas and extreme class-consciousness. Class barriers were translated into personal affront in the blink of an eye. The atmosphere of New

South Wales at the end of the transportation period was summed up in
1839 by "A Settler," writing pseudonymously but with piercing insight
in the *Sydney Morning Herald*:

> People come here to better their condition, many with limited means,
> their tempers a little soured with privations and disappointed expecta-
> tions (for all expect too much); cut off from the ties of kindred, old friend-
> ships, and endearing associations, all struggling in the road of advancement,
> and no-one who reflects will be surprised that they jostle one another.
> *Every man does not know his own position so well as at home.* [Italics
> added.][2]

One speaks of "colonial gentry" as though there were gentlemen
in early Australia; but there were not. Frontiers have a way of
killing, maiming or simply dismissing gentlemen. In any case, most
folk with settled estates have no reason to go to a raw, new country.
They can invest in it later, without needing to break their bodies on
it now. To succeed on the frontier, a man needed the kind of violent,
grabbing drive that only failure or mediocrity in his former life could
fuel.

The male society of early New South Wales could be roughly sorted
into three kinds of people. There were opportunists struggling to be
gentlemen; convicts and outcasts waiting to be opportunists; and the
failures, who would never become anything. Social life thus displayed a
crude, insecure face, which the cosmetic application of airs and graces
could not altogether hide. The mixture of ambition and social pretension
wearied many a visitor. The relentless deployment of tooth and claw
against the tentative mobility of the lower orders would impress Charles
Darwin himself with its unpleasant naïveté when he arrived in Sydney
on the *Beagle* in 1836.

The colonial elite after 1800 had arrived at an idea of gentility that
was already becoming, if not obsolete, then certainly old-fashioned in
England. It was feudal and rural. It belonged more to the 1720s than the
1820s. It parodied an ideal of privilege they had never had and, moreover,
was distinguished by its absolute inability to relax. English gentility
defined itself in relation to an aristocracy above and a peasantry and
serving classes below. But its vision of the "good yeoman" did not apply
very well in convict Australia, whose peasantry was, by definition, not
good.

The Exclusives had come from nowhere in a generation or two. They
were determined to prevent other men, also from nowhere, from getting
what they had. Hence their stubborn resistance to the gathering social

demands of the Emancipists and their Australian-born children. It was a campaign fought with extreme punctilio. When Governor Lachlan Macquarie, who correctly believed that some of the ablest men in the colony were Emancipists, invited four of them to dinner at Government House in 1810, the Exclusives were outraged. When he went further and appointed two of these men, the merchant Simeon Lord and the landowner Andrew Thompson, as trustees and commissioners of the new turnpike road that was to be built between Sydney and the Hawkesbury River, the third proposed trustee—the Reverend Samuel Marsden, senior chaplain of the colony and one of its biggest landowners, a merciless pharisee—was so piqued in his clerical dignity that he refused to serve. This in turn sent the governor into one of his military rages, and the feud between the two men poisoned relations between Church and State in New South Wales for the rest of Macquarie's term.

The Exclusives could define their sense of class against the despised Emancipists, but they were snobbish as only provincials could be. The tone was faithfully echoed as late as the 1840s by Louisa Anne Meredith, a clergyman's wife who wrote a delectably acerbic account of her five years in Australia (1839–44):

> The distinctions in society here remind me of the "dock-yard people" described by Dickens. . . . Thus—Government officers don't know merchants; merchants with "stores" don't know other merchants who keep "shops"; and the shopkeepers have, I doubt not, a little code of their own, prescribing the proper distances to be obseved between drapers and haberdashers, butchers and pastrycooks. . . . [T]his pride of place is so very ridiculous and unbecoming in such a community, that were not its tendency so mischievous, it could only provoke a smile.[3]

All colonial standards—of rank, etiquette, taste and the "interesting" —were English. Until well into the 1820s, the word "Australian" was a term of abuse, or at best of condescension; it carried an air of seediness on the rim of the Pacific. Sydney's was a heliotropic society, and the sun it faced—distant, abstract but commanding—was the Royal family, seen through its viceroy the governor. He was an autocrat presiding over a police state with certain social trimmings. His power was all-encompassing, as befitted the man who ran a continent that was also a jail. It had been so since 1788, when Arthur Bowes Smyth, hearing Captain Phillip's commission read at Sydney Cove, found it "a more unlimited one than was ever before granted to any governor under the British Crown," while Ralph Clark noted that he "had never heard of any single person having so great a power invested in him."[4] All political decisions ran through his hands; who got land, where and how much; who got labor; who was pardoned, freed or sent to a penal station; what religions were celebrated, other than the established rites of the Church of England, and at what hours; who filled administrative positions; what could be said in the colony's embryonic press—a thousand matters, loaded or trivial, down to the vexed question of which side of the road the chaotic, ever increasing traffic of Sydney should move on (Macquarie chose the left, as in Britain). Nowhere in the British Empire did a proconsul have wider social power than in penal Australia.

It was in the person of the governor, therefore, that the class divisions of the colony found their basis, their reassurance. If a governor leaned toward populism, showing favor to small farmers or ex-convicts, immense resentments could be released, as they were against Lachlan Macquarie. It is not easy to exaggerate the entrenched mentality of the dozen or so clans, starting with the Macarthurs and their allies like Samuel Marsden, who made up the leading free families of Australia between 1800 and 1840.

John Macarthur (1767–1834) and his wife Elizabeth Veale (1767–1850) were the founders and prototypes of the colonial gentry. Macarthur was the son of a Plymouth mercer and corset-maker, a choleric man with a rage for gentility, who saw plots and insults everywhere and was as touchy as a Sicilian. He wasted half his life in imbroglios. Known to Emancipists as "Jack Bodice"—a nickname that reduced him to rage— and to his administrative enemies as "the perturbator," he quarreled furiously with judges, clergymen, sea captains and traders, and with a succession of governors from Hunter to Darling. From prison in 1808, he masterminded (if that is the word for so half-cocked and rash a gesture) the Rum Corps's *putsch* against Governor Bligh.[5]

The fruit of his spleen was exile; he had to spend all but four years of the period 1801–17 in England, while his wife Elizabeth, most resourceful and levelheaded of women, bred their sheep and ran their growing estates by the Nepean River in Camden. Off the land, Macarthur was a poor businessman, betrayed by his enthusiasms and his hatreds alike. He was rarely conscious of any line between private and public interest, except when scrutinizing the behavior of his enemies. He died mad. None of this tarnished Macarthur's name as the doyen of Australian pastoral conservatism.[6]

Macarthur had come out as a New South Wales Corps ensign on the Second Fleet in 1790 with his wife, their baby son and a maid. Francis Grose, the army governor, favored him and made him paymaster of the Rum Corps. Macarthur started small, with a mixed-breed herd of about a thousand sheep. He got all the land and convict labor he wanted from

Grose and his successor Paterson. But the next two governors, Hunter and King, were navy men who saw no reason to do inside deals with Macarthur or to give him special patronage. "Jack Bodice" took this to mean war. IIis basilisk campaigns of innuendo against Government House reached their climax in September 1801 in a quarrel, and then a pistol duel, with his own colonel, whose allegiance Macarthur had tried to suborn from Governor King. He winged the colonel in the shoulder, and King, incensed by the doings of "this perturbator," arrested him for trial. But he could not be given a court-martial in Sydney, because—King believed—his fellow officers would have supported the Rum Corps against the Navy with an acquittal. So he was sent back to be tried in England. This, by one of the bizarre flukes that often seemed to govern colonial life, made Macarthur's fortune.

His sole punishment for shooting turned out to be a free ticket to London, with wool samples. King's strategy backfired, as the English court-martial acquitted Macarthur. Before leaving, Macarthur had bought 1,250 more mixed-breed sheep from a brother officer, Major Foveaux, thus making him the biggest sheep-owner in Australia. The main source of first-class wool for the growing English textile industries had been the merino flocks of Saxony and Spain. But Europe was under naval blockade and the English woollen industry was in crisis. It looked as though no more merino fleeces would be reaching England. Even with his coarse hanks of colonial wool, Macarthur's timing was perfect. He found the government more than willing to encourage the raising of fine wool in Australia. He got Treasury permission to buy and export some merino sheep from a small specimen flock owned by George III. He also persuaded Lord Camden to give him a special land grant on which to raise these aristocratic beasts—2,000 acres around Mount Taurus, by the Nepean River, an area called the Cowpastures, the finest known grazing land in New South Wales (which he later renamed Camden). Macarthur sailed back in triumph in 1805 on his own whaling ship, rechristened the *Argo* after the vessel in which Jason sought the Golden Fleece.[7]

The pure merino, two centuries ago, was a tricky and delicate animal, a pompous ambling peruke, unused to Australian heat and Australian grass. Its virtue lay in the size of its fleece and the quality of its wool. But to flourish in Australia the strain had to be cross-bred. Although Macarthur did not, as he often claimed, introduce the merino to New South Wales (both pure and cross merinos were owned by "Little Jack" Palmer and the Reverend Samuel Marsden before him), he turned it into the staple of Australian export by crossing it with hardier types, Bengal and Afrikaner Fat-Tail, while conserving a pure merino flock to improve the strains.[8]

Before long, "pure Merino" was colonial slang for any member of the pastoral elite, starting with the Macarthurs; and by 1808, when he had to run for England and stay there nine years, leaving his stud in charge of Elizabeth and his growing sons, Macarthur was the largest sheep-owner in New South Wales. In his absence, Elizabeth bought, built and bred their holdings far beyond the original Cowpastures grant, to 60,000 acres.

Few ways of life, one would think, demand more evenness of temper, perseverance, instinctive sympathy and financial prudence than stock-farming. Yet the curious fact is that both the founders of Australian sheep-farming were melancholics, given to attacks of extreme anxiety— the very opposite of the contented squire. Alexander Riley (1788–1833) was a genial Irishman most of the time, but his black fits were almost as bad as Macarthur's. Riley had followed his two sisters, who married Rum Corps officers, from Ireland to Australia. He began as a general trader, raising sheep on the side at his station, Raby, near Liverpool. His coup, which would transform Australian grazing, was to bring in Saxon merino sheep, a better stapled and hardier strain than Macarthur's Spanish me-rinos. In 1825 he landed a whole flock of them, each like a woolly pasha in its own padded pen. He wheedled from the government a grant of 10,000 acres of prime land, but further out, near Yass, on the western limits of settlement. He called this station Cavan, after his family's district in Ireland. The essential bloodlines of Australian sheep-breeding run back to Camden and Cavan.

Riley and Macarthur were very different men. Macarthur had a plan-tation mind and could not keep his fingers out of politics. Riley shied away from public affairs and expected the convict system to wither away, leaving a society of free men whose elite were graziers. The contrast between them reminds one of the dangers of generalizing about early pastoralists as though they were units in a class, not individuals. And yet the values of most well-off free men in early colonial Australia were certainly closer to Macarthur's than to Riley's, especially since very few of them were Irish.

What was the ideology of the Merinos and those who aspired to their company—of the Exclusives in general? Mainly, gut Tory conservatism, reinforced by the doctrines of the established Church of England. Like the English squires they emulated, they hated all things French and were apt to treat any kind of Emancipist restiveness as unbridled Jacobinism.

They thought themselves uniquely fitted to hold power in the colony —indeed, that no others were suitable. Not the Emancipists or their children, for the "taint" of convictry was ineradicable and hereditary; stock-breeding encourages a rigid view of genetic inheritance. Not the growing class of city traders and entrepreneurs, no matter how much money they were beginning to make, for trade was ignoble beside land, although much could be forgiven for a suitable dowry. Not the new-chum settlers, who were coming in growing numbers after 1820, for their roots in the land did not go deep enough, and they did not have the big holdings. Not being able to idealize their origins, the early Exclusives fetishized their achievements fiercely and rigidly, seeing themselves as an island of order in a lake of *arrivisme* and crime. They knew that what was good for them was good for the country.

They felt threatened by the rise of new money, generated by trade and property deals. Prudently, they married their offspring into the merchant families, crossing their lines as they had crossed their sheep for economic hardihood. Less realistically, they tried to cripple the Emancipists politically.

Was their conservatism nothing better than an exploitive, "un-Australian" style of baronial laissez-faire? This was the picture created by the Emancipists from 1815 onward—the pseudo-squire in an antipodean landscape, owning the land but not belonging to it; but it was mainly a rhetorical device.

In the 1830s this rhetoric was inflamed by the exacerbated quarrels between colonial conservatives—mainly landowners who had settled the Hunter River Valley in the 1820s—and their liberal governor Richard Bourke (1831–37). Appointed to office by the Whigs in England, Bourke had pushed through a number of reforms that endeared him to the Emancipists, the chief one being a new law which, in 1833, allowed criminal cases to be tried by civil juries and permitted former convicts to serve as jurors. This important enlargement of Emancipists' rights was viewed with horror by conservatives. What anarchy, they asked, might not be unleashed by courts which allowed felons to try criminals? Bourke also restricted the power of landowners over their assigned servants, by decreeing that disciplinary sentences of flogging for offenses against the labor code now had to be given by two magistrates, not one, and setting their limit at 50 lashes instead of 100. Getting two magistrates to judge such cases was not a problem in the settled districts, but up in the Hunter River Valley it took time and trouble. There, a plantation mentality reigned among the big settlers, and they were furious at Bourke for his "leniency." Emancipists and colonial liberals sided with Bourke, and in the crossfire of insult and polemic Bourke's critics were painted as iron-souled blimps, men who would have been more at home among slaves on the banks of the Mississippi than in New South Wales.

The emblematic figure was "Major" James Mudie (1779–1852), cashiered marine lieutenant and failed medal publisher, now a rich man and a colonial magistrate, who called his homestead Castle Forbes and was said to have treated his assigned men so badly that they were driven to rebellion.* He pictured Governor Bourke as a shallow and misguided humanitarian, practicing (as Mudie later termed it) an "anti-penal, anti-social and anti-political system" which would lead the colony to "unbridled crime and lawless anarchy, and . . . its violent and sanguinary separation from the Empire."⁹ (Moderation in attack was not a colonial habit, and certainly not Mudie's.) In 1836 Bourke struck back by depriving Mudie (along with thirty-six others) of his magistracy. This loss of caste was too much for Mudie, who sold up and returned to England, vowing revenge. It came in the form of a hastily written book with the felicitous title *The Felonry of New South Wales* (1837). "Felonry," Mudie explained, was his own word, encompassing all of the "criminal population" of the colony, including the Emancipists, no matter what their wealth or professional standing. It corresponded, he said, to the orders of the old world—"the tribe of apellatives distinguished by the same termination, as *peasantry, tenantry, yeomanry, gentry, cavalry, chivalry,* &c." Such people, he argued, were "for ever infamous . . . infamous *in law* . . . unworthy of future trust"; they and their offspring should be disenfranchised forever. There was not the slightest chance that Mudie's tirade could affect social relations in the colony, or be taken seriously outside a small group; but it certainly reinforced the Emancipist claim that men like Mudie were foreigners to New South Wales and outsiders to its social realities.

Yet most Exclusives, however rapacious and snobbish they were, identified themselves with Australia while drawing their models of hierarchy from England. The idea that egalitarianism was a true index of patriotism is mere piety. The Exclusives were more than marsupialized Englishmen; and against the boasts and toasts of the Emancipist party,

---

* In 1833, six convict runaways, most of them assigned to Mudie, went on a rampage at Castle Forbes. Led by a skilled and relatively privileged convict carpenter named John Poole, they robbed the house, shot at Mudie's son-in-law, plundered another property in the district and flogged the master of a third farm. They were soon captured, and the case became a *cause célèbre.* Conservatives greeted the "Castle Forbes rebellion" as proof of the anarchy that had to follow Bourke's liberal attitudes. The defense, marshalled by Emancipist and emigrant friends of Bourke, argued that the convicts had been driven to rebellion by flogging and starvation. Unhappily for the liberal argument, it developed that rations at Castle Forbes were good and discipline moderate (about half the sixty assigned servants there had never been flogged); the discontent arose more from the incompetence of Mudie's son-in-law, John Larnach, who managed the estate during Mudie's own prolonged absences. Despite the facts, the case tarred Mudie with a permanent reputation, which he greatly resented, as the Simon Legree of the Hunter River. See John Hirst, *Convict Society and its Enemies,* pp. 182–84. One may also note that champions of the Emancipists could get a very bad name for cruelty among their assigned men. Robert Wardell, barrister and first editor of Wentworth's pro-Emancipist newspaper *The Australian,* was shot dead by one of his servants, John Jenkins, who declared on the scaffold that he had murdered Wardell for his tyranny.

one might set this, from James Macarthur in London to his aging father in 1829:

> I shall now sit down peaceably and contentedly amongst our sheep-folds and under the shade of our own fig-trees . . . putting more trust in our own efforts, than in the acquaintance and connexions who have too many troubles of their own in this Country to think of the complaints of poor Australians. . . . [T]here are few people in England with whom I would willingly change places.[10]

Eden as property. It is hardly a populist utterance, but one cannot deny its Australian-ness.

In any case, no one held the exclusive rights on ambition or greed. It was William Charles Wentworth, the Emancipists' trumpet, who in 1852 came round to lobby with James Macarthur for the creation of a hereditary colonial *noblesse*, the "bunyip aristocracy," which, fortunately, the Crown saw no reason to create. No Merino ever came close to the kind of transaction that Wentworth, once cursed by them as a republican, a Jacobin and a leveller, attempted in 1840, when he and some associates gulled seven Maori chiefs into selling them about one-third of New Zealand—the largest private land deal in history. (It was, however, quashed by government order.) When it came to dividing the colonial pie, Whigs could behave exactly like Tories, Emancipists like Exclusives.

i i

RILEY DIED in 1833, Macarthur a year later. Neither lived to see the wool industry dominate Australia's economy. That did not happen until well into the 1830s, and when it did the graziers would be "home on the sheep's back," as the phrase went, for the next century. Wool became so big an export, so essential a part of the Australian imagination, that it is hard to imagine as a secondary industry. Yet for most of the convict period in New South Wales, it was. Between the failure of the naval-supply plans for flax and timber, and the enthronement of the sheep— that is, for about the first half-century of white settlement—much of Australia's export wealth came from whaling and sealing, both trades dominated by Emancipists and their sons, the "Currency lads," native-born white Australians.

"The fisheries," as sealing and whaling were collectively known, were of an abundance hardly imaginable today. The southern oceans were a vast, undisturbed sanctuary for the black whale, the sperm whale and the fur seals. Every season, the huge cetaceans cruised north from Antarctica in millions, to mate and calve in the tranquil bays and estuaries along the coasts of New Zealand, Van Diemen's Land and southeastern Australia. In the early 1800s, Hobart's estuary was dangerous for small boats, which could scarcely steer between the pregnant and calving black whales. Whalers could sally out in dories and kill thousands a year. Because it did not need large vessels, bay-whaling was a cheap trade and easy for Emancipists to get into. It had been plied in Australian and New Zealand coastal waters since the 1790s; the first whalemen came on the Third Fleet.

Whaling in Australian waters could not, of course, be confined to colonists. In 1803 Pitt's administration opened the whole Pacific Ocean east of 180° to unlicensed whalers. Scores of whaling ships, reeking and storm-battered, years out of Nantucket and Sag Harbor, came in for the killing. Colonial whalers learned from the American captains, those driven ancestors of Ahab, pressed on by flinty Quaker fleet-owners. By the 1820s, exports of whale oil and whalebone were paying for much of the iron, cloth, tools, salt provisions, tea, rum and Far Eastern luxury goods that came into the colony. The rest was bought with profits from sealing.[11]

Every beach of the Tasman Sea, each wild promontory of Bass Strait, every rock west of Kangaroo Island off South Australia bore teeming rookeries of seals and sea lions. They had no natural enemies and knew nothing of man except for the occasional Aborigine hunter. Tens of millions of them were wiped out in less than thirty years.

The sealers killed year-round, clubbing their prey to death. Because there was no closed season in mating and pupping time, pregnant seals were killed in myriads and the pups were left milkless on the rocks to starve. Disturbed in their ancestral rookeries, which soon became bogs of putrefaction—for the sealers took only the skins and left hills of flayed carcasses behind—the seals stopped breeding and abandoned their haunts. "The whole of this valuable trade is threatened with a speedy & total annihilation," an official warned Lieutenant-Governor Arthur in 1826. The idea of appealing to the sealers was, of course, a joke. Most were the scum of the System, escaped convicts gone wild on a bitter shore:

> The Islands . . . afford constant shelter, and secure retreats, for runaways and villains of the worst description. Amost every rock throughout the strait has become the habitation of some one or more amongst the most desperate and lawless of mankind. The whole of the Straits seem to present one continued scene of violence, plunder and the commission of every species of crime.—Natives, chiefly black women, are occasionally

stolen from the mainland and actually *sold* to the leaders. . . . [F]rom 10 to 15 children, the offspring of these poor Creatures and of their oppressors, are now or were lately to be met with on the several Islands.[12]

There were many more than that. The rapparees and bolters who formed their bloody, troglodytic island colonies kidnapped hundreds of black women from their tribes not only because they needed sex, but because many coastal Aborigines were expert seal-hunters.[13]

Convicts could easily escape from Van Diemen's Land on sealing vessels. By 1820 Hobart had become the main port and market for all whaling and sealing in the southern ocean. It was hard to monitor the passage of crews between ship and shore; and any convict could bluff his way past the wharf guards with a forged ticket-of-leave. Hundreds of men went through this loophole into the sealing trade. It was an excellent arrangement for the masters of the "fisheries." Once aboard, the convict could not return to land without risking the gallows; he was shanghaied into another sort of captivity, masquerading as freedom. By the 1830s the southern bays and refuges, from the Bay of Islands in New Zealand to the Recherche Archipelago on the west coast of Australia, were littered with criminal flotsam left by the dying pursuit of seals and whales.

The first colonist to make money on the "fisheries" was a free Scottish merchant, Robert Campbell—"just and humane and a gentleman," in Governor Bligh's view, and no ally of Macarthur's. To preserve its monopoly, the East India Company had arranged that no Australian-based trader could export whale or seal products direct to London. (Other "Southern whalers," who were not actually based in Australia, were exempt from this ruling.) Campbell was determined to break this unfair restraint on trade, which in effect denied that New South Wales had any functions but penal ones. In 1805 he sailed to England with his family in his ship *Lady Barlow*. In her hold were 260 tons of oil rendered down from sea-elephant blubber and 13,700 sealskins. A few months behind her sailed the *Honduras Packet*, laden with 34,000 skins. The East India Company reacted predictably by seizing Campbell's ship and cargo. The ensuing fracas, which Campbell handily won, led at last to free exports from Australia to England, bypassing the East India Company. Campbell returned to New South Wales a trader-hero, "father of the mercantile community."[14]

Free colonial trade destroyed the chance that there would ever be another rum monopoly. Some Emancipists could plough their profits from whaling and sealing back into property. They became—on the balance-sheet, at least—the equal of an Exclusive.

In the early 1800s most sealing and whaling in Australian waters was run by three men: Henry Kable, Simeon Lord and James Underwood. All three were ex-convicts. Kable (1763–1846) was a burglar who came out on the First Fleet under a death sentence that had been commuted to fourteen years' transportation. He became an overseer, then a rum trader, selling liquor to convicts the officers were too haughty to deal with directly.

Some time before 1800, Kable met up with James Underwood (1776–1844), another convict who possessed the inestimably useful skill of knowing how to build boats. Ships of any kind were in short supply in the colony, even then. Kable and Underwood built a sloop, *Diana*, and fitted her out for sealing in Bass Strait. Before long they had sixty men working for them and were skinning 30,000 seals a year; Underwood's shipyard, at the head of Sydney Cove, was turning out vessels up to 200 tons in burthen.

In 1805 they took on a a third partner, Simeon Lord (1771–1840), who had been transported in 1790 for stealing several hundred yards of calico and muslin. His offense was a juvenile one and he never repeated it. A ruthless stone-squeezer of a Yorkshireman, Lord too had come up through the rum trade. Doubtless the officers felt that by using such shady men as distributors, they were saved from demeaning contact with convicts and Emancipists. In fact, they were creating just the social anomaly they feared. Lord was an entrepreneurial genius and fast as a dingo. By 1798 he had his own warehouse, and by 1799 his first ship. He cultivated Robert Campbell, who gave him useful introductions to important people in the sealskin market in London. Lord "traded up" from rum to iron and timber, and then to manufacture. In workshops staffed by assigned convicts, he made the consumer goods that were still in such erratic supply, and so costly, in Sydney: candles, soap, glasses, stockings, cloth, harness, boots and leather hats. Between 1806 and 1809 Lord, Kable and Underwood sold over 127,000 sealskins in London, more in China and Calcutta. Sealing led naturally to Pacific trade in sandalwood and other commodities.

In 1803 Simeon Lord built himself a mansion in Sydney, the largest private house in the colony. It had three stories and a basement, and an elegant veranda carried on slender columns over the street; it was built of sandstone bound with imported mortar. "Lord's palace" was to commerce what Macquarie's estate was to landholding. His social betters passed it with distaste, unable to ignore this irrefutable monument to social permeability. "Mr. Lord (formerly a horse stealer) has built a house that he lives in that cost 20,000£," sniffed a visiting naval surgeon in 1810, "but still these men are despised and any free settler would not deign to sit at their tables. . . . Most of these men have made their money by *trading*."[15]

"These men" were not all men. Mary Haydock (1777–1855), convicted and transported at the tender age of thirteen for horse-stealing in Lancashire, married a young free merchant and shipowner named Thomas Reibey in 1794, learned the business of shipping and sealing from him and aggressively expanded her holdings after 1811, when he died and left her with seven children. She owned warehouses and trading brigs as well as seven farms on the Hawkesbury River and numerous buildings in the growing center of Sydney. This alert and formidably tenacious woman was the exception that proved the rule: No other convict woman made a success, or even a passing stir, at business in the male-dominated society of penal Australia, and it is unlikely that Reibey herself, for all her drive and cunning, could have done it without the start her husband gave her.

The most spectacular of the ex-convict merchants, and the most detested by the Exclusives, was Samuel Terry (1776–1838). Terry began as an illiterate Manchester laborer who was transported for seven years for stealing 400 pairs of stockings and became known to his contemporaries as "The Rothschild of Botany Bay." Freed in 1807, he set up in Sydney as a pubkeeper and moneylender. Many nasty stories, some of them perhaps true (though none proven), were told of his exploitation of drunken Emancipists and ticket-of-leave men—how he would let them booze on credit for days and weeks and then seize their farms as payment. Whether by trickery, frugality or a judicious mixture of both, by 1820 he owned 19,000 acres, or 10 percent of the land possessed by all the eight hundred or so Emancipist landowners put together. He also held more mortgages on property than the Bank of New South Wales, in which he was a principal shareholder—about one-fifth of the total value of mortgages registered in the colony. Later in life, he turned to charity and politics, becoming an enthusiastic backer of Emancipists' rights. His convict servants remembered him warmly as one who never had them flogged and never forgot the class bonds of his own past. When he died in 1838, Terry received the most lavish funeral ever held in Australia, complete with flags, full Masonic panoply and—to the disgust of his enemies—a procession through the crowded, silent streets of Sydney led by the military band of the 50th Regiment. "It is a piece of important news, certainly," ran a letter to the London *Times*, "for the criminals of England, that military honours have given lustre to the obsequies of one of their most successful chums."[16]

But the Terrys, Reibeys and Lords are memorable precisely because they were exceptions. Very few ex-convicts made big fortunes after 1821, although many of their free descendants would. Most Emancipists survived as handymen, "mechanics," butchers, bakers or small farmers. These "dungaree settlers," so called for the coarse cloth they wore, clung to the land by their fingernails until they were shaken loose by drought or debt or drink. Their truck-gardens produced the fruit, vegetables and chickens that the exalted Merinos would not condescend to raise except for their own kitchens; they feared the space and melancholy of the bush, and stuck to the land around Sydney while other settlers, more adventurous and better endowed with slave labor, pushed outward. Often they drank their small acreage away and died paupers. And yet, as Peter Cunningham remarked, they served "like the American backwoodsmen" —a breed not yet mythologized in 1825—"the office of pioneers to prepare the way for a more healthy population": their own children, the Currency.

If the colony's economy depended on ex-convicts, so did its professional and cultural communities. In Macquarie's time, there was not one lawyer in Australia who had come there as a free man. No respectable lawyer would have contemplated going there to practice. But colonial life was bitterly litigious, and much of the suing and pleading therefore had to be done by fallen solicitors who had been struck off the rolls in England and Ireland.

Their status as lawyers was, to put it mildly, uncertain. But because Ellis Bent, Macquarie's deputy judge-advocate, did not want to waste court time with the meandering, amateurish pleas of litigants acting as their own attorneys, he cautiously allowed three ex-convict lawyers to bring civil cases. Two of them built up quite flourishing practices, for a time. One was George Crossley (1749–1823), who, after twenty-four years' blameless practice as a solicitor, had been transported for perjury.[17] Governor King conditionally pardoned him in 1801, two years after he arrived; by 1803 he owned more than 400 acres on the Hawkesbury River and was handling cases for other settlers, despite a flurry of writs from newly acquired creditors. He advised Governor Bligh, who knew the law of the sea better than that of the land, on his legal dealings with the Rum Corps. Macarthur's cabal, after their *putsch* against Bligh in 1808, had him arrested as a supporter of their "Tyrant" and sent to slave in the dreaded coal mines near Newcastle. Macquarie freed him to practice civil law again, but by 1821 he was crushed by debts and a last conviction, at the age of seventy-two, for perjury. He died two years later. His colleague, Edward Eagar (1787–1866), a Dublin attorney under life sentence for forgery, did slightly better: After getting his conditional pardon in 1813, he practiced law for two years. But then his and Crossley's right to plead in court was struck down by the judge of the newly created Supreme Court of Civil Judicature, Jeffrey Bent.

Bent proved to be an idle, haughty drone, whose conservatism even embarrassed some of the Exclusives. He and Macquarie detested one another on sight, and the friction between them rendered the new court unworkable. Bent thought of Emancipists as permanent helots, and refused point-blank to hear any cases brought by ex-convict lawyers.[18] Naturally, this was a catastrophe for the likes of Eagar and Crossley. Macquarie protested, but in vain. In May 1815 it was ruled that no lawyer disbarred in England could plead in Australia. Macquarie then wrote to the colonial secretary, Lord Bathurst, threatening to resign if Jeffrey Bent and his ailing brother Ellis, the colony's judge-advocate, were not both recalled. Bathurst, realizing that the whole relationship between the government and the bench was about to break down, gave in. Ellis Bent solved half of the problem by dying a few months later, and soon after that Jeffrey Bent left Australia. Nevertheless it would be some time before an Emancipist lawyer could plead with much chance of being taken seriously by an Australian court. This legal disability continued to be one of the most potent weapons in the Exclusives' armory of social discrimination.

Ex-convict doctors fared better than lawyers. One could hardly say that harried, shady writ-pushers like Eagar and Crossley, however badly they were victimized, founded Australian law; but William Redfern (1774–1833), another ex-convict, was certainly the father of Australian medicine.

A spirited and deeply altruistic man, Redfern began his career as a naval surgeon and was tried in 1797 for supporting the mutiny of British sailors on the fleet at the Nore. He was accused as a leader of the rising, although his only role in it was to exhort the tars "to be more united among themselves." The court sentenced him to hang, but he was reprieved, due to his youth and rashness, and spent four years in prison before being transported to New South Wales in 1801.[19]

In a colony short of doctors, beset by grave problems of diet and sanitation, with a high accident rate and laws enforced by flogging, Redfern had plenty to do. He began as assistant surgeon on Norfolk Island, where he got a free pardon from Governor King in 1803. Returning to Sydney in 1808, he was made assistant surgeon to the colony and put in charge of the squalid and chaotic hospital on Dawes Point in Sydney. In 1816 he took effective charge of Macquarie's new "Rum Hospital," and by then his practice was the largest and most popular in the colony.

For Redfern, much of the social prejudice against ex-convicts was suspended. He was clearly the best surgeon in the colony; moreover, his forte was obstetrics, which meant that every family, "good" or not, needed him. He delivered Governor Macquarie's only son Lachlan in 1814, and he was also the family doctor to the Macarthurs in Camden. Respect for Redfern's skills was one of the very few matters on which Macquarie and Macarthur wholeheartedly agreed. Yet despite the strength of his connections at Government House and Camden, Redfern was not content merely to be a "social" doctor. He never forgot that he, like other convicts, had come in chains to Australia. He spent as much time on the convicts' dysenteries, broken bones, eye-sores, infected lash-cuts and bastard births as on the diseases of the rich. He was always accessible to them and ran an outpatient clinic for gang laborers at the back of the Rum Hospital. Above all, he fought to improve conditions on convict transports. Public health in Australia began with Redfern. Many convicts and Emancipists, therefore, considered him their savior; this gave the later political actions of this brusque, kindly and incorruptible man a real constituency.

Early colonial Sydney was not a cultivated town, and even its poor poet laureate Michael Massey Robinson was driven to metaphors of in-fancy and sunrise when he contemplated it. Cultural life among the better classes of Sydney society existed in a larval way, producing an occasional recitation or watercolor; but mostly it struck both visitors and residents as jejune and provincial. "A land without antiquities," complained the well-named Judge Barron Field, who had come to Aus-tralia in 1816 to replace Jeffrey Bent. To Field, it was a place so raw as to be, except for a few oddities like the kangaroo, culturally invisible:

> . . . where Nature is prosaic,
> Unpicturesque, unmusical, and where
> Nature reflecting Art is not yet born;—
> We've nothing left us but anticipation,
> Better (I grant) than utter selfishness,
> Yet too o'erweening—too American;
> Where's no past tense, the ign'rant present's all.

Sydney, he felt, was "a spireless city and profane." The only evocative object in sight is a ship:

> . . . poetry to me
> Since piously I trust, in no long space,
> Her wings will bear me from this prose-dull land.[20]

The only free professional artist to visit Australia before 1825 was John Lewin (1770–1819), a natural-history painter who, sensing that English interest in Australian exotica might make a journey worthwhile, arrived in 1800 to start work on two fine (and now exceedingly rare) illustrated books, *Prodromus Entomology* (1805), on Australian lepidop-terous insects, and *Birds of New Holland* (1808).[21] Lachlan Macquarie adopted this modest and uncomplaining young man as his quasi-official painter, taking him to do watercolors of the scenes on his gubernatorial "progress" across the Blue Mountains on the new convict road in 1815, and commissioning "transparencies" from him for the ballroom at Government House. He also gave Lewin a sinecure of £40, later £80, a year by appointing him coroner, which was as close to a direct subsidy of the infant arts as any governor could do.

Educated convicts—known as Specials—took pride in their literacy and their distance from the brutish laboring mass of felons, and Lewin was a source of comfort to them; his presence suggested that they were not totally severed from culture. "I view, admire, and venerate the Man," cried the convict John Grant, in an an exclamatory panegyric on this "tender Genius,"

> Lewin: rare, beauteous plant in Genius' Vale!
> Painter! Engraver! Nature's Wooer! Hail!
> Courage! [22]

Lewin apart, all artists in the early colony were in the literal sense counterfeiters—or thieves, or fallen clerks, or obscurely disgraced pupil-teachers. Australia was not short of convict painters. One of them, Joseph Lycett (ca. 1774–?) came under Macquarie's erratic patronage. A mere "limner" in England and a helpless alcoholic, Lycett in 1811 received fourteen years for forgery. In Sydney he was made a post-office clerk. There, he had access to the post office's small printing press. Lycett scrounged some copper plates and a burin, and before long the colony was flooded with dud five-shilling notes. He was sent to the penal station at Newcastle. Very luckily for him, the commandant was Captain James Wallis, an amateur painter himself; and instead of hewing coal in darkness, Lycett was set to designing a church and painting a triptych, long since lost, for its altar.

Wallis arranged a conditional pardon for Lycett in 1819, and then Macquarie—anxious, as always, to promote the beauties of Australia and attract free emigrant settlers—encouraged him to wander across the colony, sketching its landscapes. The watercolors became a volume of *Views of Australia*, published serially from 1824 on; these colored engravings were dedicated to the colonial secretary, Lord Bathurst, and presented an Arcadian image of Australia hardly distinguishable from the Cotswolds or a picturesque park. [23] They proclaimed how the benign hand of the "Patriot-Chief," Lachlan Macquarie, had transformed the harsh antipodes. "Behold," the advertisement for the *Views* adjured its readers, "the gloomy grandeur of solitary woods and forests exchanged for the noise and bustle of thronged marts of commerce; while the dens of savage animals, and the hiding places of yet more savage men, have become transformed into peaceful villages." There was something elegantly appropriate about setting a forger to such a task.

Although the list of convict artists is fairly long—from Thomas Watling (b. 1762) in Sydney Cove to William Buelow Gould (1801–1853) in Hobart—it contains no men (and of course no women) of more than local interest, except for the celebrated "painter-poisoner" Thomas Griffiths Wainewright (1794–1847), an epigone of Henry Fuseli who had mixed in London literary circles with Lamb, Hazlitt, De Quincey and the young Dickens. His reputation for poisoning heiresses was a posthumous canard (invented in part by Dickens: so much for literary friendships); in fact, he was transported for forgery. But most convict painters were obscure limners who struggled as best they could in a society without opportunities, lived drunk and died disheartened.[24]

Much of the same was true of writing, which, beyond the level of official dispatch, the legal opinion and the family letter, led a thin erratic life. Professional writers were of course unheard-of. There were convict balladeers, and no shortage of writers of "pipes" or anonymous pasquinades (the curious word came from their author's habit of pushing them under doors, rolled in a cylinder) directed against Authority. Most of these were awkward expostulations, railing against well-known targets to whom they gave easily decodable names—"Parson Rapine," for instance, for the sanctimonious Dr. Samuel Marsden.[25]

The first Australian publisher was a former shoplifter, George Howe (1769–1821), whose bastard son would go on to start the first newspaper in Van Diemen's Land.

The first play produced in Australia was George Farquhar's Restoration comedy *The Recruiting Officer*, performed by an all-convict cast in 1789. Its prologue, supposedly written by some nameless felon bard, was to become famous in and beyond Botany Bay:

> From distant climes o'er wide-spread seas we come,
> Though not with much eclat or beat of drum,
> True patriots all; for be it understood,
> We left our country for our country's good;
> No private views disgrac'd our generous zeal,
> What urg'd our travels was our country's weal,
> And none will doubt but that our emigration
> Has prov'd most useful to the British nation.

Alas, later research has shown that this was not penned by a convict in Port Jackson, but by Henry Carter, a hack journalist in London, well after he heard the play had been performed; he also spread the tale that it had been spoken by the famed pickpocket George Barrington. (Nevertheless, even without its imperishable second couplet, the "Barrington prologue" deserves to be remembered as the first of a long series of gibes directed by the supercilious Pommy at cultural efforts in Australia.)

The most important cultural figure to emerge from the ranks of the convicts was, however, the architect Francis Howard Greenway. He was a touchy, arrogant, painstaking and uncompromising man, and these qualities ensured both his successes and his failures. Without that stubborn egotism his talent could scarcely have survived the humiliations of convict life intact, but his outspokenness about the poor taste, graft, incompetence and bad workmanship that surrounded him made so many enemies that after Macquarie, his patron, returned to England, his career soon withered. To call Greenway an innocent victim distorts the record; much of his reputation for greed and extravagance was deserved. For example, after drawing his salary for six years as Macquarie's architect, he had the cheek to present a further bill for £11,000, which he claimed as his commission fee (about 5 percent of construction cost) on government work for which he had already been paid. He lost his official post when Macquarie left and got no real jobs after 1828; ten years later, Australia's finest Georgian architect died a pauper and was buried in an unmarked grave.

Three major Greenway buildings survive in their intended form: St. Matthew's Church in Windsor, and the Hyde Park Barracks and St. James's Church in Sydney, whose grave and spare pedimented façades face one another at the south end of Macquarie Street. Greenway had a genius for turning the relative poverty of colonial architectural resources —the lack of skilled carvers, for instance—to good account. He had to concentrate on proportion and material texture, rather than ornament: the simple-looking (but closely accounted) use of Palladian bays, with plain pilasters—brick on the Barracks, tawny sandstone on St. James's— firmly stating the ratios of the walls. His Doric detailing, straightforward and masculine, suited the hard clarity of Australian light as well as the limitations of convict masonry skills. As in early American churches, the direct speech of Greenway's idiom reinforced the content of the rituals: nothing Romish, every brick reflecting (as J. M. Freeland put it) "a vehemently evangelical society which saw all hope and cause for pride and pleasure in the unchallengeable rightness of the Protestant ascendancy."[26] The political engagement between Church and State was unambiguously put by the sole inscription in the cartouche on St. James's pediment: not a motto or a Biblical text, just Lachlan Macquarie's name, facing the same name in the same place on the Barracks a hundred yards away.

Architecture is a social art *par excellence*. A citizen sees his city's buildings every day, whether he wants to or not; their speech is quiet but pervasive. Greenway's public buildings publicly epitomized one of the "distasteful" facts of penal Australia—that free birth did not confer a monopoly of talent. For all the Exclusives' obsession with status, and despite the armored barriers of class raised against the Emancipists, the free still had to employ an ex-convict to form and condense their desire for urban elegance and ceremonial space. To worship God in a house built by a forger, while across the way more criminals were confined in another house of equal elegance—this was a piquant contradiction, not to be dwelt on. It summed up the peculiar insecurity of the signals respectable people in Sydney devised to distinguish themselves from their Others.

In their desire for signs of status, the colonial Australians developed some unlikely fixations, refuting entirely the idea that remote societies are robustly free of snobbery. Of course, the reverse is true: It is the provinces that fix on style and "correctness," since their fate is to reflect distant prototypes. Hence the attention the early Australian gentry paid to form, and their contempt for the pretensions of new Emancipist money. Louisa Anne Meredith, the recording angel of the antipodean drawing-room, took one of her finest flights on the subject of risen convicts:

> Wealth, all-powerful though it be, —and many of these emancipists are the richest men in the colony, —cannot wholly overcome the prejudice against them, though policy, in some instances, greatly modifies it. Their want of education is an effectual barrier to many, and these so wrap themselves in the love of wealth, and the palpable, though misplaced, importance it gives, that their descendants will probably improve but little on the parental model. You may often see a man of immense property, whose wife and daughters dress in the extreme of fashion and finery, rolling home in his gay carriage from his daily avocations, with face, hands and apparel as dirty and slovenly as any common mechanic. And the son of a similar character has been seen, with a dozen costly rings on his coarse fingers, and chains, and shirt-pins, glistening with gems, buying yet more expensive jewelry, yet without sock or stockings to his feet; the *shoes*, to which his *spurs* were attached, leaving a debatable ground between them and his trowsers! Spurs and shoes are, I imagine, a fashion peculiar to this stamp of exquisites, but among them very popular.[27]

But how to distinguish oneself from the spur-and-shoe men? Much ingenuity was expended on the problem. Beyond drink, social climbing and fornication, the amusements of the upper crust of New South Wales were not the same as they are today, and generally not of a distinctively "Australian" kind. Superior people did not, for instance, swim in the sea or even go to the beach; sea-bathing bore the taint of the imprisoned, because when Sydney convicts washed they usually had to do it in the salt water. To get a tan, for a woman, was to plummet from gentility to coarseness; sunburned skin suggested convict labor and carried overtones of the despicable black savage. "Few ladies venture to risk their complexions to the exposure of an equestrian costume, and accordingly few appear on horseback."[28]

The desire not to resemble convicts even affected diet. Mrs. Meredith was puzzled by her hosts' refusal ever to serve fresh fish at lunch or dinner, despite the superb quality and variety of Sydney seafood. Instead, she was given smoked salmon or dried cod brought from England. This aimed to invert the convict diet. Convicts traditionally ate salted meat —which signified lack of property, for only the landed could enjoy fresh beef or lamb—and fresh fish. The ceremonial food of the free must therefore be fresh meat and salt fish.

One could live grandly in early Sydney, given the money and the adminstrative power. The extreme example was Captain John Piper (1773–1851), a very unthrifty Scottish Lucullus who had come out with the New South Wales Corps and obtained the plum job of chief naval officer in Sydney, giving him the right to take a percentage of all excise on spirits and customs dues exacted on imported goods. This was worth more than £4,000 a year to him, and with it he built Henrietta Villa— otherwise known as the Naval Pavilion—on a 190-acre harborside promontory granted to him by Macquarie and known today as Point Piper. "He lives in a beautiful house," reported George Thomas Boyes, Governor Brisbane's deputy-assistant commissary-general in Sydney,

> but it stands alone for there is nothing like it in the Colony. He has laid out immense sums and no expense had been spared to ornament this fairy Palace. . . . He does the thing properly, for he sends carriages and four and boats for those who like the water, and returns his guests to their homes in the same manner. He keeps a band of music and they have quadrilles every evening under the spacious verandahs. At the table there is a vast profusion of every luxury the four quarters of the globe can supply, for you must know that this fifth or pick-pocket quarter contributes nothing of itself. . . . There is no honour in dining with Piper for he invites everybody who comes here.[29]

The respectable classes loved horse-breeding and horse-racing; Australia's equine fixation was fully formed by 1820. They held lavish balls, which some pastoral families would ride 200 miles to attend—these being the main displays of the colonial marriage-market. The dancing was segregated, with Emancipists at one end of the room and Exclusives at the other, sometimes with different orchestras. Some gentlemen did what English gentry were known to do—they rode to hounds. But there were no foxes in Australia, and so the "Cumberland Hunt," as it called

itself, donned pink coats amid the old scribbly gray of the bush and went
baying, belling and tallyhoing after dingoes. Rarely can Oscar Wilde's
definition of hunting as "the unspeakable in pursuit of the uneatable"
have applied so forcibly within the British Empire.

The aim was to be as English as possible, and to speak of England as
"home." But the settlers could not follow the change of English fashion;
their conservatism was underscored by the great antipodean time lag.
Ships would bring out-of-date magazines and newspapers, ancient Court
news, obsolescent ladies' clothes and overpriced luxury goods. There was
a faded pleasure in gossiping about the Prince of Wales's debts when, for
all one knew, they might have been paid before one heard of them; or
about the unwonted pregnancy of a county heiress if the baby had presumably already been born. The poverty of conversation could drive an
intelligent visitor to despair. Louisa Meredith lamented that none of the
colonial elite seemed to have read anything:

> An apathetic indifference seems the besetting fault; an utter absence of
> interest or enquiry beyond the merest gossip, —the cut of a new sleeve,
> or the guests at a late party. "Do you play?" and "Do you draw" are
> invariable queries to a new lady-arrival. "Do you *dance?*" is thought
> superfluous, for everybody dances; but not a question is heard relative to
> English literature or art; far less a remark on any political event, of how-
> ever important a nature:—not a syllable that betrays *thought.*[30]

And so the image of England slowly dimmed to a nostalgic wraith, a
film of imperfect memory. What filled up the horizon, as in small isolated communities it always does, was local news. And the convicts were
the necessary low-water mark to which all social heights were compared.
The gentry needed them for self-definition, not just for labor.

iii

ONE SAW GANGS of convicts everywhere. All around Sydney, on the
Blue Mountain roads, or south toward Bowral, Goulburn and the Monaro
plains, the visitor heard the colonial carillon of ringing leg-irons partly
muffled by leather and coarse wool—the sound of chained men hewing
the sandstone, dragging their fetter as though wading in air. Free settlers
tended to conventionalize the sight, to turn these sweating, shuffling,
unknowable Others into voids, mere yellow uniforms, man-shaped holes
in the social landscape. One half-averted one's eyes: There, but for the
grace of God, go I.

In most sketches and paintings of these landscapes, even those by convict artists, the convicts do not appear. When they do, as in the former purse-stealer Charles Rodius's sketch of *Convicts Building the Road to Bathurst*, 1833, they are reduced to inconspicuous *staffage* figures against the notch of Western plain that opens promisingly to view. Much less common are sketches like Augustus Earle's somewhat earlier *View from the Summit of Mount York, Looking towards Bathurst Plains* (ca. 1826–27), where the road gang moves into close-up and there is as much interest in its work and garb as in the immense landscape behind: a man in punishment irons carrying water, three felons hewing sandstone, an imperious—though in Earle's drawing, rather limp—gesture from the military guard. The laboring convict, unlike the Neapolitan fisherman or the Provençal peasant, never became a picturesque feature in the landscape whose social use he typified. He was a pictorial embarrassment, since his known propensity for evil prevented any kind of idealization. He was not so much "brutalized" (in the modern sense: deformed by ill-treatment) as he was "a brute," whose criminal nature was written on his very skin. He was a kind of abstraction to the traveller. "The villainous countenances of the greater number, the clank of their chains, and the thought of how awful an amount of crime had led to this disgraceful punishment, made me positively dread passing or meeting a band of the miserable wretches," wrote Louisa Meredith of her journey across the Blue Mountains.[31]

The otherness of the convict was further reinforced by his language, for his argot declared that he came from another society, an Alsatia of the mind. The linguistic class barriers in penal Australia were absolute —the very opposite of today, when all classes share the robust vernacular of Australian slang. English criminal cant, an entire sub-language, immediately branded its users and the aspiring Emancipist had to unlearn it or stay where he was. Purely colonial terms like *scrubbing brushes* (bad bread full of chaff), *smiggins* (prison soup thickened with barley), *canary* (a sentence of 100 lashes) or *sandstone* (a weak man, who crumbled under flogging), classified the speaker as plainly as the broad-arrow stamped on all prisoners' clothes. The fantastic richness of Australian slang, its power of invective and its curious metaphorical twists, are ultimately traceable to convict days, although the full blossoming of Australian language belongs to the later nineteenth century. Among themselves, old lags used the cant of transportation: They had "been married together" (gone fettered in a chain), "piked across the herring pond," or been "on my travels," or "marinated," or "napped fourteen penn'orth" (drawn a sentence of fourteen years' exile). Because such a sentence was a blow that knocked the wind out of the victim, the transported felon called himself a "bellowser." But there was also a great need for euphemism, because class was such a sensitive issue. In the ears of

Emancipists and their descendants, "convict" was a fighting word. In the 1820s, the polite form was *government man* or *legitimate*, and these were later displaced by *exile* or even *empire-builder*. Such usage was part of what amounted to a social agreement to soften the rub of convict status. One did not throw his bondage in a man's face. Until 1840 and the end of transportation, few (if any) emigrants to New South Wales would have thought of calling themselves "Australian"—a British colonel in Bombay would have as soon called himself "Indian." One was British, and it demeaned one's own standing within the conventions of British society to think that New South Wales was radically different from a "normal" civil community. Of course it was not normal, but to make it seem so the convicts had to be treated, in law and language, as belonging to such a community, lest the free emigrant colonists come to regard themselves as parasites on a jail. To its settlers, New South Wales was *not* a jail but a free community with rather a large preponderance of prisoners in it. This seemingly casuistical point had important social consequences. One sees them, for instance, in the policy that prevented governors sending prisoners, at will and without trial, from assignment to the secondary settlements. A man had to stand trial and be convicted again before losing his rights as a member of the civil community and going to Norfolk Island. If New South Wales had been thought as much a jail as Norfolk Island, no trial would have been needed—it would have been a technical matter, like moving a prisoner from one cell to another. Convicts arrested and held on suspicion in New South Wales could apply for *habeas corpus*, and in granting it a Supreme Court judge named John Stephen remarked that "the rights of prisoners were as sacred in the eye of the law as those of free men." This was no idle figure of speech. In the same spirit of civil conciliation, judges in New South Wales (especially those of the Supreme Court) could be extraordinarily careful of convicts' and former convicts' rights—so much so that one judge in 1838 ruled it improper for the attorney-general to ask a witness, "What were you sent for?" This, said the judge, invited the witness to degrade himself in court. Thereafter, even if witnesses were known to be ex-convicts, they could not be questioned about their past and their convict origin could not be mentioned.[32]

Outside the courts, in the private sphere, a particularly sensitive area of contact between bond and free lay in the use of convicts as maids, nannies, stewards and even teachers. The very idea of assigning convicts as personal servants "for the purposes of Luxury" gave later governors qualms[33]; but, since no butler or groom in London was likely to emigrate to raw Sydney to ply his skills, there was no socially acceptable alternative. For domestic service, preferences were altered. The farmer on his station might crave the labor of a horse-thief or a rick-burner. But in

Sydney, the idea of some "barn door gentleman," an untutored hayseed, big-booting nervously about the drawing-room and breaking the china, filled matrons with horror. Thus, there was a demand for city convicts, preferably refined and literate forgers, who might know from which side to pass the roast; or, if not forgers, at least thieves, who could protect their masters' property:

> It is very seldom that any thieves is sent up the country, as most of the gentlemen resides in Suydney, and would sooner take for his servant a man that he knows has been a regular thief at home, than one of them barn dore gentlemen; why is it, he knows he can depend on them, for they won't see no tricks play'd with his master's property, nor play none himself; you never hear of a thief getting into any trouble.[34]

The servant problem was "as common a topic of conversation with the ladies . . . as the weather," remarked the Catholic prelate William Ullathorne in 1838. "Whenever persons meet it is a constant topic." There were more than enough domestic horror-stories of drink, impropriety and clumsiness—particularly drink—to go round.[35]

The mistress of the house had to lock everything up—the "tantalus" (security-frame for the decanters), the cellar, the pantry, the dressing-table, the desks, the sewing-kit. Sometimes she had to put up with insults from her servants unknown in England, for convict women in domestic service were "very much in the habit" of raking their mistresses with curses and oaths of such obscenity that a proper lady could not repeat them to her husband, much less in evidence to a magistrate in court; so the foul tongue could not be punished.[36]

Given the choice, colonists would have preferred free servants. Sir John Franklin, when he was lieutenant-governor in Van Diemen's Land, proposed in 1837 that all assigned persons—including domestic help—should wear a distinguishing badge or patch on their clothes; the governor, Sir George Gipps, held back on applying this idea in New South Wales because he feared repercussions from rich colonists who did not want the splendor of their flunkies' uniforms dimmed by this mark of infamy.[37]

A few settlers in Van Diemen's Land managed to keep a domestic staff of free people, but they were scarce and apt to leave without warning; there was, in any case, little difference of quality between convict and free male servants. However, up to the mid-1830s, most efforts to bring in respectable women as nurses or governesses failed utterly. For women convicts seemed particularly uncontrollable. (Respectable settlers supposed that their own mercies ensured this.) Parents were plagued by the fear that the running of their households was in the hands of

vengeful and immoral women.[38] Convict nannies and nurses would corrupt those innocent bearers of the Australian future, its children. The
everyday peculiarities of growing up in a penal colony were striking
enough, and domestic scenes like those set down by Marcus Clarke in
His Natural Life must have been enacted many times:

> "You're an impertinent man, sir," cries Dora, her bright eyes flashing.
> "How dare you laugh at me? If I was papa, I'd give you half an hour at the
> triangles. *Oh*, you impertinent man!" And, crimson with rage, the spoilt
> little beauty ran out of the room.
> Vickers looked grave, but Frere was constrained to get up to laugh at
> his ease.
> "Good! 'Pon honour, that's good! The little vixen! —half an hour at
> the triangles! Ha-ha! ha, ha, ha!"
> "She is a strange child," says Vickers, "and talks strangely for her age
> . . . [H]er education has been neglected. Moreover, this gloomy place, and
> its associations—what can you expect from a child bred in a convict
> settlement?"

In a society where violence against the person was all-pervasive and
institutionalized, children were bound to acquire strange habits that
mimicked those of their elders. They played flogging games and judgment games as freely as their descendants would play bushrangers. "I
have observed children playing," wrote one colonial observer in 1850,

> at the Botany Bay game of Courts of Petty Sessions, and noted the cruel
> sentences which were uniformly pronounced on those who were doomed
> to be "damned," and the favour and partiality which was extended to
> others! Justice appeared never to be thought of:—the gratification of a
> licentious and an unlimited Power being all they sought.[39]

Childhood became even more a theater of coercion in Australia than
in England. On one level, children could threaten their parents' convict
servants in grotesque omnipotence: where else could a spiteful brat
promise a nurse or a butler 25 lashes? On another, the habit extended
into—and was reinforced by—adult society. As the Scottish penal reformer and future commandant of Norfolk Island, Alexander Maconochie, observed, "The total disuse . . . of moral motives in the domestic
relations of life, and the habit of enforcing obedience by mere compul-
sion, give a harsh and peremptory bearing in all transactions." Children
learned contempt for others early. "Being very much in the hands of
assigned servants," Bishop Ullathorne testified, "they of course are aware
of the condition of these servants; they look down on them with contempt. This creates an early habit in the minds of the children of looking

down on those who are placed over them; it creates altogether . . . an insolence of feeling and of bearing towards their elders."[40]

The female convict's alleged revenge was to teach the tots bad habits, from swearing to sexual precocity. "They do . . . much damage to the rising generation," John Russell told the 1838 Select Committee on Transportation, "being generally most mischievous in attempting to seduce or contaminate the daughters of settlers." The committee's witnesses, anxious to depict the antipodes as Sodom and Gomorrah, told stories of how colonists' girls had seen female convicts "in connexion" with their satyr-like lovers, and how the three daughters of one family had been so deranged by this penal primal scene that each went forth and got pregnant "by a connexion of her own, which was just the result of being left . . . to the tuition of a convict servant maid."[41]

No wonder, then, that Specials—educated convicts—were much in demand as servants. Because such people were uncommon (less than half, probably no more than a third, of the prisoners arriving in Australia at any stage of its penal history could sign their names), they were of value to government, which by the mid-1820s needed a small army of clerks to keep track of convicts' records. The bureaucracy of New South Wales and Van Diemen's Land was almost wholly made up of forgers, none averse to palm oil. Governor Darling complained that "these people are guilty of all sorts of nefarious practices, altering and interpolating the Registers, and cannot be restrained by any fear of punishment or disgrace . . . [T]hey cannot resist a bribe." But there were few free clerks, and so government demands meant that few Specials were assigned.[42]

Nevertheless, private influence sometimes worked. Thus, several wealthy families boasted their convict tutors, who steered the children through *mensa* or tinkled away the eucalyptus-scented afternoon on a slightly warped Broadwood. The first grammar school in Sydney was started by a ruined Irish clergyman, Laurence Halloran (1765–1831), transported at the age of forty-six for forging a tenpenny frank. Certainly he was a better pedagogue than John Mortlock, a former officer in the British Army who had seen service in India and who was made headmaster of a small Hobart grammar school in the 1850s: "To impress myself with a sense of my dignity, and to lighten my spirits, I immediately belaboured several of the boys (particularly those whose parents had never been transported). This refreshed and consoled me."[43]

Because they had known respectability, most Specials found it very difficult to accept their fate. They looked down on the "decent" society of New South Wales and Van Diemen's Land. Some of them were utterly convinced of their own innocence and could not perceive themselves as criminals: How could the mere alteration of a document be compared to house-breaking or mugging? The shock of transportation caused a reflex

of denial, leaving them with an aggrieved posture of superiority to convict trash. They tried to believe that transportation had not ruined the
class position they had sinned to hold.

One such man was a would-be poet, John Grant (1776– ?), whose
character typified the Special's occasional sense of unreality. He was the
unstable son of a landed English gentleman in Buckinghamshire, who,
trying to better his lot, wooed a titled heiress but found his efforts frustrated by a lawyer in his family circle. In a fit of rage, he shot the solicitor
with a pistol in the buttocks, in full daylight on a London street. His
family connections saved his life; a petition was sent to the daughters of
George III and instead of hanging, he sailed. Grant arrived in Sydney in
May 1804 and within months was asking Governor King for a ticket-of-
leave. Rebuffed, he wrote again: "Why hesitate, Governor King, to do an
act of justice? If you had presented to me the freedom of the Colony as
soon as I landed, you would only have rescued a much-injur'd Gentleman
from Highwaymen and Housebreakers." King took no notice. "You must
feel with me," Grant lamented to his mother,

> the cruelty of keeping one thus upon the footing of the Highwaymen I
> came with in the eye of the Law. . . . But there is in this colony a disposi-
> tion to humble those who come here, on the part of the Civil and Military.

If one ponders the last sentence, it could be no surprise that Governor
King thought Grant quite mad. This opinion was self-fulfilling. King
banished him to Norfolk Island, where he could tell the cormorants
about his innocence and his pretensions to gentility. Grant collapsed
under the stress of three years' isolation and ill-treatment on this remote
settlement, and was invalided back to Sydney in 1808; Macquarie in his
mercy pardoned him, and he returned to England in 1811.[44]

Now and then a Special's sense of superiority would be flavored with
a touch of irony. "Our society now became somewhat improved. Though
I did not hear of any naval or military officers, barristers or doctors of
medicine," wrote John Mortlock, who had been transported for the
attempted murder of his uncle, a clergyman of Christ's College in
Cambridge,

> I could count two Protestant clergymen convicts, one of them a doctor of
> divinity, several solicitors, including one of them an ex-mayor, and many
> Chartists. What a sensation would be caused by the transportation of a
> bishop! The colony was also honoured by the advent of an ex-member of
> parliament, a gentleman at no time treated as an ordinary offender.[45]

Giving themselves airs and graces, most Specials were disliked—and
some detested—by laboring convicts for their flashness and arrogance.

Officialdom could make life difficult for those suspected of freethinking. It was especially sweet to see these uppity nobs reconvicted and sent to a punishment gang on the Blue Mountain roads or at Port Macquarie. "Many of them were so flash that they used to look down on the other class of men, and try to play a game of 'bluff,' " recalled the convict whose memoirs were published under the pseudonym of "Woomera":

> Their hands were very soft . . . [T]hey schemed and wasted their time. In the middle of work I often heard them commence to talk about the fine wine they had drunk at some of the big inns in London—"The Angel at Islington," "The Hole in the Wall," or "The Elephant and Castle," for instance, and some of them had never tasted wine in their lives. At night they began to "blow" about how they had done some of the honest merchants in England out of large and small sums of money. But it was a different tale now—they saw very little money in the road party.[46]

Probably the rank-and-file convicts' resentment of Specials helped consolidate the prejudice, long to be felt in Australia, against brain-workers as "bludgers" or social parasites. Be that as it may, the question of the Specials (who never formed more than a tiny minority of the convicts) bears directly on the much-vexed question of convict solidarity. Here, at least, was one group of convicts that received no trust from the majority and gave no loyalty to it—which only means that the existing class divisions of English society were preserved, as one might expect, among transported felons of all stations.

Much ink has been spilt by Australian historians arguing whether or not convicts in general not only sympathized with one another but also brought these sympathies, tempered by mutual suffering, to the point of "class solidarity." Did they stick by one another as members of an oppressed class? Or were their loyalties so atomized by self-interest as to have no collective reach at all?[47]

At moments of famine and stress, convicts could and did behave ruthlessly to one another. The weak went to the wall among the bond as well as among the free. The Reverend John Morison heard an ex-convict in Van Diemen's Land utter the significant words, whose *reductio ad horrorem* was the cannibalism of Pearce: "What is the use of a friend, but to take the use of him?" "Very comforting doctrine, this," he commented, "and the friendships of some people are more to be dreaded then their enemies."[48]

Convicts were seen to treat one another with special ruthlessness in the chain gangs and the outer penal settlements, such as Macquarie Harbor, Norfolk Island and Moreton Bay. The official strategy of breaking

down their trust in one another by encouraging convict informers undoubtedly worked in these places. "Trusty" convicts, promoted to overseers, could be as brutal as the guards—and worse. Absolute punishment,
such as existed on Norfolk Island under Lieutenant-Colonel James Morisset or at Moreton Bay under Captain Patrick Logan, degrades absolutely; as men are treated, so will they become. But only a tiny fraction
of those transported to Australia spent any time in those penal stations.
Most convicts lived under conditions that sustained and often increased
their sense of mutual oppression; so that, from the earliest days of the
settlement, whole groups of prisoners would stand mute rather than
surrender one of their number to authority, whatever the promised bribes
and rewards. When someone in the late 1790s burned down the only
church in Sydney, Governor John Hunter offered the colossal incentive
of a free pardon, a passage home and £50 to anyone, even a lifer, who
informed on the culprit. "One would have thought that irresistible," he
recalled some years later. "But it brought no evidence; I never learned
who it was; it was a designed thing."[49]

The church was Anglican and the arsonist was undoubtedly Irish.
The Irish convicts had brought a "primitive" collectivism with them on
the transport ships, a common will to stick together that had nothing to
do with ideology (although it would greatly affect the tenor of socialist
movements in Australia a hundred years later) but everything to do with
kin and clan. They were seen, and despised, by English authorities in
Australia as tribal people whose allegiances were not touched by the
work-ethic of Protestant individualism. They were "depraved beyond
conception . . . designing and treacherous," ranted the Reverend Samuel
Marsden from the depths of his bigotry; and their loyalty to one another
could not be broken:

> they consider their Engagements to each other of whatever nature they
> be, as sacred; and when any are detected in the Commission of any Capi-
> tal Crime . . . they will suffer death before they will give Information of
> any of their Accomplices: and when brought to the fatal Tree, will deny
> their Guilt with their last Breath. . . . Thus many of them live and die in
> the most hardened and impenitent State.[50]

The Irish were the largest and most cohesive white minority in penal
Australia, and their folkways were bound to make a deep mark on the
ethos of all convicts and their descendants. The cohesion of the group is
what resists pressure from outside it, and the clannish solidarity of Irishmen seems to have been experienced by many convicts who were not
Irish as a way of resisting the overwhelming power of the organs of State
discipline. Crime is by definition anti-social; criminals are *lumpen* indi-

vidualists. But as Russel Ward pointed out, "When the criminal becomes a long-term convict, his scope for exercising individual cunning is very severely limited, while the forces impelling him towards social, collectivist behavior (within his own group) are correspondingly strengthened."[51] From this rude collectivism, set against the harsh environment of the country and the framework of inquisitorial law, emerged the basic traits of Australian mateship.

There is no doubt about the ties of mutual recognition, sometimes amounting to a non-ideological sort of class loyalty, that could bind convicts together. Strong friendships were forged by repression, and they were so plentiful that one example must do for all. When the convict Mellish had served out his time in Macquarie's New South Wales, he "left the bay" as servant to a married Emancipist couple, who had made their pile in New South Wales and were returning to England. He soon found there were six convict fugitives stowed away on board, two of them friends of his. "The reason I was unhappy was, I could not do by those men as I could wish; I was oblig'd to go out a thieving every night for provishions for those men; to be shoor I brought some tools with me such as would unlock any of the harness casks where the meat was kepd." He stole for them for a month, at great risk, before he was caught and subjected to six weeks of appalling privations, chained in the darkness of the hold. When the ship reached Cape Town, "my flesh was black and blue, and all around the wastebands of my trousers was scratch'd to pieces. . . . I have never so to say been right well since." Yet there is not a breath of resentment in his memoir against the fellow convicts he had kept alive. "They were men that I had a very great respect for, and I do mean to say, that no man will leave behind him a friend in bondage, if they choose to chance the consequences of it."[52]

Visitors to Australia noted what Alexander Harris called the "mutual regard and trust engendered by two men working together in the otherwise solitary bush"—the typical situation of convict shepherds on far out-stations. "Men under these circumstances often stand by one another through thick and thin; in fact it is a universal feeling that a man ought to be able to trust his mate in anything."[53]

Such feelings of trust and recognition could readily run between men who had shared the same experience of servitude. Harris described how, in his wanderings in the Hawkesbury district, he met an Emancipist farmer and public-house keeper who, "like most of those who have risen from the ranks of the prison population by their own efforts" had "a sort of open sturdy manliness about his character which was very agreeable."

> He had several convict-servants, who I could see were governed in quite a different manner from those I had met with in my Illawarra jobs under

free settlers. The free settlers governed their men with capriciousness and by terror, and so could never trust them beyond their sight; whilst these settlers, who had once been prisoners themselves, seemed rather to obtain a willing obedience, founded on respect for their judgment and fairness; and consequently they could trust their men as well out of their sight as in.[54]

Governor Bligh told the Select Committee in London in 1812 that "the convicts unite with one another, and get on very well." Commissioner Bigge in 1822 pointed out that Emancipist settlers tended not to punish their assigned men out of "sympathy with that condition which was once their own." Ten years later this had not changed; Governor Bourke in 1832 reported that most assigned men hoped to work for Emancipists, preferring "their coarse fare to being better fed and Cloathed with a More opulent Master and less liberty." Such utterances (and there were many more) can only suggest that loyalties between convicts, throughout the life of the System, regularly went beyond personal friendship.[55]

iv

OF COURSE Australia was marked for glory, some wag said (and the saying would be repeated for generations), for its people had been chosen by the finest judges in England.

And clearly, one of the things its people did best was breed. A rough census of New South Wales in 1807 showed a total population of 7,563 people. Of these, 1,430 were women, mostly convicts or Emancipists, and one woman in three was married. But the number of children was very high: 807 legitimate, 1,025 not. One person in four in the colony was a child; more than half the children were illegitimate; and most of them were the offspring of convicts.

In 1828 the first official census revealed that there were at last more free people (20,870) than convicts under sentence (15,728) in New South Wales. Almost half the free population were ex-convicts who had done their time, received their pardons and stayed. Most of the rest were children born in Australia, whose parents were either ex-convicts or "came-free" settlers—soldiers, marines, officials large and small, settlers, emigrants of every kind. This first generation of Australians were born free but were raised in a police state. The term for these native-born "Currency lads" and "Currency lasses" came from monetary slang— "currency" meaning coin or notes that were only good in the colony, makeshift stuff, implying raffishness or worse, unlike the solid virtues of the "Sterling," the free English immigrants. The Currency also called themselves "natives," a word not applied to Aborigines, only to locally born whites.

From England, the identity of these people looked simple: They were seen in a bald, one-dimensional way as "the children of the convicts," heirs of a depraved gene pool, from whom little good could be expected. That many of them did not have convict parents; that many of those who did were not raised by stereotyped villains and whores; that crime may not run in the blood—none of this affected English opinion very much. Sin must beget sin, and the "thief-colony" was doomed to spin forever, at the outer rim of the world, in ever worsening moral darkness. This idea was epitomized in 1819 by one of the many experts who had never been there, the Reverend Sydney Smith, the clerical wit who founded the *Edinburgh Review* and, unfortunately, was sometimes consulted on colonial matters by Peel:

> There can be but one opinion. New South Wales is a sink of wickedness, in which the great majority of convicts of both sexes become infinitely more depraved than at the period of their arrival. . . . It is impossible that vice should not become more intense in such [a] society.[56]

Almost everything that was said about the native-born in England, and by English visitors to Australia up to about 1835, tended to assume that they formed a homogeneous group, the "children of the convicts." However, the native-born did not think of themselves that way—not because they felt up to denying the facts of the colony's birth, but because their society was so much more intricate than England's "instrumental" view of Australia as a convict dump, a society defined by criminality, would allow. In this real society, the children of the free were inextricably mingled in a web of social and economic relations with those of Emancipists. The poor were not all convict-born, the rich were not all free; menial workers as well as Macarthurs had come there free, and there were rough Midases as well as sober tradesmen and illiterate, broken helots among the transported. Some children of convicts grew up fighting for crusts, others had private tutors or went to ladies' schools in Parramatta. Because the native-born were the sons and daughters of all conditions of people, bond and free, they were at every level of colonial Australian society by 1825 and could not be treated as a "class" on their own.[57]

Thinking and writing of them as "the children of the convicts" exposed them to condescension. The very word "convict" carried a crushing load of moral opprobrium. "Atrocious" crimes had put the parents in Australia, with predictable results for the native-born. Few of the observers of colonial life, from generally sympathetic ones like Peter Cunningham to prejudiced Tories like John Bigge—let alone choleric bigots like James Mudie—made allowance for the fact that many of their parents had been transported for small crimes. Such folk were not habitual criminals, still less limbs of that chimera the "criminal class," but ordinary sinners without much opportunity, who had offended the law once and had been caught. But to their moralizing observers, simply to be in Australia against one's will was a proof of wickedness.

In particular, the moral prejudices invoked against convict women—the stereotypes of their boozing, promiscuity, rebelliousness and lack of talent for motherhood—distorted the picture of Emancipist family life, suggesting that the native-born were reared on rum and abandoned to fate. Some of the native-born shared this prejudice against their social "inferiors." They were the smallest group: the sons and daughters of the Exclusives, the high officials and the wealthy free settlers, who believed they were a colonial aristocracy.

The idea that, in the words of a colonial judge in the 1850s, "crime *descends*, as surely as physical properties and individual temperament," was the very axis of the idea of a "criminal class"; it was also, of course, the key reason for all social discrimination by "respectable" Australians against their Others, the Emancipists. But it turned out not to be true. Despite all the jeremiads directed against their origins, despite the widespread perception of a permanent groundswell of crime for which they were supposed to be responsible, the first generations of the native-born turned out to be the most law-abiding, morally conservative people in the country. Among them, the truly durable legacy of the convict system was not "criminality" but the revulsion from it: the will to be as decent as possible, to sublimate and wipe out the convict stain, even at the cost —heavily paid for in later education—of historical amnesia.[58]

This was to be confirmed by the crime statistics in New South Wales. In 1835 W. W. Burton, judge of the New South Wales Supreme Court, speaking at length on the prevalence of crime, declared that it was as though "the whole colony were continually in motion towards the several Courts of Justice." But five years later, reflecting on his experiences on the colonial bench—and on the sensational revelations about Australian vice that had filled the ears of the Molesworth Committee—he protested that the Molesworth report "no more represents the true state of society in New South Wales than an enquiry into the horrible particulars of an ill-regulated gaol in England would represent the state of society in the county in which it is situated."[59]

For instead of growing up depraved, the Currency showed the lowest crime rate of any group. Out of 827 men he had tried in the years 1833 to 1838, 450 (54 percent) were convicts under sentence, 241 (29 percent) were Emancipists, 50 (6 percent) were free emigrants, and only 30 (4 percent) were Australian-born. Moreover, none of the Currency had committed murder or grand larceny; and he had never even heard of one being charged with rape. Of the 30 Currency defendants, 13 (nearly half) were up for horse-stealing or cattle-rustling—which, like poaching in England, ordinary Australians hardly thought were crimes at all.[60]

Then how did the cankered stock of English criminality produce such fresh, green shoots in Australia? Observers like Bigge pondered this and came up with a theory. The children had a "natural aversion" to the spectacle of sin. They "neither inherit the vices nor the feelings of their parents," he reported in 1822. They "felt contempt for the vices and depravity of the convicts *even when manifested in the persons of their own parents*" [emphasis added].[61] The Currency lasses, Cunningham thought, were "anxious to get into respectable service . . . [to] escape from the tutelage of their often profligate parents." So there must have been a general rupture between parents and children, a fissure that traversed whole generations—the young, en masse, rejecting the old, and exiling felonry from their lives as it had been exiled from Mother England. They were so hurt by the behavior of their parents that they resolved, no matter how difficult it was, to be as little like them as possible—to go straight. Thus the "viciousness and indolence" of the parents could be squared with the "honesty and industry" of their children.

But there is little to support this idea. Australia was not only a country of opportunity for the Merinos and their friends—men like John Macarthur, in England a draper's boy, a dynast in the antipodes; it was a frontier society that rewarded hard work at any level, to a degree undreamed-of by the English or Irish poor. The out-of-work blacksmith, reduced to petty theft by lack of opportunity, could soon become a flourishing tradesman in Sydney once his sentence was completed. Hope, effort and luck enabled thousands of Emancipists to make a second start in life, better than anything they had known in their British lives. The difference was biggest of all for unskilled workers, whose chances in England had been nil.

To read what these people said about themselves, instead of what their superiors like Bigge and Cunningham said about them, is to get a different impression. Its main source is the "Memorials," or petitions to the governor asking for land grants, which had, of course, to be accompanied by character references from magistrates and chaplains. By the first census, in 1828, one native-born man in three owned land, and the surviving Memorials (written by men on their own behalf, or by fathers seeking land grants for their sons) show a consistent pattern of family ties: Parents asked for land for their sons, sons petitioned for land grants close by their fathers' farms, and this somewhat confutes the "assumption of parental abandonment and neglect" among the native-born.[62] The language in which the memorials are couched always speaks of fathers as "tender," "respectable," "loving," "honest"; of the sons as "deserving," "sober," "devoted." Part of this, no doubt, is the standard language of scribes making formal addresses; one would not expect to find a petition asking the governor to give sixty acres to the "lazy, brutish, undeserving" son of a "drunken, dissolute, hard-hearted" ex-convict. Yet one may feel that the language reflected social facts as well as epistolary conventions.

By 1828, about one adult Currency man in three owned land, but not all the native-born aspired to. The landless did not want to become agricultural laborers either, since that carried the stigma of working alongside assigned convicts. It was noticed that the Currency shunned farm labor "partly from a sense of pride: for, owing to the convicts being hitherto almost the sole agricultural laborers, they naturally look upon that vocation as degrading in the same manner as white men in slave colonies regard work of any kind, seeing that none *but* slaves *do* work." By the same token, the Currency did not look to the sea for work. The harsh regime on board ship, the absolute authority of the captains and their way of keeping discipline with a rope's end was too much like convict life for their taste.[63]

The great area of opportunity was skilled labor and small trade. It took patience to succeed as a farmer. But a carpenter, joiner, bricklayer, wheelwright, cooper, cobbler or blacksmith—in short, any artisan skilled at one of the basic trades on which transport, construction and storage depended—had success at his fingertips in colonial Australia. There was little demand for luxury trades; the colony could support any number of house-carpenters but not many ivory-turners, perfumers or bookbinders. At the end of the 1820s, a good carpenter could make 7s. 6d. a day in Sydney, whereas his counterpart in London might manage to earn two-thirds that. This was the main reason why, despite the seasoning of "political" workers transported to Australia for their protests against trade and labor conditions in England, no radical ideas took root and no trade-union agitation of any note was heard from either the Emancipists or the Currency in New South Wales. Sweated free labor and the exploitation of child workers were equally unheard of there; it was the convicts who sweated and were exploited. Pay and conditions for skilled workers were so much better there than in England that, relatively speaking, they had no gripes.

The native-born Australians did not look like their parents and grandparents, those dark and often stunted emanations of English slums and mills. As children, they were well if plainly fed, cradled in sunshine, and grew into tall and stringy cornstalks, "like the Americans," the resident naval surgeon Dr. Peter Cunningham remarked in the 1820s, "generally remarkable for that Gothic peculiarity of fair hair and blue eyes." They did not have the typically apple-red cheeks which, some etymologists think, were the origin of that mysterious and durable Australian slang term for an Englishman, "pommy." Their complexion was sallow, and they lost their teeth early. They were punctiliously honest and sober, with "an open manly simplicity of character . . . little tainted with the vices so prominent among their parents."[64]

The men were very "clannish"; mateship and class solidarity were absolutely fundamental to their values. They were great street-fighters. One in, all in: "If a soldier quarrels with one, the whole hive sally to his aid; and often they have turned out at Christmas-time, and beat the *redcoats* fairly into their barracks." The Currency lasses tended to be gauche, pretty, credulous, sexually precocious (virginity had no special value for the "lower classes" on the marriage-market of penal Australia) but astute in improving their lot through matrimony. They married early, "and do not seem to relish the system of concubinage so popular among their Sterling brethren here." They spent a lot of time at the beach and swam "like dab-chicks." They were, in short, very like their seventh-generation descendants.

The Currency were also warmly patriotic. "You cannot imagine," wrote George Thomas Boyes, the sensitive and irritable colonial diarist, from Van Diemen's Land to his wife Mary in far-off England in October 1831,

> such a beautiful Race as the rising generation in this Colony. . . . As they grow up they think nothing of England and can't bear the idea of going there. It is extraordinary the passionate love they have for the country of their birth. . . . There is a degree of Liberty here which you can hardly imagine at your side of the Equator. The whole country round, Mountains and Valleys, Rock Glens, Rivers and Woods, seem to be their own domain; they shoot, ride, fish, go bivouacing in the woods—hunt Opossum and Kangaroos, catch and train parrots. . . . They are in short as free as the Birds of the Air and the Natives of the Forests. They are also connoisseurs in horses, cattle, sheep, pigs, and wool . . . and this they all understand before they can speak that two and two make four.[65]

This would become a common theme of visitors: In the midst of all the constraints of a penal colony, the native-born had developed for themselves a sense of *physical* liberty and kinship with the landscape—like Australians in the 1950s, accepting all manner of censorship, Grundyism and excess police power, but feeling like the freest people on earth because they could go surfing at lunch-time.

Surgeon Peter Cunningham was startled to find that most of them thought Australia's "very miserable-looking" gum trees more beautiful than any oak or elm. (It was contagious, for after a time, he wrote, "I myself, so powerful is habit, began to look upon them pleasurably.") The Currency lad who visited England could hardly wait to get back and tell his friends what a dull time he had, how thin the beer was and how slow the horses. Most of them did not want to visit England at all, because it was so full of thieves.

They also had by the 1820s a peculiar accent, lacking both the euphony of standard English and the glottal patter of Cockney: twangy, sharp, high in the nose, and as utterly unmistakable as the scent of burning eucalyptus.

They shared certain grievances with the Emancipist stock from which so many of them had sprung. The prime one was the general attitude of the colonial Exclusives to labor. Convictry had induced the Exclusives to think of all labor as with "supercilious intolerance." Masters used "to tell [convicts] they have no rights, and to taunt and mock them if they talk about seeking redress for any ill treatment. . . . The habit and the feeling have become rooted in their very nature; and they would wish to treat free people in the same way." Women behaved similarly: "It is most laughable to see the capers some of our drunken old Sterling madonnas will occasionally cut over their Currency adversaries in a quarrel. It is then, 'You saucy baggage, how dare you set up your *Currency* crest at me? I am *Sterling*, and that I'll let you know!' "[66]

By far the most galling manifestation of this—the point at which the colony's penal, police-state nature rubbed incessantly against the free-born—were the restrictions of movement and the farm-constable system. Many Currency lads were wanderers, constantly "on the wallaby track." They would roll their swag and go from one end of New South Wales to the other, picking their work. Most of them carried no identification and, being free, were not required to. Nor did they want to: The convict's pass or ticket, much folded and tattered, was as plain an image of servitude as a scarred back. But fear of escaped convicts had led, by the 1830s, to an oppressive patchwork of regulations, chief among which was the Bushranging Act. Under it, anyone could be arrested on suspicion of being an absconder; and the primitive communications in the outback (and records in the towns) made it hard to prove one's identity. Since police were thinly scattered, most of the arrests were made by "farm constables," "trusty" convicts still under sentence, who knew their sentences would be shortened if they could bring a bolter in.

The result was a widespread system of arbitrary arrest, without *habeas corpus* for innocent men fettered in the crude farm lockup with the "log on their toes." Alexander Harris, whose books *Settlers and Convicts* was the only substantial account of life in penal Australia from the free worker's side, told of one "native lad" who had to spend seven weeks out of three months marching in handcuffs under the Bushranging Act; arrested by a farm constable in a distant area of the Hunter River, he had to walk at a horse's stirrup 250 miles to Sydney. Once cleared, he set out in the opposite direction—southwest, toward the Murrumbidgee—and was arrested again and forced back to Sydney, to prove his name all over again. Such exasperations were so common that the Currency did not even sue for wrongful arrest—but then, they were workingmen and did not have the money to litigate, so they grumblingly accepted their fate in what would become the usual Australian manner: cursing authority, but obeying it all the same. "Whole shoals of men, both emigrant and freed, are daily passing to and fro from one police office to another 'for identification,' " Harris noted. "Yet I have never seen one syllable [written] on the subject."[67]

Common oppressions make common causes, and by the end of Macquarie's governorship, Emancipists and Currency were ranged together against the Exclusives. The Anglophile "aristocracy" was scorned as a thin, derivative elite whose standards had little of benefit to add to the emerging folkways of life in New South Wales. The Currency felt they were disenfranchised and the Emancipists knew they were. Looking for a tribune, they soon found him—a slouching, copper-haired, rasping mixture of Irish rage, English manipulation and pure Australian brashness named William Charles Wentworth (1790–1872), "the Great Native." Wentworth's birth had put him neatly between all factions. He was a Currency bastard begotten by a free man on a convict woman, with more than enough property to qualify as a Merino. But his father, D'Arcy Wentworth, was only free by a hair, and conservatives thought of him as an Emancipist.

The Wentworths came originally from Yorkshire and were related to one of the great English families, the Fitzwilliams. D'Arcy Wentworth, son of a Protestant pub-keeper in Northern Ireland, had been born in Armagh around the year 1762. He grew up a man of great charm, cheerful, gregarious, and liberal in his political views. After duty as a medical ensign in the Irish Volunteers, he went to London to continue his medical studies. The Fitzwilliams gave him social introductions and soon this personable lad was living far beyond his means. He came up on three charges of highway robbery at the Old Bailey in 1787. Acquitted of all three, he was haled before the court again in 1789 on yet another robbery charge. At the start of this fourth trial, Wentworth, who cannot have been too sure of his innocence, asked his counsel to tell the judge that he was going to Botany Bay anyhow; in fact he had got a post as an assistant surgeon. He was acquitted a fourth time, but now he had given his word and had to go. He sailed on *Neptune,* the hell-ship of the Second Fleet. A third of her five hundred convict passengers died, but Wentworth survived and so did a twenty-year-old girl named Catherine Crowley, transported for stealing cloth. By the end of the voyage she was heavily pregnant by D'Arcy Wentworth. Their son, William Charles, was probably born at sea on the way to Norfolk Island, where D'Arcy Wentworth became an assistant in the hospital.

D'Arcy Wentworth went on to make a fortune in land, rum and trade. As a doctor, he was mediocre; but as a public figure, he stood large in the tiny colony. When he died in 1827, the funeral cortege was a mile long. With tact and care, he had managed throughout his life to avoid the crab-basket quarrels and ignore the slights of colonial society. Not even the censorious pen of John Bigge could accuse him of social climbing. "Mr. Wentworth has very rarely mixed in the society of New South Wales altho' he has always been distinguished by propriety of demeanour when invited to partake of it and has been observed to shun rather than court attention."[68] In private, there was plenty of courting. He sired (and supported) at least seven other children by various mistresses in Australia, and his tombstone bore the sly scriptural text, "In my Father's house there are many mansions."

From the beginning, the Exclusives disliked him as a rake, a liberal and a convict manqué. His son William Charles, idolizing his father, heard and resented their whispers. The boy went to school in England and came back to New South Wales in 1810, a rawboned lad with thin skin and blood in his eye, just in time for the first clashes between Macquarie and the Exclusives over the Emancipists' rights to serve as jurors and magistrates. He wrote "pipes" against John Macarthur and Macquarie's lieutenant-governor, Lieutenant-Colonel George Molle of the 46th Regiment, whom Wentworth thought a hypocritical anti-Emancipist. His couplets offered "dirty, grovelling Molle" "some bum-tingling kicks" and a "mutton fist upon thy bleeding nose." No doubt Wentworth, who moved gracelessly but had shoulders like an Irish ox, could have made good on this threat. But since the verse was anonymous and not printed, there was little Molle could do.[69]

In the meantime, William Charles had larger matters on his mind—in particular, the crossing of the Blue Mountains, a feat that he accomplished with Blaxland and Lawson in 1813. He was a public figure in the colony by then, and one of its largest landowners (Macquarie, never adverse to the exercise of patronage, granted him 1,750 acres at Parramatta in 1811 and a further 1,000 for penetrating the ranges). In 1816 he set off to England again to study law. His aims were large: He would study the British Constitution so that he could draft one for Australia; and in the meantime he hoped to marry Elizabeth Macarthur, daughter of John, so as to form a great colonial dynasty, Merino inseminated by Currency. In this he was rashly overconfident, since the fierce, aging John Macarthur well knew that young Wentworth had written an anonymous "pipe" against him before quitting New South Wales.

By 1819, his marriage plans had foundered and his touchiness about his father was more inflamed than ever. When Henry Bennett, an English MP, publicly insinuated that D'Arcy Wentworth had been transported as a convict, William Charles bullied a public retraction from Bennett. Thus, the future "Emancipists' friend" could explode at the mere suggestion that he was an Emancipist's son. He remained hypersensitive about his family name for the rest of his life: "I will not suffer myself to be outstripped by any competitor and I will finally create for myself a reputation which shall reflect a splendour on all who are related to me." In his deeper heart, Wentworth believed as strongly in the "convict stain" as any Englishman or Exclusive, and part of him longed to be English; hence the frustrated ambition of his later life, the creation of a new nobility, derided by his opponents as the "bunyip aristocracy" and modelled on the Whig aristocracy of Georgian England.[70]

At first the Emancipists were not so much his friends as his enemies' enemies. But Wentworth saw that the issue of Emancipists' rights could levitate him quickly into the public eye, since Currency so far outnumbered Sterling in Australia. So he wrote a tract, arguing that Australia should cease to be a jail and become, instead, a free colony with its own elected government, rivalling America in its attraction for the English emigrant. "A native of New South Wales," he put on the title page—the first time an author had claimed Australian identity. Inside, he argued for government by a legislative council, nominated, and a small assembly, elected. Ex-convicts should be able to vote for any candidate and stand for any office. But Wentworth's own conservatism rejected the principle of "one man, one vote"; the legislative council would bear "many resemblances to the House of Lords" while landed property was "the only standard by which the right of electing, or being elected, can in any country be properly regulated." He defended Macquarie's Emancipist policy and bitterly attacked the Exclusives:

> The covert aim of these men is to convert the ignominy of the great body of the people into a hereditary deformity. They would hand it down from father to son, and raise an eternal barrier of separation between their offspring, and the offspring of the unfortunate convict.[71]

His book ran through three editions in Sydney but fell flat in England. "A Botany Bay parliament would give rise to jokes," the Reverend Sydney Smith sniffed in the *Edinburgh Review*, and as for juries, what settlement in New South Wales could produce four dozen men fit to serve on one? [72]

But Wentworth began lobbying in London. Soon after he got there, the King's Bench invalidated all pardons, conditional or absolute, granted by past governors of New South Wales. This was a disaster for the Emancipists (for one thing, it invalidated all their titles to property), and in 1821 they met to draft a petition to the Crown, pointing out the "infinite danger and prejudice" to which it exposed them and demanding the restoration of their rights. "It has been by their Labour, Industry and Exertions," the ex-convicts begged to remind George IV, "that this Your Majesty's Colony . . . has been converted from a barren Wilderness of Woods into a thriving British Colony." [73] Governor Macquarie forwarded the document with strong endorsements to London. It bore 1,368 signatures—a quarter of the Emancipist population of New South Wales.

The secretary of its drafting committee was the ex-convict lawyer Edward Eagar, whose modest practice in New South Wales had been wiped out by Jeffrey Bent. Eagar brought the petition to London, and his fare was paid by the Emancipist doctor William Redfern, who went with them. Wentworth helped them lobby the government for validation of colonial pardons, trial by jury and representative government. They did not succeed—at least, not immediately—but their presence in London helped plant the awareness that Emancipists were not just inferior social abstractions in a distant colony but people of British blood with a cause. Lobbying and letters mattered a great deal in shaping official English policy toward Australia. This was the unintended result of setting up an authoritarian, penal regime there. New South Wales had neither free press nor parliament; English officials did not suppose its governor's reports told the whole sociopolitical story; and so unofficial letters from the antipodes to men of influence soon found their way to upper Tory and Whig circles. Only a free assembly in Australia could have reduced this exaggerated power of private correspondence, by supplying a record of debate on issues. Failing that, lobbyists had to pull what strings they could reach.

In 1823 Wentworth wound up his law studies in London and went to Cambridge. This was merely to brown the crust, as he did not work for a degree. His time was taken up writing a lengthy poem in heroic couplets, his entry for the chancellor's gold medal, whose set subject that year—by a happy coincidence—was "Australasia." If he could win this, he reasoned, he would become a public literary man as well as a lawyer and political aspirant—the thirty-three-year-old Byron of the antipodes. Alas, the Native's verses, creaking with trope and figure, came in second. Yet second place was better than none, especially when viewed from Sydney; and Wentworth's peroration, in which Britain sinks in decadence while her old values rise brightly in Australia, would be quoted there for years to come:

> And, oh Britannia! shouldst thou cease to ride,
> Despotic Empress of old Ocean's tide:—
> Should thy tam'd Lion—spent his former might—
> No longer roar the terror of the fight;—
> Should e'er arrive that dark disastrous hour,
> When bow'd by luxury, thou yield'st to power;—
> When thou, no longer freest of the free
> To some proud victor bend'st the vanquish'd knee;—
> May all thy glories in another sphere
> Relume, and shine more brightly still than here;
> May this, thy last-born infant,—then arise,
> To glad thy heart and greet thy parent eyes;
> And Australasia float, with flag unfurl'd.
> A new Britannia in another world.

The poem sank without a trace in England, along with its dedication to Lachlan Macquarie and its defiant signature, "by W. C. Wentworth, *an Australasian.*"[74]

He sailed back to Sydney in 1824 with a printing press and started a newspaper, *The Australian,* the first of a line of nationalistic, pro-Currency, pro-Emancipist journals whose eventual heir in the 1890s would be *The Bulletin.* It was meant to compete against the moribund *Sydney Gazette,* whose every word was vetted by Government House.

Two years earlier, Lachlan Macquarie, hailed in departure as the "Patriot-Chief," had retired to England, and to his obsessive, time-wasting efforts to rebut the criticism of the Exclusives' allies, chiefly Bigge and Marsden. His successor was another Scottish protégé of Wellington's, Brigadier-General Sir Thomas Brisbane (1773–1860). Brisbane had one main thing on his mind. He had been instructed to carry out Bigge's recommendations that security and discipline be tightened up in the colony, so that it would once more become a place of dread and cease to be seen by the poor as one of possible opportunity. Macquarie's detractors had accused him of granting too many tickets-of-leave too early; Brisbane would cut down their number and make sure that sentences were fully served. He had Norfolk Island reopened as a place of terrible secondary punishment, "the *ne plus ultra,*" as he put it "of convict degradation." But at the same time, he realized that the colony had grown to the point where not every detail could be overseen by the governor's office. To the dismay of the Exclusives, he decided to free the press, thus giving Wentworth his inch.

The Native Son promptly grabbed a mile. In a few months *The Aus-*

tralian became so popular that most native-born Australians and every Emancipist accepted him as their tribune. Nobody in Australia had ever built a political base so strongly or so fast. In speeches and editorials, Wentworth hammered away at the issues of jury trial and political representation for Currency and Emancipists, at the prejudices and pretensions of the Exclusives. On the thirty-seventh anniversary of white settlement in Australia, January 26, 1825, eighty of the leading Currency met at a Sydney hotel for a banquet given by Wentworth and Redfern. Michael Massey Robinson, the convict bard who had been Macquarie's poet laureate (to his pique, the post was not renewed by Brisbane) was seventy-nine now and doddery from years of rum; but he roused himself to compose an Emancipists' toast in jingling couplets. It disclaimed Republican sentiments; the Emancipists were Britons reclaiming their ancient rights. Mercy and Justice made the allegorical appearances and agreed to foil the plans of the Exclusives: "Your names shall, unstain'd, to your children go forth / Distinguished for virtue—remember'd for worth." It ended with glasses raised to Australia:

> Then to *thee* shall our hearts' purest homage be given,
> And the toast that succeeds be: *"The land, boys, we live in,"*

Governor Brisbane sympathized, up to a point, with such feelings. He hardened the line on convicts under sentence, but his policy toward the Emancipists was virtually an extension of Macquarie's; and he thought Exclusivist attitudes not only pretentious but unworkable, given the human material of which Australia was composed. He was also tolerant in religious matters. Although he was not fond of Irish Catholics, to whose "barbarous ignorance" he ascribed "every murder or diabolical crime that has been committed in the Colony since my arrival," he felt the best way of saving them from barbarism was for the government to subsidize the building of their long-delayed diocesan church in Sydney to the tune of £3,000, a proposal that struck horror into Protestant hearts.[75] He also incurred Marsden's wrath by suggesting that the Protestant clergy should live on their stipends, not their trade. For these reasons as well as his amateur passion for astronomy, the Exclusives nicknamed him "the stargazer" and bombarded their official contacts in London with hate-letters about him. He was recalled to England at the end of 1825, but he tacitly showed his opinion of the Macarthurs and Marsdens by allowing Wentworth and his friends to hold a public meeting in Sydney whose object was to frame a farewell address to him.

This was the first public political meeting of any kind ever held in Australia, and Wentworth made the most of it, turning it into a forum from which to dare "the yellow snakes of the colony" (meaning the

Exclusives) to come out of their holes. The Exclusives had pursued Macquarie and now Brisbane with "a deadly hostility," "a system of persecution," private calumnies of every sort, turning the public and ministry of England into "the dupes of their habitual and filthy misrepresentations"; but now, where were they? Not "manfully" opposing him and his majority, but skulking in silence. All this robust invective, and more, was duly reported in *The Australian.*

But the reforms that the Emancipists and Currency wanted were slow in coming. In 1823 a British Act of Parliament had created legislative councils for both Van Diemen's Land and New South Wales, whose administrations were formally separated. This was a slight gain, for it meant that the governor was no longer a complete autocrat. But the councils were tiny, appointed by the governor himself, and could do no more than advise; only the governor could initiate a new law in the colony. In 1828 another act increased the size of the legislative council to fifteen people, none elected, all appointed. Not until 1842 did the legislative council acquire members who could present issues for public debate—twenty-four men out of thirty-six. But each representative had to own at least £2,000 in landed property, so that, even if all its members were not "pure Merinos," they had to be as rich as one before getting elected. As a democratic body, this "Squatters' Council" left much to be desired. Wentworth, irresistible in coarse oratory and an expert on procedure, became its de facto leader. But transportation to New South Wales had been abolished in 1840, and the convict presence in New South Wales, which stood around 45 percent of the total white population at the time of Brisbane's departure, had dwindled to a mere 12 percent. The social tensions of convictry were winding down (though not in Van Diemen's Land) and the role of the Emancipists' tribune was less politically useful. The issue of Emancipists' rights fizzled out before it could create an Australian democracy.

Meanwhile, the prospects for the convicts themselves had grown considerably worse. Brisbane had begun to re-convert Australia into a place of dread for the lower classes of Britain. The process did not stop with him. Between 1825 and 1840, the separate colonies of New South Wales and Van Diemen's Land found their penal systems refined, expanded and rendered ever more efficient and excruciating. This work was begun by two military martinets: Lieutenant-General Sir Ralph Darling, who governed New South Wales from 1825 to 1831, and Lieutenant-Colonel Sir George Arthur, who ran Van Diemen's Land from 1824 to 1836. Vast differences—of character, ideals and methods—lay between these two men. But their styles of oppression and philosophies of reform shaped Australia during the last years of the Georges.

II

To Plough Van Diemen's Land

IN CONVICT LORE, Van Diemen's Land always had the worst reputation for severity. Its name induced a *frisson* that later became integral to Australian culture, and earlier ballads refer to it with a kind of passive dread lacking in the more defiant convict-songs of New South Wales. It was the very quintessence of punishment:

Come all you gallant poachers that ramble void of care,
While walking out one moonlit night with gun and dog and snare,
With hares and lofty pheasants in your pocket and your hand,
Not thinking of your last career upon Van Diemen's Land.

It's poor Tom Brown from Nottingham, Jack Williams and poor Joe,
They were three daring poachers, boys, the country well did know;
At night they were trepanned by the keepers hid in sand—
For fourteen years transported, boys, upon Van Diemen's Land.

The very day we landed upon the fatal shore,
The planters they stood round us full twenty score or more;
They ranked us up like horses and sold us out of hand,
They roped us to the plough, brave boys, to plough Van Diemen's Land.

The cottage that we lived in was built of sods and clay,
And rotten straw for bed, and we dare not say nay,
Our cots were fenced with fire, to slumber when we can,
To drive away wolves and tigers come by Van Diemen's Land.

It's oft-times when I slumber I have a pleasant dream:
With my pretty girl I've been roving down by a sparkling stream;
In England I've been roving with her at my command,
But I wake broken-hearted upon Van Diemen's Land.

Come all you gallant poachers, give hearing to my song:
I give you all my good advice, I'll not detain you long:

O lay aside your dogs and snares, to you I must speak plain,
For if you knew our miseries you'd never poach again.

The reputation of Van Diemen's Land as the convicts' hell was gradually acquired. At first the place seemed equally miserable for bond and free, in the way that any new Australian settlement did: coarse, dangerous, and plagued by shortages. Its reputation for severity began modestly with Lieutenant-Governor Thomas Davey (1758–1823), who ran Van Diemen's Land from 1813 to 1816.

Davey was a Devon man, a lieutenant-colonel in the Royal Marines, who, a quarter-century before, had sailed to Botany Bay as an eager young first lieutenant on the First Fleet. By the end of 1792, he was back in England; but the colonial bug had bitten Davey, and by 1810, when he learned of the death in Hobart Town of his old marine comrade David Collins, he thought the antipodes might offer a way of advancement. Davey got Lord Harrowby, a liberal Tory cabinet member who came from the same Devon village as himself, to lobby for his appointment as lieutenant-governor of Van Diemen's Land. It was confirmed, and he arrived in Sydney in 1812 with John Beaumont, the son of his patron, in tow as his secretary (but without his luggage, which had gone on another ship and been captured by an American privateer).

Administratively, Van Diemen's Land was an appendage of New South Wales, not a separate colony; much depended on good relations between Davey and his governor, Lachlan Macquarie. The two men hated one another on sight. Davey thought Macquarie a Scottish prig; and Macquarie considered his new lieutenant-governor a wastrel and a drunk, who manifested "an extraordinary degree of frivolity and low buffoonery in his Manners."

So he did. Davey marked his arrival in Hobart Town in February 1813 by lurching to the ship's gangway, casting an owlish look at his new domain and emptying a bottle of port over his wife's hat. He then took off his coat, remarking that the place was as hot as Hades, and marched uphill to Government House in his shirtsleeves. Nicknamed "Mad Tom" by the settlers, he would later make it his custom to broach a keg of rum outside Government House on royal birthdays and ladle it out to the passersby.[1]

In the past, Davey was said to have tampered with his regimental payroll. Macquarie was given explicit orders from London that Davey could not have a free hand with public money, and he set out with gusto to cramp his lieutenant-governor's style. Davey was not even allowed to draw treasury bills, construct buildings or make contracts for shipping without Macquarie's approval, which, given the distance between Hobart and Sydney, would take months to get. Consequently, Macquarie was furious when Davey, in his zeal to suppress bushranging—which seemed ready to take over Van Diemen's Land by 1814—proclaimed martial law throughout the island without consulting him. Davey, for his part, was sure that Macquarie had encumbered him with regulations out of spite; that he did not understand the problems of Van Diemen's Land (as his ill-worded offer of amnesty to bushrangers in May 1814, unintentionally giving them carte blanche to commit any crime short of murder until the end of the year, indeed suggested); that he was hamstringing the island's economy by buying wheat from India instead of Van Diemen's Land; and that he used the island as a dump for hundreds of Sydney convicts who were too turbulent, lazy or brutish to be useful in New South Wales.

There was truth in all these grievances, but Macquarie went on papering Downing Street with reports denouncing Davey until, in 1816, "Mad Tom" was relieved of his lieutenant-governorship and put out to pasture as a farmer, at which he failed. He left behind him, as much through Macquarie's mistakes as his own, a sub-colony with a growing reputation for unmanageability and violence, where bushranging had become so flagrant as to border on a general convict uprising. However, the administrative chaos, the lack of records and the prevalence of embezzlement in Hobart were of Davey's own making.

It fell to the next lieutenant-governor, William Sorell (1775–1848), to repair the damage. He summed up the state of the island in a pessimistic memo in which he declared that it held "a larger portion, than perhaps ever fell to the same number in any Country, of the most depraved and unprincipled people in the Universe," and was dragged down by

> its long disordered state from a Banditti which has subsisted for years, with connexions ramified throughout the Country; the retransportation of the worst Convicts from Sydney; the great influx of Convicts to a Colony of such limited institutions, and their diffusion all over the Island; the difficulty attending the punishment of serious Offences, and . . . the want of a court of Criminal Judicature; and the Insufficiency of the Lower Police, in which (from the difficulty of obtaining with the present rate of payment the service of respectable people) Convicts are unavoidably too largely employed.[2]

Sorell was a far better man than Davey, with no weakness for the bottle. He too was a soldier, and had served with the 31st Regiment since 1790. In 1807, he was made deputy adjutant-general of the British forces at the Cape of Good Hope, which gave him some previous administrative experience. Skillful, tactful and patient, but with a steel backbone, he seemed an ideal choice to run a fractious place like Van Diemen's Land, with its bloody-minded population and long delays in orders. His only flaw, which Macquarie reluctantly overlooked, was a taste for fornication; he had abandoned his wife and seven children and had taken up while at the Cape with a Mrs. Kent, the wife of a brother officer, who bore him several more offspring and, to the scandal of many, was installed in Government House as the lieutenant-governor's lady.[3]

Sorell broke Michael Howe's gang and hanged most of its members, thus stemming the tide of banditry that seemed set to sluice all law-abiding people off the island. With troops and police, he made the rich farmland of the upper Derwent and the Clyde at least partially safe for settlers. He systematized land grants and cleaned up the Augean stables of government bookkeeping Davey had left. He tried, but failed, to regulate the chaotic slippages of debased currency. He built convict barracks and laid the foundations of the "system of perpetual reference and control" over convicts that would become the bureaucratic masterpiece of his successor, George Arthur. Under his rule, the free population of Van Diemen's Land (including Emancipists) rose from 2,546 in 1817 to 6,525 in 1824; the total population, from 3,114 to 12,464. This meant an enormous proportional increase in the convict population. At the start of Sorell's regime, convicts made up not quite 18 percent of the white populace of Van Diemen's Land; by 1822, the figure was 58 percent. New means of terror had to be devised to keep them docile, and Sorell came up with an effective one. In 1821 he founded a small penal settlement at Macquarie Harbor, as a "Place of Ultra Banishment and Punishment" for convicts who had committed second crimes in the colony and appeared to be turning into bushrangers. For ten years, this would be the worst spot in the English-speaking world.

ii

MACQUARIE HARBOR lies at latitude 42° 14' S., longitude 145° 10' E., on the west coast of Tasmania. As you approach it, sea and land curve away to port in a dazzle of white light, diffused through the haze of the incessantly beating ocean. All is sandbank and shallow; the beach that stretches to the northern horizon is dotted with wreckage, the impartial boneyard of ships and whales. No one has ever lived there or ever will. To starboard, there is a sharp jumble of rocks.

To enter the harbor, you must steer between this headland and another rock, Entrance Island, that marks the southern tip of the sandbars. There is no more than fifty yards between them, and at full tidal flow, the neck of water has a glossy, swollen look, ominous to seamen. Macquarie Harbor is one of the few large bodies of tidal water in the world (covering some 150 square miles), with a bottleneck entrance that faces west. Moreover, it looks directly into the Roaring Forties; the prevailing winds are northwesterly, and the waves of the Southern Ocean have the entire circumference of the world in which to build their energy before they crash on this pitiless coast. And so, when tide sets against wind and millions of tons of water a minute come boiling through the entrance, frightful seas rise. Worse, there is a sandbar dead across the entrance, with only eleven feet of water over it at spring tide. For these and other reasons, the place is called Hell's Gates. It was the first thing that Irish and English convicts saw when their transport ship sailed in, a hundred and sixty years ago.

Sorell made no bones about the purpose of Macquarie Harbor. He commissioned its first commandant, Lieutenant John Cuthbertson of the 40th Regiment, with powers as magistrate and justice of the peace, so that he could hear and determine all charges against convicts and punish them with solitary confinement up to 14 days and floggings not in excess of 100 lashes. The place, he wrote, was for "the most disorderly and irreclaimable convicts," and the system must be "strict and uniform." "You will consider," he wrote in his standing orders,

> that the constant, active, unremitting employment of every individual in very hard labour is the grand and main design of your settlement. They must dread the very idea of being sent there.... You must find work and labour, even if it consists in opening cavities and filling them up again. ... Prisoners upon trial declared that they would rather suffer death than be sent back to Macquarie Harbour. It is the feeling I am most anxious to be kept alive.[4]

To achieve this "grand and main design," the Macquarie Harbor convicts would be loaded at Hobart into ships without bunks or hammocks; they had to sprawl as best they could on the stone ballast in the hold:

> If they had a blanket it was all very well; but I think ... out the 35 men they mustered 4 blankets. I recollect on one occasion ... there was one prisoner who had neither jacket nor trowsers; the commanding officer gave him a bit of canvas, and I have frequently, when at Macquarie Harbour, seen men, 30 or 40 in that state, who have been on board the vessel for five or six weeks.[5]

Those weeks were spent at sea, beating north to Macquarie Harbor against the prevailing winds. Once off Hell's Gates, stuck in a northwesterly, it could be days before a ship could get in. The Quaker missionary James Backhouse went there in 1832 and described the midwinter passage through the Gates. His ship had to wait close-reefed in a storm outside the sandbar while the semaphore on Entrance Island waggled its message, through relay signals, to the distant settlement. At last the harbor pilot appeared in a six-oared boat rowed by convicts, and when he came aboard

> he commanded the women and children to go below . . . and advised me to go below too. I replied, that if we were lost I should like to see the last of it, for the sight was awfully grand. . . . The pilot went to the bows, and nothing was now to be heard through the roar of the wind and the waves, but his voice calling to the helmsman, the helmsman's answer, and the voices of the men in the chains, counting off the fathoms.

As the vessel bore in toward the sandbar, albatrosses circled her; then the bar itself was seen, a pale blurred whaleback in the dark water.

> The fathoms decreased, and the men counted off the feet, of which drew 7½, and there were but 7 in the hollow of the sea, until they called out 11 feet. At this moment a huge billow carried us forward on its raginghead into deep water. The pilot's countenance relaxed; he looked like a man reprieved from the gallows, and coming aft, shook hands with each individual, congratulating them on a safe arrival in Macquarie Harbor.[6]

Past the entrance, past another rust-streaked rock named Bonnet Island, the harbor opens to view. It is so long that its far end is lost in the grayness. The water is tobacco-brown with a urinous froth, dyed by the peat and bark washed into it by Australia's last wild river, the Gordon, which flows into the eastern end of the harbor. The sky is gray, the headlands gray, receding one behind the other like flat paper cut-outs. It is an utterly primordial landscape of unceasing interchange, shafts of pallid light reaching down from the low sky, scarves of mist streaming up from impenetrable valleys, water sifting forever down and fuming perpetually back. Macquarie Harbor is the wettest place in Australia, receiving 80 inches of rain a year.

The settlement was twenty miles back from the harbor entrance. One sailed to it past ironic names: Liberty Point, Liberty Bay, the Butt of Liberty. As their boat moved slowly to its anchorage—there was no hurry now, for prison time had superseded the time of the real world—the convicts must have begun to realize their final imprisonment in great space. Then coastal scrub, dreadful in its monotony, was so thick that a cat could hardly get ashore; the iron-laden rocks would tear the soles off your feet. Beyond them the hills rose, tier on tier of them, dominated by the 4,700-foot peak of Frenchman's Cap—named, in irony, after the

Phrygian headgear that had symbolized liberty, equality and brotherhood to the French a generation before. Below its smooth half-dome of basalt, veiled most of the year by clouds, the trees began.

The logging of these trees was the economic purpose of the settlement, and before the convicts arrived no man had ever touched them. The most prized kind was the Huon pine, *Decydium cupressinum*, which grew in great stands along the Gordon River. They attained a height of 70 feet and a circumference of 15 feet, and some of them had been saplings when Augustus Caesar was a child. Huon pine was the best ships' timber on earth—springy, close-grained, easy to work, and so rot-proof that there are still Huon trunks felled by convicts in the 1820s and bearing their ax-marks lying intact along the shores of Macquarie Harbor today. In one year, 2,869 of these trunks were felled, sawn up and loaded for transport to Hobart.[7] There were other valuable trees as well: lightwood *(Acacia melanocylon)*, a lovely semi-hard timber that worked like walnut and had the grain and figure of Spanish mahogany, much prized by colonial shipwrights; celery-top pine *(Podocarpus asplemfolius)*, good for masts and spars; and myrtle *(Betula antarctica)*, whose wood resembled beech and was used by wheelwrights.

The prisoners were quartered on an island in the middle of the harbor, known as Sarah Island (now Settlement Island). Today the trees have reclaimed it, and the pink underfired bricks of its walls have all but dissolved back into their original clay; here and there one can make out the plan of a cell or a passage, and fragments of carved lintel repose like fragments of a botched, weak culture among the embrangling thickets. In the 1820s, however, the island was bare of forest, covered with buildings, fenced with sawn paling fences and protected against the northeast gales by tall lath windbreaks. It had sawpits and shipbuilding yards, a stone penitentiary, a bakehouse and a tannery, and trim, cold barracks. Of all the sites that could have been chosen for a settlement at Macquarie Harbor, this was the most windswept and barren; even the water and firewood had to come by boat from the mainland. But it was also the most secure.

At 6 a.m., the convicts were herded into boats and ferried to the mainland to cut timber. The settlement had no draft animals, because horses and bullocks rarely survived the voyage from Hobart and, in any case, there was not enough grass there to feed them. So the ponderous trunks, some weighing twelve tons, had to be hauled down a crude corduroy slipway of logs, known as a "pine-road," laid on the forest floor. At the tideline, the logs—sometimes a hundred at a time—were chained together in rafts and towed behind whaleboats across the harbor to the sawpits. When they got the raft back to Sarah Island, the worst part of the prisoners' work began: grappling the logs ashore with handspikes, struggling for hours up to their waists in icy water.

A small minority of luckier prisoners was chosen to build boats on the Sarah Island slips under the eye of Mr. Hoy, the master shipwright. Over the eleven years of its existence, the Macquarie Harbor settlement turned out a surprising number of vessels, all made from local timber. Hoy alone was responsible for the 200-ton bark *William IV*, four brigs of 130 tons each, three 50-ton cutters, five 25-ton schooners, twenty-two launches of 5 to 10 tons, and forty-six small craft of various types.

The convict's daily ration was 1 pound of meat, 1¼ pounds of bread, 4 ounces of oatmeal or hominy, and salt. The meat was brine-cured pork or beef, two or three years old; Surgeon Barnes noted that it often had to be destroyed "as being too bad for the convicts to consume," and that in his own eighteen months at Macquarie Harbor he himself had eaten fresh meat no more than six times.[8]

The officers would vary their diet by shooting kangaroos. The hunt "relieved the dreariness and monotony of a Station and Duty, which must otherwise in numerous instances have originated discontent and probably insubordination." They also ate wombats, which they roasted like piglets ("a most delicious dish," one visitor wrote) and the echidnas, or spiny anteaters, which with a stuffing of sage and onion were vaguely reminiscent—if one closed one's eyes—of roast goose.[9] Fish could not live in Macquarie Harbor; the peat washed down by the Gordon River poisoned them. The river had big eels in it, and a giant freshwater crayfish *(Astacopsis gouldii,* named after the convict artist William Buelow Gould, who was the first to draw and describe one), and mud crabs with fifteen-inch claws.

The convicts, of course, never got fresh meat, let alone the other exotica of Macquarie Harbor; nor did they get greens. Sorell urged Cuthbertson to grow as many vegetables as possible "as the sure mode of preventing scurvy," but the incessant rain defeated most efforts at gardening in the mean, gravelly soil of the settlement. Hence scurvy was endemic there. It abated somewhat toward the middle of 1822, when lime juice and potatoes arrived from Hobart, but by January 1823 "it was again increasing rapidly, and in short there were very few who had not more or less of the disease."[10]

By ferrying topsoil and humus across to Sarah Island, which had little good earth, convicts did manage to grow vegetables "of a quality and size which would not have disgraced the stalls of Covent Garden," but these small crops were all reserved for the officers and the civil establishment. Phillip Island, about four miles down the harbor from the settlement, had better soil and potatoes were grown there—about forty tons a year, which were not issued to the prisoners either.[11] They could have as much water as they wanted, Surgeon Barnes added with no conscious effort at irony; but "other sources of comfort or luxury could not be provided, as it was an insulated situation."[12]

Such was light punishment, routine at Macquarie Harbor. If a convict was balky or insolent, he would be deprived of meat and forced to perform the same work on a protein-free diet. That was the second grade of punishment, and the third was to be ironed with clumsy leg-fetters, weighing 12, 18 or up to 45 pounds, riveted round his ankles and linked by a chain. An ironed man was issued leather gaiters to keep the basils, or rings, from wearing through his flesh. Before long, however, the wet chafing of the iron and the stiff hide started ulcers and scraped their ankles down to the bone.

By far the worst work was driving piles, under water and in chains, for the slipways. If that did not break a man down, he could be left overnight on tiny Grummet Island, half a mile off Sarah Island. According to a convict named Davies (his given name is lost) who spent several years at Macquarie Harbor, it was

a perpendicular Rock Fifty Feet above the levil of the Sea about 40 yards long and 8 wide—a rude stairs in the cliffs is the only road to a truly Wretched Barracks Built with Boards and Shingles (the timber quite green) into which 79 men were often confined in so crowded a state as to be scarcely able to lay down on their sides—to lay on their backs was out of the Question.[13]

To sleep on this rock, in Surgeon Barnes's view, was "very severe indeed, although it was considered a minor punishment." No convict could land on Grummet without being soaked, so he had to sleep either naked or in wet clothes, without fire or blankets.

Half-starved, chilled to the bone, forced to labor twelve hours a day in winter and sixteen in summer, sleeping on a wet rock under the driving rainsqualls of the Southern Ocean, aching with rheumatism and stinking from dysentery, afflicted by saltwater boils and scurvy, some convicts nevertheless remained defiant.[14] Hence flogging was a daily event, and Davies noted down the sentences handed out in his time by Cuthbertson, "the most Inhuman Tyrant the world ever produced I think, since the reign of Nero. . . . Oppression and Tyranny was his motto, he had neither Justice nor compassion for the naked starved & wretched, Humanity was a virtue he did not acknowledge." Neglect of work got 25 lashes, insolence 25. Losing an item from one's "slops"— the cotton duck government-issue work clothes—meant 50 lashes and three months in irons, even if the garment had been stolen by another prisoner. Tools, in that remote settlement, were irreplaceable, and so 50 lashes and three months' irons were meted out to anyone who broke "a Saw, Axe, Spade, Oar or any other tool no matter how, as [Cuthbertson] did not admit Accidents, he would say it was Carelessness." For robbing the stores, or attempting to escape, or striking an overseer, a convict got 100 lashes and six months in irons. Davies's manuscript gives a vivid picture of the daily blood-ritual:

> The Cats and the way they were made and used were the most Dreadful things that can be thought of. They had 9 tails or rather thongs, each four feet long, just 3 times the thickness of the Hobart Town cats. Consequently it took 3 pair [of regulation cat-'o-nine-tails] to make one at this settlement.... [E]ach tail had on it seven Overhand Knots and was whipped, some with wire ends some with waxed ends. It was left to the decision of the Commandant which should be used.
>
> The place of punishment was a low point almost levil with the sea, and just above high water mark was a planked Gangway 100 yards long. By the side of it in the center stands the Triangles to which a man is tied with his side towards the platform on which the Commandant and the Doctor walked so that they could see the man's face and back alternately.
>
> It was their costome to walk 100 yards between each lash; consequently those who received 100 lashes were tied up from one Hour to One Hour and a Quarter—and the moment it was over unless it were at the Meal Hours or at Nights he was immediately sent to work, his back like Bullock's Liver and most likely his shoes full of Blood, and not permitted to go to the Hospital until next morning when his back would be washed by the Doctor's Mate and a little Hog's Lard spread on with a piece of Tow, and so off to work . . . and it often happened that the same man would be flogged the following day for Neglect of Work.[15]

On an average, over the five years 1822 to 1826, there were 245 prisoners at Macquarie Harbor. Of these, seven men in ten were flogged for various offenses, mainly "rebelliousness," "insolence" or "refusal to work." In that period the scourgers inflicted a total of 33,723 lashes—6,744 per year, meaning a little over 40 per man, each stroke meticulously noted in the commandant's ledger.

Convicts distrusted one another, because the system was astute enough to use convicts as guards. All the constables at Macquarie Harbor were convicts, pressed into service by the military commandant. So were the floggers, the chief constable and the chain-gang overseers. The result was "the most tyrannical system that can be imagined." If a convict constable failed to report some insubordination, word of his cover-up would usually get back to the military command and he would be flogged. If he did report it, and the disobedient convict was flogged, the other prisoners would hate him all the more. The worst thing the military could do to a convict constable, therefore, was to strip him of his rank and throw him back unprotected, among the prisoners. To survive at all, the constables had to ride an ascending spiral of vigilance and brutality; and the taste of arbitrary power was an elixir to men who had lost every other source of self-esteem:

> There was a man of the name of Anderson at Macquarie Harbour, and that individual seemed to delight in seeing his fellow-convicts punished; and I believe scarcely a day passed over without four or five, and in some cases 16 or 17 individuals, being flogged on the report of that man. . . . Any man that he had a spite against, he would go before the commanding officer and swear that he had been idle; of course the man . . . would receive a flogging.[16]

The officers at Macquarie Harbor tended to be mediocre and harassed men whose skills, in the Army's view, deserved no better reward; nobody who could get a better post wanted this one, and so "it was a most difficult matter to select individuals from a regiment to fill such a post."[17] So they tended to run the settlement by the book, and endless abuses were possible within the formal chain of command. Yet the more capricious the convict-overseer system was, the better it "worked," since it demoralized the convicts as a group and made them weaker.

The jailers found other means to atomize the convicts, "to divide them as much as we could" and so frustrate their obsessive conspiracies to escape:

> It is only the keeping their minds and their bodies constantly exercised that will prevent the commission of crimes. We invariably found, if the convicts were allowed to be idle, that there was always some new plan, either an attempt to make an escape or a personal injury to the other convicts in agitation; it was not in apportioning their work so much as it was in distributing them in various gangs, so that a man who was in one gang today should not be in the same gang tomorrow.[18]

There was reason to watch the refractory, because a convict would occasionally incite his mates to defiance and try to call a strike. In one twenty-man logging gang in 1825, Commandant James Butler reported to Arthur, an Irishman named William Pearse "stepped out and urged the others not to labour any more—that the Commandant would not flog but merely confine them, which they could well bear, tho' they could not stand flogging—and called the Constables a damned set of villains." Butler gave him 25 lashes.[19]

Prisoners would go to extreme lengths to get away from Macquarie

Harbor, even for a little while. For example, two men would arrange for one to gash the other with an ax or a hoe; the victim would then swear out a charge and other convicts would step forward as witnesses. Since there was no court at Macquarie Harbor, they would all have to be shipped back to Hobart for trial. In court, their testimony would become vague and contradictory, and in the fog of lies the case would have to be dismissed. Prisoners detained on capital charges, waiting for the ship back to Hobart, could not by law be flogged or otherwise punished for a lesser offense until they had been tried for the hanging crime; hence "they become turbulent and insolent, cut their irons and injure the Gaol walls, besides setting an extremely bad example in a Station like this."[20]

If a man was so fortunate as to be sent back to Hobart as a witness in a capital crime, he had a good chance of never returning to Macquarie Harbor. The strict *omertà* among convicts there virtually ensured that he would be beaten up or killed for ratting on a mate. In 1827 nine prisoners were charged with the murder of a particularly hated convict constable, George Rex. Down they went to Hobart, where the attorney-general's case against them failed on a technicality. The five convict prosecution witnesses at once begged Lieutenant-Governor Arthur to be transferred to other settlements. "Our circumstances is at present very Critical and not safe, agoing to Macquarie Harbour again—there are such Characters there that would do us a great injury if not Terminate our Existence, as we was sent up to prosecute those men for Murder." Three of them, "through the intercession of friends" who knew Arthur, were transferred to other penal stations; the other two went back to Macquarie Harbor, where they were indeed killed.[21]

Other prisoners would simply murder an overseer or a prisoner so that they could be hanged in Hobart. T. J. Lemprière, who worked for a time as storekeeper in the commissariat at Macquarie Harbor, described how one such man, by the name of Trennam, had reasoned this out. Trennam stabbed a fellow prisoner on Grummet Island and was in jail awaiting transfer to Hobart and the gallows. Why, the chaplain asked, had he done it? Because he was "tired of his life," Trennam answered, and hoped to hang. Then why did he not drown himself, instead of murdering a fellow creature?

> "Oh," he replied, "the case is quite different. If I kill myself I shall immediately descend to the bottomless pit, but if I kill another I would be sent to Hobart Town and tried for my life; if found guilty, the parson would attend me, and then I would be sure of going to Heaven." He was asked if he had any animosity towards his victim; he replied in the negative. Would he have killed any of the officers? Certainly, if they had given him the same chance. Would he have killed his interrogator, the Chaplain? "Yes, as soon as anyone else."[22]

Even starker mutations were seen in the moral void produced by
Macquarie Harbor. A group of prisoners were being led in single file
through the forest when, without provocation or warning, one of them
crushed the skull of the prisoner in front of him with his ax. Later he
explained that there was no tobacco to be had in the settlement; that he
had been a smoker all his life and would rather die than go without it;
so, in the torment of nicotine withdrawal, he had killed the man in order
to be hanged himself. At least he could get a twist of nigger-head shag in
Hobart before he died.[23]

Such bizarre events became so common that the commandant, with
the permission of the lieutenant-governor, ordered a public hanging at
Macquarie Harbor. The gallows were raised, the felons were all mustered
and the three condemned prisoners were marched forth; but, alas for the
majesty of Law and the moral power of the spectacle,

> their execution produced a feeling, I should say, of the most disgusting
> description. . . . So buoyant were the feelings of the men who were about
> to be executed, and so little did they seem to care about it, that they
> absolutely kicked their shoes off among the crowd as they were about to
> be executed, in order, as the term expressed by them was, that they might
> "die game"; it seemed . . . more like a parting of friends who were going
> a distant journey on land, than of individuals who were about to separate
> from each other for ever; the expressions used on that occasion were
> "Good bye, Bob" and "Good bye, Jack," and expressions of that kind,
> among those in the crowd, to those who were about to be executed.[24]

Macquarie Harbor would remain a colonial benchmark for some time
—the nadir of punishment, until it was shut down and then exceeded by
Norfolk Island. Sorell himself left Van Diemen's Land in 1824. His reputation had been very much undermined by colonial gossips, particularly
by a malevolent former officer in the Rum Corps named Anthony Fenn
Kemp, who had risen to wealth as a grazier and trader in Van Diemen's
Land and out of sheer obsessive contentiousness had appointed himself
Sorell's *bête noire*. Perhaps it was Kemp's snarling recitations of the
lieutenant-governor's sexual laxity, in letters to the English authorities,
that did the trick; whatever the cause, Sorell was never to get another
administrative post in the British Empire, and he died after twenty-four
years of virtual idleness in 1848.

His successor had already been chosen before Sorell left Hobart. He
remains one of the most controversial figures in early Australian history:
Sir George Arthur (1784–1854), the archetype of the pious colonial
strongman, charged by the British Government with the task of rendering all transportation a perfect terror to the criminal classes of Great

Britain. "The most powerful, skilful and ruthless figure in the colony," L. L. Robson's judgment on him runs, "hated with an intensity of which only the neurotic and grasping settlers of Van Diemen's Land were capable."[25]

Arthur was a military man through and through. He had seen service against Napoleon with the 35th Regiment around the Mediterranean, from Calabria to Egypt; in 1815 he took on the post of superintendent and commandant of British Honduras, a slave state with some passing resemblances to the society he would later rule in Van Diemen's Land. During his eight years there, Arthur showed himself to be a reformer, not by any means a populist but certainly more on the side of the slaves than of their choleric and arrogant owners. Reports of his work in Honduras won him the admiration of William Wilberforce.

He returned to England in 1822. Honduras had given him a taste for colonial administration. It was his vocation; what other field could give him the same proconsular scope, the same free hand to take a small remote country and re-mold its life in a way acceptable both to King and to God? There was not a trace of hypocrisy in Arthur. He believed it was his duty to make men moral—high and low alike. He was an evangelist who had chosen soldiering as his medium. Soon, through friends in London, he heard that the lieutenant-governorship of Van Diemen's Land was open.

When, after much lobbying at the Colonial Office, Arthur was chosen as Sorell's successor, he insisted on running Van Diemen's Land as a separate colony and having the effective powers of governor, though he remained lieutenant-governor in title. Shrewdly, he realized even before he got there that Sorrell's and Davey's inability to move without permission from Sydney had done endless harm to convict discipline. He persuaded the Colonial Office to frame his commission so that he could draft laws, make land grants to settlers, directly control government money, extend pardons, remit sentences, appoint his own staff and report directly to Downing Street without referring to the governor in Sydney. This was done, and by 1825 the Government went further: It turned Van Diemen's Land into a separate colony from New South Wales, with its own legislative council—which, in practice, was a rubber stamp for Arthur's wishes. His Utopia of punishment and reform would be an autocracy.

iii

A FEW MONTHS short of his fortieth birthday, when he stepped ashore from the *Adrian* in Hobart on May 12, 1824, Arthur seemed distant, cold and aloof. His tall frame was stooped; the pallor of his face had not been changed by months at sea. His mouth was thin and compressed, the corners turned down. He rarely smiled in public. In conversation he would fix you with his wide, glaucous, interrogatory gray eyes, and he did not seem to blink as much as other people. He radiated an impression, not of wolfish severity, but of unshakable and vigilant moral calm. If there was ever an Australian governor who had no trouble distinguishing right from wrong, it was George Arthur.

This was not only due to his military background. Arthur's serenity came from religion. He did not like to be called a Methodist; that smacked of "enthusiasm" and hence irrationality, and suggested links with the lower orders. But ever since he had a revelation of faith amid the tropical heat of Honduras, he had known that only God was the great emancipator. The Calvinist Evangelicalism he professed was not a private matter. Arthur had been put on earth to impose his values on others; that was the burden and duty of leadership.

He knew human nature was born and saturated in wickedness and could be redeemed only by prostration before Christ, by participating in the sacrifice of his Crucifixion in a complete surrender of faith. All social amusements that stood in the way of the Savior's work were vain, and to be shunned. He was, as the vernacular of a later Australia would express it, a God-bothering, blue-nosed wowser. "Would the forerunner of Christ," he asked his sister in a letter from Honduras, "ever have allowed himself the madness of the quadrilles?" (The image of the Baptist, goatskins a-whirl, treading nimbly across the polished teak at a regimental dance in Honduras has a certain charm, but not to Arthur.) Like most fundamentalists, he was stiffly censorious in matters cultural. He read mainly to reject: The philosopher David Hume was a "wretched infidel," and the net effect of Alexander Pope's didactic satires had been to make the young cynical and self-righteous. Social encounters with Arthur and family at Government House were marked by prayer and scriptural readings and were enlivened only by tea, although he permitted himself some port with his colonial secretary. Colonists, in the presence of this martinet and his starchy wife, realized that the days of "Mad Tom" Davey and adulterous Sorell were far behind them. Few people could extract much pleasure from Arthur's company; but none could doubt that here was the most incisive and vigilantly ordered mind ever to immerse itself in the problems of running a convict colony in the antipodes.

Arthur meant to close all the loopholes in the system of convict punishment and turn the island into an ideal police state where surveillance was constant and total—a Panopticon-without-walls. Moreover, his new system of punishment and incentive would have the inexorable character of a machine, of Bentham's idea of "a mill for grinding rogues honest." Arthur came to believe that his system was so perfectly mechanical that it became cybernetic, or self-correcting. The convict's fate was determined entirely by himself—by his own obedience and tractability, or lack of them. All the officials of the Convict Department had to do was tend the machine and stoke it with paper. As long as it was running, the disposal of the convicts and the severity of their punishment became automatic. That, at least, was the theory; for machines are dispassionate, not vindictive, and Arthur wanted to purge the grit and slop of emotion from his. Weakness led to cruelty; neither befitted a man of God.

In one respect, Arthur was surprisingly modern. He thought crime was a kind of sickness. Criminals suffered from a "mental delirium," caused by seeing reality through a "false medium," a scrim of illusions and distortions. The solution was to train them by drill and rote—he compared his prisoners, more than once, to unbroken horses—backed by the total exclusion of choice from their daily lives. Hard labor and, above all, the boredom of repetition was the only way to get convicts into the passive frame of mind where reformative teaching could pierce and dispel their "delirium."

To enforce this "enlightened rigor," as he called it, Arthur devised an extraordinarily complete system of social control. Van Diemen's Land was a police state; he made no bones about that. But under Arthur, it also became the closest thing to a totalitarian society (though small and in some ways inefficient) that would ever exist within the British Empire. Arthur wanted to control his island utterly, settlers as well as convicts. His system had the logic of his given premise, which was that Van Diemen's Land was first and foremost a jail, and that any free people who lived there must put up with the inconveniences of a penal society (the galling apparatus of police, spies, travel passes, trade restrictions, a muzzled press and crackdowns on the right of assembly) if they were to enjoy its benefits—free land grants and cheap assigned labor.

He divided Van Diemen's Land into nine police districts, each with a police magistrate in charge of a force of constables and field police. Each police magistrate reported back to the chief police magistrate in Hobart, who in turn reported to Arthur. In his own district, however, the police magistrate was boss, judge, coroner and recording angel. He kept minute registers of births, behavior, proper transactions and deaths of the free and bond in his district. He issued travel passes to convicts. All applications from settlers for assigned servants and all petitions from convicts for "indulgences," remissions and tickets-of-leave had to go through him. And he controlled the local police force, which ran from the chief district constable down to the rank and file of the field police, who were recruited from among the serving convicts. To get into the field police was considered a fine indulgence, and Arthur knew perfectly well what effect these government turncoats would have on the morale of convicts: "a mistrust and jealousy had already been infused into the prisoner Population which gives a Security to the free inhabitants."[26]

Every convict, Arthur insisted,

> should be regularly and strictly accounted for, as Soldiers are in their respective Regiments. . . . [T]he whole course of their Conduct—the Services to which they are sent, —and from which they are discharged—the punishments they receive, as well as instances of good conduct they manifest—should be registered from the day of their landing until . . . their emancipation or death.[27]

In 1826 he ordered a transported law-stationer named Edward Cook, under the direction of the muster-master as registrar, to start this gigantic compilation with the 12,305 prisoners who had arrived in Van Diemen's Land since Collins founded the colony. The result was the "Black Books"—ponderous leather-bound tomes three feet high, containing the name, physical description, sentence, details of transportation and assignment, jail and surgeon's reports, punishment and conduct record of every convict sent to Van Diemen's Land. By 1830, Van Diemen's Land had the most thorough files on its inhabitants, bond and free, of any community in the world—a mastaba of paper raised on the miseries of skewed, truncated lives, falling or rising through the levels of Arthur's system.

Arthur made sure that each convict was interrogated on arrival, so that the muster-master had full particulars of them all.* He often went down to the Hobart Penitentiary to meet the prisoners as they arrived, and spoke to them in person. James Backhouse, the Quaker missionary, recounted the homily with which Arthur greeted them:

> He alluded to the degraded state into which they had brought themselves by their crimes; this he justly compared to a state of slavery. . . . [He told them] that their conduct would be narrowly watched, and if it should be bad, they would be severely punished, put to work in a chain-gang, or sent to a penal settlement, where they would be under very severe discipline; or their career might be terminated on the scaffold. That, on the contrary, if they behaved well, they would in the course of a proper time,

---

* This had not always been done before; under Davey and Sorell, thanks to lackadaisical record-keeping in England, whole shiploads of prisoners would come into the Derwent without any records of their crimes and sentences, so that, as Arthur protested in 1827, "we stand in the extraordinary predicament in a Penal Colony of not being able to *prove* that the offenders transported from England *are* Convicts."

be indulged with a ticket-of-leave; . . . that if they should still persevere in doing well, they would then become eligible for a conditional pardon, which would give them the liberty of the colony: and that a further continuance in good conduct, would open the way for a free pardon, which would liberate [them] to return to their native land.[28]

From that moment the prisoner's life became a strictly regulated and automatic game of snakes and ladders. "The spirit of the convict," their new ruler would declare in the summation of his penal philosophy, *Observations Upon Secondary Punishment* (1833),

> is not subdued by unmingled severity. Encouragement forms part of the plan by which he is reclaimed. . . . There is presented to him the choice of two opposite paths. The one will lead him to the possession of a ticket of leave. The other . . . will conduct him by a short cut, to the government gang or the penal settlement where he will be subjected to every privation. . . . Thus it is that every man has afforded him an opportunity of in a great measure retrieving his character and becoming useful in society.[29]

Arthur's system set up seven levels of punishment between its extremes of freedom and the scaffold. In growing order of severity, they were: [1] holding a ticket-of-leave; [2] assignment to a settler; [3] labor on public works; [4] labor on the roads, near civilization, in the settled districts; [5] work in a chain gang; [6] banishment to an isolated penal settlement; and [7] penal settlement labor in chains.

A prisoner sank by bad conduct, and went up the rungs by good—after a time. But he always had to conform perfectly for a part of his sentence before he had any chance of a ticket-of-leave. A man with a seven-year sentence could apply for his ticket after four years of proven good behavior; a fourteen-year man, after six years; a lifer, after eight. He might also shorten his sentence by exceptional services—by catching an escaped fellow convict, for instance, or capturing troublesome Aborigines or serving as a convict constable in Arthur's detested field police.

His progress up the ladders and down the snakes would be decided by full reports on his conduct, gathered from settlers, police magistrates and other witnesses, compiled at the police station in his district and forwarded to Arthur's colonial secretary. Every offense and sentence, each change of place and labor, would be noted by "a firm and determined, but mild and consistent supervision," which would also scrutinize the convict's attitudes to authority and work, his state of conscience and degree of remorse. Thus the prisoner would live without refuge from the eye of authority.

Arthur's belief in his system was absolute, and it distressed him to have its workings disturbed by direct orders from England. The Quaker missionary George Washington Walker called at Government House one day in 1834 and found Arthur "extremely chagrined" at an order that had just come on the transport *Moffatt* from Smith Stanley, the secretary of state for the colonies, enjoining him to take thirty of its four hundred newly arrived prisoners and work them in chains for seven years, instead of giving them the milder punishment of assignment. This draconic and arbitrary sentence, Stanley hoped, would spread the terror of Van Diemen's Land in England. None of the unfortunate men had done anything to deserve it; they had all been submissive and quiet on the voyage; and Arthur was at a loss to know what to say to them. "They naturally ask why are we treated thus? What have we done?" wrote Walker.

> [But] All the Lt.-Governor is able to say is, "such is the order from home, it is out of my power to help it. However, let me recommend you as your friend to submissively acquiesce: to resist w^d only be to render y^r situation worse; & I will write home & endeavour to obtain some mitigation of your sentence, until any bad conduct, exhibited in the colony, renders you deserving of this punishment." Common equity, let alone humanity, prompts this language, which has actually been used tow^{ds} them by the Governor.[30]

Arthur was certainly a martinet, and sometimes a suffocatingly pious one, but in no sense was he a sadist. That taint would be foisted on him later by a hostile colonial press, and fixed in literature long after his death by the Victorian tales of penal Grand Guignol written by Marcus Clarke and Price Warung. His real aim on Van Diemen's Land was reformatory, not vindictive, like the aims of the Panopticon that Jeremy Bentham had set before the French National Assembly more than thirty years earlier.

All convicts entered the board at level [2], as assigned labor. Those not assigned to settlers were put on the public works, for which there was a constant demand, for Van Diemen's Land always needed more jails, barracks, piers, bridges and roads to cope with the growing convict population and the spread of settlement. In 1827, after three years of Arthur's regime, there were 2,500 men employed at punishment labor (levels [3] through [7]) on public works in Van Diemen's Land, or 43 percent of the convict population (as against 577 men, or 32 percent in 1820); this reflected the urgent need for new government buildings of every kind.[31]

But most of the convicts in that year and all others (2,750 or 46 percent in 1827) were in level [2], the norm, as assigned servants. Assignment was the backbone of Arthur's system but also—as he was well aware—its weakest point. The idea that *any* system could smoothly and automatically convert an undifferentiated mass of criminals into the permanent underclass of repentant, tractable cottagers who were the ideal end product of transportation to Van Diemen's Land, was chimerical. To see the common reality one must turn, for a moment, from the administration to one of its thousands of subjects, whose claim to attention is that, unlike the great majority of his fellow convicts, he wrote an uncommonly frank clandestine letter, which has survived.[32]

George Taylor was transported for life to Van Diemen's Land in 1826 for stealing a pocketbook, and in 1832 he tried to smuggle a letter describing his ups and downs to his "dear Brother" John Thompson, another convict serving time in Macquarie Harbor. On first landing at Hobart, he was sent to work in a government vegetable garden "under the Superintendence of a Cruel and Vindictive tyrant where I remained for a fortnight." Then he drew assignation to a free settler named Tennant. "Here I was again unfortunate for altho I received a good Caracter from the Cleark of the prisoners barracks as a hard working industrious man Still I had no sooner got to my master than he began to discover [i.e., disclose] the disposition of a Hardhearted Wreach." After seven months Taylor started scheming to get away. He hoped to provoke his master into bringing him before the local police magistrate on a minor charge, so he started a go-slow strike, only doing "that part of my work which I thought proper." Tennant haled him before the magistrate "two or three times," but the charge was not bad enough to warrant returning Taylor to government work. So Taylor "persued a diferant line" by feigning sickness and asking, as was his right, to be sent to the doctor—who discovered "that I was sailing under false Collors and gave me a note to take to my Master to that effect." Taylor opened, read and destroyed the note. He stayed in a fellow convict's hut for three days and then told his master, on returning, that he had been in the hospital. This flimsy story came apart, of course, the next time Tennant saw the doctor. Tennant took his assigned man to the police magistrate, who sentenced Taylor to the chain gang at Bridgewater. There, convicts in levels [3] through [5] were sweating to create one of Colonel Arthur's favorite public works— a causeway and bridge over the River Derwent, part of the main trunk road from Hobart to Launceston. The facilities provided there to reform the likes of Taylor included cells that were more like animals' lairs, seven feet long and less than three feet high; the men crawled into them at night and were padlocked there, behind a stout lattice, unable to stand or sit. Taylor spent two months at Bridgewater but did not seem chastened enough. His next "automatic" descent was to chain-gang labor at the Kangaroo Point jetty in Hobart and on the roads. "You may be sure my Sittuation is not very enviable," he wrote to his friend, "for it only makes me think more of my Liberty than ever and I am determined to try the first opertunity to gain it by some means or other if possible."

Unluckily for him, his letter was intercepted by the authorities. It had been folly to write it in the first place, and after due inquiry, Colonel Arthur banished him to level [6], an isolated penal settlement. "Let Him then be removed forthwith to Port Arthur," he decreed in a note on the offending document. This was done by the end of 1832. Later, good behavior extracted Taylor from Port Arthur and moved him up again to level [5], this time in a chain gang at Launceston. But the desire for freedom still burned in him; in 1836 he vanished from Arthur's records with the laconic notation "Run," meaning that he had escaped. Whatever else Arthur's system had done for him, it had not made Taylor any more docile. There were many Taylors.

Nevertheless, Arthur had to make his system as perfect and uniform as he could. His task, in conformity with John Bigge's advice to the British Government, was to run an island of punishment, a place of terror to English criminals. He therefore had to keep assignment in Van Diemen's Land from becoming the ill-supervised lottery it had become in New South Wales.

But the free clay of his island varied as much as the criminal. Like New South Wales, Van Diemen's Land had kind and cruel settlers; vigilant and negligent ones; men who would work their assigned servants to the bone, and others who would let them eat at the same kitchen table; above all, men who by temperament and sense of moral obligation would stick to the lieutenant-governor's rules of convict management, and others who would not, and in between those who, like most people anywhere, would bend the rules if they wanted to and thought they could get away with it. All of them must be brought into line, levelled before the System.

Without assignment, there could have been no colony in Van Diemen's Land. Its economy would have died because, as in New South Wales, there was no labor but convict labor. Hence, in Arthur's view, the mere fact of living as a free settler in a penal colony meant that a man must accept the paramount values of penal discipline. Free settlers were as integral a part of Arthur's machinery of punishment as policemen or government clerks. Assignment was a bargain a man struck with the government and if he did not play by the government's rules he lost his convict servants. And the rules were far stricter than they had been under Lachlan Macquarie's more liberal (and, to Bigge, more muddled) system in New South Wales. They went with a larger and ever-growing police force, and a complete denial of any political say to Emancipists and free settlers alike. Throughout his term of office, which was as long as Macquarie's New South Wales—twelve years, from 1824 to 1836—George Arthur never lost sight of the fact that to control a state's labor supply is to control its political life. So Arthur's "red list" of settlers who could not get assigned convicts was, in plan and in detail, a formidable social weapon.

Whole groups were automatically put on it. Arthur would show none of the encouragement Macquarie had given to Emancipists in New South Wales. His view tallied exactly with Bigge's. Ex-convicts, he thought, made bad masters—and of course there was evidence to support it. Either they were too lenient to their men and despised the police, thus jamming Arthur's "objective" machinery of punishment; or else the psychological need to wield power, after their grinding years of servitude and degradation, turned them into sadists and so aborted their servants' prospects of reform. Hence, with very few exceptions, no one who had been a convict in Van Diemen's Land could get convict labor. In this way, Arthur tried to enforce the ideal of Bigge and the Exclusives—that of a permanent ruling class of free descent, with the descendants of convicts as their helots. Refusing labor to Emancipists in Van Diemen's Land could only deepen the gulf between wealthy (or at the very least, "unstained") Exclusive families there, and the convict-descended majority. There were only three passably wealthy ex-convicts in all of Van Diemen's Land at the time Arthur arrived, and he was not anxious to create any more. David Lord, who had inherited an estate worth £50,000 from his convict father James and by 1827 was said to have so multiplied it that he "knows not the extent of his riches," was not only an inveterate enemy of Arthur but also a complete social anomaly.[33]

Some trades found it hard to get convict servants. Arthur despised rum and those who sold it, and would rarely assign a convict to an innkeeper. Believing that the city was wickeder than the country— which it was, given the number of its taverns and the floating population of "loose" women it harbored—Arthur preferred to assign convicts to farmers rather than tradesmen in town.

Arthur expected masters to make their servants pray and scrupulously observe the Sabbath. They must buy Bibles for their men, if the men could read, but few masters actually did so. Few things irked Arthur more than a master's failure to instill religious habits in his convicts. Besides, he wanted to leave Van Diemen's Land covered with a brown mantle of Anglican churches and Wesleyan meetinghouses. He did all he could to bring in clergymen, missionaries and other catechists. The Wesleyans did particularly good work at the foot of the scaffold with condemned criminals, of whom there was no shortage under Arthur. One preacher, the Reverend Carvosso, helped fourteen men to lament and exult their way through the noose into the portals of eternity within a space of thirty hours.[34]

Wherever a town coalesced in the "settled districts" of Van Diemen's Land, Arthur wanted a chapel to be built, usually a plain stone box with

lancet windows and a pitched roof in the Gothic manner, without much
in the way of crockets and stone foliage, where the Lord could be praised
in metrical psalms. There were four churches in Van Diemen's Land
when he arrived in 1824, and eighteen when he left. The church and the
police magistrate's office were the architectural symbols of his regime,
and one served the other. Official religion was a means of penal control.
The mandatory Sunday muster of convicts had to finish with a service
and a clerical harangue. But it was not easy to make sure masters kept
their men's noses to the moral grindstone. Some would work their convicts on the Sabbath, tolerate their propensity to vice and give them rum
as an incentive. If he found out about that, Arthur withdrew their assigned men and left them economically crippled.

He discouraged all intimacy between bond and free. One settler found
himself red-listed for letting his convicts eat Christmas dinner with his
family. In 1831, when a leading settler, George Meredith, defied the strict
letter of police regulations by treating his assigned men to a drink on
New Year's Eve, Arthur ordered his colonial secretary to warn him that
another dram of rum down a felon's throat "will lead to the immediate
removal of all his servants."[35]

If a settler had an affair with a convict woman, and Arthur found out
about it through his district police magistrate, all his servants would be
reassigned. Even if a free man married an ex-convict woman—and most
of the women in Van Diemen's Land had been transported, so there was
not much choice for the small settler—he would lose his assigned servants at once. The situation that often arose in New South Wales, where
a convict might be assigned to a relative, was rarely allowed here. Sometimes Arthur would let a wife emigrate to Van Diemen's Land to join her
convict husband, provided that the man had his ticket-of-leave or that
his master would give her domestic work. But he would not, of course,
pay for her passage.

One exception was reluctantly made for "Ikey" Solomon, the celebrated Jewish pickpocket and fence on whom, legend (perhaps incor-
rectly) insists, Charles Dickens had based the character of Fagin. His
wife Ann, daughter of an Aldgate coachmaster named Moses Julian, had
been transported for receiving stolen goods. She landed in Hobart in 1828,
with four small children between the ages of three and nine. She was
assigned as a servant to a police officer. Meanwhile the intrepid "Ikey,"
who was tried and sentenced for theft in 1827 but had escaped from the
Black Maria on his way to Newgate (the vehicle, as the authorities discovered all too late, was driven by his father-in-law), had fled to Den-
mark, to the United States, to Rio and finally to Hobart under an alias to
join his wife. He bought land and a house and he started a business,
which flourished. Everyone in Hobart knew who he was (the town was

small, and of course full of his former colleagues) but a peculiar technicality saved him: Arthur, who always played by the book, had received
no warrant for his arrest from the Colonial Office in London and could
not touch him until one arrived. Thus, with the backing of some fellow
traders, Isaac Solomon put up a bond of a thousand pounds and Arthur
reluctantly allowed his wife to be assigned to him. Their family idyll was
rudely disrupted in November 1829 when Arthur at last received the
warrant from England. Even then, the *ur*-Fagin made one last wriggle to
dislodge the hook, and with effrontery worthy of his fictional counterpart
he petitioned Arthur from his jail cell for an official job:

TO:
>   His Excellency Colonel George Arther
>   L⁺ Govener of V D Land &c &c &c

Sir,
>   I beg leave to state the following . . . I some time back detected A Man
> with A Forged note on the Bank of the Derwent I had him taken into
> Custedy; he was Convicted and sent to Mackquarrey Harbour. I allso beg
> Leave to State that theire Was a Greate Many forged Note in Circulation
> before I detected this Man; & I have not heard of Any being in Circulation
> since I detected this Man; I theirefor now offer my Serveses to The Gov-
> ernment in detecting all Such Offences or Any thing Else that the Gover-
> ment may Appoint me to do to the Hutermost of my Obility.

>   I have the honor to subscribe
>   Your Excellencys Most humble Servant,
>   Isaac Solomon.[36]

But Arthur was not swayed. "I presume," he frostily noted on the verso,
"this is from the Person commonly called 'Ikey Solomon'—no notice
need be taken of his Memorial." So Isaac Solomon was returned to England amid cries of protest from the Hobart opposition press, who thought
it a breach of *habeas corpus*. There he was tried and sentenced to fourteen years' transportation; by the end of 1831 he was back in Hobart; and
in 1835 he got his ticket-of-leave and was reunited with his family. By
then, unfortunately, they all loathed one another.*

It was essential to Arthur's system that the settlers who had convict
labor assigned to them carry out his rules to the last detail. Judging their
moral fitness to preside over the punishment of prisoners was perhaps

---

* Solomon and his wife quarrelled incessantly and in 1840, when she got her pardon, they
broke up. "Ikey" died ten years later. His old gift for making money had deserted him and
he did not—as another legend had it—contribute to the founding of the first synagogue in
Van Diemen's Land. His estate was only worth £70.

the most ticklish problem that faced the Convict Office. The price of having assigned servants was full participation in Arthur's system of convict management. It made all free settlers into jailers—"auxiliaries," in John West's words, "hired by royal bounties to co-operate with the great machinery of punishment and reformation."[37] The settler was expected to shut up about "rights," stay at home on his farm and do exactly as he was told. A master could lose his assigned labor if he let his men idle, or used convict rather than free overseers or lent a man to another settler. In particular, it was forbidden to transfer convicts as though they were private property, as sometimes happened in New South Wales. To abuse a servant was to lose him, and assigned convicts had the right to complain to the police magistrate at any time. But it was equally forbidden to indulge them, and any delay in bringing a mulish, rebellious or backsliding convict before the magistrate would get the master (or mistress) in trouble. The only play in these regulations came from the supply of assignable convicts. When the demand for them was high, Arthur could take them away from settlers who infringed the rules, just as he pleased. But convicts had to be put somewhere, and so when there was a glut of assignable felons, more settlers found they were let off with a reprimand and could keep their men.

The key to Arthur's scheme of total surveillance was, of course, the quality of the police. "It is extremely desirable," he declared, "that either through the Police or Principal Superintendent's Department, the most conclusive information should always be obtained of the character of the applicant [for] assigned labor and all circumstances."[38] To assure this, Arthur had to make certain that his police force was run by men who had no allegiance to either settlers or convicts and were responsible only to him; and that its rank and file had no reason to favor anyone either. He cunningly did both by appointing army men as district magistrates and by putting upward-moving convicts in the field police as a reward for good conduct and a step toward freedom. This was a bureaucratic master stroke. The convict constables were anxious to distinguish themselves, could be kept in line by the merest threat of demotion, knew they had no second chances and doubtless took a certain pleasure in bossing the settlers around. One could expect dog-like obedience—and canine ferocity—from them. The army police magistrates might not know much about civil law; often they looked on the settlers with disdain, and on convicts with contempt. But they were impervious to criticism from civilians and despised the press. Their background had trained them to handle the laborious, detailed paperwork of reports and to carry out every quillet of Arthur's copious, inflexible orders with military zeal. They believed in the chain of command as implicitly as Arthur did.

Not everyone resented the methods used by Arthur's police. They had cleaned out the bushrangers, destroyed the Brady gang and made the roads safe for trade; thousands of people could sleep easier because of them. Nevertheless, they poisoned the social air. Tempers had always been short in Van Diemen's Land, frictions magnified, manners gross. Bitching and backbiting were the favorite sports of Hobart society—as of Australian society in general. Among the "dirty pack of unprincipled place hunters" whom Arthur's auditor-general, the waspish George Boyes, saw occupying the upper rungs of Van Diemen's Land, "lying, slandering, every hatred and malice are their daily ailment and their consumption is incredible." Now the stew of ill-will was thickened by spying and the fear of denunciation. By 1830, Van Diemen's Land was fast becoming "a community of slanderers and slaves."[39]

Besides, Arthur was a committed nepotist. He knew what a small pool of administrative talent he had in Van Diemen's Land, and he needed people he could trust—loyalty being an acceptable substitute for imagination. If he was an autocrat, and he was, he had partly been made so by distance: He faced a year's delay in obtaining instructions from London, and up to four months' lag in getting them from Sydney. This gave him even wider discretion than the governor enjoyed in New South Wales, and he used it with a sovereign contempt for "liberal" and "democratic" principles. Never apologize, never explain.

Arthur made no bones about the scope of his patronage or his bias toward military men. Given the quality of some of the civil officials the Crown sent, one can hardly blame him. Dudley Fereday (1789–1849), a bankrupt coal magnate's son whom an English lord's patronage had made sheriff of Van Diemen's Land in 1824, turned out to be a relentless usurer, lending money at 35 percent interest. Arthur soon got rid of him, and of his uncompliant attorney-general, Arthur Gellibrand, and of anyone else who seemed either disobliging or short on moral fiber. He went after the customs collector, Rolla O'Farrell, who had arrived penniless in Hobart but amassed a fortune of more than £15,000 by creative venality. This man, Arthur told London, was a debauchee with the morals of a stoat, who lived with one of the prostitutes off the *Princess Royal* and had been fined for harboring and seducing female convicts. In 1831 England sent Arthur a judge, Alexander "Dandy" Baxter (1798–1836), whose ignorance and paranoiac sadism (while serving as Darling's attorney-general in New South Wales, he had battered his wife with a poker after she gave birth to twins) were such that Arthur would not have him in his colony. "I found him," he declared, "in a high state of neurotic excitement and such an habitual sot that it would have been a violation of all public decency to have suffered him to take his seat on the Bench."[40] In 1826 Arthur received John Burnett (1781–1860) as his first colonial secretary—a mewing, forgetful creature, who confessed to Arthur soon after getting to Hobart that "so extremely sensitive is my nervous system that everything which agitates my mind immediately affects my bodily health, and brings on illness."[41] Not without some difficulty, Arthur replaced him with John Montagu (1797–1853), a blunt, thrusting ex-officer of the 40th Regiment, a veteran of Waterloo who— no incidental point—had married Arthur's niece.

In the end, Arthur always got his way with appointments and managed to cripple most of the enemies his purges made. "The Government of the Colony is nominally vested in the Lieutenant Governor and an Executive Council," wrote Boyes. "I say nominally, because the Executive Council as a body is powerless. The real government is composed of Colonel Arthur [and] his two nephews." The "nephews" were Montagu and the chief police magistrate, Matthew Forster (1796–1846), a half-blind former captain in the 85th Regiment who had had the excellent sense to marry another of Arthur's nieces.

Another Arthur favorite was Roderic O'Connor (1784–1860), a "red-hot Irishman," the son of a rich landowner, who had sailed to Hobart on his own ship with his two bastard sons in 1824. O'Connor was tough, outspoken, pragmatic and arrogant—a man Arthur could use, despite his atheism and his taste for the grog. He appointed him to the survey and valuation commission, whose task it was to oversee the division of Van Diemen's Land into counties and parishes, to assess unoccupied Crown land and survey the route for the north–south trunk road, the spine of the colony, which convicts would build between Hobart and Launceston. It was the right job in which to gather some land of his own. In 1824 Arthur gave O'Connor 1,000 acres; by 1828, he had 4,000 and as much convict labor as he wanted—when assigning men to his favorites, the colonel never stinted. In 1836, when Arthur left Van Diemen's Land, O'Connor was one of the half-dozen richest men in the colony, adamantly opposed to any alteration in the system of slavery that had created his wealth. He was not liked (Lady Franklin, the wife of Arthur's successor, complained that he was "bound by ties of I know not what nature to the Arthur faction . . . a man of blasted reputation, of exceedingly immoral conduct and of viperous tongue"), but he was very much feared, and at his death he owned 65,000 acres of Tasmania and leased 10,000 more from the government.[42]

Meanwhile, under Arthur's organizing hand, the economy of Van Diemen's Land was surging. In 1824, when he arrived, Van Diemen's Land had a white population of about 12,000 and its exports were worth £45,317. In 1836, the year he left, they stood at £540,221, and there were 40,000 bond and free. Most of the settlers were men of capital, for Arthur discouraged free workers, even mechanics, from emigrating to Van Diemen's Land; a free labor market would have diminished the social control that flowed from his power to allocate convict labor. Wealthy settlers —the "planters" of folksong—ruled the Vandemonian roost and despised mere traders and merchants. By 1830, Van Diemen's Land had a wool boom, a wheat boom, a boom in real estate and agricultural land and a severe loansharking problem; members of Arthur's own Legislative Council were rumored to be lending out money at illegal rates of 15 and even 50 percent. Thrifty and ruthlessly astute, the colonel himself knew of every project in advance, made a fortune from land investment and lived like a tea-drinking, psalm-intoning nabob. He stayed within the letter of the law, but the law was easier then, and respectable folk were more apt to avert their eyes from conflicts of interest. Thus when he had the causeway and bridge over the Derwent River for the Hobart–Launceston road built at Bridgewater, Arthur owned most of the land around it; and when he picked the site for a new Hobart wharf, he was accused (though not conclusively) of increasing the value of his property next to it from £800 to £12,000.

After a few years of dictatorial, God-fearing nepotism there was plenty of reckoning and questioning. It came from settlers, who chafed at the intrusions of his police and were furious when Arthur withdrew their convict servants for infractions of his code; from merchants, who were treated as low money-grubbers by Arthur's landed gentry; and from all who felt that, as Englishmen in a far colony but Englishmen still, they should have the constitutional rights their "tyrant" denied them. They liked having convict labor but disliked living in a jail. Van Diemen's Land could not be run simply as a jail forever, but Arthur was determined to do so until the Crown changed his orders. The opposition was weak and tetchy. Its attempts to make itself heard—public meetings in 1831 and 1832 and a constitutional association in 1835—were ignored in Government House. But it had an irksome and at times hysterically abusive voice: the press, which Arthur detested.

The newspapers of Van Diemen's Land were rough, choleric and short —a few columns of news and editorials, some letters and official business, tacked onto a mass of advertisements. They tried to win their petty circulation wars with stilted, lurid rhetoric. In short, they were as poor and vindictive as most early nineteenth-century American newspapers. But they were the only forum of popular opinion—as distinct from the printed mandates of the government—in the colony. Everyone read them.

Such journalism goaded Arthur to folly. In 1827, he tried to quash the liberty of all printing on the island by proposing a Licensing Act, so that any editor's right to publish could be cancelled at the lieutenant-governor's pleasure. He coldly offered his all-purpose justification. Van Diemen's Land was a jail, and in jail opposition should have no voice.

Compared to the absolute need for "security and tranquillity," the free settlers' unanimous desire for a free press must go unsatisfied. Behind this, of course, lay Arthur's implacable vanity; he could not stand criticism of any kind, especially not from civilians, and least of all from ex-convicts.

When he looked at Vandemonian journalists, Arthur saw, not a Fourth Estate struggling for freedom of the press, but a swarm of semi-criminal gadflies sent to harass him personally. There was Robert Murray (1777–1850), ex-soldier, journalist and reputedly the bastard son of an English peer, transported for bigamy in 1815 and by 1825 editor of the *Hobart Town Gazette*, who wrote sharp attacks—or gross slanders, depending on which side one took—on Arthur's policies under the name "A Colonist." (He fell into line after 1832 and became a sycophantic tool of Arthur's patronage.)

Another was Murray's colleague Andrew Bent, sent out for burglary in 1810, now editor of the *Colonial Times:* an unrestrained seditionist, Arthur thought. Henry Melville, an eccentric Freemason obsessed with the occult, published the first Australian novel set in Australia (*Quintus Servinton*, 1830–31, by the transported forger Henry Savery) and, to Arthur's intense displeasure, wrote an entire book against his administration, *History of the Island of Van Diemen's Land from the Year 1824 to 1825*, which had to be smuggled out of the colony and published in England. Then there was William Goodwin, editor of the *Cornwall Chronicle*, a harsh transport captain turned venomous hack, whose attacks on Arthur and other pillars of the Vandemonian establishment seemed, unlike those of these other editors, to have no basis at all beyond his own opportunism.[43]

Some of these men bore unmistakably personal grudges against Arthur. One was Gilbert Robertson, the mulatto son of a Scottish sugar-planter in British Guiana, who had twice failed as a farmer: first in Scotland (where falling wheat prices ruined him), and then on a 400-acre grant in Van Diemen's Land. He was jailed for debt in 1824 and then worked for Arthur as superintendent of a government farm. In 1829 he struck out on his own again on Woodburn, a fine grazing property in the Richmond district. This time Robertson seemed set. Arthur had made him district constable and the farm prospered; but in 1832 he made the mistake of indulging his convicts too much. For a celebration after the February harvest, he gave them a barrel of wine, invited in another eight assigned servants from farms nearby and left twenty-five convicts carousing while he went to perform his police duties. All the convicts got drunk and one was mortally wounded in a brawl. This time, Arthur acted with surprising leniency. He did not withdraw all Robertson's assigned men; he merely red-listed him from getting any more. But that was enough for the choleric Scot, who switched to journalism to get his revenge on Arthur and emerged as editor of a daily paper, *The True Colonist*. Through this sheet, Robertson was able to heap accusations of fraud, peculation, favoritism and tyranny on Arthur for the last two years of his office.

Arthur's running battle with the press lasted throughout his administration. The British Government refused to let him have his Licensing Act; so Arthur felt he had no recourse but to sue his critics for libel, bombarding them with litigation to the point where, harassed and short-staffed, they would no longer be able to publish their broadsides against him. Arthur did this with such methodical zeal that Murray, Robertson, Melville and Bent all spent time behind bars. They protested their treatment, in and out of print. There is a particularly indignant letter from Henry Melville to Arthur, protesting the "torture" inflicted on him in the Hobart jail:

> I am writing this in the condemned cell where the notorious man-eater Pierce and some score of other murder[er]s have been confined. In this cell I passed the night (after being locked up by British convicts!) with swarms of bugs, which precluded the possibility of my sleeping.
>
> I ask for suitable appartments chiefly on account of my wife, who has expressed her determination to remain with me as many hours as possible, and if the authorities have a wish to be revenged on a political opponent at all events the chief ruler ought to have some feelings for an unoffending woman who suffers more from the incarceration of her husband than [he] does.[44]

Naturally, they were seen as martyrs. Andrew Bent was defended in court in 1830 as "this Nimrod of printers, this [Benjamin] Franklin of the Southern Hemisphere." Arthur could put them in jail, but not all his autocratic powers could keep them there forever. What especially irked him was the attitude of his own attorney-general, Joseph Tice Gellibrand (1786–1837), a close friend of Robert Murray. Gellibrand several times refused point-blank to sue for libel on the Crown's behalf; he even helped write editorials for Murray's paper. Arthur could not endure this and laid siege to Gellibrand's reputation in England. As Gellibrand was one of the few genuinely acute and honest lawyers ever to hold public office in early Australia, Arthur could not nail him for incompetence; but he created a cloud of allegations of fiscal dishonesty, and in 1826 a dispatch from Lord Goderich removed Gellibrand. His successor as attorney-general was a feeble anorexic named Thomas McCleland, whom Arthur found much easier to control. Gellibrand at once became editor of *The Tasmanian* in Hobart.[45]

And so, through his moral arrogance and his inability to understand or sympathize with civilian tempers, Arthur soon found himself facing a raucous phalanx of opposition papers. Part of their strategy was to contrast the suffering convict with the cold, rhadamanthine lieutenant-governor. To show the "tyrant" at his worst, they harped on the dreaded nadir of Arthur's system, the secondary penal settlements: first Macquarie Harbor, and then Port Arthur.

iv

UNTIL 1832, the only place in Van Diemen's Land fit for the severest levels of Arthur's punishment system was Macquarie Harbor, reserved for those who had committed serious crimes after landing in the colony. Its name reeked of fear and woe; all convicts feared it; but Arthur thought it had defects as well, and these came to look worse as both the convict population and the number of secondary convictions grew.

Despite its wealth of Huon pine, Macquarie Harbor was expensive. Being so remote from Hobart, it was hard to run. Ships took as long as six weeks to reach it, and no overland route had been found. The sandbar at the mouth of Hell's Gates was silting up, making entry to the harbor even more perilous than it already was. Arthur's orders were slow in reaching it, and the commandant's replies were delayed. Food ran short; scurvy was endemic; the barracks on Sarah Island, with a capacity of about 370 prisoners, was too small. Furthermore, a new speculative venture called the Van Diemen's Land Company was trying to open up the west coast for stock-grazing, and it looked as though the utter isolation of Macquarie Harbor, its best feature, might be on the wane.

There was another, far milder, penal settlement on Maria Island, three miles off the east coast of Van Diemen's Land. Arthur had it set up in 1825 to receive convicts "whose crimes are not of so flagrant a nature to induce the Magistrates to sentence them to Macquarie Harbour." The convicts lucky enough to be sent to this sweetly idyllic place wove cloth and cobbled shoes, and although flogging and solitary confinement were common punishments, their life escaped the miseries of Macquarie Harbor.[46]

But it made no sense and cost too much to keep two isolated secondary-punishment stations, one severe and one not; the levels of Arthur's system did not call for light punishment in remote places. Arthur decided to shut both of them down and to open a new penal settlement on the ragged tip of the Tasman Peninsula, closer to Hobart. The place was called Port Arthur. It is his monument, and perhaps no British proconsul has a more impressive one.

Today Port Arthur is easily visited by road; it is sixty miles from Hobart, and every season thousands of tourists in buses and cars stream down the Arthur Highway below Mount Forestier, glimpsing the bright planes of Blackman Bay and Norfolk Bay like burnished pewter struck and feathered by shafts of light, framed by dark headlands. Outcrops of cream and green fibro cottages, neat with garden gnomes and carports, cling to this melancholy coast. The hamlets of this peninsula look feeble and intrusive; their modest grafts of suburbia do not belong in a landscape so drenched in sublimity and misery. One soon forgets them, looking down on the mosaic shore at Pirate's Bay, cracked into hexagonal tessellations by the cooling of the lava flow; or gazing into the vertiginous depths of the Blowhole where, beneath a slender natural arch of rock, the sea two hundred feet below thunders across the jostled slabs of basalt on the cavern floor, saturating the air with a permanent, clinging mist.

In convict days, of course, there was no road. The inaccessibility of the Tasman Peninsula was what commended it to the System, and the best way to sense this is to go there, as prisoners did, by sea. One sails down the Derwent estuary from Hobart and turns into Storm Bay, once the calving-ground of thousands of black whales but now empty; from Cape Direction, where Australia's oldest lighthouse still winks its beam, the long humpy profile of the Tasman Peninsula lies on the southeastern horizon. Its furthest southern point is Cape Raoul, which as one rounds it appears as the western arm of Maingon Bay, the sea-gate that opens the way to Port Arthur—the eastern arm being Cape Pillar. Both capes are of towering basalt pipes, flutes and rods, bound like fasces into the living rock. Their crests are spired and crenellated. Seabirds wheel, thinly crying, across the black walls and the blacker shadows. The breaking swells throw up their veils. When the clouds march in from the Tasman Sea and the rainsqualls lash the prismatic stone, these cliffs can look like the adamantine gates of Hell itself. Geology had conspired with Lieutenant-Governor Arthur to give the prisoners of the crown a moral fright as their ships hauled in.

But once inside the landlocked bay of Port Arthur, the impression melts. Or so it does for a modern visitor, who sees green lawns, the ivy-covered remains of a Gothic church and the enormous bulk of the penitentiary. In its soft tones of pink brick, far gone in crumbling, it seems an almost maternal ruin. It did not seem so to the convicts, but the shudder it reliably evokes in the modern tourist comes from the contrast between its mild, pastoral present—*et in Arcadia ego*—and the legends of its past. Australia has many parking lots but few ruins. When Australians see the ruin of an old building, our impulse is either to finish tearing it down or to bring in the architects and restore it as a cultural center, if large, or a restaurant, if small. Port Arthur is the only major example of an Australian historical ruin appreciated and kept for its own sake (although local entrepreneurs have tried, and so far failed, to refurbish it as Convictland). It is our Paestum and our Dachau, rolled into one. Far more than Macquarie Harbor or even Norfolk Island, Port Arthur has always dominated the popular historical imagination in Australia as *the* emblem of the miseries of transportation, "the Hell on earth."

Moreover, its reputation was terrible right from the start. To have served time there was to receive an indelible stain. "There is something so lowering," remarked Arthur's successor as lieutenant-governor, Sir John Franklin, "attached to the name of a Port Arthur man."[47] Yet the records clearly show that Port Arthur, though certainly a place of misery for its prisoners, was by no means as bad as either Macquarie Harbor or Norfolk Island.

Its main difference from other secondary stations lay in the hermetic regularity of its discipline. It was conceived and run as a purgatorial grinding-mill rather than a torture chamber. "The most unceasing labour is to be exacted from the convicts," Arthur's Standing Instructions emphasized, "and the most harassing vigilance over them is to be observed."[48] But his regulations for the settlement were equally strict on the behavior of its guards. The commandant's authority was absolute, and he answered directly to the lieutenant-governor through the colonial secretary in Hobart. He could, and did, inflict punishment without trial, immediately after the offense, so that the convict would "learn his lesson" without delay. But the sequence of offense, detection and punishment must show a machine-like regularity, to which vindictiveness and pity were equally alien. Arthur's regulations were framed to leave no scope for the exercise of sadistic practices by prison personnel that made a convict's life at Macquarie Harbor or Norfolk Island so vile. Thomas Lemprière (1796–1852), who served as a commissary officer at Port Arthur (as well as Macquarie Harbor and Maria Island), felt that Arthur's enemies exaggerated in calling it an "Earthly Hell." But he did not bridle at phrases like "the abode of misery." "To this cognomen we do not object," he remarked with a certain brisk realism, for

> a penal settlement is, and ought to be, an abode of misery to those whose crimes have sequestered them from the society of their fellow-creatures. Were it a place of comfort, the very object for which such establishments are formed, the punishment and reform of malefactors, would become nugatory.[49]

"*And* reform"—this was a crucial phrase. Port Arthur existed to punish its men purposively. It would be the clamp that held the rigid structure of Arthur's social system together at the bottom.

Arthur had been thinking about the place since 1827, when the colonial brig *Opossum* took refuge there from a storm on the way back from Maria Island to Hobart and came back with news of a deep sheltered inlet, surrounded by colossal stands of timber. Arthur sent her captain back with a surveyor to make a detailed report on the place: its merits as a port, its water supply, and above all its forests, since the demand for timber for buildings and furniture kept rising, and logging was an ideally harsh punishment.

The report was good, and Arthur decided to put a settlement on the bay that, "from profound respect," had been given his name. He did not mean to transfer all the convicts from Macquarie Harbor at once. Some of the less evilly inclined ones could be put there as a form of probation, on their way back up the ladder of his system. But the basic population of Port Arthur would be men re-convicted of minor offenses, and others fresh from England.

The first group, thirty-four new English prisoners with fifteen soldiers to guard them under the command of Dr. John Russell, assistant surgeon of the 63rd Regiment, was landed there in September 1830. More followed; by mid-1831, the convict population was about 150. Dr. Russell would later list "a few well-known characters . . . mixed with the general class of housebreakers, pickpockets and felons":

> There was the famous Ikey Solomons; there was Collins, the old sailor, who threw a stone at the King—he died at Port Arthur; there were those men for agrarian disturbances, for setting fire to haystacks, a circumstance that occurred about 1830 or 1831; there was a clergyman from Scotland, and an attorney from Ireland; there were a number of boys sent to learn trades.[50]

A heterogeneous crew—which, as always at new penal outposts, had great difficulty surviving at all. Rations were miserably short and scurvy widespread. Medical supplies were so inadequate that at one point the doctor had to operate on a man's "stricture" with a piece of sharpened whalebone for a scalpel. Convicts went half-naked from want of uniforms. "I had great difficulty in punishing the men," Russell recalled, "in fact, I was living in the bush myself, and I therefore struck off the irons of every man that came down, and made it a punishment to put them on again." He could not use solitary confinement at first, for want of cells; but later the "most effectual" punishment proved to be hard labor in irons, with all meals and rest hours in solitary.[51]

Russell's pleas to Hobart went unanswered, because Arthur was obsessed with the field strategy of his military campaign to round up the remaining black tribes of Van Diemen's Land. And when the first group of convicts from Macquarie Harbor was moved to Port Arthur, Russell soon saw their influence on the prisoners fresh from England: "They exercised a complete tyranny over them, and shortly rendered them as hardened, as reckless, and as hypocritical as they were themselves." With Arthur's attention distracted, the colonial government ruined morale by not keeping its word to the better prisoners:

> Promises were sometimes held out through the commandant to well-conducted men, that their sentences should be shortly remitted in case of good conduct; that very good conduct rendered the men more useful in the settlement, and then the government detained them much longer. . . . The men, finding good conduct useless, reverted to bad practices, being rendered desperate.[52]

Little by little, a settlement rose at Port Arthur. At the end of 1832, Lieutenant-Colonel Logan of the 63rd Regiment made a tour of inspection of Tasman's Peninsula and reported that, once it had a fast patrol boat that could cruise the shore looking for absconders, the place would be ready to take over from Macquarie Harbor.[53] Two months later, in February 1833, the man who was to give Port Arthur its true penal shape disembarked at Hobart with a detachment of the 21st Fusiliers. This was Charles O'Hara Booth, destined to fulfill Arthur's hopes by taking "the vengeance of the Law to the utmost limits of human endurance" on Tasman's Peninsula. He would remain commandant at Port Arthur for eleven years. In 1833, when he took command, there were 475 prisoners on the Tasman Peninsula; by 1835 there were nearly 950; and the total number of convicts received by Port Arthur up to 1844, the last year of Booth's command, was 6,002. About 6,000 more had gone there by 1853, the year transportation to Van Diemen's Land ceased. All told, about 12,700 sentences were served at Port Arthur during its half-century of active life—about one in six of the 73,500 convicts transported to Van Diemen's Land. (Some prisoners, however, went there more than once.) The place was therefore of great importance in the penal scheme and played a much bigger part in the punishment of habitual criminals, or recidivists, than Macquarie Harbor or even Norfolk Island.[54]

Charles O'Hara Booth was a tough, vigilant man, whose taste for iron discipline was mingled with a liking for puns, Frenchifications and music-hall jollities. He had a strong sense of his job as role. In his journal, he called the Port Arthur convicts his "lions"; their tamer needed a certain histrionic poise. "Put on my annihilating countenance," he wrote one evening when he had to face down 375 insubordinate prisoners on his own. "Raised my Stentorian voice and made them quake."[55]

He was innately conservative and had no illusions about his ability to reform the Port Arthur convicts. He was there to discipline them and make them work, but any moral change seemed an unlikely bonus. He made his opinions clear to a French visitor, Captain Laplace, in 1839. How, Laplace inquired as they paced the night rounds of the settlement with Booth, had he achieved such quiescence with such minimal means —a dozen or so guards to supervise several hundred men, a low-security jail building? "By severe punishments, he replied, by impartial justice, as impassive as that of fate; by untiring vigilance; by demanding absolute silence from the prisoners." Booth added that he saw to it that convicts were never insulted or sworn at, and that he rarely had them flogged because the lash "often exasperates them and drives them to crime instead of reforming them"; he preferred solitary confinement, which, "much dreaded . . . subdues them through boredom." They came out of solitary "better than they went in," but only for a little while; "the banter, the bad examples of their companions, a fatal pride, soon make them forget their good resolutions, and they become just as dangerous as before." When depressed, as he sometimes was by illness, he would feel doubts. "Sick at Heart from the number of Boys obliged to punish," he noted in his journal in 1838, after a particularly taxing day among the refractory juveniles of Point Puer. "Would that we had persons to work the system—with firmness but temper and Patience to witness the results of perseverance—find myself breaking constitutionally rapidly— this is a trying situation . . . but great good may be effected by firmness tempered with kindness and unremitting perseverance." This was the only opinion on the aims, as distinct from the means, of prison policy that Booth committed to his diaries in Port Arthur. His journals were full of notes on hunting, which he loved; sixteen brace of quail bagged one day, nine kangaroos another, duck on the lagoon; the making of a purse from a kangaroo's scrotum, or "pebble case" as he archly called it, "it being a very fine specimen from a 'Fighting Buck.' " But of reflection on his job and the moral values it entailed, there is hardly a trace. Booth was not a reflective man.[56]

He had a name for justice, and even humanity, among his subordinates at Port Arthur. "We know he detests the use of [the lash]," Lemprière wrote, "and it is with regret, when he is compelled by the necessity of inflicting strict discipline, that he causes corporal punishment to be inflicted."[57] But when he used it he laid it on, handing out sentences of up to 100 lashes. Convicts regarded the Port Arthur cat-o'-nine-tails as unusually cruel—although the same had been said about the tools of flagellation at Macquarie Harbor. One of Port Arthur's political prisoners, the Chartist John Frost (he had been sentenced to be hanged, drawn and quartered for leading an ill-armed band of insurrectionary miners from the Monmouth Hills against the English town of Newport

after the mass arrests of Chartist leaders in 1839, but this was commuted
to life transportation) claimed that "twenty-five lashes at Port Arthur . . . produced more suffering than 300 would have produced as they
are inflicted in the Army." In Van Diemen's Land in the 1840s, "politicals" were relatively privileged, and Frost was never flogged. But his
description of the hateful ritual, with "the flogger using every means in
his power to break the spirit of those who suffered, and the sufferers
determined to sustain the punishment unflinchingly," was vivid enough:

> The knout was made of the hardest whipcord, of an unusual size. The
> cord was put into salt water till it was saturated; it was then put into the
> sun to dry; by this process it became like wire, the eighty-one knots
> cutting the flesh as if a saw had been used.

Charles O'Hara Booth, Frost claimed, "would often witness this punishment with as much indifference as if he were looking at some philosophical experiment."[58]

He would also muster the convicts to witness floggings, a practice
that the Quaker missionaries Backhouse and Walker felt "has an exasperating effect upon bystanders" and risked provoking a general mutiny, "in spite of the military Guards; the Prisoners present at these
times being between six and seven hundred and the Guard but forty
in number."[59]

Booth had solitary cells built, and special punishment cells, 7 feet by
4 feet and pitch dark, where "the occupant is not even allowed a knife to
eat his food. . . . They throw in to him in the dark, as they would to a
dog, a little food, and there is nothing but an old rug for him to lie upon.
If he is wet he is obliged to remain in his wet clothes until the following
morning." Nights are cold on the Tasman Peninsula. For less "atrocious"
offenders there were boxes like dog-kennels where the prisoner was
chained, breaking stones from a pile in front of him; and if the irons were
not heavy enough to suit his sins, he would go with "the log on his toes,"
with a heavy balk of timber attached to his ankle-irons that he dragged
as he walked.[60]

To scrutinize into the punishment records of Port Arthur men is to
look into a microcosm of harsh, bureaucratic tedium. Its horror comes
not from unrestrained cruelty (as the Gothic legends and popular horror
stories of the place insisted) but rather from its opposite, the mechanical
apportioning of strictly metered punishments designed to wear each prisoner down into bovine acceptance—Arthur's criterion of moral reform.
It is like looking into the memory of some dull god interminably counting fallen sparrows on his fingers. Here, as a sample, is three years from
the punishment record of a Scottish horse-thief named Robert William-

son, born in 1812, who was sentenced to fourteen years' transportation at Inverness in 1832, arrived in Van Diemen's Land on the *John Barry* in 1834 and later that year was sentenced to seven years in Port Arthur for the extreme unwisdom of stealing a pea-jacket and other nautical gear from Arthur's former attorney-general, now a judge of the Supreme Court and passionate amateur yachtsman, Algernon Sidney Montagu:

1835

JAN. 3RD: Having a file in his possession: 6 weeks in Chain Gang.

FEB. 21ST: Neglect of Duty while at work: 6 weeks in Chain Gang.

MARCH 28TH: Breaking gaol and absenting himself without leave from the Public Works at Port Arthur . . . and remaining absent until apprehended this day at Sympathy Point [sic] by a party of Constables and Military: 75 lashes.

MARCH 28TH: Same date—having a variety of Government tools in his possession for the purpose of aiding him in his Escape from the Penitentiary . . . the Settlement Workshop having been broken into: 10 days Solitary Confinement in a Cell at the Coal Mine.

SEPT. 4TH: Absenting himself from his Gang: 10 days Solitary Confine'.

NOV. 6: Absent from his Gang for several hours: 10 Days ditto.

DEC. 3RD: Endeavouring to excite prisoners to Abscond: 6 months in Irons.

DEC. 19: Tampering with his Leg-Iron: 36 lashes.

1836

AUG. 13: Fishing contrary to orders: 3 weeks in Irons.

SEPT. 6: Having a quantity of Vegetables in his Possession: 1 month on chain gang.

SEPT. 20: Idleness: 3 Days Solitary Confine'.

OCT. 10: Idleness: To lodge in a Cell 10 nights.

OCT. 20: Fighting at Work: 48 hrs. solitary Confine'.

DEC. 28: Absenting himself from his Gang without leave: 14 days No. 1 Chaingang.

DEC. 29: Having a Knife improperly in his possession: 3 Days Solitary Confine'.

1837

JULY 15: Having a Towel improperly in his possession: 14 Days No. 2 Chaingang.

SEPT. 18: Making use of a most Grossly Indecent Expression and subsequent malicious Conduct towards a fellow prisoner: 10 Days Solitary Confine'.

OCT. 4: Absenting himself when going to the Hospital: 1 month in No. 2 Chaingang.

Nov. 28: Having a Crayfish in his possession and endeavouring to convey
it into the Gaol: 1 month No. 2 Chaingang.[61]

Charles O'Hara Booth was an active commandant, roaming on foot
and horseback through the bush of the Tasman Peninsula to drive his
favorite projects along: a coal mine; a semaphore system that could communicate with Hobart; and the first Australian railway, powered not by
steam but by convicts. But first he had to attend to the security system
at Eaglehawk Neck, where Arthur had posted a permanent guard-station
in 1831, after prisoners started escaping in numbers two years before
Booth's arrival. This wasp-waisted isthmus between the surf of Pirate's
Bay and the calm of Norfolk Bay, less than 100 yards wide, was the key
to Port Arthur; it was and still is the only way a man could leave the
Tasman Peninsula by land. Getting across it, therefore, became an obsessive focus of convict ingenuity. They walked, crept, ran, waded and even
hopped. One prisoner, a former actor named William Hunt, "who in his
younger days had belonged to a company of strolling mountebanks,"
disguised himself as an enormous "boomer" or male kangaroo. He nearly
got across to Forestier's Peninsula before two picket-guards, thinking he
really was a kangaroo, spotted him and gave chase, levelling their muskets. "Don't shoot, I am only Billy Hunt," the nervous marsupial
squeaked, to their consternation.[62]

Booth soon put a stop to such doings. His "prudent measures," Lemprière acknowledged, "have . . . rendered every attempt futile, nor does
it appear that any man effected the passage across." Eaglehawk Neck was
dotted with sandy hummocks, which gave cover to an escaping man
creeping by; and the surf blotted out the sound of footsteps. In 1832,
before Booth arrived, the ensign in charge of the guard there had the
smart idea of putting a string of nine tethered guard dogs across the Neck.
To this line he added a row of oil lamps, which shed their light on a
white band of crushed cockle-shells; these primitive searchlights made
it still more difficult for a bolter to pass at night without his shadow
being spotted, even if he got past the dogs. Booth increased the guard to
twenty-five men, built guardhouses and sentry-boxes, and doubled the
number of dogs. "Whether Port Arthur is an 'Earthly Hell' or not," Lemprière ponderously quipped, "it has at all events its Cerberus . . . [T]hese
dogs form an impassable line."[63] When convicts started trying to wade
out into the water to get past the line, Booth put more dogs on platforms
out from the shore. There may have been some truth to the legend that
the guards habitually dumped offal and blood off the beaches to draw
sharks, since there was a slaughtering-station a few miles away on
Forestier's Peninsula. But perhaps they just told the convicts they did.

To warn of escapes and crises in Port Arthur, and to receive messages from Hobart, Booth set up a chain of signal stations, the first long-range communication system in Australia. It was a "telegraph" without electricity, run by semaphores: tall poles set on hilltops and islands, each carrying three sets of double arms like railway signals. By a system of chains, each arm could be set at various angles, and each angle was allotted a numerical meaning. The number-groups translated into words, phrases and whole sentences through a codebook. Booth spent years of midnight oil on his signal book, which eventually contained thousands of number-groups referring to such matters as names, weather, runaway prisoners, supplies, tools, weapons, disease, food, places, measurements and distances. By 1844, the book listed 11,300 signals, which could be sent to Hobart through a relay of twenty-two stations perched on coastal headlands and islands around Storm Bay. In clear weather, it took less than half an hour to waggle a message to Hobart from Booth's transmitter, a wooden pole as high as a ship's mast, which dominated the settlement at Port Arthur. Local semaphores on the Tasman Peninsula could flash the news of a bolting convict from Port Arthur to Eaglehawk Neck in one minute flat.[64]

Deep in the sandstone about fifteen miles from Eaglehawk Neck, on the western side of Norfolk Bay, there was a seam of coal. What more chastening form of extra punishment than to turn convicts into miners, condemned to hard labor, darkness, extreme confinement and hourly fear of cave-ins? So Arthur reasoned, and told Booth to sink shafts there, worked by the most refractory prisoners. Before long, the commandant had built a large stone barracks for 170 men, whose apricot-colored ruins, fretted by wind and weather and underpinned by cramped, half-collapsed isolation cells, still gaze picturesquely over Norfolk Bay. The mineshafts, behind, are long closed. Working in them was much dreaded. Only eleven miners could attack the seam at a time, and each had to hew 30 trolleys-full or 2½ tons of coal a day. The deeper of the shafts was 100 feet below sea level, and seepage was a constant problem. Lumps of Port Arthur coal kept alight "for an incredible length of time," but "when at first lighted they crack and throw out small pieces in great quantities, to the detriment of carpets, furniture, ladies' gowns, etc." Nevertheless the fuel sold in Hobart for one-third the price of New South Wales coal and was in great demand.[65]

Booth's inventiveness shone forth, however, not from his mines but from his railway. It was a true curiosity, a small landmark in the history of transportation—in either sense of that word. It connected the dock at the head of Norfolk Bay, by Eaglehawk Neck, to the main settlement at Port Arthur some 4½ miles away. On it, supplies and people could be taken to the coal mines and the Neck without a long detour by sea around the peninsula. It was laid along a switchback route through the dense gum-and-fern forest; sawn hardwood rails about 6 inches by 3 inches were nailed to rough sleepers bedded in clay. Wooden bridges carried the line across the gullies. It had no engine; the power was supplied by convicts, propelling it at a trot, pushing against crossbars at front and rear. Its carriages were four-passenger carts, running on cast-iron mine-truck wheels. Such was the first passenger railway in Australia. It embarrassed some visitors, but on the other hand it was better than walking, especially for the ladies. The trucks of Booth's railway could rattle downhill at 30 mph, a terrifying velocity at a time when people seldom went faster than a trotting horse. Colonel Godfrey Mundy, a visitor to Port Arthur in 1851, described how the convicts pushed the cart up to the top of "a long descent,"

> when, gettting up their steam, down they rattled at tremendous speed—
> tremendous, at least, to lady-like nerves—the chains around their ankles
> chinking and clanking as they trotted along.... [T]he runners jumped
> upon the side of the trucks in rather unpleasant proximity with the pas-
> sengers, and away we all went, bondsmen and freemen, jolting and sway-
> ing ... a man sitting behind contrived, more or less, to lock a wheel
> with a wooden crowbar when the descent became so rapid as to call for
> remonstrance.

In a more pensive mood, Lieutenant-Governor Sir William Denison rode a similar convict railway at Ralph Bay Neck while on an official tour of inspection of Tasman Peninsula in 1847: "I must say that my feelings at seeing myself seated, and pushed along by these miserable convicts, were not very pleasant. It was painful to see them in the condition of slaves, which, in fact, they are, waiting for me up to their knees in water."[66]

It must have given the children pause, too. For Port Arthur was not only a prison for the errant mature; it was also a school for young boys.

v

THE VISITOR to Port Arthur in the 1830s and 1840s rarely failed to take a boat across Opossum Bay to a neck of land named Point Puer, where he could see, "climbing among the rocks and hiding or disappearing from our sight like land-crabs in the West Indies," a colony of ragged pale-faced lads.[67]

Point Puer was aptly named, *puer* being Latin for "boy." It was a prison for children between nine and eighteen years of age who, caught in the inexorable mechanism of British law, had been transported to Van Diemen's Land. "Little depraved felons" was Arthur's word for them. By the mid-1830s, they were arriving in disconcerting numbers, as the gross influx of transported felons steadily grew. Thus, out of 1,434 convicts disembarked at Hobart between January and September 1834, 240 were juveniles. In all, more than 2,000 such boys were transported to Van Diemen's Land and went to the reformatory at Point Puer.[68]

The problem for Arthur and his three-man Board of Assignment was what to do with them. They were, to the last boy, either too young or too ignorant to have a trade or to be of the slightest use to a settler. These bewildered tykes, many of them hardened in theft and flashness, for whom no place could be found in the assignment system, were a dead weight on the government. Some were helpless, Arthur recognized, from "having been thrown upon the world totally destituted, others have become so from the tutelage of dissolute parents—and others have been agents of dexterous thieves about London—but all are objects of compassion."[69]

In 1833, sixty-eight such lads were vegetating in the Prisoners' Barracks in Hobart, and Arthur's "compassion" expressed itself by sending them all to the Tasman Peninsula. They arrived in January 1834, all of them drunk, for on the ship they had broken into a six-dozen crate of wine and shared it with the adult convicts on board. After a sharp lecture from Commandant Booth, they were put in a large, drafty temporary barracks rigidly segregated from the main settlement, so that the adult prisoners would have no chance to "contaminate" them. Point Puer was well isolated, with a shoreline consisting mainly of sixty-foot cliffs and the sea around it full of boiling rips and dangerous currents—"a wretched, bleak, barren spot without water, wood for fuel or an inch of soil that is not . . . utterly valueless." It would improve along with its inmates, or so the System assumed.[70]

The juvenile population at Port Arthur climbed rapidly. By the end of 1834, Booth had 161 boys under his eye; in 1836, 271; and in 1837, a special transport ship, the *Frances Charlotte*, was dispatched from England at the benevolent suggestion of Lord John Russell, with 139 boys and 10 adult overseers on board. By 1842, there were 716 lads on this dismal neck of land, and a jumble of barracks, workrooms and schoolrooms had grown up to shelter them.

They were to be schooled, taught trades, instructed in the truths of Christianity, and punished. "Keep in mind that these boys have been very wicked," wrote Arthur to Booth in 1834, in the ominous accents of Dickens's Wackford Squeers; "the utmost care should be taken to enforce upon their minds the disgraceful condition in which they are placed, whilst every effort should be made to eradicate their corrupt habits." He did not want to see too much time wasted in "instructing the boys in reading and writing." They needed practical skills, which would make useful assigned servants of them. They would acquire these from a hard daily grind. Up at 5:00 a.m., fold hammocks, assembly, Bible reading and prayer; breakfast at 7:00, hygiene inspection, muster, and classes in practical trades like joinery or bootmaking from 8:00 to 12:00. At midday, ablutions and another inspection; at 12:30, dinner; from 1:30 to 5:00, more apprentice work; wash and inspection again, and supper at 5:30; muster for school at 6:15; then school lessons for an hour, followed by evening prayers and Scripture reading, and bed at 7:30. Later the time for schoolwork in the evening was increased to two hours; it made little difference, however, as most of the boys were by then too fatigued to learn anything much.

The most successful part of this regime was the trade instruction, which was remarkably diverse. By 1837 it included baking, shoemaking, carpentry, tailoring, gardening, nail-making and blacksmithery. Enrollment in trade classes was limited, and most boys wanted to get into them. "As vacancies occur," reported Booth, "the better disposed are selected to be placed at a trade, which is eagerly sought after." They were anxious to get out of the laboring gangs, where every new arrival at Point Puer was introduced to "the use of the spade, the hoe and the grubbing-axe." Boys in the laboring gangs did the donkey-work of Point Puer—the cleaning and scrubbing, the fetching and carrying—and they were worked hard; it may be no coincidence that, out of thirty-eight boys who died at Point Puer in the years 1834 to 1843, twenty-two were laborers. To be a sawyer or a joiner was far better. It also meant free skilled (or semi-skilled) labor for the Establishment, of the kind noted in the Port Arthur returns:

> Construction of wheel-barrows, four cells, five coffins, 390 hammer-handles, six barrack stools, 13 school desks, 4 garden gates, and one set of stocks, and a pillory.
> Turning of 216 masons' mallets, 20 hat-pins, 50 belaying-pins, 2 bed-posts, and 243 ships' blocks.
> Making 17 pairs of Wellingtons @ 11s. pr., 24 Bluchers @ 5s. a pr., 2 prs. ladies' shoes @ 3s. a pr., 1788 boots, prisoners', @ 4s. pr.

Point Puer boys made the nails, sewed the convicts' "canary" uniforms of yellow and gray wool, painted the fences, forged the ax-heads and shaped the sledgehammer handles with their drawknives; the stonemasons among them laboriously cut the ashlar for the round security towers of Port Arthur, chiselled the moldings and ornamented keystones for the stone arches, hewed the angles of the pediments. The carpentry class made the elaborate pulpit and pews for the large neo-Gothic church, and in 1844 the thirty-four brickmakers turned out 155,000 bricks, some of which—bearing the thumb-marks left by those long-dead adolescents as they pushed the bricks from the sandstock molds—still lie scattered among the ruins of Point Puer.

There is no question that Point Puer boys received a trades education as good as (and probably better than) any they could have hoped to get in England in the 1830s. But their intellectual schooling was rudimentary. In 1842, some boys who had been there two or three years had difficulty reading words of one syllable; their arithmetic was no better. The only readers the pupils had were Bibles, supplied by a Wesleyan mission, and there were a few spelling-books and primers, but never enough; for eight hundred pupils there was "one very small blackboard seldom used" and not even a map of the world. The state of religious instruction was not much better. At first, it had been in the hands of Methodists, who reported in 1836 that "considerable attention is given to the boys' religious instruction and several have been brought under the saving influence of the Gospel"; Backhouse and Walker, the visiting Quakers, vehemently dissented, finding the boys' morals in "a most degraded state." The Wesleyans were replaced in 1837 by an eager young Anglican catechist, Peter Barrow, fresh from running an orphanage for black foundlings on the coast of Sierra Leone. He thought a chaplain could reclaim half or even two-thirds of the Point Puer boys. He failed. Five years later, a few of the boys could parrot bits of an Anglican catechism, but none could recite the Commandments in correct order or show much grasp of scriptural history. Even their hymn-singing had declined, to the point that "the screaming is almost intolerable to any person whose ears have not been rendered callous."[71]

The likelihood of producing good little Christians at such a place was slight. Like any borstal or boarding-school, Point Puer had not one but two social systems: an official one imposed by the commandant and the chaplain, and a tribal one invented by the boys. Benjamin Horne, reporting on the place in 1842, mentioned "a sort of tyranny of public opinion amongst themselves which every boy in the place must submit to as a slave, almost at peril of his life . . . [T]he maxim of the whole fraternity was that everyone must tell as many lies [to overseers and other authorities] as may be necessary for himself and the community."[72]

The boy who ratted on his fellow prisoners would be persecuted and hazed half to death. The Point Puer boys had no reason to like their jailers; and although conditions there were at least no worse than an English orphanage or ragged-school, they were little better and its inmates loathed them. In particular, the boys hated the convict overseers as tyrants. If an overseer fell asleep on night dormitory watch, the lads would put out the lights and empty the communal chamber pot over his head. One especially unpopular overseer was so battered in such a nocturnal scuffle that he spent three months in the hospital. In 1843 one overseer, Hugh McGine, was murdered by a pair of fourteen-year-olds named Henry Sparks and George Campbell.[73]

If a boy at Point Puer found a middle way between the strictures of Authority and the pressure of his peers and managed to learn a trade, he could come out with a better chance of making good than most assigned men; if not, the System would simply grind him down. So it was with Thomas Willetts, a stunted boy of sixteen from Warwick, transported in 1834 for filching some stockings and garden vegetables, who in the course of five years at Point Puer and Port Arthur racked up a total of 35 lashes from the full cat-o'-nine tails, 183 strokes of the cane on his butt and 19 sentences of solitary confinement.

THOMAS WILLETTS N° 1809

tried 12 March 1833, arr^d V.D.L. Augt 1834.

Trade: None.	Height: 4 ft. 11 in.
Complex^n: Dark	Head: Small
Hair: Brown	Whiskers: None
Visage: Small	Forehead: M. Ht.
Eyebrows: Brown	Eyes: Grey
Nose: Small	Mouth: Med. Wide
Chin: Small	Remarks: Pockmarked, scar on Rt. Arm.

Arrived in Van Diemen's Land August 1834.
Convict. 7 Years' Transportation.
Tried at Warwick, transported for stealing Stockings.
Character—*Very Bad.*

1834

DEC^r 30TH: Assaulting fellow prisoner & attempt to deprive him of his bread: 24 lashes on the breech.

1835

SEPT. 9: Transferred to Port Arthur.
SEPT. 28: Improper & riotous conduct in the Cells: 15 lashes on the breech.
OCT. 21: Swearing, etc.: 7 days solitary confinement.
NOV. 18: Having Tobacco: 5 days ditto

1836

FEB. 22: Having turnips, 5 days ditto
NOV. 3: Insolent conduct to Overseer, 4 days ditto

Nov. 7: Talking in cells, 3 days ditto

Dec' 26: Most improper conduct to the Ass' Sub-Constable in the Execution of his Duty: 36 stripes.

1837

Jan 26: Fighting in the Schoolroom, 3 Days Solitary, Bread & Water.

Feb. 18: Disorderly Conduct in School on Sunday, 5 Days ditto, ditto.

March 20: Having a pair of Fustian Trowsers in his possession and most Improper Conduct towards the Assist. Sub-Constable: 36 Stripes on the Breech.

Same date: Most Contemptuous Conduct in laughing immediately on leaving the Office after Sentence for the preceding Offence: 7 days' solitary confinement on bread & water.

May 29: Having a pair of Boots improperly: 4 Days Solit' Conf'.

June 26: Smoking in his hut contrary to orders: 3 weeks in No. 2 Chain Gang.

Sept. 2nd: Gross Misconduct & Violence to Schoolmaster: 36 Stripes on the breech.

1838

Jan 17: Insolence: 3 Days solitary Confinement, Bread & Water.

March 16: Gross insolence, 7 days ditto.

April 19: Improper Conduct towards a fellow Boy: 10 days ditto.

June 25: Talking in church during Divine Service, 48 hrs. sol' conf' on B^d & W'.

July 7: Striking a fellow prisoner: 36 Stripes on the breech.

July 28: Talking in the Cells and Insolence when checked, 3 days solitary, B^d & W'.

August 3: Having his Face disgracefully disfigured, 48 hrs. sol' conf^mt.

August 16: Gross indecency on his going to the cells, 4 days ditto.

October 1st: Absenting himself without leave from Public Works at Port Arthur and remaining absent until apprehended and brought back: 7 days ditto.

1839

March 5: Absconding: 35 lashes.

March 20: Absconding: 2 years hard labour in Chain Gang, Port Arthur —conduct to be reported to Lieutenant Governor.

July 18: Disorderly Conduct: 24 hrs. solitary conf'.

Oct' 9: Having a Silk Stock in possession improperly: 1 month on No. 2 Chain Gang.

Dec 5: Neglect of Duty and refusing to work: 1 month ditto.[74]

On skins like his, the flaws of Arthur's system were glaringly inscribed. But however wretched the life of the "incorrigible," the "fractious" and the "refractory" could be made at Port Arthur, their sufferings were slight compared to the fate of the Tasmanian Aborigines under Arthur's reign.

vi

COLONEL ARTHUR'S last big problem was the Tasmanian blacks; and he was theirs. By 1824, the year he came to Van Diemen's Land, a vicious, undeclared and seemingly unfinishable guerrilla war had been dragging on between whites and blacks for two decades. Its first shots were fired at Risdon Cove in 1804, a few months after the first landing. Years later, Edward White, a former convict, told a Committee for Aboriginal Affairs how it had been. On May 3, 1804, he was hoeing ground by the creek when a party of some three hundred Aborigines, men, women and children, came out of the bush, driving a mob of kangaroos before them. The blacks were strung out in a big crescent, between the 'roos and the water. They carried clubs but no spears, and White saw that they were not a war-party; all they meant to do was kill the cornered game, build their fires and have a corroborree. He remembered how "they looked at me with all their eyes . . . [they] did not threaten me; I was not afraid of them." Nevertheless he ran off to tell the soldiers, who loaded their muskets and marched on the tribespeople. "The Natives did not attack the soldiers; they would not have molested them." Nevertheless the soldiers trained a carronade on them point-blank and blasted them with grapeshot. Nobody counted how many of the unarmed blacks were slaughtered, but at the end of the massacre the colonial surgeon Jacob Mountgarrett, prompted by some anthropological whim, salted down a couple of casks of their bones and sent them to Sydney.[75]

There may have been four thousand Aborigines in Van Diemen's Land when the whites landed; by Arthur's time there were considerably fewer, although it is hardly possible to guess how many. Perhaps ten blacks were killed for every white, perhaps twenty. At first the dirty little war sputtered its way around Hobart and the banks of the Derwent, as settlers in the starvation years competed against blacks for the kangaroos. Sometimes whites killed blacks for sport. In 1806 two early bushrangers, John Brown and Richard Lemon, "used to stick them, and fire at them as marks whilst alive." Another escaped convict, James Carrott or Carrett, abducted an Aborigine's wife near Oyster Bay, killed her husband when he came after them, cut off his head and forced her to wear it slung around her neck in a bag "as a plaything."[76] There were rumors that kangaroo-hunters would shoot blacks to feed their dogs. Two whites cut the cheek off an aboriginal boy and forced him to chew and swallow it. At Oatlands, north of Hobart, convict stock-keepers kept aboriginal women as sexual slaves, secured by bullock-chains to their huts. On the Bass Strait coast, marauding sealers would try to buy women from the tribes; the usual offer was four or five sealskins for a woman, but if the Aborigines would not sell, they would shoot the men and kidnap the women. When one of these women tried to run away from the sealers, they trussed her up, cut off her ears and some flesh from her thigh and made her eat it. All this and more, the convict pioneer James Hobbes remarked, with some understatement, "was known by the tribes, and operated on their minds."[77]

The pattern of violence between black and white in Van Diemen's Land was fully established by 1815. It went on against a background of proclamations by the lieutenant-governor—Collins, Davey and Sorell all issued them—enjoining the settlers not to provoke or persecute the blacks and stressing that they had the full protection of English law. Their utterances weighed nothing against the reality of invasion: The whites were on the blacks' land, and grabbing as much of it as they could. No colonists were prepared to consider such two-legged animals as beings with prior rights.

So the war of random encounter inexorably changed into one of extermination, as the settlements and the stock-pastures spread. The late 1820s began a roaring boom in sheep-farming and wool exports. Some stock-breeders got three lambings every two years. In 1827 there were 436,256 sheep in Van Diemen's Land. By 1830 there were 682,128, an increase of more than 55 percent. By 1836 the ovine population had risen by another third, to 911,357—20 sheep for every white person in the colony. The export figures, in pounds sterling, tell their own story of growth:[78]

YEAR	GROSS EXPORTS	WOOL EXPORTS
1825	£ 44,498	£ 12,543
1827	59,912	9,089
1830	141,745	57,724
1832	152,967	63,145
1836	540,221	220,739

This new prosperity affected the look, the self-esteem, the very fiber of Vandemonian life. "Trade flourishes exceedingly," wrote Richard Stickney, a Quaker emigrant, to his sister Sarah in 1834; there are

rows of shops in the first London style and elegant houses are springing up like magic. The Sperm Whale fishery is carried on successfully and to a great extent, whilst Wool is becoming a greatly increasing article of export. The peach tree is loaded with fruit without the aid of a gardener. . . . I don't think England has a colony where everything appears so much like home as this. The scarcety of the Black Natives, . . . the excellent roads, the fashionable appearance of the well-dressed inhabitants, carriages without number and good horses. It really has not the dull look of a Colony at all but the bustle and activity of an English seaport. A stranger might easily fancy himself in England.[79]

In 1829 the "scarcety of the Black Natives" was not so pronounced, and no savages would be allowed to interfere with growth. But the sheep were destroying the Aborigines' food base by displacing kangaroos and other game. By the late 1820s, retaliatory raids by tribesmen against sheep had become a constant nuisance: They speared the stock and left them dead on the ground, often without eating them, as a sign of contempt; they robbed and burned outlying huts and, although frontal attacks on homesteads were rare, they kept convict shepherds in continuous terror. Out of these scattered forays, by 1829, a general strategy seemed to be emerging. The idea that they had developed "a systematic plan of attacking the settlers and their possessions," thought Archdeacon Broughton, chairman of a committee convened in 1830 by Arthur to inquire into the causes of black hostility to white settlers, "has been but too completely verified by the events of the last two years. . . . It is manifest that they have lost the sense of the superiority of white men, and the dread of the effect of fire-arms."[80]

The Aborigines had learned not to attack en masse, charging into the muzzles of the settlers' guns. Instead, they harassed the periphery of settlement, the stock-huts and shepherds' cottages. In the first three months of 1830, there were almost thirty such incidents, involving the death of eight whites. The tribesmen set fire to thatched roofs to drive the whites into the open. They lured stockmen into the bush away from their huts where they could be more easily killed, and the undefended hut was plundered and burned. Then the blacks would melt away into the hills, where few whites could catch up with them. One settler, Gilbert Robertson, complained that there was no "effectual mode of pursuing them. . . . [T]hey cannot be surrounded by several parties coming upon them; they go all over the whole island; they always keep regular sentries, and pass over dangerous grounds, and by the brinks of the most dangerous precipices." He had a low opinion of the soldiers' ability to pursue the black marauder, declaring that they were "quite useless . . . they will not exert themselves." Settlers, police and convicts did better. Sometimes they hunted tribal groups down like kangaroos, shooting them from horseback; but the efficient way to catch up with the Aborigines was to follow them by night and mark their campfire smoke in the morning. One party of five or six constables from Campbell Town, according to Robertson (although his story was indignantly denied by other whites), ambushed an encampment of natives in a gully between two cliffs and slaughtered seventy of them; and when the gunsmoke cleared, they went down among the rocks, dragged out the terrified women and children and brained them. This, he thought, put paid to the whole tribe.[81]

When whites did such things, they showed necessary rigor; when Aborigines threw their spears from ambush, they proved their treachery. Whites "defended their interests," while blacks "perpetrated atrocities" and "committed the most wanton and unprovoked acts of barbarity." Faced with the black resistance, the settlers began sliding toward panic. Arthur, after a long and searching field trip among the agitated settlers of the outer districts that had borne the brunt of aboriginal resistance, noted a curious passivity in them. "The indifference . . . is quite remarkable, and strikingly manifests that people are always much more ready to complain of evils than disposed to exert themselves to overcome them." Instead of whingeing, he thought, they should get guns and learn to use them—"the only security which can be given, unless a safety-guard were placed in every dwelling, a thing which is impossible."[82]

Arthur's Committee for Aboriginal Affairs knew where the real blame for this ghastly situation lay, and declared that "every degree of moderation and forbearance" was due to the "ignorant, debased and un-reflecting" blacks, so cruelly wronged by "miscreants who were a disgrace to our name and nation." But on the other hand, one had to admit that "the Natives are now visiting the injuries they have received, not on the actual defenders, but on a different and *totally innocent* class." This reflected Arthur's own delusion that the only people to blame for the murder and harassment of the Aborigines were escaped convicts, sealers and other colonial trash—never the respectable settlers, who "always" showed "kindness and humanity."[83]

Some of these colonial innocents aired brisk and strong views on how to handle the blacks. "They must be captured or exterminated," opined John Sherwin, merchant, whose house on the River Clyde near Bothwell had just been burned to the ground. He said that others (not he) had proposed setting up "decoy huts, containing flour and sugar, strongly impregnated with poison." He claimed he did not know of any atrocities whites had done to blacks; all that was exaggeration. But if they did not take steps soon, by bringing in blacktrackers and bloodhounds from Sydney and hunting the pests down, no one could live in the bush, for "the Natives wish to have their lands to themselves." His fellow settler George Espie wanted to see 150 armed convicts sent after the natives, with a promise of a ticket-of-leave for every two or three blacks a man brought in —"they would shoot more than they would capture." Roderic O'Connor, a red-hot Irishman who accumulated vast estates while serving Arthur as magistrate and land commissioner, growled that armed posses of convicts might do the trick; he knew of one man named Douglas Ibbets who had wiped out half the "Eastern mob" of natives with his double-barrelled shotgun. "Some of the worst characters would be the best to send after them." An elderly farmer named Brodribb claimed he knew of no rational cause for the blacks' new ferocity, that most settlers treated them kindly, that he really "cannot form an idea if the Natives are displeased at our taking possession of the country"—and so on.[84]

The Aborigines, in fact, were in their last frenzy of resistance. In 1828 Arthur reported to Goderich that "I have been pressingly called upon by the settlers . . . to adopt some measure which should free them from these troublesome assailants, and from the nuisance of their dogs."[85] He felt he had to take "some decisive step," and he thought the most likely one was to round them all up and put them—every last Aborigine on Van Diemen's Land—on one of the islands in Bass Strait, give them temporary rations, teach them to raise crops and so convert them by force from nomadic hunter-gatherers into a "stationary . . . civilization." But he realized it would not work:

> They already complain that the white people have taken possession of their country, encroached upon their hunting grounds, and destroyed their natural food, the kangaroo; and they doubtless would be exasperated to the last degree to be banished altogether from their favourite haunts; and as they would be ill-disposed to receive instructions from their oppressors, any attempt to civilize them . . . must fail.[86]

Besides, Arthur knew where the blame lay: "All aggression originated with the white inhabitants, and . . . much ought to be endured in return before the blacks are treated as an open and accredited enemy by the government."

So instead of sending them to a miserable death on an island, Arthur proposed an early form of *apartheid* to keep them out of the settled districts. His idea was to round them up and move them all to the northeast coast of Van Diemen's Land, "the best sheltered and warmest part," where they would be fed and clothed by the government and protected from the annihilating fury of white farmers.

He issued a proclamation. It repeated what everyone knew: that the whites (especially convicts: shepherds, stockmen and sealers) were the first aggressors, but that now the black resistance was making "advances in art, system and method." So ways must be found to "restrict the intercourse" between white and black "by a legislative Enactment, of a permanent nature"—putting them beyond a pale of settlement in the northeastern corner. In the meantime, there would be a line of military guard posts stationed along the confines of the settled districts, which the Aborigines must not cross:

> And I do hereby strictly command and order all Aborigines immediately to retire and depart from, and for no reason, and on no pretence, save as hereinafter provided, to re-enter such settled districts, or any portions of land cultivated and occupied by any person whomsoever, on pain of forcible expulsion therefrom, and such consequences as may be necessarily attendant on it.[87]

This magnificently festooned slab of imperial boilerplate meant nothing to the blacks, who could not read and kept striking back against their white tormentors as best they could, while suffering the "necessarily attendant" consequences.

So Arthur proclaimed martial law against the Aborigines in the settled center of the island. It would not extend to designated outer areas, to which he hoped the blacks would drift—the Tasman Peninsula, the northeast and southwest corners, all the country south of Mount Wellington to the ocean including Bruny Island, and the whole western coast.[88] This must have seemed a fair deal to Arthur, since the "settled districts" had few kangaroos left and could not support the traditional forms of aboriginal life, whereas the areas he had exempted from martial law and hoped to push the blacks into were wild, untrammelled, unlikely ever to be settled, full of game, and constituted about half the land area of Van Diemen's Land. But the Aborigines did not think it fair.

Meanwhile, the whites kept slaughtering the blacks, women and children usually first, with musket and fowling piece, cutlass and ax. By 1830, there were perhaps two thousand Aborigines left alive in Van Diemen's Land.[89] Some settlers took Arthur's proclamation of martial law as a license to kill. In February 1830 Arthur's colonial secretary tried to recall them to a sense of measure and proportion:

> The repeated orders which have been put forth by this Government must convey the idea . . . that there exists a horde of savages in Van Diemen's Land whose prowess is equal to their revengeful feelings; thereas every settler must be conscious that his foe consists of an inconsiderable number of a very feeble race, not possessing physical strength, and quite undistinguished by personal courage.[90]

But the pressure on Arthur to solve the "black problem" was intense, and he must have reflected that a solution would amend his own extreme unpopularity with the colonists, for people will love an autocrat if they believe he is a savior. Suppressing the Aborigines was the only major issue on which every settler in Van Diemen's Land was ready to work with Arthur and the military. "How cordially and entirely the whole community unite with the earnest desire of the Government!" he reported to Murray in London.[91]

Reading Arthur's reports in London, Sir George Murray, secretary of state for the colonies, had felt a tingle of premonition: "The whole race of [Van Diemen's Land Aborigines] may, at no distant period, become extinct. . . . [A]ny line of conduct, having for its avowed, or for its secret object, the extinction of the Native race, could not fail to leave an indelible stain upon the character of the British Government."[92]

Arthur decided to bring every white—settlers as well as military—into one concerted effort to expel the aboriginal tribes from the settled areas of the island, where they had become such a menace to Europeans, and bottle them up in the Tasman Peninsula, between Forestier's Neck and Eaglehawk Neck, where they could be kept imprisoned forever by a small garrison at either end. This operation was called the Black Line. He may not have expected it to succeed; it was, as Robson rightly called it, "an excellent public relations exercise to show that the highly unpopular Arthur apparently had the welfare of the colonists at heart."[93] But if he wanted to preserve any loyalty among the colonists, he had little choice. The settlements were almost hysterical with fear that the coming spring of 1830 would produce a bloodbath. The Big River and Oyster Bay tribes had become "too much enjoined in the most rancorous animosity to be spared the most vigorous measures against them."[94] In a meeting with his Executive Council late in August 1830, Arthur succumbed to the pressure and agreed to a spring offensive against the Big River and Oyster Bay tribes.

It took the form of an immense pheasant-drive, under the command of Major Douglas of the 63rd Regiment. Every white man in Van Diemen's Land, Arthur reported to London, joined in it "with the most zealous and cheerful alacrity."[95] The main line of hunters stretched across two-thirds of the island, from St. Patricks' Head on the east coast to Quamby Bluff in the Western Tiers; it was supported by two flanking lines, one in the east and the other in the southwest, to catch any Aborigines who slipped by the ends of the main line. Some 2,200 men formed the Black Line—550 troops from the 17th, 57th and 63rd Regiments, 700 convicts, and the rest free settlers. They carried between them a thousand muskets, 30,000 rounds of ammunition and 300 pairs of handcuffs with which to subdue the resistant natives. Off they set on October 7, 1830: redcoats sweltering in their woollen uniforms under the load of knapsacks and muskets, mounted dragoons plodding forward in a clink of steel and a creaking of leather, stout farmers with their fowling pieces, cornstalk boys with red faces and hard eyes. Keeping the line as best they could, they surged slowly downward toward the Tasman Peninsula along paths determined for them by the officers of the Survey Department, hallooing and cursing and beating the bush for its black wraiths, firing musketry into the air and blowing bugles. Their movements, Arthur reported, were "much better executed than could have been anticipated." At night the bush flickered with guard fires and one man in three stood sentry duty to prevent the escape of the crafty foe."

It took the Black Line seven weeks to converge, like the closing of a fishing net, on the peninsula. A few Aborigines were spotted, and there were some brief skirmishes; two Oyster Bay tribesmen were captured and two others shot, but Arthur was certain that the main mass of them were fleeing ahead of the Black Line toward the Tasman Peninsula. "The forces are now . . . moving forward in full hopes of success," he reported from the town of Sorell on November 20, 1830.

When the net closed, it was empty. The Black Line had caught two Aborigines, a man and a small boy. All the rest had slipped through. The enterprise had been a fiasco, and for once Arthur's detailed and prolix reports to London became terse, almost evasive. Yet the Big River tribe had been driven into comparative seclusion beyond the Western Tiers, and the Oyster Bay tribesmen were split up and forced from their habitual territory; so, from the whites' point of view, the episode could be called a strategic victory, even though it did not produce all the results Arthur hoped for. It also suggested that there were fewer Aborigines in the settled districts than Major Douglas had supposed.[96] This did wonders for the settlers' morale. Arthur felt he could move from a military solution to one of "pacification." This new strategy took the mild, quietly convivial and persistent form of an emigrant house-builder from London, George Augustus Robinson (1788–1866), the "Conciliator."[97]

Robinson had been interested in the Aborigines from the moment he arrived in Van Diemen's Land. He had a philanthropic vision: He would bring these chafed and resentful people, by mildness and understanding, into the fold of white law and religion—but not before he, unlike all previous missionaries and go-betweens, had come to understand their ways and language. In 1828, in the lull before the final desperate retaliations of the black tribes, Arthur had advertised for a man who might be able to conciliate them. Robinson had put himself forward and was accepted. He tried to evangelize the blacks on Bruny Island in 1829, but his real work began the following year, when he went on an arduous eight-month trek into the wilderness of the southwest and west coast searching for surviving tribal groups of Aborigines. He had a party with him made up of trusty convict servants, an aboriginal chief from Bruny Island named Woorrady and another from the Swanport district named Eumar-rah, four black tribesmen and three women.

One of the latter was a bright, promiscuous girl named Trucanini, about eighteen years old, also from Bruny Island.[98] She was very small, only 4 feet 3 inches high, and had pronounced curly whiskers; in other respects, all white witnesses agreed, she was remarkably attractive—for an Aborigine. As a child, she had seen her mother stabbed to death in a night raid by whites; later, a sealer named John Baker had kidnapped two of her tribal sisters and her blood sister, Moorina, and taken them in slavery to the tribe of white pirates that lived on Kangaroo Island, far to the west off the coast of South Australia. Her stepmother was abducted by the convict mutineers of the brig *Cyprus* and must have died as they were seeking China; she was never heard from again. Around 1828, she was crossing from the mainland to Bruny Island with several tribesmen, to one of whom she was "betrothed," in a boat manned by two convict loggers. In mid-channel, the whites seized the black men and threw them overboard; when they grabbed for the gunwale and tried to haul them-selves up, the loggers chopped their hands off and left them to sink. They then rowed her ashore and raped her. Trucanini, one would presume, had every reason to hate the whites. In fact she sought their company there-after and was busy becoming a sealers' moll, sterile from gonorrhea, hanging around the camps and selling herself for a handful of tea and sugar, when Robinson and his guide Woorrady persuaded her to come on their long, strange journey of "conciliation" to the remaining tribes of Van Diemen's Land.

They all set off in the winter of 1830, ill-equipped and badly provi-sioned, and suffered appalling hardships from exposure, hunger and scurvy. But they worked their way around the west coast, from Port Davey to Macquarie Harbor and thence to Cape Grim, the aptly named northwesternmost tip of Van Diemen's Land. From there they struck east along the coast and reached Launceston early in October, just after Arthur's Black Line had begun working south.

Robinson was to venture upon five more such expeditions, and by the end of 1834 Robinson had made contact with every tribe and group of Aborigines left in Tasmania. Always the method was the same: opening civilities with presents and food, and a winning of the shy or hostile blacks' confidence with the help of Woorrady and Trucanini; a compila-tion of their basic vocabularies; notes on their ceremonies and religious customs, as far as he could determine them; a friendly parting, and then a new visit with promises of sanctuary. If they would "come in" with him, the Conciliator told these dying and frightened remnants of their race, they would be given a safe haven where no white man would per-secute them, where they would have food and clothing and peace.

Slowly, the blacks followed him; and when he brought in the last of the once-feared warriors of the Big River and Oyster Bay tribes—a pathetic group of sixteen people—he was greeted like a Roman conqueror in Hobart. A colonial artist, Benjamin Duterreau, painted him posed with "his" Aborigines; the girl on the right, leading a doubtful native by one hand and pointing at Robinson with the other, is Trucanini, the archtraitor to her race.

Thus, by 1834, the last Aborigines of Van Diemen's Land had followed their evangelical Pied Piper into a benign concentration camp, set up on Flinders Island in Bass Strait. There, Robinson planned to Europeanize them. They were given clothes, new names, Bibles and elementary schooling. They were shown how to buy and sell things, so that they might acquire a reverence for property. They were allowed to elect their own police. In the main, however, they simply died—of accidie, deracination and new diseases. In 1835, only 150 Aborigines were left. Little by little, they wasted away and their ghosts drifted out over the water. Robinson left Flinders in 1839 and returned to the Australian mainland. His successors chose to treat Flinders Island as a jail, and its dwindling colony of Aborigines as prisoners. Occasionally a girl would be flogged, but only for moral offenses. In 1843 there were fifty-four Aborigines alive. Three years later, amid blood-curdling prophecies of a new black war from the colonial press, the survivors were returned to the mainland and settled on a property at Oyster Cove on the D'Entrecasteaux Channel, near Hobart. There they guzzled rum, which was thoughtfully provided by their keepers; they posed impassively for photographers in front of their filthy slab huts; and they waited to die. In 1855 the census of natives was three men, two boys and eleven women, one of whom was Trucanini.

The last man died in 1869. His name was William Lanne and he was described as Trucanini's "husband," although he was twenty-three years her junior. Realizing that his remains might have some value as a scientific specimen, rival agents of the Royal College of Surgeons in London and the Royal Society in Tasmania fought over his bones. A Dr. William Crowther, representing the Royal College of Surgeons, sneaked into the morgue, beheaded Lanne's corpse, skinned the head, removed the skull and slipped another skull from a white cadaver into the black skin. This gruesome ruse was soon unmasked, for when a medical officer picked the head up, "the face turned round and at the back of the head the bones were sticking out." In pique, the officials decided not to let the Royal College of Surgeons get the whole skeleton; so they chopped off the feet and hands from Lanne's corpse and threw them away. The lopped, dishonored cadaver of the last tribesman was then officially buried, unofficially exhumed the next night and dissected for its skeleton by representatives of the Royal Society. It was, one of them remarked with some understatement, a "dirty job." Lanne's skeleton then disappeared; and the head, which Crowther consigned by sea to the Royal College of Surgeons, vanished too. It seems that the ineffable doctor had packaged it in a sealskin, and before long the bundle stank so badly that it was tossed overboard.

Trucanini wept and raged inconsolably when she was told of the fate of Lanne's body. She had long been frightened of death and of the evil spirit Rowra who would exact the revenge of the dead tribes she had betrayed; but now a further terror joined those. She begged a clergyman to make sure that when she died, she would be wrapped in a bag with a stone at her feet and dropped into the deepest part of the D'Entrecasteaux Channel—"because I know that when I die, the Tasmanian Museum wants my body." By 1873, the last of her black companions was dead and Trucanini was taken to Hobart, where she lingered on in a wretched aura of colonial celebrity, invented by the whites, as the "Queen of the Aborigines." One May evening in 1876 she was heard to scream, "Missus, Rowra catch me, Rowra catch me!" A stroke felled her, and she lay in coma for five days. Her last words, as the dark peeled back for a moment from her terrified consciousness, were, "Don't let them cut me, but bury me behind the mountains."

The government arranged a funeral procession for the last Tasmanian on May 11, 1876. Huge crowds lined the pavements to watch her small, almost square coffin roll by; they followed it to the cemetery, and saw it lowered into a grave. It was empty. Fearing some unseemly public disturbance, the government had buried her corpse in a vault of the Protestant Chapel in the Hobart Penitentiary the night before. So Trucanini lay not "behind the mountains," but in jail. In 1878 they dug her up again and sloughed the flesh off her bones, then boiled them and nailed them in an apple crate, which lay in storage for some years. The crate was about to be thrown out when someone from the Tasmanian Museum and Art Gallery read the faded label. The bones were strung together, and the skeleton of Trucanini went into a glass case in the museum, where it remained until feelings of public delicacy and humanitarian sentiment caused it to be removed, in 1947, to the basement. In 1976, the centenary of her death, the authorities—not knowing what else to do with this otherwise ineradicable dweller in their closet—had it cremated, and the ashes were scattered on the waters of the D'Entrecasteaux Channel. Just 140 years had passed since the day in 1836 when the virtuous and unbending proconsul, Sir George Arthur, had been ushered weeping onto the *Elphinstone* at the New Wharf and, to the cheers of several hundred free Vandemonians, had sailed away to England, his baronetcy and the deserved gratitude of the Crown.

Metastasis

i

IN 1815, the year Napoleon was crushed and England could once more turn her strength to building an empire, the map of white settlement in New South Wales was hardly more than a patch, consisting only of Sydney and Parramatta. The rest was void, the scarcely penetrated green continuum of bush, with a few tracks winding their frail, dusty capillaries toward inland farms.

By 1825 this had changed. There were specks on the coast north of Sydney—Newcastle, Port Macquarie, Moreton Bay—scattered along a thousand miles of coastline and tenuously linked by ships; and Norfolk Island, which had been abandoned on Macquarie's orders, was resettled.

These little footholds were hamlets of punishment. They had not been created by the hopes of settlers. A growing convict population, and increased severity from the authorities, had forced them into existence. They were, as the phrase went, "the Botany Bay of Botany Bay"—enclaves of banishment in a land of exile. The flood of convicts to Australia had now begun in earnest. From 1820 to 1831 the number of convicts serving sentences there would never be less than 40 percent of the total population. The creation of the penal out-stations was a response to crisis, even though, in practice, less than one prisoner in ten ever served time in one. If Australia was going to scare English criminals, the penal out-stations would have to terrify colonial ones.

By 1825, the English authorities knew—and in fact, had come to accept—that their ways of dealing with crime had failed in the past, were not working now and would be unlikely to succeed in the foreseeable future. The crime rate in England had not dropped; thus one had to conclude that transportation did not deter. The question of "reformation" was not quite as important, since so few people came back from Australia. In 1826, for instance, only about 7 percent of the convicts freed at the end of their sentences chose to return to England, an eloquent comment on what they believed their chances were there.[1]

Nevertheless the criminal-justice system was by now addicted to transportation and had no real alternatives. In 1821 the government had built an experimental penitentiary at Millbank on the Thames, designed to hold eight hundred people—minor criminals, both men and women, whose offenses would have brought them 7 years' transportation. It cost half a million pounds and was a failure; its cold cells and defective drains killed the prisoners like flies. Neither public nor government opinion was ready for wholesale jail reform yet; and, in the meantime, transportation was far cheaper than building new prisons. Besides, the idea of the penitentiary was seen as an American invention; no Tory and few Whigs desired to mimic the ideas of that rebellious ex-colony.

In 1822 the arch-conservative Lord Castlereagh killed himself in a fit of depression and Sir Robert Peel became home secretary. Peel oversaw the removal of some hanging statutes. But what replaced hanging, as punishment, was only more transportation. Peel was a timid reformer and, when it came to thinking about the practical issues of what one did with criminals, his imagination failed. "I admit the inefficiency of transportation to Botany Bay, but the whole subject . . . is full of difficulties," he wrote to the Reverend Sydney Smith. "I can hardly devise anything as a secondary punishment in addition to what we have at present." The hulks were full to bursting with a population of four to five thousand felons. He could not use public chain gangs, for they would "revolt public opinion" and the penitentiary had failed. Only Australia was left to cope with a swelling crime wave. "The real truth is the number of convicts is too overwhelming for the means of proper and effectual punishment."[2]

There must still be a place of terror. About the volume of crime, and therefore of transportation, there was little doubt. After 1815, England began to pay the full price for its recent defeat in war, its collapsing labor relations and a succession of failed harvests. Semi-capitalized industry was destroying the old base of town manufacture, the apprentice system; enclosure and famine were sending the rural workers of England and Ireland into paupery. The crime rate leaped, and with it the numbers of transported convicts. From 1810 to 1814, an average of 678 felons a year went to Australia; this mere trickle could easily be absorbed, as unskilled labor, by the assignment system. But from 1815 to 1819, the yearly average trebled, to 2,090; from 1820 to 1824, it went to 2,756. The British Government could not have cut down on transportation even if it had wanted to. It therefore sought ways to make it more severe, more frightening—to remove the impression, as one Lord Chief Justice put it, that it was "a summer excursion." None of its policymakers had ever been to Australia and all of them saw it through a narrow band of information. John Bigge's reports, in their thorough detail and unbending class bias, were *the* authoritative text; and Bigge's message confirmed the basic intention of the government: that Australia's eventual fate as a community of free citizens mattered infinitely less than its expedient role as England's social sewer. The Tories wanted a governor who would think less—much less—about the convicts' future reclamation than about their present punishment.

Sir Ralph Darling (1775–1858) was their man: a tough, censorious, narrow-minded veteran of the Peninsular War, who arrived in Sydney at the age of fifty in 1825. Morally and intellectually, he was a duller being than George Arthur. He, too, had spent time in a hot climate as the British proconsul of a changing slave state. The prelude to his Australian service had been four years as British military governor of Mauritius, a colony of defeated France. As its virtual dictator, he had done his heavy-handed best to protect the frail rights of the 70,000 blacks on the sugar plantations against their French owners, demanding snap-to obedience and resenting every demurral from his policies. He carried these habits to Australia, where he soon alienated everyone except the Exclusives, who were cheered by his unquestioning obedience to London and his extreme dislike of anything that smacked of democracy, reform or (where convicts were concerned) ordinary mercy. "A cold, stiff, sickly person," thought Sir James Dowling, a new puisne judge of New South Wales, on meeting Darling for the first time in 1828. "He had none of the frankness and ease of a soldier, and I absolutely froze in his presence."[3]

Like Arthur in Van Diemen's Land, Darling in New South Wales was determined to carry out the suggestions of the Bigge Report to the letter. He would roll back Macquarie's liberalism, whose vestiges had lingered under Governor Brisbane. Instead of treating the prisoners on their merits, he wanted a rigid, undeviating standard of punishment, "with a view to the prevention of Crime at Home."

The basis of this standard was the cat-o'-nine tails, whose whistle and dull crack were as much a part of the aural background to Australian life as the kookaburra's laugh. "Flogging in this country," one old hand in the 1820s remarked to the newly arrived Alexander Harris, "is such a common thing that nobody thinks anything of it. I have seen young children practising on a tree, as children in England play at horses."[4]

Most floggings by then were confined to 25, 50, 75, 100 or, on very rare occasions, 150 lashes. By the standards of earlier days when punishments of 500 lashes were handed out by the likes of Foveaux and Marsden, such inflictions may sound light. But they were not; and in any case, a magistrate could stack up separate floggings for different aspects of the same deed.

Every stroke was noted and compiled, and in 1838 Governor Sir

George Gipps submitted to Long Glenelg a summary of corporal punishment inflicted on convicts in New South Wales over the years 1830 to 1837:[5]

YEAR	NO. OF FLOGGINGS	TOTAL OF LASHES	AVG. LASHES PER FLOGGING	MALE CONVICT POPULATION
1830	2,985	124,333	41	18,571
1831	3,163	186,017	58	21,825
1832	3,816	164,001	43	24,154
1833	5,824	242,865	41	23,357
1834	6,328	243,292	38	25,200
1835	7,103	332,810	46	27,340
1836	6,904	304,327	44	29,406
1837	5,916	268,013	45	32,102

Alexander Harris's *Settlers and Convicts, or Recollections of Sixteen Years' Labour in the Australian Backwoods* (1847) offers some vivid reflections on these commonplace events:

> Officers, and especially young officers, when made magistrates, get irritated at the hardihood of a class of men whom they have made up their minds to despise; and the cat being a soldier's natural revenge, they fly to it directly. . . .
> I was sent for to Bathurst Court-house. . . . I had to go past the triangles, where they had been flogging incessantly for hours. I saw a man walk across the yard with the blood that had run from his lacerated flesh squashing out of his shoes at every step he took. A dog was licking the blood off the triangles, and the ants were carrying away great pieces of human flesh that the lash had scattered about the ground.
> The scourger's foot had worn a deep hole in the ground by the violence with which he whirled himself round on it to strike the quivering and wealed back, out of which stuck the sinews, white, ragged and swollen. The infliction was a hundred lashes, at about half-minute time, so as to extend the punishment through nearly an hour. The day was hot enough to overcome a man merely standing that length of time in the sun. . . . I know of several poor creatures who have been entirely crippled for life by these merciless floggings.[6]

Even 25 lashes (known as a *tester* or a *Botany Bay dozen*) was a draconic torture, able to skin a man's back and leave it a tangled web of crisscrossed knotted scars.

The psychological damage inflicted by the lash was worse than the physical, and its traces were equally permanent. "It had the effect of demoralizing them to the very greatest possible extent," a former surgeon at Macquarie Harbor, John Barnes, would testify to the Molesworth Committee; "I never saw a convict benefited by flagellation." What the cat-o'-nine-tails instilled was not respect for discipline, but a sullen conviction of one's own impotence in the face of Authority; this could only be expunged by violence or erased by one's own death. Next to homosexual rape, flogging was the most humiliating invasion of the body that could befall a prisoner. Nothing in an ordinary man's experience compared to the rituals of the cat: to be stripped and tied to the triangle, like an owlskin nailed to a barn door; to hear, through battering pain, the quartermaster-sergeant slowly calling out the strokes; this was to be drowned in powerlessness. It left the prisoner consumed with worthlessness and self-hatred, and Barnes spoke of convicts who, on first being flogged, "have become so very much degraded by the punishment, that they sometimes told me that they should never be satisfied until they had been executed for some further offence; *they considered it a most unmanly form of punishment.*" [Italics added.][7]

The scarred back became an emblem of rank. So did silence. Convicts called a man who blubbered and screamed at the triangles a *crawler* or a *sandstone.* (Sandstone is a common rock around Sydney; it is soft and crumbles easily.) By contrast, the convict who stood up to it in silence was admired as a *pebble* or an *iron man.* He would *show his shapes* (strip for punishment) with disdain, and after the *domino* (last lash) he would spit at the feet of the man who gave him his *red shirt.* There were always more sandstones than pebbles. Ernest Augustus Slade, superintendent of the Hyde Park Barracks in Sydney in 1833–34, believed that convicts always broke down under the lash and furnished the Molesworth Committee with examples of both, culled from his past records. James Clayton, of the *Phoenix,* was given fifty lashes for being "absent without leave and neglecting his duty . . ."

> The skin was lacerated at the fifth lash and there was a slight effusion of blood; the prisoner subdued his sense of pain by biting his lip. The skin of this man was thick to an uncommon degree, and both his body and mind had been hardened by former punishments, and he is also known to be what is termed "flash" or "game." . . . [I]f all his former punishments . . . had been as vigorously administered as this last, his indomitable spirit would have been subdued.

By contrast, there was poor James Kenworthy of Camden, a pilferer:

> The first lash elicited loud cries from this prisoner; at the 18th lash the blood appeared; at the 25th lash the blood was trickling; at the end of the 32nd, flowing down his back. . . . [H]e would have been sufficiently

punished at the 25th lash. He says he was never flogged before. . . . [H]e
was very fat, with a thin skin. The sufferings of this prisoner were evinced
by his unnerved state of body when cast loose; he could hardly stand.[8]

The System in the 1830s had a passion for bureaucratic exactitude
about pain. In 1833 Governor Bourke, Darling's successor, received many
complaints from local benches that 50 lashes, the most that one magistrate could impose for a single offense, was not enough, and that the
government-issue cats were positively feeble. Accordingly, a circular
went forth to all police magistrates in New South Wales, demanding a
report on standard cats, samples of which were enclosed for consumer
testing.[9]

The answers were illuminating but contradictory.[10] George Holden,
police magistrate at Campbelltown, could give no "categorical answer"
about the standard cat except that it was too ill-made to last more than
150 lashes. The nine tails should be stiffer and lighter, but

> it involves a fearful responsibility, which I cannot bring myself to assume,
> to decide precisely how much torture ought to be systematically inflicted
> by law on any set of men. . . . I do not profess to have yet acquired the
> power of witnessing the infliction of pain with such unmoved nerves.

Besides, his flogger seemed to lay it on without "that peculiar art in the
flourish of the scourge which [is] employed . . . in Hyde Park Barracks,
and so greatly adds to the pain."

The Draco of Hyde Park Barracks, Ernest Slade, thought the standard
cats quite adequate "when properly wielded" but reminded the colonial
secretary that scourgers must not be overworked—they should give no
more than 150 lashes a day—and that, due to the nature of their unap-
preciated task, they ought to have special protection.

One "J.P." wrote in from Bathurst to say that the cats came undone
at the ends and did not cut the back enough. The Goulburn police magistrate poured scorn on the instruments. The lashes came off the handles
after 20 strokes; the thread whipping on the end of each tail came undone, so that "altho' it bruises, bleeding but seldom is caused, consequently the offender escapes that acute pain and smarting to the extent
so desirable should be experienced under the lash." The cord should be
harder, the tails a foot longer, and "it would be preferable were they to
terminate in small knots."

For Darling and his successors in the 1830s, however, flogging merely
represented the episodic peak of punishment within a consistent environment of misery. Every male convict would be put in irons on arrival
and sent out to labor on public works for time, "at the expiration of

which, I had purposed to assign them to Settlers; and in the event of misconduct, of replacing them in the Road Gangs." The taste of road-gang life would by then "have rendered their assignment to the Settlers a desirable release from a painful and degraded situation; and in proportion to their dread . . . they would have behaved to their Masters."[11]

Darling could not put this into practice; there was too much demand for assigned labor. But he did put many more convicts into government work on the gangs, pulling them out of "the very refuse of the whole Convict Population."[12] The roads absorbed this human trash. By 1828, Darling was congratulating himself on having 1,260 second-sentence men in the road gangs of New South Wales, more than in all the penal settlements.[13] All this, he proudly informed London, was very cheap: The convict overseers got a "gratuity" of around £16 a year, and with the salaries of free superintendents the complete payroll for the roads in 1827–28 was only £1,621 18s. 9d. No private contractor using assigned labor could possibly charge so little.[14]

The convict memoirist Thomas Cook found what road-gang life was like when he was sent to labor against raw bush and sandstone at Honeysuckle Flat on the Great Western Road over the mountains to Bathurst:

> With a sheet of Bark for my bed, the half of a threadbare Blanket for my covering, and a Log for my pillow, the action of the frost was so severe on my limbs that it was with difficulty I could find the use of them, and then only by frequenting the fire at intervals during each night. As I arose, after experiencing all the horrors of a restless and perishing cold Night, the rugged mountains covered with snow, and the frozen Tools for labour stared me in the face before the stars were off the skies; and many a tear did I shed, when contemplating upon my hard fate, and the slight offence for which I had been doomed to participate so largely in the bitters of a wretched life.[15]

Cook began in the lesser kind of punishment gang, an "out-of-iron gang." These did most of the road-building in New South Wales (after 1828 there were, at any time, between 1,200 and 1,500 convicts laboring in them), but they were miserably unproductive. Most of their members had either been rejected by settlers as unfit to be assigned workers or else were working out short sentences (six months or less) for petty colonial offenses. "The mere fact of their being returned on the hands of Government in a community where the demand for labour is very urgent and clamorous," wrote Richard Bourke, Darling's successor, meant that such men "must be notoriously idle and worthless." Their "trusty" convict overseers were corrupt. They would form "select parties" of gangers to go food-stealing by night. Cook reported how some of his fellow gangers frightened two fat bullocks over a cliff at Mount Victoria by rolling boulders down at them and ate steak for days. Prisoners also kept escaping from the out-of-iron gangs; they would run off into the bush, live for a while (but not, as a rule, very long) by scavenging and robbery and then get retaken. The number of these bushrangers made travel, especially over the Blue Mountains, a risky business, since most of them were more like famished muggers than the altruistic Robin Hoods of Australian folksong.[16]

Clearly, there was room for improvement, and Darling and Bourke pinned their hopes on the iron gangs. Their members (by 1834, Bourke reported, there were over 800 men serving sentences of 6 months to 3 years in them) were all twice-convicted and they worked and slept in irons. "They have no time for recreation. . . . [T]heir lot is felt by themselves as one of great privation and unhappiness." As the road advanced, the iron-gangers dragged their nocturnal prisons with them—huts on wheels, each sleeping eighteen to twenty-four convicts. Sometimes more permanent stockades and fixed huts were provided, from which the gangers had to march out to their sites in irons. The superintendent could make them run to work in double time, pricked on by the soldiers' bayonets.[17] When Thomas Cook was condemned to a year in an iron gang on the Great Western Road he and his fellow gangers suffered in this way

for some 10 or 15 days when the men (finding themselves so much advanced in debility, and their legs so far injured by the friction of the Irons that they could no longer bear against it) offered a determined resistance . . . which led to a deal of traffic in human flesh and blood, by the soldiers with their Bayonets, and the Scourgers with their Cats.

As for the summary punishments,

The mode of Trial was a mere mockery of justice. I have known instances where the Officer would not even stay one moment to enquire into the merits of the charges, but would sit on his horse and sentence 14 or 15 men standing a distance away (sometimes a whole Gang) to 50 and some 100 lashes each, without an oath, on hearing ten words from the lips of their villainous accusers. This system of severity was so rigorously pursued that some of the longer-sentenced men were goaded . . . either to end their days on the Gallows, or better their condition by taking to the Bush.[18]

Not all the recidivist convicts could go in the chain gangs. Iron gangs needed too many guards. There was a case for penal settlements whose remoteness would deter escape, whose severity and frightening unfamiliarity would instill "salutary terror."

The need for such places had been argued at some length in John Bigge's report, which took the Exclusivist, pro-rural view and stressed that Sydney was an incubator of crime.[19] Bigge claimed that in 1820 there had been one fresh crime for every three convicts in Sydney, as compared to one for every eight in Windsor and far less in the outlying districts. The answer was to get the serving felons out of the towns and into the country—to put the recidivists in distant penal stations, where they could not corrupt the others and where the news of their sufferings would be an example to all. Only thus, Bigge thought, could the government relieve the "constant pressure of new arrivals" and "the uneasiness I felt at the constant arrivals of convict ships." The convicts were silting up in Sydney, unclassified, mingling too easily with the free, and giving the lie to talk about the "terror" of transportation. "The great cause of the diminished effect of transportation has arisen from the increase in the numbers transported," Bigge argued:

> All the evils of association, the difficulties of superintendence and control, whether arising from the extension and variety of the employments, or from the more laborious duties of the magistrates and superintendents, have arisen chiefly from this source.[20]

Besides, the settled districts around Sydney were getting almost too comfortable and Bigge thought it "hopeless" to expect that they would confront convict work gangs with "all the hardships, privations and severities [of their] unsettled state." Convicts at gang labor should get no room for initiative and work only at such uniform tasks as grubbing out the giant roots of gum trees left in the ground by earlier clearing-parties. There would be plenty of exhausting work along the north coast, to which Bigge urged the government to send them. Under the fiery Tropic of Capricorn, the combination of raw bush and hostile Aborigines would be a powerful deterrent to escape. And once the bush was cleared, the convict gangs would move out and the settlers could go in.[21]

Lord Bathurst and Macquarie's successors, Brisbane and Darling, all accepted this plan of northward colonization into the punitive tropics. It was set in full motion by Brisbane and perfected by Darling. Since the fate of prisoners in such places would bulk large in the imagery of the System, they are worth considering in some detail.

ii

THE FIRST PENAL out-station on the mainland was Newcastle, founded where the Hunter River flows into the Pacific about seventy miles north of Sydney. This river mouth had been a Cretaceous swamp and, on the flat rocks at the base of the cliffs, the ocean water swilled green and blue around the stumps of petrified trees, whose growth rings could still be read. Of more interest to the early settlers, however, was another relic of that swamp: a seam of coal, three feet thick, that ran near water level through Nobby's Head, the southern jaw of the river entrance. This seam, first noticed in 1795, gave the place its first name: Coal Harbor.

In 1801 Governor King sent sixteen refractory convicts to mine coal there, under military guard. They were soon recalled, as it was too difficult to supply this tiny outpost, but in 1804, after the Irish rose at Castle Hill, King dispatched thirty-five of them to labor in the cliff seam. The convict population of Newcastle, as the place was soon named, grew fitfully. By the end of 1804, it was 128; by 1817 it was 553; and in 1821 there were 1,169 people living there, including a handful of free settlers and Emancipist farmers. By then, the economic mainstay of the settlement was no longer coal but timber.

Vast stands of cedar, the prime joinery timber of colonial Australia, grew in the Hunter River Valley. Men with crosscut saws could rip the great trunks down into tabletops three inches thick, six feet wide and as long as you wanted—the red-gold, ponderous, subtly aromatic slabs that are unobtainable today, but were then as common as pine. Cedar was a government monopoly. Contractors took their ships to Newcastle and bought it convict-sawn, at 3d. per superficial foot. The panelled doors of Macquarie's Sydney—the moldings, the dadoes and cabinets, even the floors—were made of it.

Most prisoners at Newcastle worked in the cedar gangs. By 1820, the shore forests were so depleted that the cedar-getters had to go seventy miles upstream to find large trees. These expeditions lasted a month or more and were of course overseen by military guards who supervised the task-work; the quota for a thirty-man gang was about one hundred trunks a month. Once felled and lopped, they would be lashed together into a single big raft; sheltered by a rough hut on its "deck," the whole gang would float back down to Newcastle in style.[22]

Standing orders kept the settlement isolated. If a private vessel put in there without a license, she was scuttled and her crew imprisoned. Licensed boats had to unship their rudders and surrender them to the harbormaster. These measures not only prevented escapes but discouraged cedar-poachers.

Life at Newcastle was hard, and successive commandants were ordered to keep it so. It was a dirty infant of a town, consisting of parallel rows of convict-built slab huts and a barracks holding some 250 men considered dangerous. There, they slept in cribs a little more than four feet wide, three men to a crib. (The practice of bedding the men by threes and not in pairs was supposed, optimistically, to reduce unmentionable crime.) In summer this shantytown was oppressively hot, the thermometer rising to 105° in the shade, with burning northerlies sometimes pushing it to 115°. One young guard officer, Lieutenant William Coke, a scion of the great family of Holkham Hall, found the climate deadly:

> Often at half past 7 in the Evening we cannot bear our Coats on & are laying down panting for breath, & in a quarter of an Hour afterwards on leaving the Mess we are cold, shivering and wishing for a fire. These sudden changes kill many people. Soldiers and the Inhabitants die very quick here, what with drinking & being exposed to the sudden changes of the weather.[23]

Everything in Newcastle seemed either exhausting or boring, but that was what commended it to the authorities. The wildlife lacked charm. "If a snake bites you in this country," Coke wrote home to England, doubtless meaning to make his sisters' skin crawl, "instant death follows; one of the most deadly & common Snake's bite is so bad that the person bit only shivers and falls dead immediately."[24] There were sandflies, mosquitoes, cholera, dysentery, catarrh and, as an extra irritation, a large perambulating sand dune—unwisely stripped of scrub so that escaping convicts could not hide in it—which kept creeping into the town and had to be shovelled back.

Convict diggers, some of whom had been coal miners in England, worked ten to twelve hours a day. The old exposed seam on the face of Nobby's had been abandoned after 1817, for fear that the undermined sandstone above would crash into the sea. Now the miners went down a shaft, lowered more than 100 feet by a windlass, their leg-irons jingling forlornly in the dark. Conditions in it were dreadful, what with seepage from the sea above, rockfalls and bad air. The miners suffered from "black lung," asthma and rheumatism. At the end of the day they had no change of clothes, and sometimes no blankets. They had to mine twenty tons of coal a day.[25]

The most hated labor, worse than the mine, was lime-burning. Sydney had no mineral lime for mortar. But immense beds of oysters grew a few miles north of Newcastle, and the more refractory convicts were sent to gather and burn them. This meant trudging barefoot all day in mud thick with knife-sharp oyster shells, carrying baskets of quicklime across the tidal flats to the waiting boats. When water splashed into the unslaked lime it burned their unprotected eyes and their scabbed backs. Bigge noted that the lime-burners' eyes suffered from the smoke "but not to a greater degree than in England," and thought the convicts blinded themselves to malinger. But the hospital gave little solace to the sick; it was a mere shed, without proper supplies or even soap (which prisoners had to cook up themselves from pot-grease and ashes). In 1816 there were only enough blankets there for one patient in eight.[26]

In 1818, to exhort his lime-burners to greater efforts, Lachlan Macquarie visited the oyster beds of Newcastle. He arrived in full gubernatorial fig, with a retinue of fifty people and a four-piece band. The musicians brayed and fiddled, the governor inspected, and what the convicts thought is not recorded. He and his band then went off to lay the foundation stone of a breakwater, to be named Macquarie Pier; convict gangs spent many months dragging rocks underwater to build this hated amenity but it was never finished.

The main preoccupation among the Newcastle prisoners was escape. To discourage it, the commandants made their officers treat the local Aborigines well, cajoling them with small gifts or tobacco and sugar or, for exceptional services, blankets. In this way, Bigge noted, the Aborigines had become "very active" in recapturing prisoners:

> They accompany the soldiers who are sent in pursuit, and by the extraordinary strength of sight they possess . . . they can trace to a great distance, with wonderful accuracy, the impressions of the human foot. Nor are they afraid of meeting the fugitive convicts in the woods, when sent in their pursuit, without the soldiers. . . . [T]hey wound and disable them, strip them of their clothes, and bring them back as prisoners. . . . [N]otwithstanding the apprehensions of revenge from the convicts whom they bring back, they continue to live in Newcastle and its neighbourhood, but are observed to prefer the society of the soldiers to that of the convicts.[27]

Thus the black police tracker made his first appearance in Australia; and one more grudge was added to the growing hatred of convict white for tribal black.

The prisoners bolted singly and in parties; some reached the Hawkesbury district, where they hoped to find shelter with assigned shepherds. They arrived gaunt and naked, reamed out by diarrhea, barely able to walk after a three-week diet of bugs, roots and raw snake meat. Once recaptured, some men tried again; one convict at Newcastle in 1810 had five escapes on his record. The punishments for those recaptured were "inflicted with more severity than at other settlements," Bigge thought. Other punishments included chain-gang labor, and, for women (a few of whom had ended up in Newcastle on second convictions, despite the general policy against sending women to penal stations), humiliating spiked iron collars, riveted around the neck.[28]

The symbolism of rank was jealously maintained. Tipping the cap or touching the forelock was imposed as a fetishistic ritual on the prisoners; sometimes, as at Norfolk Island, they were required (on pain of flogging for "disrespect") to salute not only any passing soldier, but certain objects associated with soldiering—an empty sentry-box, for instance. These orders came from Major James Morisset, who had succeeded Captain Wallis as commandant at Newcastle. A free trader from Sydney named John Bingle was struck by the relentless way that Morisset ran the Newcastle station; he had "never seen arbitrary power carried to such an extent . . . [I]t seemed very un-English."[29]

Death sentences for absconding seem to have been handed out with abandon by the military court at Newcastle, if young Lieutenant Coke was not exaggerating in his letters home:

> The Lieutenants and Ensigns have no duty here, except sitting on the Criminal court and seeing men hung.—The jury here is formed of seven Officers, every day we sit we get 15 shillings allowed us each for our trouble.—The Court in general consists of one Judge, one Counsel against the prisoner, & the Witnesses, seldom indeed does any person come here as a Spectator & the prisoners seldom employ a man to defend them, we sometimes condemn five in a day to be hanged: it is more in appearance like an Inquisition as the Prisoners seldom call Witnesses, & men are condemn'd with little ceremony.[30]

What is extraordinary is Coke's matter-of-factness, his assumption that the convicts had no rights. Why did the prisoners not defend themselves? Because they believed they had no chance with the "deliberations" of this military Star Chamber. Not all the hangings seem to have been carried out; the usual procedure by the late 1820s was to commute the capital sentence or, in some cases, to send the third-time offender straight to Norfolk Island, a punishment in some ways worse than hanging. But such a passage suggests how the System could degenerate once minor officials felt that a governor like Ralph Darling cared little for "convict rights."

However, by the 1820s the usefulness of Newcastle as a place of secondary punishment was waning. The place was no longer isolated, because more and more free settlers were anxious to farm the rich plains of the Hunter River Valley. The cedar forests were vanishing and, although the coal mines were still being worked by convicts—including some Chartist political prisoners[31]—in the 1830s, they could not absorb very much labor. Besides, Bigge reported to his government, the good farmland along the Hunter River made the convicts' lives too easy. In earlier years, when the settlement only spread a mile or two inland, all crops had to be raised on the poor, sandy coastal soil, so that Nature combined with Authority "to render hard labour an indispensable condition of existence." Fertile soil contradicted the purpose of the settlement. So after 1823, Newcastle was thrown open to free trade and settlement. Its convicts stayed on—there were more than 1,600 by 1827 —but it was no longer simply a jail for the twice-convicted. That role was assumed by a new settlement started in 1821, 270 miles north of Sydney: Port Macquarie.

Port Macquarie (not to be confused with Macquarie Harbor) was meant for incorrigible life-sentence prisoners convicted of second offenses in New South Wales. Discipline under its first commandant, Francis Allman, was severe; a man could get 100 lashes for trying to smuggle a letter out, or a month in the cell for merely possessing a piece of writing paper. (One sees why convict diaries were nonexistent, and convict memoirs rare.) One veteran of the Port Macquarie iron gang recalled how

> the hills [we] cut through were so steep that a man could not comfortably ascend one of them without irons on his legs, let alone with them—but the hills had to be broken down by men with sore backs, and if one man happened to collide with another who had recently been flogged, it would be—"Oh, G—! Mind my sore back." Those were hard times; hard worked and half starved.[32]

The rubbing of the leg-rings on their flesh, Port Macquarie men used sardonically to say, "put plenty of iron in the blood."

Port Macquarie had a high proportion of Specials. Darling had them sent there so that they could not make trouble in Sydney; he did not want literate convicts adding to the rhetoric of Wentworth and the Sydney *Monitor*. Some of them were harmless creatures, like the Irishman James Bushelle, who, in cahoots with "a broken-down French gambler," had toured the jewelry shops of London masquerading as a Polish prince, with gum on his fingertips, substituting fake diamonds for real ones. He drew life in New South Wales, and on being reconvicted at Port Macquarie he found a niche as a tutor to some of the free settlers who had begun to trickle in after 1830, "instructing the young ladies both married and single," as he put it,

> in music, dancing, French and Italian . . . who met occasionally to enjoy the pleasure of a German Waltz or a Spanish Quadrille in this recent Emanation from the forest; where hitherto the sound of music, or the voice of merriment, had never been heard; where no sounds, but the cooees and howlings of the Black man, the groans of the convicts under

the excruciating Lash, or the croaking of the wild Cockatoo, ever pierc'd
the Skies or disturb'd the Ambient Air.[33]

Thus, the first uncertain pipings of the Muses were heard at Port Macquarie.

But among other Specials, "relaxation, petty traffic and abuse"
reigned. They seized every privilege they could get; they truckled to
authority ("When an overseer spoke to him," it was said of one Special,
"he had the appearance of a goose looking down a bottle") and made
tyrannous overseers themselves. Solidarity might rise between prisoners
on the run or men who had been through the assignment system; in the
penal stations, rarely. Convict overseers in such places—and on the
chain gangs—were notoriously cruel. "The worst wretches that a man
could be put to work under were those who had been sent to the country
themselves. They were far worse than men who came out free."[34]

As at Newcastle, escape attempts were common. But few succeeded,
particularly since the Aborigines proved eager to help catch bolters. As
the area opened up to free settlers at the end of the 1820s, security
faltered and after 1830 the place became a grotesque mixture of jail and
infirmary, "a *demi* penal settlement."[35] The crippled, the mad and the
blind were dumped into it along with the Specials. In the late 1830s, Port
Macquarie boasted a gang of one-armed stonebreakers and another of
blind men, who in 1835 could be seen "manacled to a chain, and so
marched to and fro on the causeway facing the window of the Commandant's quarters for 2 or 3 successive days for his amusement." The "blind
mob" had a high reputation as thieves, deft enough to ease a man's rolled-
up trousers from under his head as he slept and take the coins from his
pocket, or grope melons out of an officer's garden patch by moonlight.
Cross one, and he might put a tiger snake's head, fangs up, in your boot.

Most conspicuous of all were the "men on timber," amputees with
wooden legs who were unsuitable for gang labor elsewhere in the colony.
They served as delivery men, humping packages inland for free settlers.
When not employed, they would lie sunning themselves and gazing at
the sea, guzzling rum, of which there was plenty at Port Macquarie,
cooked up in illicit convict stills from the sugar cane that flourished
there. Real men drank it laced with tobacco juice, a mixture believed to
kill the pain of a flogging.

One of the amputees' main recreations was fighting. Since they could
not stand toe-to-toe like regular pugilists, their friends would perch them
face-to-face on the thwarts of a dinghy; each combatant was propped up
by a man at his back, "and in this fashion they would fight away in great
style" until one of them could no longer sit up. They also played practical

jokes. The overseer of the one-armed stone-cutting gang was a Jew with
two wooden legs. One day, as he lay dozing drunk in the sun, another
Jewish prisoner

> collected a quantity of old maize stalks and other fuel, and set fire to his
> wooden legs. . . . They were not burning long, however, before he awoke
> and found one to be shorter than the other; and it was a sight for sore eyes
> to see him walking down to the Old Broken Barracks, singing out to
> everyone that he met—"That Jew-looking bugger down there has burnt
> my legs nearly off."[36]

Other pranks involved animals. Convicts would wire two tomcats' tails
together and drape them over a doorknob at night. They would slide a
live shark into a drunkard's bed. Almost anything would do to relieve
the tedium of Port Macquarie, where Brueghel would not have lacked
subjects.

Discipline in the 1830s was uneven but harsh. Thomas Cook, sent
there from the iron gang as a Special in the summer of 1835, found a
commandant who (he alleged) thought nothing of flogging old men and
cripples, and boasted "that he would make the Deaf to hear, the Dumb
to speak, the lame to walk, the blind to see, and the foolish to understand" with his colonial cure-all, the lash. Soon after arriving, Cook came
down with dysentery, but he did not report to the surgeon "for the name
he bore among my fellow prisoners as a Butcher." For this, he was heavily
ironed and ordered by the commandant "in a voice like thunder" to extra
labor, under the eye of Roach, the chief flogger. But there was some pity
in Roach. Not all such men were the blood-boltered sadists of convict
lore:

> At this time the Scourger (whose calling one would have supposed had
> long since excluded almost every kindred feeling from his breast) was
> begging of me to keep my Tool in motion, until the Commandant took
> his ride out, and promising to do my work for me. In about an hour the
> Commandant left the settlement, and the Scourger, putting down his
> arms, worked excessively hard so as to save me from the Punishment
> with which I must otherwise have been visited.[37]

Nevertheless Cook was sure he would die at Port Macquarie and
decided to flee, "under the impression that there existed some hope of
my being able to effect a final escape to England." There was none. He
walked out of the settlement, which had no wall but the bush, and went
eighty miles south before realizing he was totally lost. Sick with the flux,
he survived a week on roots and wild nettles until the Aborigines caught
him and gave him to an armed search-party of constables. That did not

deter him; in all, Cook tried three times to escape from Port Macquarie, with no success.

iii

GOVERNOR BRISBANE decided to plant another penal station on the mainland, so remote that its prisoners would give up all hope of escape. It would be in the Deep North, as Australians call Queensland, where the sun's heat would bake and baste the sin out of them. In 1823 Brisbane sent an exploring party under his surveyor-general, John Oxley, to look at Moreton Bay, a big coastal inlet noted by Cook fifty years before. It was 450 miles north of Sydney, far enough to discourage any bolter. If it had a river, it might be settled.

Oxley and his men reached Moreton Bay by sea without incident and carried out a rough survey. They found a river, rich soil, plenty of fresh water, and friendly Aborigines. The shallow bay teemed with fish; they could wade out and catch mullet and snapper with their hands. The mangroves were encrusted with little milky oysters in ruffled shells, and in the ooze between their roots lived regiments of huge, delicious mud crabs. Up the river, as a former convict would remember in years to come, "it looked as though some race of men had been here before us, and planted this veritable Garden of Eden." The riverbanks were tropical jungle, laced with blue-and-white flowering vines; stately white lilies grew in masses from the tidal mud. Colonies of black Funereal Cockatoos stared from the palm trees, nodding their wiry crests and occasionally flapping clumsily into the air, like croaking umbrellas. Kingfishers flashed through the deep shade.[38]

It looked almost too good for convicts, and surely survival would not be a problem: The first human beings Oxley and his men encountered, to their stupefaction, were two naked, scarred and sunburnt white men, who had been wrecked on the coast a year and a half before and were "in healthy state and plump condition," thanks to the local Aborigines, who had adopted them. In fact, Oxley's report on Moreton Bay was so encouraging that when it reached London, Lord Bathurst decided that the area should be thrown directly open to free settlers. But his opinions on this took months to reach Sydney, and in the meantime Governor Brisbane had given orders to start a penal settlement there. He wanted it "to receive and maintain a great number of persons." The convicts' slave labor was "the best means of paving the way for the introduction of free population, as the example of Port Macquarie abundantly testifies."[39] He put it in charge of Lieutenant Henry Miller of the 40th Regiment. In September 1824, Miller sailed north with fifty settlers, thirty of whom were convict volunteers who hoped to win an early ticket-of-leave. They started on the edge of Moreton Bay, at the present site of Redcliffe.

Governor Brisbane expected the new settlement to become self-sufficient within two years, by growing maize. However, because of the inefficiency of penal labor, it did not; one cannot build an economy quickly with work designed to punish the builders. Work performed quickly was not punishment enough; the labor had to be "arduous." Miller had the convicts working twelve hours a day, dawn to dusk. Horses, draft animals and ploughs were all proscribed. As in the "starvation years" in Sydney, every inch of ground had to be inefficiently tilled with hoes, which kept breaking, and there was no animal manure. The convicts became afflicted with scurvy, and conditions were so squalid that they also fell victim to filth diseases like dysentery and trachoma.

Pioneering was bad enough, but doing it under such handicaps was absurd. The Eden-like prospect of Moreton Bay disintegrated fast, as such fantasies always did in Australia. The soil at Redcliffe was poor and the first seeds died in the ground; there was not enough building timber, and even the grass for thatch had to be dragged for miles; medicine ran out, and the place was infested with flies, ticks, scorpions and venomous snakes. Lieutenant Miller was driven near to distraction by all this, but he soldiered on:

> Nothing was undertaken that I did not plan, nothing was carried on that I did not inspect, literally, under a burning sun earning my bread in the sweat of my brow; I passed toilsome and miserable days, anxious and restless nights, and underwent privations . . . greater than any I had been called upon to sustain during years of [army] service.[40]

But toward the end of 1824, Governor Brisbane visited the Brisbane River, flatteringly named after him, and decided that the settlement should be moved to its banks. After several months of indecision he ordered Miller to make the move in February 1825. The huts were laboriously dismantled—every iron nail pulled out, straightened and saved— and the commandant's official residence, a prefabricated cottage brought in kit form from Sydney, was taken down and stowed. In July, they took everything twenty-seven miles up the river to the present site of Brisbane, Queensland's capital. "The difficulties of this task," Miller sighed, "with my original few [convicts] wasted and enfeebled by sickness, were so many and so great that none but an eye-witness could in the least form an opinion of them." Then the governor dismissed him. "I was removed to cover the mistakes of others," Miller protested, and in fact he had been: Brisbane needed a scapegoat for his own failure to equip the settlement properly.[41]

His successor, Captain Peter Bishop of the 40th Regiment, was a fairly humane man by colonial standards. He saw that the convicts would never work well under the severe discipline and the gruelling heat unless they had "a little reward for it," an ounce or two of tea or sugar. (Such gifts had also cemented good relations with the Aborigines around Brisbane Town, who, as at Newcastle and Port Macquarie, soon learned to catch runaway convicts and bring them in.)[42] But he had only two hundred convicts, few of them skilled tradesmen; and although some crops grew, only twelve acres were cultivated, because no one had enough farming experience to be superintendent of agriculture. When Bishop left Brisbane Town in March 1826, it was still only a straggle of cockeyed, leaking slab huts, without a hospital, a granary or even a jail. But the new commandant would change all that. He was Captain Patrick Logan of the 57th Regiment, and his regime would reflect the ironclad severity that the new governor, Ralph Darling, who appointed him, was determined to impose on the prisoners of Australia.

Between his arrival at Moreton Bay and his violent death there four years later, Logan became a legend among the convicts—so much so that he was the only commandant of an Australian penal station to have a whole ballad dedicated to him, "The Convict's Lament on the Unfortunate Death of Patrick Logan," which was called "Moreton Bay," for short.

> One Sunday morning as I went walking, by the Brisbane's waters I
>   chanced to stray,
> I heard a prisoner his fate bewailing, as on the sunny river bank he lay:
> "I am a native of Erin's island, but banished now to the fatal shore,
> They tore me from my aged parents and from the maiden I do adore.
>
> "I've been a prisoner at Port Macquarie, Norfolk Island and Emu Plains,
> At Castle Hill and cursed Toongabbie, at all those settlements I've
>   worked in chains;
> But of all those places of condemnation, in each penal station of New
>   South Wales,
> To Moreton Bay I've found no equal: excessive tyranny there each day
>   prevails.
>
> "For three long years I was beastly treated, heavy irons on my legs I
>   wore,
> My back from flogging it was lacerated, and often painted with crimson
>   gore,
> And many a lad from downright starvation lies mouldering humbly
>   beneath the clay,
> Where Captain Logan he had us mangled on his triangles at Moreton
>   Bay.

"Like the Egyptians and ancient Hebrews, we were oppressed under
   Logan's yoke,
Till a native black who lay in ambush did give our tyrant his mortal
   stroke.
Fellow prisoners, be exhilarated, that all such monsters such a death
   may find!
And when from bondage we are liberated, our former sufferings shall
   fade from mind."

Preferably sung *a capella* in a high nasal drone, this survived in many
variants and was perhaps the most popular anti-authoritarian ballad of
colonial Australia. Ned Kelly, last and greatest of the folk-hero bushrangers, the son of poor Irish Currency, put it into prose in his "Jerilderie
Letter." Openly addressed to the people of Australia, in 1879

> Port McQuarrie Toweringabbie Norfolk island and Emu plains and in
> those places of tyranny and condemnation many a blooming Irish man
> rather than subdue to the Saxon yoke were flogged to death and bravely
> died in servile chains.

Of all the Australian camp commandants, it was Logan who had the
worse reputation for cruelty. The convicts regarded him as an ogre and
his subordinates as grotesque monsters. Stories—almost certainly untrue
—were told about his chief flogger, a man with deformed legs named Old
Bumble (because he staggered along like a bee walking), who would wash
off the bloody thongs of his cat-o'-nine-tails in a can of water and drink
the contents. Logan was said to have flogged men to death for the pleasure of it and driven "hundreds" into the grave by working them in
chains until they dropped. The convict resister, wrote a former Moreton
Bay prisoner named William Ross in a pamphlet written after Logan's
death,

> would be tortured with flogging and slavery until the spark of life had
> fled, when he would be buried like a dog. . . . Such conduct is horrid, and
> ought not to have been permitted; but unfortunately, Logan had the great-
> est interest with the never-to-be-forgotten Governor D[arling], who
> backed him in every tyrannical work.[43]

Such was the Logan to frighten children, the infamous Beast of Brisbane. In later years, efforts would be made to exonerate him as a capable
explorer who battled against shocking conditions. The best likeness of
Logan offers few clues to him. What is one to read in Logan's stern face
with its pale, high cheekbones, level stare and slightly twisted mouth,
raised on its formal Georgian plinth of white linen? Only that he looks
as authoritarian as any other man of his day, rank and calling. Soldiers

liked to be depicted like that—and Logan, before he was anything else, was a soldier.

He had been born in Scotland in 1792, and he joined the 57th Regiment at the age of eighteen. For the next fifteen years he served his King all over the world: against Napoleon in Spain and France, in the American War, on garrison duty in Ireland, and finally in Australia, where he arrived in 1825. Because his whole life had been shaped by the army, Logan—like almost any other career officer—took for granted the army's assumptions about human nature; and the chief of these, in the early nineteenth century, was that the motley rabble who comprised the rank and file could only be turned into soldiers by unremitting discipline backed up by summary flagellation and the threat of the firing squad. Drill and the cat, not mercy or appeals to esprit de corps, had made the machine that defeated Napoleon. Logan's own regiment was noted for its severity. Why soften this proven system for worse scum, the convicts? "A little severity," Logan wrote a year after taking command at Moreton Bay, "was absolutely necessary to convert the settlement into anything like a place of punishment."[44]

On paper the commandant's powers were strictly limited. Logan could inflict summary punishments to 50 lashes, but standing orders warned that extra labor and solitary confinement should be preferred to the lash. However, the more detailed instructions he received from Governor Darling in 1829 made "every person, whether free or bond . . . subject to his orders" and gave official sanction to an inescapable fact: At distant places like Moreton Bay there was no way to keep an eye on the commandant, and therefore he could rule his small kingdom of pain as an absolute despot. He was the only magistrate, and through him all justice—other than trial for new felonies, which had to be held in a full Sydney court—was interpreted. His officers would stand behind him whenever questions were asked; so, as a rule, would free settlers (especially since Logan had absolute and summary power over their movements and could expel any one at will). Convicts, of course, had no voice. No convict could hope to persuade a Sydney court of the commandant's tyrannies; most of them were illiterate, and in any case all affidavits had to be sworn before Logan.[45]

When Logan arrived, he had a labor force of about one hundred convicts. By the end of 1826, it had doubled; in 1828 he had 415; and by February 1829, he had 772. The peak convict population was 1,020, in 1831[46] Thus, although the labor supply grew steeply during Logan's reign, it was never large enough for ambitious building programs—a problem compounded by Darling's vacillations about the nature of the settlement and whether it should have free settlers or not. Under these conditions, Logan found it hard to make long-range plans. Yet by mid-1827, he had

120 acres under wheat and another 300 prepared for maize, while on the bank of the Brisbane River a town was shaping up, with a grid of beaten-earth streets, compacted by the soldiers' boot and the dragging of the prisoners' irons, and with a hospital, barracks, stores, and even a few stone cottages among the warped timber hovels.

It was done at a certain cost, which the convicts paid. Many of them worked as naked as Aborigines in the sun, except for their irons, and had to eat "Snakes, Pigs that have died of disease, Cabbage leaves . . . and every filth that was thrown into the streets."[47] An older hand, who escaped so often that he served a total of 26 years on a 7-year sentence for petty larceny, spent 7 years at Moreton Bay alone:

> I lost one of my eyes and the use of one of my hands. I suffered a great deal of hardship because I was unable to do the work allotted to me, and the punishment was very severe . . . [M]ost of the men at the Settlement were in irons . . . I had chains on my leg for four years . . . [I]t was through being ill-treated by the overseers that I lost the use of my hand—they struck me with whatever was handiest.[48]

Although the punishment registers for Moreton Bay in Logan's time are lost, its seems clear that Logan habitually worked prisoners in irons, whatever their sentences.[49] He was also a relentless flogger. One sample record of the floggings he handed out has survived; they were noted in a journal kept by some convict clerk for Peter Spicer, the superintendent of convicts, and show that from February to October 1828, Logan ordered 200 floggings, for a total of 11,100 lashes.

The flogging cannot have abated much after October 1828, because Logan was facing an explosive situation in his settlement. The crops failed in the summer of 1828–29. And there were epidemics of trachoma and dysentery. The crude death rate at Moreton Bay shot up to 35 per 1,000 per month, and Logan chose this of all moments to put the settlement on half rations. In the midst of this social catastrophe, there was a great rise in the number of convicts hospitalized for the special affliction of Moreton Bay, coyly Latinized in the records as *"flagellatio."*[50]

Logan's subordinates, to be sure, were not much help. Peter Spicer was a ludicrous incompetent, while Henry Cowper, the settlement's surgeon, appeared to his newly arrived assistant in 1830 as

> a most uncouth individual, an excessive grog-drinker and smoker, and the most ill-tempered and quarrelsome man I ever saw . . . I really think he is half insane. However, he is aware of his dreadful temper, for he speaks about it and says he is quite sure he will yet be confined in a madhouse.[51]

No wonder, then, that the prisoners tried to run away. Any chance of escape, no matter how thin, was preferable to life in this Georgian snake pit where even their turds were inspected for undigested kernels of stolen corn. In 1828–29, 126 prisoners (about one in ten) bolted into the bush and headed south, clutching what pitiful supplies of flour, fat and corn they had managed to steal and save, prepared to risk being killed (and, most of them believed, eaten) by Aborigines. Sixty-nine of them walked or were dragged back to the settlement, half-dead from exhaustion, to face 100, 200 or even 300 clawing strokes of the cat and be loaded with 20-pound irons for the rest of their sentences, to which Logan (as magistrate) would usually add another three years. (This was illegal and fell outside his powers as magistrate; but it drew no rebuke from Darling.) The fate of the rest is unknown. Most died. No prisoner was ever officially said to have reached freedom from Moreton Bay. Some may have done it, for several actually got as far down the coast as Port Macquarie before they were taken.

Meanwhile relations got worse with the Aborigines, whose stance toward the colonials by the late 1820s had changed from curiosity to open hostility. Convicts were ready to kill any black they met in the bush, if they could; the spiral of violence grew, and by early 1828 Logan had to report that armed bands of Aborigines, sometimes fifty men at a time, were attacking the maize fields.[52] However, the convict tradition that Logan retaliated for these crop raids by shooting an Aborigine and hanging up his stuffed skin in the maize fields as a warning may be unfounded—although similar things were done in New South Wales.[53]

Governor Darling countenanced what Logan was doing at Moreton Bay, but word of it leaked out into the community. Almost certainly it was meant to: the settlement needed a terrible reputation among convicts if it was to become a deterrent. The problem was not so much Logan's severity as his rumored capriciousness. By 1830, voices in Sydney were asking what was really going on at Moreton Bay. The leading voice was that of Edward Smith Hall (1786–1860).

Hall, the son of a minor English banker, had emigrated to New South Wales in 1811. Even in England he had involved himself in religious and social work, and he was a friend of the Abolitionist William Wilberforce. This recommended him to Lachlan Macquarie, who granted him more than 2,000 acres of pastoral land over the years. Hall failed utterly as a farmer, and his record as an officer of the fledgling Bank of New South Wales was not much better. But to a man of hot conscience and philanthropic instincts, penal Australia—especially after Macquarie left it— offered a vast acreage to rake muck in. Hall found his vocation as a newspaper editor. In 1826 he and a partner in Sydney founded the *Monitor*. Its broad political aims were like those of Wentworth's *Australian*: trial by jury, government by representative assembly, and the defense of civil liberties against Darling the martinet. More than the *Australian*, whose constituency was the Emancipists, the *Monitor* was concerned (or seditiously obsessed, some officials thought) with the plight of convicts under sentence whether privately mistreated as assigned servants or officially ground down on the chain gangs and at the penal stations.

Darling was Hall's bête noire. His leaden autocracy, Hall editorialized, had made New South Wales "singularly prone to espionage, suspicion, and a servile dread of offending the higher authorities." Through the *Monitor* and in a series of open letters to the colonial secretary in England, he accused him of negligence, unconstitutional disregard for the "ancient mild Laws of England," graft, favoritism to rich colonists, jury-packing, indifference to "proven" cases of official torture, and "prostituting his Authority and influence as Governor to feelings of private resentment."[54]

Hall's first big clash with Darling on events, rather than policies, came in 1826 over the Sudds-Thompson case. Joseph Sudds and Patrick Thompson, privates in the 57th Regiment, had come to believe (like many of their comrades in New South Wales) that the life of a serving convict, bad as it was, was still easier than a rank-and-file soldier's. A soldier who committed a crime in Australia faced transportation to a penal settlement. To get out of the army, Sudds and Thompson robbed a Sydney shop and made no effort to escape arrest. They were tried and sentenced to 7 years in a penal settlement.

This enraged Darling, who felt the news that His Majesty's soldiers preferred the life of a condemned convict would make either the army seem brutal (and discourage enlistment) or transportation mild (thus encouraging crime). He took it on himself, quite illegally, to cancel their prison sentences and send them to the iron gangs for 7 years. This was preceded by a ceremony of disgrace: dressed in the convicts' "canaries" (the yellow and gray uniform of felonry) and wearing massive spiked collars linked to their leg-fetters by 13-pound chains, Sudds and Thompson were drummed out of their regiment and into jail, where they languished in their irons. But to Darling's great embarrassment, Sudds— who had suffered from "dropsy"—fell ill from this treatment and died a few days later. Darling had not known Sudds's medical history, if only because he had not asked about it; certainly he did not mean to kill the man. But the results of his "exemplary" punishment made such measures seem Draconian and provoked a wave of revulsion among all Emancipists. From the *Australian* and the *Monitor*, Wentworth and Hall accused the governor of murder, torture and Nero-like perversions of justice.

Darling fought back stiffly but as best he could against Wentworth ("a vulgar, ill-bred fellow") and Hall ("a fellow without principles, an apostate missionary"). From that point on, all criticism was sedition. "The opposition papers," he complained to Bathurst, "must destroy that Confidence which the people generally ought to place in the Government, and in a Colony composed as this is produce, if not checked, anarchy and revolt."[55] He saw, as anyone could, that the Sudds-Thompson case was a heaven-sent lever for the "democrats" to press their claims for trial by open jury and a representative assembly. So he made a clumsy lunge against the opposition press. He tried to muzzle the *Australian* and the *Monitor* by imposing newspaper licenses, which would be withdrawn if they printed a "blasphemous or seditious libel." John Macarthur also urged him to kill their circulation with a stamp duty of 4d. per copy. Both measures had already been proposed by the autocrat of Van Diemen's Land, George Arthur. But all legislative bills had to be reviewed by the chief justice of the colony, Sir Francis Forbes.

Forbes thought his narrow-minded zealot of a governor had "less knowledge of the laws of his country than any gentleman filling his high official station whom it was ever my fortune to meet." He took most of the bite out of Darling's acts, until they could no longer silence the press —although they could certainly harass it. Hall, in return, kept up his invective against Darling and the Merinos and suffered seven prosecutions for criminal libel. In 1829 Darling at last managed to imprison him, but Hall continued to edit the *Monitor* from his cell and send long diatribes against the governor to officials in England. And it was in the Sydney jail, in March 1830, that Hall was handed the document that he believed would topple Captain Logan, disgrace Darling and force reform at Moreton Bay.

It was a manuscript left in the condemned cell of Sydney Jail by a convict named Thomas Matthew; he had left it hidden when he was taken out to be hanged. Matthew had been a "troublesome" convict. On the way from Sydney to Moreton Bay, he plotted a mutiny on the transport *City of Edinburgh*; the plan failed, because a prisoner named John Carrol ratted on the ringleaders. Matthew bided his time and smashed Carrol's skull with a pickax at Moreton Bay. He was brought down to Sydney, tried and cast to die.

His death-cell letter explained that his own life was of no value to him. It told of life at Moreton Bay under "such a herd of tyrants that never met together in one place before." The convict overseers "murder many a bright man," but the prisoners could bring no charges against them, because they had to be made to Logan. The jail gang overseer, named Trenand, killed a prisoner with a spade in front of ten convict witnesses, "but such was their terror [that] none of them dared to mention it, for fear of being flogged to death." Overseers stole the prisoners' bread; men died in the fields and the cells "from want of attention and

food" and were flogged to death "for stealing a cob of corn." Some convicts were so weak that they had to crawl out to field labor. And Logan
in one of his "mad fits" had all the cripples dragged from hospital and
flogged "in their crutches." Matthew claimed he had seen men so broken
by the first half of a flogging that they had to be brought back to the
triangles the next day in a wheelbarrow to be strung up for the second
half.

Hall published this letter in the *Monitor* on March 27, 1830. He also
declared, from jail, that he would prosecute Captain Logan for the murder
of a convict named William Swann, who (Hall alleged) had died of ill-
treatment at Moreton Bay in 1827. But here he was wrong, for Swann
had died of dysentery in the hospital—or so surgeon Cowper swore in an
affidavit.[56] Captain Logan now wrote a stiff note to the colonial secretary
demanding Hall's prosecution for criminal libel. In June, the Executive
Council questioned both Reverend Vincent, the former Moreton Bay
chaplain, and Surgeon Cowper. Cowper denied outright that there had
ever been any cruelty, let alone murder, at Moreton Bay, and said nobody
named Trenand had ever been an overseer there. The clergyman did
remember Trenand, "who was said to be of a cruel disposition, and in
the habit of beating and abusing the prisoners," but denied that he had
heard of him killing a prisoner with a spade. Asked whether men were
killed unofficially by guards there, he hedged. "Certainly not to justify
the statement in the paper," was his strange reply.[57] Neither man remembered seeing cripples flogged or confirmed the more lurid accusations of arbitrary torture in Matthew's gallows document. Prompted by
Darling, the Executive Council advised the attorney-general to issue yet
another writ for criminal libel against Edward Hall, that spreader of
"sedition and levelling."

The case never came to trial. Logan was about to leave for India—a
posting now made necessary by the terrible reputation his regime at
Moreton Bay had earned from the Emancipist press. By October 1830, his
successor as commandant, Captain James Clunie of the 17th Regiment,
was already learning the ropes at Moreton Bay. But Logan was not to
leave Australia until he had given his sworn testimony in the trial of
Hall and the *Monitor*, and while awaiting this call to Sydney he filled in
time making exploratory sorties into the Brisbane Valley, upriver from
Moreton Bay. On October 17, during one of these rides, his party lost
him in the labyrinth of scrub.

Four days later a search-party found his saddle, its stirrup-leathers cut
with a stone ax. Bands of convicts, led by Cowper and others, combed
the bush for another week. In a clearing that bore the marks of many
aboriginal feet, as though a wild dance had been held there, they found
some pages of his notebook trampled in the dry grasses, along with a

The degradation of the fringe-dwelling Aborigines of Sydney, with their hand-me-down English rags and rum bottles, is recorded c. 1830 in the Augustus Earle's lithograph *Natives of New South Wales*. (*Mitchell Library and Dixson Collections, Sydney*)

An iron-gang of Government men seen outside the Sydney Barracks by Augustus Earle's unsympathetic eye, during the governorship of Sir Ralph Darling, c. 1830. (*National Library of Australia, Canberra*)

A road-gang in the bush near Sydney, c. 1838. The pinched and sallow look of the chained prisoners is probably nearer the truth than are the sturdy, brutalized Irish stereotypes of Earle's lithography. (*National Library of Australia, Canberra*)

Gang labor on the Great West Road across the Blue Mountains: Augustus Earle's *View from the Summit of Mount York, Towards Bathurst Plains*, c. 1826. (*National Library of Australia, Canberra*)

The road nears its completion, and "boundless regions open to our sight." Charles Rodius, *Convicts Building the Road to Bathhurst*, 1833. (*National Library of Australia, Canberra*)

ABOVE: "That place of tyranny"—
Macquarie Harbor. The ruins of
the stone jail on Sarah Island, photographed by J. W. Beattie in the
1860s. (*National Library of Australia, Canberra*) LEFT: Sarah Island from the south, by the
convict artist C. H. T. Costantini,
c. 1830. The main wharf and boat-
yard are in the center; note the tall
sawn-log security fences. (*Allport
Library and State Museum of Fine
Arts, Hobart*) BELOW LEFT: Crews
of convicts towing a raft of felled
Huon pine logs to the sawpit at
Sarah Island, Macquarie Harbor.
Grummet Island is at right, with
its crude punishment hut and,
below, the dark opening in the
rock used as a solitary cell. Sketch
by T. J. Lemprière, c. 1830. (*Allport
Library and State Museum of Fine
Arts, Hobart*)

ABOVE: *A View of Hobart Town, Van Diemen's Land*, c. 1823, by George W. Evans. In the foreground, convicts are working, rather lackadaisically—note the two men at center chatting and smoking —under the supervision of an architect. This loose discipline was what Lieutenant-Governor Arthur dedicated himself to abolishing. Evans, the artist, was forced by Arthur from his post as surveyor in Van Diemen's Land after allegations of bribery. (*National Library of Australia, Canberra*) RIGHT: The unbending proconsul of Van Diemen's Land, Lieutenant-Governor Sir George Arthur (1784–1854). Anonymous miniature. (*Mitchell Library and Dixson Collections, Sydney*)

ABOVE: Port Arthur in the 1860s. The four-story building with attics and stone quoins at right is part of the huge flour mill converted in 1857 to a penitentiary. The round castellated tower halfway up the hill to the left is the guardhouse. (*National Library of Australia, Canberra*) LEFT: "Impartial justice, as impassive as that of fate": Captain Charles O'Hara Booth (1800–1851), Commandant of Port Arthur from 1833 to 1840. Portrait by T. J. Lemprière. (*Tasmanian Museum and Art Gallery, Hobart*)

RIGHT: Sir John and Lady Franklin inspect the line of guard dogs at Eaglehawk Neck. (*Mitchell Library and Dixson Collections, Sydney*) BELOW LEFT: "The Polar Knight," Lieutenant-Governor Sir John Franklin (1766–1847). Anonymous miniature. (*Mitchell Library and Dixson Collections, Sydney*) BELOW RIGHT: *Et in Arcadia Ego:* instruments of Port Arthur discipline and bureaucracy, surrounded by native wildflowers. Tourist postcard by J. W. Beattie, c. 1870. (*Mitchell Library and Dixson Collections, Sydney*)

TOP: Eaglehawk Neck, the only land-bridge to the Tasman Peninsula, photographed by J. W. Beattie in the 1870s. Guardhouses are in the foreground. (*Launceston Museum and Art Gallery, Tasmania*) ABOVE: "The adamantine gates of Hell itself" —Cape Raoul, at the entrance to Port Arthur, with its towering black basalt flutes. (*Launceston Museum and Art Gallery, Tasmania*)

THE

MUSTER MASTER.

A CHAPTER OF COLONIAL HISTORY

BY

AN OLD VAN DEMONIAN.

1874.

ABOVE: The first Australian railway, convict-powered, designed and installed by Commandant Booth, carries visitors through the primeval forest of the Tasman Peninsula. (*National Library of Australia, Canberra*) LEFT: Propaganda against the memory of the System. On the title page of "The Muster Master," published thirty years after transportation to Tasmania stopped, a convict is flagellated while a low official exhorts him to "keep up." At right, a magistrate remarks, "I'll give the wretch 100 lashes and send him to be hanged." The hangman, by the gallows on the hill, exclaims, "It's complete butchery but I must do it, I suppose." In fact, such combinations of corporal and capital punishment were proscribed. (*Mitchell Library and Dixson Collections, Sydney*)

ABOVE: Benjamin Duterreau's "National Picture," *The Conciliation*, c. 1835. George Augustus Robinson is seen "bringing in" the surviving mainland Aborigines of Van Diemen's Land. Seated to his left, Trucanini points at the Conciliator and draws a hesitant tribesman toward him. Note the imagery of "reconciliation" naively expressed in the coexistence of a wallaby and some kangaroohounds. (*Tasmanian Museum and Art Gallery, Hobart*) LEFT: The last pureblood Aborigines of the Tasmanian mainland, facing the end in European finery: from left to right, Trucanini, William Lanney and Bessie Clarke, photographed by J. W. Beattie in 1866. (*National Library of Australia, Canberra*)

Arthur's policy on race relations, c. 1828: a notice-board promising equal justice to blacks and whites alike, addressed to Aborigines. (*Tasmanian Museum and Art Gallery, Hobart*)

OPPOSITE ABOVE: The rituals of the cat: a flogging at Moreton Bay, from William Ross's pamphlet inveighing against Captain Logan's regime, *The Fell Tyrant; or, the Suffering Convict,* 1836. (*Mitchell Library and Dixson Collections, Sydney*)

OPPOSITE BELOW LEFT: The martinet of the mainland: Sir Ralph Darling (1775–1858), Governor of New South Wales from 1824 to 1831, oversaw the expansion of "secondary" penal colonies from Newcastle to Moreton Bay and the revival of Norfolk Island as "the *ne plus ultra* of convict degradation." Portrait by John Linnell. (*Mitchell Library and Dixson Collections, Sydney*)

OPPOSITE BELOW RIGHT: "Fellow prisoners, be exhilarated/That all such monsters such a death may find": Captain Patrick Logan, 57th Regiment, Commandant of Moreton Bay. Anonymous portrait. (*Mitchell Library and Dixson Collections, Sydney*)

ABOVE: The remains of a "dumb cell" in the main prison at Kingston, Norfolk Island. Note the thickness of the walls, through which no sound could pass. Since this photograph was taken (c. 1870), the site has been levelled, and little trace of these structures survives. (*Launceston Museum and Art Gallery, Tasmania*)

RIGHT: Gravestone of a mutineer hanged after the convict rising of 1834 against Commandant Morisset on Norfolk Island. (*Author's collection*)

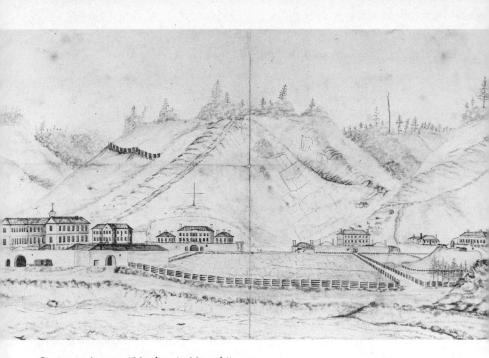

OPPOSITE ABOVE: "Murderer's Mound," the mass grave outside the consecrated ground of the Norfolk Island cemetery, where the convict mutineers of 1846 were buried. (*Launceston Museum and Art Gallery, Tasmania*) OPPOSITE BELOW LEFT: Captain Foster Fyans (1790–1870), Morisset's second-in-command on Norfolk Island, who suppressed the 1834 mutiny. (*Mitchell Library and Dixson Collections, Sydney*) OPPOSITE BELOW RIGHT: "One of the durable ogres of the Australian imagination": John Giles Price (1808–1857), Commandant of Norfolk Island from 1846 to 1853. (*Royal Society of Tasmania*) ABOVE: Unknown artist's sketch of the main settlement at Kingston, Norfolk Island, in 1838. The prisoners' barracks and mess are at left; behind, at the foot of the hill, the Military Barracks; at right, Government House. (*Mitchell Library and Dixson Collections, Sydney*) RIGHT: Maconochie permits dignity to the dead: the convict-carved headstone of Samuel Jones, shot for his part in an attempted hijacking of the *Governor Phillip* off Norfolk Island, 1842. (*Author's collection*)

Products of the System: some of the remaining "old crawlers" or veteran convicts at Port Arthur, photographed in 1874. (*Archives Office of Tasmania*)

bloodstained tatter of his waistcoat and a part of his compass, broken and discarded by prying stone-age fingers. The next morning, about a mile away, the searchers found Logan's horse dead and swollen in a creek-bed, with sticks incomprehensibly strewn over it. Up the steep bank of the stream was a shallow grave. Logan's bare feet, partly eaten, protruded from the earth and his boots lay to one side. The blacks had speared him to death and buried him facedown, but the wild dogs had begun to dig him up; now he was black with flies and beyond eating. When his body was brought back to Moreton Bay, the convicts "manifested insane joy at the news of his murder, and sang and hoorayed all night, in defiance of the warders."[58]

So anxious were they to claim his death as their own revenge that they invented a different version: The hated commandant had been seized by his own convict servants in the bush, flogged nearly to death, finished off with a stone and buried facing downward, "looking down to Hell, for that's where he's going." Then came the ghost stories. On the day Logan died, it was said, he appeared immobile and silent on his ghastly horse on the far bank of the Brisbane River; but when the ferryman rowed over to collect him, no one was there. Thus, Patrick Logan began to pass into popular legend at the moment of his death; the ballads came soon after. There was no libel trial for Edward Hall, this time. In fact Governor Darling, perhaps hoping to reduce the hail of innuendo and invective from the colonial press that beat around his head, took a deep breath and made the sole placatory gesture of his governorship: He freed Hall in November 1830, soon after the news of Logan's killing reached Sydney.

But Hall was not grateful; nor did the Sydney democrats think this gesture outweighed Darling's record of cruelty to convicts and favoritism to colonial Tories. Darling might have remained in office despite his colonial enemies—for Australians had not put him there, and they could not remove him—but England itself was moving away from the Tory extremism that Darling, an army man serving this arch-reactionary government of Wellington, embodied.

By 1830, the movement for parliamentary reform had percolated from working men to the very middle classes who, in 1819, had reacted indifferently or timidly to the Peterloo Massacre and who distrusted the idea of "reform." And as the English middle classes became more aware of the appalling inequities built into the power structure—symbolized by the postwar sufferings of the countryside and the scandal of the "Rotten Boroughs"—so the social base of the reform movement broadened, and the Whigs, led by Lord Charles Grey, could move against the Tories' monopoly of power. There was, moreover, the example of the French Revolution of 1830, which persuaded some liberal Whigs that populist moves, led by bourgeois interests, did not—as the Tories had warned since 1789—lead to Jacobinism and tumbrils. Lafayette and Louis-Philippe were plainly not the same as Marat and Robespierre. In November 1830, Wellington's government fell and the new king, William IV, instructed Lord Grey to form a government. Under Grey, the Reform Bill passed, though only by one vote.

Grey was not liberal: "There is no one more decided against annual parliaments, universal suffrage, and the ballot than I am," he told the House. "My object is not to favour, but to put an end to such hopes and projects." [59] But his son, Henry George Grey, known as Viscount Howick, did not share all the father's views. In particular he had been fired by Wilberforce's campaign against slavery, and he was not unaware of the comparisons drawn between slavery and convict transportation. Nepotism put Howick in his father's ministry in 1830 as under-secretary for the colonies, under Viscount Goderich. In Howick, the stream of complaints from Australia about Governor Darling found a sympathetic ear. The world had moved somewhat, and even at the limits of Empire there was less room for a a dull, gold-braided martinet who believed more in the lash than the ballot-box. Howick particularly disliked Darling's attempts to muzzle public speech in New South Wales; and when the governor's six-year term ran out in 1831, there was no move to renew it. So Darling left Australia.

His departure was marked by wild jubilations from the Emancipists. Hall's *Monitor* announced that an "illumination" would rise over its editorial office the night Darling sailed, bearing the incandescent phrase "He's off." "THANK GOD—We have shaken off the *incubus* at last!" Wentworth exclaimed in the *Australian*, and held open house for every Emancipist in the colony on the grounds of his estate at Vaucluse, overlooking Sydney Harbor, whose perimeter had been surrounded by a shallow trench filled with Irish earth to keep the Australian snakes out. Some four thousand people converged on Vaucluse House by gig, horse, donkey and Shank's pony, and hoed into a feast more Brobdingnagian than Lucullan, involving a whole roast ox, twelve sheep, thousands of loaves of bread and incalculable quantities of ale and spirits. The pro-Darling newspaper, the *Sydney Gazette*, asked its readers to imagine

> the roaring, bawling, screeching, blaspheming, thumping, bumping, kicking, licking, tricking, cheating, beating, stealing, reeling, breaking of heads, bleeding of noses, blackening of eyes, picking of pockets, and what not . . . the orgies of the lowest rabble of Botany Bay, congregated in the open air, shrouded by the curtain of night, released from the eyes of the police, and *helewated* by the fumes of *Cooper's gin* . . . [T]hese contemptible proceedings have excited universal disgust and abhorrence among decent people.[60]

But that night the Emancipists and Currency voted obstreperously with their bellies; there were few tears when Darling sailed, and no new appointments for him when he reached England.

Darling's departure, and his replacement by the comparatively liberal Richard Bourke, made convict life at Moreton Bay slightly better—but not much. Thanks to Logan's slave-driving, the settlement now had better buildings and a regular supply of water (whose pipes were each laboriously hollowed from an ironbark log); accordingly, the disease rate slowed down, although trachoma would linger among convicts and then among poor-white settlers on the Brisbane River for half a century longer. Logan's successor, Clunie, was a flogger but a less capricious one, and the convicts did not think him such a tyrant. Fewer of them tried to escape, but that was because they had given up hope: Relations between whites and blacks at Moreton Bay had degenerated so far that convicts now expected to be killed by the natives if they went bush. Allan Cunningham, who had been there in 1828–29, later reported that escaped convicts had been "taking liberties with"—raping—aboriginal women.[61] This must have been the last straw. However, the territories of those offended tribes lay south of Moreton Bay.

Other convicts went north, in the hope of reaching China, and at least one of them not only survived but became famous for his escape (although he did not reach China). This was John Graham, a resourceful Irishman who had been transported in 1824 for stealing a few pounds of hemp from a linen-maker. Assigned at first to a master in Parramatta, he got to know the local Aborigines and learned from them some tricks of survival in the unfamiliar bush. Then, for a second offense, he was transported to Moreton Bay in 1827. After a few months of Logan's brutalities he bolted north, managing to avoid the Aborigines and live, unaided, off the land. When at last he did blunder into contact with a tribe, he had the improbable luck to be greeted by one of its women as the white ghost of her dead warrior-husband. Thus he entered the tribe and lived with it from 1827 to 1833, before walking back to Moreton Bay and surrendering to the surprised Clunie. No convict, other than Buckley in Victoria, had ever acquired such intimate, detailed knowledge of aboriginal life and ritual, but it did not make Graham any more sympathetic to the blacks once he was back in white company. He denounced them as "frightful clans and hordes of cannibals and savages," hoping to convince the authorities that he had suffered so much among them that his sentence should not be prolonged.[62]

Under Clunie, Moreton Bay took shape as a town, the embryo of the city of Brisbane. Its crude economy of forced labor had diversified, expanded by artisans from the "First Class" of convicts—minor offenders who had shown an unblemished record over their first years of imprisonment there. Tailors sewed gray-and-yellow uniforms out of the coarse, felt-like "magpie cloth" or "canary stuff"; and there were cobblers, tanners and candlemakers, smiths, coopers, joiners and wheelwrights—a thriving little economy that contained the seeds of surplus and trade, and whose labor was exploited in various ways by the overseers and officers. The convicts had more food now and placed an enormous value on small luxuries like tea and sugar. The tea was coarse green stuff full of twigs, known as "posts-and-rails"; the brown sticky sugar was nicknamed "coal tar," but it would improve a sweet potato duff and give strength to the insipid mock-coffee the prisoners made from burnt corn kernels.

By the end of 1835, when Captain Foster Fyans of the 4th (King's Own) Regiment succeeded Clunie as commandant, the old starvation days under Logan were just a memory—though a bitterly preserved one in convict lore. But the rest of prison life went on much as before beneath the shadow of the triangles. Fyans took a sardonic pleasure in describing the rituals of the cat-o'-nine-tails to George Walker and James Backhouse, two Quaker missionaries on a tour of the Australian penal colonies:

> "Friend," said Friend Backhouse, "I wish thee much to explain the punishments. First, friend, the number of stripes in whipping?"
> My reply was, from twenty to a hundred or two hundred lashes, that was our limit:—when two long and hollow groans followed. "The first lash, Friend, the skin rises not unlike a white frost, Friend. The second lash, Friend, often reminds me of a snowstorm. . . . [T]he third lash, Friend, the back is lacerated dreadfully." Half a dozen of groans. "The painful feelings then subside, Friend, for the blood comes freely." Long groans and heavy moans, and the Friends said some prayers; when out the notebooks came. . . . I then proposed to flog a fellow that they might see the process, and be better able to judge. "No, Friend, we thank thee."[63]

But by then the main form of punishment at Moreton Bay was not the lash, but the treadmill. In 1827, Logan had built a windmill there (it still stands, though converted into an observatory, and is one of the few remaining buildings of the convict period in Brisbane); and two years later a treadmill was added to it, so that convicts could grind corn when the wind did not blow—a practical machine that doubled as an instrument of mass punishment. The treadmill was like a waterwheel, but it was forty feet long, with wooden treads nine inches wide. As many as fifty convicts could be punished on it at once. The convicts' names for it were expressive: the *everlasting staircase* or, because the stiff prison clothes scraped one's groin raw after a few hours on it, the *cockchafer*.

The prisoners went up a flight of steps and stood ready on the horizontal blade of the mill. They had a fixed handrail to hold. The overseer pulled out an iron bolt and the wheel began to turn: "You would hear the 'click, click' of their irons as they kept step with the wheel, and those with the heaviest irons seemed to have a great job to keep up. Some poor wretches only just managed to pull through until they got off."[64] The mill stood for progress—the rationalization of punishment. It was a more philosophical instrument than the cat.

From 1835 on, the exclusively penal nature of Brisbane Town and its outlying settlements began to fade. The lash could still be heard in the streets, and the centipedes of ironed men, their chains rusty with tropical dew, still shuffled from barracks to work, their heads bowed; but their numbers were declining, and when Fyans took over there were only about four hundred male convicts there. By 1840, the prisoners' barracks and the Female Factory stood empty. All convicts still under sentence had been recalled to Sydney, and the assignment system had been discontinued. Now the free settlers of Brisbane had to manage without government-sponsored slave labor, for the place was no longer isolated. It even had a post office. And the broken, marginal Aborigines, stupefied with cane liquor, dozing like lumps of shadow in patches of shade, confirmed the total victory of white civilization. By 1840, squatters had found a stock route north to the rich plains of the Darling Downs, inland from Brisbane. So the pastoral economy of modern Queensland began with the emancipation of Brisbane, for "Nature has pointed out that spot," the *Australian* editorialized in 1842, "as the site of the northern capital of Australia." A week later, Governor Gipps formally declared that Moreton Bay was no longer a penal settlement. Settlers and visitors could come and go as they pleased. Military rule was over. So ended the last of the penal stations on the Australian mainland; and when the first Queensland Parliament was convened some years later, it met, by an irony that Logan might have appreciated, in the upper floor of the largest building in Brisbane—the old convict barracks, built to house a thousand men. But soon this unloved souvenir, like so many buildings that spoke of Australian darkness, was razed.

i v

THE SPOT THAT now represented the quintessence of punishment was Norfolk Island. Governor Brisbane had turned his attention to it in 1824, the year Morcton Bay was settled. After reading the Bigge Report, Lord Bathurst had ordered him to prepare a place of ultimate terror for the incorrigibles of the System. As long as convicts were on the mainland, they could escape; and so Bathurst told Brisbane to re-occupy Norfolk Island, which had been abandoned ten years before at the merciful behest of Governor Macquarie. This speck of land, floating in the infinite waste of the Pacific a thousand miles east of Sydney and four hundred miles north of New Zealand, would once more serve as "a great Hulk or Penitentiary," the nadir of England's penal system. Its old form had been bad enough. As Governor Hunter declared in 1812, its prisoners "felt [it] was a very severe sentence; they would sooner have lost their lives." Now it would get worse, and although no convict could escape from it, rumor and reputation would. In this way, the "Old Hell," as convict argot termed it, would reduce mainland crime by sheer terror.[65]

Brisbane wrote to England, outlining his new kakotopia. On Norfolk Island, the genial stargazer promised, all pretense at reform would be dropped. Its sole purpose would be to provide "the *ne plus ultra* of convict degradation." The island could not support many prisoners, and those it contained must be the absolute worst of those double-damned by the System. Hence, most of them would be men convicted of fresh hanging crimes in the colony, whose sentences had been commuted to life imprisonment. "The felon, who is sent there, is forever excluded from all hope of return," and although mainland convicts in government service or on the assignment system had some legal rights, those on Norfolk Island "have forfeited all claim to the protection of the law." To ensure their reduction to mere ciphers, Brisbane urged that

> if it were not too repugnant to the Laws of England, I should consider it very fitting to have Norfolk Island completely under Martial Law, which would not only form part of the punishment in itself, but save the complicated machinery of Civil Courts, or sending people for trial [to Sydney]. . . . My experience convinces me that there is nothing so effectual in dealing with convicts as Summary Proceedings.[66]

This, Bathurst would not grant; but in practice, the future commandants of Norfolk Island were invested with such sweeping powers short of arbitrary hanging that their rule was all but absolute.

The prisoners must be promised nothing and given only the dimmest sense of a goal toward which they could work. "No hopes of any mitigation of their sentences . . . should ever be held out to them," and they could only get off the island after a minimum of 10 years, whose last 5 must show a perfect behavior-sheet.[67] That record, of course, could be wiped out by the whim of an officer, the merest grudge-word of an informer. And even if the prisoner finished his Norfolk Island sentence and returned to the mainland, he must serve out the rest of his original sentence in full. *Lasciate ogni speranza, voi ch'intrate*—Dante's words on the adamantine gate of Hell became the obligatory text quoted by educated visitors to Norfolk Island (not that there were many of them) over the next fifteen years. The island would be a machine for extinguishing hope.

For this purpose it was ideal, for it concentrated and epitomized the sense of delusive beauty, beauty empty at the core and flaking into viciousness, uselessness and indifference, that had been part of English reactions to Australian landscape ever since the arrival of the First Fleet. From an approaching boat, Norfolk Island is an apparition, a rolling cap of green meadow and spiring trees, raised out of the Pacific on pipes and pillars of basalt as though offered to one infinite blueness by another. It was no harbor. Most of its coast is sheer cliff, black planes of rock laced with red oxides. There are only two landing-places. One is at Cascades Bay on the northeast side, where boats and crew have to be plucked from the water by a derrick. The other, chiefly used in convict days, is at Sydney Bay, where the ruins of the Kingston penal settlement stand. A reef blocks the whole approach to the shore; ships stood off and unloaded their freight of chained convicts into whalers, which had to be rowed over the reef through its boiling cross-rips—a terrifying ordeal for all but the stoutest tar.

They struggled ashore in Paradise. There was a little crescent beach of white sand where, still by an arm of the reef, the water lapped in aquamarine clarity. Green hills encircled the flat, swampy table where the first settlement had been pitched forty years before; their folds ran down to the sea, and in them ran cascades of bright water shaded by hibiscus and palms. Great ropes of jasmine, on stems thick as a man's wrist, hung in swags from the branches of the Norfolk Island pines. There were groves of sugar cane, figs, guavas and lemons, the wild descendants of specimens brought by the First Fleet from Rio and the Cape in 1788. The Norfolk Island birds had forgotten man had ever been there; one could pick them out of the bushes, like fruit. Even today, a walk along the cliffs—where the green meadow runs to the very brink of the drop and the bushes are distorted by the eternal Pacific wind into humps and clawings that resemble Hokusai's *Great Wave* copied by a topiarist—is a fine cure for human adhesiveness. One sees nothing but elements: air, water, rock and the patterns wrought by their immense friction. The mornings are by Turner; the evenings, by Caspar David Friedrich, calm and beneficent, the light sifting angelically down toward the solemn horizon. "My object," wrote Governor Darling in 1827, "was to hold out that Settlement as a place of the extremest Punishment, short of Death."[68]

The first party of convicts—fifty-seven of them, picked for their skill as artisans—landed in June 1825 and began setting up new quarters out of stone and plank scavenged from the abandoned Kingston settlement. Over the next five years, the population grew and an unremarkable succession of military officers ran the island.* The authorities did not fix on a long-term commandant until 1829. The man they chose was a lieutenant-colonel of the 80th Regiment, James Thomas Morisset (1780–1852).

Morisset had proven tastes and abilities for the work. At the age of forty-nine he was an old soldier; in fact, the army had been his entire life, from the age of eighteen, when he joined the 80th and began a steady rise through the ranks of service in India and Egypt. He was a career officer with no family money to buy him a commission. In the Napoleonic Wars, he fought as a captain in Spain and was gravely wounded at the battle of La Albuera. In 1817 he was posted with his regiment to New South Wales, where he took over command of the Newcastle penal settlement from Captain James Wallis. Through what Hall would later call "the timidity and suspicion of his natural temper, and his proneness to severity," Morisset soon became a terror to the convicts, infamous for the harshness of his punishments. As commandant he was also magistrate, and in order to spare settlers up the Hunter River the bother of coming to Newcastle in order to bring charges against their assigned servants, he would make excursions upstream in a boat with two flagellators and a portable set of triangles so that he could hand out summary lashings on their farms.

No portrait of Morisset survives, and his appearance would have taxed the meager resources of any colonial artist. He was slender, elegantly dressed (by Buckmaster, one of the more fashionable London military tailors) and fond of gold embroidery; even his forage cap was covered with it. But the look of the military dandy was brusquely contradicted by his face. At La Albuera, a 32-inch mine-shell had exploded near him and left him with the mask of an ogre. His mouth ran diagonally upward and made peculiar whistling noises when he spoke. One eye was normal, but the other protruded like a staring pebble and seemed never to move. The cheekbone and jaw on one side had been smashed to fragments and, without cosmetic surgery, had re-knit to form a swollen mass like "a large yellow over-ripe melon"; he would defiantly thrust this cheek forward in conversation, as though daring his interlocutor to look away.[69] For Morisset was not without bravado, and he was determined to convert his wound into a badge of bitter honor in the eyes of his equals and superiors.

---

* They were, in order: Captain Turton, 1825–26; Captain Vance Young Donaldson, 57th Regt., 1826–27; Captain Thomas Wright, 39th Regt., 1827–28; Captain Robert Hunt, 57th Regt., 1828–29; Captain Wakefield, 39th Regt., 1829. Only Wright stayed longer than a year.

For his inferiors, the convicts, more dangerous sublimations lay within the dapper frame and the twisted gourd of shiny tissue. He "knew" them; and when he returned to London on leave after eight years in Australia—the last two as commandant at Bathurst, beyond the Blue Mountains—he could not get the convicts out of his mind, for their management had become an obsession. He went every day to Bow Street; he haunted the police offices; he learned to talk underworld cant. "I am the man to keep these scoundrels in order," he boasted later. "I assure you, Sir, if the Duke of Wellington searched through the Army of Great Britain he could not equal me; I understand all their priggings."[70] And while in London, he waited on Lord Bathurst and begged for Norfolk Island.

Bathurst knew talent when he saw it. He was worried about the rabble's changing attitude to transportation. Too many letters had come back from Emancipists and from assigned convicts who had found easy masters, praising the conditions of life in New South Wales and Van Diemen's Land, where wages were high and a man could make a new life for himself with his two hands. Bathurst did not want Australia to lose its reputation. Morisset seemed just the man to help Darling put a dose of iron back in the convict soul. The increase of terror (a word Bathurst used often in dispatches to Darling) must begin from the bottom of the System, which meant Norfolk Island. So Morisset went back to Australia as a lieutenant-colonel in 1827. There was some delay in getting him to Norfolk Island. He had married a young woman named Emily Vaux in 1826, but Darling wanted no women in Norfolk Island, because their presence would confuse the schematic purity of discipline in that Mount Athos of English misery. "I laid it down as a rule," Darling explained, "that women should not be sent to the Settlement, and the few free women . . . belonging to the troops and the people there, were accordingly withdrawn."[71] He was reluctant to have only one woman, the commandant's wife, in residence there. Yet it seemed unfair to separate Morisset from the meek young bride whom—with some difficulty, one may surmise, considering his looks—he had wooed and won and then brought so far to Australia. In February 1829, the Morissets sailed for Norfolk Island with their two children. These infants were to see strange sights.

Norfolk Island

i

W H E N Lieutenant-Colonel Morisset left to take up his new duties, the *Monitor* in Sydney ran an editorial about his future
on "Norfolk Island, late Gomorrah Island," exhorting him to
run it with mercy and restraint. To the powerless and passive convicts
"he will be as a God," and so

> let him therefore put himself in the place of Deity, and let his mind
> become imbued with magnanimity, considering that his power was given
> him, not for his own pleasure and benefit, but for the benefit of the
> wretches under his sovereign control (for such is a Commandant's will at
> penal settlements).
>
> Let the biting scourge be inflicted seldom, and then in merciful quan-
> tities; and let no other part of an Englishman's body be subjected to this
> ancient, though still brutal torture, but the *back*.[1]

Morisset may or may not have read this advice; it hardly mattered,
for he knew what his chief, Governor Darling, thought of the *Monitor*
and its editor. People often suppose that penal systems recruit sadists.
But cruelty is an appetite that grows with feeding, and few people receive
an epiphany of their own sadism in the abstract; they must see their
victims first. It is most unlikely that Morisset's habits were known in
advance and so ensured him the command of Norfolk Island. If anything,
the authorities concluded from his conduct at Newcastle that he was
conscientious, stern, but not unjust. Lachlan Macquarie, the Emancipists' friend, had praised his work there (and even named a lagoon after
him in 1821; 150 years later, more fittingly, a lunatic asylum would
receive his name). The *Sydney Gazette* extolled him as an opponent of
hanging.[2] Both Bathurst in London and Darling in Sydney thought they
had found in Morisset a tough, reliable line officer who would run the

settlement with a heavy hand but by the book. But this description also fits the men who have run the Gulags of our own time.

The essence of any sadistic relationship between a bad prison boss and his prisoners is that the latter should be (in the word so often used of Australian convicts) "objects." The System's distinction between "objects" (prisoners) and "subjects" (the free) was no mere grammatical quirk: It implied the convict's expulsion from the domain of rights. "Felons on Norfolk Island have forfeited all claim to protection of the law," wrote Governor Brisbane in 1825, meaning every word. "Port Macquarie for first grave offences; Moreton Bay for runaways from the former; and Norfolk Island as the *ne plus ultra.*"[3] There was no point of exile beyond this island; its convicts were at their ultimate distance from reasoned legality and open transaction. The only refuge of their criminality was within their bodies, from whose inaccessible centers the meek silence craved by the System could be trumped by mute defiance. This was the silence of the "pebble," the "stone man," as prisoners of unusual endurance were called—a panting and glaring silence, that of a fox gone to earth. On Norfolk Island, that silence would be broken. On May 26, 1829, Morisset landed on Norfolk Island. A year and a half later, the only convict to leave a first-hand account of life under Morisset also arrived there. His name was Laurence Frayne.[4]

Frayne was sent to Norfolk Island in his sixth year of transportation. He was an Irishman, convicted of theft in Dublin in October 1825. He arrived in Sydney on the transport *Regalia* with 129 other Irish convicts at the end of 1826; he may have been implicated en route to Rio in an abortive mutiny plot that failed because—as a young officer on board recounted it—"an Old Man whom we favoured a little came & confessed all the plot. . . . [The soldiers] would have been so enraged they would have murdered every convict on board."[5] In 1828 Frayne was reconvicted for "repeatedly absconding" and was sent to Moreton Bay. There, he still kept trying to escape and his behavior was so untameable that he was sent down to Sydney in January 1830, reconvicted by the Supreme Court, sentenced to death, had his sentence commuted and was put on the *Phoenix* hulk, awaiting transportation to Norfolk Island.

The hulk, an unseaworthy old transport moored in Lavender Bay, had served as an antechamber to the far penal settlements since 1824. She was a stationary hellship, "that receptable of Filth and place of Cruelty and Starvation."[6] Prisoners on board were kept half-starved by the guards, who withheld their rations of flour and "salt horse" to sell on shore; the head warden was an alcoholic who later died in delirium tremens. Frayne tried to escape from the *Phoenix*, but he was caught slipping over the side and was given 50 lashes; then he cursed the overseer and received 150 more. Other convicts on the hulk fared just as ill.

Thomas Cook, held there in May 1836 en route to Norfolk Island, was
seized by the head keeper for sharing a pipe of tobacco with his nine
cellmates. The ten men were stripped naked,

> and after manacling each of our hands behind our backs, he reefed the
> legs, which were heavily Ironed, to the upper part of the Iron Stanchions
> of the Cell . . . with the whole weight of our chains and bodies pressing
> on our Shoulder Blades for the night, in a state of perfect nudity. By the
> following morning, and for two days afterward, I could scarcely regain the
> use of my arms.[7]

Prisoners were silenced with a gag, or by sluicing them down with
sea water; in winter, this brought on pneumonia. On the voyage to Norfolk Island their ill-treatment continued. James Lawrence, the convict
son of a London diamond broker who had been transported for fraud in
1836 and sent to Norfolk Island almost as soon as he arrived in Sydney,
recalled that on this thousand-mile voyage in the brig *Governor Phillip*,
there were "Seventy-Five of us in cross irons, our clothes taken from us
with the exception of our Shirts, and then rove on a chain in a small
prison scarce able to breathe, our passage was dreadful in the Extreme."[8]
Frayne, cut to ribbons by the lash, had to make the voyage to Norfolk
Island on the *Lucy Ann* in October 1830 with maggots crawling in his
back and no chance of a wash or a bandage:

> My shoulders were actually in a state of decomposition the stench of
> which I could not bear myself, how offensive then must I appear and
> smell to my companions in misery. In this state immediately after my
> landing I was sent to carry Salt Beef on my back with the Salt Brine as
> well as pressure stinging my mutilated & mortified flesh up to Longridge.
> I really longed for instant death.[9]

As soon as they landed at Kingston, the convicts went to work. Norfolk Island had no free settlers and no assignment system; hence, the
convicts worked only for government, constructing buildings or growing
food. Every structure on the island, from the sentry-boxes to the high
stone security walls around the main compounds at Kingston, was convict-built. Few skilled masons were to be found among the twice-convicted "incorrigibles" in exile there, but the last drop of crude labor was
wrung from them in iron gangs. They made bricks, burned coral into
lime for mortar and ripped the Norfolk Island pines into planks. The jail
gang, made up of some thirty-five multiple offenders crammed in a filthy
hovel of a prison near the jetty, hewed stone in the quarry wearing double
or even triple irons. As a special punishment, men were assigned to the

"wet quarry," a reef partly covered by the sea at the edge of the cemetery, to cut stone under water.

The workday was sunrise to sunset, with an hour off for the midday meal. Every morning and evening, all irons were inspected for signs of tampering—nick-marks, ovalling of the leg-ring, a loose rivet. At unpredictable times, the convicts would be mustered, counted and given full body-searches with inspections of the mouth and anus. Their daily rations were 1½ pounds of cornmeal, 1 pound of salt beef, 1 ounce of sugar, ½ ounce of salt, and a tiny morsel of soap. At dinner, the superintendent was to issue each "mess" of six men a mess kit (knife, fork, spoon, pannikin) which they used in rotation and handed back. But there were never enough utensils to go round, so that they had to eat in a way "disgusting to any man possessing the slightest degree of decency. . . . The provisions were brought out to the various Gangs in wooden or large tin Dishes and set down as before a Hog or a Dog and [they had] to gnaugh it just the same." If a man dared to make his own utensils, especially a knife, he would be flogged at once and jailed.[10]

The basis of prison discipline was the informer. On Norfolk the policy of splintering the convicts as a class, dissolving solidarity in mutual suspicion, was taken to extremes; the authorities felt, quite correctly, that if the prisoners were given the smallest chance to combine there could be a bloody uprising, even a general massacre. Thus *not* to inform became suspicious in itself, and hardly a week passed without the disclosure of elaborate plots, complete with lists of names, as convicts competed for trivial favors from Morisset and his officers by denouncing one another. "Indulgence," Frayne noted, "was only got by such traffic in human blood." The quality of the information mattered far less than its quantity. Informers had their quotas of denunciation to fill and were "capable of any act of purfidy or blood no matter how Black or horrifying such a deed might be." Any Norfolk man could be flogged on suspicion, as long as he was charged; and since prisoners were tried summarily, by tribunal and not by jury, they had no effective defense. In this way the "normal" relations between guilt and punishment mutated into a continuous sadistic fiction, whose sole aim was to preserve terror.

Frayne described what these punishments could mean. He was brought before Morisset for breaking a flagstone in the quarry. "As usual I found my defence useless," and thus was sentenced to 100 lashes:

> After the sentence I plainly told the Commandant in the Court that he was a Tyrant. He replied that no man had ever said that about him before. I said they knew the consequences too well to tell him so.—But I tell you in stark naked blunt English that you are as great a tyrant as Nero ever was.

The moment I expressed these words I was sentenced to an additional 100 & to be kept ironed down in a cell for Life and never to see daylight again.[11]

The floggings were spaced. Frayne got 50 lashes on his back. In four days, the cuts were partly scabbed over and he got 50 more. On the eighth day, he got 50 on the buttocks; and on the twelfth day, the last 50. Morisset supervised all this "specially to see the infliction . . . given as severe as the scourgers could possibly inflict it," so that

> new and heavier Cats were procured purposely for my punishment, & the flagellator threatened to be flogged himself if he did not give it me more severe. He replied that he did his utmost and really could do no more. . . . The Super[intendent] who witnessed the Punishment swore when I was taken down that i was a Brickmaker, meaning that I was like an Iron Man past all feelings of the punishment. Alas, delusive idea!—I felt too acutely the full weight scourge & sting of every lash but I had resolution enough accompanied by inflexible Obstinacy not to give any satisfaction. . . . I knew my real innocence and bore up against it.[12]

Morisset, insulted to his face, sought new pretexts to break this stiff-necked young Irishman. Nine or ten weeks later, Frayne was up before him again, charged with assaulting a convict informer named Harper. "What have you to say for yourself?" the Commandant asked, and Frayne began a tirade:

> I replied that I would leave it to you to judge whether I am guilty or innocent; you know the character & conduct of the informer; you also know mine. It is useless for me to gainsay anything. . . . If you actually knew my innocence yourself I well know that you would punish me. . . . If you acquit me for the assault you will flog me for what I have now said to you, but I disreagard both you and all the punishment you can give me.
> His very next expression was, "I will give you 300 at three different whippings, you damned Scoundrel."
> I said, "I am no Scoundrel no more than yourself, but *I don't think I can take that punishment.*" This I said out of derision and ironically, with a sneer at the Colonel.
> I and the other man was taken out and we received our first 100 in slow time and with heavy cats. The flagellators were almost as much besmeared with blood as even we. . . . When I was taken down an overseer who assisted to loosen the cords said, giving me a Fig of Tobacco, "You are a *Steel Man* not a Flesh-and-Blood Man at all, you can stand to be sawn asunder after all that skinning and mangling."[13]

Frayne and his fellow convict were jailed for a week until their backs scabbed over; then Morisset sent the island surgeon, Dr. Gamack, to see if they could take their second hundred. Frayne begged the surgeon to get on with it: "I am ready to be scarified alive again," as long as the other man (who "had tender flesh") could take his flogging too.

> Gamack says, "Do you wish to expire under the lash?" I said, "I want to get it over and have done with it & all thought of it, being here injures me more than the flogging."[14]

He got his second 100 and went back into solitary, without any medical treatment. To alleviate the pain from his mangled back Frayne had to pour his water ration on the stone floor of the cell, piss in it to enlarge the puddle, and lie down

> with my sore shoulders on the exact spot where the water lay. . . . I was literally alive with Maggots and Vermin, nor could I keep them down; to such a wretched and truly miserable state was I reduced, that I even hated the look & appearance of myself. . . . The trifle of soap allowed me to wash our persons & shirts was stopped from me, as I thought to spur me to abuse the Gaol authorities and thereby again subject myself to more cruelty . . . knowing as they all did my hasty temper.[15]

Before he could undergo the third part of his flogging, Frayne was reprieved; the colonial secretary in Sydney issued an executive order limiting all floggings to 100 lashes. Morisset then clapped him in the "dumb cell," a totally dark, soundless stone isolation chamber, for two months. No sooner did he come out, disoriented and staggering in the sudden blaze of Pacific sunlight, than he got in trouble again.

There were two assigned convict women working as servants at Government House. They had been briefly jailed for some trivial offense. One of them was not only Irish but came from the same town as Frayne. "Strange to say (and equally true as strange) I purposely got into Gaol if possible to get to them, and while they were walking in the Yard for Air I shewed myself through the Bars. . . . I told them they might expect me to pay them a visit at all Hazard, & I would put up with the consequences if it was 300." That night he did contrive to sneak into the women's cell and hide under their bedding. "They knew too well the Colonel's feelings towards me. . . . They were equally as anxious as myself to annoy the Colonel." So Frayne and the two women had their night of sexual comfort, the only tenderness, perhaps, that any of them had received or given in years. He was found out, of course, and haled before Morisset once more:

I plainly told the Commandant that it was the only opportunity I had ever had or perhaps ever would have of spending a night in Womens company; it was a very natural offence in a twofold degree. "How do you mean twofold?" asked the Commandant. "The first," I said, "is too obvious to need explanations, the second is that they are both your servants —now you can do as you please, that is all I have to say."

"Well then," said the Commandant, "I will give you 100 lashes in slow time so that you shall pay for your creeping into the women's cell."

I said, "I hope you will send me back to gaol right after it, and you can give me another 100 tomorrow for the same offence if that will gratify you or give you a pleasure."[16]

Frayne got his hundred, in slow time. So it went on: "I am an oppressed convict," he raves at Morisset, "oppressed by your Tyranny, & sacrificed by your base Informers & blood hunters, & my hunger and your cruel torture gives you the greatest pleasure & gratification." But nothing changes; defiance calls forth the lash, torture demands resistance, each side defends its territory, neither will budge. How many men like Frayne were there among the seven hundred Norfolk prisoners under Morisset in 1834? How much implacable, hopeless courage was summoned up to confront the iron machinery of discipline? Frayne spent three years "loaded with French or exceedingly heavy Irons" in the jail gang, reefed to a chain cable every night. Certainly, few convicts can have been like him—otherwise the island would have been uncontrollable.

More normal was the experience of John Holyard, who had come to Norfolk Island on the same boat as Frayne in 1830. He, too, had had his sentence for a capital crime commuted, but he learned quite early that to truckle was to survive; and so he became an informer. In the miseries of the *Phoenix* hulk, he "learned a lesson which I trust will never be forgot, viz., Submission to the Authorities." On Norfolk Island, "the exaggerated accounts told of the misery existing on the Island . . . wrung tears from me as I got out of the Boat." Yet he found

to my great consolation, that to a well-conducted prisoner even on Norfolk Island there is kindness shewn; misery certainly stares the majority of them in the face, but their own doing is the true source of it. . . . I found that although it is a settlement of hardship and privation, yet not altogether so insupportable as I imagined.[17]

Holyard was writing to a clergyman who kept assigned servants and had given him a "character" to one of the Norfolk Island officers, so his tone is predictable. But anyone who rose above passive docility was pounced on, and Frayne was clearly not alone in feeling that the rules and those who applied them were meant "to harass and torture me in a manner repugnant to & not consistent with British Law." Authority was absolute and capricious, lacking any proportion between the acts it forbade and the punishments it meted out. Frayne knew he had been singled out as a "bush lawyer"—"the leading man among my fellow prisoners particularly among the litigious & disaffected." Despite his formidable inner resources he began to sink into despair, believing God himself was against him:

> I began to think that the Almighty had decreed that my life should be made a life of infamy & turmoil & degradation, a life to be perpetually harrow'd up & goaded with such inhuman, barbarous and algerine brutality. This place I considered worse than the blackest dens and caverns of Hell. . . . I began to question in my own then-perverted mind the infinite mercy, nay the justice, of Deity itself.[18]

He recoiled from this idea, reminding himself that God "was shewing me as forcibly as possible the truth of holy Writ." So he resorted to the Bible, particularly the 88th Psalm, which he knew by heart. Ironed down to the jail floor as the Pacific boomed without end on the Kingston reef, each percussion causing a faint shudder in the flagstones, he recited it over and over:

> I am counted with them that go down into the pit:
> I am as a man that hath no help:
> Cast off among the dead,
> Like the slain that lie in the grave,
> Whom thou rememberest no more;
> And they are cut off from thy hand.
> Thou hast laid me in the lowest pit,
> In the dark places, in the deeps.

The decisive way out of this misery was suicide. "If ever it once had entered my mind that a Self-Murderer could obtain salvation I would not have seen a 10th part of the misery I underwent." But religious instruction was so basic to the rearing of many convicts, especially the Irish, that suicide was unthinkable. By killing themselves, they believed they would exchange the pains of the island for a real and eternal Hell, from which there would be no release. And so most of the prisoners who felt, like Frayne, "heartsick of my own existence," still could not bring themselves to "that climax of human depravity, to take away my own life with my own hands." They were caught between God and Commandant, condemned by their will to survive.

Yet in Morisset's time, a remarkable usage emerged on the Island. It turned suicide into an act of solidarity, not of solipsism and despair. A group of convicts would choose two men by drawing straws: one to die, the other to kill him. Others would stand by as witnesses. There being no judge to try capital offenses on Norfolk Island, the killer and witnesses would have to be sent to Sydney for trial—an inconvenience for the authorities but a boon to the prisoners, who yearned for the meager relief of getting away from the "ocean hell," if only to a gallows on the mainland. And in Sydney, there was some slight chance of escape. The victim could not choose himself; everyone in the group, apparently, had to be equally ready to die, and the benefits of his death had to be shared equally by all survivors. Suicide by lottery thus acquired a Roman tinge of disinterestedness.

There are several references to such suicides in the 1830s. Thus William Ullathorne, the Catholic vicar-general of Australia, visited the island in 1834 and remarked that

> so indifferent had even life become, that murders were committed in cold blood; the murderer afterwards declaring that he had no ill-feeling against his victim, but that his sole object was to obtain his own release. Lots were even cast; the man on whom it fell committed the deed, his comrades being witnesses, with the sole view of being taken . . . to Sydney.[19]

But one full account of such a ritual survives. It was written by Captain Foster Fyans, Morisset's second-in-command, who had questioned the survivors of the event.[20]

One day in 1832 or 1833 a gang of 16 convicts was marched out from the Kingston barracks to labor on a road. At the site they seized and manacled their overseer to the only "outsider" in the gang, an unnamed Jewish prisoner, remarking that "Jews are not to be trusted."[21] The gang leader, Fitzgerald, produced a makeshift knife and harangued his mates:

> "Now gentlemen to business. You all know the plot, is anyone against it? Nil. I have sixteen straws in my fist—the long straw will gain a prize, and the short will be his mate, and here is as good a piece of Hoop Iron as any on the island, and what is more it would shave a Bishop—fair play is a jewel, who draws for Lazarus?"
> "Oh my Codd almighty, spare my life, Gentlemen," cried the poor Jew.
> "Fair play is a jewel, come Mr. Jew, you shall have first prize."
> "So help me Codd, spare me"—the Jew fainted, when all cried out for the overseer to choose for the Jew. With some difficulty he was forced by kicks and threats to draw; he did so, the others following, when Fitzgerald was left with the longest straw, and the other with the shortest; either were to suffer a cruel death on the spot.

The long straw now drew against the short "for who was to suffer." Fitzgerald himself won, and made a brief speech to his comrades:

> "I am sorry boys that I am leaving you, but I am not the man either to peach or tell a lie—you'll have fine fun before you going to Sydney, and a chance of giving them the go-by. Think of me, boys, you'll all get off alone. Tell old Dowling the judge that it's my own free will, and that Pat Larkins sticks me. I am all ready now. Come on, my heartys . . . now quick, please yourself and give me as little pain as you can."[22]

At this, Pat Larkins drove the hoop-iron knife into Fitzgerald's stomach "up to his fist" and disemboweled him, there in the dust of the road. The gang ran away; the Jew and the overseer found the key to their handcuffs in the dying man's pocket and freed themselves; after two days of anguish Fitzgerald died in the hospital. Later, most of the gang "with some other aspiring youths for the gallows" were shipped back to Sydney for trial. Clearly, Fyans was impressed by the stoic courage of Fitzgerald's death; he was a soldier and could respect the clan-bound toughness of such men.

We do not know how many such deaths were enacted on Norfolk Island. Fyans's wording suggests that it was part of a pattern, as when he has Fitzgerald begin his speech with the words "You all know the plot." Such rituals evolve through custom; they are not simply invented. But in cheating suicide of its stigma, they covered its traces. Officially, the victim had to be classified as murdered by other convicts. It may be that some other moments when a group of prisoners suddenly killed a convict who was not obviously an informer were, in fact, suicide pacts of this kind.

Convict killings were common on Norfolk Island by the end of 1833, so common that Governor Richard Bourke realized he had to close the loophole. "There has appeared abundant reason to suspect," he wrote to England,

> that Capital crimes have been committed [on Norfolk Island] from a desperate determination to stake the chance of capital conviction and punishment in Sydney against the chances of escape, which the passage might afford to the accused and the Witnesses summoned to attend the trial. The number of the latter has been much augmented by the Sinister endeavour of convicts to procure themselves to be summoned.[23]

He proposed that a session of the Supreme Court with hanging powers be held whenever it was needed on the island, the judge to be any barrister of three years' standing and the jury composed of five military officers

—a kangaroo court if ever there was one. This was not done, but from time to time a judge accompanied by a crown prosecutor, a defense solicitor and a hangman did visit the island to represent the Supreme Court. The first session of this kind was in September 1833; the judge was James Dowling, the second chief justice of New South Wales. He tried and hanged some convicts for murder. From then on, no Norfolk Island convicts were sent to Sydney for trial.

ii

THE CONVICTS' only chance of relief from Morisset's regime now lay in open rebellion. There can have been few who did not sometimes dream, like Laurence Frayne, of revenge:

> I should certainly have taken his life . . . & many a time I prayed, if I knew what prayer was, that the heaviest curses that ever Almighty God let fall on blighted man might reach him, for blood will have blood, and in no depth of earth or sea can we bury it; and the blood of several of my fellow-Prisoners cryed aloud & often to Heaven to let fall its vengeance on this wholesale Murderer and despicable White Savage.[24]

Through the summer of 1833–34, the prisoners' barracks seethed with rumors of a coming outbreak. According to Frayne, Morisset was on the point of flogging confessions out of him and other convicts, as the Reverend Samuel Marsden had done thirty years before to the Irish at Parramatta. But the commander of the garrison, Captain Charles Sturt—whose deeds as an explorer of the Australian hinterland included the discovery of the continent's largest river, the Murray, and who was known for his decency to convicts—dissuaded him.

By then, Morisset could barely handle the routines of his duty. He was prostrated by bouts of pain from his old head wound, which struck so fiercely that he could only lie in bed unable to speak, with his eye bulging like a hen's egg. He stared at failure, a man of fifty-one with nothing to show but this remote post, a brood of unmarriageable daughters and a whistling mask of scar tissue that even the convicts sniggered at. He decided to sell his commission. He wrote to Sydney, announcing that he must remove his daughters from "an abode so unfit for them"; perhaps the colonial secretary could get him a better civil post?[25] Then he took to his bed again, glaring at the wooden ceiling and listening to the enveloping drone of the sea wind in the Norfolk Island pines.

The running of the island now devolved on his second-in-command, Foster Fyans, who had two main informants among the convicts: a prisoner named Bullock and an overseer, Constable Price. Fyans was worried, for something was brewing. An anonymous note was dropped in the soldiers' barracks warning them to "beware of poison"; and Fyans held fresh in his memory a poison plot hatched two years before by one of the convicts on a ship to Norfolk Island. The man was John Knatchbull.[26] Knatchbull, alias Fitch (1792?–1844), was one of twenty children of a baronet in Kent who had married three times. With no inheritance coming, Knatchbull joined the navy and rose during the Napoleonic Wars to the rank of captain. Down on his luck in peacetime, he was arrested, tried and transported for fourteen years in 1824 for stealing a pocketbook with two sovereigns in it from a reveller in Vauxhall Gardens. By 1826, Knatchbull was a convict constable on the Western Road at Bathurst. He had his ticket-of-leave by 1829—won for bringing in eight runaways under the hated Bushranging Act—but two years later he forged a check and was caught. Knatchbull was sentenced to hang, but the sentence was commuted and he was shipped to Norfolk Island in 1832. Once on board, he conspired with fifteen other convicts to lace the crew's and guards' food with white arsenic, seize the ship and escape. An informer gave the plan away, and a whole pound of the deadly stuff was found hidden in their quarters. But because no one was actually poisoned, Knatchbull was not tried, as it was too much trouble to ship the conspirators back to Sydney for trial. So they remained on Norfolk Island, admired by their fellow convicts and known, collectively, as the "Tea-Sweeteners."

Fyans was right to suspect Knatchbull. He was helping them make plans. The only way off the island was by ship, and only Knatchbull knew how to run one. On August 1, 1833, before lights-out in the prisoners' barracks, Knatchbull was stretched on his mat when a convict named George Farrell "laid himself on the mat next to me, when he said I should shortly hear something." Another lifer, an eighteen-year-old Irish lad named Dominick McCoy, joined them.

> "What do you mean?" asked Knatchbull.
> "Tell him," said McCoy.
> "The men outside," Farrell began, "are all mad for their liberty; it is such a gift, especially after the last boat went."[27]

He explained the plan. At dawn muster in the convict barracks yard, they would rush Fyans and his soldiers and overpower them. If any of the guard managed to barricade themselves in the guardhouse, the prisoners would set fire to it and flush them out. Meanwhile the jail gang (made up of prisoners under special punishment in the rickety old calaboose 150 yards away) would likewise rush their own guard as they were being mustered for work in the stone quarry. They, too, were "ready at any time to do anything for their liberty." Then the convicts would break for Government House, capture Morisset, seize the 18-pound cannon there, slew it around and blow the military barracks down. If the soldiers surrendered they would be spared; if not, they would hang, along with all the hated convict constables, overseers and informers. The convicts would force Morisset to hand over his code book of signals, so that they could flag false messages to the next ship that hove to off the reef. Thus, before the captain realized what was happening, they could get on board in the overseers' blue jackets and seize the vessel. They could avenge themselves at leisure. Morisset and Fyans "should be put to a lingering death of torture." Skinned alive by his own cat, the colonel would hang for three days, then be quartered, and the fragments of his carcass would dangle on four trees until the sea birds had stripped them. The women on the island were to be "taken and distributed" to the ringleaders, and Knatchbull wanted the colonel's timid and neurasthenic wife Emily Vaux. After the orgies, the convicts meant to build a decked launch to hold forty or fifty people, which they would sail to New Caledonia. Knatchbull would pilot the hijacked ship to America, for "if he once got there, the Americans would not allow them to be given up again."[28]

So the plan grew, a poor unlikely project nourished by whispers and swollen by fantasies of vengeance. It linked convict to convict in the lumber yard and the sawpits, at the limeburners' kiln and the stone quarry, where the convict Redmond Moss, who carried messages between the various gangs, begged Knatchbull to "learn him the compass" before they all sailed gloriously off into the blue. The very thought of escape, however farfetched, gave new hope to the Norfolk Island long-sentence men. (Of the 137 rebels eventually charged with mutiny, half were lifers and another third had sentences of fourteen years.) They devised a password and countersign: "You carry a load." "Yes, but relief is at hand."

Rumors of rebellion filtered back to Fyans through his informants. They were vague about time and strategy, and so Morisset contemptuously dismissed them as a pack of lies. Fyans believed them, however, and slept badly. He pored over the uselessly long list of two hundred names his informers had given him, men they had seen whispering together, whom they had grudges against, or who were merely Irish. But there was no sign from the convicts until January 15.

That day, a Wednesday, dawned in fog and pale gray light. Soon after the 5 a.m. reveille bell, a downpour swept Kingston. Through the rain, Fyans and his men in the military barracks heard a distant clinking of iron fetters from the seaward side of the jail. They could see nothing. There were shouts and the flat bang of a musket, followed by a ragged volley. The mutiny had begun.

The timing was nearly right. At the dawn muster in the prisoners' barracks, an unusually large number of men—thirty-eight in all—had reported sick and were marched off to hospital by a warder, John Higgins. Once inside the hospital lockup, the men turned on Higgins, overpowered him and locked him in a sickroom. The prisoners burst into other wards; one convict named William Groves found the camp constable from Longridge lying ill in bed. "Here's old Howley the dog," Groves cried, "and we ought to settle with him now." The leaders of the hospital revolt, Dominick McCoy, Lawrence Duggan and Henry Drummond, told Groves to leave the sick man alone.

Soon they struck off one another's irons and armed themselves with makeshift weapons, from chair legs to scalpels and a poker; some found axes. They massed in the entrance of the hospital, ready to fall on the jail guard when it came by, and waited in silence.

A hundred yards away this guard was mustering the jail gang—about thirty convicts under the eye of a corporal and twelve privates of the 4th Regiment. The soldiers formed them up in a column by the jail gate, under the gallows. At this moment the jail wardsman looked toward the beach and saw Laurence Frayne helping a guard empty a night-tub of urine into the sea. Frayne looked toward the sawpits and cried, "Are you ready?" At that moment, the guard corporal ordered the prisoners to march. They would not budge. They stood there, rattling their chains: a signal. Seconds later, a gang of convicts from the sawpits—another forty or fifty men—ran yelling at the rear of the guards around the corner of the jail, while the hospital gang burst from hiding and attacked their front. Suddenly, the dozen guards were trapped in a melee of some 120 convicts. Taken utterly by surprise, they could not get their weapons to their shoulders; the convicts, one of the soldiers recalled, "were within the bayonets of the Guard, before they were aware of them."[29] Their muskets, nearly six feet from buttplate to bayonet tip, were not designed for hand-to-hand combat, and for a few moments the convicts and guards stood locked, grappling for the guns. Two convicts knocked Private William Ramsay down and tried to wrench the musket from his hands. In a daze he heard one of them, Patrick Glenny, shouting "Kill the bugger!" while another named Snell cried that he acted "like a bloody dog over the gang." Ramsay begged for his life, and Snell, kneeling on the soldier's arm, said he would spare him if he surrendered his gun; he did, and he lived to testify. Snell stood up but was immediately shot and bayoneted by Private James Oppenshaw. Private Pearson lost his musket to Robert Douglas. "Shoot the bugger, shoot him!" other prisoners yelled. But the gun missed fire; Douglas wheeled on a hated free overseer named Phipps and snapped the hammer six or seven times at him without result. Clutching the musket, Douglas fled into the sugar cane with Phipps in hot pursuit. Henry Drummond, another ringleader, grabbed the musket of Private William Parham, going for his throat with a knife as he did so. The gun was smashed in the struggle, but Parham wrenched free, swung its heavy barrel and brained another convict named Wilson.[30]

The guards began shooting, and their shots alerted the barracks far away across the swamp. They backed into the gateway of the jail, frantically loading and firing while their comrades kept the lunging convicts back at saber-point. The rebel Henry Drummond fell, under the gallows at the jail gate. Several others went down and, as suddenly as it began, the melee broke up. Dazed by the firing and the sudden red spouts where the balls struck home, they scrambled back into the refuge of the jail-yard: James Shields, the jailer, guessed that ten or fifteen of them "who would not have anything to do with the soldiers" rushed by him to temporary safety. Later, the rebel George Farrell would bitterly complain that their cowardice lost the mutiny. The rest of the convicts, driven back by the guard, started retreating in the direction of Longridge, away from the sea.

The clash had only lasted a few minutes. Half a mile away in Quality Row, where the barracks and officers' houses stood, Foster Fyans and his soldiers had come scrambling out in cap and shirts, buckling on their cartridge-belts as they ran; they had not even had time to lace up their boots. They double-timed down the road to intercept the mutineers and formed up panting breathlessly on a small rise, probably where the Norfolk Island war memorial now stands. The convicts came on, but they faltered when they saw the long barrels levelled at them. Fyans gave the order to fire, and when the black-powder smoke cleared, fifteen rebels were seen stretched on the ground while most of the others had plunged into the sugar cane that grew beside the road; only the remnants of the jail gang stood dumbly in surrender, hampered by their irons. Any rebel who tried to head uphill to Longridge was shot. Soldiers followed the escapees into the vegetable gardens and sugar cane. "The men were very keen after these ruffians," Fyans recalled with some relish. "It was really game and sport to these soldiers . . . 'Come on out, my Honey'—with a prick of the Bayonet through both thighs or a little above." Leaving them to this work he led a detachment up the hill to deal with the convicts at the agricultural station at Longridge.

Up there, the morning had begun casually. The convicts had lookouts planted where they could see the Kingston jail buildings and signal the start of the mutiny. Walter Bourke, the leader of the Longridge rebels, was in the toolhouse sharpening hoes when these "cockatoos" burst through the door, shouting "Turn out, my lads—now is the time for Liberty." Convicts came crowding exultantly around, and with a swing of his hoe Bourke smashed the lock on the main toolchest and started passing out axes and pitchforks to the men. "Come on, my boys, follow me," he shouted. "I do not value my life more than I do that piece of dirt —if you think you can do any good follow me."[31] Crying "Death or glory!" "Liberty or death!" and "Huzza for liberty!" about eighty convicts followed him down the road to Flagstaff Hill, pausing only to crack off one another's irons with their axes.

Foster Fyans and his men heard them coming, as a thin straggle of cheers carried over the crest of the hill in the wind. The Longridge men expected to see a victorious crowd of their fellow rebels surging to meet them. Instead they saw two men stumbling up the hill, one of them wounded, and behind them, the redcoats in pursuit. The huzzahs died away, and the surge of adrenaline turned to panic. The soldiers fired a few rounds, but the range was too great. Soon, they closed in and beat the rebels back to Longridge, taking twenty-eight prisoners on the way; with difficulty, Fyans kept the soldiers from bayonetting them to death on the spot, and felt later that "perhaps such lenity is ill bestowed."[32] Nevertheless the soldiers kicked, stabbed and beat the rebels so hard that Fyans himself broke his sword in pieces hitting them with the flat of it.

Within a couple of hours, all of the Longridge rebels were subdued and bound together with cord in a line, which the soldiers marched down the hill to Kingston. At the foot of Flagstaff Hill, they found the youngest ringleader, Dominick McCoy, dying on the ground; cut down by musketballs, he had been repeatedly bayonetted in the lungs, liver and diaphragm. Now Fyans gave the order to drag him by his chains to the Police Office; and when Dr. Gamack protested and demanded McCoy be carried to the hospital, Fyans told his men to wheel right and drag him there, his head bumping across another 200 yards of stones and mud. Other soldiers, with blood in their eyes, came up and threatened to shoot the doctor.[33]

By noon, Fyans had the mutineers behind walls in the main prison barracks—"nearly one thousand Ruffians," he wrote later, although it was more like two hundred.[34] A few were still missing, among them Robert Douglas, who was found later on the other side of the Island at Anson's Bay, groping along but still carrying a musket with ninety rounds of ammunition wrapped in a palm leaf. A bayonet thrust had destroyed his left eye, and infection blinded the other a few days later. Fyans interrogated him daily in the hospital, but Douglas refused to say a word about the rebellion. The final tally of casualties was light: five rebels dead, and about fifty crippled. No guard was killed until the night after the mutiny, when two military search parties met in a cornfield while looking for rebels still at large and, each believing the other to be convicts, opened fire. One fluke shot killed both a civilian constable and a young private of the 4th Regiment, Thomas York.

So ended the Norfolk Island mutiny of 1834. It had been the only mass convict uprising in the history of transportation to Australia since Castle Hill in 1804. It was ill-planned, badly coordinated, and a failure. It was over in seven hours, but the vengeance of the prison authorities lasted for months. When Captain Fyans, a sweaty, dishevelled figure with his double-barrelled gun on one shoulder and an old rusty dragoon sabre in his hand, reported to Colonel Morisset (who was still in bed from his migraine attack), Morisset gave him carte blanche, saying—as Fyans remembered it—"Glad I am that I am not responsible. Do as you like."

In a prolonged sadistic fury, Fyans and the soldiers of the 4th set out to make the mutineers wish they had never been born. It took the blacksmiths nine days to make new irons for the prisoners: they were double or triple weight, with the inside of the basils jagged to lacerate the flesh.[35] Rebels locked in the jail awaiting trial were kept naked in a yard so crowded that not a third of them could sit at a time. For the next five months, while the reports went back to Sydney and arrangements were being made to send a judge to Norfolk Island, the rebels were kept locked to a chain cable and "disciplined in a state of nudity for four hours each day, with their arms up and fingers extended, and such of them as betrayed the slightest emotion of pain, were either stabbed by the Military or flogged on the spot."[36] One of the soldiers' amusements, encouraged by Fyans, was to choose a prisoner at random and get one of the floggers, for a plug of tobacco, to thrust a stick into the cord that bound his arms, twisting it round and round until blood burst from his fingertips.

The main torture, inevitably, was the lash. In these weeks after the mutiny, Fyans earned his enduring nickname among the convicts, "Flogger Fyans." So many lashes were inflicted that the government cats were not equal to the task, and they kept unravelling; they were "ridiculous, and the flogger nearly as bad," Fyans grimly complained. Besides, the prisoners took their usual pride in being "stone men" and endured the triangles in awesome silence. Fyans wanted new, special cats made "to strike terror into these hardened-minded fellows: prisoners of this description cannot be treated as a Gentleman's Servant in Sydney." The mass floggings went on into the evening by the light of flambeaux, until the "desperate lawless and listless mob" had been battered into submission. Some convicts, weary of their "acute and intolerable sufferings," planned to commit group suicide: they would throw stones at the guards "and thus call forth the Fatal Ball." But this came to nothing.[37]

It took Fyans and his staff five months to interrogate all the witnesses and take their depositions for trial. There was, of course, a cataract of self-serving evidence from informers. The formal charge of mutiny was brought against 137 men, but only 55 came to trial because only known informers spoke against them, and the Crown solicitor considered them "characters . . . of the foulest description, upon whose uncorroborated testimony no conviction could take place."[38] The Supreme Court judge, a deeply religious Anglican named William Westbroke Burton, sailed with Chambers, the Crown solicitor, in June 1834 to hold his court on Norfolk Island. On arrival, Burton was puzzled by the discrepancy between the looks and the contents of the place. Why, he wondered, should its "soft beauty . . . not have its effect on hearts not wholly hardened by the searing effects of Vice"? Why should the convicts seem "to gather no heartening effect from the beauties of the Creation around them, but to make a Hell of that which else might be a Heaven"?[39] Here, Romantic belief in the therapeutic power of landscape (which had become an *idée reçue* of educated men across the world in the 1830s) had to be suspended, a distressing anomaly to the judge.

The trial went on through July 1834, and Burton's dislike for the main source of prosecution evidence, the informers or "approvers," mounted. He was moved by the evident honesty of the rebels, in contrast to the shiftiness of the witnesses—particularly of Knatchbull, who had tried to incriminate everyone else while saving his own skin. The Crown solicitor had wanted to indict Knatchbull, but "the jury rejected the evidence of the approvers and there being no *other* evidence against [him] I did not bring him to trial."[40] Burton gave Fyans a severe reprimand from the Bench for accepting any confession from Knatchbull: "He was the chief of the mutineers, the man you should have named first. . . . You have saved his life, or prolonged it. He never can do good."*

By contrast, some of the rebels on trial were praying to die. The oldest of them was only thirty-five years old, but after six months' retribution from the 4th Regiment they came before Burton "grey, wizened and shrunken, their eyes dull and unseeing, the skin stretched taut on the cheeks; they spoke in whispers and were awful to behold." One of them declared in the simplest terms that he and his friends had been condemned to death before and had been reprieved and sent to the island: "We wish we had been executed then. It was no mercy to send us to this place. I do not ask for life, I do not want to be spared. . . . [L]ife is not worth living on such terms."[41]

In the dock, Robert Douglas impressed Burton with his "singular ability and uncommon calmness and self-possession under circumstances so appalling to ordinary minds." He turned his scarred face and

---

* He was right; Knatchbull ended on the Sydney gallows in 1844, having summoned enough phlegm to write his memoirs in the condemned cell. After his release from Norfolk Island in 1839 he got his ticket-of-leave, drifted in and out of seaman's work, and murdered a Sydney widow for her savings. His lawyer made him a small footnote to legal history by attempting, for the first time in a British court, to raise the defense of "moral insanity" that would later be codified as the McNaughton Rules. It did not save him.

blinded eyes to the judge, uttering the words that remain the final judgment on the *ne plus ultra* of the System: "Let a man's heart be what it will when he comes here, his Man's heart is taken from him, and he is given the heart of a Beast."

Other convicts begged to be shriven: "Oh, your Honour, I have committed many crimes for which I ought to die, but do not send me out of this World without seeing my Priest." But Norfolk Island had no Catholic priest, and later Burton would glimpse this Irishman in his cell "in miserable agony . . . embracing and beating himself upon a rudely constructed figure of the Cross."

By now, he was beginning to feel the System was worse than its "objects." The trial had provoked a crisis of conscience in him, a "sad meditation," a gush of pity to which "the Human Heart could not be insensible." Who, under these conditions, would not rebel? The military jury found thirty of the thirty-five mutineers guilty, but Burton could not sentence them to death. In a wholly unprecedented step he reprieved them all until he could lay their case directly before the governor, Richard Bourke, and bring a Catholic priest to Norfolk Island so that the condemned could receive their last sacraments.

Back in Sydney, Burton pleaded so eloquently to Governor Bourke and his Executive Council that sixteen of the thirty convicted mutineers had their sentences commuted to hard labor for life. The remaining fourteen, however, were to hang; and so two clergymen—one Catholic, the other Anglican—were dispatched there. This was to have far-reaching effects for the System, for the Catholic priest was the vicar-general of Australia, William Ullathorne, later to be a chief witness in the inquiry that helped abolish transportation to New South Wales.

Arriving in September, Ullathorne went straight to the jail; he had five days to prepare the rebels for death. The turnkey told him to stand back, and he opened the first cell. "There came forth a yellow exhalation, the produce of the bodies confined therein," Ullathorne later wrote.

My unexpected appearance . . . came on them like a vision. I found them crowded in three cells, so small as barely to allow their lying down together—their garments thrown off for a little coolness. They had been six months looking at their fate. I had to announce life to all but thirteen*— to these, death. A few words of preparation, and then their fate. Those

---

* In fact, fourteen. They were: Michael Anderson, James Bell, John Butler, Walter Bourke, Robert Douglas, Henry Drummond, Patrick Glenny, William Groves, Thomas Freshwater, Henry Knowles, William McCullough, Robert Ryan, Joseph Snell and John Toms. The headstones of 8 of these men (Anderson, Burke, Butler, Drummond, Glenny, Knowles, McCullough and Snell) still stand in the Norfolk Island cemetery but other graves have presumably been covered by the creeping dune sand.

who were to live wept bitterly; whilst those doomed to die, without exception, dropped on their knees, and with dry eyes, thanked God that they were to be delivered from such a place. Who can describe their emotions?[42]

Ullathorne baptized four more of them as Catholics; they prayed with him, and then prayed alone, as the vicar-general strolled lost in thought by the cemetery "closed in on three sides by thick, melancholy groves of the tear-dropping manchineel, while the fourth is open to the restless sea."[43]

The hangings took place in two sessions, on September 22 and 23. Each time, half the prison population was mustered in front of the gallows, while the rest looked on from the upper story of the barracks. The condemned men "manifested extraordinary fervour of repentance," Ullathorne wrote. "They received on their knees the sentence as the will of God. Loosened from their chains, they fell down in the dust and, in the warmth of their gratitude, kissed the very feet that had brought them peace." In a silence broken only by the cry of birds and the solemn concussion of surf on the Kingston reef, they mounted the scaffold, dressed in white like bridegrooms. The oldest, Henry Knowles, was twenty-nine. The youngest, William McCullough, had just turned twenty-one. They gazed at the horizon, at the iron rocks of Phillip Island in the circling blue. The hoods went over their heads. "Their lives were brief," wrote their priest, "and as agitated and restless as the waves which now break at their feet, and whose dying sound is their only requiem."

iii

MORISSET WAS long gone. Months earlier, he had gone back to the mainland, convalescent and unofficially disgraced. He sold his army commission and invested the proceeds, all he had, in the newly formed Bank of Australia, which then collapsed, taking his money with it. He lived on in obscurity as a police magistrate in Bathurst, making £6 a week, part of which was garnished to satisfy his creditors. He died in 1852, leaving four sons, six daughters and his wife Emily totally unprovided for. He never wrote a line of reminiscence about Norfolk Island.[44]

His successor there was Major Joseph Anderson (1790–1877) of the 50th Regiment, another career veteran of the Peninsular War, a grasping, vigilant and pious Scot, with a face like an irritable osprey—bleak sunken eyes, a blade of a nose, a wiry bush of white whiskers. "Potato Joe" Anderson's command of Norfolk Island lasted from March 1834 to

February 1839. Opinions about him were divided. Ullathorne, no friend
to cruelty, praised his "prudence and solicitude" in encouraging good
prisoners, in contrast to the "wanton tyranny" of Morisset. In his own
memoirs, Anderson claimed to have reduced floggings from Morisset's
1,000 sentences a year to a mere 70 or 75.[45] This might have surprised
the convicts themselves. Thomas Cook, who arrived on Norfolk Island
in 1836 and lived through most of Anderson's regime, thought that

> his measures were of a most severe and harassing description. . . . [T]he
> tide of Informing had uninterrupted scope, and anything beyond an ex-
> pressed suspicion . . . was not required by his System. . . . It drew no dis-
> tinction between the well-behaved and the notoriously bad-disposed
> prisoner.[46]

Anderson once gave five men 1,500 lashes before breakfast. He punished two loafing prisoners who neglected to sow corn properly with 300
lashes each for the Biblical-sounding offense of "robbing the Earth of its
seed," as though their crime was vegetable contraception. Prisoners
could run up heavy punishment records, like William Riley's during two
years in heavy irons after the mutiny:

100 lashes	For saying "O My God" while on the Chain for Mutiny.
100 lashes	Smiling while on the Chain.
50 lashes	Getting a light to smoke.
200 lashes	Insolence to a soldier.
100 lashes	Striking an overseer who pushed him.
8 months' solitary confinement, on the chain	Refusing to work.
3 months ditto	Disobedience of Orders.
3 months' Gaol	Being a short distance from the Settlement.
100 lashes before all hands in the Gaol	Insolence to the Sentry.
100 lashes	Singing a Song.
50 lashes	Asking Gaoler for a Chew of Tobacco.
100 lashes	Neglect of work.

In all, this came to 1,000 lashes, eleven months' solitary and three
months' jail in two years. Another prisoner, Michael Burns, got the stupendous total of 2,000 lashes in less than three years from Anderson: his
crimes, like Riley's, included "Singing a Song"—presumably one of the
Irish "treason songs."

Anderson exacted harsh extremes of labor from the prisoners. Thus, when a field was to be hoed, a line of convicts began hacking across it and the strongest workers were picked to be the pacesetters at either end; those in the middle would be punished if they lagged and made to work after hours until they dropped.

Anderson was a builder, too, and his architectural memorial is the Commissariat Store (since converted to a church), a massive, coarsely detailed three-story building surrounded by a tall security wall. It draws its peculiarly dogmatic character from the exaggerated rhyme between its pediment and the ziggurat-like flight of steps that leads up to the entrance. In a plaque on that pediment, and in a cartouche above the main building of the New Military Barracks (1837) next door, he had a convict mason chisel his name: *Major Anderson, 50th Regt., Commandant.*

He also planned a new jail, to replace the foul, rickety structure in which the mutineers had been crammed. To get its foundations up above the swampland that lay between the sea and Military Row (where the administrative buildings, barracks and officers' quarters stood), he had all the landfill from the excavations for the Commissariat Store and New Military Barracks moved to the new gaol site, dumped and levelled. Thus the convicts, having hacked a slice off the flank of a hill 300 feet deep, 40 feet high and 700 feet long, now had to carry some 150,000 cubic yards of earth nearly a quarter of a mile in handcarts. Apart from some stretches of the Blue Mountain roads, this must have been the toughest building job in the history of the Australian convict system.[47]

Labor was aimed at punishment, not production; the conditions robbed exertion of its meaning. No ploughs were allowed on Norfolk Island "under the idea of making the work of the prisoners laborious"; so all the convicts responded with the "Government stroke." Everything went at a snail's pace, despite the threat of the lash, and the result was an almost parodical inefficiency. The harder the overseers and guards pushed, the more the convicts malingered. They feigned sickness or induced it, poisoning themselves with lye and nightshade berries; they raised ulcers with manchineel juice or got friends to cut their toes off with a hoe. Anderson had such malingerers flogged, but sometimes sick men came up for a flogging, too, and died. Thus, in October 1836 a prisoner named Barrett, gravely weakened by dysentery, was taken for a malingerer and sentenced to 200 lashes; he collapsed and died after the first 50.[48]

Deranged by cruelty and misery, some men would opt for a lifetime at the bottom of the carceral heap by blinding themselves; thus, they reasoned, they would be left alone. This was the passive end of the moral anarchy that pervaded Norfolk Island; its active end was the "demoniz-ing" of prisoners by an authority whose own capricious brutality could offer no road back from their abasement. For, as Laurence Frayne put it,

> If you endeavour to take out of [a prisoner] that manly confidence which ought to be cherished in every civilized human being, you then begin the work of demoralization; and it will end in the very Dreggs of debasement & an insensibility to every species of integrity & decency, and eradicate every right feeling in the human breast. You make him regardless of himself, and fearless as to the consequences of doing wrong to oth-ers. . . . There is a certain pitch to which you can work upon man to bring him to fear . . . but exceed that and you make him reckless. Begin to treat him as beneath [your] care and notice, and they then think that you put God, his laws, his omniscience, his providence, as though they were mere nominal attributes and not virtual & real.[49]

Norfolk Island, Frayne argues, wrecked the social contract. Authority was supposed, by sinner and saint alike, to draw its value from its mir-roring power—its role as a reflected sign of God's mercy as well as His justice. Bad authority strips all men of hope by showing them a cracked glass, a different truth about hierarchies:

> They at once throw off all restraint & regard for either God or man, and consider everyone over them as acting under the influence of Hypocrisy and Imposture, usurping a power never delegated or sanctioned by the Almighty. They say you make man the slave of man. They resist and cavil at every trifle, and multiply every little departure from rectitude as a premeditated scheme to bilk & gull them into submission . . . because they are under the operation of the LAW, and cannot seek or obtain redress.[50]

Missionaries on Norfolk Island were struck by the state of mind that oppression bred in the convicts. Judge Burton had praised the beauty of the place, and Ullathorne was enraptured by it as he watched the evening sun on the pines "like the bronzed spires of some vast cathedral, flooded in golden light." Like Burton, he wondered why such beauty did not reform the soul, on this island where "man wanders, the demoniac of the scene":

> The devout man, like David, will muse on these His works, until he kindles like a fire; but perverse hearts will never see fine days. . . . [W]e find the foulest crimes always staining the fairest lands. Those five crim-inal cities, on whom the Lord rained down his fire and his fury, were

placed in a very beautiful country, and Norfolk Island is the modern representative of these guilty cities.[51]

Norfolk Island resembled Sodom sexually, but the likeness went deeper. It seemed to have become the epitome of *all* inversions, to breed that final hopelessness held by theologians to be the worst torment of Hell: a place where—in those words of Milton used by Edmund Burke in an early Commons debate on transportation—"all life dies and all death lives." It completed the myth of the antipodean inversion of nature by projecting it onto human society. Within its unspeakable microcosm language itself was reversed:

> So corrupt was their most ordinary language . . . that, in their dialect, *evil* was literally called *good*, and *good*, *evil*—the well-disposed man was branded *wicked*, whilst the leader in monstrous vice was styled *virtuous*. The human heart seemed inverted, and the very conscience reversed.[52]

Ullathorne had never heard this kind of argot on the mainland. Who could help such men as would use it? The Catholics (about a third of the prisoners at the time of Ullathorne's second visit there in 1835) were desperately grateful for any priest's visit, for only a priest could hear their confessions and so enable them to die in a state of grace. But the Protestants no longer kept up their religious observances; there was no chaplain on Norfolk Island until 1836, because no respectable clergyman would sacrifice his career on such a remote altar. The first one was an unordained missionary, the Reverend Thomas Atkins, an erratic young man of twenty-eight with a burning sense of indignation at official cruelty, who took the convicts' side from the start, quarrelled sharply with Major Anderson, accused him of sadism and graft, and was stigmatized by Governor Bourke as "highly indiscreet and improper." The convict Thomas Cook, by contrast, called him "the brightest star that ever shone on this depraved island." He lasted less than three months. The more normal view of God and religion among the prisoners on Norfolk Island was described by James Backhouse, writing in horror of a prisoner of "great recklessness," "chafed in his mind," who "doubted the being of a Deity, but wished, if there was a God in Heaven, that he would deprive him of life." Such men had one obsession: escape. "Their passions, severed from their usual objects, centred in one intense thirst for liberty, to be gained at whatever cost. Their faces were like those of demons."[53]

None of them did escape. Some tried to capture boats and row them across the Kingston Reef to the open sea; they broached to, were sunk by musket fire, or were chased and caught. Others tried to build escape vessels in secret, with stolen lumber, working at night in caves of the island; they were always betrayed by informers. The "demonization" of the prisoners continued under Anderson's successors, Major Bunbury of the 80th Regiment and Major Ryan of the 50th. They eased some of Anderson's more gratuitous punishments—Bunbury, for instance, replaced the hoe with the plough, which almost doubled farm production in the first year—and the pace of building slowed. But for all that, the System ground on; it was too deeply moored in the habits and appetites of guard, overseer and officer to be fundamentally changed by a few leniencies.

In any case, its reputation had to be kept up. Norfolk Island held a thousand convicts, but its real use was the intimidation of tens of thousands more. If it was not "demonic," it would have been as useless a deterrent as a gallows with no rope. Mercy on the mainland needed the background of terror elsewhere. Such was the official position. It had no lack of sanction from those who might have been preaching mercy. The Reverend Sydney Smith of the *Edinburgh Review*, so clubbable and so jolly, had gone on record for himself and thousands of like minds with the view that a prison should be "a place of punishment from which men recoil with horror—a place of real suffering painful to the memory, terrible to the imagination . . . a place of sorrow and wailing, which should be entered with horror."[54]

But in England, opinion was changing, especially among the Whigs. From 1835 on, such voices as Ullathorne's, resonant with moral outrage, were added to a growing chorus of liberal indignation against the transportation system. Any system that could create a Norfolk Island—no matter how small a percentage of the mainland convicts were actually sent there—seemed iniquitous and fit to be abolished. But while the upper-class reformers were promoting their belief that transportation should cease, the opinion of the lower classes kept drifting the other way. The belief, or hope, that a convict could make his or her fortune in Australia (or at least, a better living than could be scratched from England) had become fixed in the popular imagination. Meanwhile, little by little, the reformers gained ground. It was in 1840 that transportation to New South Wales ceased; and in that year, a new commandant also found himself in charge of Norfolk Island, a prophetic reformer, a noble anomaly in the theater of antipodean terror and punishment: Alexander Maconochie.

14

Toward Abolition

i

THE MAN SENT to replace Arthur in Van Diemen's Land was an early Victorian hero, Sir John Franklin (1786–1847), fresh from the howling wastes of ultima Thule. As a boy in 1801, he had sailed to Australia with his uncle by marriage, Matthew Flinders, in the *Investigator*, a three-year voyage of discovery, charting the unknown south coast from the Great Australian Bight to the present border of Victoria. In these virgin waters, where the thick red plate of the Australian desert snaps off into the sea and only Antarctica lies to the south, young John Franklin's passion for geography, hydrography and exploration was born; it would pursue him to his death.

By the end of 1804, he was back in the Royal Navy, serving under Nelson at Trafalgar on the *Bellerophon*. After the peace, routine duties followed; but in 1818 he had his first stab at Arctic discovery when he volunteered as second-in-command on the Admiralty's expedition to find the "North-West Passage," linking the polar seas to the North Pacific. Blocked by ice, his ship had to turn back; but the north had laid its frozen word on Franklin, and he was to lead two more Arctic expeditions—the first across Canada to Arctic America between 1819 and 1822, a 5,000-mile journey of almost inconceivable hardship, and the second, to Arctic America again, between 1824 and 1828. He published narratives of both, which were avidly consumed by the public. Thus, by his early forties, this gallant English explorer found himself dubbed a knight, promoted to captain and pursued as a social celebrity; he was the muffled figure in W. M. Praed's delicious satire on the foibles of London society, "Goodnight to the Season": "the Lion his mother imported / In bearskins and grease, from the Pole."

He had also found a second wife (his first having died while he was in the Arctic). Lady Jane Franklin (1791–1875) was a restless, indefatigably curious, highly intelligent and slightly neurasthenic woman, a silk-weaver's daughter given to consuming projects—mainly, advancing her husband's career as hero. After 1833, no imperial sea wars were being fought, but Franklin still had to find a post worthy of his talents. Lord Glenelg, Melbourne's secretary for war and the colonies, was persuaded that there could be no better man for Van Diemen's Land. Accompanied by Lady Jane and his private secretary, Captain Alexander Maconochie, Sir John Franklin stepped ashore in Hobart from the *Fairlie* in February 1837.

His fame had preceded him. He was greeted with relief and good will: illuminations, balls, teas, eulogies, each more florid than the last. Every bottle-nosed, favor-grubbing colonist who could stand up at table seemed to have a toast in him. When Sir John Franklin entered Launceston at the northernmost point of his first official progress across the island, three hundred horsemen and seventy carriages turned out to escort him. After reeling off the speeches Alexander Maconochie wrote for him and receiving tumultuous applause each time, he felt "both oppressed and delighted with the signs of popular joy."

For although Franklin was guileless and did not (at first) question the motives of the colonists he had been sent to rule, he was not blind. He soon saw that these outpourings from the middle class of Van Diemen's Land had something behind them. Many free Vandemonians had assumed, on no authority but their own wishful thinking, that the "polar knight" had come to give them representative government. They were sick of Arthur and his placemen. They expected Franklin to cancel the axioms of Arthur's rule and somehow convert the island into a democracy without taking away the pleasures of assigned labor. There was no ground for this, and Franklin told them so. He might have liked to make Van Diemen's Land self-governing, but the Crown had given him no power to change its constitution.[1]

Besides, he had to work with the officials he had inherited—the "Arthur Faction," a much-detested but certainly able administrative team who knew Van Diemen's Land far better than he did. These included Matthew Forster, Arthur's chief police magistrate and head of the convict establishment, a brutal man and a cunning political survivor ("When I stick my harpoon into a man," Lady Franklin heard him remark, "I don't take it out again")[2]; John Montagu, the colonial secretary; John Gregory, the colonial treasurer; and Sir John Pedder, the chief justice. All four had got their money and power from assigned labor and Arthur's nepotism; none had any time for the airy-fairy liberalism of a new lieutenant-governor who, however intrepid he may have been in the Arctic, seemed in the antipodes not only soft on convicts but governed by the petticoats of his interfering wife. While Arthur's lady had never uttered a peep about the running of the colony, Lady Franklin never ceased to share her views on the matter with guests at Government House and grill them on theirs. She displayed an unwonted interest in the experiences, and even the welfare, of convicts. She corresponded at length with the great English humanitarian and penal missionary Elizabeth Fry, sending her regular (and by no means flattering) reports on Van Diemen's Land. Jane Franklin was particularly concerned about women convicts, who were shamefully treated at the Female Factory in Hobart and often reduced to government-subsidized whoredom in assignment. In 1841 she formed a "Tasmanian Ladies' Society for the Reformation of Female Prisoners," which was mercilessly ridiculed by the Hobart papers, lapsed for two years and was revived—though never very effectively—in 1843.

She asked a great many questions about the System (too many, people thought) and, when accompanying her husband on his first visit to Port Arthur in March 1837, she startled the officers there by asking to try on a set of convict irons. Commissary Lemprière obligingly produced a pair of light handcuffs and snapped them on her wrists. Lady Franklin bore this for a short while but then had a mild attack of anxiety and asked to be released.[3]

What was more, she wished to intervene in the culture and even the ecology of Van Diemen's Land. On learning that the island was infested with snakes, she offered convicts a shilling a head for them, hoping to de-herpetize Van Diemen's Land altogether. This is said to have cost the government £600—and won her great popularity among the prisoners—before it was stopped, for Van Diemen's Land had more snakes than shillings. Her efforts on behalf of intellectual life were more successful. She sponsored lectures and encouraged the faltering steps of the visual arts in Hobart (although its best artist, the unhappy convict Thomas Griffiths Wainewright, quondam exhibitor at the Royal Academy, received no patronage from Government House). She instituted a yearly regatta on the Derwent to honor the sailors on whom the colony depended. She persuaded her husband to sponsor a learned society which, in 1848, became the first colonial Royal Society for scientific studies. Devoted to the study of natural history, she set up a botanical garden outside Hobart; it boasted a natural history museum in the form of a Doric temple, which, for want of support after the Franklins were recalled to England, was turned into a storehouse for apples. As a friend of the great Dr. Arnold of Rugby, she was committed to the advance of education in the fledgling colony, and founded its state college (although its actual opening was delayed for years by the bitter religious factionalism endemic to Van Diemen's Land). As a traveller, she might have been the Lady Wortley Montagu of the antipodes: She was the first woman to travel overland from Melbourne to Sydney, to ascend Mount Wellington and to make the appallingly difficult journey from the "settled districts" overland to Macquarie Harbor (borne, however, for much of the way on the shoulders of convicts in a palanquin or litter). Her letters reveal an eager, tough-minded, nosy, idealistic and intensely loyal person, just the lioness her sometimes naïve and administratively timid lion of a husband needed. It was foreordained that the more conservative colonists would dislike Jane Franklin for being a bluestocking and resent her influence on Sir John.

Perhaps the Arthur Faction would have accorded Franklin a certain grudging respect (followed, as day by night, by undying enmity: that was the Vandemonian way) if he had purged them as Arthur had their predecessors. But Franklin did not have the stomach for that. He vacillated; as Montagu remarked in a letter to his old boss Arthur, now the lieutenant-governor of Upper Canada, "the high qualities which were so conspicuous in Sir John . . . at the North Pole, have not accompanied him to the South."[4]

Instead, he decided he had no choice but to work with the existing officials. So the Arthur Faction began to despise him as a vain, good-natured weakling, while the anti-Arthur colonists came to feel they had been sold down the Derwent. Lady Franklin was right when she wrote, in a letter to a friend, that in Van Diemen's Land "people should have hearts of stone and frames of steel." For Sir John Franklin, who as a midshipman had been unable to witness a naval flogging without trembling, this convict colony was a taxing place. Its colonists, as the English treasury official George Boyes remarked after nearly thirty years' experience,

> very much resemble the Americans in their presumption, arrogance, impudence, and conceit. They believe they are the most powerful men on the Globe, and that their little Island "whips all Creation." They are radicals of the worst kind and their children are brought up in the belief that all Governments are bad—that they are deprived of their rights, and that they are ground and oppressed by the Mother Country, and mocked by the Officers sent out from England to rule them. Their views are of the narrowest and most selfish kind. They are incapable of any generous sentiment, and ever ready to impute the basest motives to their fellow colonists.[5]

An avalanche of administrative problems was teetering behind Government House. And by a peculiar irony, the man whose voice started its descent was the best ally Franklin had in the colony apart from his wife: his private secretary, the incorruptible Captain Alexander Maconochie (1787–1860), who would emerge as the one and only inspired penal reformer to work in Australia throughout the whole history of transportation.

ii

ALEXANDER MACONOCHIE was a lawyer's son, born in Edinburgh. His father died when he was nine, and he had the good luck to be raised by a kinsman, Allan Maconochie, later Lord Meadowbank, who assured him a better-than-average education. He was expected to become a lawyer. But young Maconochie wanted to go to sea, not to the bar, and by 1804 he was a midshipman in the Royal Navy, serving for several years under Admiral Cochrane in the Caribbean. In 1810, as a lieutenant on the brig *Grasshopper*, he underwent perhaps the most significant experience of his career. The *Grasshopper*, on convoy duty in the Baltic, was wrecked on Christmas Eve 1811 off the Dutch coast, and Maconochie, with everyone else on board, was taken prisoner and handed over to the French. There ensued a forced march in the bitter cold of winter from Holland to Verdun, and more than two years' misery as a prisoner of war —at a time when, half a century before the signing of the Geneva Convention, a POW's lot was even less enviable than it is today. This was Maconochie's one traumatic taste of life in prison, and he never forgot it. Indeed, he was the only major official of the transportation system who had ever spent time behind bars.

Released by Napoleon's abdication in 1814, Maconochie rejoined the English Navy in its war against America, captaining the gunboat *Calliope*; he was promoted to commander just before peace was signed in 1815. For the next thirteen years he lived in Edinburgh, studying geography and geopolitics and writing lengthy tracts on Pacific colonization and steam navigation. (His interest in the Pacific, at this point, was somewhat abstract, as he had never been there.) He married in 1822, moved to London in 1828, and in 1830 became the first Professor of Geography at University College, London, and the first secretary of the newly formed Royal Geographical Society. From these chairbound labors he was plucked in 1837 by Sir John Franklin, who offered him the chance to see the Pacific, and England's remotest colony, at first hand. Maconochie's acquaintances in the Society for the Improvement of Prison Discipline asked him, since there was such a dearth of first-hand observers with no vested interest in the System, to complete for them a 67-point questionnaire on the treatment of prisoners in Van Diemen's Land. The Scot had no theories about the System and no prior acquaintance with it; he seemed quite unprejudiced. He agreed to make the report, a task to which neither Franklin nor Sir Henry George Grey, under secretary for the colonies, had any objection so long as he sent it through Franklin to Grey, not directly to the Society.

Maconochie's troubles began almost as soon as he arrived in Hobart. He saw that the wily colonials "read [Franklin] in a moment," while Franklin the new-chum was far too vulnerable to their flattery:

> I was a looker-on all the while, neither sharing in the applause nor . . . very likely to be imposed on by it—I read it thus at its just value, and tried to expose it equally to him, but that was hopeless—it was like trying to force a piece of barley-sugar out of a child's mouth.[6]

Montagu, Forster and the rest of the Arthur Faction quickly sized Maconochie up as a potential enemy whose influence on the new lieu-tenant-governor had to be neutralized quickly. They blew a cloud of innuendo at Franklin, calling his private secretary an ideologue—who but a man with unrealistic pro-felon prejudices would do a report for an English reform society?—a "perfect *Radical*" who "encouraged all the disaffected, and promised what he could not perform." Soon, Franklin and Maconochie began to draw apart—partly because Franklin wanted the Arthur Faction on his side, partly due to Maconochie's own blunt-ness, but mainly because Franklin's sworn duty was to run a system that horrified Maconochie. For Maconochie liked neither the harshness of Arthur's police state nor the cant of those who profited from it. The System, he roundly declared in the report that Franklin transmitted to the Colonial Office in October 1837,

> is cruel, uncertain, prodigal; ineffectual either for reform or example; can only be maintained in some degree of vigour by extreme severity; some of its most important enactments are systematically broken by the Gov-ernment itself. . . .[T]hey are of course disregarded by the community.[7]

The System, Maconochie thought, debased free and bond alike, pro-ducing "the fretfulness of temper . . . which so peculiarly characterises the intercourse of society in our penal colonies."

Much of his report consisted of social impressions and moral lucubra-tions, but it had a hard core of fact. There, he was helped by several others. The Quaker missionaries James Backhouse and George Washing-ton Walker, who had travelled throughout Van Diemen's Land between 1832 and 1834 and reported on the chain gangs for Arthur, opened their files to him. He was advised by the Scottish surveyor Alexander Cheyne (1785–1858), who had been Arthur's director-general of roads and bridges since 1835 and whom Franklin, in 1838, put in charge of the newly formed Department of Public Works. One sees the hand of Cheyne in Maconochie's criticism of convict labor on government works, which entailed so much waste and graft that "1s. 9d. is lost out of every 3s. worth of labour." Maconochie found little to commend in Arthur's graded assignment system. It did not reform convicts; it bred social malaise and blunted the moral sense. "It destroys both soul and body—both master and man—both colonial character and, I may almost say, national reputation."[8] The convicts, he movingly argued,

> have their claims on us also, claims only the more sacred because they are helpless in our hands. . . . [W]e condemn them for our own advantage. We have no right to cast them away altogether. Even their physical suffering should be in moderation, and the moral pain we must and ought to inflict with it should be carefully framed so as if possible to reform, and not necessarily to pervert them. The iron should enter both soul and body, but not so as utterly to sear and harden them.[9]

Manconochie gave his report to Franklin, who asked him to tone down some of the sharper criticisms, and he did so. Then Franklin sent the edited version to the main officials of the colony. Cheyne supported it, the others vehemently disagreed, and Franklin sent their minutes, one of his own, and Maconochie's rebuttal along with the report itself to Lord Glenelg. For fear that this mass of paper, now running to several hundred pages, should "perish in the Colonial office from [its] own intrinsic gravity," Maconochie wrote a separate summary of his case, and sent it to Lord Grey, as he had promised to do, but with a covering note asking him, if he thought fit, to show it to Lord John Russell. Russell was the home secretary, in charge of the British penal system. Franklin did not read this abstract from Maconochie, but he thought he knew what was in it. He hesitated to pass it on but gave in to Maconochie's pleas. He wrote a covering note to Grey urging him not to send any material to the Society for the Improvement of Prison Discipline before it was thoroughly vetted by the Colonial Office, lest it "give pain to many respectable inhabitants here."

Thus two reports on Van Diemen's Land—the long revised one Franklin had read, and the more pungent précis he had not—reached London by the same ship in February 1838. Grey read the précis and, on March 5, 1838, passed it on to Lord Russell. If any moment can be said to mark the peak and incipient decline of transportation to Australia, this innocuous act marked it.

For what Maconochie did not know—and could not have known, due to the long delays in official communication between England and Australia—was that Russell, an ardent critic of transportation, had already been appointed a member of a Parliamentary Select Committee, under the chairmanship of the even more dogmatically anti-transportationist

Sir William Molesworth, to inquire into the workings of the System. The Molesworth Committee had been convened in April 1837, when the dispatches were on the water. At that point, its members knew no more about Maconochie's criticisms than Maconochie knew about the committee.

Russell wanted ammunition. He sent Maconochie's précis straight to the government printer, for publication. Thus a private memo entered the public, official record. To back it up, Russell had the whole text and minutes of the longer report, as approved by Franklin, published a month later.

Both documents caused a sensation in the English press. But it was nothing compared to the hullaballoo the English papers touched off in Van Diemen's Land six months later, in September 1838, when they reached Hobart.

All of a sudden, the good citizens of Van Diemen's Land found themselves vilified in official parliamentary print as callous slave-owners, rulers of a petty kingdom raised on the exploited bodies of convicts. This was enough to bury—for a time—all differences between the Arthur Faction and the anti-Arthurians. Everyone who had ever had a convict assigned to him could now hate Maconochie, who (so the Hobart version went) had gone behind Franklin's back and smuggled his foul canards to England under the guise of official correspondence. Montagu and his friends lost no time persuading Franklin that Maconochie had betrayed him.

Franklin was not quite sure that he had. The opinions in the report were, after all, Maconochie's own, and not presented as official. But in the end he had no choice. He dismissed Maconochie, although he allowed him (with his wife and six children) to stay on at Government House until they found other lodgings. Lady Franklin was sorry. Maconochie, she wrote to her sister, had "such a freedom from colonial suspicion and narrowness of views and personal spite and hostility . . . and so much less apparent self-interest that I could not but value his union with us and deplore his separation."[10]

The Maconochies were ostracized. "We see few and go nowhere," Mrs. Maconochie wrote.

> Alexander is like a lion at bay, deafened by the barking and yelping of the curs about him, but in no other ways stirred from his steady honesty of purpose. . . . Alas, alas! I always looked forward to trials and difficulties, mystifications of every description, but no imagination could have realized the continued tissue of falsehood, suspicion and unworthy accusation continually poured forth.[11]

All this only stiffened Maconochie's fiber. He had at last found his mission in life: "The cause has got me complete," he wrote to London. "I will go the whole hog on it. . . . I will neither acquiesce in the moral destruction of so many of my fellow beings nor in misrepresentation made of myself, without doing *everything* that may be necessary or possible to assist both."[12]

He felt the deck lifting under his feet. The Molesworth Committee had brought in its verdict of guilty on transportation; public opinion in England was changing. Despite his isolation in Hobart, Maconochie had found the allies he needed 14,000 miles away, at the head of the System, among English Whigs whose slanting of the evidence had made the findings of the Molesworth Committee a foregone conclusion.

iii

THE MOLESWORTH COMMITTEE was convened "to inquire into the System of Transportation, its Efficacy as a Punishment, its Influence on the Moral State of Society in the Penal Colonies, and how far it is susceptible of improvement." It began its hearings in 1837 and laid its final report before the Commons in August 1838.[13]

The Molesworth Committee claimed to be an objective tribunal. It was in fact a heavily biased show trial designed to present a catalog of antipodean horrors, conducted by Whigs against a system they were already planning to jettison. Its real movers were the home secretary, Lord John Russell, and the under secretary for the colonies, Lord Grey, in consultation with the Colonial Office. Grey, then thirty-six years old, was later to run the Colonial Office under Lord Russell; he never made any secret of his disdain for the assignment system. Australian affairs were not a large issue for either of these men or for the British Government; they came some distance behind those of Canada, Malta, Gibraltar and the colony at the Cape of Good Hope.[14] But in 1836, Russell had already announced his intent to liberalize the criminal law, reduce the hanging statutes and abolish transportation as a punishment for simple larceny—which would have cut the number of transportees by half.[15] He thought transportation archaic and, like other "progressive" Parliamentarians, favored punishment (at least for routine crimes) in model prisons and penitentiaries on English soil. Between them, Russell and Lord Glenelg had decided to abolish assignment and step up free emigration to Australia before the Molesworth Committee had heard a single witness.

So the Molesworth Committee was formed to dramatize the need for a decision which had already been taken. Russell chose a chairman of suitably flamboyant idealism, an eager young show-pony: the member for Cornwall, the twenty-six-year-old Sir William Molesworth. He was a

"Philosophic Radical," a follower of Bentham and Hobbes (whose collected works he would turn to editing in 1839), and a staunch Abolitionist.

The committee heard twenty-three witnesses, most of whom, like the Scottish clergyman and politician John Dunmore Lang, an untiring promoter of free Protestant emigration to Australia, were already well-known foes of transportation. Others, like James Mudie, were so fiercely bigoted against convicts that their views on colonial morality were untrustworthy. Even Bishop Ullathorne had an ulterior motive in expounding on the horrors of atheism and sodomy Down Under, as he wanted to expand the power of the Catholic mission in Australia. James Macarthur, fourth son of fierce old John, who gave extensive evidence to the committee, thought the convict labor that had raised his family to immense wealth at Camden would no longer be needed if the Crown permitted the colony to get coolie labor from Asia and Crown-subsidized free emigrants from Britain.

Some of their evidence remains useful to the historian, for most of the witnesses were telling the truth as they saw it; but the effect was still tendentious, because it was not the whole truth. The committee was out to portray Australia as a colony plagued by a rising crime rate and crippled by its dependence on criminal slavery. It wanted to set the stage for the policy of controlled emigration set forth by Molesworth's intellectual mentor, Edward Gibbon Wakefield, whereby Crown lands in Australia would be sold to well-screened young emigrants at a "sufficient" or high price so that mere ex-convict laborers could not easily acquire land they could not use. "It is difficult," Molesworth noted,

> to conceive how any man . . . merely having the common feelings of morality, with the ordinary dislike of crime, could be tempted, by any prospect of pecuniary gain, to emigrate, with his wife and family, to one of these colonies, after a picture has been presented to his mind of what would be his probable lot. To dwell in Sydney . . . would be much the same as inhabiting the lowest purlieus of St. Giles's, where drunkenness and shameless profligacy are not more apparent than in the capital of Australia . . . [E]very kind and gentle feeling of human nature is constantly outraged by the perpetual spectacle of punishment and misery— by the frequent infliction of the lash—by the gangs of slaves in irons—by the horrid details of the penal settlements; till the heart of the immigrant is gradually deadened to the sufferings of others, and he becomes at last as cruel as the other gaolers of these vast prisons . . . [T]he whole system of transportation violates the feelings of the adult, barbarizes the habits, and demoralizes the principles of the rising generation; and the result is, to use the expression of a public newspaper, "Sodom and Gomorrah."[16]

Stirring stuff, and meant to be; but it ignored the facts that scores of thousands of emancipated convicts had gone on to build happy, productive and law-abiding lives for themselves and their children in Australia, that by no means all the "respectables" were opportunistic slave drivers, and that the place was not entirely a sink of atheism and inherited propensities to crime. Bishop Ullathorne summed up the committee's bias—without perhaps realizing the implications of his story—when he described a private call he made on the young chairman at home in London. "I went to his house, and was amused to find him in a dandy silk dressing-gown, covered with flowers like a garden, and tied with a silk cord with flowing tassels. He had my pamphlet before him, *and tried to coach me as to the best way of giving evidence*." [Italics added.][17]

The committee's basic charge against the assignment system was its randomness as a "strange lottery," ranging between "extremes of comfort [sic] and misery," in which a swarm of unpredictable variants—the character, temper and security of the master, the kind of work, the site —had, as Governor Bourke put it, "an unmeasurable influence over [the convict's] condition, both physical and mental, which no regulations whatever can anticipate."[18] What deterred crime, the committee argued, was not the fate of the convict in Australia but the *perception* of his fate among English criminals:

> Most persons in this country . . . are ignorant of the real amount of suffering inflicted on a transported felon, and underrate [its] severity. . . . On their arrival at the antipodes, they discover that they have been grievously deceived by the accounts transmitted to them, and that their condition is a far more painful one than they expected. For those convicts who write to their friends . . . are generally persons who have been fortunate in the lottery of punishment, and truly describe their lot in flattering terms; those . . . who really experience the evils of Transportation, and are haunted with "a continual sense of degradation," are seldom inclined to narrate their sufferings except when they have powerful friends from whom they may expect assistance.[19]

The main characteristics of transportation, the committee acerbically put it, were "inefficiency in deterring from crime, and remarkable efficiency . . . in still further corrupting those who undergo the punishment." Efficiency for evil and futility for good "are inherent in the system," which could never be improved. What of its economic benefits to the colony? The committee took a pessimistic view of these, too. Due to free convict labor, it noted, "a larger amount of wealth has been accumulated in a shorter space of time than perhaps in any other community of the same size in the world." But it was an artificial prosperity, not likely to continue. "New South Wales is suffering excessively from a dearth of labourers. The flocks of sheep are double the size they ought to be; a vast number perish for want of care; the complaints of the colonists on this subject are loud and universal." Ten thousand laborers were needed in New South Wales but only three thousand convicts were likely to arrive there in 1838, barely enough to replace those lost to the labor force by death, illness or tickets-of-leave. Hence, there had to be another source of labor. The committee rejected Macarthur's idea of importing Asian coolies; that smacked of American slavery.

Hence, the only course was free emigration, underwritten by the sale of Crown land in Australia as proposed by Wakefield. That, too, demanded the end of the System, for "Transportation has a tendency to counteract the moral benefits of emigration, while . . . emigration tends to deprive Transportation of its terrors." But with labor short, land cheap and wages high in New South Wales, it was too easy for free laborers to become small independent farmers—which they wanted to do for more than ordinary reasons, since "the employment of convicts as slaves has . . . a tendency to bring labour into disrepute." So when transportation was abolished, the price of Crown land, then as low as 5s. an acre, had to go up to at least £1, so that laborers would keep laboring.[20]

It was not these reflections, however, that maddened the colonists, but the report's strictures on their morals. Even before the full text reached Australia, word had leaked back of what some of the witnesses, especially Ullathorne, had said; it provoked much unease, and in May 1838 more than five hundred respectable citizens petitioned the Legislative Council of New South Wales to do something to counteract the talk about Sodom, Gomorrah and the rising crime rate. In July the council issued a lengthy resolution pointing out that "the character of this Colony . . . has unjustly suffered by the misrepresentations" of Molesworth, Russell and their parliamentary colleagues; that the free emigrants and the rising generation of native-born Australians "constitute a body of Colonists who, in the exercise of the social and moral relations of life . . . impress a character of respectability on the colony at large"; that many convicts were in fact reformed by assignment amid the "solitude and privations" of the outback; and that assignment generated the wealth that enabled settlers to buy Crown lands and so produce the government income to underwrite immigration, so that "the continuance of Immigration . . . must necessarily depend on the continuance of the Assignment of Convicts."[21]

The colonists feared, with reason, that by the time the Whigs had finished libelling their morals, nobody would want to come to Australia anyway and the colony would have neither convict nor free labor. To them, the report was a stunning parental rejection. They had posited their social self-esteem on a rigid class barrier between themselves and the convicts. Even the Currency had done this, burying their convict origins within a generation or two. Now, the report claimed that crime was increasing faster than population and referred to a "progressive demoralization both of the bond and of the free inhabitants"; clearly, in English eyes, there was little to choose between them. No wonder that the Exclusives—who had always insisted that the offspring of convicts bore a hereditary stain which had not touched their own lineage—reproached Mother England in bewildered denials and Oedipal tantrums and that they resolved to tighten the class line between convicts and "respectables" in New South Wales. Meanwhile, the Sydney press, which until 1838 had kept up a drumfire of scare stories about a growing crime wave in New South Wales, suddenly changed its tune; the very idea of a crime wave became, in local Tory eyes, a "monstrous caricature" sketched by English Whigs.[22]

The report had placed the colonists in exactly the double bind that defines a colonial mentality. Many of them wanted to be more English than the English; they needed the approval of the implacable parent. Instead, Molesworth gave them pages of condescending Whiggery-and-priggery about their ineradicable stain.

Once the fuss over the Molesworth Report had died down, however, the end of transportation and assignment in New South Wales came smoothly, without much political or economic strain. Even before the report hit the colony, the instructions from Downing Street were to wind down assignment and "coerce" convicts in government labor gangs instead. In October 1838, Bourke's successor, Governor Sir George Gipps, who had taken over a few months before, proscribed the assignments of convicts "for domestic service, or for the purposes of Luxury and in Towns," although they still did essential work on pastoral stations.[23]

Gipps, a gallant veteran of the Peninsular War and a strikingly prudent and humane governor, did all he could to ease the transition of the labor supply from convicts to immigrants. The "bounty system," approved by the Colonial Office in 1837, helped considerably: It gave £30 to every able-bodied migrant couple under the age of thirty, and £5 to each of their children; single men, sponsored by settlers, were underwritten to the tune of £10 each, and respectable spinsters between the ages of fifteen and thirty (if they came out under the protection of a married couple) got £15. Before long, eighteen thousand free immigrants had arrived in New South Wales on the bounty system, and over forty thousand on their own initiative. This was more than enough to fill the gap in the labor supply. The *Eden I*, the last convict transport to arrive in New South Wales under the Old System, dropped her 269 male passengers at Sydney Cove on November 18, 1840.

But what could England now do with her criminals? Molesworth and

Russell were impressed with American penitentiaries. But in 1838, England did not have any; therefore, they would have to be built—at a cost of millions. Spread over the years, that would probably be cheaper than transportation, which was costing the Crown between £400,000 and £500,000 a year. The committee urged the government not to be put off by the cost. Short sentences could be served in penitentiaries in England, longer ones in others built on suitable islands—places as diverse as Malta, Corfu and the Falklands were mentioned—but not in the far antipodes.

Meanwhile, convicts must still go abroad. But not to New South Wales or the settled parts of Van Diemen's Land, if assignment were abandoned—"which it ought to be at once." The committee felt short sentences ought to be served in Bermuda for the time being, but the only receptacles for long-sentence convicts, until the penitentiaries rose, were still those sites of ill-fame on the outer edges of Australia—Norfolk Island and the Tasman Peninsula, each a natural prison isolated from free settlement.

And there, the committee urged, Alexander Maconochie's guidelines for a new prison discipline based on incentives and clear future goals "might in part at least be attempted with advantage." Maconochie had not been idle; he never was. While seeking another post in Australia, he had bombarded Russell from Hobart with his theories of reformatory punishment, set forth in densely argued, prolix memos. And the committee was swayed. "It would be advisable," the report noted,

> to ascertain, by experiment, the effect of establishing a system of reward and punishment not founded merely upon the prospect of immediate pain or immediate gratification, but [on] . . . the hope of obtaining or the fear of losing *future and distant advantages*. . . . The great object of a good system for the government of convicts should be that of teaching them to look forward to the future and remote effects of their own conduct, and to be guided in their actions by their reason, instead of merely by their animal instincts and desires.[24]

Here, the committee was simply echoing Maconochie, whose ideas—so far in advance of their time, when they came to be tested on Norfolk Island between 1840 and 1844, containing so many of the principles of modern penology—we may now consider.

iv

ALEXANDER MACONOCHIE wanted to shift the focus of penology from punishment to reform. Of course, the State could and must punish crime, but punishment on its own, he argued, was a socially empty act without checks built into it: "Our penal science is . . . without precise rule, a mere balancing between conflicting impulses, severity for the supposed good of society on one hand, and leniency for the supposed good of the criminal on the other, in both frequently running into error." He saw no sense in punishing a criminal for his past while not training him with incentives for his future.

Because it was fixated on punishment alone, the Old System had produced mainly crushed, resentful and embittered men and women, in whom the spark of enterprise and hope was dead. So Maconochie argued. Exemplary punishment was only vindictive; it ran wild, degrading both convict and jailer. Terms like "mercy" and "remission of punishment" were to be dropped. "Let us offer our prisoners, not favors, but *rights*, on fixed and unalterable conditions."[25]

But how was this to be done? How to stop the corrosion of despair, the leakage of human possibility? Maconochie never claimed to be an original penal thinker, but he had what more "original" men like Jeremy Bentham lacked—firsthand experience of prison and humane understanding of its inmates. The basic idea for his system had first been raised by the Cambridge theologian William Paley in his *Moral and Political Philosophy* (1785). In this early Utilitarian text, Paley suggested that the punishment of criminals should be measured, not by raw time, but by work, "in order both to excite industry, and to render it more voluntary."

Within a few years, this idea of punishment by task and not by time was mooted in America. It found another advocate in Richard Whately, soon to be appointed Archbishop of Dublin. In the *London Review* in 1829, Whately urged that convicts be sentenced to give the state a measurable amount of labor in expiation of their sins, so that the quicker and better they worked the sooner they would be free: "With each additional step they took on the treadmill they would be walking out of prison—by each additional cut of the spade they would be cutting a way to return to society."

Such ideas reached the Quaker missionaries James Backhouse and George Walker and went from them to Maconochie. They, too, advocated task rather than time punishment, and argued that, as most convicts were morally childish, the penal reformer might take a cue from the discipline of "enlightened" schools, which offered rewards for good conduct rather than punishment for bad. At each monthly muster, the diligent convict would get a "ticket" and the lazy would lose one or more; getting three tickets would shorten one's sentence by a month.

Such ideas of discipline by the carrot, not the stick, were the germ of Alexander Maconochie's "Mark System." Maconochie argued that sentences should be indefinite—no more stretches of seven, ten, fourteen years or life. Instead, the convicts would have to earn a certain number of "marks," or credits for good behavior and hard work, before they got free. Six thousand marks would be the equivalent of a seven-year sentence, seven thousand would correspond to ten years, ten thousand to life. They would buy their way out of prison with these marks. To buy, they must save.

Hence the length of his sentence was, within limits, up to the convict himself. Marks could be exchanged for either goods or time. The prisoner could buy "luxuries" with his marks from the jail administration—extra food, tobacco, clothing and the like. They were "just wages, and will equally stimulate to care, exertion, economy and fidelity." Maconochie hoped to abolish rations, "whose moral effect is always bad, by taking the care of a man's maintenance out of his own hands." Ideally, the convict would pay for everything beyond a bare subsistence diet of bread and water with the marks he earned.[26]

Maconochie believed his Mark System would be objective. As things stood, prisoners were at the mercy of their overseers for "indulgences," which "corrupt and debilitate the mind." Official freedom to remit sentences led the convicts to lie and curry favor. It made them servile or evasive, and usually both. Only measurable actions could measure reform:

> The term "remission of sentence" should be banished. . . . There should, in truth, be none whatever; but the duration of the sentences being made measurable by conduct under them, and not by time at all . . . no power should anywhere even exist in a subordinate authority to remit a fraction of it; but on the other hand, there should not be less certainty in the result of good conduct. *The fate of every man should be placed unreservedly in his own hands. . . . There should be no favour anywhere.*[27]

As soon as a convict entered the system, then, he would begin his Pilgrim's Progress with a short harsh stretch of confinement with hard labor and religious instruction. This was a moral aperient, punishment for the past.

The next phase, rehabilitation for the future, would begin with his advance through the stages of the Mark System, where everything he had was bought with his labor and obedience, translated into marks and entered in the commandant's incorruptible ledgers. As the convict's behavior improved and the moral lesson of the Mark System—nothing for nothing—sank in, so his environment altered by stages: first, solitary or separate imprisonment; then, "social labor" through the day and separate confinement at night; next, "social treatment both day and night"; and so on. He rose from one grade to the next automatically, with no interference from commandant or magistrates, depending on his total credit of marks. Some, of course, would slide back, losing marks or wasting them, which only reinforced the metaphor of real life. However, just as there would be no favors under Maconochie's system, so the only punishment would be the loss of marks—the mild, inescapable, all-seeing accountancy that drew its attentive parallels between time and money, units of labor and moral worth.

Once the prisoner was trained to see the relation between morality and self-interest, he stood ready for the third stage of the Mark System: group therapy. Maconochie wanted to put "developed" prisoners in groups of six. They would work together and mess together. Each man in the group would be responsible for the marks of others as well as his own. If one backslid and lost marks, all would. In this way the prisoners would learn mutual dependence and social responsibility.

Nobody in England or America, let alone penal Australia, had tried such therapies on convicts before. This idea of prison as a moral hospital would not win full acceptance until well into the twentieth century. The details of Maconochie's system—that prisoners should have direct access to the commandant, through an ombudsman, for instance, or that officials should take a personal interest in individual convicts—were a century ahead of their time.

The Mark System would have stayed in Cloud-Cuckoo Land but for the Molesworth Committee, which endorsed most of Maconochie's plan except the group therapy. Recommendations passed; things moved slowly, but they did move. In May 1840, the Colonial Office suggested Maconochie's appointment to Norfolk Island. Gipps passed the matter to Franklin in Van Diemen's Land.

Sending him there struck the lieutenant-governor as a double solution. It would rid Van Diemen's Land of its intractable, idealistic gadfly and would appease the Arthur Faction, on whom Franklin relied more and more passively. Meanwhile, Maconochie's visionary penal scheme would get a fair trial. If it failed, he would sink; if not, it would hardly change things in Van Diemen's Land—not, at least, during Franklin's term of office. He offered Maconochie the post.

In fact, the Scot did not think the place at all ideal for his experiment, and he told Governor Gipps so at length. He pointed out that there were already twelve hundred twice-convicted prisoners there, hard beaten-down men who would furiously resent a second and milder system of convict discipline for new convicts; the practical difficulties of running two systems for two different groups of prisoners on such a small place would be insoluble, and it would be "extreme cruelty to mix up newcomers" with the old Norfolkers. The old lags would corrupt the new "by contagion." Besides, Norfolk Island was too remote for his purposes and (a very Caledonian thought) its soil was so fertile that "the rewards of industry may be obtained without its exertion." So Maconochie begged Gipps to let him set up a new experimental station on the Tasman Peninsula, or Maria Island, or even on King Island in the Bass Strait, rather than Norfolk. But Gipps would not hear of it.

He was not hostile to Maconochie or cynical about his plans. He knew the defects of the Old System, and its horrors plagued him. But he had to be realistic. There was nowhere to put the twelve hundred twice-convicted Norfolkers. They could not go back to New South Wales, because transportation there was ending; to have so much of the doubly damned scum of the System siphoned back to the mainland would be interpreted as a gesture of contempt for the aspirations of its free citizens and would set off a wild public outcry. At the same time, its old lags could not go to Van Diemen's Land, because Franklin would not take them and Gipps could not force him to.

So Maconochie was ordered, quite unrealistically, to keep the old Norfolkers and the new subjects of his experiment separate as best he could. By the time he took ship for Norfolk Island, with his wife and family and three hundred new convicts (all fresh from England and not even disembarked in Sydney), Maconochie was so fired with enthusiasm that he saw all difficulties melting before him like wax. He was certain that his experiment would work; he could not wait.

A few days after landing, he had the Old Hands mustered in the jailyard at Kingston and strode in to confront the collective stare of twelve hundred men, nameless to him, masks of criminality and evasion, burnt by sun and seamed by misery, the twice-convicted and doubly damned, Scottish bank clerks and aboriginal rapists, Spanish legionnaires and Malay pearlers, English killers and Irish rapparees. "A more demoniacal-looking assemblage could not be imagined," he later wrote, "and nearly the most formidable sight I ever beheld was the sea of faces upheld to me." They looked at their new commandant with utter skepticism as, exalted by the thought of laying his balm on such scars, he announced the end of the Old System and described his system of marks.[28]

He had not come as their torturer, one of the prisoners reported him as saying; but he did not have the authority to extend the Mark System to them as Old Hands. He could only try it with the new arrivals. Nevertheless,

> he felt no hesitation in saying that he should find little difficulty in obtaining such an authority, and that he would venture therefore to place us under that System with the English prisoners. . . . The cheers which emanated from the Prisoners were most deafening. From that instant all crime disappeared. The Old Hands from that moment were a different

race of beings. The notion, the erroneous notion that had been engendered in their minds by a course of harsh and cruel treatment under which they had for many years been compelled to groan, was almost entirely eradicated when they found themselves received as *men* by their Philanthropic Ruler.

At once, old feelings of patriotism stirred in the convicts:

> No sooner did they rightly comprehend the purport of his message from our Most Gracious Queen,—that Sovereign who had been forgotten by them as having any dominion over the land of their Captivity—that land in which so much blood had been spilt,—than Her Majesty reigned in their hearts and they all appeared to labor cheerfully in the one large field of Reformation.[29]

Maconochie was a zealot, but an acute one. He saw that in this terrible place the sense of a chain of authority leading back to England and its monarch had been ruptured; the men had given up hope because they believed themselves abandoned by their homeland. There was nobody beyond the prison to whom they could appeal. By reinstating the Queen as icon, with all her imagery of youth, femininity and maternal concern, Maconochie showed great insight into their predicament.

His first sight of the Old Hands seems to have dispelled the last of Maconochie's doubts. From now on, nothing but the most prompt and radical therapy could help them. Dutifully, he penned a report to Gipps announcing that he would not obey his orders to keep the old and new prisoners under separate systems. Gipps was pained. It raised his worst fears of Maconochie's "visionary" streak. Had he appointed a loose cannon who would wreck the Old System and replace it with nothing workable? The governor sent a stern rebuke to Maconochie.

It reached the island just five days before the birthday of the young Queen Victoria, May 24, 1840. The new commandant had set aside Monday, May 25, as a public holiday for everyone, bond and free. At first light, strings of signal pennants headed by the Union Jack fluttered gaily up the flagpoles while a 21-gun salute boomed across Kingston from a massed battery of cannon on the hill behind Quality Row. Turning out of bed, the Old Hands as well as the new convicts up at Longridge were stupefied to find the great gates of the walled prison compounds standing wide open. They could wander as they pleased on the island, swim in the sea, stretch and frolic on the sand—as long, Maconochie's proclamation warned them, as they showed by "retiring to their quarters at the sound of the bugle . . . that they might be trusted with safety." Thus, Cook recalled, "these men who had for many years been ruled with the Rod of

Iron and had received their hundreds for being a short distance from the Barracks, were on this loyal occasion permitted to range from the settlement . . . without the least fear of committing any depredation."[30]

They got special food, including a generous ration of fresh pork, which they cooked for themselves over festive little barbecue fires. Throughout the morning, Maconochie wandered among his prisoners, affably chatting with them. When the convicts sat down to lunch—at tables in the open air, like men, not like hogs at swill—they were further amazed to be given pannikins of rum-and-lemon, the rum paid for out of Maconochie's own pocket, with which to toast their young Sovereign. They cheered her loudly, "three times three," and then toasted their commandant's health even louder.

Then, after the meal, there was an entertainment, whose handwritten playbill survives. James Lawrence (1795–?), an educated convict —the son of a London diamond broker, who had been retransported to Norfolk Island for fraud in 1836—played the lead role of Don Caesar in the "admired Comic Opera of the *Castle of Andalusia*," supported by a cast of ten other named players and "the usual Banditti" for extras. Lawrence apparently had a taste for amateur theatricals. In the past, Major Anderson had sentenced him to fifty lashes for singing a song in the barracks, as he was "a very strict man and no lover of the Drama."[31] But now he could strut and fret his hilarious hour, amid roars of amusement from the prisoners. After the opera came a "musical melange" of glees and songs—"Prithee, Brothers, Speed to the Boat," "Paddy from Cork," "Behold How Brightly." James Lawrence gave a rendition of "The Old Commander"—a veiled reference, perhaps, to the detested Anderson— and James Porter (1807–?), one of the Macquarie Harbor convicts who had intrepidly seized the brig *Frederick* and sailed her all the way across the Pacific to Chile before being caught and sent to Norfolk Island to suffer under that "second Nero," Captain Bunbury, sang "The Light Irishman." Michael Burns, whose back bore the tangled scars of two thousand accumulated lashes, danced a hornpipe. Another convict gave the Tent Scene from *Richard III*, which Maconochie must have chosen to rebuke the indurated cynicism and despair of the Old Hands:

> My conscience hath a thousand several tongues,
> And every tongue brings in a several tale,
> And every tale condemns me for a villain.
> Perjury, perjury in the highest degree,
> Murder, stern murder, in the dir'st degree—
> All several sins, all us'd in each degree,
> Throng to the bar, crying all, "Guilty! Guilty!"
> I shall despair. There is no creature loves me,
> And if I die, no soul will pity me:

Nay, wherefore should they, since that I myself
Find in my heart no pity to myself?

In the afternoon the show was moved up the hill to Longridge and
repeated for the New Hands (who were kept segregated from the old, in
strict deference to orders). Down at Kingston there were more amusements and sports, lasting into the evening. When night fell, fireworks—
paid for, like the rum, by Maconochie himself—banged and glittered over
the prison compounds; and by the time the last spark had trailed away
in the blackness, Maconochie noted that "not a single irregularity, or
even anything approaching an irregularity, took place. . . . [E]very man
quietly returned to his ward; some even anticipated the hour."

When the good colonists of Sydney heard news of this extraordinary
day, so utterly unlike any other in the past fifty years of the colony's
history, a wave of execration broke on Maconochie's head. The scum of
the System were parading free, with rum, dances and fireworks, on the
Isle of the Damned. What further revolutions might this not presage?
What would the mainland convicts do when they heard about the felon's
picnic? How soon could this rosewater liberal of a Scot be recalled? Not
soon enough, was the answer. Gipps was embarrassed by Maconochie's
disregard of orders, but he was a principled man and had given his word
to the reformer. "My desire to see Capt. Maconochie's system tried in a
fair and proper manner remains undiminished," he wrote to Lord Russell
in June 1840, enclosing copies of his protégé's "rather voluminous" reports, but Gipps expressed his "surprise"

> that [he] had, within a week after his arrival in Norfolk Island, abolished
> all distinctions between the two classes; that he had extended equally to
> all a system of extreme indulgence, and held out hopes, almost indiscrim-
> inately, to them of being speedily restored to freedom. . . . [T]hough my
> disapproval of Capt. Maconochie's proceedings . . . was received by him
> on the 20th May, no attention whatever was paid by him to my commu-
> nications. . . . [O]n the contrary, within a few days after the receipt of
> them the whole Convict population of the Island was regaled with Punch,
> and entertained with the performance of a Play.[32]

In the meantime, Russell had written to Gipps, having second
thoughts about Maconochie and giving the governor authority to recall
the reformer if he thought proper:

> Notwithstanding the Objections which I entertain . . . to the Theory of
> Captain Maconochie, that Reformation is to be the sole Object of the
> Convict System, I still wish the Experiment to be tried under his imme-

diate Supervision; but with the clear understanding that you shall remove
him, if you should find Mischief ensue . . . from his Management.[33]

But when Gipps's account of the Queen's Birthday celebrations on Norfolk Island reached him, Russell's next letter took on a sharper note of
alarm:

> I see no Alternative but to direct that Captain Maconochie should not
> be intrusted with the management of any Convicts who have more than
> three years' time to serve before . . . they may obtain a Ticket of Leave.
> The rest of the Convicts at Norfolk Island should be gradually removed
> from under his Control. . . . Make the necessary arrangements with Sir
> John Franklin for the Reception of such Convicts in Tasman's Peninsula.
>   I have already authorised you to remove Captain Maconochie from
> Norfolk Island. . . . [I am convinced of] the necessity of leaving you full
> Discretion to supersede that Officer.[34]

Maconochie, however, cared not a fig for the colonists' prejudices. He
pressed ahead with his plans for cultural and moral reform. The first are
summed up in a shopping list he forwarded to Gipps.[35] By past penal
standards, it was outlandish. He wanted books, for instance—an encyclopedia, magazines on engineering, craft and farming, cookbooks for brew-
ers and bakers; these would help teach the men trades they had never
learned, or else forgotten. He asked for a copy of *Robinson Crusoe*, to
instill "energy, hopefulness in difficulty, regard & affection for our brethren in savage life, &c." He wanted the convicts to read travel and exploration books, starting with Cook's Voyages, because "the whole white
race in this hemisphere wants softening towards its aboriginal inhabitants." Hoping "to invest country and home with agreeable images and
recollections [which] are too much wanting in the individual experience
of our lower and criminal classes," he sent for books on English history
and popular national poetry—Robert Burns, George Crabbe, the sentimental sketches of English village life by Mary Mitford, a set of Walter
Scott's Waverley Novels to encourage national pride in Scottish convicts,
and the works of the Rousseau-tinged woman novelist Maria Edgeworth,
such as the satirical *Castle Rackrent* (1800), to do the same for Irish ones.
He also stocked this prisoners' library with moral and religious works,
some, as he put it himself, of "controversial divinity," for he wanted the
prisoners to think and argue together, not rot in their cells:

> Polemical discussions are sometimes inconvenient; but I do not dread
> them, for they are nearly always, I think, improving. Wherever a taste for
> them prevails, as in Scotland, Switzerland &c[a], it is always found accom-
> panied by other good qualities; while on the contrary, where they are

despised, as in France, or crushed, as in Spain, the national character seems to suffer. . . . I would have no fear [of controversies], even in a prison.

He included the works of Shakespeare in his island library, for their nobility; had his doubts about the reformative power of theater ("the English drama is often licentious, but substantially its tendency is moral"); and felt that theatrical training could help convicts overcome their passions. Such had been his purpose on the Queen's Birthday.

Music would be the main therapy; the Orphean lyre, once heard on Norfolk Island, would charm and soothe the savage beasts of the Old System. Music was an "eminently social occupation." It taught collaboration and disciplined obedience. It rested on strict order and subordination, and, if "national and plaintive" in character, kept its hearers affable and patriotic. "It is sometimes thought to lead to drinking," wrote this earnest Scot, anticipating objections from on high, "but this, when true at all, applies to *rude* rather than scientific music. . . . The most musical people, as the Italians or Germans, are thus sober rather than drunken." (Maconochie had never visited either country.) He put in a request for trumpet, fifes, horns, drums, cymbals and two "seraphines" (reed accordions with keyboard and bellows, invented in the 1830s and popular in small parishes that could not afford full organs). He spent £46 of the government's money on a large stock of music-paper: old, infirm and crippled prisoners would be set to copy the scores out.

Gipps worried that there was little he could do, short of recalling Maconochie altogether, to stop him running Norfolk Island as he pleased. The island was too far from the mainland. But he had his colonial secretary, E. Deas Thomson, write a blistering rebuke:

> [Your] Errors . . . appear to have been the consequence of *Your own too sanguine temperament.* . . . Deeply impressed with the Truth of your own Principles, and elated, it is not unreasonable to suppose with the Notice which your Writings had attracted in England, you appear to his Excellency to have set to work with the Idea that everything was to give way before you.[36]

He also reported to Russell, a week later, that although he could not yet

> be justified in declaring Captain Maconochie's System of Management has failed, I doubt whether he will be ever able himself to work it out, as the Nonfulfilment of the Expectations which he has encouraged the Prisoners to entertain must . . . diminish his Influence over them.[37]

Maconochie replied, with annoying airiness, that he had ignored his orders to submit all new convicts to a time of punishment labor before putting them under the Mark System because "it can scarcely be doubted that this Act [2 & 3 William IV, c. 62] will be repealed. . . . I never thought of these rules as a guide; I thought them a dead letter."[38]

But Gipps's reply, through Thomson, put the politics of the matter quite flatly. The issue was not how well Maconochie's measures were working on Norfolk Island, but their effects on the mainland:

> Whether [the Old System] was good or bad is not the question; it was a system which caused transportation to that settlement to be held in great and salutary dread by the convict population of New South Wales, and to destroy that dread before even any substitute for transportation to Norfolk Island had been devised, would be to expose this colony to risks for which [Gipps] cannot make himself responsible. I am therefore to inform you that the instructions . . . are now repeated.[39]

Gipps was pincered between his hope that Maconochie's system would succeed and his fear of the majority of influential colonists—irascible, bigoted men, haunted by the threat of a "slave rebellion," who believed that convicts should be kept in iron constraint and not given an inch. Pressed to make a public statement, he reluctantly criticized Maconochie in a speech to the New South Wales Legislative Council. This whipped the criticisms of the conservative press into a firestorm. Before long, as Gipps himself recounted it,

> every man was against him, every man derided his System. . . . The feeling in fact against him, though not so intense, and far more justifiable, was analogous to that which, a dozen years ago, manifested itself in the West Indies against any attempt to ameliorate the condition of slavery.[40]

But Maconochie, a thousand miles away, pressed indefatigably on. He argued vehemently against Russell's wish, as transmitted to him by Gipps, that "my Men" who had won their tickets-of-leave should be sent down to Van Diemen's Land to complete their sentences:

> Nothing would, I think, be more unfair to them, or more certainly tend to their second Fall. Dropping, as it were, from the Clouds, without Friends or Experience, or the Habits of Evasion and Suspicion which in existing Circumstances must and do characterize the mass of the Convict Population there,—likely to be regarded with dislike by the inferior Authorities as having been trained on with different Maxims from their own, —indifferently supported thus by their Superiors when they do get into difficulty,—and jeered and tempted, if but for the Fun of it, by their

Equals,—I can see but one fate for them, and that is too melancholy to be further dwelt on.[41]

Maconochie continued to lobby Gipps for more money, more power, an absolute scope for his Mark System. His long-winded, theory-stuffed dispatches soon palled in Sydney. Gipps's patience frayed. "His Excellency cannot lay the public Purse open to your Hands," snapped Thomson in July 1842.

> He cannot make you what, in one of your own Letters, you expressed a Desire to be,—a Dictator. . . . After a Correspondence of more than Two Years his Excellency feels he is sufficiently acquainted with your System to render unnecessary any Discussion on the first Principles of it; and he cannot help remarking, although he does it with great Reluctance, that your frequent Practice of introducing Theoretical Reasoning into your Despatches causes the Public Correspondence to be both tedious and unsatisfactory.[42]

Maconochie obviously had grave problems. He could not promise the convicts freedom under his system and be sure that the government would honor his word; his powers were ill-defined; money was short; and to keep two separate systems for two groups of prisoners on a small island was an administrative nightmare. But he kept at it, and he described his general relations with the prisoners in optimistic terms. "I deliberately claim the Merit of almost complete Success," he exulted in a lengthy dispatch to Gipps in June 1842. "I have almost made black white." He expatiated on his day-to-day relations with the convicts:

> I showed the greatest Confidence in all; walking familiarly among them; taking my Wife and Family with me to every Corner of the Island, without Protection; removing the iron bars from my House Windows . . .
> I bade them stand up like Men, whomsoever they addressed . . . [A]t one time, if a Prisoner contradicted a Free Witness against him, he was punished for Insolence. . . .
> I even frequently tried Offenders in the open Barrack Yard, and engaged the [prisoners] to act as Jurors, Pleaders, Accusers, or otherwise, as the Case might be; I derived extraordinary Advantage from this, in at once suppressing false Testimony . . . and in interesting the Body of the Men in the Administration of Justice. Their sole Object on all occasions had been to defeat it, but now they began to sympathise with it. . . .
> I told them repeatedly that I could work no miracles with them, that I had not come to be their Gaoler, but if possible their Reformer; that I could do much in this if they would assist me, but nothing without. . . . I thus omitted nothing which I thought could touch their Hearts and Feelings, and thus give them an elevated direction.[43]

Maconochie dismantled the gallows, which had stood as a permanent emblem of dread outside the gate of the prisoners' barracks. He threw away the special double-loaded cats used by the floggers. The island had never had a church, but now Maconochie built two, one for the Catholics and the other for Protestants, each accommodating 450 men. For the dozen or so Jewish prisoners, who suffered badly from the anti-Semitism of other convicts and the lack of any means to conduct their own religious ceremonies, he set aside a room in the barracks as a makeshift synagogue. He gave every man a plot of the rich soil, set up classes in vegetable and fruit gardening—"a boon to the industrious, none at all to the idle"—and encouraged them to sell their surplus produce to the officers. "I thus sought to distribute property among them, and from its possession inculcate a sense and value for its rights." It greatly reduced petty theft. He let them grow and use their own tobacco "to legalize an indulgence which it was impossible to prevent, and in which, unless forbidden, there was no moral evil."[44]

He even instituted a new policy on death and commemoration. Few convicts had ever been given headstones. The exceptions were usually rebels, such as the men executed in the 1834 rising; some of their tablets can still be read in the Norfolk Island cemetery, their inscriptions a pointed reminder to other convicts of what disobedience deserved. But to be commemorated after death, however simply, was of great importance to ordinary men; and so Maconochie authorized the placing of "headstones, or rather painted boards" on the graves of convicts.

> a privilege previously confined exclusively to the free; and our burying-ground being a somewhat romantic spot . . . near the sea, it was eventually seldom without one or more visitors reading and meditating on its stern and touching lessons and recollections.

These wooden markers are gone. But some convict headstones from Maconochie's years do remain, testifying in their elaboration to Maconochie's scrupulous refusal to deny the dead their dignity—even when they were killed in a mutiny. The gravestones of men shot in the abortive piracy of the brig *Governor Phillip* in 1842, the work of skilled but anonymous convict hands, are among the finest in the cemetery. That of James Saye bears a severe reminder:

> Stop Christian stop and meditate
> On this man's sad & awfull fate
>
> On Earth no more he breathes again
> He lied [lived?] in hope but died in pain.

But the stone of Bartholomew Kelly (an Irish convict from Kilmurray in Cork who had been transported as a mere child of twelve in 1831 and had suffered on the island since March 1834 before turning pirate at twenty-six in 1842) is adorned with emblems of mercy, two turtledoves bearing olive twigs in their beaks, between the cherub's head on top and the skull and crossbones below. And Samuel Jones, transported as a boy from Warwick for stealing rabbits eleven years before he was shot on the *Governor Phillip*, has a stone of strict and simple beauty, with an angel blowing the trumpet of resurrection while stony, leafing tendrils—shoots that promise renewal of life beyond the grave—twine upward from the ground. No convict since 1788 had been granted such exequies. Even a simple stone meant a lot. Thus Laurence Frayne, who had suffered so terribly under Morisset's regime, was allowed to set up a monument to his fellow Dubliner William Storey, officially listed as "a troublesome mutinous character," who had been shot in 1838, a year before Maconochie's arrival, after escaping into the bush. "This stone was erected by Lau[ren]ce Frayne to comemmorate his memory," the plain worn inscription reads, testifying to the solidarity between the Irish convict and his mate, a bond whose public expression only Maconochie would permit.[45]

Trusted at last, reprieved from the incessant torment of the cat-o'-nine-tails, treated like human beings instead of caged beasts, some convicts poured forth their gratitude to the man they saw as their savior. The last hundred pages of Cook's *Exile's Lamentations* are given over to describing and praising Maconochie's Mark System. Other prisoners were briefer but no less intense in their feelings. "We were relieved by an Angell and Family," wrote James Lawrence, "the well known and respected Captain Maconochie, Humane, Kind, religious and now Justice stares us in the Face, the Almighty has now sent us a deliverance—no gaol, no Flogging . . . ."[46]

Maconochie's humanity also showed in his treatment of men so broken by cruelty and neurosis that they were thought beyond help. Perhaps the most striking case was that of Charles Anderson, a mentally impaired convict who had undergone years of misery in Sydney as the butt of every colonial sadist.[47] An orphan, Anderson had passed from the workhouse into the navy at the age of nine. On active service, he was wounded in the head and suffered irreversible brain damage; after a drink or two, especially when under stress, he turned violent and hostile. During such a bout on shore leave, Anderson smashed some shop windows and was arrested for burglary. Tried and convicted, he was sentenced to seven years in Australia; he was then eighteen. Anderson was so crazed with resentment when he landed in Sydney that the penal authorities isolated him on Goat Island, a rock in Sydney Harbor. Over the next few years he escaped and swam for shore three times, and received a total of some

1,500 lashes for such "offenses" as "looking round from his work, or at a steamer in the river, etc." He spent two years tethered to a chain on the rock, naked and sun-blackened. His only shelter was a coffin-shaped cavity hewn out of the sandstone; at night he would lie down in it and the warders would bolt a wooden lid, pierced with air holes, over him till morning. His food was put on the rock and pushed at him with a pole, like a wild beast's rations. Prisoners were forbidden to speak to him, on pain of flogging. The welts and gouges torn in his back by the cat never healed and were infested with maggots. He stank of putrefaction and Sydney colonists found it amusing to row up to his rock, pitch crusts and offal at him, and watch him eat. Eventually Governor Bourke, ashamed by the light this public spectacle cast on the people of Sydney, had Anderson removed to the lime-kilns of Port Macquarie. He escaped again and joined a black tribe; was recaptured and savagely flogged; and killed an overseer, hoping to be hanged. The authorities sent him to Norfolk Island instead, and he was still there—a man of twenty-four, looking twenty years older, relentlessly persecuted by the Old Hands—when Maconochie took command.

His therapy for Anderson was simple: he gave the poor, crazed man some responsibilities by putting him in charge of some half-wild bullocks, and freed him from the taunts of the Old Hands by letting him stay with them out of range of the barracks every day. He hoped, rather fancifully, that "bovine" characteristics would rub off on Anderson, making him more tractable. But the man did tame the bullocks, and found himself—for the first time since leaving England—congratulated and spoken kindly to. Then Maconochie moved him up to a new job, managing the signal station on top of Mount Pitt, which he did "with scrupulous care." Anderson could never be fully rehabilitated—his earlier brain damage was too severe for that—but when Governor Gipps visited Norfolk Island in 1843, he recorded his amazement on seeing the former wild beast of Goat Island bustling about in a sailor's uniform, open and frank in demeanor, returned to his human condition. This was the most striking success, but not the only one, of Maconochie's occupational therapy, an idea unheard-of in the English penal system until then.

A man of such radical views was bound to make enemies wherever he went, and his system was sure to be attacked.* The first complaint

---

* Maconochie's critics especially relished, as light relief, the fate of his eldest daughter Mary Ann, or Minnie. It only showed how this Caledonian do-gooder, the felon's friend, could be hoist with his own petard: Minnie's education had been entrusted to an educated convict, a young and handsome Special transported for forgery. The nineteen-year-old girl (bored stiff, one may surmise, by the social horizons of Norfolk Island) had shown a tender and deep sentiment for her tutor. It is not known whether he actually seduced her. But

from a minor official on Norfolk Island was, of all things, that he had become a tyrant, applying his system in the teeth of regulations. In August 1842, Governor Gipps forwarded to London a letter from a "demi-official," Maconochie's commissariat officer, J. W. Smith. It claimed that

> Captain Maconochie fancies himself supreme. . . . He has contended for absolute Power . . . [A] most radical Change is wanted here immediately. The Place bears no more Resemblance to what a Penal settlement should be than a Playhouse does to a Church. The Public works are neglected for want of mere Labour; the Roads which were made with so much Pains [sic] are falling into Decay; . . . the Crops are wholly insufficient to supply the Establishment. Idleness and Insubordination prevail to a shameful extent.[48]

Both the shortage of food and decline of labor came from events beyond Maconochie's control. In 1841 blight struck the staple crops on Norfolk Island. They failed, and hunger lowered the prisoners' resistance to disease. Dysentery swept the island, and killed off a number of the "New Hands" from England. Smith mentioned none of this.

There were also rumors, impossible to quash from Norfolk Island, of escapes and near-rebellions facilitated by the lenient new system. All were untrue, but they became arguments against Maconochie. Once in 1842, a group of twelve convicts (all twice-convicted Old Hands) seized the brig *Governor Phillip* at sea off Norfolk Island and held her for half an hour before the military guard rallied, killing five of them and capturing the rest. But since this piracy happened several miles offshore, it could only be blamed—as Gipps was prompt to recognize—on the negligence of the vessel's captain and guards, not on Maconochie's Mark System.

It was hard for Governor Gipps to formulate a policy for Norfolk Island and make it stick. Lord Russell had told him to stop sending twice-convicted criminals there from New South Wales and to keep the island solely as a prison for new offenders, fresh from England, subject to Maconochie's system. All very well, but where was he to put the 250 or so recidivists who, each year, were condemned to second sentences and would normally have been sent to Norfolk Island? Russell had airily suggested putting them on Goat Island in Sydney Harbor. Gipps had to point out that Goat Island was less than a mile from Sydney Cove and now held the military magazine; putting twice-sentenced convicts on

---

when the story got out, it sent the colonial conservatives into fits of sniggering delight and filled the Sydney and Hobart papers with columns of innuendo. Minnie, bereft, was packed off to England and the care of an aunt; she died there, a spinster verging on old-maidhood, at the age of thirty-two. Gipps to Stanley, July 8, 1839, HRA, Series 1, vol. 20, pp. 217–18, and October 13, 1841, HRA, Series 1, vol. 22, pp. 541–42.

this (literal) powder-keg "excited much apprehension among the colonists." Gipps devised a new holding-pen for them, on Cockatoo Island in Sydney Harbor north of Balmain, "surrounded by deep water and under the very eye of Authority." It was solid rock, and could supply Sydney with building stones as the Sing Sing quarries did New York. Among the structures Gipps had the "hard cases" build there were twenty bottle-shaped wheat silos, hewn into the living sandstone.[49]

But Cockatoo Island could not hold more than four-fifths of the recidivists. Where to put the rest? Russell had told Gipps to send no more second offenders to Norfolk, but the law (3 William IV, c.3) forbade him to send them anywhere else. Only an act of the New South Wales Legislative Council could change that. But the Legislative Council, Gipps well knew, would not allow any Old Hands back to contaminate New South Wales. It would only send them to Van Diemen's Land—where Lieutenant-Governor Franklin did not want them either and would not permit them to land. And unless the twelve hundred Old Hands could be removed from Norfolk Island and put somewhere, there was little prospect that Maconochie's new system would get its fair trial. But was it working at all? Or should it simply be abandoned? On this point, Gipps felt torn between the pressures of the colonists and his own sympathies for Maconochie.[50]

Dutifully, Gipps kept the Colonial Office posted on all the main criticisms of Maconochie and his system. In 1840 Russell had empowered him to cancel Maconochie's appointment "whenever the public good might . . . require such an exertion of authority." By mid-1842, he felt fairly secure he ought to do so. He confessed the difficulty of getting at the truth, between the rancor of Maconochie's critics and the commandant's own lofty and long-winded certainties. Some good, Gipps agreed, had come out of the new system. There was less murder and violence among the prisoners, and Maconochie's acts of leniency did awaken "the good feeling implanted in them by nature." Punishment was rare, task work light, the New Hands "idle and listless," the Old Hands "uneasy and scheming." Maconochie had given out too many tickets-of-leave, so that the amount of work done for the government had fallen—convicts were always scurrying off to tend their vegetable-gardens. The validity of these tickets-of-leave was restricted to Norfolk Island, which raised another problem: If and when their holders were transferred to Van Diemen's Land, they could not keep their tickets. Gipps doubted if the currencies of punishment could be exchanged between Van Diemen's Land and Norfolk Island. So he advised the secretary of state for the colonies, Lord Stanley, that unless he received orders to the contrary by March 1843, he would move all the Norfolk Island New Hands down to Van Diemen's Land and declare Maconochie's experiment cancelled. "The best thing to do with Norfolk Island," Gipps concluded, encompassing the end of the Mark System with a gloomy stroke of the nib, "will be to let it revert to what it was, prior to the year 1840."[51]

But Gipps was a fair-minded man, and the idea of erasing Maconochie's project on the mere word of the man's enemies gnawed at his conscience. Thus, just before the deadline of March 1843, he decided to visit Norfolk Island—without warning its commandant. He arrived there on the *Hazard* in the Pacific autumn of that year, and on landing he was agreeably surprised. Far from being an anarchic holiday-camp for criminal loafers, as the critics had suggested, the place semed perfectly in order, the convicts "respectful and quiet." Digging deeper, he privately interrogated "every person having any charge or authority, however small" in the absence of Maconochie, taking notes and keeping the answers from the commandant. During his six-day visit, he "minutely inspected" every building of any significance on the island and spoke to many convicts.[52]

All his findings pointed to one conclusion: Maconochie's critics were mostly wrong, and the new system, though imperfect, was in some respects working better than the old. The elimination of disease, the main source of administrative troubles, lay outside the reach of any commandant; among the New Hands at the Longridge settlement, those sent directly from England to Norfolk Island as Maconochie's guinea pigs in 1840, one in nine (11 percent) had died of dysentery in the past three years. Most of the survivors seemed listless, less healthy than the Old Hands, and (understandably) obsessed with the hope of being retransported to Van Diemen's Land—anything would be better than death by the flux. "When I explained to them," Gipps reported,

> that, owing to the Scarcity of Employment in Van Diemen's Land, their Condition would probably not be improved by being removed from it, they replied "Perhaps not", but that . . . they wished to get away from the Place where they had seen so many of their Comrades die; that they would rather go to New South Wales than to Van Diemen's Land, but that they would go anywhere rather than remain on Norfolk Island.[53]

That seemed to dispose of the charge of mollycoddling. However, Gipps could not "pronounce any decided Opinion" on the all-important question of whether the New Hands, after three years of Maconochean treatment, would be more likely to behave better when off Norfolk Island than "an equal number of men taken promiscuously from the Convict Population of New South Wales." The convicts seemed to take a fairly opportunistic view of the Mark System; they thought accumulating marks would "be of little Avail to them" except by getting them, perhaps, off the island sooner. Most of the New Hands, 509 out of 593, had accumulated the 6,000 to 8,000 marks needed for a ticket-of-leave; many had racked up thousands of marks beyond that, theoretically redeemable on release at a penny a mark in cash, and Gipps doubted whether the government would ever foot this bill, running (in the case of one unusually virtuous convict, a millwright named Elliott) as high as £37 10s.

Their morale was fair, no more. They had not suffered from "the chance of that Severity"

> which often brutalizes a Man in New South Wales, where a Convict's life is one of extreme chances, yet they have become in Norfolk Island familiarized with one detestable Crime, before unknown to them, and addicted (especially of late) to one very demoralizing vice: the Vice is that of Gambling, —the Crime, the one most repugnant to Human Nature.[54]

The New Hands, Gipps thought, gambled more than the Old (although this seems unlikely, it was "admitted by all persons on the Island"). He found sodomy to be widespread: Between 5 percent and 12 percent of the New Hands practiced it (this Maconochie denied); it was "said to prevail almost exclusively among the Prisoners of English birth. . . . [T]he Irish are (to their honour) generally acknowledged to be untainted with it."

Gipps's objection was that the "Social System" had not really been tried. Maconochie's "sanguine and hasty" enthusiasm about the prisoners' reform, the governor crushingly remarked, had distracted him from "the sterner parts of his own System, which are nevertheless the Foundation of the Whole":

> Nothing is more clearly laid down by Captain Maconochie than that Punishment should precede Probation, —that before Prisoners under his System should be distributed into social Parties on the principle of mutual responsibility, they should go through a Period of severe, though not vindictive, Punishment. But . . . he entered at once on the Second Part of his own System, overlooking altogether the first Stage of it; and this was the more remarkable, as it was no less contrary to the express Directions of Her Majesty's Government, than contrary to his own System.[55]

Gipps believed that Maconochie's "marks" had become inflated currency through his goodwill. He had handed them out too lavishly. Some prisoners had worked "like tigers" to accumulate the number of marks that would make them free—"but when after they had acquired their full Number of Marks, and they found that they nevertheless were not removed from the Island, the Stimulus no longer existed, and Marks gradually came . . . to be considered valueless." Disappointment and cynicism followed.[56]

The "Experimental Prisoners," then, had not done so well under the new system. But Gipps wrote with "almost unqualified Approbation" of its effects on the Old Hands: "These men had suffered, and suffered severely. . . . [T]heir minds had consequently been brought to a State in which the Manifestation of Kindness on the Part of their Ruler was likely to make the best Impression on them." The changes had been "Great and merciful," and had only good results. The Old Hands worked twice as hard as the new; they were cleaner, healthier, had better morale, and had responded to the religious training Maconochie offered: "I cannot speak but in commendation of them, and bear witness to the humanizing effect which [Chapel] seems to be producing." Their morale, Gipps thought, was less due to the diminished use of irons and the lash than to many small mercies, "the importance of which can hardly be estimated by anyone who has not been on the Island." They could rove about, fish and swim in the sea, sleep out of barracks sometimes, grow food in their own garden plots, and even carry knives.

This "mildness," Gipps felt, was justified by the fundamental misery of being on this distant island,

> so entirely cut off from Society, or even from a View or a Glimpse of Society, and more especially from the Society of Women. The yearning of their Hearts towards Society is indescribable; it constitutes their torment; it is a punishment greater than the Lash, or any other that Man can inflict on them. . . . In Assignment a Man is a Slave, but he is still a slave in *Society*.[57]

Here, perhaps without altogether realizing it, Gipps answered his own objection to Maconochie's way of running the island—that the prisoners were not given a taste of punishment first. Maconochie clarified this some years later:

> It may be said that I . . . overlooked, or even sacrificed, the great object— that of punishment . . . [but] I carried into effect the full letter and spirit of the law, and merely did not indulge in excesses beyond it. Every man's sentence was to imprisonment and hard labour; the island was his prison; and each was required to do his full daily Government task before bestowing time on either his garden or education. What I really did spare was the unnecessary humiliation.[58]

Gipps was against the Mark System being used "indiscriminately" among the Old Hands, because even if they won enough marks to expiate their second or "colonial" conviction in Norfolk Island and went back to the mainland, they would still have to serve out their first sentence in the usual way in New South Wales. He feared the social impact on New South Wales of 876 felons coming en masse from Norfolk Island. "I cannot contemplate the Possibility of their return without alarm; by the Colonists generally I am certain it would be viewed with Terror."

But the prison population was falling so fast that Gipps doubted whether Norfolk Island could keep supporting itself. No more twice-convicted men had been sent there from New South Wales since 1840; because Old Hands were being transferred to Van Diemen's Land, their number on Norfolk Island had dropped from 1,278 to 876 in three years; and the "Experimental Prisoners" would also be going to Van Diemen's Land. Thus, if a large group of new prisoners did not go to Norfolk soon, Maconochie would not have the labor force "to maintain the cultivation of it, and to keep in repair the numerous buildings."[59]

So what would Her Majesty's Government do with Norfolk Island? "The Decision . . . is of pressing Importance." Clearly, if it remained a penal island, there should only be one system of management on it, not the two that Maconochie had been ordered to maintain. Maconochie still thought Norfolk Island "ill-adapted" to his system and, Gipps added, "I must admit, as I ever have done, that if his System is to be tried it . . . should be tried in a Locality which he approves." Moreover, "I feel it right to say that I should regret to see the Experience wholly thrown away . . . [H]e fully admits that in the Distribution of Marks (the great Engine of his System) he has hitherto been too lavish."[60]

So Maconochie had received at least a guarded vindication from Gipps. The cost of running the island, Gipps saw, was not—as Maconochie's fiercest critics had put about—the result of some inherent extravagance, but simply due to the failure or success of crops. Such variations were beyond the control of any commandant.[61]

Gipps wrote his long report, and dispatched it to Lord Stanley on April Fool's Day, 1843. Maconochie had every reason to hope that now, at last, the government would ignore his critics and give full backing to his system. What happened was the exact reverse. Powerful lobbying from the Arthur Faction throughout 1842 had convinced Downing Street that Franklin was a disaster and Maconochie worse. In any case, the Colonial Office had believed Gipps's earlier criticism of Maconochie, and it was too late for the report to change Stanley's decision: to recall Maconochie. The Colonial Office was under growing pressure from the Treasury to cut the expenses of the transportation system. Sir James Stephen, the under secretary for the colonies, felt no commitment to Maconochie's theories of penal reform. It was all unimportant stuff, happening on the "remote, anomalous" dark side of the world. Maconochie had no defenders in the Colonial Office, and Lord Russell's curiosity about his ideas had waned in the six years since his reports had helped the Molesworth Committee. He could be dropped to placate the Treasury, and he was. On April 29, 1843, before the ship carrying Gipps's report had even crossed the equator, Stanley sent a dispatch ordering the end of the Mark System and the recall of Maconochie. It was carefully worded so as not to cast too black a shadow on his career. It gave Maconochie "the fullest credit" for his exertions and probity. "I gladly acknowledge," Stanley wrote with icy unction, "that his efforts appear to have been rewarded by the decline of crimes of violence and outrage, and by the growth of humane and kindly feelings in the minds of the persons under his care." It was the coup de grace.[62]

The dispatch contained good news for the prisoners, Old and New hands alike. All the men to whom Maconochie had promised a discharge at the end of their sentences would get it; everyone holding an "Island ticket-of-leave" would go on probation to Van Diemen's Land, where after a year or two of good behavior they would be issued a fully valid ticket-of-leave.

With it, on the same ship, came Stanley's choice as the new commandant. He was Major Joseph Childs (1787–1870) of the Royal Marines, a harsh, blundering turkey-cock bearing orders to make the island a place of exemplary terror once more. Yet the signs were that Maconochie's mildness had done more to reform the Norfolk Island men than any amount of terror. Throughout his administration, Maconochie had discharged 920 of the twice-convicted prisoners to a new life in Sydney. Despite the hysterical agitation against former convicts, and especially against men with the Norfolk Island taint, by 1845 only twenty of them —a mere 2 percent—had slid back and been convicted again.

But the moment of reform clanged shut. Alexander Maconochie and his family began their long trip back to England. He was fifty-six now, and his great opportunity to raise his fellow men from degradation had been taken from him, never to be handed back. The Colonial Office did not give him another post. In England, he kept campaigning for prison reform; but, although the English ardor for transportation was rapidly ebbing, the authorities were not interested in his views. "Captain Maconochie," wrote James Stephen, "has not much that is really important to urge." There was no point in punishment without terror.

For once again, English authorities were anxious about a crime wave. The number of males committed for trial for serious offenses at Assizes and Sessions had nearly doubled in less than two decades, from 170 per 100,000 population in 1824 to 326 per 100,000 in 1842. Over the same period there had been a steady tightening of prison discipline at home as well as in Australia. Its aim was to crush the criminal subculture, to deprive the individual convict of the support of his "family felons." The day of the American penitentiary had come to England. It had two alternative forms, each named for its American model: The Auburn (or Silent) System, and the Philadelphia (or Separate) System. The Auburn System had prisoners working in gangs, but under a rule of absolute silence, whose least infraction was punished by summary flogging. By contrast, the Philadelphia System was based on monastic solitary confinement. It took away a prisoner's name and past, reducing him to a number; not even the warder who brought his food knew his name or his crime. In haggard anonymity, masked in a black hood whenever he was brought from his cell for exercise, he lived out the sand grains of his sentence. He had no visitors, received no letters, and saw no human faces except those of his warders. He could never talk to a fellow prisoner; even his shoes were felted, to make his presence the more ghostlike. In old Newgate, criminals had been jammed together in social chaos, yelling, talking, weeping, wheedling, plotting, like cats in a great stone bag. But in the new penitentiary, this sense of criminal *community* was voided: All other prisoners were silent, invisible abstractions to the man in his solitary cell. The republic of crime was vaporized, and all social sense along with it, leaving only a disoriented, passive obedience. The young Charles Dickens was horrified by the great Eastern Penitentiary at Philadelphia, which he visited in 1842 in order to see the Benthamite machine of benevolent punishment at first hand:

> I believe that very few men are capable of estimating the immense amount of torture and agony which this dreadful punishment, prolonged for years, inflicts. . . . [T]here is a depth of terrible endurance in it which none but the sufferers can fathom. I hold this slow and daily tampering with the mysteries of the brain to be immeasurably worse than any torture of the body; and because its ghastly signs and tokens are not so palpable to the eye and sense of touch as scars upon the flesh; because its wounds are not upon the surface . . . therefore the more I denounce it, as a secret punishment which slumbering humanity is not roused up to stay.[63]

Such was the new engine of reform, begotten by Utilitarianism on Idealism, to which English authorities were turning for relief from the uncertainties of transportation. The conversion of the prisons from mere incarceration to punitive brainwashing, through solitary confinement, dumb cells, crank labor and the treadmill, proceeded throughout the 1830s. In 1834 the great Coldbath Fields House of Correction in London doubled its ratio of guards to inmates and adopted a system of perpetual silence and inspection. Other prisons followed suit. By 1842, England had its first Panopticon; the ideas of Jeremy Bentham had at last completed their long loop across the Atlantic, to Philadelphia and back, creating the 450-cell "model prison" on the Caledonian Road in north London known as Pentonville. Its orthodoxy filled the horizon of penal thought, and left no room for Maconochie's more humane ideas.[64]

Unable to get a hearing, Maconochie settled down to write a book: *Crime and Punishment, The Mark System, framed to mix Persuasion with Punishment, and Make their Effect Improving, yet their Operation severe* (1846). Although it would later become one of the classical reforming texts of modern penology, it was largely ignored—except by Dickens —in Maconochie's lifetime. In 1849, through the friendship of the Recorder of Birmingham, a liberal barrister named Matthew Hill, he secured a post as governor of a new prison in Birmingham—but could not control its sadistic deputy-governor, a naval officer named William Austin. After two years of reversals and humiliation, Maconochie was dismissed. By then he was sixty-four, and in failing health: erect, prematurely aged, refined in bearing, with snow-white hair, a bitterly disappointed man too proud to bear the outward marks of self-pity. Too obscure to be given more than a brief death-notice in *The Times*, he died in 1860 at the age of 73.

v

THE REVERSES Maconochie had endured at the hands of the System were bad enough. But those suffered by his former chief, Sir John Franklin, were even more stinging. The former officials of Arthur's regime through whom Franklin had decided to govern—chiefly the able and insidious John Montagu, his colonial secretary—thought him weak. Since he could not trust them (he found that out too late, as good-natured men do) and Maconochie was gone, he naturally relied more and more on the advice of the one person in the colony he could trust, his wife. Lady Jane Franklin was highly intelligent, but the thought of a Sir taking private lessons in statecraft from a woman was appalling to the Arthur Faction—and to most of the other colonists, case-armored in dogmas of masculine ascendancy. Franklin's leanings toward pity and mildness— not only to convicts, but to the dying Aborigines as well—were proof of effeteness. He was besieged by lobbyists, but whenever he did anyone a favor he created one ingrate and ten malcontents.

Worst of all, he was blamed for events over which he had little or no control. In 1840 the economy of Van Diemen's Land began to slide into a five-year depression. Banks and businesses failed; Hobart, Launceston and the townships between were silted up with unemployed workers. At the same time, the end of transportation to New South Wales meant that the whole yearly exodus of convicts was directed to Van Diemen's Land.

In 1839, less than 1,500 convicts had arrived there. By 1842 the figure was over 5,300. The machinery could not handle them, and the island could not absorb them. Worst of all, in the midst of the confusion, it was Franklin's Sisyphean task to change the whole apparatus of convict management. The Colonial Office, under the new management of Lord Stanley, had decreed that from 1842 onward the assignment of convicts to private settlers in Van Diemen's Land must cease. It would be replaced by something Lord Stanley had cooked up in his office in Whitehall: the so-called Probation System, whereby they would all be worked in government gangs distributed at outer stations around the island (see Chapter 15). Now, the settlers could not only blame John Franklin for the depression that was bankrupting them; they could also curse him for taking away the free labor on which the whole economy of the island had depended.

It would be tedious to list the innuendos against Franklin that John Montagu and his colleagues poured into the ears of Whitehall. At the start of 1842, Montagu had written Franklin an impertinent letter, suggesting in thinly veiled terms that he was getting soft in the head. At this, Franklin's patience snapped. He suspended Montagu from his job as colonial secretary. The Iago of the Derwent took himself to England and appealed to Lord Stanley, citing Franklin's "dependence" on his wife as the cause of the myriad harassments that had gummed up the administration of Van Diemen's Land. He won. Franklin found himself censured; and his letter of recall came in 1843. When he reached England, he found that the whispers of petticoat domination had preceded him—a searing humiliation for a man who loved his wife but who had also been a brave sailor and an indefatigable explorer.

To clear his name, Sir John Franklin returned to his old love, the clean cold place he had known before his country had dropped him into the vile antipodes. Once again, in 1847, the Admiralty was equipping an expedition to the Arctic, in search of the Northwest Passage. At fifty-nine, Franklin was too old for exploring in the world's high latitudes, but his daemon would not be assuaged. Reluctantly, but in a spirit of obligation, the Admiralty gave him command. This time Sir John Franklin did find the Northwest Passage, dying of starvation with the rest of his men within sight of it, on their iced-in ship the *Erebus*. In doing so, he not only expunged his failure in Van Diemen's Land but entered the Victorian pantheon of explorers (despite evidence of cannibalism in the last weeks of the expedition) as one of the heroic legends of the Arctic. Which, all in all, was more than his luckless successor at the other end of the earth could claim.

A Special Scourge

i

LORD STANLEY had never been to the antipodes or met a felon, but he glowed with ideological confidence in his new plan for mending the morals of both. It was meant to benefit England first, the convicts second, and Van Diemen's Land not at all.

Stanley took the whole matter of convict discipline to be "an Imperial interest," to whose running the interests of local free settlers were quite irrelevant. Let them complain about losing their cheap labor; that was not the Colonial Office's problem. He only wanted to get criminals out of Britain cheaply, while satisfying the much louder and closer chorus of English MPs, clergy and editors, most of whom wanted the assignment system buried forever.

Stanley dispatched his plan in November 1842 and it reached Hobart early in 1843. It cancelled the last area in which convicts could be assigned—service on farms. Instead, the felons were to pass through five stages on their way to reformation and liberty.[1]

The first was detention on Norfolk Island, usually for a year, to instill discipline. This penal antechamber could only take 750 new convicts a year direct from England. Hence, Norfolk Island was kept for long-sentence men, mainly lifers who, Stanley reasoned, were more apt to be desperate and so would need more isolation and discipline to make them tractable. The rest would go straight to Hobart, where, along with the current crop of men emerging from their time on Norfolk, they entered the second stage: the probation gangs.

Each of these gangs was to be made up of 250 to 300 men, laboring in the "unsettled districts," on long, arduous government projects—building roads and bridges, clearing Crown land to improve its sale value or logging on the Tasman Peninsula. The gangers would need special religious instruction (for which Stanley wanted Franklin to gather more penal chaplains), but, if properly supervised on long-term projects, they might grow their own food. Stanley figured that if England sent out 4,000 men a year (the actual numbers were close to that: 4,819 men in 1842; 3,048 in 1843; and 3,959 in 1844) and the average term of probation gang-labor was 18 months, then twenty gangs of 300 men would absorb them all. Each man would cost about £18 to ship to Van Diemen's Land, and £27 a year to feed; reckoning in £35,000 for the costs of Norfolk Island and £10,000 for overheads, Stanley thought the Probation System could maintain about 35,000 convicts in government service and continuous punishment for less than £300,000 a year, half the estimated cost of building penitentiaries for them all.[2]

That would be England's only expense. After their probation labor the prisoner received a "probation pass," which meant he could work for wages for an approved settler or for the local government of Van Diemen's Land. The Crown would not contribute a penny to these wages. The convicts could work or starve—that was up to them and to their prospective employers. The probation pass led to the last two stages: the normal ticket-of-leave (allowing the man to choose his own master without a say-so from Hobart) and, lastly, a conditional or absolute pardon.

So much for the men. With less relish, Stanley turned to the women and children. Boy criminals would begin with a term of 2 to 3 years in Parkhurst Prison. "Every boy who enters Parkhurst," declared one of Stanley's underlings in Whitehall to the prison authorities there, in words that rang of iron and cold corridors,

> is doomed to be transported; and this part of the sentence passed on him is immutable. He must bid a long farewell to the hopes of revisiting his native home, of seeing his parents, or of rejoining his companions. These are the hopes and pleasures which his crimes have forfeited. . . . [H]is future prospects in life depend entirely on his conduct at Parkhurst.[3]

If he behaved well at Parkhurst, the boy would get a ticket-of-leave on landing in Van Diemen's Land "and virtually be pardoned," although Whitehall did not explain how he was expected to survive thereafter. If his conduct was indifferent, he would start with a probationary pass, "which is far short of freedom." A bad boy went to Point Puer at Port Arthur, where "every hardship and degradation awaits him, and where his sufferings will be severe."[4]

As for the punishment of women, Lord Stanley entrusted his thoughts on this "more difficult subject" to Franklin in November 1842. Though as depraved as men, they could not be worked in probation gangs. The government could lock them up in Van Diemen's Land or "permit them to enter, in some mode or other, into the mass of the population." It could hardly revive assignment for them, because "respectable" settlers

did not want them and, were they to be "assigned to the less scrupulous
and less moral portion of the community"—namely, Emancipists—
"they must continually be exposed to criminal solicitation, to grievous
oppression, and often to personal violence." Moreoever, they would confront Authority with their own version of the Cretan paradox, because
even if they were solicited, oppressed and beaten, "little confidence is
placed, or can be placed, in the truth of their complaints."[5]

Nor could Franklin keep them in the existing Female Factories at
Hobart and Launceston, which (Stanley had learned) were chaotic sumps
where evil "is constantly perpetuating and increasing itself." They held
three classes of female convict, each as bad as the next: those who could
not be assigned at all, those who were returned from assignment to the
government for punishment, and helpless women pregnant with bastard
offspring who were thrown back on the government's hands. Conditions
in such places, and in the Queen's Orphan School in Hobart which took
in illegitimates, were "sufficient to make the blood run cold," wrote a
clergyman who knew them well, the Reverend Robert Crooke (1818–
1888). Crooke had been a catechist with the Convict Department in
1843, and he described the life of the seven hundred inmates of the
Queen's Orphan School. Pale and sick, these young prisoners were segregated, kept on low coarse rations and frequently punished.

> The slightest offence, whether committed by boy or girl, was punished by
> unmerciful flogging and some of the officers, more especially females,
> seem to have taken a delight in inflicting corporal punishment. . . . The
> female superintendent was in the habit of taking girls, some of them
> almost young women, to her own bedroom and for trifling offences . . .
> stripping them naked, and with a riding whip or a heavy leather strap
> flagellating them until their bodies were a mass of bruises.[6]

Such institutions were jam-packed, so all the lieutenant-governor
could do to house the newly arriving women convicts was rent secure
buildings in Hobart, or else detain the ship they came on and keep them
on board "until you shall be able to effect more permanent arrangements." The long-term plan, on which Franklin was to start at once, was
to put up a women's penitentiary for at least four hundred prisoners
within twenty miles of Hobart, whose construction the Home Government would pay for. Here, every female prisoner would spend at least six
months on arrival and then receive a probation pass. The penitentiary
was not built.

Stanley's Probation System looked impressively machine-like and rational on paper, but it proved a cruel and wretched failure because it
ignored both the economic facts of Van Diemen's Land and the quality

of its administrators. To succeed, it needed at least a prosperous economy and a strong cooperation between the Government House and the settlers. Neither existed in the last years of Franklin's governorship. But Stanley, in his anxiety to have no one sully his plan, chose as Franklin's successor a person so devoid of initiative that he hardly cast a shadow.

Sir John Eardley Eardley-Wilmot (1783–1847) was a Warwickshire baronet of sixty, whom scarcely anyone in public life except Stanley had even heard of; and Stanley, his patron, was indiscreet enough to call him (though not in public) "a muddle-brained blockhead." Until his appointment in August 1843, Eardley-Wilmot had not devoted a moment's thought to the colonies in general or to Van Diemen's Land in particular. His qualifications were three: His duties as a county magistrate had given him an amateurish, paternal interest in prison reform and juvenile offenders;[7] having been to Oxford with Stanley, and having joined Stanley's embryonic third party on quitting the Whigs, he had a place on the Old Boy network; and he was dull enough not to be disloyal. To back him up, Stanley appointed as comptroller-general of convicts a leftover from Arthur's day, the harsh and choleric Captain Matthew Forster. Such was the team that Stanley relied on to run the penal system and to keep at bay the colonists of Van Diemen's Land, irate at being denied both assigned labor and self-government.

Under such conditions, the angel Gabriel himself would have been an unpopular lieutenant-governor. When the "battered old beau" (as one Hobart lady described Eardley-Wilmot on first glimpse) appeared with his three sons Augustus, Charles and Robert, all of whom promptly got public offices in Van Diemen's Land, no one took to the new proconsul.

He could not persuade the settlers that Whitehall knew or cared what it was doing to their economy. The trade depression that had begun in Van Diemen's Land in 1841 was still worsening. One black day in 1843, Eardley-Wilmot learned that there was only £800 left in his treasury, and he had to borrow £20,000 from banks and the military chest to pay the wages of pass-holders in government service. Every year the government revenues of Van Diemen's Land fell by £20,000, and Eardley-Wilmot had to keep borrowing "in the style of a man continuing to sign checks before his bank manager caught up with him."[8] Across the Bass Strait, in New South Wales and the Port Phillip region, vast, cheap and fertile acreage beckoned the settler. In Van Diemen's Land, grazing land was expensive, and the best of it was already taken up; so the government's revenue from the sale of Crown land dwindled to almost nothing.

As with the public sector, so with the private. By 1844, it was cheaper to import cattle from the mainland than to buy locally raised animals. Sydney imported wheat from Valparaiso but charged a duty on grain coming from the "Tainted Isle," Van Diemen's Land. Men could not sell their farms, for there were no buyers; they could not hire labor, for they had no money. The farmers were even worse placed than the government to absorb the huge labor surplus that Stanley's Probation System had created. At the low point of Eardley-Wilmot's office the island had 16,000 unemployed prisoners and ex-convicts stranded in its collapsed economy —7,000 holders of probation passes, 5,000 ticket-of-leave men, and 4,000 of the conditionally pardoned.

Meanwhile, the flow of immigrants had dried up. In 1842, 2,446 emigrants had landed in Van Diemen's Land; the next year there were 26, and in 1844 exactly one emigrant arrived. (In 1843–44, 3,618 people had emigrated from England to New South Wales.) In Launceston alone, 264 houses stood empty, abandoned by their owners, who had fled to the mainland to begin their lives again. In the first six months of 1845, 1,628 settlers left Van Diemen's Land, a loss of some 5 percent of its free population.[9]

There was also a great deal of alarm about fugitives from the probation gangs, who were said to be roaming the roads and valleys of Van Diemen's Land unchecked, plundering at will, spreading misery and vice like a contagion everywhere. Some of them were tattooed like South Sea Island chiefs and would have stood out in "respectable" company. The description on a "wanted" poster of one such absconder, Charles Stagg, a twenty-three-year-old laborer from Norwich who ran from the Seven-Mile Creek probation station in March 1843, enumerates his tattoos, which included the initials of most of his family as well as his past sweethearts:

> Mary Stagg, Thomas Stagg, crucifix, 5 dots, shoe, crucifix, WS, man with stick, HK, dog, Gwynson, X Mary Robinson, Liberty, bracelet on right arm, Eliza Smith, O Sun and blue marks and rings all over right hand; man and woman, two men fighting, TS WS LS LHHS 1842, anchor, MSCS on left arm, blue dots and rings on fingers of left hand, H Stagg, William, crucifix, sun and moon on breast, ABCDEFGH on left leg, large scar on upper right arm.[10]

It would seem, however, that the tales of marauding gangs were somewhat exaggerated, for the poster listed some 465 convicts at large, cumulative since 1831. Many of these must long since have died, escaped on sealing boats or made their way across the Bass Strait to the mainland.

A further source of irritation was that Eardley-Wilmot had been ordered to go after free settlers for the arrears on their quit-rents. These small sums had mounted up, having remained unpaid for years on land granted in Arthur's time or earlier; Stanley felt that collection of these taxes could offset the drop in Crown land sales. The settlers bridled at that, and even worse was the demand for taxes to carry the cost of both the judiciary and the police. The Van Diemen's Land police force was huge in ratio to the free population. The costs of the police, the judiciary and the maintenance of paupers came to £52,437 a year, or nearly a pound a head for every man, woman and child, free and bond, in Van Diemen's Land.[11]

The colony was sliding into bankruptcy. Eardley-Wilmot bore all the blame for this and was even more execrated than Arthur. Yet the sad fact was that he sympathized with the plight of the settlers and took their side in his dispatches to Whitehall, much to Lord Stanley's annoyance. He urged Stanley to drop the minimum price of Crown land below £1 an acre, as an inducement to new settlers; and he tried to get credit to use the mass paid labor of otherwise unemployable pass-holders on public works, to be underwritten by Britain but paid for, in time, by tolls and service charges. He also pressed the Treasury to pay the cost of the jail and police system; eventually, in early 1846, it agreed to pay two-thirds.

This gesture came too late to appease the settlers. Between October and November 1845, Eardley-Wilmot faced a political crisis in his Legislative Council. The Legislative Council of Van Diemen's Land was not an elected body, and, since Arthur's day, it had usually been content to act as a rubber stamp. It consisted of the lieutenant-governor, six government officials and eight non-official members drawn from the ranks of free citizens, usually opulent ones. Six of the latter—the "Patriotic Six," as their supporters called them—resigned over the police-funds issue and left the council without a quorum. They claimed they had been refused information on police budgets and convict administration, and that when they pressed for it Eardley-Wilmot and the official members had called them "factious" and "disloyal." Although Eardley-Wilmot managed to replace the six, he could not keep a lid on the demands for representative government and the end of transportation, which by now had fused into the single obsessive issue of political life in Van Diemen's Land.

But Whitehall would not listen. All Eardley-Wilmot could show after two years of pleas was a lengthy rebuke from Stanley, complaining that he had not filed proper reports on the working of the Probation System. By then, Van Diemen's Land boasted sixteen probation stations: four (mainly for logging and coal-mining) on Tasman's Peninsula, five for agriculture on the coast of the D'Entrecasteaux Channel, one to build the female penitentiary at Oyster Bay, two on Maria Island, one on the east coast and three, whose gangers labored to build roads and bridges, in the interior of the island. There were eight hiring depots from which the free settlers could recruit pass-holders, but traffic through them was sluggish. All this presented a lot of ground for reports to cover. Eardley-Wilmot did not take to scrambling down the coal mines or through the forests of Tasman's Peninsula to see how well the probation gangs were shedding their vices by splitting shingles and felling 150-foot eucalypts, and so he was often content to scrawl mere covering-notes on the detailed statistical reports of his comptroller-general of convicts, Forster. But Stanley's complaints typified his imperial and solipsistic view of the antipodes. To him, Van Diemen's Land was not a complex little society with severe economic problems; it was more abstract—a receptacle, a social void whose sole purpose was to swallow criminals. He did not want to hear that "his" convicts could not be fully employed in "his" colony. Realizing that the Probation System was about to fail, and that he might be blamed for it, Lord Stanley got ready to fling Sir Eardley-Wilmot to the Tasmanian Devils. He would make sure that the chaos in Van Diemen's Land was seen not as his system's fault but as the proconsul's.[12]

Stanley gave the draft of his strongly critical dispatch to the government printer, who published it for the House of Commons in February 1846. The first Eardley-Wilmot saw of it was in print. He was aghast at Stanley's maneuver, which denied him the chance to have his letters of rebuttal printed along with the Colonial Office's criticisms and pilloried him before government and press as incompetent, lazy and vague. Eardley-Wilmot dug in.

The Colonial Office was getting set to dismiss him when, in 1845, Lord Stanley quit the Colonial Office for a larger political sphere. He was replaced by the thirty-six-year-old junior minister William Ewart Gladstone. Gladstone depended for his knowledge of Australian matters on the permanent under secretary to the Colonial Office, one of the preeminent civil servants of the nineteenth century (and the grandfather of Virginia Woolf), Sir James Stephen. Stephen felt Britain had been wrong in overloading Van Diemen's Land with convicts, and he was very skeptical of Stanley's Probation System. But he was also sure of Eardley-Wilmot's incompetence and he took up the issue which, he knew, would turn the morally priggish Gladstone against the foundering lieutenant-governor.

Ever since the Probation System had been installed, lobbyists had been harping on a subject peculiarly repugnant to the Victorian sense of public morality: that, thanks to those isolated bush gangs of toiling, degenerate men, Van Diemen's Land was now a hotbed of sodomy. Letters and witnesses came across the oceans to Whitehall, testifying to the collapse of all moral values in the stained island. They made Van Diemen's Land under Eardley-Wilmot sound infinitely worse than Capri under Tiberius.

Francis Russell Nixon, Bishop of Van Diemen's Land, carried the most weight among them. The epidemic of unnatural crime, he assured

Lord Grey, "unless sternly arrested in its growth, must not only ensure the moral degradation of the colony, but draw down divine vengeance upon it." Nixon believed that all the convicts, without exception, left the probation gangs worse than they entered them. He quoted letters to him from despairing gang chaplains. "I cannot depict the horrors committed here daily by miserable men, who know better, but who cannot escape from their wretched condition." Parties of convicts slunk off together into the bush to gratify their lusts. In the "tench" or penitentiary (in fact, an ordinary prisoners' barracks) in Hobart Town, where twelve hundred were kept, "The most disgusting crimes that ever stained the character of man are perpetrated . . . and without the least possible way of preventing it." In the coal mines near Port Arthur, two men had raped a boy convict, "an offence hitherto, I believe, unheard-of in a Christian country." They hanged for it, but the medical officer at the mines, Dr. Motherwell, found twenty men "labouring under disease from unnatural crimes." The spread of rectal gonorrhea, Bishop Nixon warned, was "a special scourge" from God, "a mark of his increased wrath, for the yet greater abomination."[13]

Nor was the evil confined to men. The Female Factory at the Cascades in Hobart swarmed with lesbians. In August 1841, Franklin had set up a committee of inquiry to review the facilities for discipline of female prisoners in this dank, miserable and overcrowded building, along with its twin institution in Launceston. Its semi-confidential report appeared in February 1843, with its descriptions of women convicts in the "very act of exciting each other's passions—on the Lord's Day in the House of God—and at the very time divine service was performing."[14] By then the local press was printing stories about the "fiendish fondness" of Sapphic practices in the factories, and in November 1843 Eardley-Wilmot sent a secret dispatch of his own to London on this subject. He told Stanley that women in the Female Factories "have their Fancy-women, or lovers, to whom they are attached with quite as much ardour as they would be to the other sex, and practice onanism to the greatest extent."[15]

At least one convict, the Chartist exile John Frost (and he can hardly have been alone in his opinion), believed that the British Government maintained the probation gangs in all their turpitude in order to crush the spirit of class resistance. "The authorities of Van Diemen's Land were indifferent to the commission of this great offence," he told a shocked English audience some years after his release. "Smoking was deemed a greater offence than that of Gomorrah, and published with greater severity."[16]

Eardley-Wilmot, far away in Hobart Town, protested that although the vice denoted by asterisks in the Parliamentary Papers certainly existed in Van Diemen's Land, one found it in the army and navy, too, and in all "large assemblies of the male sex." In vain, he relayed to Stanley the opinions of the medical officers on the probation and hiring stations, as diligently collected by his comptroller-general. They showed only seventy cases of the sexual disease in a gang population of 10,000 men. Seven in one thousand, he agreed, were too many, but even so, the scare-stories had largely been made up by his critics to discredit the Probation System.[17]

None of this appeased the local press, the clergy, the settlers or the Colonial Office. In July 1846, twenty-five Van Diemen's Land clergymen (most of its Anglican establishment) signed a petition to Grey begging for the end of the Probation System, as an incubator of homosexuality.[18] In London, embarrassing stories had been current in the press for some time. "Van Diemen's Land is in a bad state," wrote an anonymous pen in the London *Naval and Military Gazette* in October 1845. "Crimes the most horrible are of daily occurrence. All the females have left the bush and have taken refuge in the towns, and . . . are subject to every kind of insult. Sir Eardley-Wilmot sets a bad example himself. No people of any standing will now enter Government House except on business. No ladies can." Satires and moral versicles made their clumping appearance:

> Shall fathers weep and mourn,
>   To see a lovely son
> Debas'd, demoraliz'd, deform'd
>   By *Britain's filth and scum!*
>
> Shall mothers heave the sigh,
>   To see a daughter fair
> Debauch'd and sunk in infamy
>   By *those imported here!*
>
> Shall Tasman's Isle so fam'd,
>   So lovely and so fair,
> From other nations be estrang'd—
>   The *name of Sodom* bear?
>
> Till Nature's GOD, provok'd,
>   Stretch forth His mighty arm;
> And in relentless fury, pour
>   His *righteous judgments down.*[19]

It was not exactly—the anonymous tongues now began to whisper—that the man in Government House condoned this frightful state of affairs; still less that he himself, despite the loneliness he must feel now and then in the antipodes without a wife, was touched by the hot breath of the Cities of the Plain. It was just that his behavior gave rise to idle rumors about quirks that, though doubtless innocent in themselves, clouded his office. He gave dinners in Lent, to the scandal of Bishop Nixon, who had already quarrelled with Eardley-Wilmot over the lieutenant-governor's right to appoint religious instructors to the probation gangs. He had been seen putting his arm around girls' shoulders on the sofa in Government House. He had flirted at a formal dinner party with Julia Sorell, the granddaughter of a leading settler and future grandmother of Aldous Huxley. Manifestly, there must be some ratio between this permissiveness at Government House and the unspeakable, furtive ecstasies of the probation gangs. Fish rot at the head.

Gladstone's reaction to all this was predictable. He flew into a moral rage, and at the end of April 1846 he wrote two letters of dismissal to Eardley-Wilmot. The first one was public, announcing that in view of the lieutenant-governor's utter failure to safeguard the morals of the convicts under the Probation System, he was dismissed. The very absence of external signs of the vice of Sodom that Eardley-Wilmot had reported, Gladstone wrote with crushing illogic, showed how deep-rooted it was, how well sheltered from the light. Eardley-Wilmot was not being fired for mismanaging the transition from assignment to probation (anyone, Gladstone seemed to imply, could have failed at that) but for not displaying enough "assiduity," "anxiety" and "prudence" in moral reform. Accordingly, Gladstone was transferring Charles La Trobe, the superintendent of Port Phillip, to Hobart to take over until a new lieutenant-governor was named.

The second letter was private, short and even nastier. It told Eardley-Wilmot that in view of unspecified rumors circulated by unnamed persons regarding aspects of his unofficial conduct which it was "perhaps unnecessary" that Gladstone should discuss, he must not expect another official post.[20]

Thus the "battered old beau" with his flirtatious post-prandial ways was at last broken on the iron wheel of Gladstone's sanctimony. He tried to defend himself; he protested against the "grossest falsehoods that ever oppressed an English gentleman," "the most extraordinary conspiracy that ever succeeded in defaming the character of a Public Servant"; he appealed to Gladstone to name his accusers and state their charges; he forwarded petitions in defense of his character, bearing many respectable signatures. It was all to no avail. In February 1847, a few weeks short of his sixty-fourth birthday, Sir John Eardley Eardley-Wilmot slipped beyond the reach of his tormentors in the Colonial Office and died in Hobart, reputedly of a broken heart. At once, the *Colonial Times* declared that he had been "murdered." The settlers who had detested and abused him performed a brisk volte-face, awarding him a state funeral with a solemn procession through the crepe-decked town, during which

Anglican clergy and Catholic priests fell over one another in their haste to lead the hearse. They then subscribed for a spindly stone monument in the Neo-Gothic style, the largest tomb ever erected to the memory of a governor on Australian soil. By the time it had been installed above the remains of Sir Eardley-Wilmot, the interim governor Charles La Trobe had come to Van Diemen's Land, made his report and returned with almost palpable relief to his duties across the Strait in Port Phillip. He told Lord Grey what everyone, in and out of the colony, knew by now— that the Probation System was an utter fiasco, that "whatever principle of reformation might be included in the theory," its only result in practice was to degrade, that it was "vicious . . . a fatal experiment," and that the sooner it ended the better for the credit of the nation and of humanity.[21] In 1846, Her Majesty's Government suspended all transportation of convicts to Van Diemen's Land for two years. By then, the last lieutenant-governor to preside over the System on that island, Sir William Denison, had arrived in Hobart to confront the problems that had defeated Eardley-Wilmot and would in due course baffle him. Among the thorniest of these was the management of Norfolk Island.

ii

THE ADMINISTRATIVE CONTROL of Norfolk Island passed from New South Wales to Van Diemen's Land in 1844, and by then an ill wind had blown through the barracks at Kingston and Longridge. Captain Alexander Maconochie had been recalled from the island in 1843, and replaced by the last military commandant of that ill-omened rock to be appointed from New South Wales: Major Joseph Childs, a fifty-six-year-old marine officer. He was Maconochie's opposite in every way—a dull, vacillating military hack, distinguished only by his severity.

For severity was what Lord Stanley wanted—and he wished to see it directed, in particular, against "crimes unattended with violence": namely, sodomy. From the second-hand reports Gipps wrote before he actually saw Maconochie's system for himself, Stanley concluded that the new "leniency" of Norfolk Island incubated all crimes, but especially the unmentionable ones. Since going there in February 1843, Gipps had changed his mind—but too late to change Stanley's. Work them till they drop, skin them alive if they get out of line and make no exceptions— this, in essence, was the formula he transmitted to Gipps as the first stage of his Probation System for men on Norfolk Island. "Nothing but constant vigilance and inflexible rigour in enforcing the appropriate Punishments will be sufficient to restrain the immoralities to which I refer."[22]

The idea that two thousand men, mostly in their twenties and thirties, could be incarcerated on a distant island, deprived of any contact with women, treated so harshly that their only emotional solace could come from one another and then "restrained" from sodomy by incessant flogging is a curiously abstract one; but it seemed real to Whitehall. All their evil proclivities, including the sexual, could be vaporized in the tension between, in Stanley's words, "an invigorating hope and a salutary dread."

There was not much hope on Norfolk Island. From the moment Childs was rowed through the foaming reefs of Kingston from the *Maitland* in February 1844, the trust Maconochie had struggled to establish between convicts and Authority caved in. There was no longer the sense of a responsive chain of command, or of access to the commandant. Childs's idea of authority, formed in the harsh mold of the British Marines, destroyed part of that; and the rest was annihilated by his lazy habit of leaving summary punishments to the turnkeys, the overseers and to his resident stipendiary magistrate, Samuel Barrow. Barrow, twenty-eight years old when he arrived from Van Diemen's Land in August 1845, had been a junior barrister in London. His real talent, however, was less for legal argument than for gross arbitrary sadism. For that, he was the right man in the right place at the right time. If the ornate diction of Lord Stanley's dispatches provided the theory of Norfolk Island after Maconochie, Childs and Barrow between them supplied the practice, and the treatment of prisoners there became as bad as it had been in the "murdering times" of Morisset. All the men on Norfolk Island were, in Childs's apoplectic language, "the worst men that the annals of criminal jurisprudence can hold forth to the world as an example of all combined evil."[23]

One did not treat such demons softly, although in fairness to Childs one should note that not all of them were handled with equal severity. One convict who passed through Childs's regime on Norfolk Island, the former military officer John Mortlock, would describe Childs as "a gallant marine officer" who gained the "entire respect" of the convicts with his "discreet management." Perhaps all that this judgment shows is that military officers shared the same views on discipline; and Mortlock was never flogged. All the same, he recalled, it was thanks to the "delightful scenery and heavenly climate" of Norfolk Island "that I do not look back upon my residence there with unmixed horror."[24]

"Many of my shipmates were flogged daily," Mortlock recalled, "in the barrack yard, under my windows, on complaints often made with a wicked purpose by their overseers; though I could shut my eyes, the horrid sound of the 'cats' upon the naked flesh (like the crack of a cartwhip) tortured my ears. . . . Petty 'dogs in office,' in order to strike terror, would commonly threaten 'to see the back-bone.' "[25] Thomas Rogers, a curate from Dublin who was posted from Van Diemen's Land to Norfolk Island in September 1845 as its sole religious instructor (such convict-department comforters being stipulated by Stanley's Probation System), claimed that Childs had 26,024 lashes inflicted in the last sixteen months of his command. On some mornings

> the ground on which the men stood at the triangles was saturated with human gore as if a bucket of blood had been spilled on it, covering a space three feet in diameter and running out in various directions in little streams two or three feet long. I have seen this.[26]

But it was in the summary punishments—inflicted by Barrow and his underlings without interference from Major Childs—that the crude ingenuity of the new regime showed itself. The cat was banal; the elite of convicts, the "pebbles" or "iron men," had their own infrangible code of contempt for it. One prisoner in Childs's day had a message to the "skinner" tattooed on his back: FLOG WELL AND DO YOUR DUTY.[27] "Salutary dread" required something more. In a report made to Eardley-Wilmot in October 1845, Childs had bewailed the limits of punishment set by the Colonial Quarter Sessions Act, as they were "too confined for the class of men we now have to deal with, for whom chains have no restraint, and the lash no terror."[28] He turned a blind eye while Barrow and his men devised methods of summary discipline. The main ones were the "tube-gag," the "spread-eagle," the "scavenger's daughter" and the water-pit.

The tube-gag was an adaption of that ancient English instrument of torture for women, the "scolds' bridle." It looked like a small leather head-harness, except that instead of a bit it had a cylinder of hardwood, four inches long and an inch and a half in diameter, fastened into a broad leather strap that buckled across the face. When this gag was forced into the victim's mouth and the straps cinched, the man could only breathe through a small hole in the wooden plug, with great difficulty, emitting what the Reverend Rogers described as a "low indistinct whistle" accompanied, if he had resisted the gag and lost a tooth or two, with some red foam. The first prisoner on whom Rogers saw the tube-gag used was blind; for talking in his sleep, he was dragged from his cell, gagged and left for three hours with his arms shackled around a post behind him and tears streaming from his sightless eye-sockets.

The "spread-eagle" was simpler, though often used in concert with the gag. The prisoner was ironed to three ringbolts, arms fully outstretched, feet together, face to the wall, and left in this tiptoe crucifixion for six to eight hours. Some remained paralyzed for days afterward. A more refined implement for inflicting a similar torture was a raised iron frame six feet by two, on which the victim was strapped with his head and neck projecting unsupported off one end. If he tried to keep his head up, he would suffer anguish from muscular cramps. If he let it flop down, he would suffocate. The "scavenger's daughter" consisted of binding the convict with his head against his knees and leaving him until he fainted from the pain of cramps. The water-pit was an underground cell with salt water to waist height; men were left there in darkness for days at a stretch, unable to sleep for fear of drowning.

No wonder, then, that all sense of contract with authority disappeared and that the island lurched toward anarchy. In 1846 the Reverend Thomas Rogers's predecessor, an Anglican clergyman named Thomas Begley Naylor who had been chaplain on Norfolk Island from 1841 to September 1845, wrote a detailed report on Childs's regime to Lord Grey. "Revolting things have been done, in silence and without remedy," things for which "nothing else but the complete isolation of the island can account for." All was favoritism, spying and evasion, and chaos prevailed beneath Childs's claim to have restored an order "lost" by Maconochie's misplaced compassion. Villains were put in soft clerical jobs,* while harmless and indeed innocent prisoners, such as the unfortunate lawyer William Henry Barber, wrongly transported for a fraud on the Bank of England and later to be exonerated by Parliament, were given the filthiest and most degrading tasks. Childs had no system of discipline "conscientiously or intelligently carried out"; all he did was feed and clothe the demons and keep them nominally busy.[29]

Far from repressing homosexuality, Naylor reported, the overcrowding and lack of segregation on Norfolk Island encouraged it. "A parade of separation is kept up, but the communication is complete, and at times unrestricted." The bad apples always contaminated the good, in "a heterogeneous mass of moral pollution painful to contemplate." First-time offenders and even innocent men "are immediately on their disembarkation thrust among the veriest monsters of crime, from the cold-blooded murderer trebly convicted, to the wretch whose enormity Blackstone characterises as 'inter Christianos non nominandum,' without a possibility of escaping." In the end, Naylor warned Lord Grey, in the tone of eschatological prophecy that would soon become a common trope in discussions of the Probation System, "the curse of Almighty God must sooner or later fall in scorching anger upon a nation which can tolerate the continuance of a state of things so demoniacal and unnatural."[30]

The report horrified Lord Grey. Naylor had hoped to publish it as a

---

* In contravention of Clause 38 of the standing regulations: "No convict shall be employed as clerk in the Commandant's or any other office, or have access to the records kept therein."

pamphlet (and Maconochie, to whom it was delivered, dissuaded him from doing so) but its private impact in Downing Street was immediate. One could not read, he noted, such a litany of "guilt, wretchedness and mismanagement," on which a clergyman had staked his name, without intense disquiet; Naylor's revelations were "too probable" to pass over. The new lieutenant-governor, Sir William Denison, was on the point of sailing from Portsmouth for Hobart. At the end of September 1846, Grey's instructions went to Denison. Her Majesty's Government must not even take the chance of prolonging evils so fearful in their nature. Denison must evacuate Norfolk Island and bring all its prisoners to Tasman's Peninsula "with the least possible delay." But he had second thoughts in November, and warned Denison that "practical difficulties, not to be foreseen at this distance" might defeat the move. They did, and Norfolk Island was not "broken up" for another decade.[31]

But meanwhile, before Gladstone's ax fell on him, Eardley-Wilmot had asked for a report of his own. He knew nothing of Naylor's damning letter but was worried by the rumors in the hostile colonial press. His own morals were under attack and he could not afford to seem dilatory. In April 1846, Eardley-Wilmot's comptroller-general of convicts, William Champ, directed an investigator to sail there and, as he delicately put it, report on the "many points . . . which might naturally fail to attract the attention . . . of Major Childs." The investigator was a magistrate in the Van Diemen's Land convict department, Robert Pringle Stuart, and he arrived at Norfolk Island in May 1846. He completed his investigation in two weeks, and his voluminous report reached Eardley-Wilmot by the end of June.

Little is known of Stuart's character, beyond the fact—obvious from his report—that he had an avid eye for detail, considerable skill in sifting and marshalling evidence, and knew the general penal environment well. One historian recently complained that his report "reads like that of a man without humour,"[32] but to wring laughs from such material would have taxed the most determined comedian.

His findings parallelled Naylor's. The physical state of the system on Norfolk was miserable—the rations underweight, the grain foul, the meat of the poorest quality, the maize-flour bread (known as "scrubbing-brushes" for the inflammation its abrasive bran produced in the prisoner's guts) scarcely edible. The service buildings, from the kitchens to the fouled latrines, provoked Stuart's disgust and the prisoner's simmering, mutinous resentment. Ophthalmia, gonorrhea and dysentery were endemic. The jail was an unventilated pigsty and the main barrack building at Kingston a *bagnio*: more than eight hundred men were locked in the barracks every evening after work, the lights went out, and what went on afterward was not the guards' business. Stuart paid it a surprise visit at eight o'clock one hot night and saw a flurry of "men scrambling into their own beds from others, in a very hurried manner, concealment being evidently their object." Prostitution was widespread; lads sold themselves for tobacco, new boots, or a lump of bread kneaded together with fat. Rape was not merely common, but inevitable.[33]

What especially shocked Stuart (and its effect on the officials who read his report may be gauged from the fact that, when it was eventually printed for the Lords and Commons in 1847, nearly all references to homosexuality were edited out) was that the virtuous forms of sexual life were parodied and inverted on Norfolk Island—not just rape and whoring, but marriage. "The association is not unusually viewed by the convicts as that between the sexes is ordinarily regarded; is equally respected by some of them; and is as much the source of jealousy, rivalry, intrigue and conflict . . . in others." Some of the demons were faithful to one another, and "the natural course of Affection is quite distracted. . . . [They] manifest as much eager earnestness for the society of each other as members of the opposite sex." In general, it was the English who turned to sodomy; the Irish Catholic prisoners abjured it.[34]

Despite the hysterical level of official violence, general discipline was poor. The morning muster was "unseemly, disorderly . . . in fact the mere nomination of the members of a promiscuous crowd," with "English and colonial prisoners intermixed, some lounging about with folded arms, others standing with their hands in their pockets, all either in conversation, uninterrupted, or otherwise engaged at their pleasure." When new men arrived from England, gangs of twenty to thirty Old Hands would pick the locks on their ward, rush in, beat them up and steal their belongings. No one stopped these forays, even when a group of bewildered New Hands just off the transport *Mayda*, when escorted down to the sea to wash, were plundered on the beach "notwithstanding the efforts of the constabulary." Convicts swore most opprobriously at their guards and got away with it; houses were robbed in broad daylight; one hardened Old Hand (as Naylor had reported) actually knocked down the commandant himself, bruising him severely. Most extraordinary of all, the convicts—or a hard core of them, numbering perhaps one hundred—often went on strike, openly refused to work and submitted "only when terms had been arranged to their satisfaction." Not one of them was punished or even tried. Their usual complaint was inedible food. On February 25, 1846, they struck over a different issue: The day was Ash Wednesday, a Catholic holiday, and they would not go to work until a military party levelled its muskets and made ready to shoot them. Childs's civilian officers, however, were not up to enforcing regulations without the help of the military, which could not be invoked every day. "The spirit of disobedience thus strengthened in the refractory," Stuart gloomily noted, "is, from impunity, reflected by the many, and provokes imitation." The hard-core men carried knives openly, threatened their overseers with them, and ruthlessly avenged any "peaching" by other prisoners. Anyone who betrayed a fellow prisoner to Authority was denounced as a traitor or "dog," and his punishment was swift: The men would kill him, or at least mutilate him by biting his nose and ears off, an operation known as "taking the dog's muzzle."

As the guards and overseers had so little control over what went on inside the barrack walls, the prisoners were able to create their own rule. Its center was the enclosed lumber-yard, a building next to the main barracks compound which also held the kitchens. It became a sanctuary where few guards or officers dared to go. The yard was ruled by the "Ring," a carceral mafia whose control over the lives of prisoners was both inescapable and minutely enforced. Its members did not fear to kill constables when they brought evidence against them; one such informer was found eviscerated in the bush near Longridge, his guts replaced by the entrails of a sheep. Later tales of the System, as composed by Marcus Clarke and Price Warung, surrounded the Ring with the awful glamour of a secret society, a freemasonry of evil, complete with elaborate initiation ceremonies, distinguishing tattoos (stamped on the neophyte's hide with needles and gunpowder) and a communal chant or oath:

> Hand in Hand
> On Earth, in Hell,
> Sick or Well,
> On Sea, On Land,
>   On the Square, Ever.
>
> Stiff or in Breath,
> Lag or Free,
> You and Me,
> In Life, in Death,
>   On the Cross, never.[35]

Such are the embellishments of fiction, but there is no doubt that the Ring had existed on Norfolk Island since the late 1830s and that it was very much feared. It gave the hardened and depraved, Stuart wrote,

> an absolute power, which is exerted in the most tyrannical manner over the majority, many of whom, I firmly believe, desire to conduct themselves becomingly, but have not sufficient courage to enable them to defy the threats, rendered more alarming by the almost hourly exhibition of them being carried into effect, or to resist the determined, vicious confed-

eracy by which they are oppressed. There are no means of protecting a
man who may have brought himself odium on account of good conduct,
or . . . having given evidence against any member of the so-called "Ring."
A more miserable position than that of such a man cannot be conceived.[36]

There was more, in the same vein. When Stuart finished his report to
Champ, and Champ "with the deepest regret" laid it before Eardley-
Wilmot, and Eardley-Wilmot called a special meeting of the Executive
Council on July 1, 1846, to consider what to do about it, that was the
end of Major Childs. The council voted unanimously to get rid of him at
once. Against Eardley-Wilmot's protests, they agreed to relieve Major
Childs without notice, lest "matters might be brought to a crisis, and
the island be subjected to all the horrors of an open mutiny."[37]

And in fact, as they sat in council on July 1, a mutiny did break out
on Norfolk Island. It was a food riot. The prisoners never had enough
food, and what they got gave them dysentery. The wretched victuals on
Norfolk Island were a permanent and galling proof of Britain's contempt
for them. In July 1846, it only took a pinprick to release an explosion of
hatred.[38]

July 1 was the date of the half-yearly survey of all stores and equipment. William Forster, the superintendent, was in charge of the inventory, and on June 30 he went into the lumber-yard and its cookhouse to
look for kitchen gear and cookpots. He did not want to make trouble
with a close search, but he thought many dishes and mess-kits were
missing (the inmates cut up large vessels and tinkered them into small
ones, for sale to guards or other prisoners) and decided to come back after
the eight hundred convicts were locked in barracks. That evening he
found "a great number" of pots, pans and knives hidden around the
lumber-yard, along with hoards of maize-meal that members of the Ring
had skimmed for themselves from the regular rations. Foster had it all
carried to the convict barracks store and locked away for the night, for
inventory.

Next morning the prisoners turned out for their breakfast and found
that "their" kettles and pans, along with their private hoards of flour,
were gone. Their loss maddened the elite of the ring and they surrounded
the muster officer, Patrick Hiney, shouting confused threats. Then, no-
ticing the open gate of the lumber-yard, a mob of men ran outside, made
for the barracks store, broke the locks and returned in triumph with their
maize-flour and cooking gear. They settled down to boil water and make
porridge. None of the guards interfered. But half an hour later, as constables and overseers gathered outside the gates to march the prisoners
off to the day's labor, there was a shout from inside the lumber-yard:

"Come on, we will kill the——."* For the second time that morning, a mob of fifty or sixty men came boiling from the gates, led now by one of the hardest cases in the Ring, a twenty-six-year-old twice-convicted bushranger from Van Diemen's Land named William "Jackey-Jackey" Westwood. They grabbed whatever weapons lay to hand—axes, shovels, slabs of wood for clubs—swinging furiously at their guards as they rushed at the constables' cottages and then toward the house of the hated stipendiary magistrate, Samuel Barrow. They left four corpses behind them, men who had barely been able to react before their skulls were caved in by the mutineers. But they had no plan, and as they charged gasping and cursing toward Barrow's cottage they saw a line of soldiers bearing down on them, muskets levelled and bayonets fixed. The mutineers faltered, turned, and ran back to their only haven, their "Alsatia" (as Stuart's report had termed it), the lumber-yard. The bloody episode had lasted only minutes, but the reprisals were thorough. Barrow arrested more than fifty prisoners, and they crammed the filthy old jailhouse (which had not been enlarged or improved since Morisset's time) to bursting. Most of them were summarily sentenced to a year's hard labor in chains, and the presumed ringleaders were loaded with iron and reeved by their fetters to a long chain cable to await the arrival of a judge who could hold the necessary trial. Before the mutiny there were nine men in the lockup on other capital charges, and Childs had already sent for a criminal court justice. He arrived on the *Lady Franklin* a few weeks later, not knowing the mutiny had happened and unprepared for the sight of several dozen capital defendants. His name was Francis Burgess, and on board with him was the newly appointed commandant of Norfolk Island, John Price.

Burgess fell ill a few days after the hearings started. He had to go back to Hobart on the *Lady Franklin*, and the court opened again in late September before a new judge, Fielding Browne. In the meantime Barrow and Price between then had developed the prosecution as a perfect opportunity to break the Ring. They indicted all the known Ring members they could, committing twenty-six men to trial; eventually, fourteen were tried on five counts of murder and abetting. Despite the protests of the chaplain, Thomas Rogers, none of them was allowed a defense lawyer; and when Rogers helped the prisoners draft a petition to the judge asking for counsel, the request was ignored. Several defendants were illiterate and could not read the depositions against them. The "jury" was only a tribunal of five military officers. Twelve witnesses were heard from the Crown but none for the defense, and as they gave their evidence

* Expletive deleted, in the Parliamentary Papers.

the men in the dock hooted and cursed at them, trying as best they could to mock the processes of this kangaroo court. On October 5, twelve men out of fourteen were sentenced to death. No reprieves were given, although "Jacky-Jacky" Westwood wrote for the Reverend Rogers a last declaration exonerating four of the accused:

> I, William Westwood, wish to die in the communion of Christ's Holy Church, seeking the mercy of God through Jesus Christ Our Lord, amen. I acknowledge the justice of my sentence; but as a dying man I wish to say that I believe four men now going to suffer are innocent of the crime laid to their charge, namely Lawrence Cavenagh, Henry Whiting, William Pickthorne, and William Scrimshaw. I believe that I never spoke to Cavenagh on the morning of the riots; and those other three men had no part in the killing. . . . I die in charity with all men, and I ask your prayers for my soul.

Rogers had persuaded Westwood and other condemned men to write out their last statements instead of declaiming them, as was the custom, from the scaffold; Price, Barrow and the guards feared that their speeches might spark another riot.

On October 13, the men were hanged in two sets of six on the gallows that looked over Kingston beach and the Pacific beyond, before the assembled convicts, with all the military standing by with primed muskets to crush any restiveness.* No voices were raised but those of the condemned, who joined together in singing a hymn. Rogers had sat up all night with them, praying; he and the Roman Catholic chaplain, Father Bond, walked with the men to the scaffold, where their irons were struck off although their arms remained "severely pinioned." The trapdoor crashed, the bodies fell, the ropes thrummed on the beams. The mutineers' corpses were cut down, coffined, loaded unceremoniously into bullock-carts and dumped in an old sawpit outside the consecrated ground of the cemetery, by the sea's edge. Rogers, cassock flying, trotted up too late for the burial; by the time he reached the edge of the mass grave, where the new commandant had stood grimly staring at the remains of the Ring, the gravediggers had done their work and the coffins were already under earth. As a token of infamy, the sawpit was unmarked, but the hump of earth over the bodies remained clearly visible decades later; it received the name of "Murderers' Mound."

---

* In all, seventeen men were hanged on various charges, some not connected with the July mutiny, over the next week. It was the largest gallows-session ever held on Norfolk Island, and one of the largest in Australian penal history.

iii

WITH THIS MASS execution, the career of the most notorious of all
the commandants of Norfolk Island began.

John Giles Price (1808–1857) was the fourth son of a Cornish baronet,
Sir Rose Price of Trengwainton. A family fortune had been raised on
sugar and slaves in the Caribbean, but by John Price's time it was all
dissipated and he was only one of fourteen children begotten by this
philoprogenitive minor aristocrat. Out he went to the colonies in 1836,
a man in his late twenties armed with good letters of introduction but
little capital. But in the pathologically snobbish society of Hobart Town,
letters and a dash of noble blood counted for a lot. Lieutenant-Governor
Arthur gave Price a generous land grant on the Huon River and more
assigned servants than most new arrivals could expect. In 1838 Price
married the niece of Arthur's successor, Mary Franklin. His farm was
successful and his skill at running assigned convicts was noted. He was
appointed muster-master of the Convict Department, then assistant police magistrate. His wife bore him five children in rapid succession.
Price's colonial future was assured, despite a bout of illness after he
moved to Hobart Town to take up his administrative duties. He was
praised for his abilities as a classical scholar, athlete and oarsman; he
was a skilled carpenter, turner, blacksmith, locksmith and tinker; he
could even cook and sew; and, like some camp commandants in Europe
a century later, he loved children. But it was his reputation for being
tough and methodical that caused poor Eardley-Wilmot, in casting
around for someone to redeem Norfolk Island from the miseries of
Childs's incompetence, to pick Price. Eardley-Wilmot got more than he
bargained for.

John Price has remained one of the durable ogres of the Australian
imagination for more than a century now. This was largely because he
was the original of the brutal island commandant Maurice Frere in the
Great Australian Novel of the nineteenth century, Marcus Clarke's *His
Natural Life*. Clarke could hardly have invented a more interesting vil-
lain than Frere, but he hardly needed to; the lineaments of the man
Australians have loved to hate ever since were traced in the official
correspondence of Norfolk Island, in the indignant letters of Price's main
opposition there, the Reverend Thomas Rogers, and in the various Parliamentary Papers that refer to him or contain his views on convict management. Clarke drew copiously on all of these, particularly on Rogers's
Correspondence Relating to the Dismissal of the Rev. T. Rogers from his

Chaplaincy at Norfolk Island (1849), which remains a source of unre-
mittingly pejorative information on Price. (In *His Natural Life*, Norfolk
Island's frail, morally tormented, alcoholic chaplain, the Reverend James
North, who unsuccessfully opposes the demonic energies of Frere, is
based on Rogers, and most of his reflections are taken verbatim from
Rogers's letters.) The habits of Frere the character were essentially those
of Price the prototype, and so was the appearance: six feet tall (unusually
tall for an Englishman in the mid-nineteenth century), with Herculean
shoulders and a thick bull neck, his legs slightly bowed like those of a
pit bull, "a round bullet head of the true Legree type," a strong flushed
face, sandy-red hair oiled in waves, and a cold gray stare through a monocle jammed in his eye. Price's monocle looked incongruous and struck
more than one prisoner as a sign of "flashness," a puzzling intrusion of
lower-class vulgarity into the world of Authority. This was confirmed by
his dress. "He was dressed something after the style of a flash gentleman," recalled a former Norfolk Island lag named Henry Beresford Garrett, who had remained so obsessed with Price that in the 1870s, years
after both had left the island, he wrote a lengthy manuscript about him
called *The Demon*:

> On his round bullet head a small straw hat was jauntily stuck, the
> broad blue ribbon of which reached down between his shoulders, a glass
> stuck in one eye, a black silk kerchief tied sailor fashion around his
> bullneck, no vest but a bobtail or oxonian coat, or something like a cross
> between this and a stableman's jacket seemed to be bursting over his
> shoulders. A pair of rather tight pants completed his costume, except for
> a leather belt, six inches broad, buckled around the loins. In the belt two
> pepperbox revolvers were conspicuously stuck.
>   . . . [A]ssured by the presence of the soldiers and the guard, he struck
> an attitude by placing his arms akimbo, and again spoke.
>   "You know me, don't you? I am come here to rule, and by God I'll do
> so and tame or kill you. I know you are cowardly dogs, and I'll make you
> worry and eat one another."[39]

Such were Price's first words to his "lambs," on his first visit to the
Kingston barracks in 1846.

When Clarke changed Price's name to Frere in his novel, it was not a
casual gesture. *Frère*, of course, means "brother," and Price's peculiar
relationship to the convicts fascinated Clarke. Unlike all previous commandants, Price went to great lengths to deal with them as an insider.
He learned their flash argot and always spoke to them in it, with none of
the slips and malapropisms that betray a man using a foreign tongue.
How had he learned it? Nobody knew, and many of the prisoners on
Norfolk Island apparently believed that he had "done time" himself. He
was rumored to have lived a Jekyll-and-Hyde existence in the doss-

houses and kens of Hobart Town, mixing freely with hard cases who accepted him as one of them. There were also some missing years in England, from 1827 (when he matriculated at Brasenose College in Oxford, though without taking a degree) to 1836, when he sailed for Van Diemen's Land. It may be—although the evidence for it, as we shall see, is ambiguous and circumstantial—that Price was homosexual and had picked up his fluent criminal slang when cruising for rough trade.

Price was extremely proud of his reputation for special insight into the "criminal mind," which he believed gave him special latitude. To confirm it, he would air weirdly contorted views on the irremediable and uniform evil of the prisoners under his charge. There was, for instance, no doubt that the brief mutiny of July 1, 1846, was a protest against semi-starvation. Price knew this perfectly well, for his first act after the mutineers were hanged was to increase the rations at the Kingston barracks. But at the end of 1846, Price cynically explained to William Champ, the comptroller-general in Van Diemen's Land, that the outbreak was caused by sodomy. Without their confiscated kettles, the prisoners could not make culinary treats for "the objects of their lusts, and . . . this aroused their savage and ferocious passions to a pitch of madness."[40]

By turns fascinated and repelled by the spectacle of convict evil, Price set himself up as its authoritarian mirror and, as his biographer John Barry remarked, entered "a psychopathological love-hate relationship" with the prisoners of Norfolk Island. He had to dominate them by their own standards, to show that he was their master, even without the backing of the System. Hence his obsession with knowing the convicts: their slang, the way they thought, their desires. To speak their language was to demoralize them, to show that their world was open to him while his remained closed to them. To this end, he deployed the jocular, domineering, fake-egalitarian cruelty that is still one of the bad dreams of Australian life. Price was certainly bad and possibly mad, but no one could have called him stupid. No wonder Australians still remember him, though they have forgotten Morisset the blundering martinet and Maconochie the humane reformer.

Price had no time for Maconochie's "soothing system," to which he attributed all the disorganization he inherited on Norfolk Island. He ruled by terror, informers and the lash, to which he added the public force of his own indomitable character; he was known to walk into the lumber-yard unescorted and, before five hundred hostile men, face down a convict who showed signs of rebellion. He once stared down a convict who snatched the pistol from his belt, taunting the man as a coward and a dog, until the prisoner handed back the weapon and fell beaten to his knees.

The informer system had been usual on Norfolk Island long before

Price arrived there; so, of course, had the lash. The question in assessing Price's regime is how far he went in arbitrary cruelty and despotic abuse, beyond the degree of "responsible" brutality that the government expected a Norfolk Island commandant to deploy.

The main evidence came from two clergymen. The first was Thomas Rogers, who witnessed the first months of Price's regime up to early 1847, when he was recalled to Van Diemen's Land by Dr. J. S. Hampton, the new comptroller-general of convicts who favored Price and wanted to protect his position. Fired from the Convict Department, unable to move the authorities against Price and widely dismissed by officials from Denison down as a slandering crank, Rogers was nonetheless supported by some of his church superiors. In 1849 he published his *Correspondence*, which described what he had seen on Norfolk Island in prolix, indignant but convincing detail. Significantly, neither Price nor Denison made any effort to refute it, although Rogers was reprimanded for using official documents without permission.

The second clerical witness to Price's regime was Robert Willson (1794–1866), a priest from Nottinghamshire who had risen, by 1844, to become the first Roman Catholic Bishop in Tasmania. Willson visited Norfolk Island three times: in 1846 (when Childs was still commandant), in 1849 and in 1852. In 1849 he was struck by the success Price had had in cleaning up the chaos of Childs's regime. Not until 1852 did his doubts about method really surface, in a long and appalling report he laid before Lieutenant-Governor Denison. Price, it seems, implored him not to send it. "I am sorry to see you carried away by the stories of these men; you know what a miserable lot they are; do not permit their stories to make any impression upon you." Willson was outraged: "When I was last in England I told the Government to take away one third of the convicts on the island, and now I will recommend the Government to take the whole." At this, Price burst into tears and begged Willson "not to ruin him."[41]

Rogers's first charge was that Price's transactions with the convicts on Norfolk Island were cynical. Price did not believe that reformation was possible; he assumed that good behavior was a sham and that everything any prisoner said about his own state of mind or moral progress was a lie. "Whenever a fellow is recommended to me by the religious instructor or the surgeon superintendent," Price declared, "I always set that fellow down as the greatest hypocrite of the whole lot." In 1846 the transport *John Calvin* landed its 199 prisoners on Norfolk Island to begin their trudge through the Probation System, and one convict was recommended by the surgeon superintendent as "an inoffensive man with very fine feelings." "Oh, I'll soon take *them* out of him!" Price replied.[42]

On the other hand, he wanted the worst men he could draft as constables and overseers. "In selecting men for the police one day," Rogers related,

> Mr. Price asked a man what he had been at home, the man replied he had been a farm servant; "well then," was the remark, "you are not thief enough for me." Another who professed to have been an "honest traveller" in England, i.e., a thief by profession, was made a police man.

Price defended such appointments on the well-worn ground that one must set a thief to catch a thief, but the consistency with which he put "hard" men in minor offices and kept "soft" ones underfoot was perverse. No less so was his purge of the civil officers on Norfolk Island. Everyone who showed signs of opposing his autocratic rule was suspended or recalled to Hobart, until no one stood between Price and the prisoners. Rogers, before he had to leave in 1847, recorded the pervasive terror of informants Price fostered and the capriciousness with which prisoners could be punished. One prisoner was flogged for mislaying his shoelaces. A man named Peart got seven days in chains for saying "good morning" to the wrong person. Another was seen walking along waving a twig; a constable saw him and demanded to know what he was up to and where he was going. "Why, I might be after a parrot," the prisoner replied, and was flogged. A cart-driver came before Price on the charge of "having a tamed bird" and got 36 lashes. A stockman named Higson was passing by a garden plot when the gardener asked him to "give this tree a push, I want to roll it down the hill to mend the garden fence where your bullocks come in." Obligingly, the stockman did so and was seen by a constable, who charged him with "pushing a tree with his foot." Price awarded him 36 lashes on the back and 36 on the buttocks, and within less than two weeks after that he was flogged twice more, once with 100 lashes for having tobacco and hiding in the bush. It had been the custom among the convicts to wash the back of a newly flogged man, to press down his mangled skin and dress it with cool banana leaves; Price had anyone seen with a banana leaf in his possession summarily punished.

Punishments for less trivial offenses were in proportion; and Price's orders were meticulously carried out by his chief constable, a ticket-of-leave man named Alfred Essex Baldock (1821–1848), whom Rogers called "of most unprincipled disposition . . . perfidious and unfeeling towards his fellow-prisoners . . . the servile creature of the commandant in everything." Some men, after flogging, would be laced into a strait-jacket and tied down to an iron bedstead for a week or two, so that their backs mortified and stank. Others were "strapped down" without a flogging, but for as much as six weeks at a time, after which the victim "looked more like a pale distended corpse than a living being, and his voice . . . could scarcely be heard." For striking Baldock, a convict named Lemon was bludgeoned unconscious by the constables, tube-gagged, and chained up with his arms, one broken, behind him around a lamp post. Cells were frequently whitewashed to cover the blood which, Rogers alleged, spattered the walls to a height of seven feet. In one fetid punishment cell, known as the "Nunnery," Price would keep a dozen men with a latrine-bucket in a space six by twelve feet when the outside temperature was 100°F.; "I had to step out into the yard at first," Rogers confessed, "to save myself from fainting." Men were sentenced to work "on the reef," cutting coral in water up to their waists, in 36-pound leg-irons; they were condemned to fourteen days' solitary for "having some ravelling from an old pair of trousers," or "being at the privy when the bell rang."

Price defended his "severities," without (of course) going into detail about them, on the ground the prisoners were wild beasts who would rise and take the island if they got an inch of slack. Rogers disagreed: Except for some twenty or thirty "villains," the two thousand prisoners "were as manageable by the common methods of just and firm and rational government as the peasantry of Kent or Devon."

The commandant had his wife and children on the island, but his "constant companion," according to Rogers, was Baldock, who went "riding with him to out-stations and shepherds' huts in the bush, and attending him and advising him constantly." Rogers seems to have thought that the two men were lovers, and that this explained Baldock's invulnerability to reproof. In Van Diemen's Land, former officers of Baldock's probation gang assured Rogers that "he was so strongly suspected of being addicted to unnatural crime that he was ordered to be placed at nights in one of the sleeping cells." There is no conclusive evidence of a liaison between Price and Baldock, although when the chief constable was drowned (to the unbounded joy of the prisoners) after his rowboat turned turtle on the Kingston reef, Price set up an unusually large and elaborate gravestone to him, much in contrast to the mass grave of Murderers' Mound, with the grieving quatrain:

'Tis His Supreme prerogative
O'er subject Kings to reign.
'Tis just that he should rule the world
Who does the world sustain.

The Reverend Rogers's strictures on the "subject Kings" of Norfolk Island, however, were not acknowledged by Sir William Denison when his *Correspondence* was printed in 1849. Price was shielded by another friend, the dismally cynical opportunist (and future governor of Western

Australia) Dr. J. S. Hampton, who wrote a whitewashing report on the prisoners' condition and strenuously denied that anything odd was happening.

Yet the suspicion that the commandant was out of control, that the island's remoteness from Hobart had permitted some cancer of his soul to metastasize wildly, could not entirely be allayed. Price's rule grew worse as his paranoia thickened, and in 1852 he received a dispatch from Denison's desk querying the enormous inflictions of the lash he himself had reported. His Excellency, Price learned, "regrets very much that you should have considered such punishment necessary to so great an extent" and "trusts that you may . . . adopt . . . means of enforcing proper discipline without recourse to such frequent infliction of this mode of punishment."[43]

In reply, Price railed against the character of the convicts—"cullings," "incorrigibles," "desperadoes," among whom "persuasion is useless, advice is thrown away." He defended the "beneficial effect" of flogging. "Stringent the regulations are," he wrote, "and stringent they must be, but they are not more so than those imposed on soldiers, indeed on boys at public schools in England."[44]

But in that month, March 1852, Bishop Willson was moved by rumor and report to make his third visit to Norfolk Island. He was appalled by what he saw there and penned a thirty-page report to Lieutenant-Governor Denison. It described mass floggings, blood-soaked earth, and an atmosphere of "gloom, sullen despondency, despair of leaving the Island." He saw hideously overcrowded cells, men loaded with 36-pound balls on their chains, wizened pallid creatures staring at him "with their bodies placed in a frame of iron work." He found the sole medical officer so much in cahoots with Price that he claimed a desperately sick prisoner had to be kept in an airless cell because ventilation would be "prejudicial" to him. Hampton, in turn, tried to discredit Bishop Willson's report with obfuscations and quibbles. Price burst into tears and begged the Bishop to suppress his report. But Willson filed it, placing the blame squarely on Price and "the system which invests one man at this remote place with absolute, I might say irresponsible power of dealing with so large a mass of human beings."

Price had tendered his resignation once, at the end of 1850, citing the difficulty of bringing up his children well in "this Lazar house of crime." He got a raise in salary instead. But by now, Denison feared he might become a serious embarrassment to the Crown. He felt that there was a connection between Price's "illness"—whose nature was not specified in official correspondence—and the morbid ferocities of his rule. Denison had already cut the size of the convict population of Norfolk Island by half in 1847, in deference to Grey's wish to abandon the island altogether; most of the probation prisoners had gone down to Van Diemen's Land, leaving a hard core of about 450 "colonial" or twice-convicted offenders. But the military force on Norfolk Island had not been reduced, and very expensive it was, while civilian officers could not be found at any price, because of the rush to the newly discovered goldfields of Ballarat and Bendigo.* In any case, Denison could read the larger political signs, all of which pointed to the abolition of transportation to Australia. It would be better to get rid of this remote penal outrider and concentrate all the management of convicts on Van Diemen's Land. Denison therefore ordered his Convict Department to start drawing up plans for a maximum-security penitentiary at Port Arthur, modelled on the Separate System of Pentonville—which would receive the hard cases of Norfolk Island.[45]

John Price was happy to leave; he had been there more than six years, he was sick of the eyes of prisoners, and he had a garden to cultivate in Van Diemen's Land. No censure was passed. The new secretary of state for the colonies, the Duke of Newcastle, scanned Bishop Willson's report and its accompanying drafts of exculpation from both Price and Hampton, and concluded that since Norfolk Island was about to be abandoned, one need investigate no further. Let the dead stay dead; let old wounds not be re-opened. John Price had done his duty according to his lights, with indefatigable prowess. He had been a good servant of the Crown, if a touch zealous. But excess of zeal in defense of penalty was no crime, the secretary of state reflected, closing the books on Norfolk Island.

Price farmed for a while, but he could not keep away from prison management. Within a year, in January 1854, he accepted a job on the mainland as inspector-general of penal establishments in Victoria. One of his tasks was to run the five prison hulks moored in the port of Melbourne, at Hobson's Bay off Williamstown. The regime on these vessels became a new byword for ferocity. The worst of Norfolk Island had come to the mainland: the tube-gagging and spread-eagling, the bludgeon-handle jammed in the mouth in tobacco searches, the rotten victuals, the loading with irons, the beatings, ringbolts and buckets of sea water. Before long, a warship had to take up station next to the hulks, its guns double-shotted so that, if the prisoners mutinied and the guards had to flee, it could sink the hulk and send its ironed men to the bottom.

On March 26, 1857, Price paid an official visit to the quarry at Williamstown where gangs of hulk convicts were laboring. He had come, as his office demanded, to hear their grievances; and with his usual bravado, he walked straight into the midst of them, escorted only by a small party of guards. A hundred prisoners watched him marching up the tramway

---

* For the gold rush and its consequences for transportation, see the next chapter.

that bore the quarried stone from the cutting-face to the jetty. Quietly they surrounded Price, and their circle began to close. There was a hubbub of hoarse voices, a clatter of chains, a scraping of hobnails on stone. Rocks began to fly. The guards fled; Price turned and began to run down the tramway when a stone flung from the top of the quarry-face caught him between the shoulderblades and pitched him forward on his face. Then, nothing could be seen except a mass of struggling men, a frenetic scrum of arms and bodies in piebald cloth, and the irregular flailing of stone-hammers and crowbars.

iv

PRICE'S REIGN on Norfolk Island had been the last paroxysm of the System's cruelty, a nightmare sweated out by a dying organism. Elsewhere, the transportation of convicts to Australia was winding down. But the process was slow, because Britain did not want it to end. In Whitehall and Downing Street, after 1846, there was still the hope that it might be kept alive. Her Majesty's Government was not going to cave in before the colonial abolitionists just because the Probation System had failed. England still had to purge itself of convicts, the "excrementitious mass" Jeremy Bentham had written of a generation before; it needed space for thousands a year. Most judges, bishops and politicians agreed that transportation was still the way to get rid of them, given the surge in penal convictions. The Report of the 1847 Select Committee on Criminal Laws, Juvenile Offenders and Transportation was quite categorical on that: "The punishment of transportation cannot safely be abandoned."[46] So various projects were mooted, with a view of relieving the pressure on Van Diemen's Land and sneaking the convicts onto the mainland through the back door. The first of these was promoted by Gladstone during his six-month term as secretary of state for the colonies, in early 1846.

Gladstone proposed drawing a line across the map of New South Wales at 26°S., just above Brisbane. The land north of it would form a new and separate colony, North Australia. The "Gladstone Colony" would be a vast low-security jail, settled by convicts with conditional pardons and tickets-of-leave who would be moved up from Van Diemen's Land. Prisoners from England would get conditional pardons as soon as they stepped ashore. In this way, Van Diemen's Land would find room for more freshly transported felons from England.

Naturally, this struck the island's free settlers as a very poor solution. Van Diemen's Land was saturated with convicts. By 1846, almost half its total population were criminals under sentence; out of 66,000 people,

30,300 were bond. If one reckoned in the number of former convicts among the free population (perhaps another 15,000), prospects for the Exclusive minority looked bad. They saw themselves as a small archipelago of decency in a rising sea of moral pollution; anything that let in new convict blood had to be opposed.

The Gladstone Colony was even more unpopular in Sydney, since its plan did not include a convict-proof fence along the 26th parallel. What would stop a new seepage of outcasts into New South Wales? Yet it was tried. Early in 1847, settlers landed at its intended capital, Port Curtis, just south of the Tropic of Capricorn. But it did not take root: Short of food, harassed by Aborigines, tropical rain, baking sun, bad water and whining clouds of insects, the colonists succumbed to despondency.

Meanwhile Gladstone moved upward from the Colonial Office and his place was taken by Lord Grey, who—to the immense relief of its settlers, who heard the glad news in April 1847—ordered the evacuation of Port Curtis. If Gladstone's scheme was meant to place convicts as pioneers in the wilderness, Grey explained to Parliament, it would have been better to put them in the wild parts of Van Diemen's Land; but his predecessor's "real object . . . was to send them through North Australia as it were through a sieve into New South Wales." It was one thing for emancipated convicts to start a new life in neighboring colonies; "this cannot, with justice, be prevented." But it was quite another, and most unfair, to dump them next to New South Wales and let them percolate south into a society that did not want them.[47]

But Grey had some tricks of his own up his sleeve. Realizing that no more convicts could be sardined into Van Diemen's Land, he announced in 1846 that transportation would be suspended for two years. In 1845, 2,870 prisoners of both sexes had landed there. The figure for 1846 was 1,126; for 1847, 1,269; and for 1848, 1,434. More than a thousand of the male convicts arriving in Van Diemen's Land during 1847–48 had been relocated from Norfolk Island, so the cut in transportation from England was large.

However, Grey in 1847 had told Lieutenant-Governor Denison that "it is not the intention" of Britain to resume transportation when the two years were up; and his under secretary, Sir James Stephen, told the Treasury a few days later that "Her Majesty's Government have decided upon altogether abandoning the system of transportation to Van Diemen's Land."[48] Denison, on reading Grey's dispatch, assumed that it meant what it said and that abolition was just around the corner; so, to their joy, did the free settlers of Van Diemen's Land. Both were wrong. Grey, speaking for perfidious Albion, had a new system in mind, euphoniously called "assisted exile."

His idea was to combine penitentiaries at home with transportation abroad. Let the sinners first do time in Pentonville; once subdued by its awful mental rigor, let them have conditional pardons and be sent to Australia to complete their sentences. Even if Van Diemen's Land (whose economy, by 1847, was showing distinct signs of revival) could not absorb them, then the labor-hungry pastoral settlers of New South Wales and Port Phillip certainly could. The sequence would be: first, "separate confinement" in England followed by a spell of "associated labor" in the naval dockyards; then "assisted exile" to the antipodes. Once there, the men would not be exposed to the evils of the Probation System; they would be dispersed to settlers across the country districts and the outback. They could also take their wives and families, if their moral qualities seemed adequate. Thus the colonists could not complain of being deluged, once more, in transportation. "The penal system known as transportation will not be renewed," Grey told Denison in 1848. "The *diffusion* of men, instead of placing them in Penal and Probation Gangs, totally changes its character."[49] And since Grey had a politician's sense of an acceptable name, the subjects of his penal experiment would not, under any circumstances, be called "convicts"; instead, they would be "exiles."[50]

This idea had been revolving in Grey's mind for almost ten years. He first produced it during the sessions of the Molesworth Committee on transportation, where in 1837, as Viscount Howick, he suggested it to James Macarthur, the pastoral king of New South Wales. "Suppose," he asked, "criminals were to be punished in England with a certain number of years' imprisonment, and after that to be banished to New South Wales, [where they would] be placed under the surveillance of the police in the same manner of ticket-of-leave men, what do you think would be the effect?" "In a modified shape, the same as . . . transportation," Macarthur replied.[51] Before Grey received the seals of the Colonial Office, the experiment had already begun. In 1844, the transport vessel *Royal George* had landed twenty-one convicts at Port Phillip Bay, the first felons to arrive in the future state of Victoria since the abortive attempt at a convict settlement there back in 1803. They had all done terms in Pentonville, the new penitentiary in Britain.

These "Pentonvillains," as they were promptly nicknamed, were snapped up by labor-hungry settlers, who asked for more. Edward Curr, a rock-ribbed conservative who had become the manager of the ill-fated Van Diemen's Land Company twenty years before and, after it failed, had taken up wide acres in the Port Phillip district, led the settlers' case. Free labor was not to be had, so wages were high, and this attracted "whole shoals" of former convicts from Van Diemen's Land and the "Middle District" of New South Wales. It would be better to have the Pentonville men, who might have been partly reformed by the penitentiary machine, than these frequently dubious characters. The grand question, Curr argued, was the need for cheap labor, and neither he nor his fellow squatters stood ready to be "ruined for virtue's sake."[52]

Others disagreed. In the view of the Melbourne editor and alderman William Kerr, the "Exiles" threatened to depress not only the wages but the moral tone of the colony; and their introduction, "free of all manner of restraint," would be a wanton injustice to all free citizens.[53]

Thus the lines of class conflict over the arrival of Exiles were drawn. It was city versus country, worker versus squatter. The prospect that transportation to mainland Australia would begin again bypassed the old and by now demographically feeble division between Exclusive and Emancipist in the vast territory of New South Wales. Some Emancipist families were now very rich and wanted cheap convict labor; many a free emigrant rebelled at the idea of losing wages to a flood of Exiles. Even among the sons and daughters of "old" Exclusive families, who preened themselves on having been in the colony for fifty years or more, the convict presence was no longer pervasive, no longer a threat to order; out of a total population of 187,000 people in New South Wales in 1846, fewer than 11,000 were convicts still under sentence. Compared to the dark taint of Van Diemen's Land, convictry (in the eyes of those who wanted more of it) was a mere tinge, rapidly fading. It was time to think about its advantages again.

Thus, on the issue of Exiles, the squatters won—at first. In 1845–46, 517 "Pentonvillains" disembarked at Melbourne and found instant employment. Late in 1846, a committee set up by the New South Wales Legislative Council reported to Gladstone that the "vast solitude" of outback New South Wales seemed "to have been assigned by Providence to the British nation as the fittest scene for the reformation of her criminals."[54] The Legislative Council itself disagreed at first, but when Grey offered to send one free emigrant for every convict, and wives and families of the Exiles as well, it changed its mind. The stage was now set for the wholesale revival of transportation to the Australian mainland, even to Sydney, under the name of Grey's Exile scheme. In 1847, 536 convicts arrived in Port Phillip; in 1848, 455.

But then, hitches began to appear. The "vast solitudes" no longer seemed quite so empty, because England's general economic depression of 1847 caused a surge of free emigration. From 1847 to 1849, some 30,000 emigrants sailed from England to take their chances in New South Wales. It was no longer so easy to find work for the Exiles who came to Port Phillip in 1847–48; the demand for convict labor had ebbed. Moreover, given the low state of the British economy, Grey did not feel he could ask the Treasury to pay for the plan of sending out a free settler for every Exile. So he dropped that part of his agreement with the Legislative Council of New South Wales. Instead, in August 1848, he secured an Order-in-Council declaring that convicts could once more be sent to New South Wales at the will and pleasure of Her Majesty's Government, and he dispatched a transport loaded with 239 male prisoners, the *Hashemy*, direct to Sydney. She was the first convict ship to enter the immense gates of Sydney Harbor in a decade, and the splash of her anchor on June 11, 1849, at Circular Quay—where, like some stained cuckoo, she nested amid five ships loaded with more than 1,400 new-chum immigrants—was promptly taken as the sign of a complete breach of faith between Lord Grey and Queen Victoria's loyal subjects in Australia.

It provoked the biggest show of mass public indignation in the colony's short history. In driving rain, crowds assembled at the Quay—five thousand by the Abolitionists' count, seven or eight hundred according to the police. The governor, Sir Charles Fitzroy, watched them pouring down George and Macquarie Streets; the shopkeepers along the quay prudently locked up their shutters as soldiers with fixed bayonets took up their stations outside Government House and the perimeter of the Quay, by now a squelching bog, was ringed with police. But there was no violence. Speaker after speaker clambered on top of the improvised dais (an omnibus) harangued the crowd and was rewarded with thunderous cheers. Robert Campbell, nephew of the great colonial merchant whose brick warehouses and wharf stood nearby, a man who had been campaigning against transportation for twenty full years, declaimed that "they would be content to subdue the land and replenish it without the introduction of British crime and its attendant British misery." John Lamb, a retired naval commander and now a leading businessman with a seat on the Legislative Council of New South Wales, moved the first of the anti-transportation resolutions, drafted by a rising Australian politician named Henry Parkes—a "deliberate and solemn protest" against transportation:

FIRSTLY—Because it is in violation of the will of the majority of the colonists, as is clearly evinced by their expressed opinions on this question at all times.

SECONDLY—Because numbers among us have emigrated on the faith of the British Government, that transportation to this colony had ceased for ever.

THIRDLY—Because it is incompatible with our existence as a free colony, desiring self-government, to be the receptacle of another country's felons.

FOURTHLY—Because it is in the highest degree unjust, to sacrifice the great social and political interests of the colony at large to the pecuniary profit of a fraction of its inhabitants.

FIFTHLY—Because . . . we greatly fear that the perpetration of so stupendous an act of injustice . . . will go far in alienating the affections of the people of this colony from the mother country.

An English emigrant barrister, Robert Lowe, the future Viscount Sherbrooke, a half-blind albino with a stentorian voice and a feel for the main vein of popular sentiment, scrambled onto the bus roof to declaim that "the stately presence of their city, the beautiful waters of their harbour, were this day again polluted with the presence of that floating hell—a convict ship." He denounced "this attempt to impose the worst and most degrading slavery on the colony" as the outcome of "that oppressive tyranny which had confiscated the lands of the colony—for the benefit of a class," the squatters. This meeting, he shouted into the brief lulls between the cheers of the crowd, was the prelude to an Australian republic, as the Boston Tea Party had been to the American. "In all times, and in all nations, so will injustice and tyranny ripen into rebellion, and rebellion into independence."[55]

The meeting wound to its end, by which time (some of the more perceptive listeners noted) not a single Emancipist or descendant of a convict had spoken; and the anti-transportation orators went to Government House and asked to present their petition to Governor Fitzroy. He agreed to see them the next day. Fitzroy told Lowe that he would pass their protest on to Her Majesty, but the convicts from the *Hashemy* would stay; on that, there could be no negotiation. So another monster rally was called at Circular Quay for June 18, to ask for the dismissal of Lord Grey. Lowe moved for dismissal, and Henry Parkes rose to speak against Grey, "a nobleman who never bestowed a thought upon New South Wales in his life, till some political chance or accident gave him his ministerial position." But because there had been a buzz of speculation about a Yankee-style revolt in Australia, he added that he did not see what good would come from such comparisons. Free Australians "were not at a state of advancement to be benefited by separation from the mother country, even if we had cause to desire separation. . . . We possessed little of the stern and sturdy spirit of the old American colonists." So much, in Parkes's view, for the legendary independence of Australians. He was righter than even he could have supposed, for a century and a quarter later Australia would continue to cling to the British Commonwealth.

Fitzroy wrote to Lord Grey, assuring him that the anti-transportation lobby in Sydney was merely a faction, whose sole audience was the mob.

Their notion that the secretary of state for the colonies had committed a breach of faith with the colonists was quite unjust, Fitzroy thought.[56] And indeed, the political crisis over the *Hashemy* did die out quite soon. When yet another convict ship, the *Randolph*, arrived in Port Phillip with 295 convicts, the citizens of Melbourne persuaded La Trobe to bar it from anchoring—but her captain merely sailed north and unloaded his bedraggled cargo in Sydney, without provoking a single meeting or speech. After that, two more vessels, the *Havering* and the *Adelaide*, disembarked a total of 593 Exiles at Sydney Cove. They were the last, and they caused no incident.

Nor did their passengers perceptibly degrade the tone of the colony. They were quite like ordinary people. "Dear Wife you can come out to me as soon as it pleases you," one of them wrote after he was settled with a master upcountry.

> I will provide for you a comfortable Situation and Home as good a one as ever lies in my power. . . . When you come ask for me as an emigrant, and never use the word Convict or the ship Hashemy on your voyage, *never let it be once named among you, let no one know your business but your own selves.* . . . Dear Wife this is a fine Country and a beautiful climate it is like a perpetual Sumer, and I think it will prove congenial for your health, No wild beast or anything of the sort are here, fine beautiful birds and every thing seems to smile with pleasure. . . . [T]his is just the country where we can end our days in peace and contentment when we meet.[57]

This encomium from a satisfied Englishman was printed in the most popular English magazine of the time, *Household Words*, whose editor was none other than Charles Dickens. To say that Dickens "edited" it is to understate the degree to which his views permeated the publication. On Australia, which he never visited, he had a most explicit line; and it had been given him by a journalist who had never been there either, although he pretended he had: Samuel Solomon (1813–1883), who wrote extensively on railways and agriculture under the pen name of Samuel Sidney. Sidney was quite well-informed about Australia (his brother had settled there and come back in 1847), and his many readers knew so little about it that for ten years they accepted him as an expert—indeed, as *the* popular authority—on matters Australian. He published a magazine, *Sidney's Emigrant's Journal* (1849–50), as well as a number of books, beginning with *A Voice from the Far Interior of Australia* (1847), and ending with *The Three Colonies of Australia* (1852), subtitled "How to Settle and Succeed in Australia," which—coinciding as it did with the discovery of gold—was a roaring popular success. Sidney was an engaging mélange of social idealist and literary con man, like many another influential journalist. His heart yearned for the vision that the Industrial Revolution was banishing from England; pastoral Arcadia inhabited by sturdy forty-acre yeomen. He believed this paradise of the common man could be revived in Australia, by emigration. "There are thousands in this country pining in indigénce, who if removed to a suitable colony would be able to attain decent independence."[58]

For this picture of Australia, Sidney drew heavily on Alexander Harris's *Settlers and Convicts* (1847), the first book on the life of free workers there—anti-System, anti-squatter, squarely on the side of self-help, extolling the comradeship of hard labor among farmers and cedar-getters in the bush. The yeomen of England had fallen into the decay foreseen by Cobbett; they were the fretful prey of agitators, Chartists, ideologues of every kind. On the vast democratic grasslands of Australia Felix they would find their natural station.

Such arguments were endorsed by reformers better-known today than Sidney: by Harriet Martineau, and the brave Roman Catholic philanthropist Caroline Chisholm, "the emigrant's friend," who had labored immensely from 1840 to 1846 in New South Wales, meeting every migrant ship, finding jobs for their bewildered women passengers, setting up shelters and employment agencies throughout the interior for newly arrived immigrants, and tirelessly escorting groups of "new chums" into the bush on her white horse, Captain.[59] On her return to London, Mrs. Chisholm won the ear of Lord Grey and Sir James Stephen, the permanent under secretary at the Colonial Office. In 1849 she formed a Family Colonization Loan Society, underwritten through Coutts Bank at the behest of the philanthropic Baroness Burdett-Coutts, with a board of London merchants; it lent migrants their passage money, found them work in Australia, and collected the loans in small installments at no interest. She had interviewed hundreds of immigrants in Australia and their words became the first-hand stuff of her pamphlets. Chisholm was fervently committed to yeoman emigration and small farming. She had a natural ally in Samuel Sidney. Both found a mutual one in Dickens, who spread their opinions in every issue of *Household Words* and enthusiastically incorporated them into his novels. It was exactly along the lines of emigration proposed by Chisholm and Sidney that the feckless and debt-ridden Wilkins Micawber, at the happy end of *David Copperfield* (1849–50), took his chances in Australia along with Mr. Peggotty, Em'ly and Gummidge, finding a happy haven at Port Middlebay, Dickens's name for Melbourne. Micawber is redeemed by the work of his hands. "I've seen that theer bald head of his, a-perspiring in the sun, Mas'r Davy, till I a'most thowt it would have melted away," says Peggotty, the Yarmouth fisherman who knows what work is. "And now he's a Magistrate."[60]

Dickens, Sidney and Chisholm: a formidable team of persuaders, backed by such sympathizers as Harriet Martineau and Edward Bulwer-Lytton, who was himself to become a strikingly inept secretary of state for the colonies in 1858. They knew who deserved their sympathy—and who did not: the villains in the drama of colonial opportunity they were writing, the graziers of Australia, the selfish squatters, nostalgic for cheap slave labor and bitterly determined to preserve transportation. "Unlock the land!"—such was the cry, both in England and New South Wales, on behalf of the forty-acre yeomen. Were the big pastoralists deliberately sabotaging free immigration? In hindsight, it seems that they were not; they were desperate for labor much of the time, and paid for it when they could get it—but there was little doubt that the most reactionary would rather have had convicts. However, experience had also shown that, although Australian prospects could be seen by Englishmen (and sometimes, under the spell of Dickens's prose, by Australians as well) through a rosy haze of Pickwickian stereotypes, small farmers in 1850 remained as vulnerable to drought, fire and flood as they had been along the Hawkesbury in the days of Governor Bligh. The land was not Arcadia; the bush could flare up and incinerate ten years of a forty-acre man's work in a day; even in good times, it took three acres to sustain one sheep. But such realities were moved into the background by the largely urban polemicists who now urged the abolition of transportation not just as a moral good in itself but as a blow against land monopoly, a condition of successful emigration and a cure for England's discontents.

In Australia, the focus was different. The image of the earnest yeoman frustrated by squatters' greed was politically potent, sure enough, but the stereotype of convict evil was fixed beyond the power of any individual's experience to alter it. Get rid of convictry, keep the imperial attachment —such was the local reformers' tune. No bunyip Demosthenes preaching abolition would open his mouth against the pollutions of English crime without unfurling a long red-white-and-blue preamble assuring Her Gracious Majesty, Queen Victoria, of his undying, wholehearted and grovelling fealty to the British Crown. The end of transportation was reached through a cumbersome accommodation between morally indignant colonials who could not make good on their threats and imperialists who felt weary of an obsolete penal system and yet could not cancel it at a stroke for fear of seeming malleable to Australian pressure. Anti-transportation views, by the late 1840s, were a commonplace of every pulpit sermon and most political meetings. Abolition was, as one British officer in New South Wales remarked, "the only movement at all resembling a popular *émeute*" in "the usually drowsy, well-fed and politically apathetic Sydney."[61] The same was true in Melbourne, and in Van Diemen's Land, where in 1849 an Anti-Transportation League was formed under the leadership of the island's leading publisher, Henry Dowling, Jr. (1810–1885), the landowner Richard Dry (1815–1869) and John West (1809–1873), a fervidly eloquent Congregationalist minister who, when not inveighing against the System from lecture halls and pulpits throughout the island, wrote the first and for many years the best history of Van Diemen's Land.

But for all the protests, the meetings and the airing of grievances at the enforced Stain, there was never any question of secession. Nobody, in or out of the League, wanted that. Meanwhile, Grey's two-year moratorium on transportation to Van Diemen's Land ran out in 1848, and the machinery of exile, obedient to his Lordship's peevishly stubborn character, began once more to roll in the direction of Hobart and Launceston. Sir William Denison, the lieutenant-governor, could do no more than pooh-pooh the "moral pretensions" of the League and find what work could be found for Lord Grey's Exiles. He also tried, with less success, to assure the free settlers that the new arrivals—having done their stint in Pentonville—were of better stuff than the old and that eight or ten convict ships a year did not mean a breach of faith by the Colonial Office. As the economy of Van Diemen's Land struggled erratically out of its catastrophic slump, Denison grew optimistic about the number of convicts it could absorb in private employment: first 1,500 a year, then 2,000. The actual arrivals were 1,434 men and women in 1848, 1,847 in 1849 and a leap to 3,406 in 1850. "I have succeeded in getting back the assignment system in a modified form," he boasted. Grey, however, did not wish to hear about assignment; and the Abolitionists did not want to have it, modified or no. The League's work played a large part—larger than it is usually credited with—in killing transportation to Van Diemen's Land. But what finished it off was Lord Grey's retirement from the Colonial Office, and the discovery of gold in Australia.

16

The Aristocracy Be We

AMONG THE FORTUNE-HUNTING optimists who set sail from Sydney across the Pacific to San Francisco when the news of the California gold rush reached New South Wales at the end of 1848 was a corpulent bull-calf of a man named Edward Hammond Hargraves. He was thirty-one when he reached California, and with a fellow "Sydney Duck" he trudged, scrambled and panned for two years, not finding so much as an ounce of gold. English by birth, he had lived in Australia and knew the terrain west of the Blue Mountains, near Bathurst. Gradually, the conviction seized him that the Wellington district of New South Wales, 170 miles west of Sydney and about 50 miles from Bathurst, with its tawny hills, quartz outcrops and gullies, was very like the gold regions of California. At the end of 1850, having bottomed out like so many thousands of other Forty-Niners, Hargraves spent his last dollars on a passage back to Sydney. But he took his pan and rocking-cradle with him, and on February 12, 1851, he and his guide, John Lister, rode down Lewes Pond Creek, a tributary of the Macquarie River near Guyong outside Bathurst.

As the horses picked their way along, Hargraves felt—as he put it later—"surrounded by gold." He got down into the creek-bed with his pick and trowel, and scratched some gravel and earth from a dike of schist that ran athwart the gully. Four pans out of five produced gold. Hargraves was overcome. "This," he exclaimed to Lister, "is a memorable day in the history of New South Wales. I shall be a baronet, you will be knighted, and my old horse will be stuffed, put in a glass case, and sent to the British Museum!"[1]

None of these happened, but something of infinitely greater consequence did. Australia was convulsed with gold fever. In April 1851, Hargraves bestowed on his district the biblical name of Ophir, and in May the newspapers announced it to be "one vast gold-field." By May 24, a thousand diggers were tunnelling, cursing and exulting on the banks of Summerhill Creek, and the road over the Blue Mountains was choked with a footsore, sluggishly winding column of men: clerks and grooms, grocers' assistants and sailors, lawyers and army deserters, oyster-sellers and magistrates, government officials and ex-convict shepherds, trudging beneath the weight of tents, blankets, crowbars, picks, shovels, pans and billycans hastily bought at gougers' prices, stumbling toward unheard-of wealth in mud-balled boots under the driving rains of the Australian autumn. It was as though a plug had been pulled and the male population of New South Wales had emptied like a cistern, in a rush toward the diggings. Business, the Bathurst and Sydney newspapers reported, was "utterly paralysed. . . . A complete mental madness appears to have seized almost every member of the community."[2]

By June the Ophir district was an impacted mass of clay-colored men, shoulder to shoulder, hacking in delirium at the fickle earth. Prospectors that month moved northeast to the banks of the Turon River and struck gold there, even more of it. An aboriginal stockman, who was not prospecting but idly chipping with his tomahawk at an outcrop fifty miles from Bathurst, found a mass of quartz that yielded 1,272 ounces of gold, the largest reef nugget in recorded history, bigger than anything found by the Forty-Niners in California. "Men . . . stare stupidly at each other, talk incoherent nonsense, and wonder what will happen next. . . . [A] hundred-weight of sugar or potatoes is an every-day fact, but a hundred-weight of gold is . . . beyond the range of our recorded ideas—a sort of physical incomprehensibility." The Aborigine was not allowed to keep the gold but his employer, a Dr. Kerr, on whose land it was found, gave him and his brother some sheep, two horses, provisions and a few acres as a consolation prize.[3]

As the gold fever spread, prospectors realized that, geologically speaking, the newly constituted state of Victoria was simply an extension of New South Wales. In July, gold was found at Clunes, a hundred miles from Melbourne; and in September 1851, a septuagenarian digger named John Dunlop discovered the richest field of all, at Ballarat, a mere 75 miles west of the Melbourne Post Office. The word ran back to Melbourne that gold was everywhere. It lay scattered on the rocks and between the wiry tussocks, glistening as it had done for unregarded thousands of years; now the deepest obsessions of a frontier society would clamp themselves to it, and it would transform that society beyond recognition.

The gold belonged to the government, which demanded an exorbitant license fee of 30 shillings a month from the Victorian diggers. Nevertheless, by November 1851 more than 6,500 Victorian licenses had been issued and a cataract of gold was pouring from Ballarat as well as the Turon diggings, into the stout canvas bags, down to the holds of the waiting ships. The first gold shipment to London, on the *Thomas Ar-*

buthnot, was a mere 253 ounces. By the middle of 1852, there were perhaps 50,000 people on the diggings and the average weekly shipment on the gold-escorts from Ballarat and Bendigo was more than 20,000 ounces—half a ton a week. The Times declared, in November 1852, that the flood of Australian gold had become "perfectly bewildering"; by then, a single ship (the Dido) was expected with 280,000 ounces, or ten and a half tons, on board. All this was from the Victorian diggings, which in the month of August 1852 alone, despite nearly continuous winter rain and bitterly difficult working conditions for the diggers, had yielded 246,000 ounces of the "yellow stuff."[4]

By then, Melbourne was both a ghost-port and a continuous saturnalia. Port Phillip Bay had become a Sargasso Sea of dead ships, rocking empty at anchor through a hundred tides and then a hundred more, bilges unpumped, their masts a bare forest. When a vessel arrived with her gold-hungry passengers and her hold crammed with mining tools and cheap furniture, the crews (and often the captains too) would desert as soon as she was unloaded, joining the thick human stream for Ballarat and Bendigo. Employers, stranded without labor, locked their offices and went on the road. "Cottages are deserted," reported the lieutenant-governor of Victoria, Charles La Trobe, In October 1851,

> houses to let, business is at a stand-still, and even schools are closed. In some of the suburbs not a man is left, and the women are known for self-protection to forget neighbours' jars [quarrels] and to group together to keep house. . . . Fortunate the family, whatever its position, which retains its servants at any sacrifice, and can further secure supplies for their households from the few tradesmen that remain . . . all buildings and contract works, public and private, almost without exception, are at a standstill. No contract can be insisted upon under the circumstances.[5]

Shanty towns and bark huts proliferated to house the thousands of emigrants, frantic with hope, who poured off the ships from England and Ireland.

In the grog-shops and hotels that lined the filthy, traffic-jammed streets of the young city, where a man could sink up to his knees in mud and ordure merely by stepping off the curb, a round-the-clock orgy was conducted by "the worst-looking population eyes ever beheld"—the diggers and their hangers-on, their mates and their flushed doxies, drinking the gold away. One man, who had never tasted champagne before, bought a hotel's entire stock of it and emptied every bottle into a horse trough, inviting all and sundry to suck it up. Miners lurched up and down the luxury shops, jamming huge tawdry rings on their girls' fingers, demanding the most expensive dresses, lighting their pipes with £5 notes and pouring gold dust into the cupped hands of hackney-drivers. "They are intoxicated with their suddenly-acquired wealth, and run riot in the wildness of their joy," noted an English gold-seeker, John Sherer. They were "just like so many unbroken horses caught in a desert where they never knew anything but hunger, and suddenly thrown into a rich paddock where they find nothing but plenty."[6] They treated their women like crude pashas, even the ones who seemed to have few prospects, like "Biddy Carroll," fresh from Ireland: "Exceedingly stupid, lazy, and dirty, poor Biddy could make no friends," and resembled "an unripe potato just dug from the soil with its jacket flying." But soon she found her digger, and soon after that an acquaintance noticed in the saloon of a steamer

> the simple, stupid, potato-like face of Biddy Carroll . . . the very perfection of a lucky, thoughtless, gold-digger's bride. Her bonnet was of white satin, with a profusion of the most exquisite flowers, the whole enveloped in the folds of a rich white veil. She wore a superb lavender-coloured flowered satin dress, with a gorgeous barège shawl . . . a massive gold brooch . . . a massive gold chain, and her wrists encircled with handsome silver bracelets.[7]

The Biddies were not just amusing objects of condescension. In their gaudy store-bought finery, they were signs of class rupture. Gold disturbed the order of Anglo-Australian society—from pastoral "aristocrat" down to convict—with shudders of democracy. Gold wealth was not "democratic," but it did expand the existing oligarchy. It would diversify both Australian markets and Australian production and help create the Australian bourgeoisie. The clay-stained digger, a butcher in his former life, who still carried the grease-stink of tallow in his hair and the argot of the diggings on his tongue, would soon have his Axminster-carpeted drawing room in Toorak. The cash his gold set in circulation would construct suburbia. His spending habits would raise more merchants to comfort. Fortunes were made by diggers—and extracted from them. Gold did respect class. It slightly favored the low: A horny-handed navvy, miner or seaman with muscles hardened by years of manual work could sink a shaft twenty feet to the blue auriferous strata of Bendigo in the time that it took a refined "new chum," his hands pulpy and blistered, to scratch away three feet of earth. "Everything had assumed a revolutionary character," wrote Sherer, adding that

> all the aristocratic feelings and associations of the old country are at once annihilated. Plebeianism of the rankest and . . . the lowest kind at present dwells in Australia; and as riches are now becoming the test of a man's position, it is vain to have any pretensions whatever unless you are sup-

ported by that powerful auxiliary. It is not what you were, but what you
are that is the criterion.[8]

"We be the aristocracy now," miners were heard to say as they rollicked
in the Melbourne grog-shops, "and the aristocracy now be we."

ii

THERE WAS, however, a specter at this feast of truculent egalitarianism: the Old Hands, or ex-convicts. Victorians took a considerable, indeed an exaggerated pride in the thought that their colony had not—or
at least, not primarily—been a convict settlement. In 1835, the pioneering land-grabber John Batman had "bought" some 600,000 acres in the
Port Phillip Bay area, including the present site of Melbourne, from three
chiefs (confusingly named Jagajaga, Jagajaga and Jagajaga) for some blankets, knives, shirts and mirrors. Pioneers had gone south from the "Middle District" of New South Wales with their bands of assigned men; and
nearly 2,000 Exiles had landed at Port Phillip in the 1840s. But until
then, Victoria had no institutions for exploiting convict labor; this
helped its free population feel more virtuous than the raffish Sydney-
siders and tainted Vandemonians. Some settlers—not gold-seekers, but
more sober and conscientious men—had gone there partly because it had
no "convict taint," expecting security and a low crime rate.

They were not merely dismayed but outraged when gold brought a
rush of emancipated convicts from Van Diemen's Land. Thousands of
criminals—for in the eyes of the "respectable," an ex-convict was a felon
still—were flooding into Melbourne and fanning out all over Victoria.
Nobody knew exactly how many there were, because they were all free
and did not have to present passes when moving from one colony of
Australia to another. The pessimistic guess was that one digger in ten
had been a government man. Soon, every unsolved crime in Victoria (and
not a few in New South Wales) was automatically blamed on the "Vandemonians," or simply the "Demons," as these undesirables from Van
Diemen's Land were called. And in fact, an unusually high number of
offenders convicted for crimes in Victoria between 1851 and 1853 turned
out to be ex-convicts who had crossed Bass Strait.

For most of the Vandemonians, the gold rush was their last desperate
gamble. The economy of Van Diemen's Land was so primitive compared
to that of the mainland, and the chances of getting enough land to compete against the established pastoral families so remote, that any man
with blood in him would rather try for gold across the Strait. The depression was past but the labor market for ex-convicts stayed badly shrunk.

On the goldfields, expirees might get rich, and even when poor they carried a certain glamor in the eyes of impressionable "new chums":

> The new chum sits on the logs about the fire listening to the tales of crime and adventure of some "old hand" or convict. Some of these men have now great quantities of Gold and now that they are independent, boast of their former bad deeds. The greater the criminal the more he is respected.[9]

The Victorian authorities sided with the Anti-Transportation League of Van Diemen's Land. In February 1851, the mayor of Melbourne had congratulated two of its prime movers, the historian and Congregational minister John West and the pastoralist William Weston—who had come there to form a "League of Solemn Engagement" of the Australian colonies never to accept convict labor again—on their "patriotic exertions." Victoria, too, the Mayor declaimed, was making "efforts to avert the attempt made by our fair Province with the outpourings of British crime," and

> the proximity of our colony to yours gives us a vital interest in assisting you to stem the tide of convictism now flowing in upon Van Diemen's Land. Rest assured that the colonists of Victoria will go with you heart and hand.[10]

Naturally, when Victoria became a separate colony a few months later, anti-convict sentiments rose higher still. In February 1852, the mayor, aldermen and citizens of Melbourne wrote a petition to Queen Victoria, protesting against transportation of "Criminals of the deepest dye" to Van Diemen's Land, whence, after "a brief period of probation," they crossed to the colony which bore her own name, contaminating and degrading it:

> The unlimited influx of manumitted convicts from Van Diemen's Land is an intolerable grievance calculated rapidly to alienate the affections of Your Majesty's dutiful subjects. . . . [W]e should be guilty of deceit if we withheld from Your Majesty the fact that there is a large and increasing population growing up to maturity amongst us who have no such feelings [of loyalty] towards the Parent State; who feel deeply the disgrace of belonging to a colony which is regarded by other nations as a portion of Britain's great emunctory of crime.[11]

There was silence from Balmoral and a perfunctory reply from Downing Street. But the tone of the mayor's address was not feigned. The grievance ran deep, and it soon produced an obnoxious law, passed with bellows of popular acclaim by the newly formed Legislative Council of Victoria in September 1852: the "Convicts Prevention Act." It was framed, as La Trobe remarked in forwarding it to London, with "zeal and haste," and it ignored "many salient principles of constitutional liberty"; but it was so popular, the crime rate was so high and the expenses of the police so ruinous that he had signed it anyway.

Anyone coming to Victoria from Van Diemen's Land now had to prove he was unconditionally free. The penalty for not doing so was three years' hard labor in irons. The particular injustice of the act was that it discriminated against holders of conditional pardons, convicts who by law were allowed to go anywhere within the Australian colonies, so long as they did not go back to England. It condemned them to stagnate in the economic backwater of Van Diemen's Land. In the wide powers of arrest and search it granted the Victorian police, it resembled the hated Bush-ranging Act of thirty years before. But in the atmosphere of Melbourne in 1852, it bordered on political suicide to speak for the "rights" of ex-convicts. The fear of a real rupture between the colonists and the Crown made La Trobe think it "highly desirable . . . to show every disposition to co-operate heartily with the Colonists . . . under the extraordinary circumstances of the times."

Not all interests in Australia agreed—especially not the graziers, who had been hardest hit by the flight of labor to the goldfields. The gold rush, even in winter, was draining pastoral labor; by spring, the shortage would be catastrophic. The only thing that could save these northeastern estates from the drain of labor into the "middle districts" of New South Wales was a prompt infusion of felons, who would not be able to quit their assigned posts to hunt gold. "At no previous crisis in the history of this Colony was a large and continuous supply of such a class so much required, or so likely to be productive."[12]

The lack of cheap labor for the sheep- and cattle-runs of Queensland had been apparent even before the gold rush. In January 1850, a son of one pastoral clan, the Leslies, reported to his father that they had held public meetings to ask the secretary of state for convicts, as "we must have more labor than Emigration will supply. . . . The Emigrants we get are the sweepings of the parish workhouses, not a bit more moral than the Exiles, and much lazier & independant; we ask for half & half Exiles & Emigrants, and if we do not get them we will send for Chinese."[13]

The issue split the Queenslanders, as it did the rest of white Australia: on one side, the squatters and pastoralists, wanting convicts; on the other, the free country workers, the clergy, the shopkeepers and almost everyone else from the town of Brisbane, agitating against the Stain and the Taint. But at the national level, the pastoralists were outnumbered. Although they could discount "unwashed" hands raised in their own woolsheds, they could not pretend that, in real political life, those hands were invisible.

Everywhere else in Australia, with one exception, it was the same. Victoria was dead set against the Stain, and so was South Australia, which in December 1851 had sent its own petition to Lord Grey reminding him that the appearance of ex-convicts from Van Diemen's Land within its boundaries was ruining the morals of its people.

The exception, of course, was Van Diemen's Land itself. It had had no gold rush. It had not benefitted from immigration; few people wanted to start a new life in the colonial source of the Stain. Too many of the young, the hard-handed, the energetic and the ambitious had been sucked out of it by the gold rush. Van Diemen's Land was an economic cripple; there, it was convictry or beggary, a point made over and over again by the pastoralists. The Anti-Transportation League could afford the luxuries of moral indignation and preach as it pleased—but the fact remained that every convict who arrived in Van Diemen's Land was eagerly snapped up by the graziers. There was no waiting-list for convict servants in Hobart before mid-1851, but when 292 prisoners arrived on the *Fairlie* in mid-1852 there were 1,259 applications for their services.[14]

Social prejudices remained, a "phalanx of antipathy," as one Hobart paper called it in 1851, among landed gentry against convicts and Emancipists. Most employers would take a free worker over a convict one any time, given the choice. But they did not have the choice, because the free workers had gone to the diggings. Thus the oligarchs of land—such families as the O'Connors and Lords, the Bisdees and Talbots, the Headlams and Bayleys, who between them disposed of more than a quarter-million acres of the green sullen island—stolidly dispatched their petitions to London; one of these respectful memorials in defense of the plantation society was signed by 459 graziers and merchants.

The Australasian Anti-Transportation League did not doubt the justice of its mission. Its letterhead was a flag with the Southern Cross and the extravagantly righteous motto *In hoc signo vinces*. These had been the words spoken in a dream to Constantine the Great, "In this sign you will conquer"; and under the aegis of the Cross, he had gone on to defeat the pagan armies of Maxentius at the Mulvian Bridge in 312 A.D. Likewise, the Leaguers intended to defeat what passed for Rome in Australia, the Colonial Office. The League's rhetoric, its tub-thumping about defilement and the Stain, went down like cream in the other colonies—except among the descendants of Emancipists, who resignedly kept their peace when the adjectives rained on their fathers and grandfathers from the platforms of abolition. But the Vandemonians choked on it. Too many of them—perhaps four people out of five by 1850—were related to convicts on one or both sides of their lineage, and although this was a social embarrassment to be passed over, if possible, in silence, they did not want to listen to harangues on the extent of their own pollution. As a result, the League was obliged to pack the empty seats at its dinners in Hobart and Launceston with free tickets; Vandemonians did not want to pay good money to hear their parents insulted.[15]

The battle between the League and the government of Van Diemen's Land, over the issue of the unfair Convict's Prevention Act that had been sponsored by the League's branch in Victoria, inflamed a real class struggle in Hobart. Its theater was the campaign for the Van Diemen's Land Legislature elections, due in January 1853, whose chief issues were the shift of responsibility to local, municipal government (which Denison favored) and the ending of transportation (which he opposed). The 1851 elections had been won by men sympathetic, in the main, to abolition— friends of the Australasian League. Could the Leaguers in Van Diemen's Land repeat their victory?[16]

One could not be sure. The Victorian Convicts' Prevention Act had put them in an awkward bind. Many of them did not want to offend the Crown with a law that, in effect, denied the validity of conditional Royal pardons for convicts. It seemed, and was, a tyrannous statute, unfair to other Tasmanians. Sir William Denison's government saw its perfect opportunity to reverse anti-transportation propaganda by depicting the Leaguers, through the government-aligned press, as reactionaries who wanted to keep conditionally pardoned convicts in permanent subjection, as oligarchs ("former merciless white slave drivers, and now new-fangled Leaguers") in liberals' clothing.[17] As the spring of 1852 gave way to the early Tasmanian summer, long-suppressed political emotions in Hobart boiled over in a way that recalled the bitter disputes of Emancipists and Exclusives in Sydney forty years before, in the time of Macquarie. All the euphemisms in which local political discourse had veiled the convict system and its class divisions were dropped, as Denison's supporters found an alliance with the ex-convict interest against the League. Insults and propaganda flew. During the campaign, readers of government-sympathizing newspapers like the *Guardian* were switched to a diet of pro-Emancipist sentiments and even treated to surveys of Australian history in which the convicts emerged as the sole heroes. At meetings, speakers for the League were howled down by what one of the Leaguers' journals, the *Times*, called "The Slumocracy," which "the patronage of Sir William Denison raised . . . into vigor." The Leaguers accused their lieutenant-governor of fomenting "a war of classes" and called his administration—in a bizarre foretaste of later political rhetoric —"the Red Republican Government of Van Diemen's Land."[18] But when the votes were counted in January 1853, the tallies showed a heavy majority for Denison and the lower-class ex-convicts whose feelings he had adroitly manipulated.

Nevertheless, the British Government did listen to the League, to critics at home and to the wealthier mainland colonies. It rebuked Denison for his "partiality" when he reported the election as a proof of his popularity. In England, the pressure to transport was slackening and, for the first time in living memory, there were actually vacant cells in government prisons at home. The government had built more jails in 1851, for instance, the grim commodious prison of Dartmoor opened, and a new jail had been built at Portsmouth to replace the crowded hulks. By 1852, there was prison space for 16,000 convicts in England.

Prison was cheaper than transportation by now, at least for short sentences. It cost £100 to keep a man in Van Diemen's Land for the run of his sentence, but prison in England cost the government £15 per man per year. Since only a small minority of British prisoners drew sentences of more than a year in home prisons (only 5,000, in all, between 1842 and 1850, as against 30,000 men and women transported for 7 to 10 years to Van Diemen's Land in the same period), it was now feasible to reduce transportation by stepping up the length of sentences in English prisons. The penitentiary, for which Jeremy Bentham had beaten the philosophical drum so long and tiringly fifty years before, was clearly destined to replace Botany Bay.[19]

In April 1850, Lord Grey rose in the House to make one of the last defenses of transportation. He still planned to send his Exiles out when and as they were needed. In fact, to assuage the northeastern graziers, he had dispatched two ships direct to Moreton Bay, *Mount Stewart Elphinstone* in May 1849 and *Bangalore* in January 1850; and as long as the Legislative Council of New South Wales was controlled by grazing interests, he wanted to keep alive the option of sending felons there. Convicts had created the economic base that made free emigrants want to go to Australia—and 31,000 such emigrants had gone there in the last year. Grey conceded that "confinement and penal labour . . . ought to be chiefly inflicted at home," and that "free colonies have a right to expect that convicts should not be sent to them without their own consent." But he was not going to abandon transportation on principle—especially not to Van Diemen's Land. The island had been founded as a penal colony; it had never had any other purpose. England had spent "millions" equipping it as a jail, and

the free population which has established itself there for the sake of the pecuniary advantages of that expenditure, has no right whatever to expect that the policy of this country should be altered when they think proper to demand it, and that we should be compelled again to incur the heavy expense of preparing some new settlement. . . . I conceive that authority ought to be firmly maintained and asserted, and that Van Diemen's Land should continue to be used for the reception of convicts.[20]

Whatever the justice of Grey's position—and justice it had, for all its lack of appeal to colonial feelings—his hopes (and the graziers') were overridden by the gold discoveries of 1851. Gold was the mineral that put an end to transportation, because its discovery plucked off the last rags of terror that clung to the name of Australia. With a quarter of Britain, from navvies to viscounts, clamoring for tickets to the southern goldfields, who was to think that a trip to El Dorado at government expense constituted a fearful punishment—especially if, as rumor had it, convicts got a conditional pardon as soon as they stepped ashore at Hobart? As Governor-General Fitzroy remarked, "few English criminals . . . would not regard a free passage to the gold-fields via Hobart town as a great boon."[21]

There were still people who thought of convict labor as an economic panacea. But they were mostly cranks.[22] The English press, led by the *Times*, was by now solidly against transportation. Grey had few allies in either house of Parliament, except for some of the more reactionary Law Lords; and in any case, his government lost office in 1852. His Tory successor as secretary of state for the colonies was Sir John Pakington, who acted without delay. In mid-December 1852, Pakington wrote to Lieutenant-Governor Denison in Van Diemen's Land. He pronounced himself "not unaware" of the continuing arguments for transportation. Part of the rage to abolish it "may . . . be ascribed to the prevalence . . . of one deplorable crime, in consequence of the temporary overcrowding of the convicts"—to wit, sodomy. But better arrangements had checked that; and certainly "the readiness and almost indeed the avidity" with which settlers snatched convict labor from each arriving ship proved that the demand for them was real. However, the pro-transportationists had not formed an effective lobby, and "whatever may be the private opinions of individuals who have not come forward on this question, numerous public meetings and all the legislative authorities in these colonies have declared themselves strongly against transportation." He would not provoke Australians to "a furious opposition" that would end with hatred of the Crown. Finally there was the gold, whose very existence made it "a solecism to convey offenders, at the public expense, with the intention of at no distant time setting them free, to the immediate vicinity of those very gold fields which thousands of honest labourers are in vain striving to reach."[23]

With this, transportation to Van Diemen's Land came to an end. The

last convict transport, the 630-ton ship *St. Vincent*, had sailed for Hobart
on November 27, 1852. Van Diemen's Land officially ceased to be a penal
colony thirteen months later; and with a collective whistle of relief, its
citizens proceeded (as they hoped) to get rid of the "demonic" image of
their island once and for all, by giving it the name of its Dutch discoverer:
Tasmania, for the navigator Abel Tasman.

The formal end of transportation to Van Diemen's Land came with
the Jubilee of the colony—August 10, 1853, the fiftieth anniversary of
the day the first settlement was pitched at Risdon Cove. It provoked a flutter of doggerel in the press. "Hurra for the noble Leaguers!" the *Hobart
Town Daily Courier* exclaimed,

> Hurra for our British Queen!
> Hurra for the tread of Freemen
> Where Bondsmen erst have been!
>
> Peal on, ye shrill-voiced heralds!
> Your thrilling music tells
> Tasmania's happy future;
> Peal on, ye English bells!
>
> From city hall to cottage,
> O'er all our island homes,
> Ring round your benediction!
> The Unstained Future comes!

Not to be outdone, an editor in Launceston composed a pastiche to the
tune of "God Save the Queen." Thousands of copies were printed on a
press which, mounted on a bunting-lined cart, was drawn in procession
through the town:

> Sing! for the hour is come!
> Sing! for our happy home,
>   Our land is free!
> Broken Tasmania's chain,
> Wash'd out that hated stain,
> Ended the strife and pain!
>   Blest Jubilee!

The cart, symbol of the power of the colonial press in its struggles for
Abolition against foot-dragging officialdom, was preceded by groups separated by bannermen: members of the Legislative Council, the mayor
and the corporation, a phalanx of native-born colonists marching four
abreast, public societies with their regalia, and "the hope and staff of the
colony," its children. They marched under a triumphal arch of paste-

board, decked with fronds of native wattle, to the sprightly tooting and flourishing of a brass band. There was feasting at Ross; and in the town of Oatlands whole sheep were roasted, while the colonial boys played cricket, climbed poles and fell to the breathless pursuit of a greased pig. It darted frantically among the spectators, smearing their moleskins until someone collared it. One "facetious bystander" extolled the animal as a symbol of the fight for Abolitionists' rights: "That pig, greasy, long-winded and cunning though he was, was caught at last by patience and perseverance."[24]

There were only a few sour notes. The next day, the *Hobart Town Daily Courier* reported the "ill-advised and unwarranted setting up of *an effigy* in the back of Messrs. Marsh and Chapman's timber-yard." It was removed before it could be burned. The paper did not say whose effigy it was, but everyone knew it was Denison's. He had offended the colonists, when they asked him to convey their satisfaction with the new policy to the people of England, by replying: "The people of England do not care for you one straw; the Houses of Parliament look upon you as the fly on the wheel." At this, the press branded him "a coarse-minded, vindictive, ungenerous man," but Denison had read worse. Abolition was rung in with triple bob-majors on the church bells, not saluted from Battery Point by army cannon. Perhaps the lack of unanimity was appropriate; on the other side of Australia, transportation had begun all over again.[25]

iii

THE LAST PLACE to receive English convicts was Western Australia, the western third of the continent where few had been and fewer, apparently, wanted to go: a colony with a body the size of Europe and the brain of an infant. Except for some coastal patches, it was all desert, pebbles, saltbush and spinifex—the right spot, in the Australian phrase, "to do a perish."

Its first settlement nearly did just that. In 1826, Governor Darling sent a detachment of soldiers and fifty convicts to occupy King George's Sound, the present site of Albany on the southwestern tip of the continent. In establishing a military base there, he hoped he would deter the white desperadoes—escaped convicts and Yankee whaling riffraff with their black slave-harems—who had set up their half-wild tribal communities all along the southern coast from Bass Strait to Kangaroo Island and westward to King George's Sound.

The settlement lasted five years, every day of them an ordeal. Officers went half-mad with loneliness and boredom. As for the convicts, the most that can be said is that, with hostile blacks and saltbush desert right behind them and the cobalt grin of a shark-infested ocean in front, none of them tried to escape. Eventually, Darling conceded that no free settler would ever want to go to the Sound, and that the military base was too frail to do much against the sealers. In 1831 he had the garrison and its surviving convicts withdrawn.

By then, another plan for Western Australian settlement had formed. It centered on the Swan River, and its mover was a gallant young post-captain in the navy, James Stirling (1791–1865), who had married into a family influential both in Westminster and in the East India Company. In 1826 Stirling was given a ship and told to remove the survivors of a dispirited garrison experimentally put on Melville Island, and the Timor Sea near the present site of Darwin. This northern outpost had been meant to discourage the French from landing, but they had never even tried to, perhaps because it was so far off the shipping routes. It had lasted two years and was now on its last legs, rotting from heat, dysentery and terror of the blacks. To avoid the monsoon season, Stirling took the long route around the 4,300-mile coast of Western Australia, imagining as he went a settlement that would keep the French off and be a staging-port for British ships. The mouth of the Swan looked promising, and in March 1827 he spent a delighted two weeks there. Then, picking up the Melville Island garrison, he proceeded to Sydney, composing on the way the first of a stream of memos to Governor Darling and the authorities in England. He urged a settlement at Swan River (Hesperia, he wanted to call it, since it faced the westering sun). He himself would be its lieutenant-governor.[26]

Not until 1828, with a change of government in London, did Stirling make much headway. Family influence played a major part. Both the new head of the Colonial Office, Sir George Murray, and his assistant, Horace Twiss, were friends of Stirling's father-in-law. Stirling proposed to them that a syndicate of private capitalists should raise the money to establish settlers at Swan River. The government liked the sound of this —a Crown colony developed by private funds, as Pennsylvania had been by William Penn and Georgia by Colonel Oglethorpe.

Enter, at this point, a young English landowner, the second son of a cotton-manufacturer, something of a wastrel but marked with gentility and imbued with the desire to cut a great figure on the colonial stage: Thomas Peel (1793–1865). An hour's conversation with Captain Stirling had convinced him that the Swan River held his future, and he appeared before the government with a hastily convened syndicate of investors, who offered to transfer ten thousand settlers with all their stock and gear to Western Australia in return for a Crown grant of four million acres. The government counter-offered one million. At this dampening stingi-ness the syndicate evaporated, and Peel, who had much less money than

Stirling thought, had to find a new backer. He did, but not one he wanted to acknowledge publicly: an ex-convict named Solomon Levey (1794–1833) who, transported in 1814 for stealing a chest of tea, had risen in Sydney as a merchant, banker, landowner and, eventually, philanthropist. The firm of Cooper and Levey, founded in 1826, was one of the biggest trading concerns in the South Pacific. Levey was an astute, generous man, but not—as it turned out—quite astute enough. He had always craved the respectability, the sense of access that had been twice denied him as an ex-convict and as a Jew. The chance to underwrite an ambitious imperial scheme with an aristocratic *goy*, a relative of the great Sir Robert Peel, dazzled him. Thomas Peel, for his part, insisted on keeping Levey's partnership secret, so that the Swan River scheme would not be tainted by Jewishness and felonry. The company they formed was called Thomas Peel & Co.[27]

The Colonial Office agreed to give this company 250,000 acres on the Swan, and 250,000 more after it landed 400 settlers, who would receive grants of 200 and 100 acres each. These settlers had to arrive by November 1, 1829. After twenty-one years—by mid-century—Thomas Peel & Co. was to get another 500,000 acres. Captain James Stirling, master of many ships and darling of the Colonial Office, would be lieutenant-governor of the new colony, with 100,000 acres of his choice. Peel would go with him to manage the company's affairs.

In May 1829, the frigate *Challenger* sailed into the Swan River estuary, and its master, Captain Charles Fremantle, took formal possession of one million square miles of territory,* naming it Western Australia— the first time the word *Australia* had been officially used. (Curiously enough, he was told to ask the Aborigines if they consented to this; but neither Fremantle nor anyone else on board spoke their language, and one could hardly convey so heroic a territorial concept to savages by pointing and waving.) Meanwhile, in England, the first Swan River colonists, all free men and women with promises of Arcadia dancing in their heads, were signed up, assembled and embarked on the *Parmelia*. No one had tried to survey the area or to map any part of its coastline, a fact that became embarrassingly evident at the end of the long voyage when Captain Stirling, catching sight of the mouth of the Swan River and the *Challenger* at anchor, became so anxious to make port that he steered a shortcut between an island and the shore and ran his ship, with all its colonists, onto the rocks. No one was drowned, and a few days later the young lieutenant-governor kedged *Parmelia* off. The Swan River pioneers

---

* Its eastern boundary was the meridian of 129°E.—not that this represented any "natural" boundary, but simply because it was the convenient fossil of the "Pope's Line," fixed in the fifteenth century by the Treaty of Tordesillas, which divided the world into Spanish and Portuguese hemispheres.

had their first taste of Australian life, huddled disconsolately under canvas in the pouring rain surrounded by the emblems of the civilization they were to plant in the wild: cases of flour, trunks full of nankeen and velvet, Georgian furniture, rusting shovels, an upright piano cocked listing in the sand. They slapped at mosquitoes and scratched at sand-fleas while gazing on the barren coast, the prostrate creeping plants and the steaming rocks; their hearts sank. Not being convicts, the ladies could not curse.

But Stirling was indefatigable. He named a port town, Fremantle, at the mouth of the Swan; and then led a party upstream, between embowered banks where the arch-symbols of antipodean inversion that had given the river its name, the black swans, dibbled their red bills in the water. Nine miles from the sea, he chose a spot for the main city, Perth. By December 1829, when Thomas Peel sailed in with ninety more colonists, two shantytowns marked the white man's foothold on the coast. It was typical of Stirling that, as the age of Sail turned to that of Steam, he had separated the capital from the port by a stretch of river navigable only by rowboats.

The fertility of the land proved, as so often it had done to Australian pioneers before, a mirage. Either the soil was barren, or it was so thick with trees that the work of clearing and stumping defeated all but the most iron-willed settlers. Not until 1835 did the Swan River colony grow enough wheat to feed itself. Stirling was constantly sending to the Cape for emergency supplies, but the British Government did not want to spend money underwriting what had been presented to it as a legitimate commercial speculation. Hence, the settlers lived on the edge of famine most of the time. Stirling won their gratitude, if little else, by sailing to England in 1832 to beg assistance; the Colonial Office sent Stirling back to Western Australia with a flea in his ear for leaving his post without permission.

As lieutenant-governor, Stirling had to spend every grain of his charm and authority to keep the anxieties of his "genteel colonists" at bay, so that their morale would not cave in. He never let them forget their Englishness. They dined at the vice-regal tent in formal dress, decorations optional; he presided over balls, picnics and hunts. Not without difficulty, he got Anglican chaplains to make the immense voyage to Western Australia so that their rites and sermons could furnish the little colony with its necessary social glue and spiritual comfort.

Yet such efforts were mainly cosmetic. Nothing could abolish the miseries of the land or the frictions of the harassed little community, promised Arcadia but given sand. One settler noted that the doctors were kept busy with "casualties and accidents, arising from grog drinking, and guns and gunpowder in the hands of persons not accustomed to their use till they came here." Thomas Peel, their financial promoter, disintegrated almost as soon as he arrived. His chosen acreage south of Fremantle, poor land to begin with, was swept by a bushfire; in May 1830, the *Rockingham*, carrying settlers for his land, was wrecked on the same rocks that had nearly destroyed *Parmelia*. In a paroxysm of rage, he challenged her captain to a duel and got shot in the right hand. He seemed so choleric and crazy that no one would work for him. Supplies he promised never arrived. Promissory notes on Cooper & Levey, in which many workers had been paid, were dishonored by Daniel Cooper in Sydney (without, it should be mentioned, the knowledge of Solomon Levey in London). Settlers sued Peel for their wages; he countersued for their passage money. He sent no reports to Levey and did not set aside the 125,000 acres meant to recompense his unacknowledged partner for the £20,000 he had sunk in the Swan River scheme. In 1832, Levey had to ask the Colonial Office what on earth was happening at Swan River—and the Office was loath to tell him, for it had no record of Levey's financial involvement. Peel had not revealed that his one solid backer was an Emancipist Jew.

Levey died the next year, 1833, his spirits broken by this utter fiasco. Peel lived on in Western Australia for another thirty years, slipping into poverty, juggling his land-grants, selling a few acres here and there to keep going—not that there were many takers. In his old age, he could sometimes be glimpsed riding alone through his vast acreage of worthless bush, wearing a frayed pink coat like the hunting squire he had tried, and failed, to become.

In 1832 the Swan River colony had slightly under 1,500 white colonists; five years later it had scarcely 500 more. By 1839, when Stirling left, it could support itself after a fashion, but all its wheat and flour still had to be imported from Hobart. Each year, it exported a token few hundred bales of wool to England, nothing else. In December 1850, after two decades of settlement, Western Australia had only 5,886 colonists—two-thirds of whom, according to its governor, Charles Fitzgerald, in a report to Lord Grey, "would quit this colony tomorrow." Sheep that had cost £4 to £5 a head were going begging at half a crown. The price of their wool had plummeted to 9d. or even 6d. a pound, leaving the grazier no margin at all. All was "depression, stagnation, and, I may say, despair."[28] One last possible fount of manpower remained to save them: convicts.

In 1846 some West Australians petitioned Whitehall "to make and declare their Colony a Penal Settlement Upon an Extensive Scale."[29] Grey was delighted. Here, at least, was one colony wise enough to realize that Britain's long enterprise of social excretion could do good, manuring the antipodean sand. If Western Australia clamored for felons, Grey reasoned, the Anti-Transportation League would look weaker. At least it could not claim a complete moral monopoly among the white settlers of Australia.

And so, just as transportation was drawing to a close in the east of Australia, it began in the west. The first convict ship to Western Australia, the *Scindian*, with 75 felons, 54 guards and the usual officials on board, appeared off Fremantle in June 1850. In January 1868, the thirty-seventh and last convict ship, the *Hougoumont*, disgorged 279 prisoners there—including a number of Irish Fenians, most prominent of whom was the writer and editor John Boyle O'Reilly, soon to make a spectacular escape on a ship chartered by fellow Irishmen in America. In those eighteen years, 9,668 convicts, all men and most of them able-bodied, were sent to Western Australia over the continuous protests of the other Australian colonies. They did not improve the moral tone of the raw West, but they saved its economy. As in the past, slave labor got the wheels turning.

The monument of the System in Western Australia was a long, low, white building overlooking the sea at Fremantle—the convict barracks, known as the "Establishment." It held the prisoners who had to work in chain gangs in and around Fremantle. Other groups of serving convicts, not in chains, were housed in depots at Perth and in the country districts, where they made roads, raised public buildings and in general improved the public face of Western Australia. After doing a specified part of his sentence, each prisoner became eligible for a conditional pardon—4 years for a 7-year sentence, 5 years and 3 months for a 10-year sentence, and so on.[30] He could then do wage-labor for a free settler until his time was up. Before his ticket-of-leave, he could only work for the local government.

The lash, by now only an execrated memory in the older Australian colonies, was part of the discipline here but not its basis. In 1858 the superintendent of convicts avowed that he wanted it reserved for "cases of brutal assault," not even for escape attempts, for "when we consider the utter impossibility of effecting escape in the bush, —the colony being in reality what it is commonly described to be, a vast natural prison, — we ought in awarding punishment to reflect that the unfortunate culprit has already received the most impressive of all kinds of persuasion, viz., actual suffering from starvation."[31]

The colony was greedy; it wanted to get as many "government men" as it could, and extract as much profit from their labor as possible. In February 1858 the comptroller-general's office in Fremantle asked the Colonial Office for a guaranteed one thousand prisoners a year, since "the prosperity of the Colony must mainly depend on the number of convicts sent here." With less success, it asked the British Government to pay for "materials, powder, cartage, plant, &c" in road, dock and bridge building, as well as the prisoners' transportation, food, clothing and tools. Western Australia was so poor, it added piteously, that paying for such things "is wholly out of the question." Popular as government labor was in Western Australia (both the Anglican and the Catholic Bishops of Perth fruitlessly requested convict labor to erect their rival episcopal palaces), the whole idea of its continued influx was regarded with horror and dismay back East. The Stain was powerful stuff; this "moral sewage" could cross deserts, contaminate seas, seep its noxious way thousands of miles east and surface on the newly purged coast of Australia. Where did the Western Australian convicts go when their sentences ran out? To New South Wales, Victoria and South Australia—or so indignant citizens believed. The one issue on which all the participating members could agree at the first Australian Intercolonial Conference, held in Melbourne in 1863, was that transportation to Western Australia had to stop. A British Royal Commission on Penal Discipline chose this heated moment to urge that *all* male convicts sentenced to *any* length of sentence should be sent to Western Australia.[32]

At this, the Victorian Anti-Transportation League, which had atrophied for want of a cause, sat up with a jerk and addressed a solemn plea to the people of Great Britain. "The happy homes of tens of thousands of families who were lately your neighbours," it intoned, were about to be "desolated, by the presence of a convict curse . . . productive of abominations too horrible to be named." If Western Australia could not survive without convicts, let its free settlers go elsewhere. But South Australia, Victoria, New South Wales, Queensland, Tasmania and New Zealand would no longer consent to indirectly serve as "the refuge for Britain's outcasts, the hiding places for her sin and shame." The fact that a convict had to have served his sentence before leaving Western Australia, and hence was no longer a convict but a free man, was immaterial.[33] Nobody knew how many demons and villains really came east—a popular though certainly exaggerated figure was six men in ten—but there was no doubt that it would be easily done by ship. Certainly no one ever heard of an ex-prisoner doing it on foot. And if (as one of the Macarthurs suggested in a letter to the London *Daily News*) only six hundred felons a year got into the eastern states, that was six thousand in ten years, and each of them capable of corrupting at least a dozen innocent folk.[34] The mere arithmetic was enough to freeze a man's blood.

The facts pointed another way. Only about one ticket-of-leave holder in Western Australia in three was convicted of a second offense; less than one in twenty of these offenses was "serious," and two convictions in five were for drunkenness or attempted escape. Escapes had become more frequent between 1862 and 1867, under the odious and corrupt governorship of J. S. Hampton, the former ally of John Price on Norfolk Island.[35]

But this time the Abolitionists won. Her Majesty's Government was no longer prepared to trade the convenience of draining six hundred felons a year into Western Australia for the grave risk of alienating all the eastern colonies, which had the population, the money, the resources, the trade—everything, in fact, that made a colony worth having. Early in 1865, Lord Palmerston's cabinet announced that transportation would end within three years. And so it did: On January 10, 1868, the last convict ship to Australia landed its cargo of sixty Fenian political prisoners and more common assorted malefactors at Fremantle, eighty years to the month, if not quite the day, since Captain Arthur Phillip brought the First Fleet to its anchorage in Sydney Cove.

The loss of convicts was an economic disaster for Western Australia. For two decades it had had the free labor of some fifteen hundred men, at a cost to England of £100,000 a year; and as a Fremantle editor put it, "we now awake from our normal state of apathetic indifference to find ourselves on the verge of ruin." Virtually all it had to show for those twenty years were some mines that could no longer be worked, since free labor did not want to go down them; a network of roads around Perth that petered out in the bush; some handsome Victorian public buildings, a few bridges and dredged channels, and a half-empty jail barracks at Fremantle. The population of Western Australia in 1871 was 25,447, of whom about 9,000 were convicts or their descendants.

The 1871 Census revealed that in population growth, the colonies that shed the System first (or, like South Australia, had never had it) had zoomed ahead of both Western Australia and Tasmania. In the twenty years since 1851, the white population of New South Wales had gone (in round figures) from 197,000 to 500,000; Victoria, from 77,000 to 730,000, a tenfold increase set off by the gold rush and sustained by land development; South Australia, from 66,500 to 189,000. Queensland's population had quadrupled since 1861, to 122,000 souls. But the last of the convict colonies, Tasmania and Western Australia, would be stuck for decades in their hangover from the malign indulgence of semi-slave labor.

The End of the System

THE LONG ANGUISH of the System was over. What had it achieved? It might be gratifying to claim that it had failed altogether; that this not-so-small, not-so-primitive ancestor of the Gulag deterred no one in Britain and reformed no one in Australia; that as a penal system it was quite unproductive, a botched act of sublimation.

Certainly, there were things it did not do. If one accepts the "strategic outlier" argument—that the hidden agenda of convict colonization was to protect England's Far Eastern trade with a refitting port on the coast of New South Wales—then it did fail. No big warships were rigged with the pine and flax that had so interested Captain Cook on Norfolk Island, and Australia's contribution to the balance of military and trading power in Indian waters between 1788 and 1820 was nil. Perhaps the English colony on the eastern coast deterred the French from claiming the continent—or perhaps the French were not as interested in Australia as the English, fearful of Napoleon, assumed? The west and north coasts, facing the Indian Ocean and the Timor Sea, had strategic prospects, but the French did not try to claim them, even though England did not put a garrison into Western Australia until 1826.

Some Frenchmen—though not, as a rule, those who had actually been there—did admire the English penal experiment in Australia. "Eh! qui ne connait pas le consolant spectacle," sang a penally inspired bard named Delille in 1830, in a work entitled "De La Pitié" ("On Pity"),

Qu'étale de bandits ce vaste réceptacle
Cette *Botany-Bay*, sentine d'ALBION,
Ou le vol, la rapine et la sédition
En foule sont venus, et, purgeant l'Angleterre,
Dan leur exil lointain vont féconder la terre?
La, l'indulgent loi, du sujets dangereux

Fait d'habiles colons, des citoyens heureux;
Soucit au repentir, excite l'industrie,
Leur rend la liberté, des moeurs, une patrie.
Je vois de toute part les marais désséchés.
Les déserts embellis, et les bois défrichés.
Imitez cet example: à leur prison stérile
Enlevez ces brigands, rendez leur peine utile.[1]

To foreign eyes, the long experiment on the Fatal Shore generally seemed a success, as philosophy in action: "Imitate this example, take these brigands from their sterile prison, make their punishment useful." It might have been more widely imitated, had there not been such a shortage of undiscovered continents in the early nineteenth century. France would presently pay England the sincere homage of imitation by constructing its own Pacific convict colony, a hellish one, in the New Hebrides.

The proponents of British transportation had hoped that, broadly speaking, it would do four things: sublimate, deter, reform and colonize. First, it would remove the "criminal class"—or a good slice of it—from England, and put it where it could do no further harm to the English polity and the interests of property. It was social amputation. What was the cause of crime? Criminals, who manufactured or, rather, secreted it from their inner nature, as snakes their venom or eels their slime. Get rid of criminals and you would get rid of, or at least greatly reduce, crime in Great Britain. Transportation had to fail in this, because the causes of crime lay further back in the social system: in poverty, inequality, unemployment and want, and in laws that had relentlessly created new categories of "transportable" crime. Transportation did rid England of many real sociopaths, men whose aggression and violence were built into their genetic labyrinth, but they were in a minority—and not a few were usefully absorbed by the System as overseers and floggers.

By the 1830s, the hopes of the English authorities had centered on a second aim. This was deterrence. Transportation would not only get rid of the guilty, but terrify the innocent away from crime. The problem with arguments about deterrence is the lack of figures on uncommitted crimes. One cannot know if the threat of a given punishment really did stop the thief at the windowpane.* The crime rate in early-nineteenth-century England did not drop as a result of transpor-

---

* The only plausible case for capital punishment, among those who believe the State has the right to kill in the interests of social order, is not the fiction that it "deters" people from murder—although it may indeed make some think twice—but that it gets rid of mad-dog sociopaths whose life, if preserved with even the slightest hope of eventual freedom, would be a lethal menace to innocent and ill-protected people. Obviously, few murderers belong in this category.

tation, again because its roots lay too deep for *any* deterrent to reach. But what most complicated the matter was the difficulty of convincing the lower classes of Great Britain that Australia was a terrible place to go.

This had been a problem from the start. A verse entitled "The Convicts' Departure," jocose rather than satirical, written as early as 1790, raised the possibility that Botany Bay might prove a milky land, compared to the withered dug of Mother England—a place where

> . . . every day
> Nature is kindly giving,
> Plenty to have, and nothing to pay,
> This is the land to live in.[2]

Nobody on the early fleets can have believed this, but the notion of a colonial Eden was not readily dispelled by colonial experience, since the whole Pacific was faintly tinged (if not in learned discourse, then in popular fancy) with the sweetness of Otaheite. The idea that one might be better off there than in England—that, in the words of the ballad, it was "Better to range in a foreign land / Than in a prison perish"—persisted after the time of Governor Macquarie, who gave commonsense recognition to the fact that, despite the pretensions of the Exclusives, the stock of Australian life would be, for the foreseeable future, Emancipist and Currency. After Macquarie had gone, the contrast was still confirmed by the miseries of common English life—the growth of slums, the unemployment, the ruin of smallholders. Hence the proletarian idea that Botany Bay might not be so bad survived the policies that were meant to destroy it: the increased severity of the regimes of Brisbane, Darling and Arthur; the brutality of the chain gangs; and the outright ferocity of Macquarie Harbor, Norfolk Island and Moreton Bay.

Some of this may have sprung from the bravado of prisoners sending letters home to England, playing down their sufferings to soothe the anxieties of their wives and children, or merely wishing to seem unbowed by the System. Some, no doubt, was due to wishful thinking among those at home. But by the 1830s, with due allowance made for the harshness that went with assignment, some of it was true. The convict with manual skills, if he had the luck to be assigned to a decent master in the back country, stood a chance of living a better life than he might have done amid the penury of England's rural depression. "The grand secret in the management of convicts," an emigrant's handbook of the early 1830s insisted, "is to treat them with kindness, and at the same time with firmness." Most masters knew this from experience, though

their "kindness" rarely had much sugar in it and their "firmness" could
be that of petty pharaohs. "It is true," wrote Edward Curr, superintendent of the Van Diemen's Land Company, in 1831,

> that convicts are sent out here as punishment. But it is equally true that
> it is not in the interests of the master to make his service a punishment,
> but rather to make the condition of the convict as comfortable as is
> consistent with economy. *The interest of the master essentially contra-
> dicts the object of transportation.*[3]

When he got his ticket-of-leave, the redeemed convict's work was
more in demand and his wages higher than in England or Ireland. As we
have seen, New South Wales and Van Diemen's Land held no shortage
of brutal masters, and a man could be crushed under the penal system
like a toad beneath a harrow—but he could also remake his life. Those
who went under did not write home; those who prospered sometimes
did.

Try as it might, the British Government could not stop the flow of
impressions this opened. It gave orders to increase the severity of the
penal stations, and under Governor Darling some 20 to 25 percent of all
male convicts in New South Wales suffered appalling conditions, either
in the chain gangs or in the penal out-stations. The Home and Colonial
Offices kept urging their proconsuls in Australia to make the System
harsher, more certain in retribution, more machine-like—right up to the
moment when transportation to Van Diemen's Land was abolished.

Successive governments, Whig and Tory alike, made no secret of their
view that transportation was meant to inflict relentless suffering rather
than to reform the criminal. But Britain could not come out and tell the
public at large how bad things really were in Norfolk Island or the Blue
Mountain chain gangs, for fear of looking sadistic; or how lenient they
could become in assignment, lest its System seem weak. The first was
left to the reformers, the second became a kind of folk-whisper that
sounded louder than the voice of Whitehall in the ears of hedgers or
coachmen.

This was not the first time that the low of England had balked at
believing the high, but the size of the credibility gap on transportation is
perhaps indicated by the fact that Charles Dickens should have contemplated leaping into it on the government's behalf. On July 2, 1840, he
wrote to Lord Normanby, the literary Whig home secretary, pointing out
that most English criminals now thought of transportation as a passport
to opportunity and even wealth, and offering to write "a vivid description
of the terrors of Norfolk Island and such-like places, told in a homely
narrative with a great appearance of truth and reality and circulated in

some very cheap and easy form."[4] One would like to know what Dickens would have made of Maconochie, for the Scottish reformer—brave, compassionate, fixated and priggish—was a very "Dickensian" creature; but he never went. Dickens's polemical reporting on prisons would come two years later, in his journals of a visit to America. In 1851, of course, with the discovery of gold, any lingering terrors eastern Australia might still have held for English laborers were outweighed by the possibility of making a fortune.

The only fully drawn character from penal Australia in Dickens is the returned convict Abel Magwitch in *Great Expectations* (1860); and Magwitch sums up the distaste verging on dread with which some middle-class Englishmen (Dickens included) viewed the transported convict "making good" in exile. As a child, the hero, Pip, has saved Magwitch from the gallows by helping him evade his pursuers in the fens; but Magwitch is betrayed by a "gentleman" crook and disappears to Australia, swallowed by the black hulk, "a wicked Noah's Ark." The plot turns on a mysterious benefaction that transforms Pip, in his young manhood, into a "gentleman." The money is revealed to have come from Magwitch, who has gone back to Australia, made a fortune and, in gratitude, endowed the one human being that ever showed him compassion. Magwitch is a figure edged with terror: coarse, brutalized, possibly a cannibal.* His energy is demonic, his thirst for revenge insatiable. And it turns out that his anonymous, obsessively prompted generosity to Pip is another kind of revenge, a black joke against English and colonial class relations. Pip will be his revenge on the Exclusives, who still spurn him as a risen felon. Do gentlemen make convicts? Then a convict will "make" and "own" a real gentleman, not a colonial facsimile. He will show the truth about gentility: It can be bought. He will hug the knowledge of that for the rest of his life. Under the skin of generosity, there is slavery in reverse. "And then, dear boy, it was a recompense to me, look'ee here, to know in secret that I was making a gentleman," Magwitch tells the horrified Pip:

> The blood horses of them colonists might fling up the dust over me as I was walking; what do I say? I says to myself, "I'm making a better gentleman nor ever *you'll* be!" When one of 'em says to another, "He was a convict, a few year ago, and is an ignorant common fellow now, for all he's lucky," what do I say? I says to myself, "If I ain't a gentleman, nor yet ain't got no learning, I'm the owner of such. All on you owns stock and land; which on you owns a brought-up London gentleman?" This way I kep myself a-going.

---

* Presumably Dickens read the confession of Pearce, the Irish man-eater of Macquarie Harbor, printed in the appendix to the Molesworth Report in 1838.

He tells Pip the truth about his upbringing to close the circle of revenge. Magwitch's sufferings have put him beyond taking pleasure in another's gratitude:

> Do I tell it, fur you to feel an obligation? Not a bit. I tell it, fur you to know as that there hunted dunghill dog wot you kep life in, got his head so high that he could make a gentleman—and, Pip, you're him!

It occurs to Pip that he is now a convict, too; Magwitch has been "loading wretched me with his gold and silver chains for years." No wonder that "the repugnance with which I shrank from him, could not have been exceeded if he had been some terrible beast."

Thus in the person of Magwitch, Dickens knotted several strands in the English perception of convicts in Australia at the end of transportation. They could succeed, but they could hardly, in the real sense, return. They could expiate their crimes in a technical, legal sense, but what they suffered there warped them into permanent outsiders. And yet they were capable of redemption—as long as they stayed in Australia.

The redemption of sinners came a distant third on the aims of transportation. Yet it may be that more people were reformed in Australia—in the sense that they came out of bondage meaning to work for their living and obey the law, and were not convicted again—than were ever "deterred" from crime in England. This was due to the assignment system. Assignment did give its "objects" a chance. Not evenly, or consistently, or reliably—but often; whereas the more schematized, "ideological" punishment of Lord Stanley's Probation System in the 1840s was a demoralizing fiasco, and all the worse because Her Majesty's Government tried to do it on the cheap.*

For all its flaws (and one cannot imagine a prison system without defects) the assignment system in Australia was by far the most successful form of penal rehabilitation that had ever been tried in English, American or European history. In assessing it one must remember that many of its critics, in dwelling on the cruelties and injustices that took place within it, were doing so not as objective reporters but as proponents of rival ideologies of punishment. From Bentham with his Panopticon to Lord Stanley with his Probation System, every one of them opposed

---

* And its parsimony could be extreme, at every level of the probation system. In Van Diemen's Land, prisoners who had escaped were expected to reimburse the Convict Department for any rewards paid out for their own capture (TSA, CON 67/1 # 2/1377). In May 1848 one finds a fallen merchant in the Saltwater River probation gang, Samuel Sidney Smith, asking for six sheets of paper on which to write a petition for clemency. Request refused, the superintendent gruffly scribbled in the margin: "The man . . . is an idle schemer. As the case of any man can be put upon one sheet of paper I have refused to let him have more." Here one sees the bureaucratic mind at full stretch, or rather crimp.

assignment in the name of penal Utopias which, when tried, were worse. The assigned man's work was hard (unless he was lucky enough to get work as a domestic servant or a clerk, as many did). But it was not necessarily harder than the kind of work a settler had to do for himself; and to judge by the surviving letters of assigned men who had been rural workers before, it was not worse than the labor of a farm-hand in Britain, despite the flies, the snakes and the heat. Enemies of the System got used to calling this work, and the condition of those who did it, slavery. But it was not slavery. The assigned man worked within a vigilantly sustained framework of laws and rights. Some of the masters were cruel, others irresponsible, some exploitative and a few openly sadistic. But most were none of those things; they were hard, imperfect men struggling to wrest survival or something more from the stingy Australian earth, and many of them had been transported themselves. Few of them perceived their assigned servants as a seigneur did a serf, and those who wished to were frustrated by the law.

Assignment had been the early form of today's open prison. Instead of herding men together in gangs—in which bad apples automatically dominated—assignment dispersed them throughout the bush and kept them in working contact with the free. It fostered self-reliance, taught them jobs and rewarded them for doing them right. It put them on the frontier and did not leave them to rot. Of course, one can overrate the virtues of assignment. But as a rough-and-ready way of getting convicts back into society as self-sustaining workers, it was better than the soul-crushing, totalitarian machinery of the Philadelphia System applied at Pentonville to "reform" Lord Stanley's probationers and Lord Grey's exiles before they took ship to Australia.

Its results were uneven. For a decade and more after transportation to New South Wales ended, colonial society wanted to believe that the residue of convict evil produced most of its crime. In 1835, at the peak of transportation to New South Wales, its courts had handed down a total of 771 convictions for all indictable offenses committed against property or against any person within the colony—a rate of nearly 1,100 convictions per 100,000 inhabitants. From there, the annual number of convictions fell slowly, but the population, swollen by immigrants, grew rapidly, so that by 1851 the conviction rate was just over 290 per 100,000, and by 1861 it was 122—about a tenth of its level in 1835. The conviction rate for New South Wales in 1835 had been about ten times that of England. By 1861, it was only twice as large.[5]

Without doubt, the crime rate fell as the Stain was diluted by immigration and the original felons died off. But did its fall argue reformation as well? In 1841 about three men in five in New South Wales had originally been transported. In 1851 about three in ten had been—still a lot.

Very few of the convictions (about 6 percent) were for crimes committed by the Currency (native-born Australians)—partly because so many of these were children, but largely because the Currency adults, despite the jabber about hereditary stains, were diligent family-oriented workers with a stake in their community. By contrast, convicts or Emancipists (all of whom, by definition, were adults) were the defendants in 70 percent of all criminal trials that yielded convictions in New South Wales in 1841.

As the historian Michael Sturma has shown, one should see this seeming endurance of a propensity for crime in the light of other factors. New South Wales remained a police state well after it finished receiving convicts in 1840. "Its machinery for social control was directed largely to the coercion of convicts. They were subject to more stringent regulation, kept under closer surveillance by the police, and treated differently by the courts."[6] The police leaned on Emancipists as well, legally free though they were. It was far harder for an offender to disappear in a tiny outback town or even in Sydney than in the vast and pullulating anonymity of London. Hence, ticket-of-leave men and Emancipists were more likely to be charged and convicted. They had the worst jobs, the least capital, the lowest education. Hence they were more likely to steal, fight and get drunk. In sum, Australia presented them with much the same social disabilities that had pushed them into crime in Britain, and one thing more: the unrelenting, go-getting, land-grabbing, cash-and-gold-obsessed materialism of free Australian colonists, acting in a vast geographical space but a small social one. Nowhere in the world was the Victorian equation between wealth and virtue rammed home more brutally than in mid-nineteenth-century Australia. With such a social ethic, it is perhaps surprising that the conviction rate was not higher. Indeed, such gross figures as 666 superior-court convictions in New South Wales out of a total population of 265,503 do not begin to justify the rantings and wailings of local Jeremiahs on their obsessive subject, colonial morality.

The fourth, and last, aim of transportation was colonization. Here, *si monumentum requiris, circumspice.* If Australia had not been settled as a prison and built by convict labor, it would have been colonized by other means; that was foreordained from the moment of Cook's landing at Botany Bay in 1770. But it would have taken half a century longer, for Georgian Britain would have found it exceptionally difficult to find settlers crazy or needy enough to go there of their own free will. As James Matra had pointed out before the First Fleet sailed, no one would take such a voyage to such a place "from *romantick* views." To ask what Australia would have been without convicts is existentially meaningless. They built it—if by "it" one means European material culture there—

and their mute traces are everywhere: in the peckings and scoops of iron chisels on the sandstone cuttings of Sydney, hewn with such terrible effort by the work gangs; in the fine springing of one bridge at Berrima in New South Wales, and the earnest, slightly bizarre figures carved on the face of another at Ross in Tasmania; in the zigzags of the Blue Mountain road, where traffic now rolls above the long-buried, rusted chains of the dead; less obviously, in the fruitful pastures that were once primeval gum forest:

> Shame on the mouth
> That would deny
> The knotted hands
> That set us high![7]

What these people bequeathed to Australian character, or to our sense of ourselves as a nation, is much more debatable than the economic results of their labor. Probably it was not what Australians like to think—the truculent independence on which, with shaky justification, we are apt to pride ourselves.

To see the opposite effects of the System on those who lived it out, one may consider Tasmania, which stagnated. Its population had crept from 69,000 in 1851 to 102,000 in 1871, not even doubling in twenty years. Visitors at the end of the 1860s saw apathy and depression everywhere: silent streets, building at a standstill, farmers sinking into rural solipsism, empty docks, a static populace heavy with old people and children but deserted by the young and energetic, who had gone across Bass Strait. The flood of immigrants to Victoria, Queensland and New South Wales passed Tasmania by. The island was decaying, like the Southern slave states of America after Abolition. Convicts remained an inescapable presence, a gray-and-yellow ghost in a dying house. Although Her Majesty's Government had stopped sending prisoners to Tasmania so long ago, the long-sentence men remained there and had to serve out their years of stipulated punishment; the imperial convict system was not fully dismantled until 1886.

Economic stagnation condemned the island to live with its past; long after the rough developing energies of the mainland colonies had transcended the "convict stain," the Dr. Jekyll of Tasmania remained paired with the sinister Mr. Hyde of Van Diemen's Land. Convictry lived on in a hundred pervasive ways. It seemed to be rooted in the very landscape, cankering its lavish and picturesque beauty, as the Irish political prisoner John Mitchel remarked in his journal in 1850:

> Trees of vast height wave their tops far beneath our feet: and the farther
> side of the glen is formed by a promontory that runs out into the bay,

with steep and rocky sides worn into cliffs and caves floored with silvery
sand, shellstrewn, such as in European seas would have been consecrate
of old to some Undine's love . . . and over the soft, swelling slope of the
hill above, embowered so gracefully in trees, what building stands? Is that
a temple crowning the promontory as the pillared portico crowns Su-
nium? Or a villa, carrying you back to Baiae? Damnation! It is a convict
"barrack."[8]

Instead of Paestum, Port Arthur. Instead of the train of classical satyrs,
the road gangs "harnessed to gravel-carts . . . their hair close-cropped,
their close leathern caps, and hangdog countenances . . . evil, rueful and
abominable . . . vacant but impudent."[9] Instead of Claudian or Turner-
esque nymphs in this landscape, a pass-holding woman servant in the
charge of a convict constable, "a hideous and obscene-looking creature
with a brandy-bloated face and a white satin bonnet, adorned with artificial flowers."[10] Tasmania was a place of social counterfeits and off-key
echoes, where "the convict-class is regarded just as the negroes must be
in South Carolina," and ex-convict shepherds "whistled nigger melodies
in the balmy air."[11] The main veneer, however, was Englishness. In Tasmania one found every kind of frustrated longing for British privilege and
British aristocracy, but the only proper coat-of-arms would be "a fleece,
and a kangaroo with its pocket picked; and the legend *Sic Fortis Hobartia
crevit*, namely, by fleecing and picking pockets."[12] It was, to Mitchel's
piercing though jaundiced eye, a pathetic replica accurately made from
wrong materials:

> At one o'clock up comes the Hobart Town and Launceston day coach,
> which . . . is precisely like what an English stagecoach was before the
> railroads had swallowed them all up. The road is excellent, the horses
> good. The coachman and guard (prisoners, no doubt) are in manners, dress
> and behaviour as like untransported English guards and coachmen as it is
> possible to conceive. The wayside inns we passed are thoroughly British;
> even, I regret to say, to the very brandy they sell. The passengers all speak
> with an English accent. . . . Every sight and sound . . . remains me that I
> am in a small, misshapen, transported, bastard England; and the legiti-
> mate England itself is not so dear to me that I can love the convict copy.[13]

Even allowing for Mitchel's unconstrained spleen—Tasmania was his
prison, and he an Irish nationalist—no visitors were writing of the mainland colonies in such terms by 1850.

The toxins of convictry would linger in Tasmania for another generation after 1853. There was no sudden purging of the Stain, and even its
old name stuck to it like tar; "Vandemonians," in the eyes of the free

Australian working class, were either criminal drones or tyrants. "During the last twenty years," wrote a journalist as late as 1882,

> I have been thrown among some hundred of immigrants, and I can safely say that not one in a hundred of them knows this island by the name of Tasmania; but it is well-known as Van Diemen's Land; the land of white slavery.

No new felons were coming, but the old ones remained, and the census of 1857 showed that half the adults of both sexes on the island (and 60 percent of the adult men) were either convicts or Emancipists.[14] It took the Old Hands another thirty years to die off, and in the meantime they supplied most of the crime in Tasmania. In 1848–49 convicts and Emancipists formed 68 percent of the population but committed 93 percent of its serious crimes. In 1866–67, although only about 35 percent of the adults there had gone through the System, the convicts and Emancipists were responsible for 70 percent of the crime. In this period, Tasmania had the highest crime rate in Australia: 1.72 Supreme Court convictions per 1,000 people, as against 1.3 in New South Wales, 1.18 in Victoria and 0.61 in South Australia.

Meanwhile the refuse of the System—the broken, the unhinged, the helpless, the mad and the abandoned—clogged the institutions of Tasmania. What transportation produced in them was not Victorian "manliness" but abject neurosis. Ticket-of-leave men from the Probation System were scattered all over the interior—debilitated, muttering odd-jobbers who were known, with the usual finesse of Australian slang, as "old crawlers." In 1867, a clergyman recalled meeting one of the "old crawlers" in the employ of a former naval officer. The retired salt boasted that he had had his man "flogged times without number. . . . I have put a rope around his neck, and on horseback dragged him back and forth through that pond. . . . But it was all of no use, the man will not leave my service." At which the Reverend John Morison reflected that the worn-out incorrigible "must have been so habituated to punishment that it had become a kind of necessity to him, and likely he felt at times uneasy if he did not receive any; all that was human in his nature must have been well-nigh lashed out of him, leaving nothing but . . . the nature of a spaniel dog."[15]

A few "old crawlers" did not crawl. One of the *frissons* of Anthony Trollope's visit to Tasmania was his journey to Port Arthur in January 1872. There, he interviewed one of its last fifteen or so prisoners, an Irishman from Londonderry named Dennis Doherty, one of "the heroes of the place . . . who told us that for forty-two years he had never been a free man for an hour." Doherty was tall, heavily tattooed, with a large cleft chin and one small gray eye. He had enlisted in the 16th Lancers as a boy, and he was still a lad of eighteen in May 1833 when a court-martial in Guernsey sentenced him to 14 years' transportation for desertion. From that point on, he traversed the whole of the System. In 1837 the Sydney Supreme Court sentenced him to life imprisonment on Norfolk Island as a bushranger. After four years, he feigned madness well enough to be repatriated to Sydney. He was reconvicted at Berrima Quarter Sessions, in New South Wales, for bushranging in 1841, and returned to Norfolk Island for his second life sentence. A year later, he went on the Probation System to Port Arthur. In 1844 he was sent back among the hard cases to Norfolk Island. On the way he tried to seize the brig *Governor Phillip*, for which he received his third life sentence. In 1853 Doherty returned to Van Diemen's Land, or Tasmania as it was now called, to serve out the rest of his probation. Two years later, he received his fourth life sentence for assaulting a man with a stolen gun. And so it had gone on. Over the years, Doherty told the astonished Trollope, he had received more than 3,000 lashes. "In appearance," the writer noted, "he was a large man and still powerful, well to look at in spite of his eye, lost as he told us through the miseries of prison life. But he said that he was broken at last." Doherty had made his last escape attempt three weeks before and had been brought back "almost starved to death":

> He had been always escaping, always rebelling, always fighting against authority, and always being flogged. There had been a whole life of torment such as this; forty-two years of it; and there he stood, speaking softly, arguing his case well, and pleading while the tears ran down his face for some kindness, for some mercy in his old age. "I have tried to escape; always to escape," he said, "as a bird does out of a cage. Is that unnatural; is that a great crime?" The man's first offence, that of mutiny [sic], is not one at which the mind revolts. I did feel for him, and when he spoke of himself as a caged bird, I should have liked to take him out into the world, and have given him a month of comfort. He would probably, however, have knocked my brains out at the first opportunity. I was assured that he was thoroughly bad, irredeemable, not to be reached by any kindness, a beast of prey, whose hand was against every honest man, and against whom it was necessary that every honest man should raise his hand. Yet he talked so gently and so well, and argued his case with such winning words! He was writing in a book when we entered his cell ... "Just scribbling, sir," he said, "to while away the hours."[16]

Dennis Doherty was then fifty-seven, and his conduct record, which Trollope had not been able to see, bears out what he said of his life. It is a litany of almost inconceivable suffering and defiance, pages long—lashes, chains, gang labor, solitary confinement, for offenses that ran from "Absconding" and "Mutiny" to "Having a Crayfish in his possession without authorization."

By the 1870s, Tasmania had more paupers, lunatics, orphans and invalids than South Australia and Queensland combined, concentrated in a population less than half of theirs. Despite the labor shortage, most ex-convicts were discriminated against, usually with a sullen reflexive viciousness, by the freeborn. They were regarded as lazy, improvident, unworthy to own land; and as the Victorian animus against homosexuals grew ever stronger in Australia after 1850, so did the belief that most convicts were sexually tainted. "The growing dread of the frightful practices to which it is well known many of them are addicted," remarked a Parliamentary committee in 1860, "render[s] their search for employment often tedious and difficult." In contrast to the ex-convicts of New South Wales, the felonry of Tasmania was so fettered by social prejudice that it could never rise. Moreover, the laws governing their work and their relations to their employers retained, dilute but unmistakable, the iron and gall of the System. Thus, under the 1856 Master and Servants Act, masters had the power to arrest their servants, and it was quite legal for an employer (or any member of his family) to put a hired hand in custody on suspicion of an offense and keep him confined for a week without trial. The extraordinary fact was that this law remained on the statute books of Tasmania for more than a generation; in 1882, the Legislative Council rejected efforts to repeal the employer's right of arrest. This would not have happened so late in New South Wales, with its working-class resentment of authority, its ethos of mateship and its mistrust of "boss-cockies."

By and large, Tasmanian Emancipists showed very little sense of themselves as a political group, so that "the large ex-convict component in the population probably retarded the growth of radical and working-class politics."[17] Probably this was because so few Irish convicts were sent there. Forty percent of all transported felons went to Van Diemen's Land. But in the period 1812–1853, only fifty-one transports sailed from Ireland to Hobart, an average of hardly more than one ship a year.[18] As a result, the proportion of Irish to English convicts was far, far smaller in Van Diemen's Land than in New South Wales; and the percentage of Catholics was about half that on the mainland—17 percent of the white Tasmanian population, bond and free. The Irish were not a powerful minority in Tasmania, and they never became one. The residual clan collectivism that they had brought to New South Wales, which would give such a strong root to the anti-authoritarian, stick-together ethos of the mainland workers, scarcely existed in Tasmania. The exaggerated "Englishness" of post-penal Tasmania was one result of this, since the thin colonial elite etched its values on the classes below it.

So Tasmania is a problem for those who would like to believe that most Australian bush virtues—intransigence, sticking to your "mate," distrust of judge, trap and nob, unpolished self-reliance, democratic and brusquely dissenting temper—were created by the convict system. If this were so, one would naturally expect these traits to be vividly emblazoned on the social fabric of Tasmania, the colony with the highest density of convicts and their descendants. But they were not. Workers were less sure of themselves as a class there than in New South Wales, because they were selling their labor in a buyer's market: Tasmania nearly always had a glut of hands, New South Wales a shortage. Moreover, Tasmania had little sense of the frontier and hence no context in which the "bush ethos," however sentimentalized, could flourish. It could not expand, and this marked its people. It remained a close-settled, leaf-green microcosm, where the roving bush-worker, beholden to no squatter and picking up his check where he wandered, was a complete anomaly. Nomads made respectable Tasmanians wince; they thought of escaped probation gangers.

What convictry left to the island, then, was the very opposite of its supposed legacy in New South Wales: a malleable and passive working class, paternalistic institutions, a tame press and colonized Anglophile values. The idea that rebels are the main product of oppression is a consoling fiction. In any penal society the rebel is always the exception and never the rule. Tasmania was a factory, a "mill for grinding rogues honest," which turned out an unleavened human mass, a submissive *lumpenproletariat* of men and women, cudgelled into humility by repetitive task-work and the all-pervasive threat of corporal punishment. They had learned to eat out of the hand of Authority, because Authority had always fed them. They illustrated the melancholy truth of Vauvenargues's maxim: "Servitude debases men to the point where they end up liking it." And because there were so many of them in proportion to the free population, immigration being so slight, Authority was harder on them than in post-penal New South Wales. The depth of virulence of Tasmania's obsession with the Stain still astonished visitors from the mainland in the 1890s, even though by then hardly any Old Hands remained alive.

Yet there is no doubt that bitter memories of the System were sometimes a deep source of energy of Australian independence—on the mainland. John Fawkner (1792–1869), the "Grand Old Man of Victoria," who with John Batman settled Port Phillip Bay and founded Melbourne on the Yarra River in 1835, was a convict's son, who shipped with his father to the first settlement of Hobart Town in 1803. Growing up with convicts, he sided with them as a class. When he was twenty-two, his sympathies were confirmed in blood and agony: He helped seven prisoners build a lugger to escape to South America, but it was captured and Fawkner, implicated, received 500 lashes. He carried the cat's claw-marks on his skin—the essential text of a power he loathed—for the rest of his life. But he also worked and cheated, made money, turned himself into a "bush lawyer," started newspapers of liberal-radical bias in Van Diemen's Land and then in Victoria, and campaigned vituperatively for the rights of convicts and small settlers. Fawkner spent fifteen years on the Legislative Council of Victoria as a populist gadfly, "the tribune of the people." His target was the big sheep-grazing families that had "locked up the land" for themselves, growing fat from convict labor and hungry for more. He saw transportation itself, not the transportees, as the shame of Australia; he wanted to foster a society of yeomen farmers. Fawkner's stubborn, cantankerous altruism was rooted in his experience of convict Tasmania, but it only became politically effective in the wider arena of the mainland.

By the mid-1830s, the struggle for Emancipists' rights had been won, and it would never pay another Australian politician—as it had paid Wentworth, on his long progress toward fantasies of colonial aristocracy—to campaign for ex-convicts as a group. The idea of a convicts' party was absurd, and there were no political advantages in displaying one's own convict past—or that of one's parents. On the contrary: The drawbacks were extreme. Australians, especially well-to-do and powerful Australians, retained no sympathy with or interest in the convict past. They only wanted to forget it. The exceptions were mostly working-class Irish, mainly in New South Wales, among whom convict memory was concentrated and to some degree fetishized. It survived because it linked up to an older tissue of recollection, the general pattern of English oppression of the Irish. It tended to produce a dug-in clannishness, the attitude of a "mental ghetto . . . a thought-universe of harsh conflict," as the historian Miriam Dixson called it.[19]

If it did contribute to Australian egalitarianism, then it did so in a most unamiable way. In the 1830s, astute observers like Maconochie and his associate Alexander Cheyne felt that the primary division of Australian society into two classes, the bond and the free, tended to flatten distinctions of class between free men by concentrating their hostility on the convicts below them. "The habit which most of the free contract," Cheyne told the Molesworth Committee,

> of thinking and speaking of and treating the convicts contemptuously, is, by a very natural process extended to the whole species; and hence the want of respect and deference to others which is so universally manifested.[20]

By the same token, the importance of being a free man and not a convict "has a tendency to break down the distinctions conceded in the mother country, *and thus to place the whole free population on a nearly equal footing.*" Contempt was repaid in hatred; convicts and ex-convicts "regard with settled antipathies, nearly amounting to hatred, all who have not been, or who are not prisoners; and, when not repressed by self-interest, this is plainly exhibited."

Not all the roots of Australian egalitarianism can be idealized. Bush comradeship was real, but so was the defensive, static, levelling, two-class hatred that came out of convictry. From it ran an undertow of impotent dreams of vengeance, as in the hope of Australia's republican bush poet of the late nineteenth century, Henry Lawson, that the poor man would be educated up *and* the rich man educated down. By the turn of the century, most connections between early Australian socialist temper and the resentments of the convict past were conventional matters of ritual invocation—or else, they were buried by workers who cherished their right to be respected and no more wanted to be identified with criminal ancestors than the Chartists of an earlier day in England had wished to be associated with thieves and footpads. When such connections surfaced, they took their popular, idealized form, with the convicts presented as shining innocent poachers, Chartists and apple-stealing children, and the bushrangers as Robin Hoods.

The "convict past" is a shadowy behavioral catch-all today. Thus, it made Australians cynical about Authority; or else it made them conformists. As so many Australians are conformist skeptics, the "convict legacy" is seen to be all the more pervasive. Perhaps there are roots of social conduct that wind obscurely back to the convict era, and the familiar Australian habit of cursing authority behind the hand while truckling to its face may well be one of them; it may also be that Australian sexism receives some of its force from the brutal psychic legacy of carceral life. But since the vast majority of European Australians are the descendants either of Anglo-Irish-Scots who arrived after 1850, or of Greeks, Italians, Hungarians, Balts, Poles and Germans who emigrated after 1945, this seems a sterile line of inquiry.

Would Australians have done anything differently if their country had not been settled as the jail of infinite space? Certainly they would. They would have remembered more of their own history. The obsessive cultural enterprise of Australians a hundred years ago was to forget it entirely, to sublimate it, to drive it down into unconsulted recesses. This affected all Australian culture, from political rhetoric to the perception of space, of landscape itself. Space, in America, had always been optimistic; the more of it you faced, the freer you were—"Go West, young man!" In Australian terms, to go west was to die, and space itself was the jail. The flowering of Australian nature as a cultural emblem, whether in poetry or in painting, could not occur until the stereotype of the "melancholy bush," born in convict perceptions of Nature-as-prison, had been expunged. A favorite trope of journalism and verse at the time of the Australian Centennial, in 1888, was that of the nation as a young vigorous person gazing into the rising sun, turning his or her back on the dark crouching shadows of the past. A "Centennial Song" published in the Melbourne *Argus* struck the right note of defensive optimism, coupling it with an appeal to censor early Australian history—or, preferably, not to write it at all:

> Is it manly, fair or honest with our early sins to stain
> What we aimed at, worked for, conquered—aye—an honest, noble name?
> And those scribes whose gutter pleasure is to air the hideous past,
> Let us leave them to the loathesome mould in which their mind is cast.
> Look ahead and not behind us! Look to what is sunny, bright—
> Look into our glorious future, not into our shadowed night.

At the heart of each proclamation of renewal was a longing for amnesia. And Australians embarked on this quest for oblivion with go-getting energy. They wanted to forget that their forefathers had ever been, or even rubbed shoulders with, government men; and before long, they succeeded.

Nobody could deny that convicts had once been in Australia. Indeed, some of the "old crawlers" were still alive, though only just, in 1888. But they were not invited to crawl in the parades, and the Centenary was not heavy with historical retrospection. One dipped one's brush in the Stain, to put in a little darkness behind the radiant bouquet of wattle, wheat, Union Jacks and Golden Fleeces that symbolized Australia's present and future prosperity. One hinted, in the text of commemorative albums that bore cartouches of kookaburras and paddle steamers stamped in gold leaf on their covers, that dreadful things had been done in the remote colonial days of Australia, but new pages must not be sullied; that it was time to draw the curtain at last on so much indignity and suffering and to contemplate the Dawn. "The convict stage is now forgotten as a dream," wrote one of these Centennial boosters. "Today New South Wales . . . has an annual import and export trade of nearly £50,000,000, . . . 1727 miles of railway, . . . 19,000 miles of telegraph wires." In Tasmania, "slowly but surely Nature is reclaiming her own, and is effacing the memorials of an infamy which none care to look back upon. Chapter after chapter might be written on the annals of Port Arthur, but they would be inconsonant with the tone [of] these pages."[21]

Whenever they could, the instruments of official culture tried to play down the obdurate attachment of the Australian rank and file to its bushranger folk-heroes, to the distant memory of Bold Jack Donohoe and the recent one of Ned Kelly. The memory of the English officer and his punishment-book, of the whole detested machinery and practice of forced labor and flogging, was shifted into the background as one of the things on which it was unhealthy to "dwell."

Australian politicians conceived and ran the Centenary as a lavish feast of jingoism, a tribute to the benevolent, all-embracing British Empire. Without Britain's market, Australian business could not survive; without her institutions, especially the Monarchy, Australian morality would decay; without her dreadnoughts, Australian blood would be yellowed by hordes of invading junks. Bunting, flags, parades, speeches and more bunting were rammed down the popular throat, and only republicans gagged on them.

The organ of their protest was *The Bulletin*, that anti-imperialist paper, which excoriated the whole idea of the Centennial as a slavish feast of Australian dependence. Australia, it argued, began its first hundred years as a penal colony, but was finishing them as an economic and political one. Its irons had been struck off but nothing else had changed. One of its cartoonists made this point with a pair of drawings: the first, labelled 1788, of an Irish convict dancing a jig in his chains for the amusement of an English officer; the second of a modern bush-settler in his cabbage-tree hat, doing the same dance for John Bull in 1888. In an editorial headlined "The Day We Were Lagged," *The Bulletin* called the celebrations "a feeble, fifth-rate drunk—a sort of combined scalp dance and gin conversazione—in honour of the meanest event in [our] short history."[22] The Australian Centenary was a "feeble copy" of the American one of 1876: "The elements of grandeur are entirely wanting. The great Republic rejoiced, not on account of an empty flight of years, which pass alike for man and beast . . . but in honour of the triumph of liberty over grasping tyranny. Australia, on the other hand, celebrates a century which begins and ends alike in nothing. A hundred years have left her as they found her—a name but not a nation, a huge continent content to be the hanger-on of a little island."[23] However unwelcome these sentiments, there was a good deal of truth in them, and even more in the connection *The Bulletin* drew between imperialisms past and present:

> The day which inaugurated a reign of slavery and loathesomeness and moral leprosy—is the occasion for which we are called upon to rejoice with an exceeding great joy. Yet there might be a palliation even for this, if Australia could show that she had shaken off the old fetters and the old superstitions of that dark era. . . . [B]ut the old slavish taint still clings to her garments, and her chains of iron are merely exchanged for chains of gold.[24]

English capital, the editorial went on, was imported every day to develop Australian resources—"and, naturally enough, the English capitalist takes the resources themselves for his pains." It was better to be poor and independent, *The Bulletin* urged, pointing to Chile, Mexico, Switzerland, and above all the Boer Republic, whose "little army of farmers almost exterminated the gaudy troops of England and slaughtered their aristocratic commander at Matuta Hill. . . . [E]ven the effeminate soldiers of Egypt made a gallant struggle before their native land sank into a feudatory of England, but Australia, by the mouth of such 'representative statesmen' as GILLIES and PARKES, declares herself to be something meaner than Egypt and lower than the Boer Republic. The declaration is one which fits the occasion and does honour to the anniversary of the day on which our first families were—exported."[25]

Nothing could be allowed to diminish the gratitude Australians were meant to feel for the imperial umbrella. The essence of colonization was that they could claim no history of their own. Some thirty years before the Centenary, the English gold-seeker John Sherer had complained of the historical blankness of the antipodean landscape, where nothing recognizable had happened for millennia:

> There can be no walk, no journey of any kind, more monotonous than one through the bush. . . . There is no association of the past connected with it. Your sight is never regaled with the "ruins grey" of some fine old fortress. . . . Imagination is at a standstill—fairly *bogged*, as your body may be in the mud-swamp. There are no sacred groves . . . No time-hallowed fanes, sanctified by the recollections of hospitable deeds . . . No fields, recalling the downfall of tyranny . . . Nothing whatever to visit as a spot noted as being capable of exalting the mind by the memories with which it is associated. No locality, memorable as the haunt of genius. No birthplaces of great men . . . Nothing of this kind; all is dully-dead, uninspiring mud-work.[26]

But if the landscape carried no such litany of association, Australian children would; they were made to read the novels of Walter Scott and the deeds of Sir Francis Drake, to recite like parrots the names of English kings, the dates of unexplained events like the Rump Parliament and the Gunpowder Plot, the lengths of European rivers they would never see— while, as the poet Henry Lawson complained in the *Republican* in 1888, they were shown nothing of Australian history earlier than 1850. Educators played their part, with the result that it became impossible to find, in any history book used in Australian schools up to the mid-1960s, a satisfactory or even coherent account of penal Australia. For what was this meager "history"? A chronicle of provincial misery; a minor episode in English imperial policy, best forgotten. What was distant in time and space was real; what was close had been sublimated into the substance of bad social dreams.

Amnesia and shame nibbled at the edges of the record, without altering it much. A citizen might ink over his family name in a ship's bound indent; the record books of trials and convictions at country benches in New South Wales would sometimes be burnt, so as not to inflict social pain on innocent descendants. But the mountain of paper the System left behind it was too huge to be removed.

Paper outlives stone and brick. Most of the buildings directly associated with the System in Australia are long gone. Most historically significant structures raised in New South Wales before 1835 or in Tasmania before 1850—churches, stores, town halls, courts, villas, station homesteads, bridges—were built, wholly or in part, by convict labor. Many of them remain, especially in Tasmania, which did not have enough money to pull them down and build new ones. But there seemed little point in keeping obsolete jails and barracks standing as souvenirs of a haunted past, and the few that survive only narrowly escaped a general demolition. On Norfolk Island, the pentagonal New Jail and the huge Prisoners' Barracks at Kingston, along with many lesser structures, were torn down for building-stone by the new inhabitants who moved in after the last convicts left—the descendants of Fletcher Christian's mutineers and their Tahitian women, relocated from Pitcairn Island in 1856. Except for the eroded foundations of cells that protrude illegibly from the green carpet of turf, little is left in the compound, and even the walls and gates themselves, raised so high by the sweating gangs, were narrowly saved from being bulldozed to create a picnic park in 1959. At the head of Sydney Cove, now renamed Circular Quay, nothing speaks of the convict past; a banal modern sculpture of two joined bronze ellipses, which might represent leg-irons, turns out to be an allegory of the bonds of friendship between Sydney and Portsmouth. There is no monument of any kind to the men and women of the First Fleet, and none appears to be planned for the Bicentennial in 1988.

Yet despite neglect, amnesia and a thousand unconscious acts of censorship, the System did continue to flourish in popular memory—as Grand Guignol. One of the few tourist attractions of Hobart in the 1880s was the *Success*, a convict hulk that had lain in Port Phillip Bay for years and had acquired a delectably bloody reputation, as its prisoners had joined in the killing of "The Demon," John Price. Entrepreneurs had bought her and fitted her out with dummy convicts and an imposing array of fetters, gratings, handcuffs, punishment-bands, balls, chains and cats, all genuine (such things had not become expensive colonial antiques at the time), along with the black iron armor worn by the bush-ranger Ned Kelly at his last stand at Glenrowan. When most of the population of Tasmania had trooped through her, the owners sailed *Success* to Sydney in the hope of bigger crowds. She was promptly censored: Scuttled in the dead of night by indignant citizens who did not wish to be reminded of the Stain, *Success* sank at her moorings with the loss of all waxworks.

The *locus classicus* remained unsinkable. Port Arthur was closed down in 1877. By then, its roster of inmates had dwindled to 64 convicts still serving their accumulated sentences, 126 paupers and 79 lunatics. They were transferred to Hobart; the convicts came ashore in handcuffs and leg-irons, even though most of them were old and infirm, before a gaping and giggling crowd.

In its last years it had been visited not only by Anthony Trollope but by the young Australian novelist and journalistic hackabout Marcus Clarke, who had pored over a mass of documentation on con-victry in the Melbourne Public Library and, inspired by Victor Hugo's *Les Misérables* and Alexandre Dumas's *The Count of Monte Cristo*, had decided to write his own epic of crime and punishment. Clarke's *His Natural Life* began running as a serial in the *Australian Journal* in March 1870. It ran for two years, and in the end it lost most of its readers. But its appearance as a book in 1874 revived it—and, with it, came a revival of popular interest in the System and its dreaded epitome, Port Arthur.

Clarke and his followers impressed the full character of Grand Guig-nol on the place, for they knew their audience. Why, not so long ago, did one hear "oral traditions" (tall stories for tourists) about collective sui-cides of children jumping, like lemmings, from the cliffs at Point Puer to evade the miseries of flogging and rape; about slavering convicts eating the dead in the darkness of Commandant Booth's mineshafts? Because, given the lack of serious historical writing about transportation for more than seventy years after Clarke's novel was published, its stories became "true."

Port Arthur inhumanity had been made its central myth long before —by George Arthur's enemies in the Van Diemen's Land press. In the 1870s, when Clarke and Price Warung (followed by a horde of penny-a-liners) began to write their versions of the System, the myth had be-come "reality" and so could be re-invested with fantasy. Hence Clarke's goriest episodes, such as the cannibalism of Gabbett at Port Arthur (a thinly disguised version of the escape of Pearce), were shifted from Macquarie Harbor in the 1820s to the Tasman Peninsula in the 1830s, and used to "typify" the System. Likewise, Clarke's suicide of Tommy and Billy, the little Point Puer boys who jump from the cliff, is

one of the finest heart-wringers in Victorian fiction—a penal answer to
the death of Little Nell:

> "I can do it now," said Tommy. "I feel strong."
> "Will it hurt much, Tommy?" said Billy, who was not so courageous.
> "Not so much as a whipping."
> "I'm afraid! Oh, Tom, it's so deep! Don't leave me, Tom!"
> The bigger baby took his little handkerchief from his neck, and with
> it bound his left hand to his companion's right.
> "Now I can't leave you."
> "What was it the Lady that kissed us said, Tommy?"
> "Lord have pity on them two fatherless children!" repeated Tommy.
> "Let's say it, Tom."
> And so the two babies knelt down on the brink of the cliff, and, raising
> the bound hands together, looked up at the sky, and said, "Lord have pity
> on us two fatherless children!" And then they kissed each other, and did
> it.[27]

Nothing like this ever happened at Point Puer, but the tourists loved it.
On fine weekends in the late 1870s and through the '80s, hundreds of
trippers would descend on it from Hobart in paddlewheel steamers,
shrieking with agitation as they were locked for a few minutes in the
pitch-black, stony silence of the Dumb Cells, chattering happily as their
boots crunched through the debris in the echoing penitentiary dormito-
ries. Sometimes a visitor would be able to buy a rusty leg-ring or a rotted
hobnail boot from one of the "locals" who, now that Port Arthur had
been officially renamed Carnavon and re-incorporated as a town, were
trickling back to the Tasman Peninsula. The appetite for carceral souvenirs had not been lost on a Hobart photographer named John Watt Beattie, who documented the buildings and some of the surviving Old Hands
of Port Arthur and even visited Norfolk Island. He also printed postcards
of prison emblems—elaborate still lifes of leg-irons, cuffs, keys, guards'
carbines and paraphernalia from the Model Prison, surrounded by swags
of leaves and wildflowers.

It was well that he made such records of the detested past, for not
long afterward the long-impending fate of Sodom struck the Tasman
Peninsula. First, there was an earthquake; then, in 1897, a bushfire consumed the penal settlement. It raged in the great four-story penitentiary
for two days and nights, and the Model Prison, that ominous replication
of Pentonville in the south, once the silent hive of hooded and numbered
human drones, was gutted. Many Tasmanians had difficulty concealing
their glee and wished only to demolish the ruins. The visitor today,
wandering through what remains of the penitentiary with other tourists,
can hardly grasp the isolation it once stood for. Perhaps that is easier

deduced from Nature itself, from the barely penetrable labyrinth of space that England chose as its abode of crime; and to see that, one need only go to the black basalt cliffs that frame the Tasman Peninsula, crawl through the bushes to their unfenced rim and gaze down on the wide, wrinkled, glimmering sheet of our imprisoning sea.

Appendixes

Abbreviations

Notes

Bibliography

Index

Appendixes

APPENDIX 1

Governors and Chief Executives of New South Wales, 1788–1855

Capt. Arthur Phillip, R.N. (1738–1814), Gov.	Jan. 1788–Dec. 1792
Maj. Francis Grose (1758?–1814), Lt.-Gov.	Dec. 1792–Dec. 1794
Capt. William Paterson (1755–1810), Administrator	Dec. 1794–Sept. 1795
Capt. John Hunter, R.N. (1737–1821), Gov.	Sept. 1795–Sept. 1800
Lieut. Philip Gidley King, R.N. (1758–1808), Gov.	Sept. 1800–Aug. 1806
Capt. William Bligh, R.N. (1754–1817), Gov.	Aug. 1806– Jan. 1810
Lt.-Col. Lachlan Macquarie (1762–1824), Gov.	Jan. 1810–Dec. 1821
Sir Thomas Brisbane (1773–1860), Gov.	Dec. 1821–Nov. 1825
Sir Ralph Darling (1775–1858), Gov.	Nov. 1825–Dec. 1831
Sir Richard Bourke (1777–1855), Gov.	Dec. 1831– Oct. 1837
Sir George Gipps (1791–1847), Gov.	Oct. 1837– July 1846
Sir Charles Fitzroy (1796–1858), Gov.-General	Aug. 1846– Jan. 1855

APPENDIX 2

Chief Executives of Van Diemen's Land, 1803–53

Lieut. John Bowen, R.N.	Sept. 1803– Feb. 1804
Col. David Collins, R.M., Lt.-Gov.	Feb. 1804–Mar. 1810
Lt. Edward Lord, R.M.	Mar. 1810– July 1810
Capt. John Murray, 73rd Regt.	July 1810– Feb. 1812
Lt.-Col. Andrew Geils, 73rd Regt.	Feb. 1812– Feb. 1813
Col. Thomas Davey, R.M., Lt.-Gov.	Feb. 1813– Apr. 1817
Col. William Sorell, Lt.-Gov.	Apr. 1817– May 1824
Col. George Arthur, Lt.-Gov.	May 1824– Oct. 1836
Lt.-Col. K. Snodgrass, Acting Lt.-Gov.	Oct. 1836– Jan. 1837
Sir John Franklin, R.N., Lt.-Gov.	Jan. 1837–Aug. 1843
Sir John E. Eardley-Wilmot, Lt.-Gov.	Aug. 1843– Oct. 1846
C. J. Latrobe, Administrator	Oct. 1846– Jan. 1847
Sir William Denison, Lt.-Gov.	Jan. 1847– Jan. 1855

APPENDIX 3

Secretaries of State for the Colonies, *1794–1855*

Evan Nepean, as under secretary of state to Lord Sydney in the Home Department, was chiefly responsible for the arrangements for the First Fleet and the administration of the colony up to 1794. Thereafter it passed into the hands of a succession of secretaries of state for [war and] the colonies:

	Month appointed
H. Dundas	July 1794
Lord Hobart	Mar. 1791
Earl of Camden	May 1804
Viscount Castlereagh	July 1805
W. Windham	Feb. 1806
Viscount Castlereagh	Mar. 1807
Earl of Liverpool	Nov. 1809
Earl of Bathurst	June 1812
Viscount Goderich	Apr. 1827
W. Huskisson	Sept. 1827
Sir George Murray	May 1828
Viscount Goderich	Nov. 1830
E. G. Smith Stanley	Apr. 1833
T. Spring Rice	June 1834
Duke of Wellington	Nov. 1834
Earl of Aberdeen	Dec. 1834
C. Grant	Apr. 1835
Marquess of Normanby	Feb. 1839
Lord John Russell	Sept. 1839
Lord Stanley	Sept. 1841
W. E. Gladstone	Dec. 1845
Earl Grey	July 1846
Sir John Pakington	Feb. 1852
Duke of Newcastle	Dec. 1852
Sir Henry George Grey	June 1854
Hon. S. Herbert	Feb. 1855
Lord J. Russell	May 1855
Sir W. Molesworth	July 1855
H. Labouchere	Nov. 1855

Abbreviations

ADB	*Australian Dictionary of Biography.*
AJPH	*Australian Journal of Politics and History.*
ANZJM	*Australian and New Zealand Journal of Medicine.*
Bigge NSW	John Bigge, "Report of the Commissioner of Inquiry into the State of the Colony of New South Wales," *Great Britain, Parliamentary Papers* 1822, vol. 20, paper #448.
BL	British Library
BT	Bonwick Transcripts, Mitchell Library, Sydney.
Clark *HA* 1–4	C. M. H. Clark, *A History of Australia,* vols. 1–4.
CO	Colonial Office Records, Public Record Office, London.
Col. Sec.	Colonial Secretary.
CON	Convict Department Records, Van Diemen's Land.
Con. Disc. 1, 1846	*Correspondence re Convict Discipline,* ordered to be printed February 9, 1846, containing: (1) Secondary Punishment, pp. 1–139; (2) Convict Discipline and (3) Convict Discipline and Convict Estimates, pp. 141–259.
Con. Disc. 2, 1846	*Correspondence re Convict Discipline,* ordered to be printed February 9, 1846, pp. 1–69, PP (HL) 1846, vol. 7.
Con. Disc. 3, 1846	*Correspondence re Convict Discipline,* ordered to be printed June 12, 1846, pp. 1–77, PP (HL) 1846, vol. 7.
Con. Disc. 4, 1846	*Correspondence between the Secretary of State . . . and the Governor of New South Wales, respecting the Convict System Administered in Norfolk Island, Under the Superintendence of Captain Maconochie R.N.,* ordered to be printed February 23, 1846, pp. 1–169, PP (HL) 1846, vol. 7.
Con. Disc. 1847	*Correspondence Relative to Convict Discipline,* PP (HL) 1847, vol. 8, pp. 1–250.
Con. Disc. 1850	*Correspondence Relative to Convict Discipline,* PP (HL) 1850, vol. 11, pp. 1–282.
Con. Disc. 1853	*Further Correspondence on Convict Discipline and Transportation,* PP (HL) 1852–3, vol. 18.
Cook *EL*	Thomas Cook, *The Exile's Lamentations.*
Corr. Military Operations 1831	*Copies of all Correspondence between Lieutenant-Governor Arthur and His Majesty's Secretary of State for the Colonies, on the Subject of the Military Operations lately carried out against the Aboriginal Inhabitants of Van Diemen's Land,* PP (HC) #259, pp. 1–86, September 23, 1831.

Crowley, *Doc. Hist.*	Frank Crowley, *A Documentary History of Australia.*
CSO	Colonial Secretary's Office Records, Van Diemen's Land.
DRO	Derbyshire Record Office.
FLB	Joseph Foveaux, "Letter Book, 1800–1804."
GO	Governor's Office, Tasmania.
HO	Home Office Records, Public Records Office, London.
HRA	Historical Records of Australia (Series 1).
HRNSW	Historical Records of New South Wales.
HS	*Historical Studies of Australia and New Zealand.*
JAS	*Journal of Australian Studies.*
JRAHS	*Journal of Royal Australian Historical Society.*
LF	Laurence Frayne, *Memoirs of Norfolk Island.*
LH	*Labour History.*
LRO	Lancashire Record Office, Preston, Lancashire.
MJA	*Medical Journal of Australia.*
ML	Mitchell Library, Sydney.
NLA	National Library of Australia, Canberra.
NSW	New South Wales.
NSWA	Archives Office of New South Wales, Sydney.
NSW V & P	Votes and Proceedings of the Legislative Council of New South Wales.
PC	Privy Council Papers.
PHR	*Pacific Historical Review.*
PP	Parliamentary Papers, Great Britain (Lords and/or Commons).
PRO	Public Records Office, London.
RAHJ	*Royal Australian Historical Journal.*
Robson, *Hist. Tas.*	Lloyd L. Robson, *A History of Tasmania.*
SC 1798	*Report of the Select Committee on Transportation*, PP 1798.
SC1812	*Report of the Select Committee on Transportation*, PP 1812.
SC 1832	*Report of the Select Committee on Secondary Punishments*, PP 1832.
SC 1837–38 (i)	*Report of the Select Committee on Transportation* ("Molesworth Report," part i), PP 1837.
SC 1837–38 (ii)	*Report of the Select Committee on Transportation* ("Molesworth Report," part ii), PP 1838.
Shaw *CC*	A. G. L. Shaw, *Convicts and the Colonies.*
SMH	*Sydney Morning Herald.*
SPO	State Paper Office, Dublin.
THRA, PP	Tasmanian Historical Research Association, Papers and Proceedings.
TSA	Tasmanian State Archives, Hobart.
UTL	University of Tasmania Library, Hobart.
VDL	Van Diemen's Land.

Notes

CHAPTER ONE *The Harbor and the Exiles*

1. Jeremy Bentham, *Panopticon Versus New South Wales*, p. 7.
2. The numbers given for convicts transported vary widely; Shaw *CC* gives a total of some 156,000, Robson (*The Convict Settlers of Australia*) the same, others as high as 162,000.
3. John Hunter, *An Historical Journal of the Transactions at Port Jackson and Norfolk Island*, p. 77.
4. On the prevalence of imported stereotypes of landscape among colonial artists looking at Australian nature, and their gradual resolution toward naturalism in the work of Lycett, Earle and others, see Bernard Smith, *European Vision and the South Pacific, 1768–1850*, esp. Chapter 9, "Colonial Interpretations of the Australian Landscape, 1821–35."
5. Arthur Bowes Smyth, "Journal," ML Sydney. (This has been published as *The Journal of Arthur Bowes Smyth, Surgeon, Lady Penrhyn, 1787–1789*, ed. P. G. Fidlon and R. J. Ryan, Sydney, 1979.)
6. The bloodlines of Australian animals were, by other standards, young. Fossil remains of vertebrates reaching back 200 million years have been found in other continents; in Australia, the earliest such evidence of mammalian life is only about 22 million years old, from the Miocene epoch. The three main and distinctive types of vertebrate that evolved in Australian isolation were ratites (large, flightless birds like the emu), monotremes (egg-laying mammals) and marsupials (pouched mammals).

   On other continents, mammals had increased their genetic efficiency by developing into placentals, in which the embryo grows within the mother's womb, fed by an umbilical cord or placenta. It enjoys this protection for months and so is born relatively well-developed. Marsupials, by contrast, are born when still embryos—hardly bigger than ants. The embryo remains inside the mother's body for no more than a few weeks after fertilization, until it has used up the nutrients in the egg-sac; then out it comes, groping blindly like a grub through the savannah of belly fur, heading for the mother's pouch and, inside that, her teat. There it stays until it is mature enough to get around on its own.
7. J. C. Beaglehole, ed., *The Journals of Captain James Cook on His Voyages of Discovery*, vol. 1, p. 359.
8. C. Lockhart, replying to Circular Letter from Select Committee on the Aborigines, New South Wales V & P (1849): 20.
9. Geoffrey Blainey, *The Triumph of the Nomads*, p. 17.
10. On the as yet unsolved question of the origin of the Australian Aborigines, opinion divides between the "hybridists" and the "homogeneists." A summary of their positions is given by A. G. Thorne in "The Racial Affinities and Origins of the Australian

Aborigines," in Mulvaney and Golson, eds., *Aboriginal Man and Environment in Australia*, pp. 316–25.

Throughout the nineteenth century, and on into the twentieth, it was widely assumed that the Australian Aborigines were all of one racial stock and "practically uniformly homogeneous" (A. A. Abbie, "Physical Characteristics of Australian Aborigines," in *Australian Aboriginal Studies*, pp. 89–107). The exceptions, in this theory, were the insular Tasmanians, believed to be descended from Melanesians who arrived after the rising of the Pacific and the isolation of Tasmania and who never visited the mainland.

A contrary "hybridist" argument was advanced in 1967 by the American anthropologist Joseph B. Birdsell (in his "Preliminary Data on the Trihybrid Origin of the Australian Aborigines," in *Archaeology and Physical Anthropology in Oceania*, vol. 2, pp. 100–155). He proposed that there were three distinct waves of migration from the north in the Quaternary period. The first were a light-skinned, woolly-haired people, physically similar to the hill tribesmen of the Andaman Islands in the Bay of Bengal, whom Birdsell called the Oceanic Negritoids. They were in turn absorbed or driven south by a second wave, the Murrayians (so called because their racial type was conspicuous among the Aborigines of the Murray River), who had straighter hair and sprang from archaic Caucasoid stock. The displaced Oceanic Negritoids, according to this theory, survived in a few pockets in the Queensland rain forests and, retreating south, occupied Tasmania—which was cut off from the continent soon afterward by the rising sea level.

The Murrayians, by this theory, then dominated most of mainland Australia, except for the extreme north. This area, the gateway of the continent, was then invaded by a third race, the Carpenterians, racially similar to the hill peoples of Malaya, who never moved south of Australia's tropical zone.

This theory has been disputed by other anthropologists who argue in favor of a double Australian population; but all around, the evidence is so scanty that, in the words of D. J. Mulvaney, "a century after T. H. Huxley, it remains premature to pronounce for racial heterogeneity or homogeneity" (Mulvaney, *The Prehistory of Australia*, p. 64).

11. Inland movement of coast: Mulvaney, *Prehistory*, p. 136.
12. Ibid., pp. 147–52.
13. On the distribution of tribes and territory around the area of Sydney at the time of European contact, see Norman Tinsdale, *Aboriginal Tribes of Australia*, 2 vols.; for the Iora, vol. 1, p. 193. See also Blainey, *Triumph*, p. 31.
14. Phillip to Banks, Dec. 3, 1791, cit. in John Cobley, *Sydney Cove, 1789–1790*, p. 117.
15. Watkin Tench, *A Complete Account of the Settlement at Port Jackson, in New South Wales . . .* , p. 230.
16. On aboriginal canoes: William Bradley, *A Voyage to New South Wales*, Ms. facsimile ed. (Sydney, 1969), pp. 68–69.
17. The boomerang scarcely appears in First Fleet accounts and there is no printed description of its use before 1804. Hunter does not mention it; and although a boomerang (or at least, a boomerang-like object, curved, symmetrically tapered and about 18 inches long) figures in the plate facing p. 292 of John White's *Journal*, it is described as "an humble kind of scymitar," which suggests that White cannot have seen it in action.
18. George Barrington [pseud.], *The History of New South Wales*, p. 17.
19. Hunter, *Historical Journal*, p. 60.
20. Barrington, *History*, p. 20.
21. Ibid., p. 10.
22. Phillip to Sydney, HRNSW ii:129, May 15, 1788; for the Australian Aborigine as exemplar of "hard" primitivism in contrast to the indolent and peaceable Tahitian, see Smith, *European Vision*, pp. 126–27.
23. John White, cit. in John Cobley, *Sydney Cove, 1788*, p. 30.
24. Predatory aboriginal courtship: Barrington, *History*, p. 35.

25. A. P. Elkin, *The Australian Aborigines*, rev. ed. (Sydney, 1974), pp 159–61.
26. Hunter, *Historical Journal*, p. 64.

CHAPTER TWO   *A Horse Foaled by an Acorn*

1. John Gloag, *Georgian Grace*, p. 54. This attitude is still very much with us; its recent
   monument (1985–86) was a vast and theatrical loan exhibition in Washington, D.C.,
   called *Treasure Houses of England*, in which the English country house was presented
   as the primary "vessel of civilization" and taken as epitomizing the "age" in which it
   flourished. Modern Americans, in particular, like to fantasize about being Georgian
   gentlemen.
2. Henry Mayhew, *London Labour and the London Poor*, vol. 1, pp. 342–43.
3. Robert Blincoe to Central Board on Employment of Children in Manufactories, in PP
   1833, xxi. D3:17–18.
4. Josiah Wedgwood to Peel Committee, in PP 1816, iii:64.
5. Joseph Badder to the Factory Commission of 1833, in PP 1833, xx. Cl:191.
6. Theodore Price to the Peel Committee, in PP 1816, iii:125.
7. Francis Place, cit. in Graham Wallas, *Life of Francis Place*, p. 163.
8. L. Lacombe, *Observations sur Londres . . .*, p. 180.
9. Edward P. Thompson, *The Making of the English Working Class*, pp. 59–60. This
   casual identification of any woman living out of wedlock as a "whore" would cause
   grave confusions about the actual morality of transported women convicts in Australia. The results of such assumptions are discussed in Chapter 8.
10. Henry Fielding, *An Enquiry into the Causes of the Late Increase of Robbers . . .*,
    p. 176.
11. Ibid., p. 92.
12. Jonas Hanway, *The Defects of the Police*, p. 224.
13. On Jonathan Wild, see Christopher Hibbert, *The Roots of Evil*, pp. 47–50.
       Jonathan Wild's career long predates transportation to Australia, but because of its
    effect on English views of the growth of crime it deserves a brief recapitulation here.
    Like thousands of other London toughs, Wild began as a pimp; but within a few years
    he had acquired two brothels and a circle of underground contacts—the human capital
    of the informer's trade. Not content with managing whores and informing, Wild built
    a fortune on the insight, dazzling in its simplicity, that would make all magistrates
    regard him as a national treasure: Although it was illegal to act as a receiver of stolen
    goods (a "fence"), no law forbade you to tell owners where their stolen property was,
    or to share in a reward for that information. Thus Wild set up a profitable business in
    stolen goods without ever touching a stolen object. Instead of buying the candlesticks
    or watches, he took a list of the loot from the thief, item by item. He then went to the
    owner with the news that certain items had fallen into the hands of an "honest
    broker," who had refused to buy them. The thief had fled, leaving the loot in the
    broker's hands, and Wild had been designated to find the owner and arrange for their
    return—provided the fictitious broker were decently rewarded for his honesty and
    civic spirit. This suited the thieves well, as Wild paid better than ordinary fences who
    only gave about 10 percent of value on stolen goods. It satisfied the law, as he only
    shared in a legal reward, and the sketchiness of eighteenth-century records made it
    difficult to disprove the broker's existence. It pleased the owners, because it was their
    one good chance of getting their property back. Most of all, it gratified Wild. He made
    £10,000 off it in fifteen years, the equivalent of a fairly large landed income.
       Parliament, startled by the sums he and others were pulling through this legal
    loophole, attempted to close it in 1718 with an act that made it a crime equal to theft
    to accept a reward for restoring goods without prosecuting the thief (4 Geo. I, c. 11, s.
    4). In response, Wild merely shifted his tactics a little. He told the robbed householders
    who arrived in a daily stream at his office in Cock Lane to leave their money in cash
    in a designated place, and their possessions were returned to them the same day. Thus

there was no record of Wild even handling the money, let alone the loot. Before long Wild had done business with thousands of criminals and knew them by name. He kept files on them, listing their specialties; with these, he boasted, he could hang any thief in London. His next step was to use his leverage as England's top fence to shape the raw material of English crime, marshalling the scattered efforts of thieves, cut-purses and coiners across the nation into a corporate pattern. Starting with London, Wild organized gangs in every district of England. He had specialists trained in all kinds of theft and employed his own jewelers to melt plate and break up jewelry. He set up a rental service in burglars' tools and ran stolen goods to Holland in his own cargo sloop. London was his hatchery; in it, he raised thieves like trout. There was little profit in turning in a young thief for petty pinching. Wild cajoled his recruits along, prodding them deeper into crime, appealing to their audacity until they matured as "forty-pound men," criminals who would be worth handing over to the authorities. If anyone crossed him, Wild donned his role as thief-taker and haled him into court. It made no difference whether the charge was real or trumped-up, since Wild could produce as many witnesses as he wanted who would give whatever perjured testimony he needed. In the same way, he protected his friends by providing witnesses to swear to their innocence, retaining defense lawyers (there being no public defender) and, if necessary, bribing the more corruptible magistrates. He wielded his power with ruth-less zeal, certain that the law was on his side. It was; for the authorities were more interested in the thieves he caught than the ones he raised, and as a thief-taker he was hugely successful. He boasted of sending seventy-two men to the gallows, and he secured the conviction of thousands of lesser fry. Despite its mock-official ring, the title he bestowed on himself—"Thief-Taker General of Great Britain and Ireland"— was not exaggerated: In the eyes of the London mob, the bourgeoisie, the magistrates and the penny press alike, Wild was the arm of the law.

He went down at last, in 1725, convicted under the act which for the last seven years had borne his name. At Tyburn, the bellowing crowd that had gathered to watch him die pelted him with stones and slops, and his last act was to pick the hangman's pocket.

14. De La Coste,——*Voyage Philosophique d'Angleterre Fait en 1783 et 1784*, vol, 1, p. 12, cit. in Radzinowicz, *A History of the English Criminal Law and Its Administration Since 1752*, vol. 1, p. 724.

15. Cit. in Shaw *CC*, p. 39.

16. Radzinowicz, *History*, vol. 1, p. 27, note 87.

17. Ibid., vol. 1, p. 77.

18. For a discussion of the rituals of the Rule of Law, see Douglas Hay, "Property, Authority and the Criminal Law," in *Albion's Fatal Tree: Crime and Society in Eighteenth-Century England*, ed. Douglas Hay, Peter Linebaugh and Edward P. Thompson, p. 17ff.

19. Extract from *Dorset County Chronicle* [date unknown], 1831, incl. in Withers document file in TSA, Hobart.

20. The ritual of the procession to Tyburn from Newgate lasted until 1783, and it appears to have been curtailed by the sheriffs of London and Middlesex for fear that the "mob" would take it over completely—a fear probably reinforced by the Gordon Riots of 1780. Hangings remained public for a while thereafter, but they were done in front of the entrance to Newgate. Michael Ignatieff (*A Just Measure of Pain*, pp. 88–90) com-pares this to the efforts of prison reformers to reclaim the subculture of prisons from the inmates, and to Colquhoun's proposals for a metropolitan police force—"an at-tempt to establish state hegemony over collectivities of the poor whose defiance of public authority had long been tolerated or taken for granted."

21. J. P. Grosley, *A Tour in London* (London, 1772), vol. 1, pp. 172–73, cit. in Radzinowicz, *History*, vol. 1, p. 176, n. 50.

22. Radzinowicz, *History*, vol. 1, p. 175, note 45.

23. Text of the sexton's prayer: Howard, *The State of the Prisons in England and Wales*, p. 175.

24. The fullest eighteenth-century dictionaries of criminal slang and cant are Francis Grose, *A Classical Dictionary of the Vulgar Tongue* (London, 1785) and Anon., *A New Canting Dictionary* (London, 1725). The indispensable modern guide is Eric Partridge's monumental *A Dictionary of the Underworld* (3rd ed., London, 1971).
25. James Boswell, *The Life of Samuel Johnson* (Everyman ed., London, 1920), vol. 2, p. 447.
26. Jonathan Swift, "Clever Tom Clinch Going to Be Hanged," in Harold Williams (ed.), *The Poems of Jonathan Swift* (Oxford, 1937), vol. 2, p. 399.
27. Anon., *Hanging Not Punishment Enough* (London, 1701), cit. in Radzinowicz, *History*, vol. 1, p. 235.
28. F. Gemelli, *Viaggi per Europa* (1701), vol. 1, p. 328, cit. in Radzinowicz, ibid., vol. 1, p. 182.
29. Peter Linebaugh, "the Tyburn riot Against the Surgeons," in Hay et al., eds., *Albion's Fatal Tree*, p. 83.
30. Figures from Radzinowicz, *History*, vol. 1, p. 190.
31. On mercy and patronage, see Hay, "Property," in Hay et al., eds., *Albion's Fatal Tree*, p. 23.
32. The source for these petitions, especially those relating to transportation, is in the Privy Council Papers in the Public Records Office, London, in-letters to the Home Office 1/67–92, covering the years 1819–44. I have quoted from a few of them in Chapter 5, but the immense wealth of information they offer on the social background, experiences and circumstances of individual convicts and their families awaits the attention of historians.
33. John Howard, *The State of the Prisons in England and Wales*, p. 12.
34. Ibid., p. 9.
35. Fielding, *Enquiry*, p. 214.
36. Howard, *State of the Prisons*, p. 21.
37. Brisbane to Bathurst, Nov. 29, 1823, HRA xi:181.
38. Samuel Johnson, Jan. 6, 1759, in *The Idler*, vol. 1, p. 38.
39. In 1786 Pitt wrote to William Wilberforce, who was pressing him for penal reform, to say that "The multitude of things depending, has made the Penitentiary House long in deciding upon. But I still think," he added vaguely, "a beginning will be made before the season for building is over." No beginning was made and in the summer of 1788 Pitt reassured Wilberforce that penitentiaries "shall not be forgotten." Although Sir Samuel Romilly urged the government to pursue the idea of a national penitentiary, it remained in limbo until 1812, when ground was broken at Millbank, on the Thames, for the biggest prison in Europe—seven pentagonal blocks holding 1,200 prisoners, clustered around a chapel. It was theoretically modelled on Jeremy Bentham's scheme for a centralized Panopticon, but it turned out, in practice, to be an almost uncontrollable maze. The Millbank Penitentiary was never an effective substitute for transportation. It was demolished to make way for the Tate Gallery.
40. Smith, *Colonists in Bondage*, p. 92.
41. Ibid.
42. *The Correspondence of King George III*, ed. J. Fortescue, vol. 6, p. 415ff, cit. in Clark *HA*, vol. 1, p. 64.

CHAPTER THREE *The Geographical Unconscious*

1. On the dissemination of information in the eighteenth century, see Eric J. Hobsbawm, *The Age of Revolution*, pp. 21–23.
2. Luis de Camoëns, *Os Lusiadas*, vol. 10, p. 139.
3. On the Tordesillas line, originally meant to divide the Atlantic only but soon extended into a great meridian around the world dividing Luso-Castilian zones of influence in seas as yet unknown, see O. H. K. Spate, *The Pacific Since Magellan*, vol. 1: *The Spanish Lake*, pp. 25–29. On the Dieppe maps, and presumed Portuguese encounters

with the eastern coast of Australia, see Russel Ward, *Australia Since the Coming of Man*, pp. 21–26, and K. G. McIntyre, *The Secret Discovery of Australia*.

4. There is some evidence, not conclusive, of Chinese contact with Australia in the fifteenth century. See D. G. Mulvaney, *The Prehistory of Australia*, pp. 41–44.

5. William Dampier, *Dampier's Voyages*, ed. John Masefield, vol. 1, pp. 350–51.

6. Cook's instructions from the Admiralty on the Southern Continent: James Cook, *The Journals of Captain James Cook on His Voyage of Discovery*, ed. J. C. Beaglehole, vol. 1, pp. 279–84, and J. C. Beaglehole, *The Life of Captain James Cook*, pp. 147–49.

7. On the doings of the *Endeavour's* men two centuries ago at the now hopelessly corrupted paradise of Matavai Bay on Tahiti, the literature is vast. A summary is given by Beaglehole, *Life of Cook*, pp. 172–95.

8. Joseph Banks, *The Endeavour Journal of Joseph Banks, 1768–1771*, ed. J. C. Beaglehole.

9. Banks, *Journal*, April 25, 1770. Thus the image of sterile Australia—the "old Cow" of a continent—makes its appearance at the very moment of contact.

10. Cook, *Journals*, vol. 1, p. 399.

11. Alan Frost, *Convicts and Empire: A Naval Question, 1776–1811*, p. 135.

12. John Ehrman, *The Younger Pitt*, vol. 1, p. 405. In 1781–85 Britain's exports to the East Indies were worth less than £1 million and its imports a little more than £2 million. The corresponding figures for the Atlantic countries (Caribbean, North America, Newfoundland, Africa) were £4 million and £3.5 million.

13. Harris to Carmarthen, Aug. 19, 1785, cit. in Frost, *Convicts and Empire*, p. 99.

14. Harris to Carmarthen, Mar. 7, 1786, cit. in Frost, *Convicts and Empire*, p. 104.

15. Admiral Hughes on spar shortage in India: cit. ibid., p. 66.

16. *Phormium tenax*, the New Zealand flax plant which grew on Norfolk Island, superior in tensile strength and fiber to *Gymnostatus anceps*, the wild flax plant of the mainland coast, figured in the royal instructions to Phillip on the First Fleet, which mentioned its "superior excellence for a variety of Maritime purposes" and the prospect that it "may ultimately become an Article of Export." Phillip was enjoined to "particularly attend to its Cultivation, and . . . send home . . . Samples of this Article." Phillip's Instructions, Apr. 25, 1787, HRNSW ii:89.

17. James Mario Matra's proposal, Aug. 23, 1783, HRNSW ii:1–6.

18. Ibid.

19. Addition to Matra's proposal, Aug. 23, 1783, HRNSW ii:7.

20. Howe to Sydney, Dec. 26, 1784, HRNSW ii:10. "The length of the navigation," Admiral Howe remarked discouragingly, "subject to all the retardments of an India voyage, do [sic] not, I must confess, encourage me to hope for a return of the many advantages in commerce or war which Mr. M. Matra has in contemplation."

21. Young to Pitt, enclosed in Pepper Arden to Sydney, Jan. 13, 1785, HRNSW ii:11. Young stressed the possible revenue from trade in Australian products, mainly spices, "fine Oriental cotton," sugar cane, coffee and tobacco. His main subject of enthusiasm, however, was *Phormium tenax*, "that very remarkable plant known by the name of the New Zealand flax-plant," which Young believed could be grown in limitless quantities. "Its uses are more extensive than any vegetable hitherto known, for in its gross state it far exceeds anything of the kind for cordage and canvas, and may be obtained at a much cheaper rate than . . . from Russia."

22. John Call to Pitt [?], ca. August 1784, HO 42/7:49–57, cit. in Frost, *Convicts and Empire*, p. 203.

23. Alexander Dalrymple, "A Serious Admonition . . . ," cit. in David Mackay, *A Place of Exile: The European Settlement of New South Wales*, p. 33.

24. Shaw *CC*, pp. 46–47.

25. For Rolle's pressure on Pitt to transport the felons accumulating in the Devon hulks, see Mackay, *Place of Exile*, p. 21.

26. Clark *HA*, vol. 1, p. 67.

27. For King's continuing interest in Norfolk Island flax, sustained in the face of discouraging indifference from his government, see Mackay, *Place of Exile*, p. 95.

28. In *Convicts and Empire*, Alan Frost claims a place in the Napoleonic Wars for the

infant colony of Sydney. "It is one of history's niceties," he claims, "as it is a tribute both to their percipience and their political longevity, that those who in the mid-1780s created [the colony as strategic outlier] called it onto the stage of war with the Emperor Napoleon." Yet Australia's "role" against Napoleon consisted of a passing thought by Pitt, in 1804, that Valparaiso might be attacked by a trans-Pacific expeditionary force from Sydney; and of Grenville's unexecuted plan to attack Chile, Peru and Mexico with a force that included men from the New South Wales Corps and "100 convict pioneers . . . seasoned to work in the sun." Nothing came of either. Australia's "role" in the struggle against Bonaparte was nil.

29. Nepean, CO 201/2:15 and HO 42/7:24.
30. In preparing the "Heads of a Plan" for announcement by Lord Sydney, Nepean leaned heavily on the argument and phrasing of Matra's 1783 proposal for the Botany Bay settlement. The "Heads of a Plan" on flax in 1786: "The threads or filaments of this New Zealand plant are formed by nature with the most exquisite delicacy, and may be so minutely divided as to be manufactured into the finest linens." Matra on the same, in 1783: "The threads or filaments of this plant are formed by nature with the most exquisite delicacy, and they may be so minutely divided as to be small enough to make the finest Cambrick."
31. "Phillip's Views on the Conduct of the Expedition and the Treatment of Convicts," 1787, HRNSW ii:53.
32. Charles Bateson, *The Convict Ships, 1787–1868*, pp. 96–98.
33. Phillip to Nepean, Mar. 18, 1787, HRNSW ii:58.
34. Phillip to Nepean, Jan. 11, 1787, HRNSW ii:46.
35. Philip Gidley King, *The Journal of Philip Gidley King, Lieutenant, R.N., 1787–1790*, p. 6.
36. Phillip to Sydney, Feb. 28, 1787, HRNSW ii:50.
37. Phillip to Sydney, Mar. 12, 1787, HRNSW ii:56–57.
38. Phillip to Nepean, Mar. 18, 1787, HRNSW ii:59.
39. The basic source for the identity of the First Fleet convicts is a thorough compilation from sessions papers and assizes records published by Dr. John Cobley in 1970, *The Crimes of the First Fleet Convicts*. Defects and ambiguities in the records make it uncertain how many prisoners actually were shipped on the First Fleet. Cobley's figure is 778, both male and female; Crowley's (in *A Documentary History of Australia*, vol. 1) is 736; Lieutenant King's count, before sailing, was 752; and so on.
40. "Botany Bay: A New Song" is in Ballads collection, ML, Sydney.
41. [Alexander Dalrymple], *A Serious Admonition to the Publick on the Intended Thief-Colony at Botany Bay*.
42. *Whitehall Evening Post*, Dec. 19, 1786, cit. in C. M. H. Clark, *Sources of Australian History*, pp. 75–77.
43. "Memorial from the Marines," written on *Scarborough*, May 7, 1787, HRNSW ii:100–101.
44. Phillip to Sydney, June 5, 1787, HRNSW i:107.
45. Watkin Tench, *A Narrative of the Expedition to Botany Bay*, p. 3.
46. Ralph Clark Journal, May 13–14, 1787, *Journal and Letters, 1787–1792* (Sydney, 1981).
47. Samuel Eliot Morison, *The European Discovery of America*, vol. 1: *The Southern Voyages* (New York, 1974), p. 222.
48. Tench, *Narrative*, p. 19.
49. John White, *Journal*, July 1787, p. 39.
50. Ibid., pp. 30–31.
51. Clark, *Journal*, July 3, 1787.
52. Phillip to Nepean, Sept. 2, 1787, HRNSW ii:112.
53. White, *Journal*, p. 45.
54. Arthur Bowes Smyth, Journal, Nov. 12, 1787.
55. Ibid., Dec. 10, 1787.
56. Ibid., Jan. 10, 1788.

57. White, *Journal*, Jan. 1788, p. 113.
58. Ibid., p. 114.

CHAPTER FOUR *The Starvation Years*

1. The prepossessing description of Botany Bay was given by Capt. James Cook in his Journal, Mar. 1, 1770. Joseph Banks, in his summary of the New South Wales coast written aboard *Endeavour* in August 1770 (Banks, *Journal*, ed. Beaglehole, vol. 2, p. 111ff.: "Some Account of that part of New Holland now called New South Wales"), was much more skeptical. "Barren it may justly be call'd and in a very high degree. . . . [U]pon the Whole the fertile Soil Bears no kind of Proportion to that which seems by nature doomed to everlasting barrenness. Water is here a scarce article. . . . [A]t the two places where we filld for the ships use it was done from pools not brooks. Cultivation could not be supposed to yeild much towards the support of man."

A few pages later he softened these strictures a little, remarking that "Upon the whole New Holland, tho' in every respect the most barren countrey I have seen, is not so bad that between the productions of sea and Land a company of People who should have the misfortune of being shipwrecked upon it might support themselves."

2. Lieut. Philip Gidley King, *Journal*, Jan. 20, 1788, pp. 34–35.
3. Ibid.
4. Ibid.
5. Arthur Bowes Smyth, *Journal*, Jan. 21, 1788, pp. 57–58.
6. Watkin Tench, *A Narrative of the Expedition to Botany Bay*, pp. 57–58, and John White, *Journal*, p. 117. Apparently the tune (that of "For He's a Jolly Good Fellow") was retained among the Aborigines, for George Thompson (*Slavery and Famine: An Account of the Miseries and Starvation at Botany Bay*, p. 16) would describe them paddling their canoes while singing it—"they have the French tune of Malbrook very perfect: I have heard a dozen or twenty singing it together."
7. Phillip to Sydney, May 15, 1788, HRNSW ii:121–22.
8. David Collins, *An Account of the English Colony at New South Wales*, vol. 1, p. 5.
9. Tench, *Narrative*, p. 60.
10. Jean-François de la Pérouse, *A Voyage Around the World . . . Under the Command of J. F. G. de la Pérouse*, vol. 2, p. 180.
11. Phillip to Sydney, May 15, 1788, HRNSW ii:123.
12. Ralph Clark, Journal, Feb. 1, 1788, *Journal and Letters, 1787–1792*. (The original Ms. is in ML Sydney.) On the indolence of convicts, see Phillip to Sydney, HRNSW ii:123.
13. Bowes Smyth, *Journal*, Feb. 6, 1788.
14. Ibid., Feb. 7, 1788, pp. 67–69. Bowes Smyth's opinion that Phillip's Commission was "a more unlimited one than was ever before granted to any Governor under the British Crown" was shared by other officers, including Ralph Clark: "I never heard of any one single person having so great a power invested in him." George Worgan, the naval surgeon who brought the first piano to Australia on the *Sirius*, felt that the "feeling and concern" of Phillip's delivery did honor to his humanity, "and it really is a Pity, he has the Government of a set of Reprobates who will not suffer him to indulge himself in a Lenity, which he sincerely wishes to govern them by." G. B. Worgan, *Journal*, Feb. 9, 1788.
15. Phillip in HRNSW ii:155–56, July 9, 1788.
16. On the construction of the first settlement's huts, see J. M. Freeland, *Architecture in Australia*, pp. 12–17.
17. Thomas Watling, *Letters from an Exile at Botany-Bay . . .*, p. 17. The use of sheeps' *hair* in the mortar (not wool) was inevitable; the first Australian sheep were hairy animals from the Cape, raised for their meat not their fleece.
18. Ross to Col. Sec. Stephens, July 10, 1788, HRNSW ii:173.
19. Bowes Smyth, *Journal*, Feb. 25–26, 1788, pp. 74–75.

20. HRNSW 1/ii:89. N. G. Butlin, in *Our Original Aggression*, proposes that the officers of the First Fleet, with the connivance of Phillip, deliberately infected the Aborigines with cholera as a form of germ warfare. There is no direct or persuasive evidence for this, and the distress with which the First Fleet diarists observed the epidemics among the tribespeople argues strongly against it.
21. George B. Worgan, *Journal*, May 24, 1788.
22. Ibid.
23. Daniel Southwell, HRNSW ii:666.
24. Worgan, letter to Richard Worgan, June 12, 1788, Ms. in ML, Sydney.
25. Watling, *Letters from an Exile*, pp. 7–8.
26. Ibid.
27. Ibid.
28. Collins, *Account*, vol. 1, p. 17.
29. Extract of Journal of Richard Williams (seaman on *Borrowdale*) in broadsheet Q991/W, ML, Sydney.
30. HRNSW ii:746–77.
31. Bowes Smyth, *Journal*, Feb. 23, 1788, p. 74.
32. Ross to Nepean, HRNSW ii:212.
33. Campbell to Lord Ducie, cit. in Cobley, *Sydney Cove, 1788*, p. 191.
34. Phillip to Sydney, July 9, 1788, HRNSW ii:150.
35. Clark, *Journal*, Feb. 28, 1790.
36. King, *Journal*, May 10, 1788.
37. Tench, *Account*, p. 37.
38. Southwell to Rev. W. Butler, Apr. 14, 1790, cit. in Cobley, *Sydney Cove, 1789–1790*, p. 183.
39. Collins, *Account*, p. 81.
40. Tench, *Account*, pp. 39–40.
41. King, HRNSW ii:431.
42. Clark, letter to Capt. Campbell, Feb. 11, 1791, in Clark, *Journal and Letters, 1787–1792*.
43. Clark, *Journal*, May 21, 1790.
44. Phillip to Sydney, HRNSW ii:211.
45. Kidnapped Maoris: King, *Journal*, Nov. 1793, pp. 177–78. King had made the young Maoris "a very serious promise of sending them home" [*Journal*, May 1793, p. 135] and he honored it, though not soon enough for either of them. "Woodoo like a true Patriot thinks there is no country People or Customs equal to those of his own, which makes him less curious in what he sees about him, than his companion Tooke." [*Journal*, November 1793, pp. 178–79.]
46. Tench, *Account*, p. 43.
47. Letter from anonymous convict woman dated Port Jackson, Nov. 14, 1788, in HRA ii:746–47. Rev. Richard Johnson to Henry Fricker, Apr. 9, 1790, at C232 in ML, Sydney.
48. Southwell to Rev. Butler, Apr. 14, 1790.
49. Anonymous male convict, cit. in Cobley, *Sydney Cove, 1789–1790*, pp. 165–66.
50. Tench, *Account*, p. 42.
51. Collins, *Account*, p. 88.
52. Watling, *Letters from an Exile*, p. 18.
53. "We shall not starve": Phillip to Nepean, Apr. 15, 1790, HRNSW ii:330.
54. Arrival of *Lady Juliana:* Tench, *Account*, p. 46.
55. Phillip to W.W. Grenville, HRA i:194–97, Jul. 17, 1790.
56. Collins, *Account*, cit. in Cobley, *Sydney Cove, 1791–92*, p. 129.
57. For the New South Wales Corps, see George Mackaness, *Life of Vice-Admiral Bligh*, vol. 2, p. 117–18; Herbert V. Evatt, *Rum Rebellion*, passim; Clark *HA*, vol. 1, pp. 150, 166.
58. Collins, *Account*, vol. 1, p. 187.
59. Phillip to Grenville, July 17, 1790, HRA i:194–97.

60. Phillip to Dundas, Mar. 19, 1792, HRNSW ii:597.
61. "Reminiscences of Henry Hale to Mrs. Caroline Chisholm," in Samuel Sidney, *The Three Colonies of Australia*, p. 43.
62. George Thompson, *Slavery and Famine*, pp. 35–36. Phillip to Dundas, Oct. 2, 1792, HRNSW ii:645.
63. HRNSW ii:664. I am assuming a (very approximate) conversion rate of 50:1 between modern and late eighteenth-century sterling. See Roy Porter, *English Society in the Eighteenth Century*, p. 13.
64. *Parliamentary History*, vol. 28, pp. 1222–24.
65. See Appendix 1, "Governors and Chief Executives of New South Wales During Convict Period, 1788–1855," for the various governors' dates of office.
66. Grose to Dundas, Feb. 16, 1793. HRA ii:14–15.
67. Crowley, *Doc. Hist.*, vol. 1, p. 63. Shaw *CC*, p. 66.
68. Roe, "Colonial Society in Embryo," *HS*, vol. 7, no. 26 (May 1956), p. 157.
69. S. Macarthur-Onslow, ed., *Some Early Records of the Macarthurs of Camden*, pp. 45–46.
70. John Easty, "A Memorandum of the Transactions of a Voyage from England to Botany Bay in the Scarborough Transport . . . ," Dixson Library, Sydney; entry for Sept. 30, 1792. Easty's opinion as to the severity of discipline under King on Norfolk Island is not supported by King's own journal, with its (on the whole) moderate record of flogging. A private in the Marines, and subject to harsh discipline himself, Easty showed a lively sense of injustice when noting the punishments inflicted on others. Thus at Cape Town [Nov. 7, 1787] he found the Dutch authorities "very Strict sort of People . . . they hang them for the Lest thing in the World allmost and for anything that is very Bad they rack them and Break their Bones one by one and hang them upon a Gibett like a Dog."
71. King to Dundas, Mar. 10, 1794, HRNSW ii:137.
72. King's report, in HRNSW ii:145.
73. Grose to King, Feb. 25, 1794, HRNSW ii:130–31.
74. On Maj. Joseph Foveaux, see ADB entry and Mss. catalogued under Foveaux in ML, Sydney, especially Foveaux's "*Letter Book*, 1800–1804" (ML A1444), hereafter referred to as FLB.
75. Foveaux to King, Nov. 16, 1800, FLB.
76. Robert Jones, "Recollections of 13 Years Residence at Norfolk Island," ca. 1823.
77. Ibid.
78. Ibid.
79. Ibid.
80. Ibid.
81. Foveaux to King, Jan. 13, 1801, FLB.
82. Foveaux to Duke of Portland, Sept. 17, 1801, letter at Af 48/4, ML, Sydney.
83. Jones, "Recollections."
84. On Richard Atkins, see ADB entry; John Grant, letter 15, July 13, 1804, Ms. 737, NLA, Canberra.
85. Alan Frost, *Convicts and Empire*, pp. 168–69.
86. Ibid., p. 172.
87. Liverpool to Macquarie, HRNSW vii:562–63.
88. On the numbers, distribution and tribal organization of the Van Diemen's Land Aborigines, see Robson, *Hist. Tas.*, pp. 13–25, esp. pp. 17–18. Lyndall Ryan (*The Aboriginal Tasmanians*, p. 14) follows Rhys Jones in assuming a population of 3,000 to 4,000 Aborigines at the time of European settlement. This figure is disputed, on no very clear evidence, by present-day aboriginal descendants, whose guesses run as high as 8,000 to 10,000.
89. The word "tarpaulin" is common eighteenth-century slang for "career naval officer."
90. For Bentham's pursuit of Collins, see Bentham Papers, Add. Ms. 33544, fols. 20–21, 41–42, 57–58, BL.
91. George Prideaux Harris at Port Phillip, to Henry Harris: Harris Family Papers, Add.

Ms. 45156, fols. 14–15, BL. James Grove, undated letter 2, in "Select Letters of James Grove," ed. Earnshaw, THRA, PP.

92. George Harris, Add. Ms. 45156, fol. 16, BL.
93. King to Collins, Nov. 26, 1803, HRA iii:39, and Dec. 30, 1803, HRA iii:50. Collins to King, Dec. 30, 1803, HRA iii:50, and Jan. 27, 1804, HRA iii:53.
94. Collins to King, Feb. 28, 1804, HRA iii:217–18.
95. Memo by Lieut. Edward Lord in "Select Letters of James Grove," ed. Earnshaw, pp. 38–39.
96. James Backhouse, *A Narrative of a Visit to the Australian Colonies*, p. 21.
97. William Maum to Robert Nash, Jan. 28, 1808, Calder Papers, ML, Sydney.
98. Robson, *Hist. Tas.*, p. 71.
99. Jones, "Recollections."
100. James Grove, undated letter 4, in "Select Letters of James Grove," p. 38.
101. Memo by Lieut. Edward Lord, ibid., p. 39.
102. George Harris, Add. Ms. 45156, fol. 16, BL.
103. Mary Gilmore, "Old Botany Bay," 1918.

CHAPTER FIVE *The Voyage*

1. Thomas Holden to Molly Holden, DDX 140/7:4, LRO.
2. Peter Withers to Mary Ann Withers, April 1831, TSA, Hobart.
3. Richard Dillingham to Betsey Faine, Dec. 28, 1831, letter 2, Bedfordshire County Archive.
4. John Ward, "Diary of a Convict," transcript pp. 39–40, in Ward Papers, NLA.
5. Thomas Holden to Molly Holden, DDX 140/7:8 and 10a, LRO.
6. Peter Withers to Mary Ann Withers, TSA, Hobart.
7. Ibid.
8. Deborah Taylor to Sir Robert Peel, Apr. 8, 1830, PC 1:78, PRO.
9. Jane Eastwood to Sir Robert Peel, Apr. 12, 1830, PC 1:78, PRO.
10. Ibid.
11. Isherwood et al. to Viscount Sidmouth, May 12, 1819, PC 1:67, PRO. R. Downie to Peel, Apr. 15, 1830, PC 1:78, PRO.
12. Richard Boothman to his father, Feb. 10, 1841, DDX 537:5, LRO.
13. Richard Taylor to his father, Apr. 14 and Apr. 22, 1840, DDX 505:2 and 3, LRO.
14. R. Taylor to parents, May 1840, 505:4, LRO.
15. R. Boothman to father, May 18 and June 16, 1841, DDX 537:11 and 13, LRO. R. Brown to father, May 2, 1841, DDX 505:15, LRO. T. Holden to mother, June 1812, DDX 140/7:7, LRO.
16. "The Borough," letter 18, in *George Crabbe, Poems*, ed. A. W. Ward, vol. 1, p. 458, cit. in Coral Lansbury, *Arcady in Australia*, p. 10.
17. Wentworth Papers, pp. 31–32, ML, Sydney.
18. T. Holden, DDX 140/7:8, LRO. R. Boothman, DDX 537:11, LRO.
19. Petition of Mrs. Silas Harris, May 2, 1819, PC 1:67, PRO.
20. William Tidman to Sidmouth, Feb. 8, 1819, PC 1:67, PRO. Mrs. Lycot to Sir George Paul, encl. in Paul to Sidmouth, May 12, 1819, PC 1:67, PRO.
21. Helen Guild, petition dated April 1830, PC 1:78, PRO.
22. T. Holden to mother, DDX 140/7:6, LRO.
23. T. Holden to Molly Holden, DDX 140/7:9, LRO. Henry Bennett, *A Letter to Viscount Sidmouth, on Transportation*, p. 24. Ward, "Diary of a Convict," p. 42.
24. Ward, ibid., p. 44.
25. Mansfield Silverthorpe, Ms. no. 9, Norfolk Island Convict Papers.
26. Woomera [pseud.], *The Life of an Ex-Convict*, printed extract in ML, Sydney, p. 2. Ward, "Diary of a Convict," p. 78.
27. George Lee to Sir Henry St. J. Mildmay, Jan. 24, 1803, Bentham Papers, BL, Add. Ms. 33544, ff. 14–15.

28. Little boy: Bennett, *Letter to Viscount Sidmouth*, p. 25. James Grove, letter 1 in "Select Letters of James Grove." Silverthorpe, Ms. no. 9, Norfolk Island Convict Papers.
29. John Mortlock, *Experiences of a Convict*, p. 55.
30. Bennett, *Letter to Viscount Sidmouth*, p. 30.
31. Mortlock, *Experiences*, p. 53. Ward, "Diary of a Convict," p. 83.
32. Silverthorpe, Ms. no. 9, p. 66.
33. Silverthorpe., ibid. Ward, "Diary of a Convict," p. 90. Mortlock, *Experiences*, p. 53.
34. Ward, ibid., p. 40.
35. John Nicol, *The Life and Adventures of John Nicol, Mariner*, pp. 114–15.
36. Bennett, *Letter to Viscount Sidmouth*, p. 29.
37. Simon Taylor to his father, May 1841, DDX 505:17, LRO.
38. Contract system: see Charles Bateson, *The Convict Ships 1787–1868*, pp. 12ff.
39. Death rate during the Atlantic crossing and in the Navy: see Shaw *CC*, p. 117.
40. The death rate in the early 1830s was increased by three bad shipwrecks. In 1833 the *Amphitrite* ran around near Boulogne before she even cleared the English Channel, drowning 106 women convicts. In 1835 the *George III* sank in the D'Entrecasteaux Channel, near Hobart, after a scurvy-ridden outward voyage; captain and crew slow to unbar the hatches, and 127 male prisoners drowned. The same year, *Neva* was wrecked in the Bass Strait, killing another 138 women. If allowance is made for the loss of life from these wrecks, one sees that the convicts' general death rate from disease and neglect en route had, by naval standards, become very small by the 1830s.
41. Capt. William Hill to Wathen, July 26, 1790, HRNSW ii:367.
42. Thomas Milburn, "Copy of a Letter from Thomas Milburn in Botany Bay to his Father and Mother in Liverpool," broadsheet, Aug. 26, 1790, ML, Sydney.
43. Hill to Wathen, July 26, 1790, HRNSW ii:367.
44. Rev. Richard Johnson to Thornton, HRNSW ii:387–88.
45. The design of the Great Seal: HRNSW ii:389. In England, Erasmus Darwin, poetaster and grandfather of the great naturalist, was moved to pen his *Visit of Hope to Botany-Bay* to accompany a medallion made by Wedgwood out of Sydney clay, a verse less remarkable for its social realism than for its prediction of the Sydney Harbor Bridge:

> Where Sydney Cove her lucid bosom swells,
> Courts her young navies, and the storm repels;
> High on a rock amid the troubled air
> HOPE stood sublime, and wav'd her golden hair;
> Calm'd with her rosy smile the tossing deep
> And with sweet accents charm'd the winds to sleep;
> To each wild plain she stretch'd her snowy hand,
> High-waving wood, and sea-encircled strand.
> "Hear me", she cried, "ye rising Realms! record
> Time's opening scenes, and Truth's unerring word—
> *There* shall broad streets their stately walls extend,
> The circus widen, and the crescent bend;
> *There*, ray'd from cities o'er the cultured land,
> Shall bright canals, and solid roads expand.—
> *There* the proud Arch, Colossus-like, bestride
> Yon glittering streams, and bound the chafing tide— ...

And so on. Hope was easier to see in England than in Sydney.
46. Short rations on *Queen*: Bateson, *Convict Ships*, p. 137.
47. Capt. William Hill, cit. in Shaw *CC*, p. 112.
48. For conditions on the *Hillsborough* before her departure from Australia, see Jerome Fitzpatrick to Baldwin, Aug. 25, 1801, Pelham Papers, BL, Add. Ms. 33107, pp. 407ff. A vivid account of the voyage (*Voyage to Sydney in the Ship Hillsborough 1798–99, and a Description of the Colony*, Ms. in Dixson, published for the Library of Australian History, 1978) was written by the convict silversmith William Noah, a native of

Shropshire who, at forty-three, had been sentenced to death at the Old Bailey in April 1797 for stealing two thousand pounds of lead, value £23, from a plumber in Westminster. Captain Hingston's attitude to the convicts may be gauged from Noah's account of his wife's attempt to visit her condemned husband on Dec. 4, 1798, before the *Hillsborough* sailed:

> I was very mich Suppris'd on looking thro' the port Holes of the Ship to see my Wife come Off in a Werry & a longside. I immediately wrote to Capt Hingston begging the Indulgence to speak to her on the Deck but had no Answer finding her still along side I wrote a Second Stating to him that she had Came from London with what she must have Experienc'd from the Cold & that it might be a final Leave I being banish'd to a Distant Land, this last sofed'd his Heart & after her being a Longside two Hour's I was Orderd on Deck when with a Brutal Kind of Behavior she was admitted with a Box she had brought for me. . . . [Hingston] fell in a Violent Passion askin how many Boxes I meant to have, Swearing If any thing was in it off Tools he would throw the [w]Hole into the Sea & unfortunately I had Orderd a few Ingravers & Others small tools . . . the Maj[ority] of which he found she was then Immediately Orderd out of the Ship with the Tools and I with the most Horrid Language down to my Miserable Place of Confinement no One can feel the Horror of an Unhappy Mind I was Disconsolate & felt the Horrors of Cruel Misfortunes.

49. Conditions and medical officers on the *Royal Admiral:* see Bateson, *Convict Ships,* p. 43.
50. Ibid. pp. 45–46.
51. Ibid., pp. 160–65. *Massey's Journal Book,* 1796, typescript extract at Ab. 93, ML, Sydney. Beyer was on his third voyage to Sydney; he had been Captain Anstis's surgeon on *Scarborough* in the Second Fleet.
52. Fitzpatrick to Rev. Charles Lindsey, re conditions on *Hercules* and *Atlas,* Pelham Papers, Add. Ms. 33107, pp. 200–203, BL.
53. Fitzpatrick to Pelham, ibid., p. 341ff.
54. Shaw *CC,* p. 114. Macquarie to Bathurst, Dec. 12, 1817, HRA ix:510.
55. Fitzpatrick to Baldwin, Pelham Papers, Add. Ms. 33105, BL, p. 242ff.
56. Redfern to Macquarie, HRA viii:275ff.
57. Figures from Bateson, *Convict Ships,* Appendix 7b.
58. As merchantmen, most transports had been designed to squeeze as much cargo space as possible from the tonnage laws that governed the payment of harbor dues up to 1835. The rule of thumb in this tonnage calculation assumed that a hull's depth was half its beam. Hence the owners sought to fool the tax man by building ships as narrow and deep as possible. This was fine for cargo, but terribly uncomfortable for convicts, as narrow hulls were less stable than beamy ones and rolled violently. As free emigration to Australia began to take hold in the 1830s, so the quality of convict shipping declined—for it was much more profitable for owners to take paying passengers than to accept government charters.
59. John Boyle O'Reilly, *Moondyne,* pp. 186–89.
60. George Prideaux Harris to family, n.d. [Jan. 1804], BL, Add. Ms. 45156, p. 9v.
61. Alfred Tetens, *Among the Savages of the South Seas,* p. xxii.
62. John Gorman, Log-book, untitled Ms. 1524, NLA, Canberra.
63. Mellish, "A Convict's Recollections of New South Wales," p. 49.
64. Charles Cozens, *The Adventures of a Guardsman,* p. 98.
65. Ibid., pp. 95–96.
66. Ibid., pp. 103–4.
67. John Gregg, Journal on convict ship *York,* 1862, Ms. 2749, NLA.
68. William Coke to his father, Apr. 20, 1826, Coke letters, D 1881, DRO.
69. Ibid.
70. Tetens, *Among the Savages,* p. xxiii.
71. Ibid., p. xxiv.

72. T. Holden to parents, DDX/140:12, LRO.
73. John Smith, Surgeon's log on transport *Clyde*, Ms. 6169, NLA, Canberra.
74. Murray to Smith, Sept. 13, 1838, encl. in Ms. 6169, NLA, Canberra.

CHAPTER SIX   *Who Were the Convicts?*

1. William Blake, "Vala, Night the Ninth," in *The Complete Writings of William Blake*, ed. Geoffrey Keynes, London, 1966, pp. 359–60.
2. J. L. Hammond and B. Hammond, *The Village Laborer, 1760–1832*, p. 239; G. Arnold Wood, "Convicts," *JRAHS*, vol. 8, no. 4 (1922), p. 187.
3. See C. M. H. Clark, "The Origins of the Convicts Transported to Eastern Australia, 1787–1852," HS, vol. 7, no. 26 (May 1956), pp. 121–35, and vol. 7, no. 27 (June 1956), pp. 314–27; and see also Lloyd L. Robson, *The Convict Settlers of Australia*.
4. C. M. H. Clark, *Select Documents in Australian History, 1788–1850*, pp. 406–8.
5. Robson, *Convict Settlers of Australia*, Appendix 4, table 4(e). I have rounded off the percentages.
6. Ibid., Appendix 4, table 4(d).
7. Ibid., Appendix 4, tables 4(b) and (1).
8. Gertrude Himmelfarb, *The Idea of Poverty*, p. 291. For her discussion of class language, see pp. 281–304.
9. Ibid., p. 295.
10. Henry Mayhew, *London Labour and the London Poor*, vol. 3, p. 381.
11. Patrick Colquhoun, *A Treatise on the Police of the Metropolis*, pp. vii–xi.
12. Edward P. Thompson, *The Making of the English Working Class*, pp. 59–66.
13. *Fraser's Magazine*, June 1832, pp. 521–22, cit. in J. J. Tobias, *Crime and Industrial Society in the 19th Century*.
14. *Eclectic Review*, vol. 2 (April 1854), p. 387, cit. in Tobias, ibid.
15. Himmelfarb, *Poverty*, p. 397.
16. Ibid., p. 399. "Ragged-schools" were charity schools for pauper children.
17. Petition from S. Nelson to Home Secretary, Ms. in NLA, Canberra. Isaac Nelson survived the voyage and—gentle soul—became one of the first schoolteachers in Australia, under the Rev. Richard Johnson.
18. On the wreckers' assumption of their traditional "rights," see John G. Rule, "Wrecking and Coastal Plunder," in Hay et al., eds., *Albion's Fatal Tree*, pp. 181–84.
19. Peter Cunningham, *Two Years in New South Wales*, vol. 2, p. 234.
20. Henry Mayhew, *London Labour and the London Poor*, vol. 4, pp. 25–26.
21. G. Parker, *Life's Painter of Variegated Characters*, 1789, cit. in Eric Partridge, *Dictionary of the Underworld*.
22. Partridge, ibid.
23. On Barrington, see HRA i:1–4 and ADB entry.
24. Dickens, *Oliver Twist* (London: Penguin Books, Penguin Classics, 1966), pp. 390–91.
25. Mayhew, *London Labour*, vol. 1, pp. 411 and 467.
26. Peter Gaskell, *The Manufacturing Population of England*, 1833, chapter 4.
27. Thomas Holden, letter to parents, 1812, DDX 140/7:13, LRO.
28. On Muir's trial and those of other "Scottish Martyrs," see Anon., *The Political Martyrs of Scotland Persecuted During the Years 1793 and 1794* (Edinburgh, 1795).
29. Ibid.
30. Lauderdale's objection was that the 1703 Act under which Muir and Palmer had been convicted limited their punishment to banishment, not transportation. Banishment meant only "exclusion from a community," whereas transportation "implies that exclusion executed in a compulsory and commonly ignominious Manner, always aggravated by Confinement and . . . the obligation of laborious Servitude." Lauderdale et al. to Dundas, Dec. 14, 1793, WI/5007 in Whitbread Papers, Bedford.
31. Gerrald to Margarot, 1794, Ms. at Ag. 14, ML, Sydney.
32. Muir to Moffatt, Dec. 13, 1794, Ms. in ML, Sydney.

33. Thomas Fyshe Palmer, *A Narrative of the Sufferings of T. F. Palmer*, p. 35.

34. Palmer, letters dated Apr. 23 and May 5, 1796, ML, Sydney.

35. Thomas Muir, "The Telegraph: A Consolatory Epistle," unpublished Ms. at Am. 9, ML, Sydney. "Telegraph" here means a semaphore.

36. Hill and Newton to Cooke, Mar. 12, 1797, Rebellion Papers 620/29:58 and 196, SPO, cit. in Shaw *CC*, p. 170.

37. Hugh Reid, statement in summary of evidence on *Marquis Cornwallis* mutiny, HRA i:657–58.

38. Hunter to Portland, Nov. 12, 1796, HRA i:674–75.

39. Irish convicts in Australia: HRA x:203–4. Hunter to Portland, Mar. 3, 1796, HRA i:555–56.

40. David Collins, *An Account of the English Colony in New South Wales*, vol. 1, pp. 380–81, and vol. 2, p. 57.

41. Hunter to Portland, Feb. 15, 1798, HRA i:131.

42. Number of Irish convicts in New South Wales in 1798: T. J. Kiernan, "Transportation from Ireland to Sydney 1791–1816" (M.A. thesis), p. 59.

43. James Carty, ed., *Ireland from Grattan's Parliament to the Great Famine, 1783–1850: A Documentary Record*, p. 69.

44. Cornwallis to Major-General Ross, cit. in Carty, *Ireland*, pp. 95–96.

45. Shaw *CC*, p. 170.

46. Kiernan, "Transportation," Appendix II, p. 29. Opinions differ, however, on the number of "politicals" in these Irish shipments. George Rude, in *Protest and Punishment* (1978), takes the stringently reductionist view that only 241 Irish were "politicals."

47. Hunter to Portland, Jan. 10, 1798, HRA ii:118.

48. Elizabeth Paterson to Capt. Johnson, Feb. 10, 1800, in Ms. Ap. 36:5, ML, Sydney.

49. King to Cooke, July 20, 1805, HRA v:534.

50. Hunter to Portland, Mar. 20, 1800, HRA ii:223.

51. Irish Conspiracy Papers, HRA iii:575 et seq. and 582–83.

52. Samuel Marsden, "A Few Observations on the Toleration of the Catholic Religion in New South Wales," Ms. 18, Marsden Papers, ML, Sydney

53. Hester Stroud, deposition to Marsden, Irish Conspiracy Papers, HRA iii:641.

54. Joseph Holt, "Life and Adventures of Joseph Holt . . . ," Ms. in ML, Sydney, pp. 293–95. I have corrected the distractingly erratic spelling and some of the odder punctuation of this passage.

55. King's court of inquiry into Irish insurgents: Oct. 1, 1800, HRA iii:650–51.

56. Elizabeth Patterson to "Mrs. B.," Oct. 7, 1800. Bentham Papers, Add. Ms., BL, pp. 423–24.

57. King to Portland, HRA iii:8–9.

58. Punishment of Father O'Neil: HRA iii:759. Irish efforts to get a priest to the colony, and King's eventual permission to Father Dixon to say Mass and administer the sacraments: King to Hobart, May 9, 1803, HRA iv:82–83.

59. "Situation shocking to Humanity": King to Transport Commissioners, HRA ii:532.

60. On Hassall's description of the start of the Irish rising at Castle Hill, see Castle Hill Rebellion Papers, Bonwick Transcripts, vol. 1, box 49, pp. 234–35, ML, Sydney.

61. Major George Johnston refuses to parley with Paterson: HRA iv:570.

62. Johnston to King, encl. 4 in King to Hobart, Mar. 12, 1804, HRA iv:568.

63. John Grant, Journal, pp. 47–48, Ms. 737, Grant Papers, NLA, Canberra.

64. King to Hobart, Apr. 16, 1804, HRA iv:611.

65. "Occasionally removed from one Settlement to another": King to Hobart, Apr. 30, 1805, HRA v:305. Poteen stills: HRA v:571.

66. George Rude, *Protest and Punishment*, p. 249.

67. Leslie C. Duly, "Hottentots to Hobart and Sydney: The Cape Supreme Court's Use of Transportation, 1828–1838."

68. On Canadian protesters see Rude, *Protest and Punishment*, pp. 42–51 and 82–88.

69. Eric Hobsbawm, *Industry and Empire*, p. 76.

70. Thompson, *English Working Class*, pp. 347–48.
71. Cook to Churton, Jan. 20, 1831, copy in "The Exile's Lamentations," MS at A1711, ML, Sydney, and cit. in Clune, *The Norfolk Island Story*, p. 157.
72. Thompson, *English Working Class*, p. 250.
73. Eric Hobsbawm and George Rude, *Captain Swing*, p. 262.
74. Ibid., pp. 245–46.
75. Richard Dillingham, letter to parents, Sept. 29, 1836, Dillingham Papers, Ms-CRT. 150:24, Bedfordshire County Record Office.
76. Peter Withers, letter to brother, Ms. letters in TSA, Hobart.
77. James Backhouse and G. W. Walker, *A Narrative of a Visit to the Australian Colonies*, Appendix J, letter 3.

CHAPTER SEVEN   *Bolters and Bushrangers*

1. Watkin Tench, *A Complete Account of the Settlement at Port Jackson, in New South Wales*, p. 141. Some of the "Chinese travellers," he found (*Account*, p. 138), believed that China was only a hundred miles to the north of Parramatta, and separated from Australia by a river. Others were not so sure, but they had gone along "on account of being over-worked, and harshly treated . . . [T]hey preferred a solitary and precarious existence in the woods, to a return to the misery they were compelled to undergo." The China myth, Phillip correctly thought, was "an evil that will cure itself" (Phillip to Nepean, Nov. 18, 1791, HRA i:309). For Collins's views on it and the Irish who held it, see Collins, *An Account of the English Colony at New South Wales*, vol. 1, pp. 154, 162–63, and vol. 2, pp. 54–55, 57. In 1791, according to John Hunter (*An Historical Journal of the Transactions at Port Jackson and Norfolk Island*, pp. 563–64), no less than forty of them were missing in the bush.
2. Hunter to Portland, Feb. 15, 1798, HRNSW iii:359. Collins (*Account*, vol. 2, p. 57) adds that the Irish imagined this colony of whites to lie some 300 to 400 miles southwest of Sydney.
3. King to Hobart, May 9, 1803, HRA iv:85. King to Hobart, enclosure of Govt. & General Order dated March 1803, in Aug. 7, 1803, HRA iv:337.
4. On Mary Bryant, see ADB, vol. 1, pp. 173–74; C. H. Currey, *The Transportation, Escape and Pardoning of Mary Bryant*; and F. A. Pottle, *Boswell and the Girl from Botany Bay*. For the voyage, see James Martin, *Memorandoms*. This is an edition of Martin's own "Memorandoms," acquired by Jeremy Bentham and preserved in his papers in the British Library. Martin had been sentenced to 7 years' transportation at the Exeter Assizes for stealing "16½ lb. of old Lead and 4½ lb. of old Iron property of Lord Courney powdrum cacle near Exeter." He had struck up a friendship with the Bryants both on the hulk and on *Charlotte*, and escaped with them from Sydney Harbor. When, after his adventures, he returned to London, he wrote down an account of their sufferings on the epic small-boat voyage. It found its way to Jeremy Bentham, who was collecting evidence of the injustices and failures of transportation for his *Letter to Lord Pelham* (1802) and *A Plea for the Constitution* (1803), reprinted as *Panopticon Versus New South Wales* (1812). However, there is no reference to James Martin or his "Memorandoms" in Bentham's published works.
5. Collins, *Account*, pp. 129–30.
6. John Easty, "A Memorandom of the Transactions of a Voyage from England to Botany Bay in Scarborough Transport," entry for Mar. 28, 1791.
7. All quotations are from the account of the voyage in Martin's "Memorandoms."
8. Tench, *Account*, note to p. 108.
9. On Boswell and Mary Bryant in England, see Pottle, *Boswell and the Girl from Botany Bay*.
10. For Parsons's satire on Boswell's imagined affair with Mary Bryant, see Pottle, ibid., and Brady, *James Boswell: The Later Years*, pp. 464–65.

11. Hunter to Portland, Jan. 10, 1798, HRNSW iii:346.
12. Baudin to King, May 9, 1803, HRA iv:151.
13. Macquarie to Bathurst, May 16, 1818, HRA ix:793.
14. Memo to Lt.-Gov. Arthur on Bass Strait sealing, May 29, 1826, at reel 600, NSWA, Sydney.
15. Hobart Port Regulations, Apr. 13, 1830, CSO 1/445:1922, TSA, Hobart.
16. On the sandalwood trade and escaped convicts in the Pacific, see Greg Dening, *Islands and Beaches*, pp. 119ff., 129ff.
17. Cook *EL*, pp. 177–78.
18. Hunter to Portland, Jan. 10, 1798, HRNSW iii:345. Collins (*Account*, vol. 2, p. 35) gives an account of the seizure of the *Cumberland*.
19. On the seizure of the *Harrington*, see *Sydney Gazette*, May 22, 1808.
20. *The Australian*, Feb. 23, 1827, cit. in Crowley, *Doc. Hist.*, vol. 1, pp. 349–50.
21. On the piracy of the *Cyprus*, see Arthur to Murray, Sept. 11, 1829. TSA, CON 280:31; John West, *The History of Tasmania*, p. 425ff.; Lloyd L. Robson, *A History of Tasmania*, p. 150. The version of the ballad "The Cyprus Brig" is from Gary Shearston's recording *Bolters, Bushrangers and Duffers*, CBS #BP 233288. The *Cyprus* episode forms an important part of the narrative of Marcus Clarke's *His Natural Life*.
22. On James Porter and the voyage of the *Frederick*, see Porter's "Memoirs," typescript of an unpublished Ms. at MSQ 168, Dixson Library, Sydney. All quotations of Porter are from this source. General outlines of the voyage are given in the rare Anon., "Narrative of the Sufferings ... of the Convicts Who Piratically Seized the '*Frederick*,' " ca. 1838 (copy in ML at 910.453/29A1), and in West, *History of Tasmania*, p. 429ff.
23. SC1837–38 (ii), "Papers Delivered in by John Barnes, Esq." (B, "List of Prisoners Who Absconded from Macquarie Harbour . . .").
24. Pearce's origin, physical appearance and deeds have been, due to his subsequent history, the subject of much journalistic fantasy. The one reliable study is Dan Sprod, *Alexander Pearce of Macquarie Harbour*. Primary sources are: (1) "Narrative of Escape from Macquarie Harbour" (the "Knopwood Narrative," based on Pearce's interrogation after capture by the Rev. Robert Knopwood), Ms. 3, Dixson Library, Sydney; (2) manuscript in National Library of Australia, Ms. 3323, ff. 1–5; and (3) deposition made before Cuthbertson at Macquarie Harbor and entered in SC 1837–38 (ii). Except where noted I have taken all direct Pearce quotes from (3).
25. For the chronology and route of Pearce's escape, see Sprod, *Alexander Pearce*, pp. 64–81.
26. "Knopwood Narrative."
27. W. S. Sharland, "Rough Notes of a Journal of Expedition to the Westward . . . ," in Tasmanian Parliament Legislative Council Papers, 16, 1861, as *Survey Office Reports*, 1861, 1, p. 6.
28. "Knopwood Narrative."
29. Ibid.
30. Ibid.
31. For Pearce's second escape from Macquarie Harbor, with Cox, see Sprod, *Alexander Pearce*, pp. 99–106, based on evidence of John Barnes to SC 1837–38 (ii), Appendix 1, 56(d).
32. Barnes to SC 1837–38 (ii), Appendix 1, 56(d), p. 316.
33. Pearce's "Bisdee" confession, Jun. 20, 1824, in Sprod, *Alexander Pearce*, p. 105.
34. On the emergence of Van Diemen's Land bushrangers and their relative immunity from capture and prosecution, see Robson, *Hist. Tas.*, Chapter 6, esp. pp. 79–83.
35. West, *Tasmania*, p. 364.
36. On Brown, Lemon and Scanlan, see Paterson to Castlereagh, May 7, 1818, HRA iii:685–86; Robson, *Hist. Tas.*, p. 80; and Charles White, *History of Australian Bushranging*, vol. 1, pp. 3–4.
37. Macquarie's proclamation: May 14, 1814, HRA viii:262 and 264–65. Davey's proclamation of martial law: West, *Tasmania*, p. 360, and Robson, *Hist. Tas.*, p. 81.

38. Petition to Davey by Humphrey, Sept. 30, 1815, CON 201:79. Robson, *Hist. Tas.*, p. 88.
39. Howe to Davey, CSO 1/223:5399, a contemporary copy of Howe's lost original. I have amended the spelling and punctuation slightly, for clarity's sake. Davey mentioned in dispatches that the original was "written in blood," presumably that of a sheep or a kangaroo. Of course there were few inkwells in the Tasmanian bush, but one may still admire Howe's dramatic gesture.
40. Wylde to Macquarie, encl. 2 in Macquarie to Bathurst, Jul. 17, 1821, HRA x:512–15.
41. Ibid.
42. Macquarie to Bathurst, Jul. 17, 1821, HRA x:509.
43. On Brady, see ADB entry and bibliography; Robson, *Hist. Tas.*, pp. 141–44; George Boxall, *The Story of the Australian Bushrangers*, p. 41ff; and White, *Australian Bushranging*, vol. 1, pp. 40–53.
44. John Barnes, testimony in SC 1837–38 (ii), Minutes, p. 41.
45. *The Australian*, Nov. 11, 1834.
46. T. L. Mitchell, *Three Expeditions into the Interior of Eastern Australia*, vol. 1, p. 9.
47. Bourke to Goderich, Mar. 19, 1832, HRA.
48. Alexander Harris, *Settlers and Convicts*, p. 35.
49. White, *Australian Bushranging*, vol. 1, pp. 102–3.
50. See Russel Ward, "Felons and Folksongs," passim.

CHAPTER EIGHT   *Bunters, Mollies and Sable Brethren*

1. Lloyd L. Robson, *The Convict Settlers of Australia*, pp. 77–78.
2. Ibid., Appendix 4, table 4(o), p. 187.
3. Shaw *CC*, p. 164.
4. Anne Summers, *Damned Whores and God's Police*, p. 286. Summers attributes the emblematic phrase "damned whores" to Lieutenant Ralph Clark of the First Fleet, who allegedly uttered it on seeing the *Lady Juliana*, female transport of the Second Fleet, sail into Sydney Harbor in June 1790. "No, no—surely not! My God—not more of those damned whores! Never have I known worse women." A sharp-eyed fellow, for at the time of *Lady Juliana*'s arrival he was actually a thousand miles away, stranded on Norfolk Island.
5. Sydney to the Treasury Commissioners, "Heads of a Plan," Aug. 18, 1786, HRNSW i:18. One may note, without dwelling on it, the sense of Pacific geography implied by Lord Sydney's notion that New Caledonia and Tahiti were "contiguous" to New South Wales.
6. Before he sailed for Australia, Phillip briefly considered a scheme of licensed prostitution in New South Wales. "The keeping of the women apart merits great consideration, and I don't know but it may be the best if the most abandoned are permitted to receive the visits of the convicts in the limits allotted them at certain hours, and under certain restrictions; something of this kind was the case in Mill Bank formerly. The rest of the women I should keep apart." ("Phillip's Views on the Conduct of the Expedition and Treatment of the Convicts," HRNSW ii:52.) Maybe the general promiscuity of the early settlement made this idea unnecessary. On Phillip's policy of encouraging convict marriages—most of which lasted—see HRNSW ii:52; and Watkin Tench, *A Narrative of the Expedition to Botany Bay*, p. 63: "To prevent their intercourse was impossible; to palliate its evils only remained. Marriage was recommended, and such advantages held out to those who aimed at reformation, as have greatly contributed to the tranquillity of the settlement."
7. Thomas Watling, *Letters from an Exile at Botany-Bay . . .*, pp. 18–19. Does his "*whore* and *rogue* together" indicate a reading of Dean Swift?

> Under an Oak, in stormy weather,
> I put this Whore and Rogue together:

And none but Him Who rules the thunder
May put this rogue and whore asunder.

8. Patrick Colquhoun, *A Treatise on the Police of the Metropolis*, pp. vii–xi. Mayhew conflating promiscuity with prostitution: see Mayhew and Hemyng, "The Prostitution Class Generally," in Mayhew, *London Labour and the London Poor*, vol. 4, cit. in Sturma, "The Eye of the Beholder," p. 6.
9. Sturma, ibid., pp. 8–10.
10. For a discussion of Marsden's *Register* and the effects it had on the perception of colonial "immorality," see Portia Robinson, *The Hatch and Brood of Time*, vol. 1, pp. 75–77.
11. Ralph Clark, *Journal*, June 23, 1787.
12. Ibid., June 28, 1787.
13. Ibid., July 16, 1787.
14. "Ten thousand times worse": ibid., May 16, 1787. "I would have flogged the four whores also": ibid., June 19, and July 3, 1787.
15. Ibid., July 18, 1787.
16. "Surely an angel": ibid., Dec. 9, 1787. "If they were to lose anything": ibid., Oct. 11, 1787. "I was going down to Tregadock": ibid., Nov. 20, 1787. "She was better than half dead": ibid., May 24, 1790. "I wish the almighty": June 21, 1790.
17. For Nicol's account of women convicts on the *Lady Juliana*, see John Nicol, *The Life and Adventures of John Nicol, Mariner*, pp. 111–23.
18. Ibid.
19. Lord Auckland, draft of letter, Aug. 25, 1812, in Auckland Papers, BL, Add. Ms. 34458, pp. 382–84.
20. John Capper to SC 1812, Appendix 1, p. 77.
21. S. Hutchinson to J. Foyle, Sept. 5, 1798, letter at Ab. 67/15, ML.
22. Thomas Robson to SC 1812, Appendix 1, p. 52.
23. William Bligh to SC 1812, Appendix 1, p. 32.
24. T. W. Plummer to Macquarie, May 4, 1809, HRA vii:120.
25. Castlereagh to Macquarie, May 14, 1809, HRA vii:84.
26. G. H. Hammersley, "A Few Observations on the Situation of the Female Convicts in NSW," ca. 1807, in Hammersley Papers, A 657, ML.
27. The opinion of the *Atrevida*'s lieutenant is given in Crowley, *Doc. Hist.*, vol. 1, p. 57.
28. Michael Hayes to his sister Mary, Nov. 2, 1802, ML, Sydney.
29. Ibid.
30. Bigge NSW, p. 20.
31. Ibid.
32. For general descriptions of the Female Factory in 1815, before its reconstruction by Greenway, see Samuel Marsden, "An Answer to the Calumnies of the Late Governor Macquarie's Pamphlet" (1826), p. 18ff. (Marsden Papers, ML, Sydney), and (for the Factory in 1820) Bigge NSW, pp. 68–74. For regulations of the Female Factory and classification of its inmates, see "Rules and Regulations for the Management of Female Convicts at the New Factory at Parramatta," Sydney 1821, ML, Sydney.
33. Anon., in HRA ix:198–99. Macquarie to Bathurst, Dec. 4, 1817.
34. Rev. Samuel Marsden, "An Answer," pp. 23–24.
35. R. Durie to J. T. Campbell, Mar. 3, 1811, NSW Col. Sec. in-letters bundle 5, Nos. 1–64, pp. 99–100, ML, Sydney.
36. Thomas Reid, *Two Voyages to New South Wales and Van Diemen's Land*, cit. in Margaret Weidenhofer, *The Convict Years*, p. 77.
37. J. F. O'Connell, *A Residence of Eleven Years in New Holland*, p. 54, cit. in Crowley, *Doc. Hist.*, vol. 1, p. 310.
38. Mellish, *A Convict's Recollections*, p. 54.
39. Summers, *Damned Whores*, p. 281.
40. J. E. Drabble to J. Lakeland, Hobart, May 1, 1827, CSO 1/324:1704, TSA, Hobart.
41. *Sydney Gazette*, Oct. 31, 1827, cit. in Summers, *Damned Whores*, p. 285.

42. Peter Murdoch to SC 1837–38 (ii), Minutes, p. 118.
43. Robert Jones, "Recollections of 13 Years Residence on Norfolk Island," Ms. in ML, Sydney.
44. James Mitchell, memorandum ca. 1815, typescript Ms. 27/c. in Stenhouse Papers II, ML, Sydney.
45. Joseph Holt, "Life and Adventures of Joseph Holt," Ms. A2024, ML, Sydney.
46. Ibid.
47. Ibid.
48. Ibid.
49. James Mitchell, Ms. memorandum in Stenhouse Papers II, Ms. 27/c, ML, Sydney.
50. Jones, "Recollections."
51. Lepailleur's journal, covering the years 1839–44, is in the Archives Nationales de Québec; a translation is expected for publication by F. Murray Greenwood of the University of British Columbia. On Lepailleur and his comrades in Australia, see Beverley D. Boissery, "French-Canadian Political Prisoners in Australia, 1838–39" (Ph.D. diss.), and Beverley D. Boissery and Murray F. Greenwood, "New Sources for Convict History."
52. Lepailleur, "Journal."
53. Bishop William Ullathorne, *Autobiography*, p. 152.
54. Caroline Anley, *The Prisoners of Australia*, cit. in Crowley, *Doc. Hist.*, vol. 1, p. 461.
55. *The Australian*, Apr. 7, 1825.
56. For one chronicler of homosexuality in Australia, this promise of fierce punishment was "evidence" of Phillip's own homosexuality; it was, he claimed, meant to deflect attention from "rumors" of his own supposed "interest in young seamen." (Martin Smith, "Arthur Phillip and the Young Lads," p. 15.) This is wishful thinking. No jot of evidence suggests that the *pater patriae* was homosexual, or that such rumors existed. All military governors of Australian colonies found homosexual prisoners utterly repugnant; Arthur, for instance, called one pair of convict lovers "horrible beasts" (Jan. 27, 1832, CSO 1/572:12924).
57. George Lee, letter to Sir H. St. J. Mildmay, Jan. 24, 1803, Bentham Papers, Add. Ms. 33544, BL, pp. 14–15. Jeremy Bentham, draft letter re hulk conditions, ibid., p. 105ff.
58. See, for example, Backhouse and Walker, Ms. "Reports" in ML, at B706–7, i/27:231ff.
59. Ullathorne's reflections on immoral Australia: William Ullathorne, *The Catholic Mission in Australasia*, p. iv.
60. John Stephen, Jr. to SC 1832. Minutes, p. 30. Allan Cunningham, ibid., p. 36.
61. Report of SC 1837–38 (ii), Appendix 1/57, "Return of the Number of Persons Charged with Criminal Offences," p. 317.
62. John Russell to SC 1837–38 (ii), Minutes, p. 60.
63. Ullathorne, *Catholic Mission*, p. 17.
64. Cook *EL*, pp. 19–20.
65. Ibid.
66. Ibid., p. 46.
67. Ibid., p. 41.
68. Ibid., pp. 174–75.
69. Ibid., p. 173.
70. Thomas Arnold to SC 1837–38 (ii), Sept. 27, 1837, Appendix E/45. Robert Pringle Stuart, 1846 Report to the VDL Comptroller-General, reprinted in Eustace Fitzsymonds, ed., *Norfolk Island 1846: The Accounts of Robert Pringle Stewart and Thomas Beagley Naylor*, p. 46. Ullathorne to SC 1837–38 (ii), Minutes, p. 25.
71. Thomas Beagley Naylor, "Norfolk Island, the Botany Bay of Botany Bay: A Letter . . . to the Rt. Hon. Lord Stanley, Secretary of State for the Colonies" (1846). Original in TSA, GO 1/63; reprinted in Fitzsymonds, ed., *Norfolk Island*, pp. 17–18. The reports of both Naylor and Stuart were printed by the English Government in *Correspondence Relative to Convict Discipline and Transportation, presented to both Houses of Parliament*, Feb. 16, 1847. But both were heavily bowdlerized, all proper names were omitted, and all reference to homosexual practices was suppressed—either to protect

the delicate sensibilities of Parliamentarians, or to minimize the damage to the already much-bruised name of the transportation system.

72. Stuart, Report, in Fitzsymonds, ed., *Norfolk Island*, pp. 45–46.
73. Ibid., p. 47.
74. George III's instructions to Phillip: HRNSW ii:52.
75. C. D. Rowley, *Aboriginal Policy and Practice*, vol. 1: *The Destruction of Aboriginal Society*, p. 19.
76. J. Arnold, letter to his brother, Mar. 18, 1810, at A1849, ML, Sydney. P. G. King, "Observations on the New Zealand Natives," HRA vi:7.
77. Macquarie to Bathurst, Oct. 8, 1814, HRA viii:369–70, and Mar. 24, 1815, HRA viii:467.
78. F. Debenham, ed., *The Voyage of Captain Bellingshausen to the Antarctic Seas 1819–1821*, cit. in Crowley, *Doc. Hist.*, vol. 1, p. 264.
79. Geoffrey Blainey, *The Triumph of the Nomads*, pp. 108–9.
80. Decision by J. Burton in *Rex* v. *Jack Congo Murrell* (1836), cit. in Rowley, pp. 15–16.
81. Proclamation by King, June 1802, HRA iii:592–93. Atkins to King, July 8, 1805, HRA iv:653.
82. William Walker to Rev. W. Watson, 1821, cit. in Jean Woolmington, ed., *Aborigines in Colonial Society, 1788–1850*, p. 86. "It was an observation of the Governor's that will never lose its impression on my mind," remarked the Wesleyan missionary in this letter to his colleague in London.
83. Economic warfare by Aborigines: Reynolds, *Other Side*, p. 121.
84. Aboriginal perception of white settlement and land ownership: Reynolds, *Other Side*, p. 64ff.
85. Benjamin Hurst to Latrobe, July 22, 1841, BT Box 54 in ML, Sydney, cit. in Woolmington, ed., *Aborigines*, p. 38.
86. Edward M. Curr, cit. in ibid., pp. 63–64.
87. Reynolds, *Other Side*, pp. 121–24.
88. E. Deas Thomson to James Dowling, Jan. 4, 1842, HRA xxi:655–56. *SMH*, Dec. 26, 1836, cit. in Woolmington, ed., *Aborigines*, p. 54.
89. *The Colonist*, June 20, 1838, cit. in Woolmington, ed., *Aborigines*, pp. 55–56.
90. Thomas Holden, letter to his wife, ca. 1815, DDX 140/7:18, LRO.
91. James Gunther, Journal, Dec. 30, 1837, cit. in Woolmington, ed., *Aborigines* p. 69.
92. The most famous of these was William Buckley (1780–1856), an English militiaman from Cheshire who stood 6'6" in his bare feet and had been transported for life, in 1802, for receiving stolen cloth. He absconded from the tiny settlement on Port Phillip in Victoria in 1803 and had the luck to run into an aboriginal tribe, the Watourong, who mistook him for the reincarnated spirit of their dead chief. (It was an almost universal belief among Aborigines, irrespective of tribe, that the spirits of the dead returned in the form of "peeled" men, ashen white or gray. The color white was associated with death and resurrection.) Thus, in the guise of an enormous spirit, Buckley lived with the Watourong for thirty-two years before giving himself up. The sheer improbability of this gave rise to an Australian expression that still survives: "Buckley's chance," meaning no chance at all.
93. On the conditions of inland life, and the attitudes of lower-class settlers to aboriginal tribes on the frontiers of settlement in penal New South Wales, see David Denholm, *The Colonial Australians*, p. 37ff.
94. Wentworth, in the *SMH*, June 21, 1844.

CHAPTER NINE *The Government Stroke*

1. For a critique of the idea of penal Australia as a "slave society," see John B. Hirst, *Convict Society and Its Enemies*, esp. pp. 21–25, 31, 82.
2. Robert Gouger [pseud. of E. G. Wakefield], *A Letter from Sydney*, pp. 12–13. Wakefield had not visited Sydney, and his views on the difficulties facing the uninitiated settler

in an economy where land was given away were meant as propaganda for his "sufficient price" emigration scheme, whereby the price of Australian crown land was raised so that only substantial colonists could afford it. However, his sketch of this fictional servant carried a nugget of truth.

3. Eugene D. Genovese, *The Political Economy of Slavery,* p. 43. For a contrary view on the efficiency and adaptability of southern slave labor, which argues that southern slave agriculture was 35 percent more efficient than northern family farming, see William Fogel and Stanley Enderman, *Time on the Cross* (New York, 1974).

4. Hirst, *Convict Society,* p. 65.

5. Gouger [Wakefield], *Letter,* p. 37.

6. E. G. Wakefield, *The Art of Colonization,* pp. 176–77.

7. King to Castlereagh, HRA v:748–49.

8. Meredith to Burnett Dec. 30, 1828, in Meredith, *Correspondence,* p. 8, cit. in Shaw *CC,* p. 218. On the proportion of assigned "mechanics" in Van Diemen's Land under Arthur, see Shaw *CC,* p. 217.

9. Murray to Darling, Jan. 30, 1830, HRA xv:351ff.

10. "In what can Britain show": anon. article in *Virginia Gazette,* May 24, 1751, cit. in Abbot Emerson Smith, *Colonists in Bondage,* p. 130. John Pory, cit. in ibid., p. 13.

11. Smith, *Colonists,* p. 13. For a discussion of the legal differences between the old, American system of indenture and the new, Australian assignment system, see Murray to Darling, Jan. 30, 1830, HRA xv:351ff.

12. King, General Order of Oct. 31, 1800, in NSW General Orders and Proclamations, Safe 1/87, ML, Sydney, cit. in Crowley, *Doc. Hist.,* pp. 97–98.

13. King, General Order published in *Sydney Gazette,* Jan. 14, 1804.

14. David Collins, *An Account of the English Colony in New South Wales,* p. 11.

15. Margarot to SC 1812, Appendix 1, Minutes, p. 54.

16. SC 1812, Report, p. 4.

17. Bligh to SC 1812, Appendix 1, Minutes, p. 43.

18. Richardson to SC 1812, Appendix 1, Minutes, p. 57. King to Portland, Dec. 31, 1801, HRA iv:655–56.

19. Thomas Holden, letter in LRO, DDX 140/17:18.

20. Bigge NSW, p. 77.

21. Bligh to SC 1812, Appendix. 1, p. 46.

22. John Palmer to SC 1812, Appendix 1, p. 61. George Johnston, ibid., p. 73.

23. Campbell to SC 1812, Appendix 1, p. 68ff.

24. Brisbane to Undersecretary Horton, Nov. 6, 1824, HRA ix:414–15.

25. John Broxup, *Life of John Broxup, Late Convict at Van Diemen's Land,* p. 11. Addition (by scribe) to letter from Richard Dillingham, Sept. 29, 1836, in Harley W. Forster, ed., *The Dillingham Convict Letters.*

26. Brisbane to Bathurst, Nov. 6, 1824, HRA ix:413–14.

27. John Rule, *The Experience of Labour in Eighteenth-Century English Industry,* p. 201.

28. Macquarie to Castlereagh, Apr. 30, 1810.

29. Mellish, *A Convict's Recollections of New South Wales,* p. 51.

30. Macquarie, General Order, Dec. 15, 1810, in NSW General Orders and Proclamations, safe 1/87, ML, Sydney. The towns in question were Windsor, Richmond, Wilberforce, Castlereagh and Pitt Town; Macquarie's decision to name a town after William Wilberforce, the anti-slavery leader, reflected a mutual admiration between the two men.

31. See M. H. Ellis, *Francis Greenway;* J. M. Freeland, *Architecture in Australia,* pp. 30–41; and Morton Herman, *Early Australian Architects and Their Work,* passim.

32. Macquarie to Bathurst, Sept. 1, 1820.

33. Appendix to Bigge NSW, cit. in Shaw *CC,* p. 92.

34. Macquarie to Bathurst, Dec. 4, 1817, HRA ix:507–9.

35. M. M. Robinson, "Ode for the Queen's Birthday, 1816," in Brian Elliott and Adrian Mitchell, eds., *Bards in the Wilderness,* p. 12.

36. J. D. Lang, "Colonial Nomenclature," in ibid., p. 29.

37. Figures from Shaw *CC,* pp. 98–99.

38. R. B. Madgwick, *Immigration into Eastern Australia, 1788–1851*, pp. 30–32.
39. Macquarie to Bathurst, Mar. 24, 1819, HRA x:88.
40. Mar. 18, 1825, HRA xi:549.
41. Bathurst to Bigge, HRA x:4ff.
42. Margarot to SC 1812, Appendix 1, p. 54.
43. Petition of Robert Townson, NSWA, Mechanics' Bond Accounts 4/4525, 4/1775, p. 173.
44. Gipps to Glenelg, HRA xix:604–5.
45. Bourke to Goderich, HRA xvi:625, cit. in Bigge NSW, p. 75.
46. Bigge NSW, p. 75ff.
47. Goderich to Bourke, Aug. 22, 1831, HRA xvi:330. Bourke to Goderich, May 4, 1832, HRA xvi:640.
48. Darling to Goderich, July 14, 1831, HRA xvi:299.
49. W. C. Wentworth to Committee on Police, 1839, pp. 88–96, cit. in Hirst, *Convict Society*, p. 185.
50. Bourke to Goderich, Apr. 30, 1832, HRA xvi:624–26.
51. The clothing issue was fixed at three shirts a year, two sets of jacket and trousers (wool for winter and light wool or cotton duck for summer), and a strong pair of leather shoes. The weekly food ration was 12 lb. wheat (ground by the convicts themselves, in small iron handmills), 7 lb. fresh beef or mutton, two ounces of salt and two of soap. When grain or fresh meat were short, the master could substitute maize flour and salt pork. It will immediately be seen that, though monotonous and lacking in vegetables, this was a solid diet; no one could starve on a pound of meat a day. "They can make a meal": Broxup, *Life*, p. 7.
52. Port Macquarie Bench Book, June 13, 1836, NSWA 4/5639, cit. in Alan Atkinson, "Four Patterns of Convict Protest."
53. Atkinson, ibid.
54. George Taylor, letter, CSO 1/624/14148, TSA, Hobart.
55. Deposition of James Davis, Dec. 10, 1829, HRA xv:306–7. Thomas Argent: HRA xv:305.
56. CSO 1/568/12796, TSA, Hobart.
57. *Sydney Gazette*, Aug. 18, 1825.
58. Darling to Murray, Feb. 16, 1829, HRA xiv:646.
59. Gipps to Glenelg, Oct. 8, 1838, HRA xix:604.
60. Cook *EL*, pp. 33–34.
61. *Sydney Gazette*, Feb. 1, 1826.
62. George Loveless et al., *A Narrative of the Sufferings of . . . Four of the Dorchester Labourers*, p. 16.
63. Hirst, *Convict Society*, p. 109.
64. Goodwin to Lang, Sept. 21, 1850, A2226, Lang Papers, vol. 6, pp. 492–95, ML, Sydney.
65. James Brine, in G. Loveless et al., *A Narrative*, pp. 11–12.
66. Edward J. Eyre, "Autobiography," Ms., p. 45.
67. Alexander Berry, *Reminiscences*, cit. in ADB, vol. 1, p. 95.
68. Berry to Wollstonecraft, June 7, 1823, and Oct. 13, 1825, cit. in Shaw *CC*, p. 222 from Berry Papers, xi/xii, ML, Sydney.
69. James Macarthur to SC 1837–38 (ii), Minutes, p. 164. James Atkinson, *An Account of the State of Agriculture and Grazing in New South Wales*, pp. 112–16. T. P. Besnard, *A Voice from the Bush in Australia: Shewing its Present State, Advantages, and Capabilities* (1839), pp. 20–21, cit. in Crowley, *Doc. Hist.*, pp. 478–79.
70. Eyre, "Autobiography," Ms., p. 46.
71. Parents to Holden, DDX 140/17:14, LRO; wife to Holden, DDX 140/17:16, LRO.
72. Bigge NSW, p. 76.
73. Bourke to Goderich, Apr. 30, 1832, HRA xvi:625.
74. Bigge NSW, pp. 76–77.
75. William Vincent, letter to his mother, Aug. 17, 1829, in SC 1837–38 (ii), Appendix, p. 354.

76. Peter Withers, letter to his brother, TSA, Hobart.
77. Withers, ibid.; Richard Dillingham, *The Dillingham Convict Letters*, ed. H. W. Foster (Melbourne, 1970), pp. 21–23 [Sept.–Nov. 1838].
78. Petition of Thomas Jones, Apr. 8, 1830, PC 1/78, PRO.
79. Bigge NSW, p. 103.
80. Richard Whately, "Transportation," in *Miscellaneous Lectures and Reviews*, pp. 258–59, cit. Clark, ed., *Select Documents in Australian History, 1788–1850*, p. 151.
81. [O.P.Q.] in *New South Wales Magazine*, vol. 1 (August 1833), pp. 16–17.
82. Eyre, "Autobiography," Ms., pp. 46–47.
83. John Standfield, in G. Loveless et al., *A Narrative*, pp. 5–6.
84. Shaw *CC*, p. 226, quoting Anne McKay, p. 355. Eyre, "Autobiography," Ms., p. 47.

CHAPTER TEN   *Gentlemen of New South Wales*

1. Peter Cunningham, *Two Years in New South Wales*, vol. 1, pp. 44–45.
2. "A Settler," *SMH*, Jan. 16, 1839, cit. in John B. Hirst, *Convict Society and Its Enemies*, p. 207.
3. Louisa Anne Meredith, *Notes and Sketches of New South Wales*, pp. 52–53.
4. Arthur Bowes Smyth and Ralph Clark, Journals, Feb. 7, 1788.
5. On John Macarthur, see ADB entry (vol. 2, pp. 153–59); Macarthur Papers, ML, Sydney; M. H. Ellis, *John Macarthur*; and S. Macarthur-Onslow, ed., *Some Early Records of the Macarthurs of Camden*.
6. Macarthur's attempts to broaden his business interests beyond the pastoral were almost uniformly unsuccessful, so much so that by 1812 his unwise investments in Pacific trade had all but cancelled his profits from wool. He was the worst of company men. No one could work with him and expect to be treated as an equal partner. He boasted that he had "never yet failed in ruining a man who had become obnoxious to him." His grand disaster was a chartered company set up to corner the production of wool in Australia. Macarthur had dreamt of such a monopoly since at least 1804, but not until twenty years later did he bring it into existence with the all-important backing of the British Government: the Australian Agricultural Company, endowed with a million acres of land near Port Stephens, north of Sydney, and capitalized by private subscription at £1 million. No corporation of this size had ever been set up in the Pacific, and despite its early success Macarthur wrecked it within four years. By 1828 his meddling had become so intrusive that the AAC's shares sank from their original £100 to £8.
7. Macarthur's timing: S. Cottrell to E. Cooke, July 14, 1804. Lord Camden's land grant to Macarthur: David Collins, *An Account of the English Colony in New South Wales*, vol. 1, pp. 437–38.
8. On sheep-breeding in early colonial Australia, see Eric Rolls, *A Million Wild Acres*, pp. 23–27.
9. James Mudie, *The Felonry of New South Wales*, pp. 12–13.
10. James Macarthur to John Macarthur, Sr., June 24, and July 11, 1820, cit. in John M. Ward, *James Macarthur, Colonial Conservative*, p. 45.
11. On the southern "fisheries" of whales and seals, see Alan Moorehead, *The Fatal Impact*, pp. 195–204.
12. Unsigned memo on Bass Strait sealing to Lieut-Gov. Arthur, May 29, 1826, on microfilm reel 600, NSWA, Sydney.
13. The numbers of native women kidnapped in this way cannot be accurately assessed, but the traffic had two chief results. First, it stamped the aboriginal tribes with an ineradicable hatred of whites and depleted their birthrate. Second, and paradoxically enough, it ensured the survival of the Tasmanian Aborigines. After their extermination on the main island of Tasmania, a small group of aboriginal descendants contin-

ued to exist on Cape Barren Island in Bass Strait. (See Chapter 11.) For an account of the sealers' incursions, see Anne McMahon, "Tasmanian Aboriginal Women as Slaves"; on the Cape Barren Islanders, see Lyndall Ryan, *The Aboriginal Tasmanians*.

14. On Campbell's defiance of the East India Company's embargo on oil and sealskin from Australia, see Alan Frost, *Convicts and Empire*, p. 193ff.

15. J. Arnold, letter to his brother, Feb. 25, 1810, A1849, ML, Sydney, cit. in Crowley, *Doc. Hist.*, vol. 1, p. 171.

16. London *Times*, July 14, 1838. On Terry, see ADB entry (vol. 2, pp. 508–9); P. E. Leroy, "Samuel Terry" in *JRAHS*, vol. 47 (1961). On the rumors against Terry, see Bigge NSW, p. 141: Terry was alleged to keep ready-written powers of attorney in his public house, which fuddled ex-convicts would sign when drunk. "By these means, and by an active use of the common arts of over-reaching, Samuel Terry has been able to accumulate a considerable capital, and a quantity of land . . . inferior only to that which is held by Mr. D'Arcy Wentworth." The allegations that he fleeced other ex-convicts began with the Rev. Samuel Marsden. At his death, the "Botany Bay Rothschild" (who was, in fact, a Gentile) left his widow with £10,000 a year, an estate of £250,000, and vast land holdings that included the whole of Martin Place, the hub of modern Sydney.

17. On Crossley, see ADB entry (vol. 1, p. 262). Crossley was charged with posthumously altering the will of a clergyman, on the man's very deathbed, in favor of one of his own friends. He is said to have pleaded that there was, in fact, "life" in the Reverend's body at the moment the will was doctored. He had made sure of this by popping a live fly in his client's mouth, pushing it shut, and then placing in the dead hand a pen with which the signature was written. The court surprisingly acquitted him, but before long he was on his way to Botany Bay for seven years, for perjury in another malpractice case.

18. Although Bent's sole motive was bigotry, he attempted to give his decision a legal veneer by basing his refusal to hear convict attorneys on the statute 12, Geo. I, c. 29.

19. On Redfern, see HRA i:6–10; E. Ford, *The Life and Work of William Redfern*; and E. Ford, "Medical Practice in Early Sydney," *MJA*, July 9, 1955.

20. Barron Field, "On Reading the Controversy between Mr. Byron and Mr. Bowles," in Brian Elliott and Adrian Mitchell, eds., *Bards in the Wilderness: Australian Colonial Poetry to 1920*, p. 18.

21. On Lewin, see Bernard Smith, *European Vision and the South Pacific*, pp. 158–62. A relatively large number of convict artists were transported for the crime closest to their profession, forgery. The colony also had its free amateurs: naval draftsmen like the unidentified "Port Jackson Painter," who came with the First Fleet, and George Raper; and army officers who dabbled in painting, like Capt. James Wallis of the 46th Regiment.

22. John Grant, "Verses Written to Lewin, the Entomologist," 1805, in Grant Papers, Ms. 737, NLA, Canberra.

23. On Lycett and the beguiling modifications of Australian landscape in his "Views," see Smith, *European Vision*, pp. 179–81.

24. On Thomas Griffiths Wainewright, see J. Curling, *Janus Weathercock* (London, 1838); and R. Crossland, *Wainewright in Tasmania* (Melbourne, 1954). A sickly but eager esthete and something of a Georgian dandy, Wainewright was both painter and art critic, writing for the *London Magazine* in the 1820s under the pseudonyms of Egomet Bonmot and Janus Weathercock. He exhibited paintings strongly indebted to Henry Fuseli at the Royal Academy from 1826 onward. Wainewright lived beyond his means, and his fall from grace into the Antipodes began when he forged powers of attorney in order to get his hands on a capital sum of £5,250 left him by his grandfather and transferred, in trust, to his wife. Thirteen years later he was arrested and tried for (as he saw it) taking his own money. The governor of Newgate Prison persuaded him to plead guilty in return for a light sentence. Instead, to Wainewright's horror, he was transported for life.

The unhappy artist arrived in Hobart at the end of 1837 and was put in a chain gang on the roads. His health collapsed and he was transferred to ward work in the Hobart hospital. In return for small and condescendingly given favors from the eminent of Hobart, he did watercolor portraits; some forty of these survive. A heart-rending plea for a ticket-of-leave, written to the lieutenant-governor, Sir John Eardley Eardley-Wilmot, in April 1844, is preserved (Aw. 15, ML, Sydney). Wainewright calls Van Diemen's Land "a moral sepulchre." "Deign, your Excellency! to figure to yourself my actual condition during 7 years, without *friends, good-name* (the breath of Life) or *Art*—(the fuel to it with me). Tormented at once by Memory, & Ideas struggling for outward form & realization, barred up from increase of knowledge, & deprived of the exercise of profitable or even *decorous* speech. Take pity, Your Excellency!" He reminds Eardley-Wilmot (who had probably not heard of any of them) that he, Wainewright, has been praised by "Flaxman, Coleridge, Chas. Lamb . . . & the God of his worship, *Fuseli.*" All to no avail; his ticket-of-leave was not granted until the end of 1846, less than a year before his death.

25. For an example of these "pipes," see Anon., "Alas; poor Botany Bay," in Elliott and Mitchell, eds., *Bards in the Wilderness*, p. 8.
26. J. M. Freeland, *Architecture in Australia*, p. 39. On Greenway, see ADB entry (vol. 1, pp. 470–72); M. H. Ellis, *Francis Greenway*; and Morton Herman, *Early Australian Architects and their Work.*
27. Meredith, *Notes and Sketches*, pp. 50–51.
28. Ibid., p. 39.
29. Letters of G.T.W.B. Boyes, May 6, 1824, Royal Society of Tasmania, UTL, Hobart.
30. Meredith, *Notes and Sketches*, pp. 49–50.
31. Ibid., pp. 58–59, 75.
32. Hirst, *Convict Society*, pp. 118–19.
33. Gipps to Glenelg, Mar. 29, 1839. HRA xx:74.
34. Mellish, *A Convict's Recollections*, p. 52.
35. Ullathorne to SC 1837–38 (ii), Minutes, p. 22. Domestic horror-stories: Meredith, *Notes and Sketches*, p. 128. Christmas was especially trying, she reported: "The prevailing vice of drunkenness among the lower orders is perhaps more resolutely practised at this season than any other. I have heard of a Christmas-day party being assembled, and awaiting the announcement of dinner as long as patience would endure; then ringing the bell, but without reply; and on the hostess proceeding to the kitchen, finding every servant either gone out or rendered incapable of moving, the intended feast being meanwhile burned to ashes. Nor is this by any means a rare occurrence."
36. John Russell to SC 1837–38 (ii), Minutes, p. 56.
37. Gipps to Glenelg, Mar. 29, 1839, HRA xx:74.
38. Russell to SC 1837–38 (ii), Minutes, pp. 58–59.
39. John Goodwin to J. D. Lang, 1850, Lang Papers, vol. 6, A2226, ML, Sydney.
40. Maconochie to SC 1837–38 (ii), Report, p. xxxiii; Ullathorne to SC 1837–38 (ii), Minutes, p. 23.
41. Russell to SC 1837–38 (ii), Minutes, p. 56.
42. Darling to Goderich, Oct. 2, 1837, HRA xiii: 673.
43. J. F. Mortlock, *Experiences of a Convict Transported for Twenty-one Years*, p. 92.
44. On John Grant, see ADB entry (vol. 1, pp. 469–70); W. S. Hill-Reid, *John Grant's Journey*; Grant Papers (journal and letters), NLA, Canberra. Grant's description of his efforts to extract a ticket-of-leave from Governor King is in a letter to his mother and sister, Jan. 1, 1805, Ms. 737/22, NLA, Canberra.
45. Mortlock, *Experiences of a Convict*, pp. 84–85. The former MP was William Smith O'Brien (1803–1864), member for Ennis (1828–31) and Limerick (1835–49), one of the leaders of the Young Ireland movement who, with his compatriot John Mitchel and several others, was convicted of high treason in 1848 and transported for life to Van Diemen's Land.

46. Woomera [pseud.], *The Life of an Ex-Convict*, p. 13. On official harassment of Specials who professed atheism, see James Bushelle, "Memoir." Bushelle, the son of an Irish merchant in Limerick, was transported for stealing diamonds. He served a term in the penal station at Port Macquarie, returned to Sydney, became choir-leader in St. Mary's Cathedral and instructor to the military bands; he presented these signs of respectability to Governor Bourke, hoping for an early ticket-of-leave. Alas, "Governor Bourke would not grant [me] that indulgence; having referred to [my] character on the books, and found the charge of ATHEISM affixed to [my] name." Instead, he went back to Port Macquarie for another year, bitterly lamenting the day he had succumbed to the French accomplice in crime who "in the polite and fascinating language of France and Italy . . . infused into my unsuspecting mind, that ffrench Philosophy best known in England as *ffrench Principles*, meaning those poisonous seeds disseminated by *Voltaire* and his school, founded upon Satire and Irony upon Religion and Government."

47. The first view was set forth by Russel Ward in *The Australian Legend:* "All we know about the convicts shows that egalitarian class solidarity was the one human trait which usually remained to all but the most brutalized." It was attacked by Humphrey McQueen (*A New Britannia*, pp. 126–27) on the grounds that the convicts could not have felt class loyalty because they did not form a class: "For its first fifty years at least, Australia did not have a class structure, but only a deformed stratification. . . . The convicts lacked, through no fault of their own, any feeling of class-consciousness." This late Marxist boilerplate ignores the primary social fact of colonial society, which was that convicts were treated, oppressed, and made to see themselves as a class separate from and inferior to all free settlers. They were usually called "a class" in official communications. That their behavior did not conform to Utopian stereotypes of class unity—that, like their social superiors, they competed for property and status—in no way altered their sense of separateness as a group, or their ability to stick together. In McQueen's schematic view of history, even the convicts' dislike of guard, trap, informer and beak was "essentially bourgeois in origin and content," reflecting only the hegemony of false individualism. No doubt if they had loved their Gulag, such writers would laud them as pioneer Stalinists.

48. Rev. John Morison, *Australia As It Is*, London, 1864, p. 223.

49. Hunter to SC 1812, Appendix 1, Minutes, p. 23.

50. Samuel Marsden, "A Few Observations on the Toleration of the Catholic Religion in N. South Wales."

51. Ward, *Australian Legend*, pp. 29–30.

52. Mellish, *Recollections*, pp. 63–65.

53. Alexander Harris, *Settlers and Convicts*, p. 326.

54. Ibid., p. 126.

55. Bligh to SC 1812, Appendix 1, Minutes, p. 46. Bigge NSW, p. 102. Bourke to Goderich, Apr. 30, 1832, HRA xvi:625.

56. Sydney Smith, *Edinburgh Review*, July 1819.

57. For a discussion of the complexities of origin in colonial society in the 1820s, and the inadequacy of the "children of the convicts" stereotype, see Portia Robinson, *The Hatch and Brood of Time*.

58. "Crime *descends*": Judge Alfred Stephen to James Macarthur, ca. 1857, cit. in Michael Sturma, *Vice in a Vicious Society*, p. 2. On the respectable reaction against convictism, see Sturma, p. 8: "Ultimately the community's reaction to its convict origins proved of more lasting and profound significance than convictism itself."

59. Sir William W. Burton, "State of Society and State of Crime in New South Wales . . . ," *Colonial Magazine*, vol. 1, p. 425.

60. Burton, ibid., vol. 2, pp. 51–53. Burton's general figures for crime, gathered from trials before other judges as well, show the same pattern. Translated into percentages of defendants in three sample years, they become:

		percentage of total indictments	
SOCIAL GROUP	1833	1835	1836
Free emigrants	1	11	9
Currency	2	3	5
Emancipists	43	37	41
Convicts under sentence	51	46	42
Other (incl. military and blacks)	3	3	3

61. Bigge NSW, p. 105.
62. Robinson, *Hatch and Brood of Time*, p. 12.
63. "None *but* slaves *do* work": Cunningham, *New South Wales*, vol. 2, pp. 48–49. Aversion to the sea and maritime labor: Robinson, *Hatch and Brood of Time*, p. 237ff. Bigge, it seems, was wrong in reporting (Bigge NSW, pp. 81–82) that "many of the native youths have evinced a strong disposition for a sea-faring life, and are excellent sailors. . . . [T]hat class of the population will afford abundant and excellent materials for the supply of any department in the commercial or naval service."
64. "Fair hair and blue eyes": Cunningham, *New South Wales*, vol. 2, p. 53. Other references to Currency traits also are from Cunningham, passim.
65. G.T.W.B. Boyes to Mary Boyes, Oct. 23 and 27, 1831, in Boyes Letters, UTL, Hobart.
66. "Supercilious intolerance": Harris, *Settlers and Convicts*, pp. 295–96. "Sterling madonnas": Cunningham, *New South Wales*, vol. 2, p. 53.
67. Harris, *Settlers and Convicts*, pp. 149–53.
68. Bigge NSW, Appendix. CO 201:142, p. 336ff, cit. in Clark *HA*, vol. 2, p. 43. On Wentworth, see Clark *HA*, vol. 2, p. 41ff.
69. William Charles Wentworth, "Where'er the sickening Muse," in Wentworth Papers, Miscellanea, ML, Sydney.
70. "I will not suffer": W. C. Wentworth, May 1, 1820, in Wentworth Letters, ML, Sydney. The term "bunyip aristocracy"—still occasionally used in Australia to deride the pretentious—was invented by the young Irish politico Daniel Deniehy in 1853, in a speech against Wentworth's self-serving proposal for a hereditary colonial *noblesse*. The relevant passage, as reported on Aug. 16, 1853 in the *Sydney Morning Herald*, runs: "Even the poor Irishman in the streets of Dublin would fling his jibe at the Botany Bay aristocrats. In fact, he [Deniehy] was puzzled how to classify them. . . . Perhaps it was only a specimen of the remarkable contrariety that existed at the Antipodes. Here they all knew the common water-mole was transformed into the duck-billed platypus, and in some distant emulation of this degeneration, he supposed they were to be favoured with a bunyip aristocracy. (Great laughter.)"
71. W. C. Wentworth, *A Statistical, Historical and Political Description of the Colony of New South Wales . . .* , pp. 349–50.
72. Sidney Smith, *Edinburgh Review*, July 1819.
73. The text of the Emancipists' petition to the Crown is given in HRA x:549–52.
74. The winner was William Mackworth Praed, who knew little about Australasia but was soon to become the wittiest writer of *vers de société* in England. Against him, Wentworth's clumping measures had little chance; but that second prize was the first cultural kudos earned by an Australian overseas.
75. Brisbane to Bathurst, Oct. 28, 1824, in "Transcripts of Missing Despatches," A1267, ML, Sydney.

CHAPTER ELEVEN *To Plough Van Diemen's Land*

1. On Thomas Davey, see ADB entry; Robson, *Hist. Tas.*, pp. 64–67 and 78–94; and J. W. Beattie, *Glimpses of the Lives and Times of the Early Tasmanian Governors*, pp. 23–25.

2. William Sorell, Memorandum in HRA iii:4.

3. In July 1817, shortly after assuming office in Van Diemen's Land, Sorell was ordered to pay damages of £3,000—a colossal sum—to Lieutenant Kent for alienating the affections of his wife. When Mrs. Kent arrived in Hobart and settled into residence at Government House, the notoriously choleric Anthony Fenn Kemp, merchant, landowner, former New South Wales Corps Captain and conspirator in the "Rum Rebellion" plot against Governor Bligh, used this "evil example to the Rising Generation" as his main weapon in a campaign to unseat Sorell. Partly because the normally prudish Governor Macquarie distrusted Fenn Kemp for his role in the Rum Rebellion, these objurgations failed.

4. Sorell to Cuthbertson, in standing orders, Dec. 8, 1821, CSO 1/133/3229, TSA, Hobart.

5. John Barnes to SC 1837–38 (ii), Minutes, pp. 45–46.

6. James Backhouse, A *Narrative of a Visit to the Australian Colonies*, pp. 44–45.

7. Pine logging statistics for the year 1827: T. J. Lemprière, *The Penal Settlements of Van Diemen's Land*, p. 39.

8. Barnes to SC 1837–38 (ii), Minutes, p. 37.

9. Monotony relieved by hunting privileges: J. Butler to Arthur, Aug. 28, 1828, CSO 1/290/6944, TSA, Hobart. Taste of echidna: Lemprière, *Penal Settlements*, pp. 43–44.

10. Vegetables against scurvy: Sorell to Cuthbertson, Dec. 10, 1823, CSO 1/134/3229. Rapid increase of scurvy: J. Spence (asst. surgeon at Macquarie Harbor) to James Scott, Colonial Surgeon, Feb. 8, 1823, CSO 1/134/3230.

11. Lemprière, *Penal Settlements*, pp. 37–38.

12. Barnes to SC 1837–38 (ii), Minutes, p. 37.

13. Davies, "Memoir of Macquarie Harbour," Ms. 8 in MSQ 168, Dixson Library, Sydney.

14. For occupational disease among the convicts and guards at Macquarie Harbor, see Spence to Scott, CSO 1/134/3230.

15. Davies, "Memoir," pp. 2–3.

16. Barnes to SC 1837–38 (ii), Minutes, p. 45.

17. Ibid., p. 46.

18. Ibid., p. 43.

19. J. Butler (commandant at Macquarie Harbor) to Arthur, June 9, 1825, CSO 1/280/5313.

20. Butler to Col. Sec. Burnett, Nov. 25, 1827, CSO 1/216/5236, p. 189.

21. CSO 1/216/5188, Minute 312, Dec. 17, 1827, pp. 239, 243, 247.

22. Lemprière, *Penal Settlements*, p. 31.

23. Ibid., p. 32.

24. Barnes to SC 1837–38 (ii), Minutes, p. 43.

25. Robson, *Hist. Tas.*, p. 137. On Arthur, see ADB entry; Anne McKay, "The Assignment System of Convict Labour in Van Diemen's Land, 1824–1842" (M.A. thesis); and W. D. Forsyth, *Governor Arthur's Convict System.*

26. Arthur to Huskisson, cit. in P. R. Eldershaw, "The Colonial Secretary's Office," in "Guide to the Public Records of Tasmania," Thrapp, vol. 15, no. 3, Jan. 1968, p. 57.

27. Arthur to Bathurst, July 3, 1825.

28. Backhouse, *Narrative*, p. 19.

29. Arthur, *Observations Upon Secondary Punishment*, pp. 27–28.

30. George Washington Walker to Margaret Bragg, May 24, 1834, Walker Papers, UTL, Hobart.

31. McKay, "Assignment System," p. 78.

32. George Taylor to John Thompson, CSO 1/624/14148, collected as No. CXXVIII in Eustace Fitzsymonds, ed., *A Looking-Glass for Tasmania.*

33. The first major landowner and capitalist of Van Diemen's Land was Edward Lord; see E. R. Henry, "Edward Lord: the John Macarthur of Van Diemen's Land." On his unrelated namesake, the convict's son David Lord (1785–1847), see ADB entry (vol. 2, p. 126).

34. On the Rev. Carvosso at the scaffold, see Robson, *Hist. Tas.*, p. 276.

35. Arthur to Montagu, January 1831, CSO 1/224/5434, CSO 1/141/2493, cit. in McKay, "Assignment System," pp. 124–25.

36. Petition of Isaac Solomon to Arthur, CSO 1/430/9642. On Isaac "Ikey" Solomon, see ADB entry.
37. John West, *The History of Tasmania*, part 3, sect. XVII, p. 138.
38. Arthur, memo, Oct. 20, 1827, CSO 1/172/4150.
39. "Slanderers and slaves": West, *Tasmania*, part 3, sect. xvii, pp. 139–40.
40. Arthur's opinion of Baxter: ADB, vol. 1, p. 75.
41. On John Burnett, see ADB entry and corr. file under Burnett, J., in TSA.
42. On Roderic O'Connor and his relations with Arthur, see ADB, vol. 2, p. 296.
43. On Goodwin, Bent, Melville, Murray and other pioneers, however flawed, of journalism in Van Diemen's Land, see ADB entries and E. M. Miller, *Pressmen and Governors*.
44. Melville to Arthur, Nov. 17, 1835, CSO 1/836/17722. In a covering note to Melville's letter, the jailer, Thomas Capon, gives an interesting side-light on public opinion of Australian journalists. He had offered Melville a cell on the side of prison reserved for debtors, but "the Debtors had expressed their great repugnance to any person connected with the Press being put on their side of the Prison."
45. On Gellibrand, see ADB entry (vol. 1, p. 437), and Robson, *Hist. Tas.*, pp. 289–92.
46. Margaret Weidenhofer, *Maria Island: A Tasmanian Eden*, pp. 18–22.
47. On the growth of the "demonic" reputation of Port Arthur, see Decie Denholm, "Port Arthur: the Men and the Myth."
48. Arthur's Standing Instructions for Port Arthur are in CSO 1/639/14383.
49. Lemprière, *Penal Settlements*, p. 61.
50. John Russell to SC 1837–38 (ii), Minutes, p. 50.
51. On early years at Port Arthur (administrations of Russell and Mahon, 1830–32) see Margaret Weidenhofer, *Port Arthur: A Place of Misery*, pp. 7–12.
52. Russell to SC 1837–38 (ii), Minutes, pp. 51–2.
53. Logan to Col. Sec., Dec. 31, 1832, CSO 1/633.1/14299.
54. For number of sentences served at Port Arthur, see Decie Denholm, "Port Arthur," p. 408.
55. Charles O' Hara Booth, *Journal*, ed. Dora Heard, May 18, 1833.
56. C. P. T. Laplace, "Considerations" p. 152, cit. and trans. in Booth, *Journal*, p. 28; Booth, *Journal*, Feb. 20, and Dec. 7, 1833.
57. Lemprière, *Penal Settlements*, p. 94.
58. John Frost, *The Horrors of Convict Life*, pp. 30–31.
59. Backhouse and Walker to Arthur, CSO 1/807/17244, cit. in Weidenhofer, *Port Arthur*, p. 24.
60. Frost, *Horrors*, p. 59.
61. Punishment record of Robert Williamson is in TSA, Hobart.
62. Absconder disguised as kangaroo: Lemprière, *Penal Settlements*, p. 69.
63. Ibid., p. 95.
64. Details of the semaphore system are in Dora Heard's Introduction to Booth, *Journal*, pp. 24–25; W. E. Masters, *The Semaphore Telegraph System of Van Diemen's Land* (Hobart, 1973); and Weidenhofer, *Port Arthur*, p. 25.
65. Characteristics of Port Arthur coal: Lemprière, *Penal Settlements*, pp. 78–80.
66. For the convict-propelled railway, see Godfrey Mundy, *Our Antipodes*, and William Denison, *Varieties of Vice-Regal Life*, both cit. in Weidenhofer, *Port Arthur*, pp. 37, 39.
67. Ross, "Excursion to Port Arthur," in *Elliston's Hobart Town Almanack* (1837), p. 91.
68. On Point Puer, I have relied on F. C. Hooper's M.Ed. thesis, "Point Puer," University of Melbourne, 1954 (subsequently revised and published as *Prison Boys of Port Arthur*, Melbourne, 1967). Unless otherwise noted, all quotations are from Hooper's thesis, the standard and only full study of this curious pedagogical experiment.
69. Arthur to Turnbull, Feb. 8, 1834, cit. in Hooper, "Point Puer," p. 21.
70. Champ to the Comptroller-General of Convicts, June 3, 1844, cit. in ibid., p. 3.
71. On the religious instruction of inmates at Point Puer, see Hooper, pp. 72–79.

72. Benjamin Horne, "The Report of B. J. Horne to the Lieutenant-Governor of Van Diemen's Land," cit. in ibid., pp. 43–44.
73. Hooper, pp. 36–39.
74. Punishment record of Thomas Willetts is in TSA, Hobart.
75. Corr. Military Operations 1831, Minutes of Evidence for Committee for Aboriginal Affairs, testimony of Edward White, pp. 53–54.
76. James Carrott: Report of Committee for Aboriginal Affairs, Corr. Military Operations 1831, p. 36.
77. Corr. Military Operations 1831, Minutes of Evidence, testimony of James Hobbs, pp. 49–50. A full account of European settlers' and sealers' aggression against the Tasmanian Aborigines is given in Lyndall Ryan, *The Aboriginal Tasmanians*, Chapters 3–7.
78. Figures from Robson, *Hist. Tas.*, p. 260.
79. Richard Stickney to his sister Sarah, June 21, 1834, Stickney Papers, UTL. The Vandemonians, Stickney thought, "are a facsimile of the Americans both in body and mind, tall, raw-boned and muscular, with a most exalted opinion of themselves.... They are mostly ignorant to the last degree."
80. Corr. Military Operations 1831, Report of Aborigines Committee (Mar. 19, 1830), p. 41.
81. Ibid., Minutes, testimony of Gilbert Robertson, p. 48.
82. Ibid., encl. 7, Arthur to Murray, Apr. 15, 1830, p. 16.
83. Ibid., p. 48. For Arthur's views on treatment of Aborigines by free settlers, see ibid., p. 16.
84. Ibid., p. 47 (Sherwin, Espie), pp. 54–55 (O'Connor).
85. Ibid, p. 4: Arthur to Goderich, Jan. 10, 1828. The dogs were not dingoes, but the descendants of kangaroo-dogs and sheep-dogs "originally purloined from the settlers," which now formed enormous semi-wild packs.
86. Ibid.
87. Proclamation by Arthur, encl. 2 in Arthur to Huskisson, Apr. 17, 1828, Corr. Military Operations 1831, pp. 5–7.
88. Arthur's proclamation of martial law and his definition of restricted aboriginal territory in Van Diemen's Land, issued Nov. 1, 1828: ibid., pp. 11–12. Arthur was careful to "strictly order, enjoin and command that the actual use of arms be in no case resorted to ... that bloodshed be checked as much as possible; that any tribes which may surrender themselves up shall be treated with every degree of humanity; and that defenceless women and children be invariably spared."
89. Robson, *Hist. Tas.*, pp. 214–15.
90. John Burnett, Government Order 2, Feb. 25, 1830, Corr. Military Operations 1831, p. 35.
91. Arthur to Murray, Nov. 20, 1830, ibid., p. 58.
92. Murray to Arthur, Nov. 5, 1830, ibid., p. 56.
93. Robson, *Hist. Tas.*, p. 230.
94. Fear of bloodbath: Anstey to Arthur, Aug. 22, 1830, CSO 1/316. "The most rancorous animosity": Report of Aborigines Committee, in Corr. Military Operations 1831.
95. Arthur, Memorandum, encl. 7, Corr. Military Operations 1831, p. 72.
96. For an account of the Black Line and its effects on the big River and Oyster Bay tribes, see Ryan, *Aboriginal Tasmanians*, pp. 110–12.
97. On George Augustus Robinson, see ADB entry (vol. 2, pp. 385–87) and Ryan, *Aboriginal Tasmanians*, Chapters 8–9.
98. For the story of Trucanini, and a useful criticism of the myths that grew up around her (including the fiction that she was an Aboriginal "Queen"), see Vivienne Ellis, "Trucanini."

    However, the most pernicious—and seemingly, the most durable—myth is the one exposed by Lyndall Ryan, in *The Aboriginal Tasmanians*: the belief that Trucanini was "The Last Aborigine," and that after her death the Tasmanian Aborigines became an extinct race. It has been repeated, with varying degrees of outrage and pathos, by historians, anthropologists and journalists for over a century, with the result that the surviving Tasmanian Aborigines—who now number about 2,500—have found themselves treated as ciphers or non-persons by conservative Tasmanian whites, and as embarrassments by liberal ones with a vested emotional interest in the tale of their "extinction." Consequently, the Tasmanian State Government recognizes neither the ethnic identity of the surviving Tasmanian Aborigines, nor any of their claims to ancestral territory or sacred sites—as other Australian State Governments, in varying degrees, grudgingly do with mainland Aborigines. What happened, as Ryan shows in detail, was that a substantial number of Aborigines survived, interbreeding with the descendants of white sealers, on the islands in the Bass Strait, especially Cape Barren Island. In 1847 the Cape Barren islanders numbered thirteen families, comprising some fifty people. Their descendants, though as racially dilute as most American blacks or mainland Australian Aborigines, form the present black population of Tasmania. It should also be noted that Trucanini was not even the last full-blood Aborigine to die; that person was Suke, an old woman who had been taken by sealers from Cape Portland in Tasmania to Kangaroo Island off South Australia, and who lived until 1888.

CHAPTER TWELVE *Metastasis*

1. Shaw *CC*, p. 142.
2. Peel to Smith, Mar. 24, 1826, cit. in Shaw *CC*, pp. 144–45.
3. James Dowling, "Norfolk Island Journal," Feb. 25, 1828, ML, Sydney.
4. Alexander Harris, *Settlers and Convicts*, p. 11.
5. Figures based on Gipps to Glenelg, Nov. 8, 1838, HRA xix:654.
6. Harris, *Settlers and Convicts*, p. 12.
7. John Barnes in SC 1837–38 (ii), Minutes, p. 37.
8. Report of Ernest Augustus Slade, Appendix to SC 1837–38 (ii), paper 518, pp. 89–90.
9. Bourke to Rice, Dec. 14, 1834, HRA xvii:604 and n.; Col. Sec. circular 33/38, NSWA, Sydney.
10. Replies to Col. Sec. circular 33/38, Oct. 1–8, 1833, at NSWA 4/2189:1.
11. Darling to Bathurst, Mar. 1, 1827, cit. in Shaw *CC*, p. 195.
12. Darling to Huskisson, Mar. 28, 1828, HRA xiv:70.
13. Darling to Huskisson, Mar. 28, 1828, ibid. There were 1,045 "colonially convicted" men at Port Macquarie, Moreton Bay and Norfolk Island put together. On the road gangs, Darling's count ran to 500 men, supervised by 22 "trusty" convict overseers, split into gangs of a few dozen at work stations along the 150-mile Great Western Road, out of Parramatta; some 400 gangers on the Great Northern Road north from Windsor; 249 on the Great Southern Road, connecting Sydney to Stonequarry and Throsby Creek beyond; and 119 on the unfinished road to Newcastle.
14. As Governor Bourke found six years later, when he tried using privately contracted roadwork "at a very high rate, notwithstanding that the bonus of an assignment of three convicts per mile has been given to the contractors." Bourke to Stanley, Jan. 15, 1834, HRA xvii:317.
15. Cook *EL*, p. 18.
16. "The mere fact": Bourke to Stanley, Jan. 15, 1834, HRA xvii:315. Two fat bullocks: Cook *EL*, p. 28.
17. "They have no time": Bourke to Stanley, Jan 15, 1834, HRA xvii:321. Iron-gangers running to work in double time: Cook *EL*, p. 58.
18. Cook *EL*, pp. 58–60.
19. Bigge NSW, p. 99.
20. Ibid., p. 155.
21. Lachlan Macquarie had proposed outward colonization by convict gangs before Bigge,

in the wake of the disastrous Nepean floods of 1816–17, when settlers were actually returning assigned convicts whom they could no longer support on their ravaged farms to the government. In May 1818, having received five ships carrying 1,046 men within a single month, Macquarie sent 450 of the new arrivals down to Van Diemen's Land and proposed, as a long-term buffer, that convicts working for the government should break ground to the south of Sydney, at Jervis Bay and Illawarra. (Macquarie to Bathurst, May 1818, HRA ix:795.)

22. James Jervis, "The Rise of Newcastle."
23. William Sacheverell Coke, letter, 1827, in DRO, D1881.
24. W. S. Coke, letter in DRO, D1881.
25. On conditions in the Newcastle coal mine, see Bigge NSW, p. 115–16. A harrowing account of both coal-mine and lime-kiln labor at Newcastle is given in the early Australian novel *Ralph Rashleigh*, written about 1840 by "Giacomo di Rosenberg," supposedly the pseudonym of the convict James Rosenberg Tucker (1808–1888?), an Essex clerk tranported for life in 1826 for writing a threatening letter.
26. Jervis, "Newcastle," p. 149.
27. Bigge NSW, p. 117.
28. Ibid., p. 116.
29. Jervis, pp. 149–50.
30. W. S. Coke, letter, Apr.–Aug. 1827, DRO D1881.
31. James Backhouse, *A Narrative of a Visit to the Australian Colonies*, p. 405.
32. Woomera [pseud.], *The Life of an Ex-Convict*, p. 6.
33. James Bushelle, "Memoir," Ms.
34. Woomera, *Life*, p. 15.
35. Bushelle, "Memoir."
36. Woomera, *Life*, p. 6.
37. Cook *EL*, pp. 79–80.
38. "The Brisbane River 100 Years Ago, by an Old Brisbaneite," *Brisbane Courier*, Mar. 22, 1930, cit. in J. G. Steele, *Brisbane Town in Convict Days, 1824–1842*, p. 28.
39. Brisbane to Bathurst, HRA xi:604.
40. Miller to Balfour, CSO 1/371/8476.
41. Ibid.
42. Charles Bateson, *Patrick Logan, Tyrant of Brisbane Town*, p. 52.
43. W[illiam] R[oss], *The Fell Tyrant; or the Suffering Convict*: in places a tendentious and biassed diatribe, although its bias, as from a former convict, is understandable. It is verifiably accurate on certain matters of routine and convict discipline, but apt to invent when it comes to names and cases. Thus Ross asserts, at one point that a prisoner named Geary "starved to death in his cell" when in fact he died of dropsy in hospital. Ross was a Special, serving time for embezzlement, and was Logan's clerk at Moreton Bay. He did not have to labor and was apparently not flogged.
44. Logan to Col. Sec. Macleay, Apr. 6, 1827, cit. in Steele, *Brisbane Town*, p. 72.
45. Darling's orders to Logan: HRA xv:104–16. Summary power over free settlers: ibid., clause 35.
46. Bateson, *Patrick Logan*, p. 96. Douglas Gordon, "Sickness and Death at the Moreton Bay Convict Settlement," p. 473.
47. Ross, *Fell Tyrant*, p. 20.
48. J. J. Knight, *In the Early Days* (1895), cit. in Steele, *Brisbane Town*, p. 181.
49. Bateson, *Patrick Logan*, pp. 81–82. In 1827 Macleay wrote to Logan enclosing a copy of a report on Moreton Bay discipline by the acting attorney-general, William Moore, and instructed him to "state both whether the prisoners are actually worked constantly in irons, as supposed by Mr. Moore, and whether hard labour may not advantageously be imposed instead of the severe corporal punishments of which he takes notice."
50. Gordon, "Sickness and Death," p. 474.
51. Asst. Surgeon J. F. Murray to Anna Bunn, NSWA 4/1966. One of Spicer's recorded efforts was to tell the kitchen overseer to replace the worn-out copper bottoms of the

settlement cauldrons with wood. "Sir," the mystified overseer replied, "the wood will catch fire, and the bottoms be immediately burned out, and the prisoners' victuals will fall into the fire." "Then, sir," Spicer is said to have told him, "let the carpenters make fresh bottoms every day, for there is plenty of wood in the settlement." (Ross, *Fell Tyrant*, pp. 24–25.)

52. Bateson, *Patrick Logan*, p. 100.

53. Thus at Glendon in the Hunter River Valley an Aborigine was shot while in custody of the mounted police, "a very singularly formed man" nicknamed Black Cato, whom "it took four men to hold." His body "was hung up by the Men on the Farm as a terror to the other Blacks," just as one would nail a dead dingo to a tree. Enclosure 3 in Darling to Bathurst, Oct. 6, 1826, HRA xii:625–26.

54. "Singularly prone to espionage": E. S. Hall, *Monitor*, Oct. 17, 1829. "Prostituting his authority": E. S. Hall to Murray, May 1830, Enclosure 1 in Darling to Murray, HRA xv:628ff.

55. Darling to Bathurst, Apr. 18, 1827, HRA xiii:262–63.

56. Affidavit of Surgeon Henry Cowper, NSWA 4/2081.

57. Affidavit of Rev. Vincent, Executive Council Minutes, NSWA 4/1516.

58. Steele, *Brisbane Town*, p. 150.

59. Lord Charles Grey, November 1830, cit. in E. P. Thompson, *The Making of the English Working Class*, p. 202.

60. *Sydney Gazette*, Oct. 22, 1831.

61. Allan Cunningham to SC 1832, Minutes, p. 40.

62. John Graham, petition in NSWA 4/2325:4. Graham helped rescue one of the minor celebrities of colonial Australian history, Mrs. Eliza Frazer, from a tribe of Aborigines near Lake Cootharaba, north of Moreton Bay. She was among the survivors of the *Stirling Castle*, wrecked on Eliza Reef, some 150 miles northeast of Gladstone, in May 1836. Its castaways (including its master, Captain Fraser) had reached Macleay's Island (since renamed Fraser Island) in a longboat and a pinnace before they were seized by local tribesmen. Captain Fraser and others were killed. In August a search party from Moreton Bay, led by Lieutenant Otter and guided by Graham, located the naked and by now partly deranged widow, "dreadfully debilitated and crippled from the sufferings she had undergone" at the hands of the natives. The ordeal of Mrs. Fraser became the subject of a number of books and accounts, from John Curtis's *Shipwreck of the Stirling Castle*, 1838, to Patrick White's novel *A Fringe of Leaves*. It was also the basis of two well-known series of paintings (1947, 1957) by the Australian artist Sidney Nolan. The best account of the wreck of the *Stirling Castle* and its aftermath is Michael Alexander, *Mrs. Fraser on the Fatal Shore* (London, 1971).

63. Foster Fyans, "Memoirs," Ms., pp. 314–15 (p. 146 in the recently published edition, *Memoirs, 1790–1870*, ed. P. L. Brown). See Chapter 13, note 20, below, for a brief account of Fyans.

64. Constance Petrie, *Tom Petrie's Reminiscences* (1904), cit. in Steele, *Brisbane Town*, p. 247. Treadwheels had been in use in English prisons since 1818; the idea had been given to the poor by the engineer and builder Samuel Cubitt, who gave the rich (among other things) the luxurious and solid architecture of Belgravia. It was a parody of labor: utterly useless work which produced nothing, merely "grinding air" as prisoners put it. Never had the alienation of producer from product been so complete—and the authorities did not need a Marx or an Engels to tell them what a torment of anomie this could inflict on the "workers." Sydney Smith hailed the treadwheel as a wonderful and salutary invention, and one judge called it "the most tiresome, distressing, exemplary punishment that has ever been contrived by human ingenuity." See Michael Ignatieff, *A Just Measure of Pain: The Penitentiary in the Industrial Revolution, 1750–1850*, pp. 177–78.

65. Bathurst to Brisbane, HRA xi:322. "Very severe sentence": Hunter to SC 1812, Appendix 1, Minutes, p. 21.

66. Brisbane to Horton, HRA xi:552–54; to Bathurst, HRA xi:604; to Bathurst, HRA xi:553.

67. Bathurst to Darling, HRA xiii:36.
68. Darling to Undersecretary Hay, Feb. 11, 1827, HRA xii:105.
69. Fyans, "Memoirs," pp. 213–14 (published edition, p. 92).
70. Ibid.
71. Darling to Hay, HRA xii:105.

CHAPTER THIRTEEN *Norfolk Island*

1. *Monitor*, Feb. 10, 1829.
2. Morisset praised by Macquarie: Lachlan Macquarie, *Journal*, Nov. 17, 1821, p. 50, A785, ML. Morisset as opponent of hanging: *Sydney Gazette*, Nov. 20, 1827.
3. Brisbane Papers, Box 4, Ms. 4036, NLA, Canberra.
4. "Memoir of Norfolk Island," Frayne's undated Ms., catalogued in the ML as "Anonymous Convict Narrative," is at p. 427 of miscellaneous papers bound in the back of NSW Col. Sec. Papers, vol. 1, Ms. 681. It was clearly written some time after the events described, a memoir (not a diary) probably composed during the Norfolk Island administration of Captain Maconochie (1840–44), who is known to have encouraged other convicts including Frayne's friend Thomas Cook to set down their recollections of the Old System—thus supplying the only first-hand accounts of the Norfolk Island regime from the convicts' viewpoint. The transcription is mine.
5. W. S. Coke, Apr. 1826 from Rio, letter 20, D1881, DRO.
6. LF, p. 1.
7. Cook *EL*, p. 100.
8. James Lawrence, "Memoir," Ms.
9. LF, p. 3.
10. Ibid., pp. 20–21.
11. Ibid., p. 15.
12. Ibid., p. 16.
13. Ibid., pp. 35–37.
14. Ibid., pp. 38–39.
15. Ibid., p. 40.
16. Ibid., p. 51.
17. John Holyard to Rev. J. Reddell, Feb. 4, 1834, in Reddell Papers, A423, p. 91, ML.
18. LF, p. 19.
19. William Ullathorne, *Catholic Mission*, p. 41.
20. Foster Fyans (1790–1870), an Irish Anglican from Dublin, was a seasoned career officer by the time he came to Norfolk Island. He had enlisted in the 67th Regiment in 1810 and served at Cadiz and in the Peninsular War for seven years. As soon as he returned to England he re-embarked, with the 1st Battalion, for India; of its thousand men only 130 survived the ravages of cholera and fighting. He bought his captaincy, and 1827 found him in England again; but like many another "Empire hand," he could not summon up the will to live there. He transferred to the 20th Regiment and in 1833 moved from Mauritius to Sydney, where he joined the 4th (King's Own) Regiment and was sent to Norfolk Island as captain of the guard under Morisset. After his repression of the prisoners' revolt there, he was posted (as commandant) to Moreton Bay.

When the 4th K.O. sailed for India in 1837, Fyans sold his commission and remained in Australia, settling in the Port Phillip district as the police magistrate of Geelong. In 1840 he was made commissioner of crown lands for Portland Bay, riding six thousand miles a year on his tours of inspection of licensed runs. He built up his own cattle-run and married in 1843. Fyans retired from government service ten years later. Up to then his hobby had been carpentry and wood-turning; it was said to be his eccentric fancy to hide jewels, purchased or looted in India, in secret compartments in the furniture he made, and a desk constructed by Fyans and sold at a country auction in the 1940s for £7 did in fact yield diamonds worth £4,000. But on retirement he turned to write his memoirs, whose 500-page manuscript reposes in the Latrobe

Library, Melbourne. Rambling, unselfconscious and full of salty humor, it is a prime source on penal Australia. All quotations have been checked against these edited memoirs (1986, ed. P. L. Brown) but were taken from a typescript copy generously furnished by the Army Museums Ogilby Trust, Connaught Barracks, Aldershot. On Fyans, see also entry in ADB (vol. 1, pp. 422–24); S. Sayers, "Captain Foster Fyans of Portland Bay District," *Victorian Historical Magazine*, vol. 40, nos. 1–2, pp. 45–66.

21. Jewish prisoners on Norfolk Island were few. In 1841, when the convict population stood at 1,400, only 12 Jews were counted. One may tentatively guess that the man in question was Israel Levey, sentenced to 7 years on Norfolk Island in 1829 and appointed a convict overseer there in September 1832, which would place the suicide pact earlier in that year. Levey played a major role as an informer and witness after the convict mutiny of 1834, and was highly commended by Fyans to the Colonial Secretary for his "zeal." This was the kind of man whom other convicts would say was "not to be trusted."

22. Fyans, "Reminiscences," pp. 233–35.

23. Bourke to Stanley, Nov. 30, 1833, HRA xvii:276–77.

24. LF, p. 65.

25. Morisset to Undersecretary R. W. Hay, Morisset Letters, Ms. AM34, ML, Sydney.

26. On Knatchbull, see ADB entry (vol. 2, p. 66); the colonial secretary's correspondence on Norfolk Island for 1833–35, NSWA 4/2244:2; Executive Council Minutes for 1834, NSWA 4/1441 and 1443; Colin Roderick, *John Knatchbull, from Quarterdeck to Gallows*; and Anon., *A Memoir of Knatchbull, the Murderer of Mrs. Jamieson, Comprising an Account of his English and Colonial History* (Sydney, 1844).

27. Knatchbull, deposition in NI Mutiny Papers, 1834, NSWA 2/8291.

28. John Jackson, deposition in NI Mutiny Papers, NSWA 2/8291.

29. James Pearson in NI Mutiny Papers, NSWA 2/8291, p. 223.

30. Narrative reconstructed from depositions of James Pearson, Elijah Sallis, William Phipps, James Oppenshaw, Charles Russell and William Parham in NI Mutiny Papers.

31. Deposition of James Fitzgerald, ibid.

32. Fyans to Col. Sec. McLeay, Feb. 16, 1834, NI Mutiny Papers, NSWA 4/1441.

33. Cook *EL*, pp. 128–29.

34. All the mutiny figures in Fyans's "Reminiscences" are exaggerated. He gave 500 (not 120) for the first attack on the jail gang guard; and 300 for the strength of the mutineers at Longridge, whereas his report to McLeay written within a month of the mutiny put it between 60 and 80. He was writing his memoir many years later, in retirement: Heroic exploits grow with age.

35. Cook *EL*, pp. 134–35.

36. Cook *EL*, pp. 130–31. This form of torture was also referred to by Rev. T. Sharpe, who was chaplain on Norfolk Island from 1837 to 1841, hence not a witness to the mutiny: Sharpe Papers, 27 ff., A1502, ML, Sydney.

37. Fyans to Col. Sec. McLeay, Feb. 20, 1834, NI Mutiny Papers, NSWA 4/1441. "Fatal Ball": Cook *EL*, p. 133.

38. Chambers to Col. Sec. McLeay, Aug. 20, 1834, NSWA 4/2245.

39. Sir William W. Burton, *The State of Religion and Education in New South Wales*, pp. 152–54.

40. Chambers to McLeay, Aug. 30, 1834, CSO 34/6236, NSWA 4/2245.

41. Burton, *Religion and Education*, p. 154.

42. Ullathorne, *Catholic Mission*, passim and esp. pp. 40–45.

43. Ibid., p. 37.

44. On the last years of Morisset, see Petition of Emily Morisset to Sir Charles Fitzroy, Governor of NSW, Sept. 13, 1852, Ms. at Am. 34, Morisset Papers, ML.

45. Joseph Anderson, *Recollections of a Peninsula Veteran* (London, 1913).

46. Cook *EL*, p. 137.

47. T. Sharpe, "Letter Book," Ms. A1502 in ML, also cit. in Phillip Cox and Wesley Stacey, *Building Norfolk Island*, p. 24.

48. James Backhouse, *A Visit to the Australian Colonies*, p. 257. It was difficult to per-

suade the skeptical authorities on Norfolk Island of the genuineness of one's injuries. In January 1834 (NSWA) the convict John Boyd petitioned for release from his chains and his life sentence: "Being totally deprived of sight . . . I most humbly intreat you to look on me with an eye of Mercy . . . the remainder of my life, shall be spent in sorrow for violating the Laws of the Land . . ." This heartrending plea did not impress Fyans, who minuted on the back: "From all I can learn of this person, he has malingered with his eyes—and has anything but a good Character."

49. LF, pp. 25–26.
50. Ibid., p. 26.
51. Ullathorne, *Catholic Mission*, p. 40.
52. Ibid.
53. Prisoner of "great recklessness": Backhouse, *Australian Colonies*, p. 266. "Their passions": Ullathorne, *Catholic Mission*, p. 41.
54. Sydney Smith, cit. in Sheldon Glueck, Foreword to Sir John Vincent Barry, *Alexander Maconochie of Norfolk Island*, p. viii.

CHAPTER FOURTEEN *Toward Abolition*

1. John West, *The History of Tasmania*, part 4, sect. 1, pp. 146–47.
2. Lady Franklin to Mrs. Simpkinson, Dec. 10, 1841, in George Mackaness, *Some Private Correspondence of Sir John and Lady Jane Franklin*, vol. 2, p. 36.
3. T. J. Lemprière, Diary at Port Arthur, Mar. 26, 1837, p. 24.
4. Montagu to Arthur, Dec. 9, 1837, cit. in Shaw CC, p. 269.
5. Diary of G.W.T.B. Boyes, June 11, 1846, cit. in Sir John V. Barry, *Alexander Maconochie of Norfolk Island*, p. 30.
6. Maconochie to Admiral Sir George Back, cit. in Barry, *Maconochie*, p. 28.
7. Alexander Maconochie, *Report on the State of Prison Discipline in Van Diemen's Land*.
8. Maconochie to Back, Mar. 14, 1839 [?], cit. in Barry, *Maconochie*, p. 52.
9. Maconochie, *Report*.
10. Jane Franklin to Mrs. Simpkinson, Dec. 26, 1839, cit. in Barry, *Maconochie*, p. 58.
11. Mrs. Maconochie to Back, Mar. 11, 1839, cit. in Barry, ibid.
12. Maconochie to Washington, May 29, 1839.
13. On Apr. 8, 1837, the "philosophic Radical" William Molesworth, Member for East Cornwall, rose in the Commons to propose a select committee of inquiry into transportation. Fifteen members were appointed, representing a fair cross-section of political views from Tories to Radicals, with Molesworth as chairman. The committee held, in all, thirty-eight meetings between its first session on Apr. 10, 1837 and its last on Aug. 3, 1838. It examined twenty-three witnesses; the most extensive testimony was given by Sir Francis Forbes, James Mudie, James Macarthur, J. D. Lang, Colonel George Arthur and the Rev. William Ullathorne. The voluminous Report of the Molesworth Committee, with minutes of testimony and appendices was published in two parts: PP vol. xix, no. 518, 1837, pp. 5–317, cited as SC 1837–38 (i), and PP vol. 22, 1837–38, pp. 1–139, cited as SC 1837–38 (ii).
14. Correspondence between Russell and the Commissioners for the Reform of the Criminal Law, *The Times* (London), Apr. 1, 1837, cit. in John Ritchie, "Towards Ending an Unclean Thing," p. 158.
15. Ritchie, "Towards Ending," pp. 159–60.
16. Extract from Molesworth's notes on Report of SC 1837–38 (ii), cit. in Sir William W. Burton, "State of Society and State of Crime in New South Wales," *Colonial Magazine*, vol. 1.
17. William Ullathorne, *Autobiography*, pp. 138–39.
18. See SC 1837–38 (ii), Report, p. viii, and Appendix, p. 77.
19. Ibid., p. xxi.
20. Ibid., pp. xxiv–vi.

21. NSW V & P, July 17, 1838.
22. On the changing perception of colonial crime in the wake of the Molesworth Report and the attitudes of "respectables," see Michael Sturma, *Vice in a Vicious Society*, pp. 27–30.
23. Gipps to Glenelg, Mar. 29, 1839, HRA xx:75.
24. SC 1837–38 (ii), Report, p. xliv.
25. Maconochie, encl. 7 in Gipps to Russell, Feb. 25, 1840, HRA xx:544.
26. Maconochie, encl. 2 in Gipps to Russell, HRA xx:532–33.
27. Maconochie, encl. 3 in Gipps to Russell, HRA xx:533–34.
28. Alexander Maconochie, *Norfolk Island*, p. 8. West, *Tasmania*, vol. 2, p. 283.
29. Cook *EL*, pp. 192–93.
30. Ibid.
31. James Lawrence, "Memoir," Ms.
32. Gipps to Russell, June 27, 1840, HRA xx:689.
33. Russell to Gipps, Sept. 10, 1840, *Con. Disc.* 4, 1846, p. 29.
34. Russell to Gipps, Nov. 12, 1840 (in response to Gipps-Russell, June 27, 1840), *Con. Disc.* 4, 1846, pp. 29–30.
35. Maconochie to Gipps, encl. 4 in Gipps to Russell, Feb. 25, 1840, HRA xx:535.
36. E. Deas Thomson (Col. Sec. Off., Sydney) to Maconochie, Aug. 20, 1841, *Con. Disc.* 4, 1846, p. 29.
37. Gipps to Russell, Aug. 27, 1841, *Con. Disc,* 4, 1846, p. 27.
38. Maconochie to Gipps, re Mark & Ticket System, June 2, 1842.
39. Encl. 1 in Gipps to Stanley, Aug. 15, 1842, *Con. Disc.* 4, 1846, p. 59.
40. Gipps to Stanley, Aug. 15, 1842. HRA xxii:209.
41. Maconochie to Gipps, Dec. 31, 1841, encl. 1 in Gipps to Stanley, *Con. Disc.* 4, 1846, p. 38.
42. Thomson to Maconochie, Jul. 29, 1842, *Con. Disc.* 4, 1846, p. 55.
43. Maconochie to Gipps, June 2, 1842, encl. 1 in Gipps to Stanley, Aug. 15, 1843, *Con. Disc.* 4, 1846, p. 54 and passim.
44. Alexander Maconochie, *The Mark System of Prison Discipline.*
45. On the convict graves in the Norfolk Island cemetery, see R. Nixon Dalkin, *Colonial Era Cemetery of Norfolk Island.*
46. James Lawrence, "Memoir," Ms. It seems to have been Maconochie's policy to encourage literate convicts to write down their experiences, both to exorcise their horrors and to supply an unofficial record of the underside of the Old System. The historian can only be grateful to him, since, if Maconochie had not given men like Thomas Cook, James Lawrence, James Porter and Laurence Frayne the means and time to describe the hells they had passed through, their reality would now be lost in administrative euphemisms, omissions and lies.

    In general, convicts' experiences were not considered worth wasting time on, and it is remarkable not only that the occasional manuscript like Cook's should have survived complete, but that the others survived in any form, however physically damaged or edited. Most, one may assume, were thrown out by archivists or embarrassed descendants. Thus the memoir of a Liverpool convict named Jones (b. 1813), probably written under Maconochie's aegis, ends after a few pages before his transport ship has left the White cliffs of Dover behind; on the last page is the notation, in a later hand, "Jones—Thief—up to his transportation for the Colonies—nothing interesting. Excerpt 1867." One could wish to see those missing pages. See memoir of Jones, item 10 at MSQ 168, Dixson Library, Sydney.
47. The story of "Bony" Anderson, the convict chained to the rock of Goat Island in Sydney Harbor, appears first in the English journal *Meliora*, vol. 4, no. 13 (April 1861), pp. 12–14. Barry (*Maconochie*, p. 121) raises the possibility that it was taken from an unpublished, and now lost, manuscript by Maconochie himself. For a full account of Anderson and Maconochie see Barry, *Maconochie*, pp. 121–24.
48. J. W. Smith to Gipps, encl. 1 in Gipps to Stanley, Aug. 15, 1842, *Con. Disc.* 4, 1846, p. 58ff.

49. Gipps to Stanley, Oct. 13, 1841, HRA xxi:542.
50. Gipps to Stanley, Aug. 15, 1842, *Con. Disc.* 4, 1846, p. 66.
51. Gipps to Stanley, Apr. 1, 1843, HRA xxii:617. Barry, *Maconochie*, p. 140.
52. Gipps to Stanley, Apr. 1, 1843, *Con. Disc.* 4, 1846, p. 138.
53. Ibid., p.142.
54. Ibid., p. 143.
55. Ibid., pp. 143–44.
56. Ibid., pp. 146–47.
57. Ibid., p. 147.
58. Alexander Maconochie, *On Reformatory Prison Discipline*, p. 26.
59. Gipps to Stanley, Apr. 1, 1843, *Con. Disc.* 4, 1846, p. 148.
60. Ibid., p. 149.
61. In 1840 it had cost £10. 18s. 4d. to keep a convict on Norfolk Island; in 1843, £13 3s. 11d., a rise of 21 percent. But in 1838, due to bumper harvests; the year's cost of a convict was £4 14s. 2d; whereas in 1839, the year before Maconochie arrived, the crops were dismal and because all food had to be imported the figure went to £17 19s. 10d —a rise of 380 percent.
62. Stanley to Gipps, Apr. 29, 1843, HRA xx:691.
63. For the Eastern Penitentiary in Philadelphia, see Charles Dickens, *American Notes for General Circulation*, pp. 68–77.
64. Pentonville penitentiary seemed, from the moment of its opening in 1842, to be "a model for prison architecture and discipline not only in England but in most of Europe . . . the culmination of three generations of thinking" (Ignatieff, *A Just Measure of Pain*, p. 3). Its purpose was to crush the will of its 450 inmates by means of absolutely inflexible routine, complete isolation and unvarying task-work, with each convict identically engaged on a 12-hour day of cobbling or weaving. Whenever the prisoner stepped outside his cell for muster or exercise, he was required to don a woollen mask with eyeholes so that he could neither recognize nor be recognized by his fellow-prisoners. The Pentonville chapel, where prisoners were assembled every day, was designed with a separate box for each prisoner; wooden partitions and a door in each box assured that no convict could see the man to right or left of him, only the preacher in the "cackle tub" or pulpit. All the main features of Pentonville—the silent cells, the spyholes, the isolation, the masks and the chapel—would be faithfully copied after 1853 in the "Model Prison" built at Port Arthur in Tasmania. (See note 45 to Chapter 15, below.)

CHAPTER FIFTEEN   *A Special Scourge*

1. Stanley's dispatches to Franklin outlining the Probation System: Nov. 25, 1842, *Correspondence re Convict Discipline*, in PP 159, 1843, nos. 175 (p. 3) and 176 (p. 10).
2. Shaw *CC*, pp. 295–96.
3. Sir James Graham to the Committee of Visitors of Parkhurst Prison, Dec. 20, 1842, *Correspondence re Convict Discipline*, Appendix to Part I, pp. 1–2, PP 1843.
4. Ibid.
5. Stanley to Franklin, Nov. 25, 1842, dispatch no. 176.
6. Robert Crooke, *The Convict*, pp. 39–40.
7. Eardley-Wilmot's loyalty to the apprenticeship system for training young artisans—which was being harried into extinction by the free labor market of the late 1820s—would be upheld in the curriculum of craft-training at Point Puer in Port Arthur in the 1840s. He blamed the increase of juvenile crime on the breakdown of the master's parental supervision of the young. "Formerly the apprentice was taken into the house of the master," he declared in 1827; "he was considered one of the family. . . . [N]ow the master has ten or a dozen apprentices and perhaps never sees them. . . . [They] are allowed to go where they please . . . and the consequence is that they are all thieves." Ignatieff, *A Just Measure of Pain*, p. 182.

8. Robson, *Hist. Tas.*, p. 418. For a general description of the depression of the Van Diemen's Land economy, see pp. 413–19.

9. Robert Pitcairn to Lord Stanley, Feb. 4, 1846, *Correspondence re Convict Discipline*, PP 1843, p. 38.

10. "Half-Yearly Return of Runaway Convicts, Authorised by J. S. Hampton, Comptroller General at Hobart." Poster, dated Jul. 1, 1850, cumulative since 1831, D356–18, ML, Sydney.

11. F. R. Nixon to Lord Grey, Feb. 15, 1847; printed in PP 1847, Memorials on Transportation, "A Communication upon the Subject of Transportation," vol. 38, no. 741, p. 2.

12. Stanley to Eardley-Wilmot, draft dispatch dated Sept. 1845, encl. 1 in J. Stephen to S. W. Phillips, Sept. 8, 1845, *Con. Disc.* 3, 1846.

13. Nixon to Grey, Feb. 15, 1847, in PP 1847, vol. 38, no. 741, p. 3ff.

14. For the incidence of lesbianism in the Female Factories in Launceston and at the Cascades, see G. R. Lennox, "A Private and Confidential Despatch of Eardley-Wilmot." The mention of lesbianism in chapel is at p. 342 of the 1841 Committee's report at CSO 22/50, TSA. One reason for Eardley-Wilmot's downfall as lieutenant-governor was that Gladstone believed he had done little or nothing to curb convict lesbianism in Van Diemen's Land. Though plans for the separate women's penitentiary Stanley had called for as part of his Probation System had been drawn up (by Major Joshua Jebb, along the lines of Parkhurst on the Isle of Wight) and sent from England, and though a budget of £35,000 had been approved for its construction, it was not, as noted above, actually built. Instead, as many newly arrived women convicts as possible were diverted from the Cascades Factory into a converted prison ship moored in the Derwent, HMS *Anson*, where (it was hoped) they would not be exposed to the factory's corrupting influence. In all, about 3,500 convict women passed through probationary instruction on board the *Anson* between 1844 and 1849, under the authority of Edmund and Philippa Bowden, superintendent and matron. To save money, however, Eardley-Wilmot planned to reverse the roles of the *Anson* and the Cascades Factory; the factory would become the reform-school, the ship a punishment hulk. This earned him the enmity of Matron Bowden; she helped persuade Gladstone (already famous for his interest in "fallen women") that her work as a rehabilitator was being undermined by the lieutenant-governor; and this, Lennox points out (p. 87), must have accelerated Eardley-Wilmot's sacking in April 1846.

15. Wilmot's confidential report to Stanley, Nov. 2, 1843, cit. in Lennox, "Eardley-Wilmot," p. 80.

16. John Frost, *The Horrors of Convict Life*, p. 40.

17. Eardley-Wilmot to Stanley, Mar. 17, 1846, *Con. Disc*, 1847, p. 46.

18. The petition of twenty-five clergymen in Van Diemen's Land to Lord Grey was couched in somber tones, inspired by "a deep sense of the responsibility of living in a land where such awful sins are committed, and where the unhappy convicts are subjected to an association leading them into such shocking corruption." Enclosure 1 (dated July 9, 1846) in Bishop Nixon to Lord Grey, May 3, 1847, *Con. Disc.* 1847, p. 44.

19. J. Syme, *Nine Years in Van Diemen's Land . . .*, Dundee, 1848, pp. 200–201, cit. in Crowley, *Doc. Hist.*, vol. 2, p. 122.

20. Gladstone to Eardley-Wilmot, Apr. 30, 1846, both private and public letters in CO 408/25.

21. C. J. La Trobe to Lord Grey, May 31, 1847, paper 941, in *Con. Disc.* 1847.

22. Stanley to Gipps, HRA xxii:695–96.

23. Childs to Champ, July 11, 1846, encl. 2 in Wilmot to Gladstone, Sept. 3, 1846, *Con. Disc.* 1847, p. 176.

24. John Mortlock, *Experiences of a Convict*, pp. 73, 71.

25. Ibid., p. 70.

26. Rev. Thomas Rogers, *Correspondence*, p. 144. Thomas Rogers (1806–1903), a graduate of Trinity College in Dublin, accepted from the Society for the Propagation of the Gospel a post on Norfolk Island as religious instructor to convicts. He arrived in

Hobart in July 1845 and by September was on Norfolk Island. His position was anomalous. Not having been appointed by Bishop Nixon in Tasmania, he had no ecclesiastical authority. He was not well-placed to argue with the island commandants, Childs and Price; but argue he did, passionately and with anguish, on behalf of the tormented prisoners. He tried (but failed) to report on Childs's misdeeds and neglect to Eardley-Wilmot in Hobart; tried (and failed again) to get Denison's ear on John Price. Naturally, this dissident friend of the convicts did not last long on Norfolk Island; he was recalled to Hobart in February 1847. In 1849 he published a book defending his stand against the System, *Correspondence Relating to the Dismissal of the Rev. T. Rogers, from his Chaplaincy at Norfolk Island.* Rogers's manuscript Letter-Book for his sojourn on Norfolk Island, 1844–46, is in the ML, Sydney.

He was less generous to his family. Over four years in Australia Rogers only sent £75, a miserable pittance, to the wife and six children he had left behind. Sarah Rogers died destitute without seeing her errant husband again. Early in 1850, friends subscribed to raise the passage money to send their children to Australia. Unaware of this, Rogers had made arrangements to sail back to Ireland to fetch them. The two ships passed each other en route; Rogers was not reunited with his offspring until he returned to Australia in 1860.

One of his sons, John William Foster Rogers, worked up his father's reminiscences and letters into a manuscript, which remained unpublished: "Man's Inhumanity— Being a Chaplain's Chronicle of Norfolk Island in the 'Forties" (typescript, with illustrations, C214, ML, Sydney). Rogers himself was the prototype of the tormented, alcoholic chaplain the Rev. James North in Clarke's *His Natural Life.*

27. Diary of Elizabeth Robertson, Ms. 163 in Dixson Library, Sydney, cit. in Margaret Hazzard, *Punishment Short of Death,* p. 189.
28. Childs to Eardley-Wilmot, Oct. 1, 1845, encl. in Wilmot to Stanley, Dec. 19, 1845, *Con. Disc.* 2, 1846, p. 48.
29. Naylor to Grey, in GO 1/63, TSA, cit. in Eustace Fitzsymonds, ed., *Norfolk Island 1846 . . .*, pp. 15–16. (Naylor's report to Stanley, edited for parliamentary publication, is printed as encl. 2 in Grey to Denison, Sept. 30, 1846. *Con. Disc.* 1847, pp. 67–76.)
30. Ibid.
31. Maconochie advises Naylor against publishing the report: Maconochie to B. Hawes, Sept. 22, 1846, encl. 1 in paper 11, *Con. Disc.* 1847, p. 67. "Too probable" to pass over: Grey to Denison, Sept. 30, 1846, paper 11 in *Con. Disc.* 1847, p. 66. Grey's second thoughts: Grey to Denison, Nov. 7, 1846, paper 12 in *Con. Disc.* 1847, p. 76.
32. Hazzard, *Punishment Short of Death,* p. 196.
33. Robert Pringle Stuart's Ms. of the report is at CON 1/5183 and GO 33/55, TSA. The censored version, with whole paragraphs missing and a copious scattering of asterisks, appeared in *Con. Disc.* 1847, pp. 84–101. The full text, as with Naylor, is published in Fitzsymonds, ed., *Norfolk Island 1846.*
34. Ibid.
35. Clarke's account of the Ring in *His Natural Life,* based on Stuart's report, is relatively unsensational, though fanciful in parts. Price Warung's "Secret Society of the Ring," in *Convict Days,* pulls out all the stops and sounds like an antipodean mixture of *Maria Monk, Juliette, The Castle of Otranto* and *Melmoth the Wanderer,* overglazed with Poe; the Ring's nocturnal conclaves are lit with blazing light from the eyesockets of a skull, producing "a diabolic effect upon weakened nerves," including the reader's. As for the language, "Were you to clothe with literary form the mouthings of the creatures led by Hebert, as thy danced round Lais and Phryne enthroned as Goddesses of Reason on the desecrated church altars of Revolutionary Paris, you would scarcely parallel it in point of blasphemous horror" (pp. 159–60). On the rhymed "Convict Oath" (presumably written by Warung), see "The Liberation of the First Three" in *Convict Days,* pp. 68–69.
36. Stuart, in Fitzsymonds, ed., *Norfolk Island 1846,* p. 67.
37. Minutes of Executive Council Meeting, Hobart, July 1–2, 1846.
38. On the Norfolk Island mutiny of July 1, 1846, see Judge Fielding Browne's Report in

Con. Disc. 1847, pp. 35–40. Price's report, with declarations and testimony from Alfred Baldock, George Bott, William Forster and others, encl. in Latrobe to Grey, Jan. 8, 1847, ibid., pp. 25–35.

39. On Henry Beresford Garrett and "The Demon," see Sir John Vincent Barry, *The Life and Death of John Price,* Appendix A. The facts of Garrett's life are unclear. According to one version, he was a soldier transported for robbing the commissariat in Nottingham. He arrived on Norfolk Island around 1845, and toward the end of Price's commandancy he was transferred to Van Diemen's Land; he escaped in 1853 and fled to Victoria, finding anonymity within the vast horde of gold-seekers. In 1854 Garrett and three accomplices "stuck up" the Bank of Victoria at Ballarat, making off with £14,300 in cash and 250 oz. of gold. With his share of the loot, Garrett returned to London but was recognized at once and re-transported to Melbourne for trial. Convicted of bank robbery, he went to the hulks in Port Phillip Bay, where he saw (and perhaps took part in) the murder of John Price in 1857. Released in 1861, he went to New Zealand, lived as a bushranger, and was sentenced in 1868 to 20 years in jail for shopbreaking. During the latter part of this sentence, before his death in 1885, Garrett wrote a number of manuscripts, including "The Demon," his 25,000-word account of John Price—a document of obsession. It survives only as a transcript made after 1948; the original notebooks, which Garrett entrusted to a Methodist lay preacher named Hall, are lost. A photocopy of the transcript is in the Mitchell Library, Sydney.

40. Price to Champ, Dec. 7, 1846, encl. 1 in Latrobe to Grey, Jan. 8, 1847, letter 8 in *Con. Disc.* 1847, p. 26.

41. Barry, *The Life and Death of John Price,* p. 37. Willson's damaging report to Denison on Norfolk Island (dated May 22, 1852) is printed in *Con. Disc.* 1853, pp. 88–95. In 1849, on his previous (second) visit, Willson had praised the improvement of rations, the "perfect unanimity" among the civil and military officers, and "the judicious conduct of Mr. Price, the Commandant" (*Con. Disc.* 1850, pp. 111–114).

42. Quotes from Rogers, unless otherwise specified, are from passages cited in Barry, *The Life and Death of John Price,* pp. 45–50, and from W. F. Rogers, "Man's Inhumanity . . . ," typescript at C214, ML, Sydney.

43. W. Nairn to Price, Feb. 2, 1852, in *Con. Disc.* 1853, pp. 88–89.

44. Price to Nairn, Mar. 15, 1852, ibid., pp. 89–90.

45. The "Model Prison" at Port Arthur was begun in 1848 and finished in 1852; it remained in continuous use until Port Arthur closed down in 1877. It was, in every way, a scale model of Pentonville, with a fraction of the capacity—48 separate cells, arranged in three wings; the fourth wing of the cross was the chapel, with its partitioned stalls so designed that convicts could not see or communicate with one another when at Divine Service. The cells, fittings, central inspection hall and schedules for work, exercise and cleaning were copied from Pentonville, as were the prisoners' cloth masks, the felt slippers worn by guards to ensure silence, the silent numbering-machine that indicated to prisoners the order in which they must leave the chapel, and much else besides. It had four dumb-cells, black isolation chambers with walls three feet thick and no less than three internal doors; when these and the entrance door were closed, as any visitor to the restored Model Prison can now test for himself, the silence and darkness were such as to exclude all sensory stimulation. The records suggest that the Model Prison produced a high level of neurosis and mental breakdown in its inmates—as did Pentonville.

46. Report of SC on Criminal Laws, Juvenile Offenders and Transportation, PP 1847 (449), pp. 3–7.

47. Lord Grey in *GB Parl. Debates,* 3rd series, vol. 110, cols. 211–12, cit. in Crowley, *Doc. Hist.,* vol. 2, p. 114.

48. Grey to Denison, Feb. 5, 1847. Stephen to the Treasury, Feb. 15, 1847, CO 280/196.

49. Grey to Denison, Apr. 27, 1848.

50. Grey to Fitzroy, Sept. 3, 1847, HRA xxv:735. In September 1847, Grey offered to send

out one free emigrant, his fares paid by the government, for every "exile" transported to Australia. However, he retracted this offer the following year.

51. James Macarthur to SC 1837, p. 218.
52. *Port Phillip Patriot and Melbourne Advertiser*, Dec. 19, 1844.
53. Ibid., Dec. 26, 1844. On William Kerr (1812–1859), editor of the radically anti-pastoralist *Argus* and champion of workers' rights in early Victoria, see entry in ADB and Garryowen [pseud. of E. Finn], *The Chronicles of Early Melbourne* (Melbourne, 1888), pp. 1–2.
54. V & P, NSW Legislative Council, Oct. 30, 1846.
55. *Sydney Morning Herald*, June 12–18, 1849.
56. Fitzroy to Grey, June 30, 1849, CO 201/414, cit. in Clark *HA*, vol. 3, p. 420.
57. Anon. letter in *Household Words* (London), Mar. 30, 1850, p. 24.
58. Samuel Sidney, *Emigrant's Journal and Travel Magazine*, cit. in Coral Lansbury, *Arcadia in Australia: The Evocation of Australia in Nineteenth-Century English Literature* (Melbourne, 1970). Prof. Lansbury's discussion of Sidney, a figure ignored by most Australian historians, is highly pertinent to an understanding of the image of Australia among English reformers at mid-century, and I have relied on it here.
59. On Caroline Chisholm, see ADB entry; M. L. Kiddle, *Caroline Chisholm* (Melbourne, 1957); and Caroline Chisholm, *The Emigrants' Guide to Australia*, (London, 1853).
60. Charles Dickens, *David Copperfield*, Chapter 63.
61. Godfrey Charles Mundy, *Our Antipodes*, vol. 3, p. 125.

CHAPTER SIXTEEN   *The Aristocracy Be We*

1. Edward Hammond Hargraves, *Australia and Its Gold Fields . . .* , p. 116. On the "Sydney Ducks," see Sherman Ricards and George Blackman, "The Sydney Ducks: A Demographic Analysis," and Jay Monaghan, *Australians and the Gold Rush*. Sydney first heard of the California gold discoveries in December 1848. The first Australian gold-seekers arrived in San Francisco in April 1849. By May 1851 no less than 11,000 Australians had sailed to California, about 7,500 of them from Sydney. (In 1852 the population of San Francisco County was about 36,000, so the proportion of the Australian gold-seekers—and hence, of ex-convicts—was enormous. The origin of the term "Sydney Duck" (or "Derwent Duck," for gold-seekers from Tasmania) is unclear. They were viewed with extreme suspicion by Americans, and the crimes of a few brought down prejudice upon the whole. Some Ducks were reported to have adapted a mode of robbery from aboriginal hunters, who would set fire to hollow trees and kill the animals as they scurried out. In San Francisco, the technique was to set fire to a building at night and wait for the occupants to run outside clutching—of course—their most valuable possessions. The California Vigilance Committees were especially hard on Australian emigrants. They were "obvious objects of persecution," due to their strange accents and presumed criminal past, even though only one in eight from New South Wales and one in five from Van Diemen's Land were Emancipists. Most of them (some 65 percent) migrated in family groups and had no criminal past or larcenous ambitions. The committees made ninety-one recorded arrests of Ducks. Of these, four were summarily hanged in front of mobs of as many as 15,000 people; fourteen were deported back to Australia, fourteen more summarily deported from California, fifteen handed over to other authorities, and the rest let off.
2. *Bathurst Free Press*, May 17, 1851.
3. Ibid., July 19, and Aug. 13, 1851. Clark *HA*, vol. 4, p. 9.
4. *The Times* (London), Nov. 24, 1852.
5. La Trobe to Lord Grey, Dec. 10, 1851, PP 1852, 34/1508, pp. 45–46.
6. John Sherer, *The Gold-Finder of Australia: How he Went, How he Fared, and How he Made His Fortune*, pp. 195–96.
7. Ibid., p. 198.

8. Ibid., p. 10.
9. William Rayment, Diary, Oct. 19, 1852, Ms. in Public Library of Victoria, cit. in John M. Ward, *The Australian Legend*, pp. 116–17.
10. Address from William Nicholson, mayor of Melbourne, to the delegates from the Van Diemen's Land Anti-Transportation League, February 1851, Ms. Aa 25/5, ML.
11. Address from Mayor J. T. Smith, aldermen and citizens of Melbourne to Queen Victoria: Dispatches from Victoria #26, Feb. 16, 1852, A2341, ML.
12. A. G. Dumas to Lord Grey, July 17, 1851, in Dumas Family Papers, vol. 1, pp. 19–34, A4453–1, ML.
13. Leslie family letters, Jan. 20, 1850, pp. 37–40, A4094, ML.
14. Robson, *Hist. Tas.*, p. 502.
15. Clark *HA*, vol. 4, pp. 28–29.
16. For an account of the 1851 elections in Van Diemen's Land and the curious alliance of Denison and the ex-convict lower classes against the Anti-Transportation League, see Michael Roe, "The Establishment of Local Self-Government in Hobart and Launceston."
17. Ibid., pp. 31–32.
18. Ibid., p. 34.
19. Shaw *CC*, pp. 348–49.
20. Lord Grey, in G.B. Parliamentary Debates, 3rd series, vol. 110, cols. 206–18.
21. Fitzroy to Grey, June 19, 1851.
22. Among these believers in the miraculous universality of convict labor was a Mr. Levinson, who appeared in Hobart with a prospectus for an irrigation canal to be dug across the continent from sea to sea, whose "stupendous nature . . . offers no obstacle to the science, ingenuity and perseverance of Englishmen of the 19th century." Convicts, guarded by sappers and miners, would do the spadework on three-year terms, and be rewarded at the end with an allotment of land and a share of all minerals discovered on the way. The water for the canal, Levinson vaguely averred, would come from the "many rivers [which] would probably be discovered. . . . Thousands of men, who fail at the diggings and do not exactly like to go to agricultural labour, would take to this work, there being a chance of gold." No investors were seduced. *Hobart Town Daily Courier*, Aug. 10, 1853.
23. Pakington to Denison, Dec. 14, 1852, PP 1852–53, 82/1601, pp. 105–6.
24. *Colonial Times and Tasmanian* (Hobart), Aug. 13, 1853.
25. "The people of England": *Colonial Times and Tasmanian*, Aug. 6, 1853. Church bells instead of cannon: *Hobart Town Daily Courier*, Aug. 11, 1853.
26. Stirling to Darling, Dec. 14, 1826, encl. 2 in Darling to Bathurst Dec. 18, 1826, HRA xii:777–80. On Stirling and the Swan River colony, see ADB entry and Clark *HA*, vol. 3, pp. 11, 17–37.
27. On Peel and Levey, see Hasluck, *Thomas Peel of Swan River*; ADB entries; and Clark *HA*, vol. 3, p. 18ff.
28. Fitzgerald to Grey, Mar. 3, 1849, in *Further Correspondence re Convict Discipline and Transportation*, PP 1849, 43/1121, pp. 246–47.
29. *Perth Gazette*, Jan. 2, 1847.
30. Kennedy to Stanley, June 12, 1858, CO 18/104.
31. Superintendent (Fremantle) to Comptroller-General (Henderson), Jan. 10, 1858, CO 18/104.
32. "The prosperity of the colony": Henderson to Stanley, Feb. 9, 1858. "Wholly out of the question": Stanley to Gov. Kennedy, Apr. 16, 1858, CO 18/104. Convict labor to erect rival episcopal palaces: Kennedy to Labouchère, Mar. 13, 1858, CO 18/104.
33. *Statement and Appeals of the Anti-Transportation League of Victoria for the People of Great Britain*, Melbourne, Oct. 23, and Dec. 22, 1853, Q041/Pa 10, ML, Sydney.
34. A. Macarthur, letter in *The Daily News* (London), Mar. 7, 1864, Macarthur Papers, vol. 29, pp. 567–77, A2927, ML, Sydney.
35. Shaw *CC*, p. 356.

CHAPTER SEVENTEEN *The End of the System*

1. Cit. in Ernest de Blosseville, *Histoire des Colonies Penales de L'Angleterre dans Australie.* The verses translate thus: "Ah! Who does not know the consoling spectacle / Displayed by this vast receptacle of bandits, / This Botany Bay, the sewer of ALBION, / Where theft, rapine and treason / Go in hordes, and, while purging England / Fertilize the ground in their far exile? / There, kindly laws turn dangerous men / Into skilled colonists and happy citizens / Stir them to penitence, stimulate industry, / And give them freedom, customs and a homeland. / On all sides, I see drained marshes / Flowering deserts, and cleared forests. / Follow this example! Take these bandits / From their sterile prison, make their punishment useful.

2. John Freeth, ed., *The Political Songster* (Birmingham, 1790).

3. Edward Curr to Directors of VDL Co., letter 162, Jan. 12, 1831, VDL Co. Foreign Letter Book No. 3, cit. in Shaw *CC*, p. 220.

4. Dickens to Normanby (unpublished), July 2, 1840, cit. in Sarah Bradford, "Forthcoming Sale of English Books and MSS," *Times Literary Supplement*, Dec. 10, 1981.

5. See Appendixes III, IV and V in Michael Sturma, *Vice in a Vicious Society.*

6. Sturma, ibid., p. 77. For a general discussion, see his Chapter 4, "Measuring Morality," pp. 64–85.

7. Mary Gilmore, "Old Botany Bay."

8. John Mitchel, *Jail Journal*, p. 231.

9. Ibid., p. 227.

10. Ibid., p. 213.

11. Ibid., p. 244.

12. Ibid., p. 210.

13. Ibid., p. 238.

14. Henry Reynolds, " 'That Hated Stain': The Aftermath of Transportation in Tasmania." I have relied on Reynolds's essay for the account of post-Transportation entropy in Tasmania that follows.

15. Rev. John Morison, *Australia As It Is*, p. 214ff.

16. Anthony Trollope, *Australia and New Zealand*, vol. 2, Chapter 2, pp. 28–29.

17. Reynolds, "Hated Stain," p. 31.

18. My count, based on figures from Bateson, *The Convict Ships*, Appendix II, "Convict Ships to Van Diemen's Land, 1812–1853."

19. See Miriam Dixson, *"Greater Than Lenin"? Lang and Labour, 1916–1932.*

20. Alexander Cheyne to SC 1837–38, *Report*, pp. xxii–xxiii.

21. Edward Willoughby, *Australian Pictures Drawn with Pen and Pencil*, pp. 78–79, 151.

22. Anon., "The Day We Were Lagged," *The Bulletin*, Jan. 20, 1888.

23. Ibid.

24. Ibid.

25. Ibid.

26. John Sherer, *The Gold-Finder of Australia*, p. 246.

27. Marcus Clarke, *His Natural Life*, Chapter 22.

Bibliography

MANUSCRIPT SOURCES

JOURNALS, DIARIES, ACCOUNTS

Bowes Smyth, Arthur. Journal of a Voyage to NSW in the *Lady Penrhyn*, 1786–89. Safe 1/ 15, ML, Sydney.

Boyes, G.T.W.B. Diary, 1823–43. Royal Society of Tasmania Library, Hobart.

Bradley, William. Journal, 1786–1792. Safe 1/14, ML, Sydney.

Bushelle, James. Memoir. Ms. 4 at MSQ 168, Dixson Library, Sydney.

Clark, Ralph. Journal, 1787–92, Typescript and *Letter Book*. C219, ML, Sydney.

Coke, William Spencer. Diary (Feb.–Sept. 1828). Brookhill Hall Collection, Derbyshire Record Office, Wardwick, Derby.

Cook, Thomas. "The Exile's Lamentations: Memoir of Transportation." Ms. A1711, ML, Sydney.

Davies,——. Memoir of Macquarie Harbor. Ms. 8 in Norfolk Island Convict Papers, MSQ 168, Dixson Library, Sydney.

Downing, J. Norfolk Island Journal. Ms. B804, ML, Sydney.

Easty, John. "A Memorandum of the Transactions of a Voyage from England to Botany Bay in the Scarborough Transport . . . ," Dixson Library, Sydney.

Eyre, Edward J. Autobiography. ML, Sydney.

Frayne, Laurence. Memoir on Norfolk Island. NSW Colonial Secretary Papers, vol. 1 (re NSW 1799–1830). Ms. 681/1, ML, Sydney.

Fyans, Foster. "Memoirs." Ms., Latrobe Library, Melbourne. Typescript copy in Army Museums Ogilby Trust, Connaught Barracks, Aldershot.

Gorman, John. Log-book. Ms. 1524, NLA, Canberra.

Grant, John. Notes and manuscripts. Ms. 737, Grant Papers, NLA, Canberra.

Gregg, John. Journal on Convict Ship *York* (1862). Ms. 2749, NLA, Canberra.

Holt, Joseph. "Life and Adventures of Joseph Holt, Written by Himself." Ms. A2024, ML, Sydney.

Jones,——. Memoir. Ms. 10 in Norfolk Island Convict Papers, MSQ 168, Dixson Library, Sydney.

Jones, Robert. "Recollections of 13 Years Residence on Norfolk Island." Ms. C/y/1/2, ML, Sydney.

King, Philip Gidley. Journal, Norfolk Island (1791–94). Ms. A1687, ML, Sydney.

Knopwood. Rev. Robert. Diaries, 1803–25. ML, Sydney.

——. "Narrative of Escape from Macquarie Harbour by Alexander Pearce." Ms. 3, Dixson Library, Sydney.

Lawrence, James. Memoir. Ms. 1 in Norfolk Island Convict Papers, MSQ 168, Dixson Library, Sydney.

Lemprière, T. J. Diary. ML, Sydney.

Lepailleur, François-Maurice. Journal, 1839–44. Archives Nationales de Québec.

Marsden, Samuel. "A Few Observations on the Toleration of the Catholic Religion in New South Wales." Ms. 18, ML, Sydney.

Muir, Thomas. "The Telegraph, A Consolatory Epistle . . . to the Honble. Henry Erskine." Ms. Am. 9, ML, Sydney.

Palmer, Thomas Fyshe. Letters. Ms. B1666, ML, Sydney.

[Pearce, Alexander.] "Narrative of Escape from Macquarie Harbour," Ms. 3, Dixson Library, Sydney.

Porter, James. Memoirs. Typescript 6 in Norfolk Island Convict Papers, MSQ 168, Dixson Library, Sydney.

Rogers, W. F. "Man's Inhumanity." Typescript C214, ML, Sydney.

Sharpe, Rev. T. Journal, Ms. B217–8, ML, Sydney.

Silverthorpe, Mansfield. Ms. 9 in Norfolk Island Convict Papers, MSQ 168, Dixson Library, Sydney.

Smith, John. Surgeon's Log on Transport *Clyde* (1838). Ms. 6169, NLA, Canberra.

Sorell, William Jnr. Diaries, 1800–1860. UTL, Hobart.

Walker, James Backhouse. Papers, 1853–98. UTL, Hobart.

Ward, John. "Diary of a Convict." Ms. 3275, NLA, Canberra.

Worgan, G. B. Journal, Jan.–July 1788. Typescript B1463, ML, Sydney.

CORRESPONDENCE AND GENERAL PAPERS

Arthur Papers. Mss. A1962, A2161–95, A2214, D292. ML, Sydney.

Auckland Papers. Add. Ms. 34458, BL.

Bentham Papers. Add. Mss. 33543, 33544, BL.

Bonwick Transcripts, Bigge NSW, Appendix, ML, Sydney.

Boothman, Richard. Letters. Ms. DDX 537, LRO, Preston, Lancashire, Eng.

Boyes, G.T.W.B. Letters. UTL, Hobart.

Bradley, William. Journal . . . 1786–1792. Ms. A3631, ML, Sydney.

Brisbane Letter Book. Ms. A1559, ML, Sydney.

Brown, Simon. Letters, 1840–58. Ms. DDX 140, LRO, Preston, Lancashire, Eng.

Calder Papers. Ms. A594, ML, Sydney.

Catton Papers. Derby Central Library, Wardwick, Derby, Eng.

Coke, William Spencer. Letters (1824–28). Ms. D1881, Brookhill Hall Collection, Derbyshire Record Office, Wardwick, Derby, Eng.

Dillingham, Richard. Letters. Ms. CRT 150/24, Bedford County Record Office, Bedford, Eng.

Dumas Family Papers. Vol. 1. Ms. A4453–1, ML, Sydney.

Foveaux, Joseph. Letter Book, 1800–1804. Ms. A1444, ML, Sydney.

Gordon, Hugh. Letter to his brother Robert, Dec. 31, 1839. Doc. 1308, ML, Sydney.

Grant, John. Letters in Grant papers. Ms. 737, NLA, Canberra.

Grieg, James. Letters, 1824–29. Doc. 2316, ML, Sydney.

Hammersley papers, A657, ML.

Harris family letters. Add. Ms. 45156, BL.

Hassall Correspondence. Ms. A1677, ML, Sydney.

Hayes, Michael. Letters. Ms. A3586, ML, Sydney.

Holden, Thomas. Letters, 1812–16. Ms. DDX 140, LRO, Preston, Lancashire, Eng.

Irish Political Prisoners' Letters. NLA, Canberra.

Jewell, W. H. Letter, May 1820. Doc. 1042, ML, Sydney.

King, Philip Gidley. Letter Books, 1788–96, 1797–1806, and papers. Mss. A1687, C187, ML, Sydney.

Lang Papers. Mss. A2221, A2226, A2229, ML, Sydney.

Leslie Papers, A4094, ML, Sydney.

Macarthur Papers. Mss. A2897, A2900, A2911, A2927, A2955, ML, Sydney.

Marsden Papers. Mss. A1992, A1998, ML, Sydney.

Morisset, J. T. Papers, Ms. Am.34, ML, Sydney.

NI Mutiny Papers. NSWA.
Peel Papers. Add. Ms. 40380, BL.
Pelham Papers. Add. Mss. 33105, 33106, 33107, BL.
Privy Council Office Papers. 1/67–92 (1819–1844). Letters and petitions from convicts and families. PRO, London.
Reddell Papers, ML, Sydney.
Sharpe, Rev. T. Papers. Ms. A1502, ML, Sydney.
Stenhouse Papers II, ML, Sydney.
Stickney Papers. UTL, Hobart.
Taylor, Richard. Letters, 1840–58. Ms. DDX 505, LRO, Preston, Lancs.
Ward Papers, Ms. 3275, NLA, Canberra.
Wentworth Papers. Ms. A751, ML, Sydney.
Whitbread Papers, Bedford.
Withers, Peter. Letters. TSA, Hobart.

PRIMARY SOURCES

[Contemporary books, pamphlets and articles, published during the transportation period or drawn from their authors' direct experience of the penal system in convict Australia.]

Anderson, Joseph. *Recollections of a Peninsular Veteran*. London, 1913.
Anon. "Anti-transportation Movement in Sydney." *Colonial Magazine and East India Review*, vol. 18 (July–December 1849), pp. 179–84.
————. *Biographical Memoir* [of John Price]. Melbourne, 1857.
————. *Great and New News from Botany Bay*. London, 1797.
————. *A Narrative of the Sufferings . . . of the Convicts Who Piratically Seized the 'Frederick' in Van Diemen's Land*. c. 1838. (Copy in ML Sydney at 910–453/29A1.)
————. *Sinks of London Laid Open*. [On slang and cant.] 1844.
————. *The Political Martyrs of Scotland Persecuted During the Years 1793 and 1794*. Edinburgh, 1795.
————. "Transportation and Convict Colonies." *Colonial Magazine and East India Review*, vol. 18 (July–December 1849), pp. 27–37.
Anon. [Edward Eagar]. *Letters to Sir Robert Peel on the Advantages of New South Wales and Van Diemen's Land as Penal Settlements*. 1824.
Arthur, George. *Observations upon Secondary Punishment*. Hobart, 1833.
————, ed. *Defence of Transportation in Reply to the Remarks of the Bishop of Dublin*. Hobart and London, 1835.
Atkins, Rev. T. *Reminiscences of Twelve Years Residence on Tasmania and New South Wales, Norfolk Island and Moreton Bay, Calcutta, Madras and Cape Town, the United States of America and the Canadas*. London, 1869.
Atkinson, James, *An Account of the State of Agriculture and Grazing in New South Wales . . .*, London, 1826.
Backhouse, James, and Walker, George Washington, *A Narrative of a Visit to the Australian Colonies*. London, 1843.
Banks, Joseph. *The Endeavour Journal of Joseph Banks, 1768–1771* (ed. J. C. Beaglehole). 2 vols. Sydney, 1962.
Barrington, George [pseud.]. *The History of New South Wales*. London, 1802.
Beccaria, Cesare. *Degli Delitti e delle Pene*, trans. as *Essay on Crimes and Punishments*. London, 1767.
Bennett, H. G. *A Letter to Viscount Sidmouth on Transportation*. London, 1819.
————. *A Letter to Earl Bathurst, Secretary of State for the Colonial Department, on the Condition of the Colonies in New South Wales and Van Diemen's Land*. London, 1820.
Benoiston de Chateauneuf, Jean-François. *De la Colonization des Condamnés*. Paris, 1827.
Bentham, Jeremy. *Panopticon; or, The Inspection-House*. London, 1791.
————. *Panopticon Versus New South Wales: Two Letters to Lord Pelham*. London, 1812.

Betts, T. *An Account of the Colony of Van Diemen's Land.* Calcutta, 1830.

Bischoff, James. *Sketch of the History of Van Diemen's Land.* London, 1832.

de Blosseville, Ernest. *Histoire des Colonies Penales de L'Angleterre dans Australie.* Paris, 1831.

Booth, Charles O'Hara. *The Journal of Charles O'Hara Booth, Commandant of the Port Arthur Penal Settlement* (ed. Dora Heard). Hobart, 1981.

Boswell, James. *The Life of Samuel Johnson,* vol. 2. London, 1920 (Everyman ed).

de Bougainville, Louis Antoine. *A Voyage Around the World* (trans. John Reinhold Foster). London, 1772.

Bowes Smyth, Arthur. *The Journal of Arthur Bowes Smyth, Surgeon, Lady Penrhyn, 1787–1789.* Ed. by P. G. Fidlon and R. J. Ryan. Sydney, 1979.

Bradley, William. *A Voyage to New South Wales, 1786–1792.* Facs. ed. of Bradley Ms. in Safe P.H. 8, ML, Sydney, 2 vols., Sydney, 1967.

Breton, William H. *Excursions in New South Wales, Western Australia and Van Diemen's Land, 1830–33.* London, 1833.

Browning. C. A. *The Convict Ship and England's Exiles.* 2nd ed., London, 1847.

Broxup, John. *Life of John Broxup, Late Convict at Van Diemen's Land.* London, 1850.

Burton, Sir William Westbrooke. *The State of Religion and Education in New South Wales.* London, 1840.

———. "State of Society and State of Crime in New South Wales, During Six Years' Residence in that Colony." *Colonial Magazine and Commercial-Maritime Journal,* vol. 1 (January–April 1840), pp. 421–40; vol. 2 (May–August 1840), pp. 34–54.

Byrne, J. C. *Twelve Years' Wanderings in the British Colonies, From 1835 to 1847.* 2 vols. London, 1848.

Chisholm, Caroline. *Emancipation and Transportation Relatively Considered; in a Letter, Dedicated, By Permission, to Earl Grey.* London, 1847.

———. *The Emigrants' Guide to Australia.* London, 1853.

Clark, Ralph. *Journal and Letters 1787–1792.* Sydney, 1981.

Collins, David. *An Account of the English Colony in New South Wales.* 2 vols. London, 1798, 1802; reprinted Sydney, 1975.

Colquhoun, Patrick. *A Treatise on the Police of the Metropolis.* London, 1797.

———. *The State of Indigence and the Situation of the Casual Poor in the Metropolis Explained.* London, 1799.

———. *A Treatise on the Commerce and Police of the River Thames.* London, 1800.

Cook, James. *The Journals of Captain James Cook on His Voyage of Discovery* (ed. J. C. Beaglehole). Vols. 1 and 2. Cambridge, 1955 and 1961.

———. *A Voyage to the Pacific Ocean.* 3 vols. (vol. 3 by Capt. James King). London, 1784.

Cook, Thomas. *The Exile's Lamentations* (ed. A. G. L. Shaw). Sydney, 1978.

Cozens, Charles. *The Adventures of a Guardsman.* London, 1848.

Cunningham, Peter. *Two Years in New South Wales.* 2 vols. 2nd ed., London, 1827.

Curr, Edward M. *Recollections of Squatting in Victoria Then Called the Port Phillip District, from 1841 to 1851.* Melbourne, 1883.

[Dalrymple, Alexander]. *A Serious Admonition to the Publick on the Intended Thief-Colony at Botany Bay.* London, 1786.

Dampier, William. *Dampier's Voyages* (ed. John Masefield). 2 vols. London, 1906.

Darwin, Charles. *The Voyage of the Beagle.* New York: Bantam paperback edition, 1972.

Denison, Sir William. *Varieties of Vice-Regal Life.* 2 vols. London, 1870.

Dickens, Charles. *American Notes for General Circulation.* London, 1850.

Fielding, Henry. *An Enquiry into the Causes of the Late Increase of Robbers . . .* London, 1751.

———. *A Proposal for Making Effectual Provision for the Poor.* London, 1753.

Fielding, John. *An Account of the Origin and Effects of a Plan of Police.* London, 1753.

———. *Penal Laws Relating to the Metropolis.* London, 1768.

Forster, Harley W. (ed). *The Dillingham Convict Letters.* Melbourne, 1970.

Frost, John. *The Horrors of Convict Life.* Preston, 1856; Hobart, 1973.

Fyans, Capt. Foster. *Memoirs, 1790–1870* (ed. P. L. Brown). Geelong, 1986.

Gaskell, Peter. *The Manufacturing Population of England: Its Moral, Social and Physical Conditions*. London, 1833.

Gouger, Robert [pseud. of E. G. Wakefield]. *A Letter from Sydney, the Principal Town of Australia*. London, 1829.

Grove, James. "Select Letters of James Grove, Convict . . . , 1803–4" (ed. John Earnshaw). Part II, the letters. THRA, PP, vol. 8, no. 2, October 1959.

Hanway, Jonas. *The Defects of the Police*. London, 1775; reprinted as *The Citizen's Monitor*, London, 1780.

Hargraves, E. H. *Australia and its Gold Fields: A Historical Sketch of the Progress of the Australian Colonies, from the Earliest Times, to the Present Day*. London, 1855.

Harris, Alexander. *The Emigrant Family: or, The Story of an Australian Settler*. London, 1849; reprint (ed. W. S. Ramson), Canberra, 1967.

———[An Emigrant Mechanic]. *Settlers and Convicts, or Recollections of Sixteen Years' Labour in the Australian Backwoods*. London, 1847; reprint (ed. C. M. H. Clark), Melbourne, 1964.

Haygarth, Henry W. *Recollections of Bush Life in Australia, During a Residence of Eight Years in the Interior*. London, 1848.

Henderson, John. *Observations on the Colonies of New South Wales and Van Diemen's Land*. Calcutta, 1832.

———. *Excursions and Adventures in New South Wales; with Pictures of Squatting and Life in the Bush*. 2 vols. London, 1851.

Holt, Joseph. *Memoirs of Joseph Holt* (ed. T. C. Croker). 2 vols. London, 1838.

Howard, John. *The State of the Prisons in England and Wales*. Warrington, 1777.

Hunter, John. *An Historical Journal of the Transactions at Port Jackson and Norfolk Island*. London, 1793; reprint (ed. J. Bach), Sydney, 1968.

Jeffrey, Mark. *A Burglar's Life*. Hobart, 1893.

King, Philip Gidley. *The Journal of Philip Gidley King, Lieutenant, R.N., 1787–1790* (ed. P. G. Fidlon and R. J. Ryan). Sydney, 1980.

Lacombe, L. *Observations sur Londres par un Athéronome de Berne*, Paris, 1777.

Lang, John Dunmore. *An Historical and Statistical Account of New South Wales, Both as a Penal Settlement and as a British Colony*. 2 vols. London, 1837.

———. *Transportation and Colonization: or, The Causes of the Comparative Failure of the Transportation System in the Australian Colonies*. London, 1837.

La Pérouse, Jean-François de Galaup, Comte de. *A Voyage Around the World, Performed in the Years 1785, 1786, 1787 and 1788, by the Boussole and the Astrolabe, under the Command of J. F. G. de la Pérouse*. 2 vols. London, 1799.

Laplace, C. P. T. "Considérations sur la Système de Colonization suivi par les Anglais," in *Voyage Autour du Monde, 1830–32*, vol. 3. 1835.

Lilburn, Edward. *A Complete Exposure of the Convict System . . .* Lincoln, n.d.

Loveless, George et al. *A Narrative of the Sufferings of Jas. Loveless, Jas. Brine, and Thomas & John Standfield, Four of the Dorchester Labourers; Displaying the Horrors of Transportation*. 1838.

Macarthur, James. *New South Wales, Its Present State and Future Prospects . . . Submitted in Support of Petitions to Her Majesty and Parliament*. London, 1837.

Maconochie, Alexander. *Report on the State of Prison Discipline in Van Diemen's Land, . . .* Hobart, 1838.

———. *Thoughts on Convict Management and other subjects connected with the Australian Penal Colonies*. Hobart, 1838.

———. *Australiana, Thoughts on Convict Management, etc.* London, 1839.

———. *General Views Regarding the Social System of Convict Management*. Hobart, 1839.

———. *Principles of the Mark System, now sought to be introduced into Transportation, Imprisonment and other Forms of Secondary Punishment*, London, n.d. [ca. 1845].

———. *Crime and Punishment, The Mark System, framed to mix persuasion with punishment, and make their effect improving, yet their operation severe*. London, 1846.

———. *Norfolk Island*. London, 1847.

———. *On Reformatory Prison Discipline*. Birmingham, 1851.

————. *The Mark System of Prison Discipline.* London, 1857.

Macquarie, Lachlan. *A Letter to the Rt. Hon. Viscount Sidmouth in Refutation of State-ments Made by the Hon. Henry Grey Bennett.* London, 1821.

Macqueen, T. Potter. *Australia as She Is and As She Might Be.* London, 1840.

Marjoribanks, Alexander. *Travels in New South Wales.* London, 1847.

Martin, James. *Memorandoms.* From 1791 Ms. in Bentham Papers, BL, London (ed. C. Blount), Cambridge, 1937.

Mayhew, Henry. *London Labour and the London Poor.* 3 vols. London, 1862.

————. *Those that Will Not Work* (extra vol. to *London Labour*).

Mellish,————. "A Convict's Recollections of New South Wales, Written by Himself." Lon-don Magazine, vol. 2, 1825.

Melville, Henry. *The Present State of Australia, including New South Wales, Western Australia, South Australia, Victoria and New Zealand, with Practical Hints on Emigra-tion.* London, 1851.

Meredith, Louisa Anne. *Notes and Sketches of New South Wales During a Residence in that Colony from 1839 to 1844.* London, 1844; facs. ed., Melbourne, 1973.

Mitchel, John. *Jail Journal; or, Five Years in British Prisons.* Glasgow, 1876.

Mortlock, John F. *Experiences of a Convict Transported for Twenty-One Years.* London, 1864–65; reprint (ed. by G. A. Wilkes and A. G. Mitchell), Sydney, 1965.

Mudie, James. *The Felonry of New South Wales: Being a Faithful Picture of the Real Romance of Life in Botany Bay.* London, 1837; reprint (ed. Walter Stone), Melbourne, 1964.

Mundy, Godfrey Charles. *Our Antipodes: or, Residence and Rambles in the Australian Colonies with a glimpse of the Gold Fields.* London, 1855.

Nicol, John. *The Life and Adventures of John Nicol, Mariner.* London, 1822.

Noah, William. *Voyage to Sydney in the Ship 'Hillsborough' 1798–99, and A Description of the Colony,* Sydney, 1978.

O'Connell, J. F. *A Residence of Eleven Years in New Holland and the Caroline Islands: Being the Adventures of James F. O'Connell, Edited from his Verbal Narration.* Boston, 1836.

O'Reilly, John Boyle. *Moondyne Joe.* Philadelphia, [188—?], p. 230.

Palmer, Thomas Fyshe. *A Narrative of the Sufferings of T. F. Palmer.* London, 1797.

Parkinson, Sydney. *A Journal of a Voyage to the South Seas.* London, 1784.

Peron, François, and de Freycinet, Louis. *Voyages de Découvertes aux Terres Australes.* 2 vols. Paris, 1807–16.

Phillip, Arthur. *The Voyage of Governor Phillip to Botany Bay.* London, 1789; reprint (ed. J. J. Auchmuty), Sydney, 1970.

————. *Extracts of Letters from Arthur Phillip, Esq.* Facs. ed., Adelaide, 1963.

Phillips, Sir Richard. *A Letter to the Livery of London.* London, 1808.

Prieur, F. X. *Notes of a Convict of 1838.* N.p., n.d.

Reid, Thomas. *Two Voyages to New South Wales and Van Diemen's Land.* London, 1822.

Ritchie, D. *Voice of Our Exiles; or, Stray Leaves from a Convict Ship.* London, 1854.

Rogers, Rev. Thomas. *Correspondence relating to the Dismissal of the Rev. T. Rogers from his Chaplaincy at Norfolk Island.* Launceston, 1849.

R[oss], W[illiam]. *The Fell Tyrant; or, the Suffering Convict.* London, 1836.

Sadleir, John. *Recollections of a Victorian Police Officer.* Melbourne, 1913.

Savery, Henry. *The Hermit in Van Diemen's Land.* Hobart, 1829; reprint (ed. Cecil Hadgraft and Margaret Roe), Brisbane, 1964.

Sherer, John. *The Gold Finder of Australia: How He Went, How He Fared, and How He Made His Fortune.* London, 1853.

Sidney, Samuel. *The Three Colonies of Australia: New South Wales, Victoria, South Aus-tralia: Their Pastures, Copper Mines and Gold Fields.* London, 1852.

Syme, J. *Nine Years in Van Diemen's Land.* Perth, 1848.

Tench, Watkin. *A Narrative of the Expedition to Botany Bay; with an Account of New South Wales, Its Productions, Inhabitants &c . . .* London, 1789.

————. *A Complete Account of the Settlement at Port Jackson, in New South Wales* . . . London, 1793.

Tetens, Alfred (trans. F. M. Spoehr). *Among the Savages of the South Seas: Memoirs of Micronesia, 1862–68.* Los Angeles, 1958.

Therry, Roger. *Reminiscences of Thirty Years' Residence in New South Wales and Victoria.* London, 1863; facs. ed., Sydney, 1974.

Thompson, George. *Slavery and Famine: An Account of the Miseries and Starvation at Botany Bay.* London, 1794.

Trollope, Anthony. *Australia and New Zealand.* Vol. 2. London, 1968.

Ullathorne, William. *The Catholic Mission in Australasia.* Liverpool, 1837.

————. *The Horrors of Transportation Briefly Unfolded to the People,* Dublin, 1838.

Wakefield, E. G. *The Art of Colonization.* London, 1849.

Wakefield, E. G. [Robert Gouger]. (See Gouger, Robert.)

Watling, Thomas. *Letters from an Exile at Botany-Bay to his Aunt in Dumfries; Giving a Particular Account of the Settlement of New South Wales, with the Customs and Manners of the Inhabitants.* Penrith, n.d.

Wentworth, William C. *A Statistical, Historical and Political Description of the Colony of New South Wales.* London, 1819.

West, John. *The History of Tasmania.* Launceston, 1852; reprint (ed. A. G. L. Shaw), Sydney, 1971.

———— [Lackland, Jacob]. *Common Sense: an Inquiry into the Influence of Transportation on the Colony of Van Diemen's Land.* Launceston, 1847.

Westgarth, William. *Australia Felix: or, a Historical and Descriptive Account of the Settlement of Port Phillip, New South Wales.* Edinburgh, 1848.

Whateley, Richard. *Thoughts on Secondary Punishment, in a Letter to Earl Grey* . . . London, 1832.

White, John. *Journal of a Voyage to NSW.* London, 1790.

Woomera [pseud.]. *The Life of an Ex-Convict.* Printed extract in ML, Sydney.

SECONDARY SOURCES

PUBLISHED BOOKS AND ARTICLES

Abbie, A. A. "Physical Characteristics of Australian Aborigines." In H. Shields, ed., *Australian Aboriginal Studies,* pp. 89–107. Melbourne, 1967.

Asbury, Herbert. *The Barbary Coast.* London, 1937.

Atkins, Barbara. "Australia's Place in the Swing to the East—an Addendum." HS, vol. 8 (1958).

Atkinson, Alan. "Four Patterns of Convict Protest." *LH,* vol. 37 (November 1979), pp. 28–51.

Australian Council of National Trusts. *The Historic Buildings of Norfolk Island: Their Restoration, Preservation and Maintenance.* Canberra, 1971.

Baker, Sidney J. *The Australian Language.* Sydney, 1966.

Barker, Sydney K. "The Governorship of Sir George Gipps." *JRAHS,* vol. 16, parts 3 and 4, 1930, pp. 169–260.

Barnard, Marjorie. *Macquarie's World.* Melbourne, 1949.

Barry, Sir John Vincent. *Alexander Maconochie of Norfolk Island: A Study of a Pioneer in Penal Reform.* Melbourne, 1958.

————. *The Life and Death of John Price: A Study in the Exercise of Naked Power.* Melbourne, 1964.

Bateson, Charles. *Patrick Logan, Tyrant of Brisbane Town.* Sydney, 1966.

————. *The Convict Ships, 1787–1868.* Sydney, 1974.

Beaglehole, J. C. *The Exploration of the Pacific.* London, 1934; rev. ed., 1947.

————, ed. *The Journals of Captain James Cook on His Voyages of Discovery.* Vols. 1 and 2. Cambridge, 1955 and 1961.

————, ed. *The Endeavour Journal of Joseph Banks, 1768–1771.* 2 vols. Sydney, 1962.

————. *The Life of Captain James Cook.* London, 1974.

Beattie, J. W. *Glimpses of the Lives and Times of the Early Tasmanian Governors.* Hobart, n.d. [1905].

Birdsell, Joseph B. "Preliminary Data on the Trihybrid Origin of the Australian Aborigines." In *Archaeology and Physical Anthropology in Oceania,* vol. 2, pp. 100–155. London, 1967.

Blainey, Geoffrey. *The Rush That Never Ended: A History of Australian Mining.* Melbourne, 1963.

————. *The Tyranny of Distance: How Distance Shaped Australia's History.* Melbourne, 1966.

————. *The Triumph of the Nomads: A History of Ancient Australia.* Melbourne, 1975.

Boissery, Beverley D., and Greenwood, F. Murray. "New Sources for Convict History: The Canadien Patriotes in Exile." *JRAHS,* vol. 71 (October 1978), pp. 277–82.

Bolger, Peter. *Hobart Town.* Canberra, 1973.

Boxall, George. *The Story of the Australian Bushrangers.* London, 1899.

Boyer, P. W. "Leaders and Helpers: Jane Franklin's Plan for Van Diemen's Land." THRA, PP, vol. 21, no. 2 (June 1974).

Brady, Frank. *James Boswell: The Later Years.* New York, 1984.

Brand, Ian, *The 'Separate' or 'Model' Prison, Port Arthur.* Hobart, 1975.

Butlin, N. G. *Our Original Aggression.* Sydney, 1984.

Cadogan, Edward. *The Roots of Evil.* London, 1937.

Calder, J. E. et al. *Some Account of the Wars, Extirpation, Habits etc. of the Native Tribes of Tasmania.* Hobart, 1875.

Campbell, J. F. "The Valley of the Tank Stream." *JRAHS,* vol. 10 (1924).

Campbell, Walter S. "The Use and Abuse of Stimulants in the Early Days of Settlement in New South Wales." *JRAHS,* vol. 18, part 2 (1932), pp. 74–99.

Cannon, Michael. "Violence: The Australian Heritage." *National Times Magazine,* March 5, 1973, pp. 16–21; March 12, 1973, pp. 28–30.

Carty, James, ed. *Ireland from Grattan's Parliament to the Great Famine, 1783–1850: A Documentary Record.* Dublin, 5th ed. 1966.

Chapman, Don. *1788, The People of the First Fleet.* Sydney, 1981.

Chapman, Peter. "G.T.W.B. Boyes and Australia: The Pursuit of a Vision?" THRA, PP, vol. 23, no. 3 (September 1976), pp. 58–76.

Chesney, Kellow. *The Anti-Society: An Account of the Victorian Underworld.* Boston, 1970.

Clark, C. M. H. *A History of Australia.* Vol. 1: *From the Earliest Times to the Age of Macquarie.* Melbourne, 1962.

————. *A History of Australia.* Vol. 2: *New South Wales and Van Diemen's Land, 1822–1838.* Melbourne, 1968.

————. *A History of Australia.* Vol. 3: *The Beginning of an Australian Civilization, 1824–1851.* Melbourne, 1973.

————. *A History of Australia.* Vol. 4: *The Earth Abideth For Ever, 1851–1888.* Melbourne, 1978.

————, ed. *Sources of Australian History,* London 1957.

————, ed. *Select Documents in Australian History, 1788–1850.* Sydney, 1977.

————. "The Origins of the Convicts Transported to Eastern Australia, 1787–1852," HS vol. 7, nos. 26–27, May–June 1956.

Clarke, Marcus. *His Natural Life* (ed. Stephen Murray-Smith). London, Penguin Books, 1970.

Clune, Frank. *The Norfolk Island Story.* Sydney, 1967.

Cobley, John. *Sydney Cove, 1788.* London, 1962.

————. *Sydney Cove, 1789–1790.* Sydney, 1963.

————. *Sydney Cove, 1791–1792.* Sydney, 1965.

————. *The Crimes of the First Fleet Convicts.* Sydney, 1970.

Conlon, Anne. " 'Mine Is a Sad Yet True Story': Convict Narratives 1818–50." *JRAHS*, vol. 55, part 1 (March 1969), pp. 43–82.

Cor, Henri. *Contribution à l'étude des questions coloniales de la Transportation* . . . Paris, 1895.

Cox, Philip, and Stacey, Wesley. *Building Norfolk Island*. Melbourne, n.d.

Cribb, A. B., and Cribb, J. W. *Wild Food in Australia*. Sydney, 1974.

Cronin, Sean. *Irish Nationalism: A History of its Roots and Ideology*. New York, 1980.

Crooke, R. *The Convict*. Reprint. Hobart, 1958.

Crowley, Frank, ed. *A Documentary History of Australia*. Vol. 1: *Colonial Australia, 1788–1840*. Melbourne, 1980.

———. *A Documentary History of Australia*. Vol. 2: *Colonial Australia, 1841–1874*. Melbourne, 1981.

Currey, C. H. *The Transportation, Escape and Pardoning of Mary Bryant*. Sydney, 1963.

Dalkin, R. Nixon. *The Colonial Era Cemetery of Norfolk Island*. Sydney, 1974.

Denholm, David. *The Colonial Australians*. Sydney, 1979.

Denholm, Decie. "Port Arthur: The Men and the Myth." *HS*, vol. 15, no. 55, Sept. 1966.

Dening, Greg. *Islands and Beaches: Discourse on a Silent Land, Marquesas 1774–1880*. Honolulu, 1980.

Department of Home Affairs and Environment. *Norfolk Island: Kingston and Arthur's Vale Historic Area Management Plan, April 1980*. Australian Government Publishing Service, Canberra, 1981.

Dingle, A. E. " 'The Truly Magnificent Thirst': An Historical Study of Australian Drinking Habits." *HS*, vol. 19, no. 75 (October 1980), pp. 227–49.

Dixson, Miriam. *The Real Matilda: Woman and Identity in Australia, 1788–1975*. Melbourne, 1976.

———. "Greater Than Lenin"? *Lang and Labour, 1916–1932*. Melbourne, n.d.

Duly, Leslie C. " 'Hottentots to Hobart and Sydney': The Cape Supreme Court's Use of Transportation 1828–1838." *AJPH*, vol. 25, no. 1 (April 1979).

Eddy, J. J. *Britain and the Australian Colonies, 1818–1831—The Technique of Government*. Oxford, 1969.

Ehrman, John. *The Younger Pitt*. 2 vols. London, 1969.

Eldershaw, M. Barnard. *Phillip of Australia*. London, 1938.

———. *The Life and Times of John Piper*. Sydney, 1973.

Eldershaw, P. R. "Guide to the Public Records of Tasmania." *THRA, PP*, vol. 15, no. 3, Jan. 1968.

Elkin, A. P. *The Australian Aborigines*. Rev. ed. Sydney, 1974.

Elliott, Brian, and Mitchell, Adrian, eds. *Bards in the Wilderness: Australian Colonial Poetry to 1920*. Melbourne, 1970.

Ellis, M. H. "Macquarie and the Rum Hospital." *JRAHS*, vol. 32 (1946–47).

———. *Lachlan Macquarie*. Sydney, 1947.

———. *Francis Greenway*. 2nd ed. Sydney, 1953.

———. *John Macarthur*. Sydney, 1955.

Ellis, Vivienne R. "Trucanini." *THRA, PP*, vol. 23, no. 2 (June 1976).

Evans, Lloyd. *Convicts and Colonial Society, 1788–1853*. Sydney, 1977.

Evatt, Herbert Vere. *Rum Rebellion*. Sydney, 1938.

Fels, Marie. "Culture Contact in the County of Buckinghamshire, Van Diemen's Land, 1803–11." *THRA, PP*, vol. 26, no. 2 (June 1982).

Firth, Marjorie M. *The Tolpuddle Martyrs*. London, 1971.

Fitzpatrick, Kathleen. *Sir John Franklin in Tasmania, 1837–1843*. Melbourne, 1949.

Fitzsymonds, Eustace, ed. *Norfolk Island 1846: The Accounts of Robert Pringle Stuart and Thomas Beagley Naylor*. Adelaide, 1979.

———. *A Looking-Glass for Tasmania*. Adelaide, 1980.

Fletcher, Brian H. *Ralph Darling: A Governor Maligned*. Melbourne, 1984.

Ford, E. *The Life and Work of William Redfern*. Sydney, 1953.

Forsyth, W. D. *Governor Arthur's Convict System*. London, 1935.

Fortescue, J., ed. *The Correspondence of King George III.* 7 vols. London, 1928.

Foster, John. *Class Struggle and the Industrial Revolution: Early Industrial Capitalism in Three English Towns.* London, 1974.

Freeland, J. M. *Architecture in Australia, A History.* Melbourne, 1974.

Frost, Alan. *Convicts and Empire: A Naval Question, 1776–1811.* Melbourne, 1980.

Gandevia, Brian. "Socio-Medical Factors in the Evolution of the First Settlement at Sydney Cove, 1788–1803." *RAHJ* (March 1975).

———, and Cobley, J. "Mortality at Sydney Cove, 1788–1792." *ANZJM,* vol. 4 (1974).

———, and Gandevia, Simon. "Childhood Mortality and its Social Background in the First Settlement at Sydney Cove, 1788–1792." *Australian Paediatric Journal,* vol. 11 (1975).

Gaskell, Peter. *The Manufacturing Population of England.* London, 1933.

Genovese, Eugene D. *The Political Economy of Slavery: Studies in the Economy and Society of the Slave South.* New York, 1965.

George, M. Dorothy. *London Life in the Eighteenth Century.* London, 1925; reprint, London, 1966.

Gibbings, Robert. *John Graham, Convict 1824; an historical narrative.* London, 1956.

Gibson, Rev. C. B. *Life Among Convicts.* London, 1863.

Gloag, John. *Georgian Grace.* London, 1954.

Gordon, Douglas. "Sickness and Death at the Moreton Bay Convict Settlement." *MJA,* September 1963.

Grabosky, Peter. *Sydney in Ferment: Crime, Dissent and Official Reaction, 1788 to 1973.* Canberra, 1977.

Greener, Leslie. "The Bridge At Ross." THRA, PP, vol. 14, no. 3 (February 1967).

Grocott, Allan. *Convicts, Clergymen and Churches: Attitudes of Convicts and Ex-Convicts Towards the Churches and Clergy in New South Wales, 1788–1851.* Sydney, 1980.

Hamer, Clive. "Novels of the Convict System." *Southerly,* vol. 18, no. 4 (1957).

Hammond, J. L., and Hammond, B. *The Village Laborer, 1760–1832.* London, 1913.

Harrison, J. F. C. *Early Victorian Britain.* London, 1979.

Hasluck, Alexandra. *Unwilling Immigrants.* Melbourne, 1959.

Hay, Douglas. "Property, Authority and the Criminal Law." In *Albion's Fatal Tree: Crime and Society in Eighteenth-Century England* (ed. Douglas Hay, Peter Linebaugh and Edward P. Thompson). London, 1975.

Hazzard, Margaret. *Punishment Short of Death: A History of the Penal Settlement at Norfolk Island.* Melbourne, 1984.

Heard, Dora, ed. *The Journal of Charles O'Hara Booth.* Hobart, 1981.

Henry, E. R. "Edward Lord: The John Macarthur of Van Diemen's Land," THRA, PP, vol. 22, no. 2 (June 1973).

Herman, Morton. *Early Australian Architects and their Work.* Sydney, 1954.

Hibbert, Christopher. *The Roots of Evil.* London, 1963.

Hill, Christopher. *Reformation to Industrial Revolution.* London, 1967.

Hill-Reid, William Scott. *John Grant's Journey: A Convict's Story, 1803–11.* London, 1957.

Himmelfarb, Gertrude. *The Idea of Poverty: England in the Early Industrial Age.* New York, 1984.

Hirst, John B. *Convict Society and its Enemies.* Sydney, 1983.

Hoare, M. H. *Norfolk Island, An Outline of its History 1774–1968.* Brisbane, 1969.

Hobsbawm, Eric J. *Primitive Rebels: Studies in Archaic Forms of Social Movement in the 19th and 20th Centuries.* Manchester, 1959.

———. *The Age of Revolution.* London, 1962.

———. *Industry and Empire.* Vol. 3 of Pelican Economic History of Britain. London, 1969.

———, and Rude, George. *Captain Swing.* London, 1969.

Hooper, F. C. *Prison Boys of Port Arthur.* Melbourne, 1967.

Howard, Derek L. *The English Prisons.* London, 1962.

Ignatieff, Michael. *A Just Measure of Pain: The Penitentiary in the Industrial Revolution, 1750–1850.* New York, 1978.

Ingleton, Geoffrey. *True Patriots All.* Sydney, 1952.

Inglis, Brian. *Poverty and the Industrial Revolution*. London, 1971.

Inglis, K. S. *The Australian Colonists: An Exploration of Social History 1788–1870*. Melbourne, 1974.

Jervis, James. "The Rise of Newcastle." *JRAHS*, vol. 21, no. 3 (1935).

Johnson, W. B. *English Prison Hulks*. London, 1957.

Johnston, Edith M. *Great Britain and Ireland 1760–1800: A Study in Political Administration*. London, 1963.

Keesing, Nancy. *John Lang and "The Forger's Wife": A True Tale of Early Australia*. Sydney, 1979.

Kerr, James S. *Design for Convicts: An Account of Design for Convict Establishments in the Australian Colonies*. Sydney, 1984.

Kiddle, M. L. *Caroline Chisholm*. Melbourne, 1957.

Kiernan, T. J. *Irish Exiles in Australia*. Dublin, 1954.

King, Jonathan, and King, John. *Philip Gidley King: A Biography of the Third Governor of New South Wales*. Sydney, 1981.

Knight, Ruth. *Illiberal Liberal: Robert Lowe in New South Wales, 1842–1850*. Melbourne, 1966.

Lansbury, Coral. *Arcady in Australia: The Evocation of Australia in Nineteenth-Century English Literature*. Sydney, 1970.

Lemprière, T. J. *The Penal Settlements of Van Diemen's Land*. Launceston, 1954.

Lennox, G. R. "A Private and Confidential Despatch of Eardley-Wilmot: Implications . . . Concerning the Probation System for Convict Women." THRA, PP, vol. 29, no. 2 (June 1982).

Levi, J. S., and Bergman, J. F. *Australian Genesis: Jewish Convicts and Settlers, 1788–1850*. Sydney, 1974.

Levy, M. C. *Governor George Arthur, a Colonial Benevolent Despot*. Melbourne, 1953.

Linebaugh, Peter. "The Tyburn Riot Against the Surgeons." In *Albion's Fatal Tree: Crime and Society in Eighteenth Century England* (ed. Douglas Hay, Peter Linebaugh and Edward Thompson). London, 1975.

Macarthur-Onslow, S., ed. *Some Early Records of the Macarthurs of Camden*. Sydney, 1914.

Mackaness, George. *Some Private Correspondence of Sir John and Lady Jane Franklin*. Sydney, 1947.

———. *The Life of Vice-Admiral Bligh*. 2 vols. Sydney, 1951.

Mackay, David. *A Place of Exile: The European Settlement of New South Wales*. Melbourne, 1985.

———. *In the Wake of Cook: Exploration, Science and Empire, 1780–1801*. Wellington, 1985.

McIntyre, K. G. *The Secret Discovery of Australia: Portuguese Ventures 200 Years Before Captain Cook*. Menindie, New South Wales, 1977.

McMahon, Anne. "Tasmanian Aboriginal Women as Slaves." THRA, PP, vol. 23, no. 2 (June 1976).

McNab, Robert. "Phillip's Views on . . . Treatment of Convicts." HRNZ, vol. 1, pp. 67–70.

McQueen, Humphrey. "Convicts and Rebels." *LH*, vol. 15 (November 1968).

———. *A New Britannia: An Argument Concerning the Social Origins of Australian Radicalism and Nationalism*. Melbourne, 1970; rev. ed., 1975.

McRae, Mary M. "Yankees from King Arthur's Court: A Brief History of North American Prisoners Transported to Canada from Van Diemen's Land, 1839–40." THRA, PP, vol. 19, no. 4 (December 1972).

Madgwick, R. B. *Immigration into Eastern Australia, 1788–1851*. London, 1937; reprint, Sydney, 1969.

Manifold, J. S., ed. *The Penguin Australian Song Book*. Sydney, 1964.

Marlow, Joyce. *The Tolpuddle Martyrs*. 1971.

Meredith, John. *The Wild Colonial Boy: Life and Times of Jack Donahoe (1808?–1830)*. Sydney, 1960.

Miller, E. M. *Pressmen and Governors*. Sydney, 1952.

Mitchell, T. L. *Three Expeditions into the Interior of Eastern Australia.* 2 vols. London, 1839.

Monaghan, Jay. *Australians and the Gold Rush: California and Down Under, 1849–54.* San Francisco, 1966.

Moore, James. *The Convicts of Van Diemen's Land, 1840–1853.* Hobart, 1976.

Moorehead, Alan. *The Fatal Impact: An Account of the Invasion of the South Pacific, 1767–1840.* London, 1966.

Morison, Samuel Eliot. *The European Discovery of America.* Vol. 1: *The Southern Voyages.* New York, 1974.

Morrell, W. P. *British Colonial Policy in the Age of Peel and Russell.* London, 1930.

Mulvaney, D. G. *The Prehistory of Australia.* Rev. ed. Melbourne, 1975.

———, and Golson, eds. *Aboriginal Man and Environment in Australia.* Canberra, 1971.

Murray-Smith, Stephen. "Beyond the Pale: The Islander Community of Bass Strait in the Nineteenth Century." THRA, PP, vol. 20, no. 4 (December 1973).

O'Farrell, Patrick. *The Catholic Church and Community in Australia, A History.* Melbourne, 1977.

———. *Letters from Irish Australia, 1825–1929.* Ed. Brian Trainor. Sydney and Belfast, 1984.

Park, Ruth. *The Companion Guide to Sydney.* London, 1973.

Partridge, Eric. *A Dictionary of the Underworld.* London, 1971.

Peyser, Dora. "A Study of the History of Welfare Work in Sydney from 1788 to about 1900: Part One." *JRAHS*, vol. 25, part 2 (1939).

Pike, E. Royston, ed. *Human Documents of the Industrial Revolution in Britain.* London, 1966.

Porter, Roy. *English Society in the Eighteenth Century.* London, 1982.

Pottle, F. A. *Boswell and the Girl from Botany Bay.* New York, 1938.

Pritchard, W. T. *Polynesian Reminiscences.* London, 1866.

Radzinowicz, Leon. *A History of English Criminal Law and Its Administration from 1750.* 3 vols. London, 1948–56.

    Ideology and Crime: A Study of Crime in Its Social and Historical Context. London, 1966.

———, with Wolfgang, Marvin, eds. *Crime and Justice.* Vol. 1: *The Criminal in Society.* New York, 1971.

Reece, R. H. *Aborigines and Colonists: Aborigines and Colonial Society in New South Wales in the 1830s and 1840s.* Sydney, 1974.

Reed, Michael. *The Georgian Triumph, 1700–1830.* London, 1983.

Reynolds, Henry. " 'That Hated Stain': The Aftermath of Transportation in Tasmania." *HS,* vol. 14, no. 53 (October 1969), pp. 19–33.

———. "Violence, the Aboriginals, and the Australian Historian." *Meanjin Quarterly,* vol. 31, no. 4 (December 1972).

———. *The Other Side of the Frontier: Aboriginal Resistance to the European Invasion of Australia.* Melbourne, 1982.

Ricards, Sherman, and Blackburn, George. "The Sydney Ducks: A Demographic Analysis." *PHR,* vol. 42, no. 1 (February 1973).

Richmond, Barbara. "John West and the Anti-Transportation Movement." THRA, PP, vol. 2 (1952).

Ritchie, John. *Punishment and Profit: The Reports of Commissioner John Bigge on the Colonies of New South Wales and Van Diemen's Land, 1822–23.* Melbourne, 1970.

———. "Towards Ending an Unclean Thing: The Molesworth Committee and the Abolition of Transportation to New South Wales, 1837–40." *HS,* vol. 17, no. 67 (October 1976), pp. 144–64.

Robinson, Portia. *The Hatch and Brood of Time: A Study of the First Generation of Native-Born White Australians, 1788–1828.* Vol. 1. Melbourne, 1985.

Robson, Lloyd L. "The Historical Basis of *For the Term of His Natural Life.*" *Australian Literary Studies,* vol. 1 (1963).

————. *The Convict Settlers of Australia: An Enquiry into the Origin and Character of the Convicts Transported to New South Wales and Van Diemen's Land, 1787–1852.* Melbourne, 1965.

————. *A History of Tasmania.* Oxford, 1983.

Roderick, Colin. *John Knatchbull from Quarterdeck to Gallows (Including the Narrative Written by Himself in Darlinghurst Gaol . . .).* Sydney, 1963.

Roe, Michael. "Colonial Society in Embryo." *HS*, vol. 7, no. 56 (May 1956).

————. *Quest for Authority in Eastern Australia, 1835–51.* Melbourne, 1965.

————. "The Establishment of Local Self-Government in Hobart and Launceston." THRA, PP, vol. 14, no. 1 (December 1966).

————. "1830–1850." Chap. 3 of Frank Crowley, ed., *A New History of Australia.* Melbourne, 1980.

Rolls, Eric. *A Million Wild Acres.* Melbourne, 1982.

Rowley, C. D. *Aboriginal Policy and Practice.* Vol. 1: *The Destruction of Aboriginal Society.* Canberra, 1970.

Rude, George, *Paris and London in the 18th Century: Studies in Popular Protest.* London, 1952.

————. *The Crowd in History: A Study of Popular Disturbances in France and England, 1730–1848.* New York, 1964.

————. "Captain Swing and Van Diemen's Land." THRA, PP, vol. 12 (1964).

————. *Protest and Punishment: The Story of the Social and Political Protesters Transported to Australia, 1788–1868.* London, 1978.

Rule, John. *The Experience of Labor in Eighteenth-Century English Industry.* New York, 1981.

Ryan, Lyndall. *The Aboriginal Tasmanians.* Brisbane, 1981.

Serle, Geoffrey. *The Golden Age: A History of the Colony of Victoria, 1851–1861.* Reprint, Melbourne, 1968.

Serventy, Vincent. *A Continent in Danger.* London, 1966.

Shaw, A. G. L. "Origins of the Probation System." *HS*, vol. 6 (1953).

————. "Sir John Eardley-Wilmot and the Probation System in Tasmania." THRA, PP, vol. 11 (1963).

————. *Convicts and the Colonies: A Study of Penal Transportation from Great Britain and Ireland to Australia and Other Parts of the British Empire.* London, 1966.

————. *Heroes and Villains in History: Governors Darling and Bourke in New South Wales.* Sydney, 1966.

————. "Some Officials in Early Van Diemen's Land." THRA, PP, vol. 14 (1967).

————. "A Colonial Ruler in Two Hemispheres: Sir George Arthur in Van Diemen's Land and Canada." THRA, PP, vol. 17 (1970).

————. "Violent Protest in Australian History." *HS*, vol. 15 (April 1973).

————. *Sir George Arthur, Bart. 1784–1854.* Melbourne, 1980.

Smith, Abbot Emerson. *Colonists in Bondage: White Servitude and Convict Labor in America, 1607–1776.* New York, 1971.

Smith, Bernard. *European Vision and the South Pacific, 1768–1850: A Study in the History of Art and Ideas.* Oxford, 1960.

———— (ed). *Documents on Art and Taste in Australia: The Colonial Period, 1770–1914.* Melbourne, 1975.

Smith, Martin. "Arthur Phillip and the Young Lads." *Campaign,* no. 19, Sydney (1977).

————. "The Emergence of a Gay Society." *Campaign,* no. 20, Sydney (1977).

Smith, Sydney. *Works.* London, 1878.

Smith, Warren B. *White Servitude in Colonial South Carolina.* Columbia, S.C., 1961.

Spate, O. H. K. *The Pacific Since Magellan.* Vol. 1: *The Spanish Lake.* Minneapolis, 1979.

————. *The Pacific Since Magellan.* Vol. 2: *Monopolists and Freebooters.* Minneapolis, 1983.

Sprod, Dan. *Alexander Pearce of Macquarie Harbour: Convict—Bushranger—Cannibal.* Hobart, 1977.

Steele, J. G. *Brisbane Town in Convict Days, 1824–1842.* St. Lucia, Queensland, 1975.

Sturma, Michael. "Eye of the Beholder: The Stereotype of Women Convicts, 1788–1852." *LH*, no. 34 (May 1978).

————. *Vice in a Vicious Society: Crime and Convicts in Mid-Nineteenth-Century New South Wales.* Brisbane, 1983.

Summers, Anne. *Damned Whores and God's Police: The Colonization of Women in Australia.* London: Penguin Books, Pelican edition, 1975.

Sweeney, Christopher. *Transported: In Place of Death. Convicts in Australia.* Melbourne, 1981.

Thomas, J. E., and Stewart, A. *Imprisonment in Western Australia.* Nedlands, Western Australia, 1978.

Thompson, Edward P. *The Making of the English Working Class.* London: Penguin Books, Pelican edition, 1968.

————. *Whigs and Hunters: The Origin of the Black Act.* London, 1975.

————, Douglas Hay, and Peter Linebaugh, eds. *Albion's Fatal Tree: Crime and Society in Eighteenth-Century England.* London, 1975.

Tinsdale, Norman. *Aboriginal Tribes of Australia.* 2 vols. Los Angeles, 1974.

Tobias, J. J. *Crime and Industrial Society in the 19th Century.* London, 1967, 1972.

Townsend, Norma. "The Molesworth Enquiry: Does the Report Fit the Evidence?" *JAS*, no. 1 (June 1977).

Tucker, Maya. "Centennial Celebrations, 1888." In *Australia 1888*, A Bicentennial History Bulletin, ed. Graeme Davidson and Ailsa McLeary, Bulletin no. 7 (April 1981).

Turnbull, Clive. *Black War: The Extermination of the Tasmanian Aborigines.* Melbourne, 1948.

Ullathorne, William. *The Autobiography of Archbishop Ullathorne, with Selections from his Letters.* London, 1891.

Walker, Robin. "Bushranging in Fact and Legend." *HS*, vol. 11, no. 42 (April 1964).

Wallas, Graham. *The Life of Francis Place, 1771–1854.* London, 1898.

Ward, John M. *Earl Grey and the Australian Colonies, 1846–57: A Study of Self-Government and Self-Interest.* Melbourne, 1958.

————. *James Macarthur, Colonial Conservative, 1798–1867.* Sydney, 1981.

Ward, Russel. "Felons and Folksongs." October 1954. Typescript in ML, Sydney.

————. *The Australian Legend.* Sydney, 1958; rev. ed., 1970.

————. *Australia Since the Coming of Man.* Rev. ed. Sydney, 1982.

Warung, Price [Astley, William]. *Tales of the Convict System.* Sydney, 1892.

————. *Tales of the Early Days.* Melbourne, 1894.

————. *Tales of the Old Regime.* Melbourne, 1897.

————. *Tales of the Isle of Death.* Melbourne, 1898.

————. *Convict Days.* Sydney, 1960.

Weidenhofer, Margaret. *The Convict Years: Transportation and the Penal System 1788–1868.* Melbourne, 1973.

————. *Maria Island: A Tasmanian Eden.* Melbourne, 1977.

————. *Port Arthur: A Place of Misery.* Melbourne, 1981.

Wells, T. E. *Michael Howe, the Last and Worst of the Bushrangers of Van Diemen's Land: Narrative of his Chief Atrocities . . .* Introd. by George Mackaness. Dubbo, 1979.

White, Charles. *History of Australian Bushranging.* 2 vols. Reprint, Sydney, 1976.

Whitley, G. "The Doom of the Bird of Providence." *Australian Zoology*, vol. 8 (1934).

Wilding, Michael. *Marcus Clarke.* Melbourne, 1977.

Willoughby, Edward. *Australian Pictures Drawn with Pen and Pencil.* London, 1886.

Wilson, Barbara Vance. *Convict Australia, 1788–1868: A Social History.* Melbourne, 1981.

Wood, F. L. W. "Jeremy Bentham versus New South Wales." *JRAHS*, vol. 19, part 6 (1933), pp. 329–51.

Wood, G. Arnold. "Convicts," *JRAHS*, vol. 8, no. 4 (1922), p. 187.

Woolmington, Jean, ed. *Aborigines in Colonial Society, 1788–1850: From 'Noble Savage' to 'Rural Pest.'* Sydney, 1973.

Wright, Gordon. *Between the Guillotine and Liberty: Two Centuries of the Crime Problem in France.* New York, 1983.

UNPUBLISHED THESES

Boissery, Beverley D. "French-Canadian Political Prisoners in Australia, 1838–39." Ph.D. diss., Australian National University, 1977.

Crowley, K. "Master and Servant in Early Australia." M.A. thesis, University of Melbourne, 1949.

Dalkin, R. N. "Norfolk Island: A History of its Government and Administration." M.A. thesis, Australian National University, 1977.

Driscoll, Francis. "How the Convict System Worked under Governor Macquarie." M.A. thesis, Sydney University, 1940.

Hooper, F. C. "Point Puer." M.Ed. thesis, University of Melbourne, 1954.

Kiernan, T. J. "Transportation from Ireland to Sydney, 1791–1816." M.A. thesis, Australian National University, 1954.

Korbell, M. J. "Bushranging in Van Diemen's Land, 1824–1834." 4th year thesis, University of Tasmania, 1974.

Leroy, Paul Edwin. "The Emancipists from Prison to Freedom: The Story of the Australian Convicts and their Descendants." Ph.D. diss., Ohio State University, 1960.

McKay, Anne. "The Assignment System of Convict Labour in Van Diemen's Land, 1824–1842." M.A. thesis, University of Tasmania, 1959.

Rosenberg, Sidney. "Black Sheep and Golden Fleece: A Study of Nineteenth-Century English Attitudes towards Australian Colonies." Ph.D. diss., Columbia University, 1954.

Watson, M. S. "Transportation and Civil Liberties in New South Wales, 1810–1840." M.A. thesis, Sydney University, 1960.

Williams, John Vernon. "Irish Convicts and Van Diemen's Land." M.A. thesis, University of Tasmania, 1972.

Index

ABOUT THE AUTHOR

Robert Hughes has been art critic for *Time* magazine since
1970. His major eight-part BBC/Time-Life television series
The Shock of the New was the basis of his 1981 book of
the same title, and he is the author of several earlier books,
including a standard history of Australian art. Twice winner of the Frank Jewett Mather Award for distinguished
criticism, he is a fellow of the New York Institute for the
Humanities. Born and educated in Sydney, Australia, he
now lives in New York City.